EXPERIENCES
IN EARTH-SPACE SCIENCE

EXPERIENCES
IN EARTH-SPACE SCIENCE

Michael A. Magnoli
Professor of Science Education
Mobile College
Mobile, Alabama

Linda S. Douglass
Teacher
Manchester Central
*   High School*
Manchester, New Hampshire

Doris M. Ellis
Earth Science Instructor
Richardson West
*   Junior High School*
Richardson, Texas

Laidlaw Brothers • Publishers   **A Division of Doubleday & Company, Inc.**

River Forest, Illinois

Irvine, California   Chamblee, Georgia   Dallas, Texas   Toronto, Canada

The New Exploring Science Program

The New Exploring Science   YELLOW
The New Exploring Science   ORANGE
The New Exploring Science   GOLD
The New Exploring Science   BLUE
The New Exploring Science   BROWN
The New Exploring Science   GREEN
The New Exploring Science   RED

Experiences in Science for Secondary Schools

Experiences in Life Science
Experiences in Physical Science
Experiences in Earth-Space Science
Experiences in Biology

To the Student

As you read this book, you will explore the long history of the earth. You will read about the changes that have occurred through the years. For example, the fossil record has provided earth scientists with much information about the earth's history. Because scientists have studied fossils, they have developed certain theories. These theories seek to explain changes in living things and in the earth itself. You will explore some of these theories in this book. As you study, keep in mind that these are theories, not facts. Science will continue to work for final answers.

On the Cover

The Office of Space Tracking and Data Systems of the National Aeronautics and Space Administration (NASA) is responsible for tracking all of NASA's flight projects. Among these flight projects are the earth-orbital missions, the lunar and planetary spacecraft, the deep-space probes, and the space shuttle program. An important instrument used when tracking flight projects is the tracking antenna. This photograph is of one such antenna, which is located at the Wallops Flight Center, Wallops Island, Virginia.
Photo by Photri

Supervising Editors Helen Frensch, J. David Johnson / *Staff Editors* Ronald A. Cwiak, Yvonne John, Dianne J. Kennedy / *Production Director* LaVergne G. Niequist / *Production Supervisor* Emily Fina Friel / *Production Associates* Nancey Epperson, Anthony Giometti, Michael J. Hruby, Bernard Shannon / *Production Assistants* Minerva Figueroa, Martha Kreger / *Photo Researcher* William A. Cassin / *Art Director* Gloria J. Muczynski / *Assistant to the Art Director* Dennis Horan / *Artists* Paul Hazelrigg; Frank Larocco; John D. Firestone & Associates, Inc.; James Teason; Lee Ames & Zak

ISBN 0–8445–5588-6

Copyright © 1985, 1983 by **Laidlaw Brothers, Publishers** ● A Division of Doubleday & Company, Inc.

Grant Heilman

NASA
Lick Observatory
California Institute of Technology

Contents

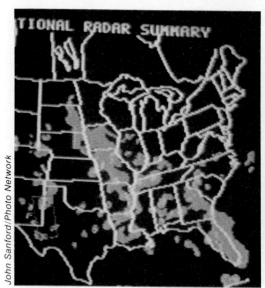

John Sanford/Photo Network

Photri

Bert Van Bork/Root Resources

Artstreet

Unit 1
EARTH

You are a traveler in space, returning home after a long voyage. As you enter the Milky Way galaxy, you point your spaceship toward the solar system. You are heading for the sun. The sun and its planets are at the far edge of the galaxy. But, in time, you are cruising through the solar system.

In the distance you see a giant ball of gas with many rings. This is the planet Saturn. Soon you are passing a giant among the planets. Jupiter and its Great Red Spot come into view. Finally, you are closing in on the most familiar of all the planets. You are nearing Earth, your home in the solar system.

Planet Earth is unlike any other planet. It is different from Saturn and Jupiter. It is different from Mars, Venus, and Mercury. What makes Earth different from all the other planets? To answer this question, you must first study the different parts of Earth. What are these parts? How do they fit together? How do they interact with one another?

Grant Heilman

8

NASA

The Apollo 8 *astronauts saw this view of the earth when orbiting the moon. Can you pick out the oceans and the landmasses of the earth?*

1   The Earth's Makeup

When the astronauts landed on the moon some years ago, they looked at the earth. There was the earth, reflecting light from the sun and becoming visible across the miles of space. The earth is 384 000 kilometers (238,080 miles) from the moon. But it can be seen from the moon, just as a full moon in the nighttime sky can be seen from the earth.

The astronauts took a picture of the earth from the moon. Their remarkable photograph shows the water and the landmasses on the earth. It also shows a cloud cover, a blanket of misty clouds in the air. As you can see in the picture, water covers much of the earth's surface. There is more water than land on the earth.

EARTH'S ATMOSPHERE

What gases make up the atmosphere?
What are the upper and lower limits of the
  atmosphere?
What are some properties of air?
How does the atmosphere interact with the
  earth's surface?
What are the elements of weather?

Gases in air

The ocean of air around the earth is known as the *atmosphere* [AT-muh-SFIH(UH)R]. Many different gases and particles make up the atmosphere. The gases that make up the lower atmosphere are mostly nitrogen and oxygen. Nitrogen accounts for more than 78 percent of dry air, and oxygen accounts for about 21 percent. Carbon dioxide is another important gas in the air. Traces of other gases account for less than 1 percent of dry air. See the table in Figure 1–1.

The makeup of the atmosphere changes at higher levels. At 960 kilometers (595.20 miles) above the earth's surface, the air is made up mostly of the gases hydrogen and helium. Hydrogen is the only gas in the air at a height of 2 400 kilometers (1,488 miles).

Find Out More

Scientists believe that the earth's atmosphere has gone through many changes before reaching its present state. Using references, find out what scientists think the atmosphere was like when the earth was first formed. How did the presence of monerans possibly change the atmosphere?

Figure 1–1. Many different gases make up the earth's atmosphere. Which gas is the most abundant? Which three gases would you say are the most important?

GASES IN THE ATMOSPHERE

Gas	Percent by Volume	Gas	Percent by Volume
Nitrogen	78.08	Hydrogen	trace
Oxygen	20.95	Xenon	trace
Argon	0.93	Ozone	trace
Carbon dioxide	0.03	Sulfur dioxide	trace
Neon	trace	Nitrogen dioxide	trace
Helium	trace	Iodine	trace
Methane	trace	Ammonia	trace
Krypton	trace	Carbon monoxide	trace
Nitrous oxide	trace	Radon	trace

Artstreet

Do It Yourself
Collect tiny bits of matter from air

The atmosphere contains tiny bits of solid matter such as soot, dirt, dust, salt from the oceans, and pollen from plants. You can collect some of these tiny bits of matter from the air. To do so, spread a light film of petroleum jelly on two or three glass slides. Put the slides outside in a place where they will not be disturbed. After several days have passed, observe each slide under a microscope. Try to identify as many of the solid particles as you can.

Mixed in with the gases are many particles. These particles cannot easily be seen, but they can be measured. Air in the lower atmosphere contains about 6,100 particles per cubic centimeter (100,000 particles per cubic inch). Among these particles are soot, dirt, dust, salt from the oceans, pollen from plants, and tiny living things known as *microbes* [MY-KROHBZ].

The atmosphere stretches from the surface of the earth to thousands of kilometers out into space. At its upper level, the air is thin. The molecules of hydrogen gas are wide apart. One by one, they escape and rise into space. Because the molecules of hydrogen gas move out into space, it is hard to determine the upper edge of the earth's ocean of air.

☐ **From where do animals get the oxygen they need?**

Properties of air

Like all matter, air has weight, and it takes up space. Air is much lighter than most other kinds of matter. The air in an "empty" drinking glass weighs less than 1 milligram (a fraction of an ounce). Still, the total amount of all the air that surrounds the earth is heavy. The total amount of air in the atmosphere weighs more than 4 trillion metric tons.

Find Out More

Using references, find out what is meant by the term "air pressure." Where would you expect the air pressure to be the greatest, at sea level or at the top of a mountain? Why?

Air has resistance. You can feel the resistance when you ride your bicycle. The faster you pedal, the greater is the amount of air resistance. Air can expand and contract. It expands when it is heated, and it contracts when it is cooled. Air can also be *compressed* [kuhm-PREHST], or squeezed. Compressed air is used to inflate automobile tires and to operate pneumatic drills.

Air moves. You can feel the air on your face when the wind blows. The sun heats the air and causes it to move. When the air is heated, it expands and becomes lighter. It rises in the atmosphere. Cool air moves in to take the place of the warm air. As the air rises and cool air moves in, the wind begins to blow.

Interaction with the surface

The atmosphere is active. That is, many different things are often happening in the atmosphere at the same time. Much of this activity comes about when the atmosphere interacts with the surface of the earth. The atmosphere and the surface act upon each other in many different ways.

Weather is an interaction between the atmosphere and the surface of the earth. Weather is a condition of the atmosphere. Among the elements of weather are wind, temperature, precipitation, humidity, and air pressure. Each of these elements acts upon the earth's surface in some way. You will be learning about the earth's weather in your study of Unit 3, "Atmosphere and Weather."

The atmosphere interacts with the surface of the earth in ways that are not so easily seen. For example, the atmosphere acts as an insulating blanket. It traps part of the heat that is given off by the earth. This heat warms the air above the earth. Without this "blanket," the average temperature on the earth would be about —29°C (about —20°F).

The atmosphere also absorbs most of the ultraviolet rays from the sun. Large amounts of these rays can harm living things. So the atmosphere acts as a shield. It protects life on the earth from harmful radiation.

Find Out More

You may have heard of the term "ozone." But what is ozone? What is the ozone layer? Why is this layer important to life on the earth? Use references such as encyclopedias and earth-science books to help you answer these questions.

Photo Trends

Figure 1–2. The Grand Canyon in Arizona is one of the most spectacular landforms of the lithosphere.

EARTH'S LITHOSPHERE

What are the three main layers of the solid earth?
How does the earth's crust differ from the mantle?
*How does the crust beneath the continents differ
   from the crust beneath the oceans?*
*How was the boundary between the crust and the
   mantle discovered?*
*How does the earth's inner core differ from the
   outer core?*

Surface of the earth

The outer shell of the earth is known as the *lithosphere*
[LIHTH-uh-sFIH(UH)R]. Within the lithosphere are soil,
rocks, and minerals, such as iron and copper. Many different landforms show up in the lithosphere. There are hills,
mountains, valleys, fields, and riverbeds. The lithosphere is
active. This activity is seen as volcanoes erupt and as earthquakes shake the land.

The lithosphere has boundaries. It begins at the surface of the earth. It extends about 100 kilometers (62 miles) into the earth. The lithosphere continues deep into the earth until rock is no longer hard. Beneath the lithosphere the rock is *molten* [MOHLT-uhn], or melted.

The deeper you go into the earth, the higher the temperature becomes. It is estimated that with each kilometer (0.62 mile) of depth, the temperature increases by 15°C (59°F). Therefore, at 100 kilometers (62 miles) down, the temperature is about 1 500°C (2,732°F). It is here that the rock is molten. Molten rock is hot and soft and is known as *magma* [MAG-muh].

Outer earth: the crust

The outermost layer of the lithosphere is called the *crust*. The crust is a layer of rocks made up mostly of two elements—oxygen and silicon. There are also other elements in the crust. Among these elements are iron and aluminum, which are mined and put to use. See the table in Figure 1–3.

The crust varies in thickness. Under the seafloor, the crust is five to ten kilometers thick (about three to six miles). It is much thicker under the *continents* [KAHNT-uhn-uhnts], the earth's large landmasses. At some places beneath the continents, the crust can be as thick as thirty to sixty kilometers (about nineteen to thirty-seven miles).

MAKEUP OF THE EARTH'S CRUST

Element	Percent of Crust's Mass	Percent of Crust's Volume
Oxygen	46.71	94.24
Silicon	27.69	0.51
Aluminum	8.07	0.44
Iron	5.05	0.37
Calcium	3.65	1.04
Sodium	2.75	1.21
Potassium	2.58	1.85
Magnesium	2.08	0.27

Figure 1–3. The earth's crust is mostly made up of eight elements. What are the names of these eight elements? Which one of these elements makes up the largest percentage of the crust's volume?

Two different layers of rock make up the crust of the earth. One layer makes up the continents. This layer is known as the *sialic* [sy-AL-ihk] *layer*. See Figure 1–4. Rocks in this layer are rich in oxygen, silicon, and aluminum. *Granite* [GRAN-uht] is the dominant rock found in the sialic layer.

The second layer makes up the part of the crust located beneath the seafloor. This layer is called the *simatic* [sy-MAD-ihk] *layer*. See Figure 1–4. Rocks in this layer contain oxygen, silicon, iron, and magnesium. *Basalt* [buh-SAWLT] is the dominant rock found in the simatic layer. Basaltic rocks differ from granitic rocks in their chemical makeup.

To Think About

What kinds of matter make up the rocks found in the sialic layer? What do you suppose the "si" and the "al" in "sialic" stand for? What, then, do the "si" and the "ma" in "simatic" stand for?

Figure 1–4. The sialic layer makes up the continents. The simatic layer is located beneath the seafloor. These two layers make up part of the earth's lithosphere. What other layer within the earth helps make up the lithosphere?

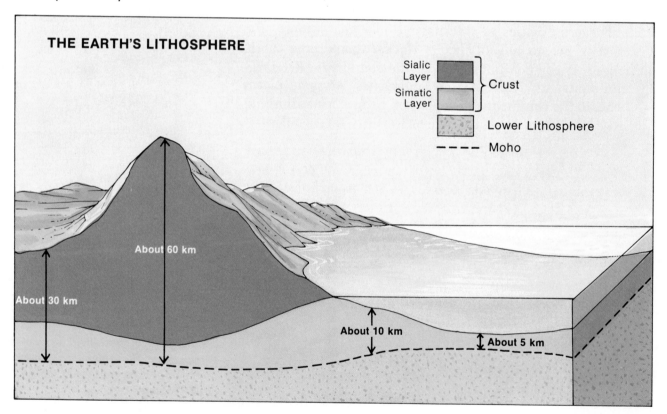

THE EARTH'S LITHOSPHERE

Sialic Layer
Simatic Layer
} Crust

Lower Lithosphere

– – – Moho

About 60 km

About 30 km

About 10 km

About 5 km

16

In comparison with other parts of the earth, the crust is a thin layer. See Figure 1–5. It accounts for only about 3 percent of the earth's mass. Although it is only a thin layer, the crust is an important part of the earth. It provides such needs as iron, aluminum, coal, oil, and natural gas. In addition, the rocks in the crust, when acted upon by the atmosphere, break down and form soil.

☐ **What is one difference between the earth's atmosphere and the earth's crust?**

Middle earth: the mantle

The next layer of the earth begins directly beneath the crust. This layer is called the *mantle* [MANT-uhl]. The mantle ends about 2 900 kilometers (1,798 miles) below the surface of the earth. It is the largest layer of the earth. The mantle accounts for about 67 percent of the mass of the earth.

The crust is separated from the mantle by a special boundary. This boundary is called the *Mohorovičič discontinuity* [MOH-huh-ROH-vuh-CHIHCH dihs-KAHNT-uhn-(Y)OO-uht-ee], or simply the *Moho* [MOH-HOH]. The boundary was discovered in 1909 by a Yugoslav scientist named Andrija Mohorovičič.

Mohorovičič made his discovery by studying earthquake waves. He observed that at a certain depth, the earthquake waves increased in speed. The waves moved faster, he reasoned, because they ran into a different kind of rock. The place at which earthquake waves change speed is the Moho. The Moho separates the crust from the mantle.

The mantle is divided into 3 layers. The first layer is the lower part of the lithosphere. The second layer of the mantle is known as the *asthenosphere* [as-THEHN-uh-SFIH(UH)R]. The asthenosphere begins where the lithosphere ends. The asthenosphere ends about 250 kilometers (155 miles) beneath the earth's surface.

The temperatures and the pressures in the asthenosphere are believed to be high enough to cause most of the rocks to

Figure 1–5. The lower lithosphere, the asthenosphere, and the mesosphere make up the mantle of the earth. At what depth does the lower lithosphere end? The asthenosphere? The mesosphere?

LAYERS OF THE EARTH

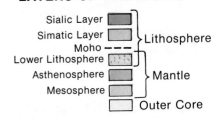

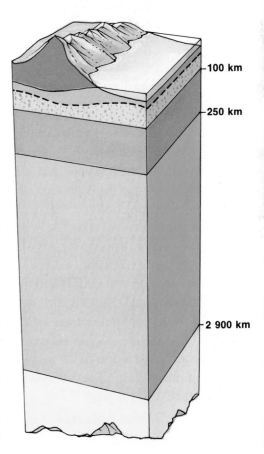

17

Figure 1–6. Castle Geyser in Yellowstone National Park is one of several well-known geysers. In a geyser, groundwater comes in contact with a heat source—such as hot rock—within the earth. This heat source causes groundwater to become heated above its boiling point and to expand, so that steam and very hot water are forced out of the ground.

Artstreet

be flexible. That is, the rocks in this layer are not as hard and rigid as the rocks that make up the crust. Instead, the rocks in the asthenosphere are like soft clay.

It is further believed that the temperatures in the asthenosphere are high enough to melt about 10 percent of the rocks. The melted rock, or the magma, flows ever so slightly because of the high pressure at this depth. The magma that erupts from a volcano at the surface of the earth is known as *lava* [LAHV-uh].

The *mesosphere* [MEHZ-uh-sFIH(UH)R] is the third layer of the mantle. It begins about 250 kilometers (155 miles) beneath the surface of the earth. It ends at a depth of about 2 900 kilometers (1,798 miles). The pressure in this layer becomes great enough to make the molten rock hard and strong once again. The boundaries of the mantle are shown in Figure 1–5 on page 17.

☐ **What do geysers and volcanoes tell you about the earth's interior?**

Find Out More

There have been many attempts to gather evidence concerning the makeup of the mantle. These include Project Mohole, Project Famous, the Deep Sea Drilling Project, and the Cayman Expedition of Woods Hole Oceanographic Institution. Using reference books and magazines, try to find out some of the goals and accomplishments of these and other evidence-gathering projects.

THE EARTH'S INTERIOR

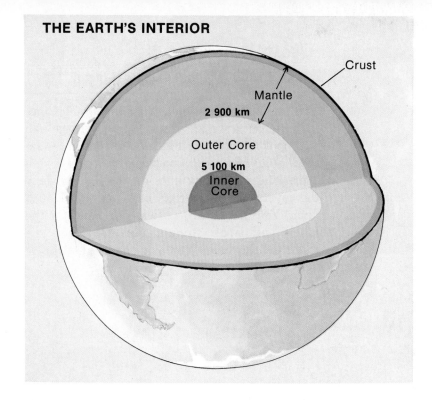

Crust
Mantle
2 900 km
Outer Core
5 100 km
Inner Core

Figure 1–7. The earth's crust is only a thin layer compared with the rest of the earth. Which layer of the earth would you say is the largest? Which layer would be the most difficult to study? Why?

Inner earth: the core

The *core* is the part of the earth below the mantle. It is not part of the lithosphere. The core begins where the mesosphere ends—about 2 900 kilometers (1,798 miles) beneath the surface of the earth. It continues to the center of the earth—about 6 731 kilometers (4,173.22 miles) beneath the surface. The core makes up about 30 percent of the mass of the earth.

The boundary between the mantle and the core was also discovered by noticing a change in the speed of earthquake waves. In fact, when scientists studied the change in speed of earthquake waves, they discovered that there is a liquid *outer core* and a solid *inner core*. See Figure 1–7.

The outer core is believed to be made up mostly of molten iron and sulfur. However, there may also be small amounts of other elements. The outer core ends at about 5 100 kilometers (3,162 miles) beneath the surface of the earth. It is here that the inner core is believed to begin. The inner core makes up the center of the earth. It is thought to be mostly solid iron.

To Think About

There have been many science-fiction stories about traveling to the center of the earth. What are some of the problems that would have to be overcome before such a journey could be possible?

Do It Yourself

Make a model of the earth's interior

Obtain a 15-cm (6-inch) Styrofoam ball. Carefully cut out a wedge of the ball so that the ball will look similar to Figure 1–7 on page 19. *CAUTION: Be careful not to cut yourself.* Using a marking pen, draw lines on the ball to show the layers of the earth. Color and label each layer. You may wish to use white paper for the labels and small straight pins to attach the labels to the ball. Which is the largest layer? The smallest?

EARTH'S HYDROSPHERE

What is the hydrosphere?
What is the most common salt found in the
  ocean?
Where can fresh water be found?

Water, water everywhere

Water covers most of the earth. In fact, the oceans alone cover about 70 percent of the earth's surface. Rivers and streams flow across the land. Fresh water also fills the lakes and ponds. The water on the earth is known as the *hydrosphere* [HY-druh-SFIH(UH)R]. Without the hydrosphere, there would be no life on the earth.

The three great oceans of the world are the Atlantic Ocean, the Pacific Ocean, and the Indian Ocean. Together, these massive bodies of water can be looked upon as the *world ocean.* As you can see on a globe, the Atlantic, the Pacific, and the Indian oceans all come together around the continent of Antarctica.

Oceans are constantly changing the land. As the waves roll in, they carry sand onto the beaches. Large waves caused by a storm can pick up boulders and hurl them to points far from shore. Waves are constantly working against the land, breaking the rocks into pebbles and sand. Shore-lines are constantly changed by rolling seas and massive waves.

Rivers also change the land. As a river flows from the mountains to the lowlands, it wears itself a channel. Rivers pick up soil and rocks. As they pass through mountains, rivers carve out deep channels and, over long periods of time, canyons can be formed. The Colorado River formed the Grand Canyon in this way. A river drops its silt at its mouth when it flows into an ocean.

Elements in the water

Chemical elements can be found in both salt water and fresh water. Water itself is H_2O, with a molecule consisting of one oxygen atom and two hydrogen atoms. The water in the oceans is salt water. The salt in the water is *sodium chloride*, or common table salt. There is little, if any, salt in fresh water. It is said to be fresh because it contains little or no salt.

Besides salt, seawater also contains sulfur, calcium, and magnesium. Nearly all the elements found in the minerals in the earth's crust can be found in the ocean. They are found in trace amounts. The proportion of salt to the other elements is about the same in all parts of the world's oceans.

Minerals in the soil and the rocks make their way into fresh water. As rivers and streams flow in their channels,

To Think About

During evaporation, some water molecules from the salt water in the ocean change into a gas—water vapor. Water vapor does not contain salt. What happens to the salt found in water from the ocean when it evaporates?

Taurus

Do It Yourself

Make a chart

Fresh water often contains small amounts of different salts. It also contains many dissolved minerals. Use references to find out what salts and minerals can be found in fresh water. Arrange the names of the salts and the minerals in a column titled "Substance." In another column, titled "Effects," tell what effect each substance may have on you or on the plumbing of your home.

21

they break apart the soil and the rocks. The streams pick up elements such as iron, calcium, and sulfur.

☐ **Why is it easier to float in the ocean than in a fresh-water lake?**

Earth's zone of life

There are many different kinds of living things on the earth. Some of these living things are plants, animals, fungi, and microbes. All the living things can be found only in one part, or zone, of the earth. This part is known as the *biosphere* [BY-uh-sFI(UH)R]. The biosphere is that part of the earth in which life exists. It includes the atmosphere, the lithosphere, and the hydrosphere.

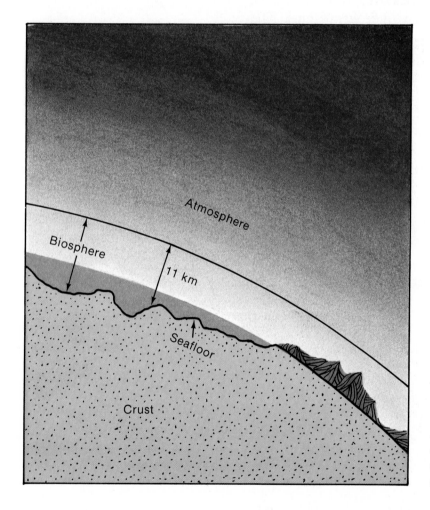

Figure 1–8. The biosphere is the layer of the earth in which living things exist. All the things needed for life are contained within the biosphere.

The biosphere is also called the earth's zone of life. It is a far-reaching zone, extending from the depths of the oceans to about eleven kilometers (about seven miles) above the surface of the earth. All the living things on the earth are found in this zone.

Many different kinds of living things can be found on the earth's surface. Among the living things are cattle on the farms, wild animals in the forest, earthworms in the soil, and insects all around. Fish and aquatic plants live in the water, and birds fly through the air. The biosphere, then, includes all the places on the earth where life can exist.

□ **In what parts of the biosphere can insects be found? Where do mammals live?**

Figure 1–9. Black-tailed deer forage for food near the timberline of many mountain ranges in the United States. Sea lions often rest on rocky shores, but they return to the ocean to hunt for fish and squid.

23

EARTH'S MAGNETIC FIELD

In what way is the earth like a bar magnet?
How can you find the directions north and south?
What does magnetic inclination tell you about
magnetic lines of force?
How is magnetic declination helpful to
navigators?
What happens in the Van Allen belts?

Magnetic poles

The earth is a magnet. It has a magnetic north pole and a magnetic south pole. The magnetic poles are like the ends of a bar magnet. Like a bar magnet, the earth is surrounded by a magnetic field. See Figure 1–10. The earth's magnetic field extends far out into space.

Have you ever used a compass to find the direction north? If you have, you have made use of the earth's magnetic field. The iron needle of a compass is mounted on a pivot, and it can swing freely. The north-seeking end always swings toward the magnetic north pole. The magnetic north pole attracts the needle. The opposite end, or south-seeking end of the needle, points toward the magnetic south pole.

The magnetic north pole is not the same as the geographic north pole. The magnetic north pole is near Bathurst

Figure 1–10. In the drawing of the earth's magnetic field, locate the magnetic north pole (MN) and then the magnetic south pole (MS). Notice how the geographic north pole (GN) and the geographic south pole (GS) differ in location from the two magnetic poles.

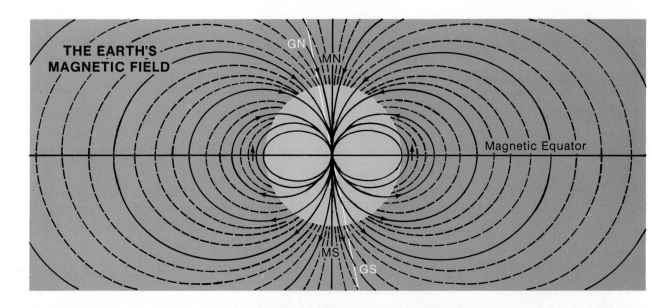

Island in northern Canada. In fact, it is 1 600 kilometers (992 miles) from the geographic north pole. The magnetic south pole is 2 570 kilometers (1,593.40 miles) from the geographic south pole. It is in Wilkes Land, a part of Antarctica.

In a way, the earth is a huge electromagnet. Its magnetism is like the magnetism of a coil of wire through which electricity flows. Earth scientists believe electricity is generated in the core of the earth. As the electricity flows outward through the earth, it forms the magnetic field.

□ **Will there someday be a change in the location of the magnetic north pole and the magnetic south pole? Explain your answer.**

Magnetic declination

As you have observed, a compass needle points to the magnetic north pole. A line could be drawn from the needle to the pole. A line also could be drawn from the needle to the geographic north pole, or to *true north*. Since the magnetic north pole and the geographic north pole are not in the same place, there would be a difference between the two lines. The angle of this difference is known as *magnetic declination* [DEHK-luh-NAY-shuhn].

At some places on the earth, magnetic declination is the same. On a map, lines known as *isogonic* [EYE-suh-GAHN-ihk] *lines* connect the places with the same declination. See the map in Figure 1–11. Magnetic declination differs at

To Think About

The prefix "paleo" means dealing with ancient forms or conditions. What do you think the term "paleomagnetism" means?

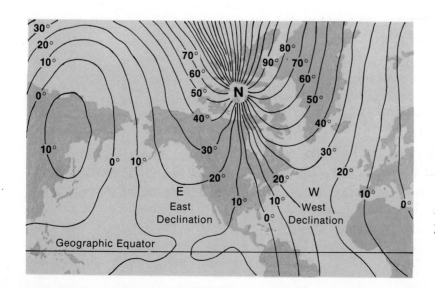

Figure 1–11. Bar Harbor, Maine, has a declination of about 20°W. That is, in using a compass at Bar Harbor, you have to add 20° to the indicated compass direction to find true north. Coos Bay, Oregon, has a declination of about 20°E. You have to subtract 20° from the compass direction to find true north at Coos Bay.

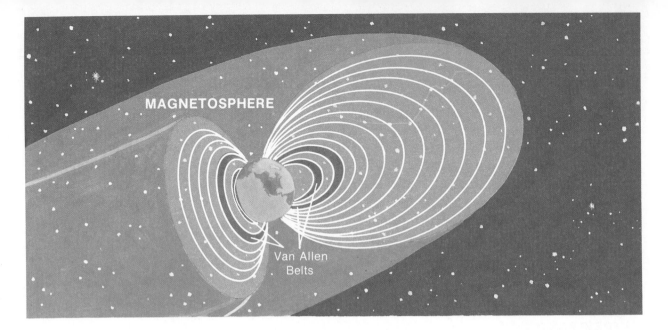

Figure 1–12. The magnetosphere is shaped somewhat like a donut. The solar wind gives the magnetosphere a "tail" on the side facing away from the sun. What is the name given to the two belts of electrically charged particles that lie within the magnetosphere?

many places around the world. The declination may be toward the east or toward the west of true north.

The navigator of a ship has to know the magnetic declination for the part of the ocean in which the ship sails. This information is needed to keep the ship on its course. The ship's compass points to the magnetic north pole. Knowing the declination, the navigator can make sure the ship is sailing in the right direction. For example, the navigator may find it necessary to sail as much as 10° east of the magnetic course.

Magnetosphere

The earth's magnetic field reaches into the inner part of the earth, across the surface of the earth, through the atmosphere of the earth, and into interplanetary space. The lines of force, however, are confined to a region surrounding the earth. The region surrounding the earth that is affected by the earth's magnetic field is the *magnetosphere* [mag-NEET-uh-sfih(uh)r]. The lines of force usually do not allow charged particles from outer space to enter the magnetosphere. But from time to time, particles do enter the magnetosphere.

Look at Figure 1–12. In this drawing notice how the earth looks as though it is surrounded by a somewhat large

(Text continues on page 28.)

To Think About

It is possible for the magnetic declination to be 0°. Where, on an isogonic map, would the magnetic declination be 0°?

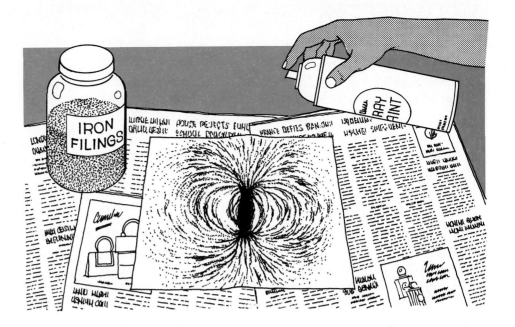

Investigate

**How can you make a model showing
the earth's magnetic lines of force?**

You will need

newspaper, bar magnet, white sheet of paper,
color spray paint other than white, iron filings

Background

Lines are often drawn in order to "see" the
earth's magnetic field. These lines are called magnetic lines of force. These lines form a picture
of the magnetic field.

One should remember that a magnetic field is
not really made up of lines. Magnetic lines of
force are imaginary. However, we make use of
these lines to help us "see" something that is
not really visible.

What to do

In a well-ventilated room, lay several sheets
of newspaper on the floor or on an old tabletop,
Place the bar magnet in the center of the newspaper. Lay a sheet of white paper on top of the
magnet. Sprinkle iron filings on the white sheet
of paper. Gently tap the white sheet of paper.

Look at the pattern formed by the iron filings.
Spray a *light* coat of paint over the iron filings.
Allow the paint to dry. Gently remove the iron
filings from the paper. You now have a model
of the earth's magnetic lines of force.

Using Figure 1–10, label the magnetic north
pole and the magnetic south pole on your model.
Also label the geographic north pole and the
geographic south pole.

Now that you have done the investigation

■ Look at Figure 1–10 on page 24. How do the
magnetic lines of force of your model compare
with the magnetic lines of force of the earth?
■ How is the earth like a bar magnet?
■ On your model, are the magnetic north pole
and the geographic north pole in the same location? Explain.

doughnut. This doughnut represents the magnetosphere. It reaches far out into space—perhaps more than 4 800 000 kilometers (about 2,976,000 miles).

The *solar wind,* which is made up of particles given off by the sun, acts upon the lines of force. As a result, farther out in space, the magnetosphere is not shaped like a true doughnut. Instead, the solar wind gives the magnetosphere a "tail" on the side facing away from the sun.

Within the magnetosphere lie two belts of electrically charged particles. These belts are called the *Van Allen belts.* They were first detected in 1958 by a Geiger-Müller counter carried aboard the satellite *Explorer I.* They were later confirmed by *Explorer III.* The two belts are named for James A. Van Allen, a physicist at the University of Iowa. Van Allen interpreted the findings of *Explorer I.*

Perhaps you have seen or heard of the northern lights— *aurora borealis* [uh-ROHR-uh ʙᴏʜʀ-ee-AL-uhs]—or the southern lights—*aurora australis* [uh-ROHR-uh aw-STRAY-luhs]. They are a spectacular sight of glittering streamers of light in the night sky. Scientists believe the Van Allen belts to be responsible for these lights. They believe the protons and electrons of the outer Van Allen belt strike the gas molecules in the earth's atmosphere, causing the gas molecules to glow.

Dr. E. R. Degginger

Figure 1–13. The aurora borealis, or northern lights, appears in the Northern Hemisphere. It is mentioned in the mythology of the Eskimos, the Germans, the English, and others. The early Eskimos saw the aurora borealis as the reflection of the dance fire of people farther north. Northern Germanic tribes saw these lights as the splendor of the shields of the Valkyries, or warrior goddesses.

Geophysicists use many kinds of instruments to help them gather information about the earth.

Careers

Geophysicist

The study of the makeup of the earth—from the core to the outer limits of the atmosphere—is known as *geophysics* [JEE-uh-FIHZ-ihks]. Geophysics is a branch of science that deals with geology and physics. Geophysicists must know something about chemistry and mathematics. The work of most geophysicists includes writing, reporting, fieldwork, and laboratory work. Geophysicists who are studying the makeup of the inside of the earth might collect rocks from volcanoes. They may also look for rocks from the bottom of the ocean. They might use instruments to gather information about the earth's gravity, rock layers, or heat flow from inside the earth. The rocks and information must then be studied in the laboratory.

Geophysicists must be able to explain the results of their work. They must be good at piecing things together. Much of the information that geophysicists gather for their research comes from indirect evidence.

Geophysicists who study the atmosphere collect air samples. They also use instruments to gather other information about the earth. For example, they might use a *magnetometer* [MAG-nuh-TAHM-uht-ur] to study the earth's magnetic field. They gather information about the conditions affecting radio signals and about radiation from the sun. The information gathered from their work is helpful in transmitting radio and television waves. It is also helpful in mapping and navigation and in studying and exploring space.

If you think you might like to be a geophysicist, you or a friend may write to the American Geophysical Union, 1909 K Street, N.W., Washington, DC 20006. Ask for information about the training and work of a geophysicist.

Reviewing and Extending

Summing Up

1. The three major parts of the earth are the atmosphere, the lithosphere, and the hydrosphere.
2. The atmosphere is a mixture of gases.
3. Weather is a condition of the atmosphere.
4. The lithosphere includes the crust and the upper part of the mantle.
5. The core lies beneath the mantle.
6. The hydrosphere includes all the parts of the earth in which water is found.
7. The biosphere is that part of the earth in which life exists.
8. The earth has a magnetic field.
9. The magnetosphere is the region surrounding the earth that is affected by the magnetic field of the earth.

Checking Up

Vocabulary   Write the numerals *1–7* on your paper. Each numbered phrase describes a term from the following list. On your paper, write the term next to the numeral of the phrase that describes it.

magma	inner core	lithosphere
sialic	outer core	asthenosphere
simatic	hydrosphere	Van Allen belt

1. outer shell of the earth that includes the crust and part of the mantle
2. includes all parts of the earth in which water is found
3. made up of molten iron and sulfur
4. layer of the crust made up of rocks that are rich in oxygen, silicon, aluminum, and magnesium
5. belt of electrically charged particles
6. molten rock
7. layer of the mantle containing molten rock

Knowledge and Understanding   Write the numerals *8–17* on your paper. Beside each numeral, write the word or words that best complete the sentence having that numeral.

8. The region surrounding the earth that is affected by the magnetic field of the earth is the _____.

9. The _____ is the outermost layer of the litho-sphere. It varies in thickness.
10. The _____ includes all parts of the earth where water can be found.
11. The mantle is made up of three layers—the lower part of the lithosphere, the astheno-sphere, and the _____.
12. The part of the earth that is made up of gases and stretches from the surface of the earth to many thousands of kilometers out into space is the _____.
13. The _____ is the part of the earth that is made up of solid rocky material.
14. The crust is made up of two layers—the sialic layer and the _____ layer.
15. On a map, lines known as isogonic lines connect the places with the same magnetic _____.
16. The earth's _____ north pole is located near Bathurst Island in northern Canada.
17. The boundary that separates the crust from the mantle is called the Mohorovičič discon-tinuity, or simply the _____.

Expressing Yourself   Write a paragraph as an answer to each of the following questions:

18. What is the biosphere? What parts of the earth are included in the biosphere?
19. What elements are believed to make up the outer core and the inner core of the earth? Why do scientists not know exactly what elements make up the core?

Doing More

1. Observe the atmosphere each day for one week. Look for changes in the atmosphere. Keep a record of the changes you observe. How has the atmosphere interacted with the surface of the earth during the week? Keep a record of the interactions.
2. Make a large terrarium using a very large glass jar and its lid. Place a layer of charcoal and pebbles in the jar. Add a layer of sand. Put water in a small plastic dish in the sand as a pond. Add soil, stones, small plants, and a twig. Moisten the soil around the plants. Add small animals such as worms, beetles, and spiders. Poke a few holes in the lid of the jar. Keep the jar in a well-lighted area, but not in direct sunlight. Observe the terrarium for several days. How are your plants surviving? Your animals? Why is it important for living things to have certain amounts of nonliving things in their environment?

The edges of many of the hot springs in Yellowstone National Park contain minerals that give the hot springs their brilliant colors.

2   Minerals

Since prehistoric times, people have made use of the materials around them. Stone Age people chipped pieces of flint to make sharp tools and weapons. Later, people learned that by striking flint against a hard metal, they could produce sparks. These sparks turned small piles of twigs into campfires.

Stone Age people also found uses for other materials. About 8000 B.C., early people began to use copper as a substitute for stone. They made ornaments and decorations out of copper. As early as 4000 B.C., Egyptians hammered copper into thin sheets to make tools, weapons, and jewelry. About 3500 B.C.,

people who lived in the region of present-day Iraq began to mix copper with tin. This mixture of copper and tin is called *bronze* [BRAHNZ].

Flint and copper, like many of the materials used by early people, are *minerals* [MIHN(-uh)-ruhlz]. To an earth scientist, minerals are solids formed in nature that have a definite chemical makeup and structure and that do not contain the remains of living things. More than three thousand different kinds of minerals are found in the earth. As you study this chapter, you will learn about minerals.

MINERAL FORMATION

How are minerals formed from magma?
What is one mineral formed from the process of evaporation? Precipitation?

Find Out More

A mineral that is also an element is sometimes called a *native element*. Native elements are often divided into three groups—metals, semimetals, and nonmetals. Use reference books to find out which minerals are native elements.

Heat and pressure

High heat and high pressure exist beneath the lithosphere. The high heat and high pressure help form magma. Magma is made up of many different kinds of matter, such as iron, copper, and oxygen. As magma cools, the different kinds of matter in the magma join together to form minerals. For example, iron may join with oxygen to form the mineral *hematite* [HEE-muh-TYT]. Most of the world's iron comes from hematite.

As magma cools, atoms of the same kind of matter sometimes join together. The atoms join together and form an *element* [EHL-uh-muhnt]. An element is a substance made up of only one kind of atom. Many elements are minerals. For example, copper is both an element and a mineral. Gold and silver are two other elements that show up as minerals in the earth's crust.

☐ **Hematite is sometimes referred to as iron oxide. Why is this so?**

Evaporation and precipitation

Rain flows along gullies and down hills during a rainstorm. Some of the minerals found in the soil are dissolved by the rain. The dissolved minerals mix with the rain and collect in streams and puddles. As the rain from the puddle evaporates, the dissolved minerals form a solid and are left behind. Water that evaporates from saltwater lakes and oceans leaves behind deposits of *halite* [HAL-YT]. Halite is known as table salt. *Gypsum* [JIHP-suhm] is another mineral formed when water evaporates. Gypsum is used to make plaster of paris.

Other minerals are often formed when matter *precipitates* [prih-SIHP-uh-TAYTS], or separates, from water.

Figure 2–1. Hematite can appear in several forms. Which of the pieces of hematite pictured would you say is commonly called kidney ore?

Runk/Schoenberger/Grant Heilman

Jacqueline Durand

Do It Yourself

Show how a salt deposit may form

Put 240 ml of water into a pan. Heat the water until it begins to boil. Slowly pour small amounts of salt into the water while you stir the water. Keep adding salt and continue stirring until no more salt will dissolve. Pour some of this salt water into a shallow bowl and set the bowl aside. Observe the bowl over the next three days. What changes do you observe? How do the changes in the bowl of salt water show what might happen during the formation of a salt deposit?

Groundwater contains many different kinds of dissolved matter, including a gas called carbon dioxide. As this gas escapes from groundwater, an interesting thing happens. A solid matter separates from the groundwater. This matter is the mineral *calcite* [KAL-syt]. Calcite helps form the stalagmites and the stalactites found in caves. See Figure 2–2.

PROPERTIES OF MINERALS

What are the five basic properties of minerals?
Why is calcium in milk not a mineral?
Why is a shell from a snail not a mineral?
What are five physical properties of minerals?

Five basic properties

All minerals, regardless of where they are found, have five basic properties in common. A *property* is a trait belonging to a particular thing. The five basic properties of minerals are so important that they are used to tell whether a certain piece of matter is a mineral.

One property of a mineral is that it is a solid. A solid, as you have learned, has a definite volume and shape. The shape is determined by the arrangement of the atoms that make up the solid.

Figure 2–2. Calcite often precipitates from the groundwater that drips from the roof of a cave. The calcite may then form stalactites and stalagmites.

James Plala/Tom Stack & Associates

A mineral also has a definite chemical makeup. Some minerals are made up of only one kind of atom. Copper is a mineral that is made up entirely of copper atoms. Most minerals, however, are made up of two or more different kinds of atoms. *Quartz* [KWAW(UH)RTS], for example, is made up of silicon and oxygen atoms.

A third property of a mineral is that it has a definite shape. That is, a mineral is made up of atoms that are arranged in a neat and orderly way. This arrangement gives the mineral an internal pattern that is repeated over and over. This arrangement is called a *crystalline structure* [KRIHS-tuh-luhn STRUHK-chur]. The silicon and oxygen atoms in quartz form a *hexagonal* [hehk-SAG-uhn-uhl] crystalline structure. Figure 2–3 shows the crystalline structure of quartz. Every mineral has one of six different types of crystalline structures. You will be reading about these six crystalline structures later in this chapter. When a mineral melts or dissolves in a liquid, its atoms lose their internal pattern and therefore no longer exist as a mineral. Calcium in milk is not a mineral. That is because calcium has dissolved in a liquid and has lost its crystalline structure.

All minerals are formed in nature. Some minerals are called gems. *Gems* are precious stones used in making jewelry. Because there is a high demand for gems, scientists have learned to make some of them in the laboratory. For example, a diamond can be made in the laboratory. Even though it has the same chemical makeup and the same structure as a diamond found in nature, the laboratory-made diamond is not a mineral. That is because it is made by people and not by a natural process.

The fifth property of a mineral is that it is *inorganic* [IHN-AWR-GAN-ihk], or without life. A mineral is not formed from living things, and it does not contain matter that was once part of a living thing. A snail uses dissolved minerals from water to build its shell. But an empty snail shell is not a mineral. That is because the shell was once part of a living thing.

☐ **Salt, but not coal, is a mineral. Why is coal not a mineral?**

Figure 2–3. Crystals of pure quartz are pictured. What color are they?

Find Out More

Many gems are minerals. For example, a diamond is a gem. Using references, find out what other minerals are considered to be gems. Pearls, coral, and amber are gems. Are pearls, coral, and amber minerals? Why or why not?

Five physical properties

When you pick up a mineral, one of the first things you may notice is its color. *Color* is one physical property of a mineral. Earth scientists can sometimes identify a mineral by observing its color. For example, *malachite* [MAL-uh-KYT] is green. Sulfur is bright yellow. The mineral *azurite* [AZH-uh-RYT] is deep blue.

Not all minerals can be identified by color. That is sometimes because an impurity has changed the color of a mineral. Pure quartz is colorless. Depending on the impurity in it, quartz may be pink, yellow, violet, or gray-brown. Some minerals may change color because their surface tarnishes when it is exposed to air. What happens to silver when it is exposed to air?

Whether or not a mineral tarnishes, it leaves the same color *streak*. When a mineral is rubbed on a hard, white piece of unglazed porcelain, it leaves a powder on the porcelain. The color of the powder is called the streak. For many minerals, the streak is not the same as the color of the mineral itself. Hematite may be either red or black in color. But the streak of hematite is always reddish brown. The streak, then, is another physical property that can be used to identify a mineral.

Another physical property of a mineral is *hardness*. Hardness is the resistance to being scratched. Friedrich Mohs, a German scientist, devised a hardness scale in 1812 that lists ten well-known minerals. Each mineral is given a number from one to ten. The softest mineral—talc—is listed first. Its hardness is 1. The hardest mineral—diamond —is listed last. Diamond has a hardness of 10. Mohs' scale of hardness is shown in Figure 2–5.

Minerals have *luster*. Luster is the shine or the lack of shine of an object. Luster can be either *metallic* or *nonmetallic*. If a mineral shines like polished metal, it is said to have a metallic luster. If it does not shine like polished metal, then it is said to have a nonmetallic luster. Gold has a metallic luster. What kind of luster do diamonds have?

The ease with which and the way in which a mineral splits or separates along a flat surface is called *cleavage*

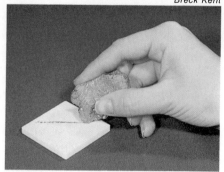

Figure 2–4. A mineral's streak is a physical property that can be used to help identify the mineral. In the picture, what is the color of the streak left by pyrite?

Find Out More

Nonmetallic lusters are given special names. Some of these names are *pearly, vitreous* [VIH-tree-uhs], *silky, waxy, greasy,* and *dull.* Use reference materials to find out the names of some minerals that have a pearly luster, a vitreous luster, and a silky luster. What does the term "vitreous" mean?

MOHS' SCALE OF HARDNESS

Mineral	Hardness	Simple test
Talc	1	Fingernail scratches it easily.
Gypsum	2	Fingernail scratches it.
Calcite	3	Copper penny just scratches it.
Fluorite	4	Steel nail file scratches it easily.
Apatite	5	Steel nail file scratches it.
Feldspar	6	It scratches glass plate easily.
Quartz	7	It scratches glass plate and steel nail file easily.
Topaz	8	It scratches quartz.
Corundum	9	It scratches topaz.
Diamond	10	It scratches corundum. It is the hardest of all minerals.

Figure 2–5. Using Mohs' scale of hardness, how can you tell if a mineral has a hardness of 1? A hardness of 8 or above?

[KLEE-vihj]. Some minerals split easily and always in the same direction. They are said to have *perfect cleavage.*

Not all minerals have perfect cleavage. Some minerals are said to *fracture,* or break up. *Spinel* [spuh-NEHL], copper, and *asbestos* [as-BEHS-tuhs] fracture. One type of fracture is called *conchoidal* [kahng-KOYD-uhl]. It looks like the inside surface of a shell. The mineral spinel has a conchoidal fracture. *Hackly* and *fibrous* are two other types of fractures. Copper has a hackly fracture. That is, copper tears and leaves little jagged points along the torn edge. These little jagged points can catch the skin of your hand when it brushes across these points. Asbestos fractures into silken threads much like some types of fiber. Asbestos, then, is said to have a fibrous fracture. See Figure 2–6.

Identifying minerals

The five physical properties of minerals—color, streak, hardness, luster, and cleavage—are used to identify different minerals. Some tests are done to find hardness and cleavage. You can use a copper penny, a steel nail file, and a small glass plate to determine the approximate hardness of a mineral. See Figure 2–5.

Cleavage can be found by gently tapping the mineral with a hammer. If the mineral breaks easily and always in the same direction, it is said to have *perfect cleavage.* The

Figure 2–6. Copper and asbestos are pictured. Copper has a hackly fracture. What type of fracture does asbestos have?

mineral *feldspar* [FEHL(D)-SPAHR] splits easily and in two different directions, at or near right angles. For these reasons, feldspar is said to have *good cleavage*. If a mineral does not split easily, it fractures or has *poor cleavage*.

The testing done to find the five physical properties of a mineral is often done at the site where the mineral is found. For this reason, these tests are called *field tests*. However, sometimes more information than color, streak, luster, hardness, and cleavage is needed to identify a mineral. In such cases, the mineral is taken to a laboratory where it can be identified by *chemical analysis* [uh-NAL-uh-suhs].

Chemical analysis is an examination of the matter that makes up a mineral. Many tests are made to find out what kinds of matter make up a mineral. Tests are also made to find out how much of each kind of matter makes up a mineral. For example, a chemical analysis of a mineral may show that oxygen and copper are in the mineral. Further analysis may show that there is twice as much oxygen as copper. If these findings are true, then scientists know that the mineral is *cuprite* [K(Y)OO-PRYT].

☐ **How does one do field testing for color, luster, and streak?**

Figure 2–7. Mica has a perfect basal cleavage. That is, it breaks to form thin, flat sheets.

CRYSTALLINE STRUCTURE

What is a crystal?
What are the six different kinds of crystalline structures in minerals?

Crystals and physical properties

As you may remember reading at the beginning of this chapter, quartz has a hexagonal crystalline structure. But just what is a crystalline structure? Why is it an important property of all minerals?

Halite is table salt. It is made up of sodium and chlorine atoms. These atoms form a solid and are arranged in a neat and orderly way. An object with such an arrangement of atoms is called a *crystal*. The way the atoms are arranged in a crystal is called the crystalline structure.

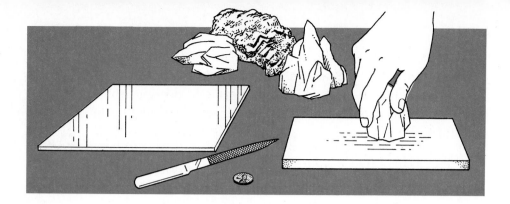

Investigate

How can you find the physical properties of minerals?

You will need

streak plate; copper penny; steel nail file; small glass plate; minerals such as talc, galena, halite, calcite, graphite, magnetite, muscovite, and quartz

Background

A mineralogist often identifies minerals in the field. To identify a mineral, the mineralogist uses five simple field tests. He or she tests for color, streak, hardness, luster, and cleavage. Sometimes it is necessary to use a laboratory test before a mineral can be identified. A chemical analysis is often used in the laboratory.

What to do

Test each sample for color, streak, hardness, luster, and cleavage. You have to look at a clean surface to see a mineral's color. Luster is also determined by means of observation. The streak is found by gently rubbing the mineral on a streak plate. A streak plate is a piece of unglazed porcelain.

Hardness is found by seeing if the mineral can be scratched with a fingernail, a copper penny, a glass plate, or a piece of steel such as a steel nail file. Hardness is also found by seeing if the mineral will scratch glass. The results of the hardness test should be compared with Mohs' scale of hardness.

Note how easily the mineral breaks to determine whether the cleavage is perfect, good, or poor. If the mineral will break when one uses only a small amount of force and if the broken part of the mineral retains a shape similar to the shape of its crystalline structure, it is said to have perfect cleavage. If the mineral will not break unless one uses a large amount of force, it has poor cleavage.

On a piece of paper make a chart with six columns. Label the columns "Mineral," "Color," "Streak," "Hardness," "Luster," and "Cleavage." Fill in each of these columns with the correct information about the minerals you are testing.

Now that you have done the investigation

■ Which minerals have a colorless streak? A white streak? A black streak?
■ Which mineral is the hardest? The softest?
■ Which of the minerals have a metallic luster? Which have a nonmetallic luster?
■ Which minerals have perfect cleavage? Which minerals have poor cleavage?

The crystalline structure of a mineral is important because it helps give the mineral two of its physical properties—hardness and cleavage. Hardness seems to depend upon the arrangement of the atoms in the mineral. Carbon atoms can arrange themselves in two possible ways. If carbon atoms are arranged in one way, one of the softest minerals is formed—graphite. If the carbon atoms arrange themselves in the other way, the hardest known mineral is formed—diamond. See Figure 2–8.

Cleavage also seems to depend on the crystalline structure. Some minerals, as you know, easily separate along a flat surface. The place where the mineral separates is the place of weak *bonds* among the atoms. Bonds hold the atoms of a mineral together. Minerals that fracture seem to have strong bonds.

The different shapes

Table salt has a certain type of crystalline structure. The sodium and chlorine atoms that make up table salt form a crystalline structure with the shape of a *cube*. No matter how big or how small a crystal of salt is, it will always be a cube. Look at some table salt under a hand

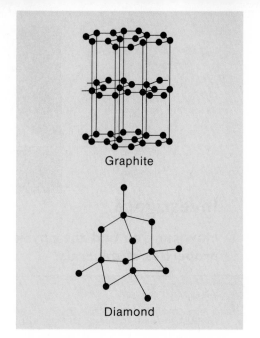

Graphite

Diamond

Figure 2–8. This illustration shows how carbon atoms are arranged in graphite and in diamond. How are the atoms arranged in graphite?

Jacqueline Durand

Do It Yourself

Grow some crystals

Place two or three charcoal briquettes in an aluminum pie pan. In an old cup, mix the following substances: 50 g of table salt, 60 ml of laundry bluing, 60 ml of water, and 15 ml of household ammonia. Stir the solution well and pour it over the briquettes. Be sure that parts of the briquettes are not covered by the solution.

Observe the briquettes and the solution pan every few hours over a period of two days. Keep accurate notes of the date, the time, the temperature of the room, and the humidity in the room. Also keep a record of the changes you observe in the briquettes. How long does it take for crystals to appear?

lens. You will see that each crystal of table salt is a cube. How would you describe the shape of a cube?

Figure 2–9 shows the six basic crystalline shapes. A crystal has three or four axes that intersect at the center of the crystal. An *axis* is an imaginary line extending from one side of the crystal to the other side. Notice that a cube has three axes that are equal in length. A tetragonal crystal has two horizontal axes equal in length. Its third axis has a different length.

Figure 2–9. Depending on its crystalline structure, a mineral is assigned to one of the six basic crystal systems. What are the names of these systems?

CRYSTAL SYSTEMS

System Name	Shape	Axes	Examples
Isometric (Cubic)	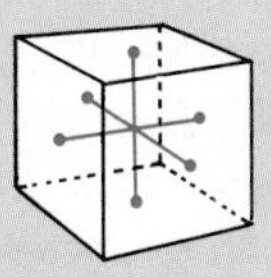	Three equal-length axes	Halite, Pyrite Magnetite 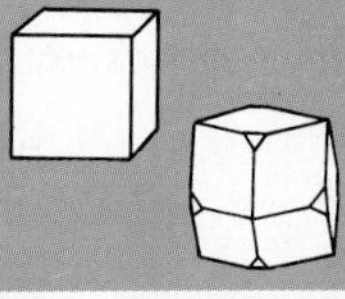
Tetragonal	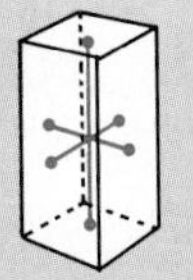	Two equal-length axes and a third axis that is either longer or shorter than the other two	Calomel Wulfenite 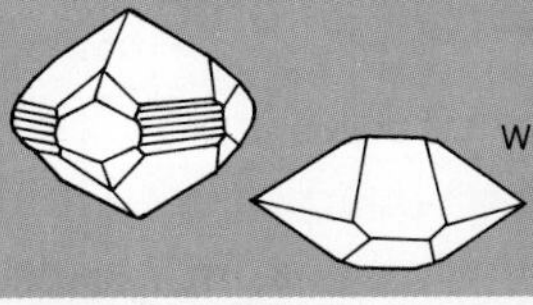
Hexagonal	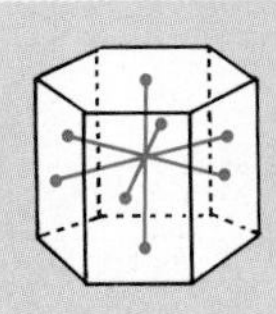	Three equal-length axes in the same plane and a fourth axis that is perpendicular to the plane of the other three	Pyromorphite Calcite, Dolomite 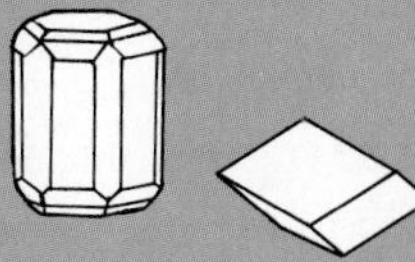
Orthorhombic	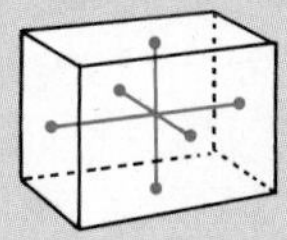	Three unequal axes	Topaz Sulfur 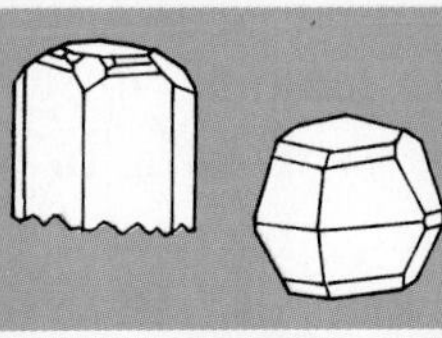
Monoclinic	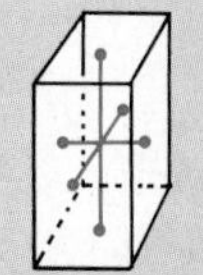	Three unequal axes	Mica Orthoclase 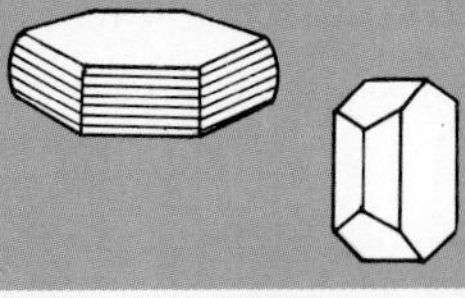
Triclinic	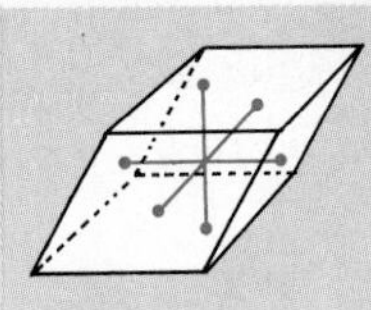	Three unequal axes	Turquoise Plagioclase 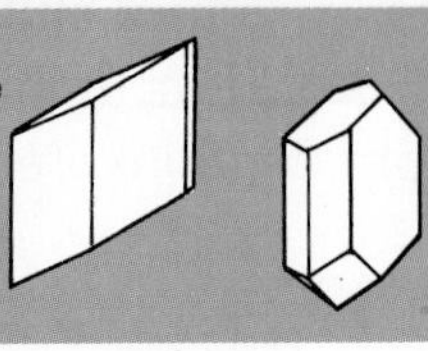

Some minerals form crystals that can be seen with the naked eye. But the crystals of most minerals are so small that they can be seen only with a microscope. A few minerals have crystals so small that they can be studied only with an electron microscope or with an X-ray machine. The mineral *kaolinite* [KAY-uh-luh-NYT] has unusually small crystals. Kaolinite is a white mineral that is used to make ceramics.

☐ **Can different kinds of minerals have the same crystalline shape?**

ORES

What is an ore?
What is a native metal?
What is a compound ore?
How are native metals formed?

Minerals as ores

You make use of metals such as aluminum, iron, and copper every day. Aluminum, iron, and copper come from *ores*. Ores are minerals that are mined or taken from the ground. There are two types of ores—*native metals* and *compound ores.*

Native metals are found as pure metal. Gold, silver, and copper sometimes occur as pure metals. Many native metals are formed as the heavier metals settle to the bottom of cooling magma. Pure metals are also formed by means of *weathering*, or the breaking apart of rocks into small pieces by wind, water, and ice.

Deposits of native metals formed by settling and weathering are called *placer* [PLAS-ur] *deposits*. Gold and silver are found in placer deposits. The gold rush to California in 1849 was caused by the discovery of rich placer deposits.

In some ores, a metal is joined with other substances, such as oxygen or sulfur. This type of ore is called a compound ore. For example, hematite is a compound ore. Hematite contains iron and oxygen.

Figure 2–10. Iron ore is being mined from this mountain in western Australia. How does the mining of iron ore change the land?

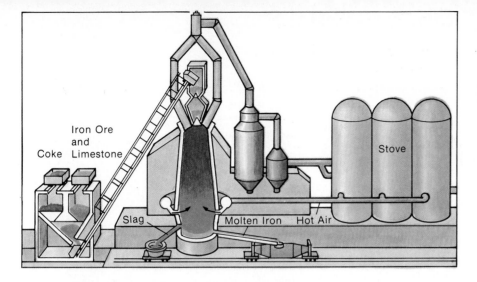

Figure 2–11. Iron ore must be refined before the iron in the ore can be used. What are the steps in refining iron ore?

Refining ores

Since it is usually the metal that is needed from the ore, most ores must be *refined,* or put into a pure state. During the refining process, the metal is separated from the other substances or impurities in the ore. For example, iron is separated from the oxygen in hematite.

To separate the iron from the oxygen, hematite is put into the top of a blast furnace along with *coke*—partially burned coal—and limestone. Inside the furnace is a roaring fire. This fire causes the coke to burn and the ore to melt. The burning coke attracts the oxygen from the iron ore.

As the melted iron ore moves toward the bottom of the furnace, the impurities in the ore combine with the limestone to form *slag.* Because the slag is lighter than the melted iron, it floats on top of the melted iron. The slag and the melted iron are then separated. See Figure 2–11.

Sometimes one metal is mixed with another metal or another substance. A mixture of two or more metals, or a mixture of a metal and another substance, is called an *alloy* [AL-oy]. An alloy of iron is *steel.* After iron ore is refined, metals such as chromium or nickel are added to the iron to make steel. Alloys of iron are important because they are stronger and more durable than pure iron.

☐ **Different ores are mined for different metals. What are some metals that come from ores? Are these ores native metals or compound ores?**

To Think About

An alloy now in common use is *duralumin.* What is the base metal in duralumin? With what other metals is the base metal mixed? Why is duralumin more useful than pure aluminum? You can find the answers to these questions in encyclopedias and other books.

COMMON USES OF SOME MINERALS

Mineral or Ore	Product	Uses
Bauxite	Aluminum	Door and window frames, screens, food containers, foil food wrap, kitchenware, alloys (for strong and lightweight metals), toothpaste tubes, appliances, insulation
Galena	Lead	Solder, plumbing, car batteries, radiation shielding, printers' type, rubber products, explosives, certain gasolines, glass, ceramics, insecticides, medicines
Gypsum	Plaster of Paris	Plaster for walls and casts, cement, wallboard, soil conditioner, paint, filters, insulation
Bornite	Copper	Electric wiring, jewelry and other ornaments, alloys (for brass and bronze hardware), plumbing, coins
Cinnabar	Mercury	Thermometers, silent electric switches, batteries (for small radios, cameras, and hearing aids)

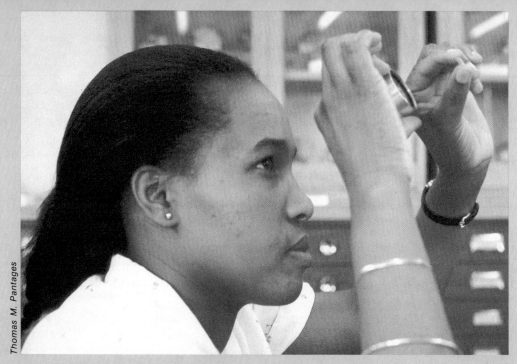

Minerals may be studied in many ways. This mineralogist is studying a sample of quartz by looking at it through a magnifier.

Careers

Mineralogist

A scientist who studies minerals is called a *mineralogist* [MIHN-uh-RAHL-uh-juhst]. A mineralogist gathers information about the physical and chemical properties of minerals. By knowing these properties, mineralogists can find industrial uses for the different minerals. For example, diamond is the hardest known mineral. Because of this one property, diamond is often used at the end of a drill. A diamond-tipped drill can quickly bore through hard metal.

Mineralogists work for mining companies. They help to locate places with rich ore deposits. Other mineralogists may work for mining companies that mine gems. They help to find the minerals that are valuable gems. They do this by studying the size, the color, and the clarity of the minerals. They also check for any flaws in the gems.

Mineralogists have a college degree. They are trained in geology, with mineralogy as a specialty. As geologists, they usually begin their careers by working in the field. They also fill jobs as research assistants.

For more information about the career of a mineralogist, you or a classmate may wish to write to the American Geological Institute, 5205 Leesburg Pike, Falls Church, VA 20041. Be sure to ask about the education and career opportunities of a mineralogist.

Reviewing and Extending

Summing Up

1. Some minerals are formed as magma cools.
2. Some minerals are formed by means of evaporation and precipitation.
3. A mineral is a solid with a definite chemical makeup.
4. The atoms that make up a mineral are arranged in a neat and orderly way.
5. Minerals are inorganic and are formed in nature.
6. The five physical properties of minerals are known as color, streak, hardness, luster, and cleavage.
7. Chemical analysis is a laboratory test used in identifying minerals.
8. Every mineral has a crystalline structure. There are six types of crystalline structures in minerals.
9. Minerals that are mined are called ores.
10. Two types of ores are native metals and compound ores.
11. Native metal deposits formed by weathering are called placer deposits.
12. A metal is separated from an ore by means of refining.

Checking Up

Vocabulary Write the numerals *1–10* on your paper. Each numbered phrase describes a term from the following list. On your paper, write the term next to the numeral of the phrase that describes it.

cube   crystal   hardness
color   element   inorganic
luster   mineral   compound ore
streak   cleavage   native metal

1. ore found as a metal joined with another substance
2. substance made up of one kind of atom
3. solid formed in nature that has a definite chemical makeup and structure and does not contain any remains of living things
4. shine or lack of shine
5. resistance to being scratched
6. color of the powder of a mineral
7. ease with which and way in which a mineral splits or separates along a flat surface
8. ore found as a pure metal
9. object with an orderly arrangement of atoms
10. type of crystalline structure

Knowledge and Understanding

Write the numerals *11–25* on your paper. Beside each numeral, write the word or words that best complete the sentence having that numeral.

11. Gold has a _____ luster.
12. Minerals that split easily and in the same direction are said to have perfect _____.
13. Precious stones, called _____, are used in making jewelry.
14. Hematite is an important ore of _____.
15. Diamond has a _____ luster.
16. Steel is an _____ of iron.
17. The softest mineral on Mohs' scale of hardness is _____.
18. Table salt is the mineral _____.
19. Conchoidal is a type of _____.
20. Table salt has _____ that are shaped like cubes.
21. The hardest known mineral is _____.
22. The mineral _____ is used to make plaster of paris.
23. Quartz is colorless, but an impurity may change the _____ of quartz to yellow or violet.
24. In the laboratory, a mineral can be identified by chemical _____, or an examination of the matter that makes up the mineral.
25. Desposits of native metals formed by the weathering of rocks are called _____ deposits.

Expressing Yourself

Write a paragraph as an answer to each of the following questions:

26. Why does the general public refer to petroleum as a mineral? Why, do you think, would an earth scientist say that petroleum is not a mineral?
27. Of the five physical properties of minerals, which one property would be considered the least reliable in identifying minerals? Explain your answer.

Doing More

1. Using photographs or drawings, make a bulletin-board display of minerals. Next to each mineral list its properties and its possible uses.
2. Try growing crystals of copper sulfate. Slowly add crystals of copper sulfate to hot water, stirring, until no more copper sulfate will dissolve. Pour the copper sulfate solution into a glass jar. Tie one end of a thread around a small copper sulfate crystal. Tie the other end to a pencil and hang the crystal from the top of the jar at a height of about 2.5 cm from the bottom of the jar. Set the jar in a warm place. Observe the jar each day for one week in order to observe any changes in the size and shape of the original crystal.

Many kinds of rock formations make up the solid part of the earth's crust. One can see spectacular rock formations in the Grand Canyon.

3 Rocks

If minerals can be thought of as the building blocks of the earth's lithosphere, then rocks can be looked upon as the products of these building blocks. A rock is usually made up of one or more minerals.

In general, rocks are combinations of two or three minerals. But some rocks are made up of only one mineral, and a few kinds of rocks do not contain any minerals. Coal is a rock, but coal is not made up of minerals. It is made up of the remains of plants.

The hard, solid part of the earth's crust is rock. At nearly all places on the earth, soil covers the rock in the crust. Trees and other plants grow in the soil. The soil itself contains bits of rock. As time passes, rocks break down and are mixed with the remains of plants and animals to form soil. Three kinds of rocks help make up soil. These are *igneous* [IHG-nee-uhs] *rocks, sedimentary* [SEHD-uh-MEHNT-uh-ree] *rocks,* and *metamorphic* [MEHT-uh-MAWR-fihk] *rocks.*

IGNEOUS ROCKS

*What is the difference between intrusive igneous
  rocks and extrusive igneous rocks?*
*Why do some igneous rocks have large crystals
  and others have no crystals?*
What is one difference between a dike and a sill?

Kinds of igneous rocks

Pockets of *molten,* or melted, rock material can be
found beneath the surface of the earth. This material is
known as *magma* [MAG-muh]. The earth's upper crust
presses down on the magma with a great deal of pressure.
Because of all this pressure, the magma is hot. It can
have a temperature of about 1 093°C (about 2,000°F).
Sometimes the hot magma rises to the surface through
cracks in the earth's crust. It can also come from a volcano.

When magma cools and hardens, igneous rocks are
formed. Igneous rocks can be formed on the surface of the
earth. They are formed on the surface when magma erupts
from a volcano or when it rises through cracks in the
earth's crust. Igneous rocks formed on the earth's surface
are known as *extrusive* [ihk-STROO-sihv] *igneous rocks.*
This kind of rock forms when the magma is *extruded,* or
forced out, onto the surface of the earth. Perlite is one kind
of extrusive igneous rock.

Many igneous rocks are formed beneath the surface of
the earth. Magma collects in pools known as *magma chambers* beneath the surface. Some of the magma in these
chambers may force its way through solid rock surrounding the chambers, but it never reaches the surface. The
magma in the solid rock and in the magma chambers cools
slowly. As it cools, the magma forms a kind of igneous
rock known as an *intrusive* [ihn-TROO-sihv] *igneous rock.*
Granite is one kind of intrusive igneous rock.

Magma deep within the earth cools slowly. It forms
igneous rocks with large crystals. Granite is formed in this
way. Granite is said to have a *coarse-grained texture.* The
crystals in granite are large and easily visible. Many of
them are as wide as thirteen millimeters (one-half inch).

To Think About

There are many sizes of rock
fragments that are formed
when pressure inside a volcano blasts the magma into
pieces. These fragments include dust, ash, cinders, and
bombs. Are dust, ash, cinders,
and bombs intrusive or extrusive igneous rocks? How
do you know?

49

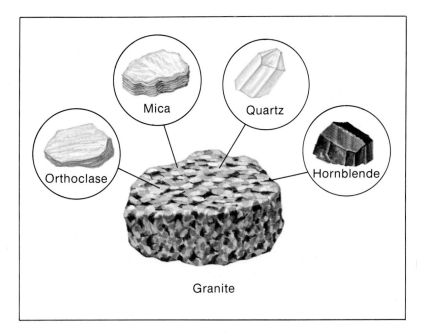

Figure 3–1. Most rocks are made up of several different minerals. What minerals make up granite?

To Think About

There are certain places in the seafloor where cracks form and are immediately filled in with lava. The lava hardens and forms extrusive igneous rock. Would this rock have large crystals or small crystals? Why?

On the surface or close to the surface of the earth, magma cools quickly. The magma then forms igneous rocks with small crystals. The crystals in basalt are small. Basalt has a *fine-grained texture*. The crystals can be seen only with a microscope.

Lava is magma that erupts from a volcano. Lava is thrown to the surface of the earth where it cools quickly. There is not enough time for crystals to form. *Obsidian* [uhb-SIHD-ee-uhn], an extrusive igneous rock, forms in this way. It has a *glassy texture*. Obsidian is as smooth as glass.

Sometimes the magma cools so quickly that steam and other gases bubble out of it as it hardens. When this happens, *pumice* [PUHM-uhs], another kind of igneous rock, is formed. This rock looks like a sponge with many tiny holes. Your dentist cleans your teeth with a powder containing pumice. Pumice is also found in soap used for scouring.

☐ **What type of texture would pumice have? Explain.**

Figure 3–2. Obsidian and pumice are pictured. Like certain minerals, obsidian has a conchoidal fracture. What type of texture does obsidian have? What type does pumice have?

Dr. E. R. Degginger

Breck Kent

50

Brent Jones

Do It Yourself

Observe the effect the rate of cooling has on crystal formation

Obtain two clean test tubes. In each test tube add 10 ml of water and 5 g of potassium nitrate. Put each test tube in a beaker of water. Using a hot plate, heat the beaker of water till all of the potassium nitrate in each test tube has dissolved. When the potassium nitrate has dissolved, use a test-tube holder to remove one test tube from the beaker of hot water. Immediately put this test tube in a beaker of ice water. Remove the second test tube from the beaker of hot water. Put this test tube in a test-tube rack. Allow this test tube to cool gradually to room temperature. How do the sizes of the crystals in each test tube compare? Which crystals represent those found in extrusive igneous rocks? Intrusive rocks?

Rock formations

Magma deep within the earth can harden into formations of igneous rock. The largest of such formations is known as a *batholith* [BATH-uh-LIHTH]. A batholith is a thick block of rock. It forms at a depth of several kilometers beneath the earth's surface. See Figure 3–3 on page 52. A batholith can be eighty kilometers (about fifty miles) wide and hundreds of kilometers long. A small batholith is known as a *stock*.

Batholiths form the cores of mountain ranges. In places where the overlying rock has been removed by erosion, thick batholiths are exposed at the surface. An example of an exposed batholith is the Idaho batholith, which has an exposed surface of 41 000 square kilometers (16,400 square miles). Another exposed batholith is the British Columbia batholith in Canada. Its exposed surface is 2 000 kilometers (1,240 miles) long and 290 kilometers (179.8 miles) wide.

Another rock formation is known as a *laccolith* [LAK-uh-LIHTH]. A laccolith is formed when magma pushes upward between layers of rock. The overlying rock is pushed

ROCK FORMATIONS

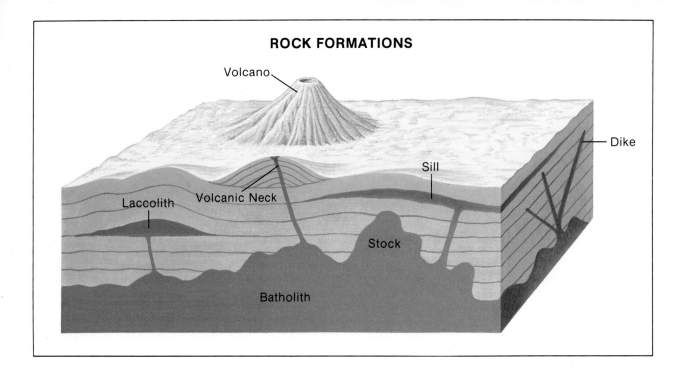

Volcano

Dike

Sill

Laccolith

Volcanic Neck

Stock

Batholith

up into an arch. The laccolith is the floor of the arch. It is a flat expanse of rock and is parallel to the layer of rock it rests on. A laccolith looks like the cap of a large mushroom. See Figure 3–3.

Sometimes magma pushes its way between layers of rock without causing the overlying rock to form an arch. When this happens, a *sill* is formed. A sill is a tablelike block of rock. See Figure 3–3. The Palisades, overlooking the Hudson River between New York and New Jersey, is an example of a sill.

Another igneous rock formation is a *dike*. A dike is formed when magma fills a crack in surrounding rock. The magma hardens and forms a dike. Dikes can be outgrowths of batholiths. See Figure 3–3.

The channel that feeds a volcano will sometimes fill with magma and then harden into igneous rock. The igneous rock that forms in the part of the channel found within the volcano itself is called a *volcanic neck*. A volcanic neck can be thought of as an extension of a dike. See Figure 3–4. A well-known volcanic neck is Ship Rock, in New Mexico.

Figure 3–3. Magma deep within the earth can harden into several different kinds of igneous-rock formations.

Figure 3–4. In time, the cone of a volcano may erode away, exposing the volcanic neck. The volcanic neck shown here is known as Ship Rock.

Breck Kent

SEDIMENTARY ROCKS

What is a sedimentary rock?
What are the three types of sedimentary rocks?
How is coal formed?

To Think About

Glaciers are able to carry boulders that weigh several tons. As the glaciers melt, the boulders are left behind as sediments. Why can glaciers carry such heavy loads?

Kinds of sedimentary rocks

Sedimentary rocks are formed when sediments harden and are packed together. But what are sediments? *Sediments* are bits of matter that settle to the bottom of lakes and oceans. Sediments are also deposited on land by water, wind, and glaciers.

There are three kinds of sediments—*clastic* [KLAS-tihk], *chemical*, and *organic*. There are also three kinds of sedimentary rocks. The names of the sedimentary rocks are taken from the names of the sediments. The three kinds of sedimentary rocks are clastic sedimentary rocks, chemically precipitated sedimentary rocks, and organic sedimentary rocks.

☐ **How do sedimentary rocks and igneous rocks differ?**

Clastic sediments

Clastic sediments are pieces of rock. They are formed mostly by weathering and erosion. Weathering and erosion break rocks into pieces of various sizes, and in this way, the sediments are formed. Examples of clastic sediments are gravels, sands, and mud.

Rivers carry clastic sediments to the ocean. As they are picked up and carried away by flowing streams, the sediments are "sorted." The first sediments to be deposited in the ocean are heavy boulders and pebbles. Later, the sands are deposited. Finally, the clays and silts are dropped into the ocean.

Over a long period of time, the different sediments on the seafloor harden and are compacted as sedimentary rocks. Pebbles and gravels form a sedimentary rock known as a *conglomerate* [kuhn-GLAHM-(uh-)ruht]. A sedimentary rock called *breccia* [BREHCH-(ee-)uh] is one kind of a

Figure 3–5. Breccia, a type of conglomerate, is pictured. It is made up of broken pieces of rock that have sharp edges. However, most conglomerates are made up of rounded pieces of rock.

Breck Kent

CLASTIC SEDIMENTS			
Sediment	Particle	Limiting grain size in millimeters	Rock
Gravel	Boulder	256	
	Cobble	64	Conglomerate
	Pebble	4	
Sand	Coarse sand	1	
	Medium sand	0.25	Sandstone
	Fine sand	0.125	
Mud	Silt	0.004	
	Clay	<0.004	Shale

Figure 3–6. The particles within different clastic sediments are listed. What is the smallest particle? What type of sedimentary rock do such particles form?

conglomerate. Broken pieces of rock are cemented to form breccia.

Sands harden together and form a rock called *sandstone*. Nearly all sandstones are made up of quartz grains, but some sandstones also contain large amounts of the mineral feldspar. *Arkose* [AHR-koHs] is a sandstone containing feldspar. Sandstones are a source of sand for making glass.

Silt and clay, when dry, are blown about by the wind. When wet, they form mud. As the mud cements, a sedimentary rock known as *shale* is formed. Because of the fine particles of silt and clay, shales are smooth. Shales have different colors. Shales with iron oxide in them are red, blue, green, or black. If they have organic matter in them, they are gray to black. If they have oil in them, they are often brown.

Figure 3–7. What mineral causes arkose to be pink? What causes shale to be gray or brown?

Do It Yourself

Make a conglomerate rock

Fill a 240 ml clear plastic cup about half full with water. Add coarse sand, silt, and pebbles to the water. Stir the mixture. Which sediments are found in the bottom layer in the cup? The top layer? Why? Pour off as much water as you can without pouring out any of the sediments. Add a small amount of portland cement to the sediments. (Under natural conditions, certain kinds of matter are present that act as natural cementing agents.) Allow the cement to dry. Cut away the plastic cup. How is this "rock" like a conglomerate rock?

Chemical sediments

As you know, some minerals can be dissolved in water. In some instances, a mineral is separated from the water by means of evaporation. When the water evaporates, the mineral is left. A mineral can also be separated from a solution as a *precipitate* [prih-SIHP-uht-uht]. A precipitate is a substance separated from a solution by means of a chemical change or a physical change. Minerals formed by evaporation or by precipitation are also known as chemical sediments.

The most common sedimentary rocks formed from chemical sediments are limestone, rock salt, and rock gypsum. Limestone is formed from the mineral calcite. At one time, the calcite was dissolved in water, but it was separated from the solution as a precipitate. Rock salt contains halite. Rock gypsum consists almost entirely of the mineral gypsum. Rock salt and rock gypsum are separated from water by evaporation.

Organic sediments

Organic sediments are the remains of once-living organisms. Shells and plants are the most common organic

Figure 3–8. The limestone in the picture was formed by the precipitation of calcite molecules.

Figure 3–9. The white cliffs of Dover, England, are pictured. Why do scientists say that these cliffs of chalk were at one time part of the seafloor?

sediments found. Coal is made mostly from the remains of once-living plants. Coal, then, is formed from organic sediments.

Many limestones are formed from chemical precipitates, but some limestones are made of organic sediments. Two types of organic limestone are *chalk* and *coquina* [KOH-kee-nuh]. Chalk is made up of the remains of microscopic marine organisms. It is soft, smooth, and fine-textured. Chalk makes up the famous White Cliffs of Dover, overlooking the English Channel.

Coquina is a sedimentary rock made up of shells. Many animals in the ocean take calcite from the water and use it to make their shells. Among these animals are clams, snails, oysters, and sea urchins. When these animals die, their shells are left behind on the seafloor. Eventually, waves break some of the large shells into small pieces. Over a period of time, the whole shells and the shell fragments harden together to form the sedimentary rock coquina.

☐ **How are coquina and coal alike?**

Coal

Millions of years ago swampy land covered much of the earth. Ferns and other plants grew during this time. As the plants died, they fell into the shallow water of the swamps and were covered by mud and by sand. With each passing year, more and more plants died.

Find Out More

Ripple marks are sometimes found in sedimentary rocks, especially sandstone. Mud cracks can be found in shale. Use references to find out what ripple marks show. How are mud cracks formed?

Peabody Museum of Natural History/Yale University

James H. Pickerell

Many layers of plants, sand, and mud accumulated. Pressure from overlying layers compressed the mud and the sand. The mud and sand eventually formed shale and sandstone. The layers of plants were also compressed. Because of this compression and because of chemical changes, the plants were formed into *coal*.

Plants are made up mostly of carbon, hydrogen, and oxygen. As the plants were compressed, much of the hydrogen and oxygen was squeezed out, leaving behind the carbon. As a result, coal has much carbon in it.

The plant layers under the least amount of pressure formed *peat*. Peat is a spongy material containing more moisture and less carbon than coal. As the layers of peat were compressed, more moisture and more hydrogen and oxygen were removed by chemical changes, leaving behind more carbon. This hard peat is called *lignite* [LIHG-NYT], or brown coal.

Lignite was also compressed to form *bituminous* [buh-T(Y)OO-muh-nuhs] *coal*, or soft coal. This coal is harder than lignite. It also has a higher carbon content than lignite. But bituminous coal was also compressed to form another type of coal—*anthracite* [AN(T)-thruh-SYT].

Anthracite is sometimes called hard coal. Because this coal was formed under the greatest pressure, it is the hardest of all coals. It also has the highest amount of carbon of all coals. That is because almost all of the moisture, hydrogen, and oxygen have been removed by chemical changes, leaving carbon behind.

☐ **Why is coal often called a fossil fuel?**

Figure 3–10. The coal that is mined today was formed from plants that lived millions of years ago. What did the area now being mined look like millions of years ago?

Find Out More

Peat is used for many different things. For example, in Ireland, peat is cut into blocks and dried. The dried peat is then burned as a fuel. What other uses does peat have?

Investigate

How can you test for calcium carbonate?

You will need

salt, chalk, shell fragment, marble, limestone, vinegar, hammer, steel file, paper towel, eye-dropper, small glass dish

Background

To find out if certain rocks and other kinds of matter contain calcium carbonate, or calcite, you can use the acid test. When a dilute acid is dropped on rocks or other substances containing calcium carbonate, you will notice fizzing or bubbling. The tiny bubbles are caused by carbon dioxide gas. Carbon dioxide gas is released by the calcium carbonate when it reacts with the dilute acid.

What to do

Place a shell fragment between two paper towels. Using a hammer, crush the shell. Put the pieces of crushed shell in a clean, dry glass dish. Add a few drops of vinegar to the crushed shell. Note what happens.

Scrape a piece of chalk with a steel file. Put the powdered chalk into a clean, dry glass dish. Add a few drops of vinegar. Note what happens.

Now put some salt into a clean, dry glass dish. Add a few drops of vinegar to the salt. Note what happens.

Scrape a piece of limestone with a steel file to form a mound of powder. Add a few drops of vinegar to the powdered limestone. Note what happens. Do the same for a piece of marble.

Now that you have done the investigation

- Which substances tested contain calcium carbonate?
- Which substances tested do not contain calcium carbonate?
- What is another name for calcium carbonate?
- Would you expect a stalactite to fizz and bubble when a dilute acid is dropped on it? Why or why not?

METAMORPHIC ROCKS

What is a metamorphic rock?
*How can rocks such as igneous and sedimentary
    rocks be changed into metamorphic rocks?*
What does the rock cycle show?

Agents of change

Metamorphic rocks are formed when existing rocks are changed into new kinds of rocks by heat and by pressure. Pressure within the earth causes rocks to undergo certain changes. This pressure may squeeze and bend rocks. Such pressure can also cause changes in the shapes of crystals. Heat from magma may cause further changes in the shapes and kinds of crystals present. Heat and pressure can also cause a change in the mineral makeup of the rock.

The change of a rock into a metamorphic rock is known as *metamorphism* [MET-uh-MAWR-FIZ-uhm]. The metamorphism of granite, an igneous rock, changes granite into a metamorphic rock known as *gneiss* [NYS]. The metamorphism of limestone, a sedimentary rock, changes limestone into a rock called *marble*. Metamorphism changes sandstone, a sedimentary rock, into a rock called *quartzite*. The quartz grains in quartzite are more tightly packed than in sandstone.

Shale, a sedimentary rock, may undergo different changes to form different metamorphic rocks. When shale is baked within the earth, it becomes a rock called *hornfels*. A metamorphic rock called *slate* is formed when shale undergoes changes caused by pressure. But a combination

Photri

Dr. E. R. Degginger

Figure 3–11. Through metamorphism, limestone is changed into marble and shale is changed into slate. The slate shown here is red because the shale from which it formed contained large amounts of iron oxide.

of heat and pressure changes shale into a rock called *schist* [SHIHST].

Igneous rocks and sedimentary rocks are changed into metamorphic rocks at depths of 12 to 16 kilometers (7.4 to 9.9 miles) beneath the surface of the earth. At this depth, the overlying beds exert a great deal of pressure on the rocks. The temperature can be as high as 800°C (1,472°F). Because of all this heat and pressure, the rocks are changed into metamorphic rocks.

☐ **Is it possible for a metamorphic rock to undergo metamorphism? Explain your answer.**

The rock cycle

Rock does not remain the same kind of rock forever. Rock near the surface is broken down into sediments. The sediments may come from either igneous, sedimentary, or metamorphic rock. They may later form into other sedimentary rock.

Rock may undergo other changes as well. For example, rock may be buried under igneous rock or under sediments. In time, the buried rock may be changed into metamorphic rock. This rock may also be melted by rising magma. The melted rock may then become igneous rock. Because each kind of rock may be changed into other kinds, scientists speak of a *rock cycle* [SY-kuhl]. See Figure 3–12. In the rock cycle, rocks are always undergoing changes.

Find Out More

Slate is a metamorphic rock formed from shale. Slate is widely used by the building industry. Use reference books to find out what slate can be used for.

Figure 3–12. The rock cycle is illustrated. It indicates various ways in which rocks form and undergo changes.

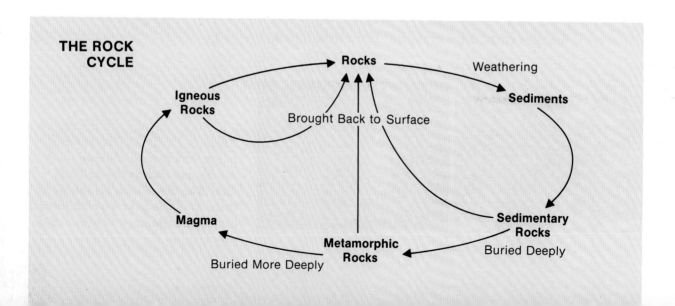

Geologists drill deep into the earth to obtain samples of rock layers. These samples are called core samples. The core samples are taken to a laboratory for further study.

Careers

Geologist

Geologists [jee-AHL-uh-juhsts] are people who study all aspects of the earth. They use rocks to help them study the origin of the earth. They try to answer such questions as, How old is the earth? What types of organisms once lived on the earth? How many years ago did these organisms appear on the earth?

Geologists also study the rocks and the minerals that make up the earth. They study the structure of the earth, too. Geologists are interested in finding out about the crust, the mantle, and the core of the earth.

To answer their questions about the earth, geologists must first gather data. They may need to drill deep into the earth to obtain samples of the material they need. They may also gather and study the material found near or on the surface of the earth. After the materials are

gathered, the geologists take them to a laboratory. There, they carry out many tests in order to analyze the materials. The results of the tests help to answer their questions.

Most geologists specialize in a certain field of geology. Petroleum geologists study rocks and features of the earth in an attempt to locate natural gas and oil deposits. Engineering geologists apply their knowledge about the structure of the earth to help solve problems arising in the building of roads and bridges. Those who study the earth's surface and the processes that change the surface are called *geomorphologists* [JEE-uh-mawr-FAHL-uh-juhsts].

If you would like more information about geologists, you or a classmate can write to the American Geological Institute, 5205 Leesburg Pike, Falls Church, VA 22041.

61

Reviewing and Extending

Summing Up

1. There are three kinds of rocks—igneous, sedimentary, and metamorphic.
2. Igneous rocks form when magma cools.
3. Igneous rocks are either extrusive or intrusive.
4. The rate of cooling determines whether igneous rocks have a coarse-grained texture, a fine-grained texture, or a glassy texture.
5. Sedimentary rocks form when sediments harden together.
6. Sedimentary rocks form from clastic sediments, from chemical sediments, and from organic sediments.
7. Coal is a sedimentary rock that has formed mostly from layers of compressed plants.
8. Metamorphic rocks form when existing rocks are changed into new kinds of rock by pressure and by heat.
9. The rock cycle shows the various ways in which rocks are always undergoing changes.

Checking Up

Vocabulary Write the numerals *1–11* on your paper. Each numbered phrase describes a term from the following list. On your paper, write the term next to the numeral of the phrase that describes it.

sills	igneous	laccoliths
dikes	organic	rock cycle
stocks	chemical	metamorphic
clastic	batholiths	sedimentary

1. large mushroom-shaped igneous rock formations
2. rock formed from an existing rock that has undergone changes brought about by pressure and heat
3. shows the various ways in which rocks are always undergoing changes
4. sediments such as shells and plants
5. rock formed from magma
6. large bodies of igneous rock that form the cores of mountain ranges
7. large masses of igneous rock that form when magma from batholiths cuts across rock layers and hardens
8. sediments such as boulders and gravel
9. small batholiths
10. rock formed from sediments
11. large tablelike blocks of igneous rock that are parallel to the layer of rock that they intrude

Knowledge and Understanding Write the numerals *12–24* on your paper. Beside each numeral, write the word or words that best complete the sentence having that numeral.

12. An igneous rock formation that can be thought of as an extension of a dike is a (*stock, batholith, volcanic neck*).

13. The metamorphic rock marble is formed when (*shale, quartzite, limestone*) undergoes changes caused by high pressures.
14. Granite is an igneous rock that has a (*glassy, fine-grained, coarse-grained*) texture.
15. Particles of sand harden together to form (*quartz, sandstone, a conglomerate*).
16. An example of an igneous rock is (*shale, obsidian, limestone*).
17. (*Peat, Lignite, Bituminous coal*) is also known as brown coal.
18. As a certain magma slowly cools, granite forms. But if the same magma cools so quickly that gases are bubbling out of it, then (*pumice, obsidian, rhyolite*) forms.
19. (*Extrusive, Intrusive, Glassy-textured*) igneous rocks form from magma that cools deep within the earth's crust.
20. The mineral (*calcite, quartz, sulfur*) is also known as a chemical sediment.
21. A rock that is important in making glass is (*limestone, sandstone, shale*).
22. Pebbles and gravel cement to form a sedimentary rock called a (*clay, grain, conglomerate*).
23. (*Shale, Slate, Schist*) is a sedimentary rock formed when moist silt and clay harden together.
24. Coquina is a limestone formed from (*gravel, shells, quartz*).

Expressing Yourself   Write a paragraph as an answer to each of the following questions:

25. Of the different types of coal, anthracite has the highest metamorphic rank. It is 92 to 98 percent carbon. Graphite is 100 percent carbon. Would it be possible for anthracite to undergo further metamorphism to form graphite? Explain.
26. Why may coal be an important source of energy in the future?

Doing More

1. Mix together some soil, sand, pebbles, and gravel. Make a sloping surface by propping up one end of a wide board with a box. Pile the mixture of soil, sand, pebbles, and gravel at the top of the incline. Slowly pour water onto the pile. As the water runs down the incline, it carries away some of the sediments. Which sediments are left at the top of the incline? At the bottom? Why?
2. Obtain two pieces of sandstone that are about the same size. Gently drop one piece of sandstone into a clear plastic cup that is about half full of water. Drop the other piece of sandstone into a clear plastic cup that is about half full of vinegar. Make sure the pieces of sandstone are completely covered by the liquid in each cup. Why do bubbles appear in the cup of water? Which cup has the most bubbles? Why does one cup have more bubbles than the other?

What surface features of the earth are shown in this photograph taken in Switzerland? How might these surface features affect the way people live?

4 Mapping the Earth

When you look at most globes of the earth, the earth is shown as a smooth, round ball. Some pictures of the earth taken from space also show the earth to be smooth and round. Most maps also show the earth to be smooth. But when you look around you, you can see that the earth is not smooth at all.

There are hills and valleys on the earth. Some areas have mountains so large that the peaks of the mountains are covered with snow year-round. Other areas have valleys so deep and narrow that they are canyons. Some areas of the earth are open plains, whereas other areas are the sites of large cities.

Hills, mountains, valleys, canyons, plains, and cities are some of the surface features found on the earth. Others are oceans, rivers, streams, and deltas. What surface features have you seen? As you study this chapter, you will learn how these surface features can be shown on a map of the earth.

SHAPE AND SIZE OF THE EARTH

> *How is the shape of the earth generally described?*
>
> *What evidence do we have that tells us about the shape of the earth?*
>
> *What do measurements of the earth tell us about its shape?*

Flat as a pancake?

The people in the cartoon are talking about an idea that was believed by many people until around 400 years ago. But things were different before then. For example, very little of the earth had been explored. No one had yet sailed all the way around the earth. People had no pictures taken from space that showed that the earth was round like a ball. Even today, as far as the eye can see, the earth still looks flat rather than round! It's not surprising, then, that long ago people believed the earth was flat.

Actually, the idea that the earth is round rather than flat is quite old. In the fourth century B.C., the Greek philosopher Aristotle observed that during an eclipse of the moon the shadow cast by the earth on the moon was

Figure 4–1. What are some other early ideas about the earth that have changed through the years?

circular. He concluded from this evidence that the earth must be round. A century later the Greek astronomer and geographer Eratosthenes made another observation. He noted that at noon on one day of the year the sun lit the entire bottom of a certain well. So, he reasoned that the sun was directly overhead. But at that same time, a tall object in a city about 925 kilometers (573.5 miles) north of the well cast a shadow. Because of this evidence, he concluded that the earth was round rather than flat. Eratosthenes used the angle of the shadow to help figure the circumference of the earth. Today we know that his calculations of the circumference of the earth around the poles were remarkably accurate!

Because of wars and a long drought in learning, known as the Dark Ages, these ideas were forgotten. It wasn't until seventeen centuries later that people gained new evidence that the earth was round. In 1519 Magellan, an explorer from Spain, set out with five ships to find a western passage to the Spice Islands (north of Australia). In 1522 one of Magellan's ships returned to Spain after having sailed around the earth. How did this show that the earth was round?

☐ **Of the evidences given in the text for the shape of the earth, which could be called indirect evidences and which could be called direct evidences? Why?**

Figure 4–2. How does this illustration help show that the earth is round?

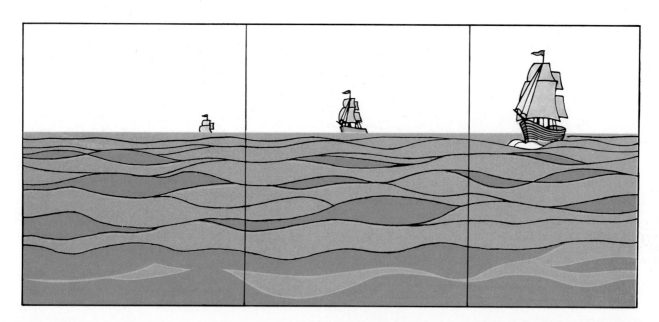

Big but not endless

The earth is generally said to have the shape of a *sphere* [sfih(uh)r], or ball. But it is not a perfect sphere. That is, the earth is not perfectly round. The circumference of the earth around the poles is 40 008.00 kilometers (24,804.96 miles). The circumference around the middle is 40 075.16 kilometers (24,846.60 miles). The difference of 67.16 kilometers (41.64 miles) gives the earth a slight bulge at the middle. But the fattest part of the earth is found along a line slightly south of the middle. Even though there is a bulge, why, do you think, does the earth still look like a perfect sphere?

Have you ever walked a kilometer or perhaps a mile? If so, that probably seemed like a long way. And when you think about the earth as having a circumference of thousands of kilometers or thousands of miles, it seems like the room on the surface of the earth is endless! But the fact that the size of the earth can be measured means that there is only a certain amount of room on the earth. That is, there are certain limits to our environment. And much like a large room that seems to get smaller as it becomes crowded, the limits of our environment seem to get smaller as more and more of the earth is explored and settled. In what ways do you think the limits of our environment seem to get smaller?

Figure 4–3. One way of dealing with the limits of our environment is to build taller and taller buildings. What are some advantages of this? Some disadvantages?

67

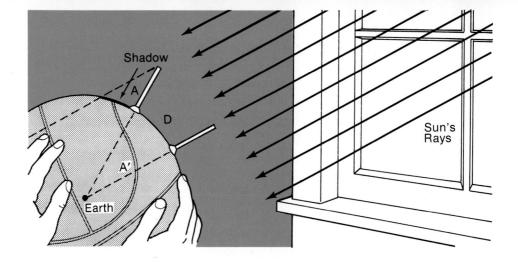

Investigate

How big is the earth?

You will need

string, protractor, chewing gum, flexible ruler, large ball (such as a basketball), 2 small sticks

Background

You can use the method of Eratosthenes to measure the circumference of a ball and of the earth. The method involves some basic rules of geometry.

What to do

With the help of the gum, place the sticks on the ball about 10 cm apart, as shown. Hold the ball close to a light so that no shadow is cast by one of the sticks (as in the well Eratosthenes knew about). Mark the end of the shadow from the other stick. Measure angle A between the stick casting the shadow and a line from the top of the stick to the end of the shadow. (Stretch a string from the top of the stick to the end of the shadow.)

Now measure distance D between the sticks along the ball. This distance represents an arc on the ball, and angle A is equal to the angle A' of this arc at the center of the ball. Since a complete circle has 360°, you can figure out the fraction of the circle represented by D by dividing 360° by angle A'. For example, if angle $A' = 30°$, then $360°/30° = 12$, or $D = \frac{1}{12}$ of the circumference of the ball.

Now calculate the circumference of the ball. For example, if $D = 10$ cm ($\frac{1}{12}$ of the circumference), the circumference would be 10 cm $\times$ 12, or 120 cm. You can check your calculations by wrapping a string once around the ball and measuring it.

Now check the earth's circumference. Chicago, Illinois, is about 11° (angle A') due north of Mobile, Alabama. The distance (D) between these cities is about 1 222 kilometers. Calculate the earth's circumference around the poles.

Now that you have done the investigation

■ How close were your calculations to actual measurements?
■ In using this method of calculation, what assumption did Eratosthenes have to make about the sun's rays? The earth?

LAND AND WATER AREAS OF THE EARTH

How much of the earth's surface is land? Water?
What is a continent, and what are some of the
  continents of the world?
What is a map projection, and what are the uses
  of some of the different map projections?

Early maps of the earth

Suppose someone were to ask you to make a map of the area in which you live. You would most likely put your house or neighborhood in the middle of your map. This was pretty much the case with early maps of the earth. Early Egyptians showed Egypt in the middle of their maps. Maps of the earth made by ancient Greeks showed Greece in the middle. Most of the first maps showed the Mediterranean Sea as the main body of water on the earth. And the land around this sea was the main part of the earth known at the time.

The 1400's and the 1500's saw much exploration of the earth, such as the travels of Columbus and Magellan.

Figure 4–4. What things does this Spanish map made around the year 1592 show?

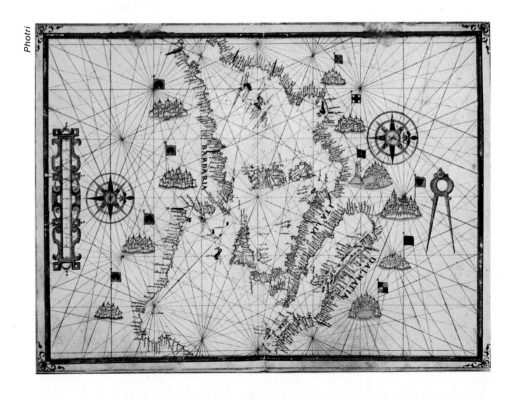

Maps of the earth became more complete and accurate. Even so, these maps showed more land area than water. Only after much more exploring and mapping was it realized that about 70 percent of the earth's surface is water and about 30 percent is land! Why do you think it is important to have complete and accurate maps of the earth?

There are many kinds of maps of the earth in use today. The kind that best shows the land and the water areas of the earth is a *globe*. Why, do you think, is this so?

Globe-trotting

It may be hard to believe that about 70 percent of the earth's surface is water and only about 30 percent is land. To gain a better idea of the size and location of the land and water areas of the earth, let's take a quick trip around the earth. Obtain a globe from home, school, or a library. Let's begin in the United States. The United States is a part of a large landmass called a *continent* [KAHNT-uhn-uhnt]. This particular continent is North America.

To the south and slightly east of North America is the continent of South America. East of South America, across the Atlantic Ocean, is the continent of Africa. Just north of Africa is Europe. To the east of Europe is Asia. Actually, Europe and Asia are part of the same landmass. But for various reasons they are often thought of as separate continents.

To the south and slightly east of Asia is the continent of Australia. At the South Pole is the continent of Antarctica. To get back to North America, you would have to cross the largest ocean, the Pacific Ocean. What other large bodies of water do you notice on the globe?

> ☐ **Which is the largest continent? The smallest? About how much of the earth's surface is covered by the Pacific Ocean alone?**

Finding certain places on the earth

In addition to finding a continent or an ocean on a globe, you might want to find a certain place on a continent or in an ocean. For ease and accuracy of finding places, a system of *grid lines* is used. Figure 4–5 shows these lines. Lines that run north and south are known as *meridians* [muh-RIHD-ee-uhnz]. Lines that run east and west are known as *parallels* [PAR-uh-LEHLZ]. Each grid line represents a circle or a half-circle around part of the earth. Grid lines are marked in degrees. This is because circles can easily be divided into degrees. The symbol for degrees is °.

The *prime meridian,* which runs through London, England, is marked 0°. The distance of any place east or west of the prime meridian is known as its *longitude* [LAHN-juh-T(Y)OOD]. This distance is measured in degrees.

The *equator* [ih-KWAYT-ur] is the parallel drawn halfway between the poles. The equator is marked 0°. The distance in degrees of any place north or south of the equator is known as its *latitude* [LAT-uh-T(Y)OOD]. Why, do you think, are both longitude and latitude needed in finding a place on a globe?

Map projections

Though a globe is the most complete and accurate map of the earth, it is not always possible or practical to use a globe. Why?

Figure 4–5. Using the grid lines on this map, how would you describe the location of the United States? Of some other places?

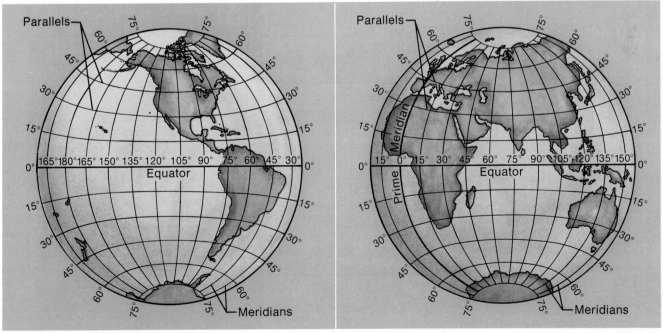

Jacqueline Durand

Do It Yourself

Locate some places on a globe

Obtain a globe that has parallels and meridians and shows major cities of the world. What city is near latitude 30° north and longitude 90° west? What city is located at latitude 60° north and longitude 30° east? What is the location of Montreal, Canada? Sydney, Australia?

By using a globe as a model, however, people can make different kinds of *map projections* [pruh-JEHK-shuhnz]. That is, the curved surface of a globe can be "projected" onto a flat map. Picture a transparent globe with a light in the center. Also picture the globe as having the meridians, the parallels, and the outline of the continents marked on it. When you turn the light on, these lines can be projected onto a flat surface, as shown in Figure 4–6.

Figure 4–6. This kind of map projection, known as a Mercator projection, was named after Gerhardus Mercator. He was a Flemish geographer who developed this kind of map in the 1500's.

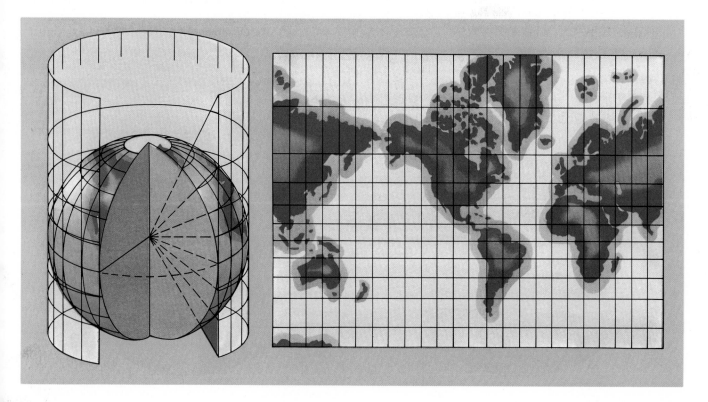

In mapmaking, however, the projection is made mathematically. The main problem with map projections is that there is always a certain amount of *distortion* [dihs-TAWR-shuhn], or error. Why might this be so?

There are many different map projections. Let's look at three basic kinds. In one kind, the projection is made as if a cylinder were wrapped around a globe, as shown in Figure 4–6. In this projection, the distance between the meridians is equal, and they do not meet at the poles as they do on a globe. Therefore, the areas near the poles are shown larger than they actually are. But, the shapes of features such as coastlines and islands are shown accurately. This kind of map is often used for world maps and navigation charts.

Another kind of map projection is made as if the surface of a globe were projected onto a flat surface that touched the globe at a single point. Polar regions are often mapped in this way, as shown in Figure 4–7. The shape and size of areas become more distorted as you move away from the center. However, a straight line between two points shows the shortest distance between these points. How might such a map be useful to people?

Figure 4–7. In what ways is this map projection different from the map projection in Figure 4–6?

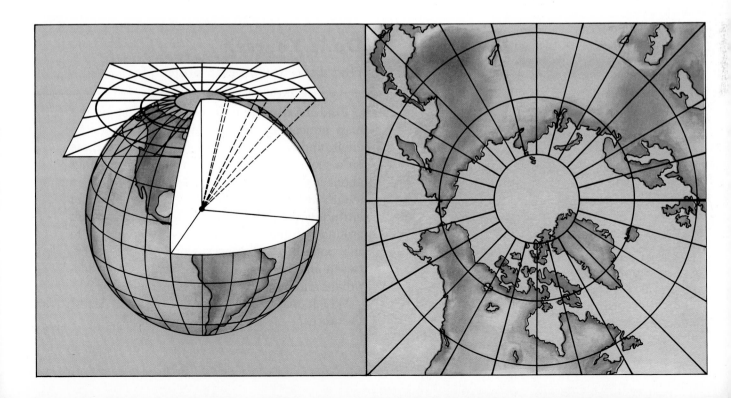

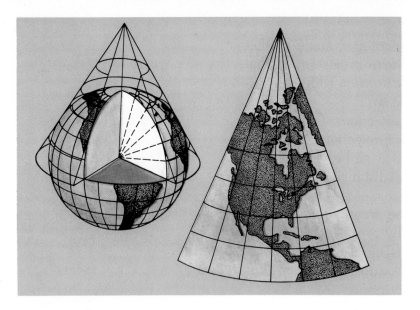

Figure 4–8. What areas of this map do you think are the most accurate? The least accurate?

The third basic kind of map projection is made as if a cone were laid over a globe and touched it along one of the parallels or other circles. Figure 4–8 shows this kind of projection. Shapes, distances, and directions are all shown fairly accurately for small areas. This kind of map is used in road maps and some weather maps. They are often used in a book of maps known as an atlas. When have you used any of the different maps that have been discussed?

Mary Elenz Tranter

Do It Yourself

Find distortion on map projections

Find the distortion of the features on various map projections by comparing meridians, parallels, and rectangles made by them with those on a globe. Keep in mind the following things about a globe: (1) All meridians are equal in length and meet at the poles; (2) all lines of latitude are parallel; (3) the length of parallels around the globe decreases from the equator to the poles; (4) distances along meridians between any two parallels are equal; (5) all meridians and parallels meet at right angles, or 90°.

Which maps show distorted shapes? Sizes? Distances?

MAPPING THE SURFACE FEATURES OF THE EARTH

*What are some of the things that make up the
   language of maps?*
*What do topographic maps show that other maps
   do not show?*

Language of maps

As you probably know, maps can be used to show many
things. Some maps are used to show boundaries between
states or countries. Some maps are used to show population or rainfall in an area. What are some other uses
of maps?

Although you might use different kinds of maps, all of
them have a certain language. That is, maps have certain
things to help you read them. For example, some maps
have grid lines marked in degrees, such as those you saw
on a globe. These lines help you find places on a map. Some
maps, such as road maps and city maps, have numbers
along the top and bottom and letters along the sides. The
numbers and letters mark off areas so that you can find
places listed in the *index* of the map.

In order to be accurate, a map must be drawn to *scale*.
The scale of a map shows how much of the earth's surface
is represented by a given measurement on the map. For
example, the scale on a map might read "1 centimeter = 10
kilometers." In other words, 1 centimeter on the map equals
10 kilometers on the earth. Sometimes the scale is shown
as a straight line with marks. The distance between each
mark represents a certain distance on the earth. Another
way of showing the scale is by using a fraction or a ratio.
The scale may be written as 1/1,000 or 1:1,000. This means
that a single unit of measurement on a map equals 1,000 of
the same units on the earth. What do you think is the
advantage of this kind of scale?

Color is also part of the language of many maps. Color
is often used to show the area of counties, states, or countries. Color is sometimes used to show the height of the

land at different places. How have you seen color used on a map?

Another part of the language of maps is *symbols* [SIHM-buhlz]. Symbols are used to show features on a map. Sometimes a symbol looks like the feature it shows. For example, a small picnic table is often used to show a rest area along a road. Sometimes a symbol does not look like the feature it shows. For example, cities are often shown by circles or dots. A *legend* [LEHJ-uhnd] found on a map explains what the symbols mean. What other map symbols have you seen?

□ **What is the advantage of using symbols on a map?**

Figure 4–9. What parts of the language of maps can you find on this map?

Do It Yourself

Study the language of a road map or a city map

Obtain a state road map or a city street map from a gas station. Practice locating places by using the index and the grid lines. What scale is used on the map? How is color used? What are some of the symbols used on the map? What other information is given on the map?

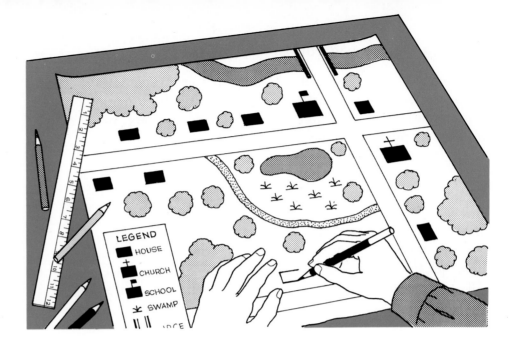

Investigate

What things can you show by making your own map?

You will need

ruler, regular pencil, large piece of paper, colored pencils

Background

One of the best ways to learn about the uses of maps and the language of maps is to make a map of your own. Perhaps you'd like to make a map of your neighborhood, a favorite area outside your neighborhood, or an area you've never been to. In any case, you may be surprised at how much you can find out about your environment by making a map.

What to do

First, decide upon the size of the area you want to show and a convenient unit of measurement. For a small area, meters may be con-

venient. For larger areas, city blocks might be used. This will help determine the scale you will use on your map. A large-scale map shows more detail than a small-scale map.

Next, draw to scale the features or symbols for the features that you want to show. Be sure to include the symbols and any other important information in your legend.

Now that you have done the investigation

■ Do you think a person using your map could find places, distances, and directions accurately? Try finding out.

■ What symbols did you use that are not found on other maps?

■ What did you learn about your environment from your map?

■ How is your map a model of your environment?

Mapping the ups and downs

Whenever you use a globe to study the earth, you are using a model of the earth. A model is usually a small representation of something. Model trains and cars are other examples of models. What other models are you familiar with?

In order to study an area of land in detail, a model of that area is sometimes used. This model is called a *relief* [rih-LEEF] *map*. A relief map is not flat like other maps. It actually has mountains, valleys, ridges, or other surface features that appear on an area of land. Surface features make up the *topography* [tuh-PAHG-ruh-fee] of an area. Any map, such as a relief map, that shows surface features is known as a *topographic* [TAHP-uh-GRAF-ihk] *map*.

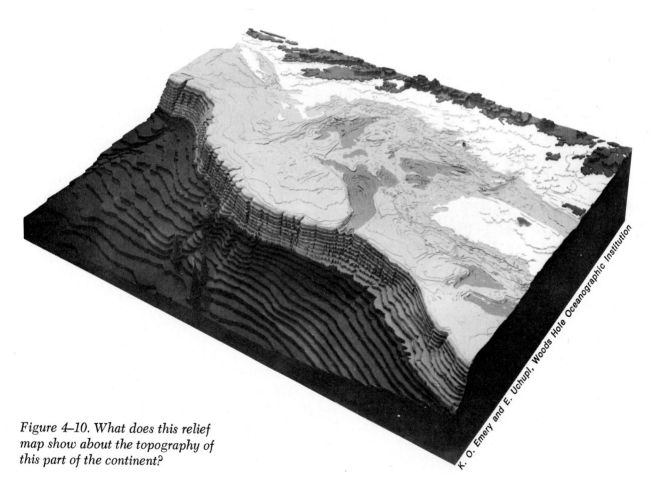

Figure 4–10. What does this relief map show about the topography of this part of the continent?

K. O. Emery and E. Uchupi, Woods Hole Oceanographic Institution

An important part of the topography of an area is the *elevation* [EHL-uh-VAY-shuhn], or height, of the land. A topographic map that shows exact elevation is the *contour* [KAHN-TU(UH)R] *map*. Though a contour map shows elevation, a contour map is flat. Elevation is shown by a series of lines, as pictured in Figure 4–11. When would it be helpful to know the exact elevation of an area of land?

Still another kind of map is used to show topography. It is called a *physical* [FIHZ-ih-kuhl] *map*. A physical map is also flat. It shows what an area of land might look like from an airplane. Surface features are shown by different shadings of color. Darker shadings of brown and green might show mountains. Lighter shadings of brown might show deserts. When have you seen or used such a map?

Figure 4–11. In what ways are the contour map (left) and the physical map (right) alike? In what ways are they different?

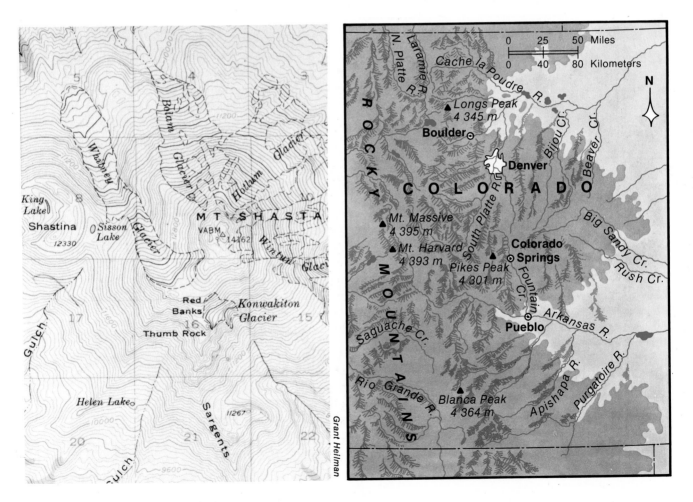

Grant Hellman

79

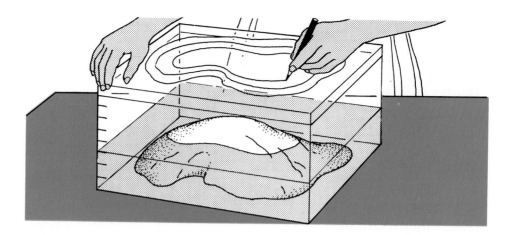

Investigate

How can you make a relief map and a contour map?

You will need

food coloring, grease pencil, modeling clay, clear plastic box with lid

Background

Each line on a contour map represents a certain elevation above or below sea level, which is marked 0 (zero). The number spacing between contour lines is known as the contour interval. In making a contour map, a mapmaker would obtain information about elevation from a surveyor. In making your contour map, you will make and use a relief map (sometimes called a relief model).

What to do

Using the modeling clay, make a relief map in the bottom of the plastic box. You can make up your own relief map, or you can make a map of an area that you know about if you wish. If your clay is water-soluble, coat your relief map with shellac or waterproof paint after it dries.

Place evenly spaced marks up one side of the plastic box. The spacing between these marks represents the contour interval. A contour interval that represents 6 m is convenient for an area of medium-sized peaks and valleys. You can choose any contour interval that is convenient for your relief map.

Add colored water up to the bottom mark. Place the lid on the plastic box. Viewing from directly above, trace the waterline of the relief map onto the lid. Add more water until the level reaches the next mark and trace the waterline. Repeat this until the relief map is covered with water. Then pour off the water. Examine your contour map to identify the features on the relief map.

Now that you have done the investigation

- What do contour lines that are close together show? Lines that are far apart?
- What do contour lines that run parallel show?
- How can you tell the highest areas?
- What features can you note by the pattern of the lines?
- When might contour lines intersect or cross?

TOPOGRAPHY AND PEOPLE

What are some of the surface features that can be found across the United States?
How do some of these surface features affect people?

Importance of topography

Think of some of the things you like to do outdoors. Do you like to play ball? To ski or sled? To swim? To ice-skate? No matter what you like to do outdoors, you most likely depend upon the topography of the area. For example, to play ball, you need a flat area. To ski or sled, you need a hill. To swim or ice-skate, you need a body of water. What other things do you do that depend upon the topography of the area?

Topography is also important to people in other ways. For example, areas that are mostly flat with good soil are suitable for farming. Many mountain and forest areas offer scenic beauty and recreation. Cities and industries are often located near rivers or lakes. Why might this be so?

Hans Schmied/ZEFA

Figure 4–12. How would you describe the topography shown in this picture? How is the topography important to these people?

As you study the topography of an area, you learn about more than just the surface features. You also become aware of the many ways that people depend upon their environment. Perhaps the best way to illustrate this is to take a closer look at the topography of some of the different areas across the United States. The next sections will help you do this.

☐ **How might studying the topography of an area help you understand people from that area?**

The East

A physical map of the United States is provided on pages 84–85. This map shows the surface features covered in the following sections of this chapter.

The map shows the East as having many miles of jagged coastline. This provides many good harbors for fishing and shipping. Many of the coastal cities, such as New York and Baltimore, have grown not only because of their coastal location but because of their location near a river as well. Why is being located near a river important for a city or town?

Figure 4–13. What surface features of the East are shown in this picture?

Grant Heilman

As you move inland from the coast, the land is hilly and rocky. This land provides pasture for dairy cows. The fertile river valleys of the East are used to grow many kinds of crops. Most of the cranberries eaten in the United States are grown in the swampy lowlands of the Cape Cod area. The East also has many mountains and lakes. How might these surface features be important to people?

The South

A large part of the South is made up of an area known as the Coastal Plain. This flat, sometimes rolling land and favorable weather make farming, such as cotton and tobacco farming, important to this area.

There are many rivers in the South. They provide transportation, recreation, and electric power. The South also has many beautiful mountain and forest areas. What cities in the South are important because of their location on a river or a coast?

Find Out More

An interesting feature known as a fall line occurs where the Coastal Plain meets the Piedmont Plateau in the South. In fact, a number of large cities have developed along this fall line. Using reference books, find out what a fall line is, which cities these are, and why they have developed along the fall line.

Grant Heilman

Figure 4–14. What surface feature of the South is shown here?

83

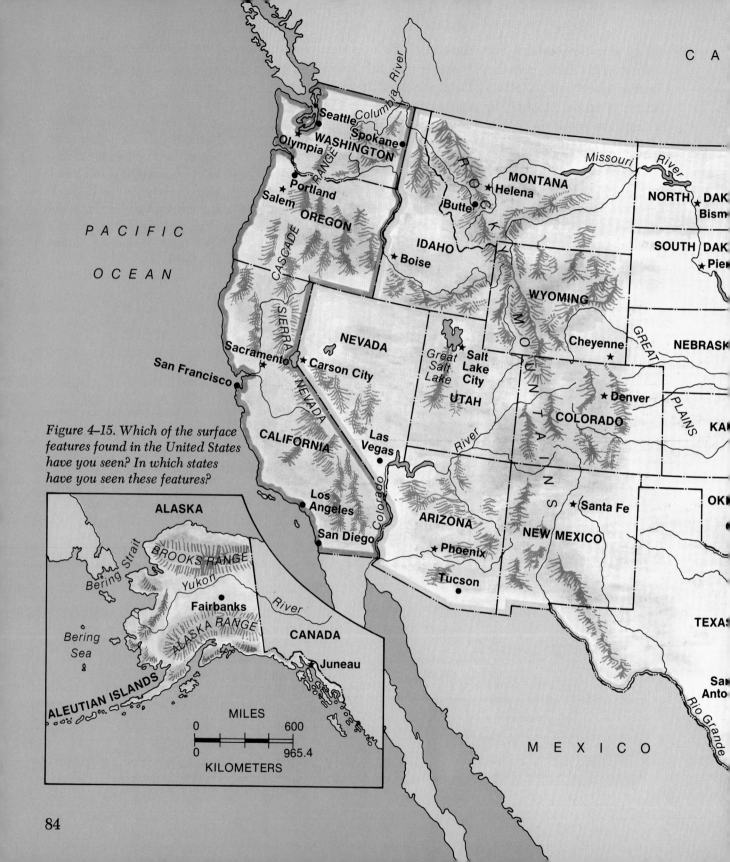

C A

PACIFIC

OCEAN

Columbia River

Seattle
Spokane
WASHINGTON
Olympia
Portland
Salem
OREGON

CASCADE RANGE

MONTANA
Helena
Butte
IDAHO
Boise

Missouri River

ROCKY

R

O

C

K

WYOMING

Cheyenne

NORTH DAK
Bism

SOUTH DAK
Pie

NEBRASK

GREAT

Sacramento
San Francisco

Carson City
NEVADA

SIERRA NEVADA

CALIFORNIA

Las
Vegas

Los
Angeles

San Diego

Colorado

NEVADA

Great
Salt
Lake

Salt
Lake
City

UTAH

River

ARIZONA

Phoenix

Tucson

M

O

U

N

T

A

I

N

S

Denver

COLORADO

Santa Fe

NEW MEXICO

PLAINS

KA

Denver

OK

Figure 4–15. Which of the surface
features found in the United States
have you seen? In which states
have you seen these features?

ALASKA

BROOKS RANGE

Yukon

Bering Strait

Fairbanks

ALASKA RANGE

River

CANADA

Juneau

Bering
Sea

ALEUTIAN ISLANDS

MILES

0   600

0   965.4

KILOMETERS

TEXAS

Sa
Anto

Rio Grande

M E X I C O

84

MILES
0   200   400

0   322   644
KILOMETERS

CANADA

Duluth

MINNESOTA

St. Paul

Minneapolis

Lake Superior

WISCONSIN

MICHIGAN

Lake Huron

Lake Michigan

Milwaukee

Madison

Lansing

Detroit

Chicago

Gary

Toledo

Lake Erie

Lake Ontario

St. Lawrence River

MAINE

Augusta

Montpelier

Portland

VERMONT

NEW HAMPSHIRE

Concord

MASSACHUSETTS

Boston   Cape Cod

Albany

NEW YORK

MOUNTAINS

Hartford

Providence

RHODE ISLAND

CONNECTICUT

IOWA

Des Moines

ILLINOIS

Springfield

INDIANA

Indianapolis

Columbus

OHIO

Cleveland

Pittsburgh   Harrisburg

PENNSYLVANIA

Philadelphia

New York

Trenton

NEW JERSEY

Baltimore

Washington

D.C.

Dover

DELAWARE

Annapolis

MARYLAND

Chesapeake

Bay

ATLANTIC

OCEAN

Lincoln

MISSOURI

Topeka

Jefferson City

St. Louis

River

Frankfort

Louisville

Ohio

KENTUCKY

WEST

VIRGINIA

Charleston

Richmond

VIRGINIA

Winston-Salem

Raleigh

NORTH CAROLINA

APPALACHIAN

Tulsa

OKLAHOMA

ARKANSAS

Memphis

Nashville

TENNESSEE

Tennessee River

Mississippi River

SOUTH

CAROLINA

Columbia

COASTAL PLAIN

Little Rock

MISSISSIPPI

Birmingham

ALABAMA

Jackson

Montgomery

Atlanta

GEORGIA

Dallas

Austin

LOUISIANA

Baton Rouge

New Orleans

Tallahassee

FLORIDA

Houston

Gulf of Mexico

Miami

UNITED STATES

- West Coast States
- Western States
- Midwestern States
- Southern States
- Eastern States

HAWAIIAN ISLANDS

KAUAI

NIIHAU

OAHU

Honolulu

MOLOKAI

LANAI

MAUI

KAHOOLAWE

Hilo

MILES
0   100

0   161
KILOMETERS

HAWAII

Figure 4–16. A cargo of coal is being unloaded from an ore boat in Duluth, Minnesota. Which of the Great Lakes borders this midwestern city?

The Midwest

The topography of the Midwest can generally be described as flat. This feature and good soil make it the largest farming area in the country. What are some of the main crops of the Midwest?

The Great Lakes are another important surface feature of the Midwest. The lakes provide easy access to coal and iron-ore deposits around the Great Lakes area. Many industrial cities have developed around the Great Lakes. Among these cities are Chicago, Detroit, Cleveland, Toledo, Milwaukee, Duluth, and Gary. What are some of the things made in these cities?

The West

The western part of the United States has a large area known as the Great Plains. The eastern part of the Great Plains is flat and suitable for farming. The western part of the Great Plains is drier and hillier. Much of this land is used for grazing cattle and sheep.

To the west of the Great Plains lie the Rocky Mountains. The lower slopes and valleys offer pastureland for sheep and cattle. The mountains themselves contain deposits of various minerals. Thus, mining is one of the important activities in this area.

The Rockies are famous for their beautiful waterfalls, canyons, and ski slopes. Campers and hikers find much to see and do in the Rocky Mountain area.

South of the Great Plains and the Rockies lies an area with a wide variety of topographic features. Rugged mountains, wide plateaus, and dry deserts are found side by side. Farming and ranching are carried out with the help of irrigation. The fast-moving rivers provide not only electric power for people but beautiful scenery as well. Many deep canyons, such as the Grand Canyon in Arizona, have been carved by these rivers.

Taurus

Figure 4–17. Fast-moving rivers help provide electric power for people in the West. Such a river is the Colorado River. The Glen Canyon Dam on the Colorado River in northern Arizona can produce up to 900 000 kilowatts of electricity.

The West Coast

Along the West Coast area of the United States you can find mountains, valleys, and deserts. The valleys provide very productive farmland. The forests of the mountain areas produce much lumber. What kinds of industries would you expect to find in these mountain areas?

The entire coastline is dotted with small fishing villages and large fishing and shipping ports. Canning and processing of fish are important activities. The southern part of the West Coast is a good resort area because of its sandy beaches, beautiful desert, and favorable weather.

Of course, there are many more surface features across the United States than were covered in this chapter. But each of these examples helps illustrate the importance of topography to people.

☐ **What surface features are you familiar with that were not covered in this chapter?**

Find Out More

Using atlases or reference books, find out what surface features are found in Alaska, Hawaii, and other parts of the world. How do these surface features affect people?

Figure 4–18. What surface features of the West Coast are shown in this picture?

Camerique

These cartographers are deciding which style and size of type to use on a map. What things do you think they need to consider in making their decision?

Careers

Cartographer

Any map is basically a means of communicating facts and ideas. This may sound easy. But making a map involves many steps and many people. First, information is gathered by observing, plotting, and photographing the land and by studying other maps. This may be done by an expert such as an explorer, a geologist, a geographer, or a historian. A surveyor may take measurements of distances, directions, and elevations.

Next, professional *cartographers* [kahr-TAHG-ruh-furz], or mapmakers, plan, design, and draw the map. A cartographer analyzes and organizes the information that best shows the theme of the map. A cartographer designs such things as size of type, width of lines, and use of color. A cartographer also puts information into symbols and draws in features so that they are attractive and easily understood. The use of mathematics and of special drafting tools and machines is important in mapmaking. The finished map is then sent to a printing company, where copies of the map are made.

Career opportunities related to cartography can be found in many organizations. These include the armed forces, the United States Geological Survey, the National Ocean Survey, other government agencies, and many commercial and private organizations, such as publishers.

Reviewing and Extending

Summing Up

1. The earth is generally said to have the shape of a sphere. However, it is not a perfect sphere.
2. There are limits to the boundaries of our environment.
3. About 70 percent of the earth's surface is water, and about 30 percent is land.
4. A globe is the kind of map that best shows the land and water areas of the earth.
5. A map projection is a way of showing the curved surface of the earth on a flat surface.
6. Things that make up the language of maps include grid lines, scale, color, and symbols.
7. Topographic maps are used to show the surface features of the earth.
8. The various surface features across the United States affect people and other living things in many ways.

Checking Up

Vocabulary Write the numerals *1–14* on your paper. Each numbered phrase describes a term from the following list. On your paper, write the term next to the numeral of the phrase that describes it.

globe	continent	parallels
scale	elevation	distortion
legend	grid line	map projection
equator	longitude	prime meridian
latitude	meridians	topographic map

1. shows the curved surface of the earth on a flat surface
2. landmass
3. shows how much of the earth is represented by a given measurement on a map
4. error on a map projection
5. grid lines that run north and south
6. shows the surface features of the earth
7. height of the land
8. line on a map that represents a circle or a half-circle around part of the earth and is marked in degrees
9. distance in degrees of any place north or south of the equator
10. part of a map that explains some of the information on the map
11. grid line that runs through London, England, and is marked 0°
12. grid lines that run east and west
13. distance in degrees of any place east or west of the prime meridian
14. grid line that runs halfway between the poles and is marked 0°

Knowledge and Understanding   Write the numerals *15–22* on your paper. Beside each numeral, write the word or words that best complete the sentence having that numeral.

15. The earth's circumference at the poles is (*greater than, less than, about the same as*) the circumference at the equator.
16. Early maps of the earth showed that the amount of land was (*more than, less than, the same as*) the amount of water on the earth.
17. The language of most maps includes (*grid lines, the International Date Line, projection*).
18. A globe best represents the earth because of its (*size, shape, use of symbols*).
19. Error on a map projection may occur in (*size, shape, both size and shape*).

20. A topographic map that is most like the surface of the earth is the (*relief map, contour map, physical map*).
21. If the scale on a map was written as 1:680, then 3 centimeters on this map would be equal to (*226.7, 680, 2 040*) centimeters on the earth.
22. You would be at the North Pole if no matter which way you faced, you were facing (*north, south, west*).

Expressing Yourself   Write a paragraph as an answer to each of the following questions:

23. Why did Eratosthenes conclude that the earth was round rather than flat?
24. How are a relief map and a contour map alike? How do they differ?

Doing More

1. Obtain a globe, some string, and a Mercator projection wall map. This kind of map is used for ship navigation charts because the distance between two points represents a direct compass route. Stretch the string between two points far apart on the map. Now stretch the string between the same two points on a globe. This represents a route known as a great-circle route. Disregarding length (because of different scales on your globe and map), how do the routes differ? Which route do you think an air navigator would use? Why? Find out what rhumb lines are and how a ship's navigator uses them in plotting a course on a navigation chart.

2. Make a survey of the different surface features in your area. Set up a chart so that you can answer the following questions about each surface feature you find: Is it natural or was it made by people? If natural, has it been changed by people? If so, how? How does each surface feature affect people? Include photographs of each surface feature if you can.

Pros and Cons

Depletion of the Earth's Resources— How Will We Meet the Challenge?

The resources of the earth have been called the life-blood of people. Without resources, people could not survive. Early in history, there seemed to be little or no need to control the extraction or the use of resources. They seemed to be plentiful. There were fewer people then. And the effects upon the environment seemed slight.

Today, the situation is much different. The discovery of more and more uses for various resources and the increase in population have increased the demand for resources. As you know, the supply of many resources is limited. Some have already become scarce. And the extraction and the use of many resources have had ill effects upon the environment.

Clearly, the tendency to use resources with little or no regard for depletion and environmental effects must end. There are many unanswered questions regarding this issue. For example: How are we going to cope with depletion of resources? Whose responsibility should this be? There is much controversy over such questions.

There are many examples that illustrate these questions

The Wilderness Society claimed that the Trans-Alaska Pipeline does not meet federal environmental safeguards. But Congress allowed the pipeline to be built. What is more important, avoiding harm to the environment or transporting oil to places where it is needed?

and raise even more. Let's look at the case of some of the ores that are in danger of being depleted in the near future. These ores include those of gold, lead, tin, zinc, and copper. Some people believe that we should begin restricting the use of metals from such ores now. If we do this, what restrictions should be placed on the use of these metals? Who should be responsible for making such decisions—governments, industries, or individuals?

Some people believe we should increase our efforts to find new deposits of these ores. But how much of our environment are we willing to dig up or scrape away to get to these ores? The use of substitutes for metals from these ores has been suggested and tried. But this sometimes puts a strain on other resources. The use of plastics as substitutes, for example, cuts into the supply of coal and oil, from which they are made. Recycling has proved fairly successful in conserving certain materials such as iron, aluminum, and glass. But how much of the cost or inconvenience are people willing to bear in collecting, returning, and processing these materials?

When all the fossil fuels and nuclear fuels are used up, there will be no more. But the sun will continue to shine. Should solar energy devices be improved and promoted now, or should they become important only after all the fossil fuels and nuclear fuels are gone?

The case of energy resources also raises some unanswered questions. Our supply of oil and natural gas is being depleted quite fast. Oil and gas from new deposits must be transported from farther and farther away. For example, deposits of oil in northern Alaska must be moved along a pipeline that stretches the length of the state. Some people say this pipeline will upset the ecological balance of a large area. Some disagree. The question is, how many unknown risks are we willing to take to get the oil and natural gas we need? It appears that the supply of coal will last a long time. But many of the new deposits must be strip-mined. How much more of the landscape are we willing to scrape away to get at these deposits?

What are your opinions regarding some of these questions? What other questions can you think of regarding depletion of resources? What are some possible solutions?

Investigate On Your Own

1. Collect different rocks from around your home or school. Use books on rocks and minerals to try to identify your rocks. Prepare a display of your rocks. Make a label for each rock, telling what kind of rock you think it is and whether the rock is igneous, sedimentary, or metamorphic. Also tell whether it is a mineral, is made up of several minerals, or is a nonmineral.

2. A property of matter that scientists often find useful in studying the makeup of the earth is density. Density is usually expressed as grams per cubic centimeter, or $D = g/cm^3$. For example, suppose you had a rock sample that had a mass of 27 g. And when you placed this rock in a graduated cylinder of water, it displaced 10 cm^3 of water. Its density would be 27 $g/10\ cm^3$ or 2.7 g/cm^3.

Get a balance and a graduated cylinder. Using the formula above, determine the density of various things around you, including some liquids. Which of the materials around you has a density of 1.0 g/cm^3? (Most graduated cylinders show milliliters rather than cubic centimeters. For most purposes, a milliliter can be considered equal to a cubic centimeter.)

Read On Your Own

Asimov, Isaac, *How Did We Find Out About Coal?* New York: Walker & Company, 1980.

This book tells the story of coal. An account of how coal is formed and of the history of coal as a fuel is given in an interesting way.

Berger, Melvin, *The New Earth Book: Our Changing Planet.* New York: Thomas Y. Crowell, 1980.

With the use of diagrams, this book discusses the layers of the solid earth along with the layers of the earth's atmosphere. A discussion about the earth's hydrosphere and the earth's biosphere can also be found in this book.

Branley, Franklyn M., *Pieces of Another World: The Story of Moon Rocks.* New York: Thomas Y. Crowell, 1972.

An interesting account of how rocks from the moon were collected by astronaut Neil Armstrong, commander of *Apollo 11,* is given in this book. The book also explains the tests that were performed on the moon rocks and the results of those tests.

Doty, Roy, *Where Are You Going with That Coal?* Garden City, New York: Doubleday & Company, 1977.

A brief history on the use of coal is presented. The importance of coal in future years is discussed in this book.

Fodor, R.V., *What Does a Geologist Do?* New York: Dodd, Mead & Company, 1977.

Geologists study the earth. They study the rocks, the mountains, the oceans, and the other parts of the earth. This book describes activities of geologists and some of the latest ideas they have developed.

Shedenhelm, W.R.C., *The Young Rockhound's Handbook.* New York: G.P. Putnam's Sons, 1978.

Start your own mineral collection. This book explains what to look for when collecting minerals and where the best specimens of different minerals can be found.

Thackray, John, *The Earth and Its Wonders.* New York: Larousse & Co., Inc., 1980.

Many colorful illustrations and photographs supplement this general book of earth science.

Zim, Herbert S., *Quartz.* New York: William Morrow and Company, 1981.

Quartz is the most common mineral. But what is quartz? This book explains what quartz is and how it is formed. The section on how quartz is used in clocks, radios, television sets, and electronic devices is interesting. One section discusses the use of quartz in making glass.

Unit 2
THE EARTH IN SPACE

Your study of earth science is not complete unless you view the earth as a part of its whole environment. When you do this, you study the earth as a planet moving in space. The earth is a planet in the *solar system.*

The earth is a small part of a large whole, the *universe* [YOO-nuh-vurs]. The earth is subject to the same laws that govern all the other bodies in the universe. The surface of the earth and its makeup have been caused by interaction with the solar system to which it belongs.

In this unit you will look at space as the earth's true environment. Learning about other planets in space in relation to the earth will help you to understand many things about the earth itself.

NASA; Lick Observatory;
California Institute of Technology

NASA

Much has been learned about the solar system since the time of Copernicus. For example, this painting shows how the Voyager spacecraft flew behind the rings of Saturn in order to photograph the rings.

5   The Solar System

Almost 500 years ago a Polish *astronomer* [uh-STRAHN-uh-mur], Nicolaus Copernicus, studied the skies and came to an important conclusion. Copernicus' conclusion changed people's view of the universe.

During the time of Copernicus, scientists looked upon the earth as the center of the universe. In their view, the sun, the moon, and the stars traveled around the earth. Copernicus thought differently. He made a model that placed the sun at the center of the solar system. In this system, the earth revolved around the sun, not the sun around the earth. It took a long time before people were convinced that Copernicus was right.

In recent years, space explorations have contributed much new information about the solar system. In this chapter, you will find out what has been learned as a result of these explorations.

PLANETS IN THE SOLAR SYSTEM

*Which object in the solar system has the greatest
   amount of matter, or mass?*
*Which object in the solar system exerts the
   greatest gravitational force?*
In what two ways do the planets move?
What is the meaning of the abbreviation "AU"?
Which planet is the farthest from the sun?

Mass and planetary motion

The solar system is made up of the sun and the objects
in orbit around the sun. The word "solar" comes from the
Latin word for "sun." Among the objects in orbit around
the sun are the earth, the eight other planets, and their
moons. The asteroids and the comets are also part of the
solar system.

In the days of Copernicus, astronomers knew of only
six planets. They had observed Mercury, Venus, Earth,
Mars, Jupiter, and Saturn. Astronomers know now that
there are nine planets in the solar system. Besides the six
known in the early days, there are also Uranus, Neptune,
and Pluto in orbit around the sun.

The solar system is huge. It is made up of a large
amount of matter, or *mass*. In order to get an idea of how
the mass in the solar system is distributed, you may want
to use a model. A basket of apples might serve as your
model of the solar system. Suppose you have one hundred
apples in a basket. These apples stand for the whole mass
of the solar system.

Now, imagine that you take an apple out of the basket
and cut it into 7 equal pieces. You will have to put 6 of
these pieces back into the basket. The 99 apples left in the
basket plus the extra 6 pieces of the cut-up apple stand for
the mass of the sun! You can see from this that 99.86
percent of the mass of the solar system is in the sun.

How is the rest of the mass of the solar system distributed? You have one small piece of the apple to represent
the mass of the rest of the solar system. What if you cut

(*Text continues on page 102.*)

FACTS ABOUT THE PLANETS

	Mass Earth = 1	Diameter (km)	Average Distance from Sun (millions of km)	Distance from Sun (AU)*	Known Moons
Mercury	.055	4 990	57.9	0.387	0
Venus	.815	12 180	108.2	0.723	0
Earth	1	12 756	149.6	1	1
Mars	.108	6 790	227.9	1.524	2
Jupiter	317.9	142 700	778.3	5.203	16
Saturn	95.2	120 000	1 424.6	9.539	17
Uranus	14.6	50 800	2 866.9	19.18	5
Neptune	17.2	48 600	4 486.1	30.06	2
Pluto	.00017	3 000	5 890.0	39.44	1

*See page 105.
**See page 103.
***See page 104.

Sun

Mercury   Venus   Earth   Mars

Jupiter

Figure 5–1. Use this chart to compare the planets.

Period of Revolution** (earth days/earth years)	Period of Rotation*** earth time	Main Components of Atmosphere	Temperature
88 da	59 da	Helium, hydrogen, oxygen	−193° to 342°C
224.7 da	243 da (reverse motion)	Carbon dioxide, argon, helium, nitrogen, oxygen, sulfur dioxide, water vapor	455°C
365.25 da	23 hr 56 min 4 sec	Nitrogen, oxygen, argon, small amount of other gases	−88.29° to 58°C
687 da	24 hr 37 min 23 sec	Carbon dioxide, nitrogen, argon, oxygen, water vapor	−124° to −31°C
11.86 yr	9 hr 55 min	Hydrogen, helium, methane, ammonia, carbon monoxide, ethane, water vapor	−149°C
29.46 yr	10 hr 14 min	Hydrogen, helium, methane, ammonia, ethane	−176°C
84.01 yr	16–28 hr (reverse motion)	Hydrogen, helium, methane	−216°C
164.8 yr	18–20 hr	Hydrogen, helium, methane, ethane	−218°C
247.7 yr	6 da 9 hr	Methane and perhaps neon or argon	About −150°C

Saturn

Uranus

Neptune

Pluto

that piece in ten equal parts. Seven of the ten parts represent the mass of Jupiter, the largest planet. Two of the ten parts represent the mass of Saturn, the second-largest planet. This accounts for nine of the ten parts of the last piece of the apple.

Most of the one remaining part of the apple can be divided among the other seven planets. If you cut the remaining part in half, the two halves stand for Neptune and Uranus. The small bits of the apple left on the knife represent Earth, Venus, Mars, Mercury, and Pluto. Only microscopic particles of the apple would make up the moons, the comets, the *asteroids* [AS-tuh-ROYDZ], and the *meteoroids* [MEET-ee-uh-ROYDZ] that are also a part of the solar system.

Mass is important in understanding motion in the solar system. The planets have been in motion since the beginning of the solar system. Everything that has mass

Brent Jones

Do It Yourself

Show how to keep an object in orbit

Run a piece of string (1 m long) through a glass tube (15 cm long). Tie 1 end of the string through a 1-holed rubber stopper. The rubber stopper represents a planet in orbit. Tie the other end of the string through about 10 iron washers. The washers will represent the sun's pull of gravity. Hold the glass tube in your hand and whirl the rubber stopper above your head. This motion represents the revolution of the planet around the sun. Control the speed of the rubber stopper so that the pull of the washers is just enough to keep the orbit of the rubber stopper from changing. Repeat this activity several times. Each time, change 1 factor—either the size of the orbit, the number of washers, or the rate of rotation. How can you change the effect of the force of gravity in this activity? What else affects the orbit of the rubber stopper?

exerts a force on the things around it. This force is known as *gravity* [GRAV-uht-ee].

The gravity of the sun is greater than that of the planets because its mass is greater. The sun's gravity pulls on the planets and the other bodies in the solar system. The balance between a planet's own motion and the pull of the sun's gravity makes a planet move in orbit around the sun. You will learn more about motion in the solar system in your study of Chapter 8, "The Earth in Motion."

☐ **Do you think the sun's gravity exerts as much force on Pluto as it does on Mercury? Why or why not?**

Rotation and revolution

If you could watch the planets from beyond the solar system, you would see that all the planets travel around the sun. The planets *revolve,* or go around the sun in an orbit. This motion is referred to as *revolution* [REHV-uh-LOO-shuhn]. The revolution of the planets is one of their two basic motions.

All the planets revolve in the same direction. The inner planets (Mercury, Venus, Earth, and Mars) seem to race

Find Out More

Astronomers have figured out many ways to determine the mass of the earth. Look in reference books to find out what some of these ways are.

Figure 5–2. The size of the sun is actually much larger in proportion to the size of the planets than is shown in this illustration. Why can't the true proportions be shown?

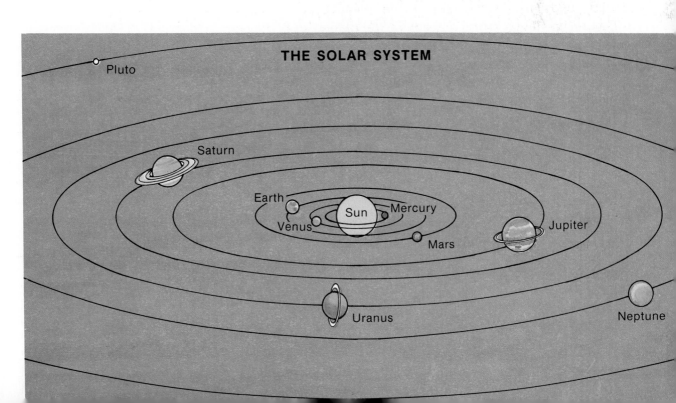

THE SOLAR SYSTEM

around the sun. The earth travels around the sun at a speed of 110 079 kilometers (68,400 miles) per hour. The earth goes around the sun once each year. A year is measured by the earth's revolution around the sun.

The outer planets (Jupiter, Saturn, Uranus, Neptune, and Pluto) seem to move more slowly in their orbit. Neptune travels at the rate of 19 698 kilometers (12,240 miles) per hour. It takes Neptune 164.8 earth years to go around the sun. Jupiter makes the trip in 11.86 earth years.

Like the earth, all the planets *rotate*, or turn around on their *axis*. An axis is considered to be an imaginary straight line about which a planet rotates. An axis is a line through the middle of a planet from its north pole to its south pole. As a planet rotates, the side facing the sun has daytime. The side facing away from the sun has nighttime. The length of one day is measured by one complete rotation.

The axis of each of the planets tilts at a certain angle. Sometimes the northern hemisphere of a planet tilts toward the sun. At other times the southern hemisphere tilts toward the sun. This tilting causes a difference in the heating of the northern and the southern hemispheres of the planets as they orbit the sun. The tilting brings about the different seasons of the year on the planets.

The overall temperature on each of the planets depends on the planet's distance from the sun and on the planet's rotation. A planet that is close to the sun receives more heat than one farther away. A planet with a fast rotation has short days and nights. A planet with short days and nights has a more even temperature than it would have if the days and nights were long.

The temperature of a planet also depends on the planet's *atmosphere* [AT-muh-SFIH(UH)R], or layer of gases surrounding the planet. Heavy clouds in the atmosphere can keep some of the sun's heat from reaching the surface of the planet. On the other hand, an atmosphere also prevents heat from escaping from the surface.

☐ **Why, do you think, is the temperature higher on Venus than on Mercury, which is closer to the sun than Venus?**

To Think About

Figure 5–1 gives you the *period,* or length of time required, for each planet to rotate on its axis and the period for each planet to revolve around the sun. Why do these periods vary from planet to planet? What similarities do you see?

Distances in the solar system

You may know that the earth is about 150 million kilometers (93 million miles) from the sun. Most of the other planets are much farther from the sun than that. Such distances are sometimes hard to work with when they are stated in kilometers or in miles. To solve this, astronomers have made up a unit of measurement based on the distance from the earth to the sun. They call the distance from the earth to the sun 1 *astronomical unit,* or 1 *AU.* They then use astronomical units to measure distances in the solar system.

For example, Jupiter is 778.3 million kilometers (466.9 million miles) from the sun. This distance is a little more than 5 times the distance from the earth to the sun. Therefore Jupiter is 5.2 AU from the sun. Pluto, the farthest planet, is 39.4 AU from the sun. See Figure 5–1 to find out the distance from the sun to each of the other planets in kilometers and in astronomical units.

☐ **How many astronomical units would you have to travel to go across the solar system? (For help, use Figure 5–1.)**

Brent Jones

Do It Yourself

Make your own unit of measurement

Astronomers use astronomical units to measure distances in space. You can make your own unit of measurement for measuring large distances. Measure the length of your classroom by unrolling a ball of string from wall to wall. Have two students at either end hold the string tight. Cut the string the exact length of the classroom. Call the string a "classroom unit."

Measure the playground in meters. Next use the classroom unit to measure the playground. How many classroom units are in the playground? How does this exercise help you to understand the advantages of using the astronomical unit?

Origin of the solar system

You know that the sun's gravity keeps the planets revolving around the sun. But you may still be wondering how all this motion got started. A look at one theory of how our solar system may have begun will help you understand motion in the solar system.

This theory states that about 5 billion years ago, the solar system may have begun from a huge cloud of gas and dust rotating in space. This cloud was made up of matter left over from stars that had died out or exploded long before.

At first the cloud rotated slowly. Then matter was pulled toward the center of the cloud by the force of the matter's own gravity. The cloud began to get smaller and to rotate faster. The faster rotation caused the cloud to become flat like a pancake. As the center of the cloud slowly became more dense, the center heated up, forming the sun. The sun continued to rotate, just as the cloud had done before. In fact, the sun is still rotating.

The outer rim of the original cloud kept revolving around the forming sun. The outer rim had been set in motion by the rotation of the original cloud. The rim was revolving fast enough to keep it from being pulled in by the sun's gravity.

California Institute of Technology

Figure 5–3. The Crab Nebula, shown in this picture, was formed when a massive star exploded. Scientists think that a similar explosion may have helped in forming our solar system.

The matter slowly grew dense in some areas of the outer rim. As the rim became more dense, it broke apart and formed the planets and the rest of the solar system. In the process of pulling more matter to itself, each planet began its own rotation. Each planet also continued to revolve around the sun, just as the cloud rim had done before.

☐ **Why, do you think, is it likely that many stars may have a solar system?**

MAKEUP OF THE PLANETS

How do astronomers find out about the makeup of the planets?
Why do the inner planets have a different structure from the outer planets?
What is the origin of the energy that Jupiter and Saturn give off?

Probing the interior of the planets

You may wonder how astronomers find out about the makeup of a planet without ever setting foot on its surface. One way they do this is to consider how temperature changes the way in which different chemicals react with one another. They know how the reactions of elements such as oxygen, hydrogen, carbon, and nitrogen are changed by temperature. This has helped scientists to understand how these elements react in differents parts of the solar system.

On the warm inner planets close to the sun, carbon often joins with oxygen to form the gas *carbon dioxide* [KAHR-buhn dy-AHK-syd] (CO_2). On the cold outer planets, carbon joins with hydrogen to form the gas *methane* [MEHTH-ayn] (CH_4). Closer to the sun, nitrogen does not unite with other elements. It is free in the form of nitrogen gas (N_2). Farther from the sun, nitrogen joins with hydrogen to form the gas ammonia (NH_3). As the temperature drops to a low reading, carbon and nitrogen tend to join with hydrogen.

Hydrogen is the most common element in the solar system. It makes up 77 percent of the sun. It also makes up almost all of Jupiter and Saturn and more than half of Uranus and Neptune. Figure 5–4 shows which planets have hydrogen in their atmosphere. Helium, the second most abundant element in the sun, is believed to be an important part of Jupiter and Saturn.

The inner planets

You may notice in Figure 5–4 that the inner planets seem to have similar structures. The innermost part, the *core,* is made up of metals in liquid form. (In the case of the earth, the core is in two parts. The *inner core* is thought to be solid, and the *outer core* is believed to be liquid.) Surrounding the core, the inner planets have a rocky layer made up mostly of oxygen, silicon, and iron. This middle layer is called the *mantle.* Three of the inner planets—Venus, Earth, and Mars—have another rocky layer, the *crust,* covering the mantle. Mercury does not have a crust.

The inner planets are made of dense matter. When the sun first began to form, more-dense matter was drawn in

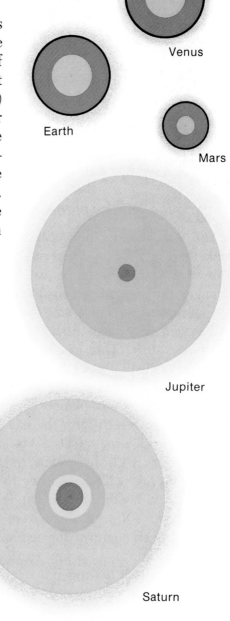

Figure 5–4. Which planets seem to be alike? Which planet is most like the earth?

STRUCTURES AND ATMOSPHERES OF THE PLANETS

Mercury

Venus

Earth

Mars

Metallic Hydrogen

Liquid Hydrogen

Metallic Core

Rocky Core or Mantle

Crustal Rock

Ice

Hydrogen, Helium, Methane, Ammonia, Carbon Monoxide, Water Vapor*

Hydrogen, Helium, Methane*

Nitrogen, Oxygen, Water Vapor*

Carbon Dioxide*

* Gaseous

Uranus

Jupiter

Saturn

Not Sufficiently Known

Pluto

Neptune

closer to the sun. Less-dense matter remained in the outer part of the solar system.

The outer planets

The large outer planets—Jupiter, Saturn, Uranus, and Neptune—have a rocky core. The makeup of their core is similar to that of the mantle of the inner planets. You may notice in Figure 5–4 that Jupiter's core is small. When Jupiter was forming, temperatures at its center may have been too high to allow much of a core to remain.

Jupiter and Saturn have a layer of what is called *metallic hydrogen*. This layer of hydrogen is called metallic because it behaves like a liquid metal. The gravity of these huge planets creates a tremendous pressure on the hydrogen layer. Such pressure changes the way hydrogen acts. Some helium is believed to be mixed with the hydrogen.

Both Jupiter and Saturn give off their own stored energy, which was made long ago when the gas and dust from which they formed contracted. Had they been ten times larger, their temperature might have risen high enough to make them both stars like the sun.

Uranus and Neptune have similar structures and nearly identical diameters. The core of each is believed to be made up of heavy elements such as silicon and iron. The outer layer of Uranus and Neptune is a mixture of icy methane, ammonia, and water.

Uranus is tilted 98° to the side. As it revolves around the sun, its north and south poles take turns pointing in the direction of the earth and the sun. This causes each of Uranus' polar regions to remain in sunlight for 42 years and then in darkness for the same amount of time.

Pluto seems to be much different from the other planets. Some scientists think it should not even be listed as a true planet, but rather as a minor one. Because of its size and its distance from the earth, little is known about the makeup of Pluto.

☐ **How, do you think, does a study of the makeup of the planets help scientists to know about the beginning of the solar system?**

Find Out More

After the discovery of the planet Neptune, Percival Lowell, an American astronomer, predicted that another planet beyond Neptune would be found. Using reference books, find out who discovered the planet Pluto. Also find out if Pluto fits Lowell's predictions.

Figure 5–5. Uranus is tipped 98° from an imaginary line that is perpendicular to its orbital path. Scientists do not understand what caused Uranus to be tilted in this way.

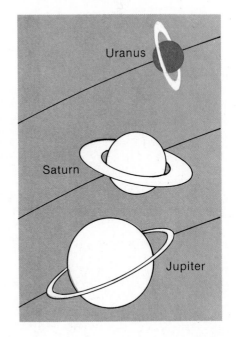

SURFACE OF THE PLANETS

What events change the surface of a planet?
Why is a heavily cratered surface a sign of an
*   ancient surface?*
Of the inner planets, which seems to have the
*   youngest surface?*

Craters, volcanoes, and mountains

After learning about the structure of the planets, you may wonder what it is like on the surface of these planets. The outer layer of Jupiter and Saturn is a mixture of liquid hydrogen and helium. The outer layer of Uranus and Neptune is a mixture of icy methane, ammonia, and water. These liquid and ice surfaces have not been studied in detail as yet. Because of this, most information about planet surfaces has been learned from studying the inner planets.

The surface of an inner planet can be changed in certain ways. Bodies the size of a small asteroid may cross the path of a planet and be pulled toward it. Impact from such bodies may cause a *crater* [CRAYT-ur], or a hollow in the surface of the planet, to form. See Figure 5–6. Many such bodies struck the planets during the early years of the solar system. When you look at a picture of the cratered surface of a planet, you see the result of something that happened billions of years ago. Some cratering has taken place in

Figure 5–6. The photograph on the left, showing the crater Eratosthenes, was taken during the second lunar landing. The drawing on the right demonstrates how a crater is formed.

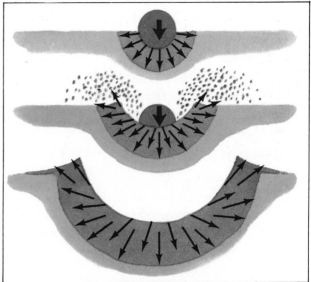

more recent times, but recent impacts are rarer than the very early ones. A large number of craters may be a sign of a very old surface.

The surface of a planet may have newer structures such as *volcanoes* [vahl-KAY-nohz], mountains, and plains. Volcanoes are openings in the crust of the planet through which hot rock and steam flow. Volcanoes, mountains, and plains formed long after the planet itself. Wherever these structures formed, they changed the surface in that place. A region that was once cratered may later have been covered by lava from a volcano. Or a young mountain range may have folded upward, burying the older surface beneath. These features tell scientists how active the planet is or has been.

Surface of Mercury

Mercury has a much-cratered surface, as seen in the images sent to the earth by the *Mariner 10* spacecraft. These images, covering 35 percent of the surface, may remind you of pictures you have seen of the moon. Mercury also has large areas of ancient plains, which show that during the period of cratering, volcanoes may have poured lava over the surface. If so, the cooled lava formed the plains.

Surface of Venus

Spacecraft also helped scientists to find out about the surface of Venus. Even though it is the closest planet to the earth, Venus' surface is completely hidden from view. It is surrounded by a dense atmosphere of carbon dioxide.

In 1975, the Soviet spacecraft *Venera 9* and *Venera 10* sent the first photographs of Venus to the earth. The pictures show the rocky surface of Venus. In 1982, *Venera 13* and *Venera 14* made soft landings on Venus. They sent back color photos of the surface.

Surface of the earth

Much of the earth's surface is covered by water or growing plants. Only about seventy craters have been found on

NASA

Figure 5–7. This mosaic is made from photographs of Mercury taken by Mariner 10. *It shows mostly the northern part of Mercury's western hemisphere.*

Figure 5–8. The information used to draw this computerized map of the surface of Venus was transmitted by the Pioneer-Venus *orbiter.*

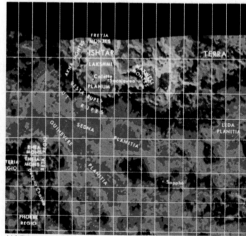

NASA

the earth's surface. However, this does not mean that the earth was not struck by falling bodies during its early years.

The earth is a very active planet in a geological sense. Therefore, much of its present surface is different from its early surface. Many mountain ranges have formed, earthquakes have rearranged areas, and erupting volcanoes have covered the surface with lava. Besides, as you will study in Chapter 21, "Plate Tectonics," the earth's crust is believed to be made up of moving plates. These plates are responsible for drastic changes in the surface of the earth.

Surface of Mars

The surface of Mars is complex. Its northern hemisphere is unlike its southern hemisphere. The surface of the northern hemisphere dips in below the average radius of the planet. The northern hemisphere has only a few early craters. Instead, there are many plains formed by lava. Some of these plains have craters superimposed.

The surface of the southern hemisphere juts out about 3 kilometers (about 1.9 miles) above the average radius. The southern hemisphere seems to be made up of 2 parts. It has a very ancient crust with many large craters and very ancient plains with few craters. The southern hemisphere also has many channels, which look like those formed on the earth by heavy flooding.

☐ **Why is the surface of the earth considered to be younger than the surface of Mars?**

Find Out More

Before the *Viking* missions to Mars, scientists had wondered if life in any forms had ever existed on Mars. To find out about this possibility, various experiments were carried out by means of the *Viking* lander. Using reference books, find out about these experiments and their results.

Figure 5–9. The rocky surface of Mars shown in this picture was photographed by the Viking 2 *lander. How would you describe the surface?*

NASA

ATMOSPHERES OF THE PLANETS

How has the earth's atmosphere changed over
the years?
How has the dense atmosphere of Venus affected
its temperature?
What are the parallel bands in the atmospheres
of Jupiter and Saturn?
What causes the green color of Uranus?

The earth's atmosphere

Most of the planets are surrounded by a blanket of gases, known as the *atmosphere*. The atmosphere of the earth is the air. Air is a mixture of nitrogen, oxygen, argon, carbon dioxide and a small amount of other gases. Nitrogen makes up almost 78 percent of air.

The earth's atmosphere has changed a great deal over the years. At one time, it had much more carbon dioxide than it now contains. Most of the carbon dioxide now on the earth is locked up in rocks such as limestone. Likewise, long ago the atmosphere contained no free oxygen, or oxygen not joined with other elements. Now, because green plants give off free oxygen when they make their food, 21 percent of the earth's atmosphere is made up of free oxygen. The earth's gravity holds the air around the earth. It keeps the gases from escaping into space.

Mercury, Venus, and Mars

The smallest of the inner planets, Mercury, has a very thin atmosphere. Most of the gas around Mercury is from the solar wind that flows past the planet. See Figure 5–1 to find out which gases are present in the atmosphere of Mercury. Mercury has a thin atmosphere. This causes the side of the planet facing the sun to be hot and the side facing away from the sun to be cold.

Venus is completely covered by a dense atmosphere. In fact, the atmosphere of Venus is so dense that it causes a pressure at the surface 90 times greater than the pressure of the earth's atmosphere. Carbon dioxide is the principal gas in the atmosphere of Venus. Sulfuric acid clouds and water clouds are also present. The dense atmosphere keeps the heat that reaches the surface of Venus from escaping. For this reason, the average temperature at its surface is 455°C (about 850°F).

The atmosphere around Mars causes only a weak pressure at the surface of the planet. Mars' atmosphere has a pressure that is 1/150 the pressure of the earth's atmosphere. Free oxygen is present in the atmosphere of Mars in very small amounts. The principal gas present is carbon dioxide.

Atmospheres of the outer planets

Since the 1930's, scientists have known that methane and ammonia are present in the atmosphere of Jupiter. About 1960, hydrogen gas was discovered there also. During the 1970's, the other gases shown in Figure 5–1 were detected. Similar gases were found around Saturn.

The atmospheres of Jupiter and Saturn form multicolored clouds, arranged in parallel bands around the two planets. These bands are caused by alternating easterly and westerly winds, which circulate storms. The storms sometimes last for hundreds of years. A part of these storms is the Great Red Spot in Jupiter's atmosphere. The Great Red Spot seems to be a cold spot. Sulfur or phosphorus in that part of the atmosphere may be responsible for the color of the huge spot. White ovals can also be seen in the atmospheres of Jupiter and of Saturn. These ovals, like the Great Red Spot, are colder than the area around them. Scientists think that the ovals are high-pressure centers. The whirling winds in the ovals travel in a clockwise direction in the northern hemisphere of the planets, as do all high-pressure centers.

The atmosphere of Uranus is cold and clear. No clouds hide Uranus from view. The green color of the planet is caused by the large amounts of methane in the atmosphere.

Neptune's atmosphere contains ice crystals and fine particles that form a haze around the planet. The haze causes the upper atmosphere to be warmed by absorbing sunlight.

Find Out More

Look in reference books to find out more about the Great Red Spot on Jupiter. How long have people known about the presence of the Great Red Spot in the atmosphere of Jupiter? Has the spot ever disappeared? How has this spot helped scientists study the atmosphere of Jupiter?

Figure 5–10. The colors in the atmosphere of Jupiter and of Saturn show that there is much chemical activity around both planets. The cloud color in the atmosphere seems to be related to temperature. Blue indicates the highest temperature; brown, the next highest temperature. Still cooler clouds are white. Red clouds are the coldest.

In fact, Neptune's temperature is about the same as that of Uranus, even though Neptune is about 1.6 billion kilometers (1 billion miles) farther from the sun than Uranus.

Little is known about the atmosphere of Pluto except that methane is present. Frozen methane is believed to be present on the surface of Pluto. This seems to imply that the planet has an atmosphere of methane and of some other heavy gas, such as neon or argon. The heavy gas helps to bind the methane to Pluto. Otherwise, the methane would escape into space.

☐ **Why has the atmosphere of the earth changed more than the atmospheres of the other planets?**

115

RINGS, MOONS, AND ASTEROIDS

Which planets have rings in orbit around them?
What are the rings made of?
How do Jupiter, Saturn, and Uranus resemble mini solar systems?
How many moons does Saturn have?
Where is the asteroid belt?
What causes some comets to have tails?

Planetary rings

In 1610, Galileo saw a blur on either side of Saturn. He thought that Saturn was made up of three separate bodies. In 1655, Christian Huygens resolved the problem. What Galileo had seen was a system of rings around Saturn. Until recently, Saturn seemed to be the only planet with rings.

In the late 1970's when astronomers were looking for a certain bright star, they found that the star was blocked from view by something in the space around Uranus. Searching that area more closely, they discovered nine narrow rings in orbit around Uranus.

In 1979, *Voyager 1*, an American spacecraft, discovered another ring, this time around Jupiter. The *Voyager 1* camera took a picture of a thin, flat ring around the planet. *Voyager 2* learned more about Jupiter's ring when it neared the planet in July 1981. From the *Voyager 2* data, scientists found that Jupiter's ribbonlike ring is only a few thousand

Photri

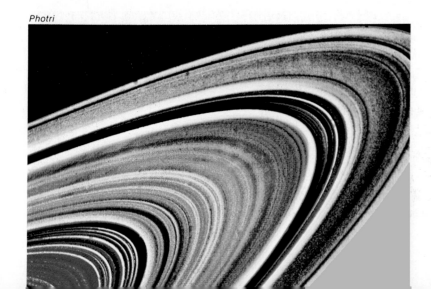

Figure 5–11. This color-enhanced photo of Saturn's rings seems to show that there are differences in chemical composition from one part of the rings to another.

kilometers wide, much narrower than the broad rings of Saturn. Neptune may have two icy rings.

The rings around the planets are different from one another in some ways. For a long time Saturn's rings seemed to consist of five or six bands. However, images from *Voyager 1* revealed that more than one thousand rings are in motion around Saturn. The rings around Saturn are made up of snow or ice particles. Uranus' rings consist of small rocky chunks. Jupiter's ring is wispy and is constantly changing. Scientists think that meteorites bombard a small moon, which is close to Jupiter. Material from this moon may continually regenerate the ring around Jupiter.

Moons of the inner planets

A moon is a *satellite* [SAT-uhl-YT], or small body that orbits a larger body in space. At least forty-four moons orbit the planets in the solar system. Only three of these moons orbit the inner planets. Mercury and Venus have no moons.

The earth's moon is quite different from the earth itself. A study of moon rocks seems to indicate that there are no *sedimentary* [SEHD-uh-MEHNT-uh-ree] rocks on the moon. You may know that sedimentary rocks form when flowing water leaves sediment in a place. The moon has no water on its surface, and moon rocks have no water inside them. The moon's rocks formed when molten lava cooled. As a result, moon rocks are all *igneous* [IHG-nee-uhs] *rocks.*

To Think About

Rings around a planet may be formed when a moon is torn apart by planetary tides, or the pull of the planet's gravity. Other planets may at some time in the future have rings. What information about a planet's moons might help scientists to predict which planets might have rings in the future?

Figure 5–12. The moons that are in orbit around Uranus and Jupiter are probably the source of the material in each planet's rings.

Some of the rocks on the moon have an apparent age of 4.6 billion years. If this is true, these rocks were among the first material that cooled on the once-molten moon. After cooling, the moon was struck by many objects in space, which caused craters on its surface. The period of cratering was followed by at least 700 million years during which volcanoes poured lava over the surface.

The two moons of Mars—Phobos and Deimos—are small and dark. It is not certain whether they were formed at the same time as Mars or were captured later by the gravity of Mars. Phobos is close to Mars and is being pulled by planetary tides. These tides may someday pull Phobos apart. Its pieces might then form rings around Mars.

Moons of the outer planets

Three of the outer planets with their system of moons and rings resemble mini solar systems. Jupiter has sixteen moons, Saturn has seventeen, and Uranus has five. See Figure 5–13 for the names and sizes of these moons.

The five moons closest to Jupiter and three small moons in an outer group orbit the planet in a counterclockwise direction. The rest of Jupiter's moons move in a clockwise direction. This has led scientists to suggest that the moons traveling in opposite directions might have different origins.

Four of Jupiter's moons were discovered by Galileo. These moons—Io, Europa, Ganymede, and Callisto—are called the *Galilean satellites*. Because these moons are quite large, they cause disturbances in one another's orbits. Io and Europa have a rocky makeup. The low densities of Ganymede and Callisto lead scientists to think that these moons are made mostly of water in some form. One model for the structure of Ganymede and Callisto suggests that they have an ice crust, a water or ice mantle, and a mineral-rich core. The difference in the makeup of Jupiter's moons may remind you of the difference in the makeup of the inner planets and the outer planets.

Figure 5–13. This chart can help you compare the sizes of the moons. Which moon is nearest to the earth's moon in size?

CHART OF THE MOONS

Planet	Moon	Moon Diameter (km)
Earth	Moon	3 476
Mars	Phobos	27 × 21 × 19*
	Deimos	15 × 12 × 11*
Jupiter	1979 J-3	40
	1979 J-1	35
	Amalthea	170
	1979 J-2	75
	Io	3 632
	Europa	3 126
	Ganymede	5 276
	Callisto	4 820
	Leda	15
	Himalia	170
	Lysithea	35
	Elara	80
	Ananke	30
	Carme	40
	Pasiphae	50
	Sinope	35
Saturn	Titan	5 140
	Iapetus	1 440
	Rhea	1 530
	Dione	1 120
	Tethys	1 050
	Enceladus	500
	Mimas	390
	Hyperion	360
	Phoebe	200
	1980 S-1	100
	1980 S-3	90
	1980 S-6	160
	1980 S-13	35
	1980 S-25	35
	1980 S-26	200
	1980 S-27	220
	1980 S-28	30
Uranus	Miranda	320
	Ariel	860
	Umbriel	900
	Titania	1 040
	Oberon	920
Neptune	Triton	3 800
	Nereid	940
Pluto	Charon	800

* Irregular shape

One of the most active and interesting moons yet explored is Io. Its surface is marked by many volcanoes. Images sent back by *Voyager 1* and *Voyager 2* show several erupting volcanoes. The heat in these volcanoes seems to be generated by gravitational tugs caused on Io by the other Galilean satellites. Steam is the driving force of volcanoes on the earth. On Io, sulfur dioxide performs this role. Io's black, red, orange, and yellow colors seem to come from sulfur and its compounds. The *Voyager* images of Io show no craters.

Europa has very few craters. It has the smoothest surface of any body in the solar system. The surface of Europa is covered with a tangle of light and dark lines that may be breaks in its ice crust. From beneath the surface, the breaks may have been filled in by water, which then froze. Callisto's whole surface is cratered. It probably has the oldest surface of all the moons of Jupiter. Ganymede is the largest of all the moons in the solar system. It has both older and younger cratered areas.

Saturn's seventeen moons fall into four classes: the giant Titan, seven medium-sized icy moons, eight small moonlets, and Phoebe, a captured asteroid. Titan is Saturn's most

NASA

Figure 5–14. Photographs of Jupiter and its Galilean satellites were taken by Voyager 1 *and then arranged in this collage. Io is located at the upper left. Europa is in the center. Ganymede is at the lower left, and Callisto is at the lower right.*

119

interesting moon. It is the second-largest moon in the solar system. It is also slightly larger than the planet Mercury. It is the only moon with a dense atmosphere. In fact, its atmosphere is ten times denser than the earth's.

Titan is the only body in the solar system besides the earth that has nitrogen as the principal gas in its atmosphere. The other gases in Titan's atmosphere are methane and ethane. Studying the atmosphere of Titan may lead to an understanding of the steps that led to the beginning of living things on the earth.

☐ **On which of the moons of the solar system might scientists look for signs of primitive life?**

Asteroids and comets

Planets are not the only bodies in the solar system orbiting the sun. Asteroids and comets are also in solar orbit. Asteroids are small planets, many of which are in orbit between Mars and Jupiter. This area is called the *asteroid belt*. Two other large groups of asteroids are trapped in the orbit of Jupiter. A recently discovered asteroid crosses the orbits of Saturn and Uranus. Comets are small, icy bodies traveling in elongated orbits. They periodically come in from the outermost part of the solar system.

Until recently, astronomers felt that an asteroid and a comet were different from each other in many ways. Astronomers are now taking another look at all small bodies. They think that asteroids and comets, and even some of the smaller moons, are different only because of where they formed in the early solar system.

Sometimes comets come close to the sun during their orbit. Heat from the sun causes some of the frozen matter to become a gas. The gas around the frozen particles scatters the sunlight and makes the comet look fuzzy. As the comet gets closer to the sun, solar radiations and solar winds put pressure on the comet. They force gases from the comet, causing its streaming tail to form. The tail is always longest when the comet is nearest the sun.

☐ **How are comets and asteroids alike? How are they different?**

Figure 5–15. The Arend-Roland Comet, shown here, was first discovered in November 1956. Since its closest distance to the sun did not occur until April 1957, astronomers had enough time to observe it.

Courtesy of California Institute of Technology

This astrophysicist can study sunspot activity by using a solar telescope. The astrophysicist can gather information about the sun without looking directly at the sun's surface.

Careers

Astrophysicist

Astrophysicists [AS-truh-FIHZ-(uh-)suhsts] are scientists whose work is a blend of astronomy and physics. Using the laws of physics, astrophysicists study the atmosphere of a planet or the interior of a star. They often make use of the observations of astronomers to find out what elements exist in the various planets and stars.

An astrophysicist is highly skilled in mathematics. James Clerk Maxwell used mathematics to conclude that Saturn's rings are made up of many small, separate particles. Mathematics helped Albert Einstein to develop his theories of relativity. Mathematics also helped in the discovery of the planet Neptune.

Astrophysicists use radio telescopes to study radio waves that are emitted or reflected by a planet or a star. Sometimes they study the pattern of wavelengths produced by the light from a star. Such a study helps astrophysicists to find out about the star's density and temperature.

Perhaps you have a strong curiosity about the planets and the stars. You may enjoy experimenting in order to find out why physical events happen as they do. You may also like to solve mathematical problems. If you have these qualities and are an independent thinker, you may want to become an astrophysicist. You will need a college degree. Most astrophysicists have advanced degrees.

To find out more about the work of astrophysicists, a student in your class might write to the Joint Institute for Laboratory Astrophysics, University of Colorado, Boulder, CO 80309.

121

Reviewing and Extending

Summing Up

1. Nine planets, at least forty-four moons, and many asteroids and comets orbit the sun in our solar system.
2. The sun has tremendous gravity because almost all the mass in the solar system is contained in the sun.
3. The overall temperature on each of the planets is affected by the planet's distance from the sun, by the rotation of the planet, and by its atmosphere.
4. Knowing the density of a planet and the way elements react at certain temperatures helps astronomers understand the makeup of the planets.
5. The inner planets are mostly rocky in structure; the outer planets are mostly liquid in structure.
6. Billions of years ago, asteroids and other small bodies collided with the planets and their moons, causing craters on the surface of the planets and their moons.
7. Newly formed mountain ranges and lava from volcanoes covered parts of the older surface of the planets and moons.
8. Much of the earth's present surface is different from its early surface because the earth is an active planet geologically.
9. The planets and some of the moons are surrounded by a layer of gases, or an atmosphere.
10. Green plants have released large amounts of free oxygen into the earth's atmosphere.
11. Comets and some asteroids may have a common origin.

Checking Up

Vocabulary Write the numerals *1–10* on your paper. Each numbered phrase describes a term from the following list. On your paper, write the term next to the numeral of the phrase that describes it.

gravity   density   asteroid
mantle   atmosphere   green plants
axis   igneous   sedimentary
mass   crater   astronomical unit

1. kind of rocks on the moon
2. layer of gases that may surround a planet or a moon
3. hollow in the surface of a planet or a moon caused by a collision with a small body in its path
4. layer between the core and the crust of a planet
5. force exerted by anything that has mass
6. distance from the earth to the sun
7. amount of matter in a certain volume
8. straight line about which a planet rotates
9. continuously add oxygen to the atmosphere of the earth
10. small body between Mars and Jupiter that revolves around the sun

Knowledge and Understanding Write the numerals *11–18* on your paper. Beside each numeral, write the word or words that best complete the sentence having that numeral.

11. The planets and other bodies of the solar system are kept in orbit because of (*their own, the sun's, the moon's*) gravity.
12. The inner planets move (*more slowly, more swiftly, at more-even speeds*) than the outer planets.
13. A planet with a fast rotation usually has a (*less even, more even, cold*) temperature.
14. (*Oxygen, nitrogen, hydrogen*) is the most common element in the solar system.
15. On the warmer inner planets, carbon joins another element to form (*carbon dioxide, ammonia, methane*).

16. The planet (*Venus, Uranus, Neptune*) is tilted on its axis 98° to the side.
17. A much-cratered surface is probably (*very old, very young, not able to be dated*).
18. The Great Red Spot in Jupiter's atmosphere seems to be a (*cold spot, hot spot, center of calm*).

Expressing Yourself Write a paragraph as an answer to each of the following questions:

19. What may cause a planet closer to the sun to have a colder temperature than another planet farther away from the sun?
20. Why is a heavily cratered surface on a planet or moon a sign of an ancient surface?

Doing More

1. Make a model of the solar system. Use various round objects to represent bodies in the solar system. Look in reference books to find a proper scale for your model. Include the more prominent moons in your model of the solar system.

2. Call a planetarium or a space center at a college in your area. Find out when a sky show about the solar system will be given. Plan to attend the show. Prepare questions you would like to ask the astronomers about the solar system.

6 Earth and Its Moon

The moon affects the earth in several ways. As this picture shows, the moon's reflected light helps brighten and beautify some of the nighttime hours.

Between the years 1969 and 1972, twelve American astronauts landed on the moon. They traveled to the moon in the Apollo spacecraft. The astronauts explored the surface of the moon and picked up many rocks from the surface. They returned to the earth with the rocks and with pictures of the lunar terrain.

The astronauts' rocks have revealed much about the moon and its surface. Geologists have studied the rocks and have learned about the moon's makeup and the moon's history. The astronauts also left instruments on the moon. Readings from the instruments have helped geologists in their study of the moon. The instruments have detected moonquakes and other phenomena.

Now the moon is viewed not only as an object in space. It is also seen as a physical body to be studied in much the same way as the earth. A study of the moon reveals much about the earth itself. The earth and the moon make up a single system. This system is known as the *earth-moon system*.

THE EARTH-MOON SYSTEM

What is meant by the earth-moon system?
How does the moon's gravity compare with
the earth's gravity?
What causes tides in the ocean?

Shared center of gravity

Five moons of other planets in the solar system—Ganymede, Titan, Callisto, Triton, and Io—are larger than the earth's moon. However, when the size of a planet's moon is compared with the size of its planet, the earth's moon ranks before the 5 larger moons. The earth's moon is one fourth the size of the earth. Its diameter is 3 476 kilometers (about 2,160 miles).

The sun's gravity exerts a force on the earth and the moon as if they were a single body. This force is exerted on the earth and the moon together even though the moon is 384 403 kilometers (about 238,857 miles) from the earth. Because of the sun's gravitational pull, both the moon and the earth remain in orbit around the sun. As the moon goes around the sun along with the earth, it is also in orbit around the earth.

The earth and the moon are considered a single system, the earth-moon system, because they share a *center of gravity.* The center of gravity is the place where the sun's gravitational pull on the earth and the moon is the greatest. This place is 128 kilometers (about 80 miles) from the center of the earth. At the center of gravity, the sun exerts a gravitational force on the earth and the moon as a single system.

Gravity and tides

You may have seen movies of astronauts hopping or even leaping on the moon. The astronauts were lighter on the moon than on the earth because the moon's gravity does not pull things to its surface with as great a force as the earth's gravity does. In fact, the moon's gravity is only

Figure 6–1. Jupiter's moon Ganymede is believed to be the largest moon in the solar system. However, Jupiter makes Ganymede look small. Jupiter's diameter is twenty-seven times larger than Ganymede's.

NASA

125

one sixth the earth's gravity. Even so, the moon's gravity has important effects on the earth.

☐ **Why, do you think, is the moon's gravity less than the earth's gravity?**

If you have been at the seashore, you may have noticed that the surface of the ocean rises at times, bringing the water closer to the shore. Then, at other times, the water falls. It moves away from the shore. The rising or falling of the water in the ocean is known as a *tide*. There are high tides and low tides.

Once it has reached a low point, the water in the ocean begins to rise. The water level rises gradually for about six hours and then reaches its peak, which is high tide. The water level then begins to fall. It falls gradually for about six hours until it reaches its low point, which is low tide. A high tide and a low tide occur every twelve hours.

The moon's gravity causes the tides. The gravity of the moon pulls on the earth and on whatever is on the earth. For example, the moon's gravity pulls on the water in the ocean. It pulls the water that is closest to the moon away from the solid part of the earth, causing a bulge in the ocean. This bulge is a tide.

As it pulls on the water, the moon also tugs at the solid earth. It pulls the solid earth slightly away from the ocean water on the opposite side of the earth, causing another bulging tide. When there is a high tide on one side of the earth, there is also a high tide on the opposite side.

The earth rotates on its axis. As it rotates, first one place and then another place on the earth is directly under the moon. The land and the water on the earth rotate together. Because of this rotation, the tidal bulges on the ocean are first at one place and then at another place.

The sun also exerts a gravitational pull on the earth. At a full moon and at a new moon, the sun and the moon are pulling along the same line. They are lined up with each other. The tides then are higher than usual. See Figure 6–2. The higher tide is known as a *spring tide*. The name has nothing to do with the season. Spring tides occur twice each month.

Find Out More

In addition to ocean tides the moon also causes *air tides* on the earth. Air tides are also called *lunar winds*. Read an article on tides in an encyclopedia to find out if air tides happen at the same time as ocean tides. Find out if air tides are as noticeable as ocean tides. Also find out the direction in which air tides blow.

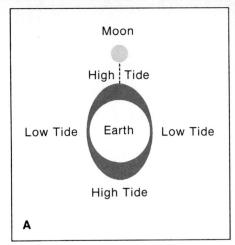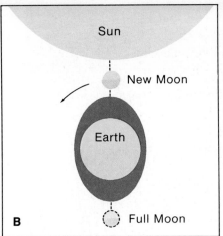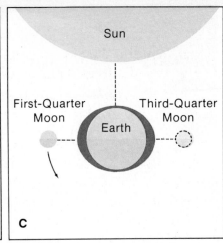

At a first-quarter moon and at a third-quarter moon, the sun and the moon are at right angles to each other. They are not lined up, and they are not pulling together on the earth. The tides then are lower than usual. See Figure 6–2. The lower tide is known as a *neap tide*. Neap tides occur twice each month.

Figure 6–2. Three kinds of ocean tides are shown here: (A) ordinary ocean tides, (B) spring tides, and (C) neap tides.

☐ **Why, do you think, does a high tide occur at a different time each day?**

MAKEUP OF THE MOON

What may have caused the moon to melt beneath the surface?
How did the lunar plains form?
How do moon rocks differ from earth rocks?
What do scientists use to study the interior of the moon?
How may mascons have affected the spacecraft that orbited the moon?

Surface of the moon

Even without a telescope you can see certain regions on the moon. Some regions look dark. These are low, level plains covered with lava. Early astronomers mistakenly thought these dark plains were seas on the moon. They called them *maria* [MAHR-ee-uh], the Latin word for seas. Other regions on the moon are light-colored. These

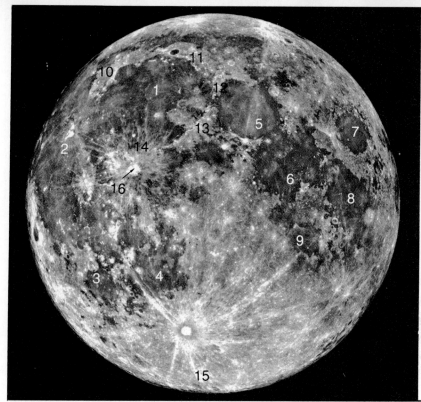

LOCATING PLACES ON THE MOON

1 Sea of Rains
2 Ocean of Storms
3 Sea of Moisture
4 Sea of Clouds
5 Sea of Serenity
6 Sea of Tranquility
7 Sea of Crises
8 Sea of Fertility
9 Sea of Nectar
10 Jura Mountains
11 Alps Mountains
12 Caucasus Mountains
13 Apennine Mountains
14 Carpathian Mountains
15 Leibnitz Mountains
16 Copernicus Crater

are the rugged highlands. With a telescope, craters and canyons can be seen.

The whole surface of the moon is covered with millions of craters. These craters are the result of collisions with small bodies in space that crashed into the moon's surface. Hundreds of thousands of craters on the moon are more than 1.6 kilometers (1 mile) wide. The largest crater, Imbrium Basin, is in the Sea of Rains. It is more than 1 100 kilometers (700 miles) wide. Widespread collisions with small bodies most likely stopped on the moon about 4 billion years ago.

The surface of the moon is covered by fine powder and broken rock. This layer was formed when small bodies struck the moon and ground up parts of the moon's surface. These ground-up parts cover the moon just as soil covers the earth. People sometimes call this layer *lunar* [LOO-nur] soil, or moon soil. Lunar soil is not true soil because it contains no water and no dead plant or animal matter.

Figure 6–3. Each numeral on this map of the near side of the moon indicates the location of a place listed at the right of the map. Where are the Leibnitz Mountains located?

Investigate

How can you recognize places on the moon?

You will need

flashlight, map of the moon, binoculars or telescope

Background

Some features on the surface of the moon can easily be recognized when a map and binoculars or a telescope are used. This is best done when the moon is almost full. Plains stand out as dark areas on the moon. They are called "seas" on most maps. Many plains are very large craters filled in with lava. Other, smaller, craters are clearly visible. Some of these are called *ray craters* because streaks surrounding these craters look like rays of light. These streaks may have formed from broken rocks scattered when the crater was made.

What to do

Locate important plains on the moon by finding them on the map of the moon. Find the following plains on the west side of the map: Sea of Rains, Ocean of Storms, Sea of Moisture, and Sea of Clouds. Try to locate each of these plains on the moon, using binoculars or a telescope.

Find the following plains on the east side of the map: Sea of Serenity, Sea of Tranquility, Sea of Crises, Sea of Fertility, and Sea of Nectar. Try to locate each of these plains on the moon.

Find these mountain ranges around the Sea of Rains: Jura Mountains, Alps, Caucasus, Apennines, Carpathians. Find the ray crater Copernicus south of the Carpathian Mountains. Notice other features on the moon. Find their names on the map.

Now that you have done the investigation

- In which hemisphere, north or south, are there more plains?
- Which hemisphere has more small craters?

After the craters were formed, other changes on the surface of the moon occurred. Radioactive elements inside the moon *decayed,* or changed into other elements. The decay caused heat to build up beneath the surface. Soon the moon's matter that was 200 kilometers (about 124 miles) beneath the surface began to melt. Then for about 500 million years lava from the melted part inside the moon flowed out through volcanoes. It flowed over many parts of the moon, forming the plains, or maria.

Much of the moon's surface has not changed because the moon has no atmosphere and no water. Only when the moon was young did much change take place on its surface. Even mountain ranges on the moon are as rough as if they had just formed.

The mountain ranges on the moon seem to be the broken rims of large craters. Many of the mountains are as tall as the highest mountains on the earth. The Leibnitz Mountains rise to an altitude of 7 920 meters (26,000 feet). They are near the moon's south pole. Another mountain range, the Apennine Mountains, has peaks that are at least 6 100 meters (20,000 feet) high. The Apennines are near the Sea of Rains. See the map in Figure 6–3.

☐ **Why would living things not grow well in lunar soil?**

Moon rocks

To find out about the makeup of the moon, scientists study the moon rocks brought back by the astronauts. Rocks on the moon are all igneous. The same minerals that make up lava on the earth are found in moon rocks. Three new minerals not found on the earth have been found in moon rocks: *tranquilityite, armalcolite,* and *pyroxferroite.* For what may the first two minerals have been named?

Moon rocks look different from earth rocks under a microscope. Since there is no water or free oxygen on the moon, its rocks are well preserved. The minerals in the rocks have remained intact, instead of forming different compounds. There is no rust or clay in moon rocks.

Find Out More

Astronauts on the moon never saw a blue sky, even though it was daytime. Look in reference books to find out why this was so.

To Think About

The atmosphere has caused great changes on the earth's surface through weathering and erosion. Suppose that the moon had an atmosphere. What do you think the moon's surface would be like?

Cameramasters

Do It Yourself

Locate Apollo spacecraft landing places on a map of the moon

Use reference books to find out where the Apollo astronauts landed on the moon. Draw a map of the moon and label its important features. Mark the place where *Apollo 11, Apollo 12, Apollo 14, Apollo 15, Apollo 16,* and *Apollo 17* landed. Write a report about the contributions to science made by Project Apollo to accompany your map.

Moon rocks brought back to the earth have to be kept from being changed chemically. They are sealed off in a special laboratory with large glass windows. All oxygen and water vapor have been removed from the air in the laboratory. Before handling moon rocks, scientists outside the laboratory slip their hands into special gloves that extend into the closed-off workroom where the rocks are. They then handle a moon rock otherwise sealed off from them.

Elements that melt at low temperatures, such as sodium and potassium, are rare in moon rocks. This has led scientists to think that the moon was much hotter when it formed than the earth was. They think that certain elements boiled off the moon but not off the earth.

Interior of the moon

Scientists have discovered many things about the interior of the earth by studying *vibrations* [vy-BRAY-shuhnz], or movements back and forth, caused by earthquakes. Vibrations give information about the kind of matter through which they pass. Vibrations travel more quickly through some kinds of matter than through other kinds.

Some vibrations on the moon are caused by meteorites striking its surface. Others are caused by moonquakes deep inside the moon. Both kinds of vibrations help scientists to understand the makeup of the moon. Moonquakes seem to be weaker and to happen less often than earthquakes. Instruments set up on the moon by the Apollo astronauts sent information about vibrations caused by moonquakes and about other vibrations back to the earth from 1969 until 1977.

Scientists can now make a model of the interior of the moon. They know that the crust of the moon is about sixty kilometers (about thirty-seven miles) thick. It is made up of rocks that are rich in calcium and aluminum. The mantle of the moon is more than twelve times thicker than its crust. The moon may still be hot and partly melted inside. It may even have an iron core like the earth's. Information about the core is not certain as yet.

The interior of the moon is not uniform. The Apollo spacecraft, orbiting the moon, registered an extra pull of gravity whenever they passed over large maria filled with lava. Then scientists developed the theory that in certain parts of the moon there is extra matter lumped together beneath the very large maria. They called these lumps of matter *mascons* [MAS-kahnz]. Some scientists think the extra mass in the mascons was caused by the large amounts of lava that filled the craters above them.

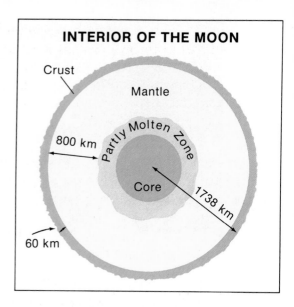

Figure 6–4. This model of the interior of the moon shows the relative size of each part of the moon. Which part of the moon is the largest?

☐ **How does the theory of mascons help to explain the change in the pull of gravity over certain areas on the moon?**

MOTIONS OF THE MOON

What is the moon's distance from the earth at perigee? At apogee?

Why does the moon have such extremes in temperature?

Why does the same side of the moon always face the earth?

What causes the phases of the moon as seen from the earth?

What is a lunar eclipse? A solar eclipse?

Moving in orbit

The earth-moon system revolves around the sun once in 365 days 6 hours 9 minutes 9.54 seconds. While the earth-moon system is revolving around the sun, the moon continues to revolve around the earth. It takes the moon 29.5 days to complete 1 earth orbit.

The moon's orbit around the earth has the shape of an ellipse, or an oval. The moon is not always the same distance from the earth. Its *perigee* [PEHR-uh-jee], or the point in the orbit at which the moon is nearest to the center of the earth, is 356 399 kilometers (221,456 miles). Its *apogee* [AP-uh-jee], or the point in the orbit at which the moon is the farthest from the center of earth, is 406,699 kilometers (252,711 miles).

Rotation of the moon

Like the earth and the planets, the moon also rotates on its axis. It takes the moon 29.5 days to rotate on its axis just once. For this reason, a day on the moon lasts 2 weeks on the earth. A night on the moon also lasts 2 earth weeks. Such long days and long nights result in extremes in temperature. During a day on the moon, the surface temperature reaches 127°C (261°F). During a night on the moon, the temperature falls to —173°C (—279°F).

The moon takes the same amount of time, 29.5 days, to revolve around the earth as it takes to rotate on its axis. Because of this, the same side of the moon always faces the earth. No one on the earth had ever seen the other side of the moon until spacecraft orbited the moon. Cameras on the spacecraft took pictures of the other side of the moon and sent them back to the earth.

☐ **If the moon had an atmosphere, how might this affect its temperature?**

Phases of the moon

You have most likely noticed that the shape of the moon seems to change slowly during a month. It seems to change from a thin slice to a full circle and then back to a thin slice again. The moon does not really change, but the amount of the moon that you can see does change.

Half of the moon faces the sun and is therefore lighted by the sun. However, the half of the moon that faces the

Figure 6–5. Numerous craters can be seen in this photo of a portion of the far side of the moon. More mountains and fewer plains than there are on the near side are also found on this side of the moon.

NASA

133

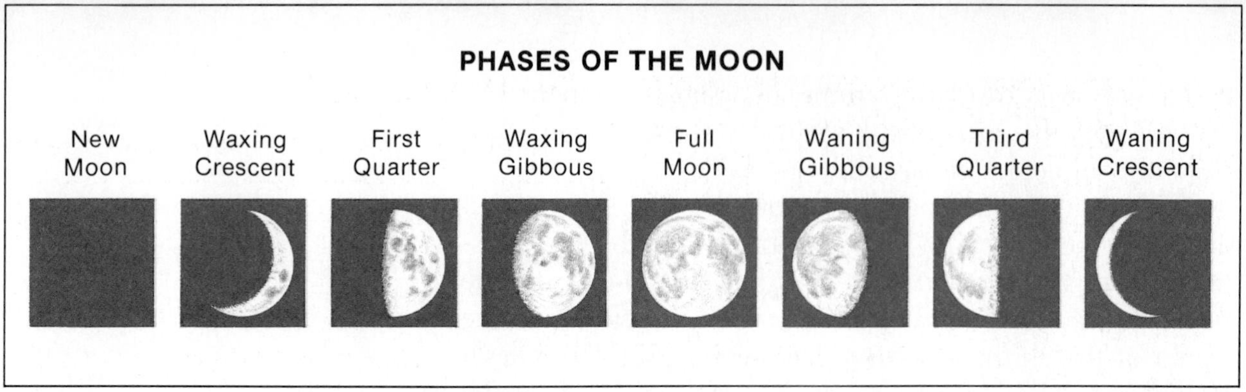

PHASES OF THE MOON

New Moon	Waxing Crescent	First Quarter	Waxing Gibbous	Full Moon	Waning Gibbous	Third Quarter	Waning Crescent

Figure 6–6. Which of these phases of the moon have you seen?

earth is not always lighted by the sun. Sometimes only a part of that side is in sunlight. Only the lighted part of the moon can be seen from the earth. Because of this, the moon is said to go through several *phases*, or changes in the way it looks from the earth, during the month.

When no part of the moon that faces the earth is lighted by the sun, the phase is called *new moon*. Each night for two weeks after new moon, more and more of the lighted side of the moon can be seen. The moon is then said to be *waxing*, or growing larger. Two weeks after new moon, *full moon* can be seen. Then each night for two weeks, less and less of the lighted side of the moon can be seen. During this time the moon is said to be *waning*, or getting smaller in size.

Find the following phases in Figure 6–6:. new moon, waxing crescent, first quarter, waxing gibbous, full moon, waning gibbous, last quarter, waning crescent. What names are given to the phases when the moon is a small slice? What phases show more than half of one side of the moon and yet do not show a full moon?

☐ **Do you think the earth has phases when seen by an astronaut on the moon? Why or why not?**

Lunar and solar eclipses

The motions of the earth-moon system result in interesting views of the sun and the moon from the earth. At certain times during its orbit of the sun, the earth moves to a position where it is between the sun and the moon. When this happens, you may witness an *eclipse* of the

To Think About

Look at a clock on the wall. Close one eye. Move a coin slowly backward and forward in front of your open eye. Do this until the coin blocks out the clock. How would you explain that a small object can eclipse a larger one?

Phil Degginger

Do It Yourself

Show what causes the phases of the moon

Paint a rubber ball (the size of a tennis ball) white. Turn on a table lamp in a darkened room. Turn your back to the light. Hold the ball at arm's length above your head so that the light strikes the ball. Notice what part of the ball is lit by the light from the lamp. What phase of the moon does this represent?

Turn slowly from right to left. Keep the ball in front of you and above your head. Stop at each one-eighth turn. Have someone draw the shape of the "moon" that is lit by the light at each stop you make. Watch the changes in the shape of the bright part of the "moon," as you make one complete turn.

moon, or a *lunar eclipse*. An eclipse happens when one body in space is hidden by the shadow of another. See Figure 6–7. During a lunar eclipse, the moon is darkened.

A *solar eclipse* happens when the moon in its orbit around the earth gets between the earth and the sun. The moon then blocks out all or a part of the sun for the people on the earth who are in the moon's shadow. During a total eclipse, the sun cannot be seen. See Figure 6–7.

☐ **What might cause an eclipse of the earth as seen from the moon?**

Figure 6–7. A lunar eclipse may be seen by most people on the night side of the earth. No danger to the eyes is involved in viewing a lunar eclipse. A solar eclipse can be seen only by people in the path of the moon's shadow. When people view a solar eclipse indirectly through a pinhole projector, they will not damage their eyes.

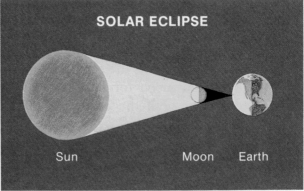

135

ORIGIN OF THE MOON

How did scientists determine the age of the moon?

What may be the origin of the moon?

Age of the moon

Many scientists think that the moon is very old. They base this idea on radioactive dating. Lunar soil contains some radioactive matter. As you know, radioactive matter decays, or changes to another kind of matter, in a certain amount of time.

Scientists measured the radioactive matter in certain lunar soil. They then found out the amount of the different matter in the soil to which the radioactive matter had changed. When they figured out how long it would take for that amount of matter to change, they concluded that the age of the moon may be about 4.6 billion years.

Origin of the moon

Although many facts about the moon have been learned in recent years, some questions still puzzle scientists. They are still not sure how the moon was formed. One theory states that the earth and the moon were formed as one body. According to this theory, the sun's gravity pulled harder on one side of the earth than on the other side. This pull formed a lump. Gradually the lump broke loose from the earth. It became the earth's moon.

Another theory states that the moon began as an asteroid. As it traveled around the sun, the asteroid came close to the earth and was captured by the earth's gravitational pull. The asteroid became the earth's moon. A third theory has the earth and moon forming at the same time. This theory states that both the earth and the moon formed from gas and dust in space.

☐ **Which of the theories about the origin of the moon suggest that the earth and the moon are the same age?**

Find Out More

Some scientists believe that it is unlikely that the moon separated from the earth. Look in reference books to find out what evidence these scientists present to prove their point.

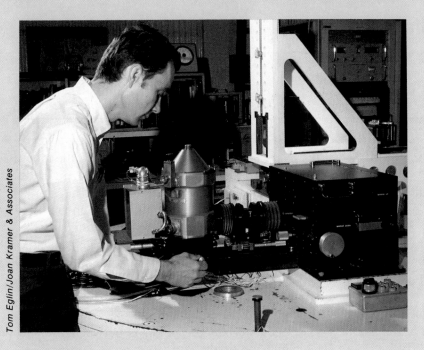

This aerospace engineer is hooking up a magnetograph to a solar telescope. The magnetograph is an instrument that can be used to record measurements of the magnetic field of an object in space.

Careers
Engineers

Much of the information you are learning in this unit was gathered by instruments that can measure pressure, temperature, or volcanic activity on the planets or their moons. These instruments are called *telemeters* [TEHL-uh-MEET-urz]. They transmit readings of different kinds of quantities by radio waves from space to stations on the earth.

Telemeters and many other useful instruments used in space were designed by *engineers.* Every phase of the space program has been worked out by engineers called *aerospace engineers,* who use their knowledge of science and mathematics to solve problems of space travel. Aerospace engineers design space vehicles and then guide their launching. Electronics and communications engineers plan control rooms and the equipment needed to track spacecraft.

If you like to design things and enjoy working out problems, you may want to become an engineer. For this you will need a strong background in science and mathematics and a college degree in engineering. Many engineers have advanced degrees.

You may also want to look into the career of *engineering technician* [tehk-NIHSH-uhn]. These technicians are trained in a certain field of technology at a community college or a technical institute. Engineering technicians work closely with engineers.

For further information about these careers in engineering, write to the National Society of Professional Engineers or to the American Society of Certified Engineering Technicians. The address for both organizations is 2029 K Street, N.W., Washington, DC 20006.

Reviewing and Extending

Summing Up

1. The sun's gravity exerts a force on the earth and the moon as if they were a single body—the earth-moon system.
2. Tides are the alternate rising and falling of the water surface on the earth, caused by the gravity of the moon.
3. Collisions with small bodies that crossed the moon's path until about 4 billion years ago have caused many large craters on the moon.
4. Radioactive decay beneath the surface of the moon caused some of the interior of the moon to melt and to flow out as lava.
5. The surface of the moon has changed little because the moon lacks water and an atmosphere.
6. On the moon, extra lumps of matter, called mascons, may be beneath large craters.
7. Because it takes the moon 29.5 days to rotate on its axis just once, a day on the moon lasts 2 weeks on the earth, and a night on the moon lasts 2 weeks on the earth.
8. Because the entire half of the moon that faces the earth is not always lighted by the sun, the moon appears to change its shape during a month. Each apparent change in shape is known as a phase.
9. A lunar eclipse occurs when the earth is between the sun and the moon; a solar eclipse occurs when the moon is between the sun and the earth.
10. The moon may have begun as a part of the earth, it may have been an asteroid captured by the earth, or it may have formed at the same time as the earth from similar gas and dust.

Checking Up

Vocabulary   Write the numerals *1–10* on your paper. Each numbered phrase describes a term from the following list. On your paper, write the term next to the numeral of the phrase that describes it.

decay	maria	tides
lunar eclipse	lava flows	solar eclipse
mascons	moonquakes	perigee
apogee	water	phases

1. alternate rising and falling of the water surface on the earth
2. name given to the plains on the moon
3. change into other elements
4. extra matter that may be lumped together beneath large craters on the moon
5. formed the plains on the moon
6. point in the orbit at which the moon is nearest to the center of the earth
7. happens when the moon gets between the earth and the sun
8. cause vibrations on the moon
9. point in the orbit at which the moon is farthest from the center of the earth
10. happens when the earth gets between the moon and the sun

Knowledge and Understanding Write the numerals *11–22* on your paper. Beside each numeral, write the word or words that best complete the sentence having that numeral.

11. The moon is (*one half, one fourth, one sixth*) of the size of the earth.
12. The center of gravity in the earth-moon system is 128 kilometers from the center of the (*earth, moon, solar system*).
13. The moon's gravity is (*one half, one fourth, one sixth*) of the earth's gravity.
14. High tides occur about every (*four, eight, twelve*) hours.
15. The interior of the moon beneath the surface melted because of heat from (*moonquakes, tides, radioactive decay*).
16. Scientists think the early moon was (*hotter than, colder than, about the same temperature as*) the earth.
17. A day on the moon lasts (*one day, one week, two weeks*) on the earth.
18. A phase of the moon that is seen for a few nights after full moon is (*waxing crescent, waxing gibbous, waning gibbous*).

19. The surface of the moon seems to have undergone little change because of its (*slow movement, lack of atmosphere and water, solid crust*).
20. Whenever the Apollo spacecraft passed over certain places on the moon, they registered an extra pull of gravity that may be caused by (*magnetism, mascons, radioactive elements*).
21. Rocks on the moon are (*sedimentary, igneous, metamorphic*).
22. A phase of the moon when no part of the moon is visible is (*new moon, full moon, waning crescent*).

Expressing Yourself Write a paragraph as an answer to each of the following questions:

23. How would you explain that high tides occur on opposite sides of the earth at the same time?
24. How have vibrations on the moon helped scientists to understand the makeup of the moon?

Doing More

1. Find out by looking in the *World Almanac* when the next new moon is expected. After the new moon, observe the moon every night for a month. Make a calendar showing the phase of the moon for each night. Predict beforehand which phase will appear.

2. Pretend you are an astronaut being sent to the moon. Look in reference books to find out the physical changes you will experience while being sent into space, while on the moon, and while returning to the earth. Write a report about these changes.

Energy from the sun makes life possible on the earth. Also, a sunrise such as the one in the picture adds splendor to the landscape.

7 Earth and the Sun

The sun contains 99.86 percent of all the matter in our solar system. The sun provides the energy needed by the living things on the earth. For these reasons, the sun is certainly the "star" of our solar system. The sun is a star in the true sense also, even though it is just a medium-size star when compared with the other stars.

The sun is large when compared with other objects in the solar system. It has a diameter of about 1 392 000 kilometers (865,000 miles), which is about 109 times the diameter of the earth. Its volume is 1.3 million times greater than the earth's volume. The sun's mass is 2,000 million million million million tons.

You have already seen how the sun's huge mass keeps the earth and the planets in orbit around the sun. In this chapter, you will learn about the makeup of the sun. You will also find out how the sun's huge mass helps it to produce large amounts of energy.

MAKEUP OF THE SUN

*What force keeps the gases in the sun from
    escaping?*
*What force keeps the mass of the sun from
    collapsing?*
*In what form do hydrogen and helium exist in
    the sun?*
What zones make up the interior of the sun?
*What is the temperature of the surface of the
    sun?*
What are the layers of the sun's atmosphere?

Balanced forces in the sun

Size sets the sun and other stars apart from most other
objects in space. The sun and most other stars are much
larger than the moon and the planets. Because the sun
was the center of the cloud of gas and dust that may
have formed our solar system, many scientists think that
the sun was able to pull most of the matter in the cloud
to itself. They think that such a large amount of matter
collapsed under its own gravity. This collapse caused the
gases that make up the sun to become hot. Gravity also
kept most of these gases from escaping into space.

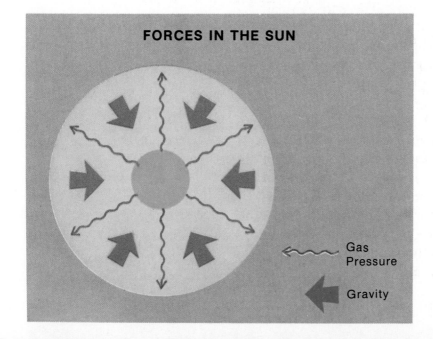

*Figure 7–1. Gases inside the sun
press outward, balancing the inward
pull of the sun's gravity.*

141

You may wonder what keeps the sun from collapsing any further. The answer is "gas pressure." You may have seen how the gases inside a balloon press outward against the sides of the balloon. Gas pressure forces the matter of the sun outward while gravity pulls the matter inward.

☐ **What happens when two equal forces within the same matter pull in opposite directions?**

Kinds of matter in the sun

Most of the matter in the sun consists of 2 elements. About 71 percent of the sun is hydrogen and 27 percent is helium. Most of the energy of the sun is produced when hydrogen is changed into helium.

Most people think of the sun as a heated ball of gases. However, in the sun hydrogen and helium form a phase of matter known as a *plasma*. A plasma is a gas with an electric charge. It is made up of electrically charged particles. The intense heat causes electrons to be pulled from the atoms that make up the sun's gases. When an atom loses electrons, it becomes electrically charged.

☐ **Why, do you think, would an atom from which electrons have been lost be electrically charged?**

The sun's interior

Like the planets, the sun has a *core*. The core is small compared with the rest of the sun, as you can see in Figure 7–2. But, although it is small, the core accounts for perhaps one half of the entire mass of the sun. The core is very dense, since so much matter is packed into such a small area. The core is the hottest part of the sun. The temperature there is 15 000 000°C (27,000,000°F). Most of the energy of the sun is produced in the core.

Outside the core is an area known as the *radiation* [RAYD-ee-AY-shuhn] *zone.* Energy is carried outward from the core through this zone. The temperature in the radiation zone is 4 500 000°C (8,100,000°F). Beyond the radiation zone is the *convection* [kuhn-VEHK-shuhn] *zone.* In the convection zone, the temperature drops to 1 100 000°C (1,980,000°F).

Find Out More

Using references, find out which parts of an atom are negatively charged, which parts are positively charged, and which parts have no electrical charge. Also, find out why an atom generally has no electrical charge.

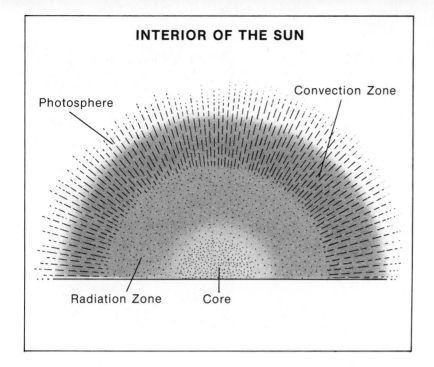

INTERIOR OF THE SUN

Photosphere

Convection Zone

Radiation Zone   Core

Figure 7–2. The temperature in the interior of the sun is highest in the core, where most of the energy is produced. The temperature is lowest in the convection zone, where the outward flow of energy causes giant bubbles of gas to rise toward the surface of the sun.

Surface of the sun

The visible surface of the sun is called the *photosphere* [FOHT-uh-SFIH(UH)R]. This layer is only 500 kilometers (about 311 miles) thick. The temperature at the surface of the sun drops to 5 700°C (about 10,300°F). This temperature may seem cool when compared with that of other parts of the sun. However, it is still hot enough to turn all known substances into gases.

Photographs of the sun show many large, bright regions on the surface. These regions are known as *plages* [PLAHZH-uhz]. The plages change often and seem to be caused by a rise in temperature when clouds of hydrogen vapor on the sun give off additional energy. Smaller bright or dark patches called *flocculi* [FLAHK-yuh-LY] can also be seen on the sun's surface. These and other features make the sun look like a bowl of cooked rice with raisins and glowing embers scattered over its surface.

The sun's atmosphere

The sun's surface is made up of gases. So, it is hard to say where the sun's surface ends and its atmosphere begins. In fact, the photosphere is the first layer of the atmosphere. The second layer of the atmosphere is called the *chromosphere* [KROH-muh-SFIH(UH)R]. Its name comes from its red color. *Chromo-* means "color."

The chromosphere extends outward from the photosphere to about 16 000 kilometers (10,000 miles). The temperature in this layer falls to about 4 200°C (7,600°F) and then begins to rise to about 9 700°C (17,000°F). Most of the chromosphere is hotter than the photosphere but is less dense and less bright.

The chromosphere is filled with *spicules* [SPIHK-yoo(uh)lz] that look like flaming fingers. Spicules are really jets of hot gases. They form a network throughout the chromosphere.

The third layer of the sun's atmosphere is called the *corona* [kuh-ROH-nuh]. It extends outward for 7 million kilometers (about 4.3 million miles). Its temperature measures about 1 100 000°C (1,980,000°F). It is not clear why the temperature rises so sharply in the corona. However, although its temperature is high, the corona is probably quite cold because of its low density. To understand how this can be so, suppose that you lit hundreds of matches, each of which burned at 1 100 000°C. If you placed the matches hundreds of miles apart, very little heat would build up when the matches were lighted.

The corona seems to have many holes. A coronal hole is a large area of the corona that has a lower temperature and a lower density than the rest of the corona. A hole looks black in X-ray photographs.

Neither the chromosphere nor the corona is visible except during eclipses of the sun. An instrument called a *coronagraph* can block the surface of the sun at any time. The chromosphere and the corona can then be seen.

☐ **Why, do you think, are the chromosphere and the corona not visible unless the surface of the sun is blocked?**

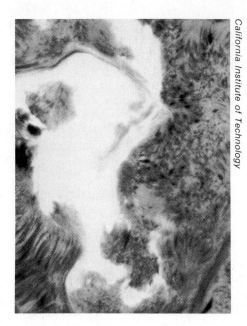

California Institute of Technology

Figure 7–3. Bright plages such as these often appear in the upper photosphere and in the dense regions of the chromosphere above a sunspot. Notice the numerous spicules also visible in the chromosphere.

Figure 7–4. The sun's brilliant surface has been blocked by a coronagraph to allow a view of the corona. The corona, which extends for millions of kilometers, has been color coded to show its different levels of brightness.

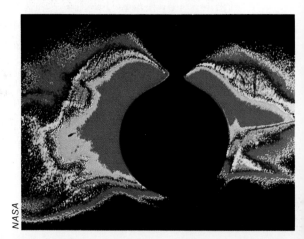

NASA

SOLAR ACTIVITY

What causes sunspots?
How long does a sunspot cycle last?
What are solar prominences?
What causes solar wind?
How does solar wind affect the sun?

Sunspots

Many interesting activities take place on or above the surface of the sun. One of these activities is called sunspots. Scientists have known about sunspots for a long time. In fact, Chinese astronomers knew about them 1,300 years ago. Galileo was aware that they seemed to move across the surface of the sun.

Sunspots are hollow places in the sun's surface gases. The floor in a sunspot is made up of gases that are cooler than the gases in the surrounding surface of the sun. Because the gases in sunspots are cool, they appear darker than the gases around them. Sunspots show up as black spots on the sun's surface. Some sunspots are small. Others may be huge areas at least 144 000 kilometers (90,000 miles) in diameter.

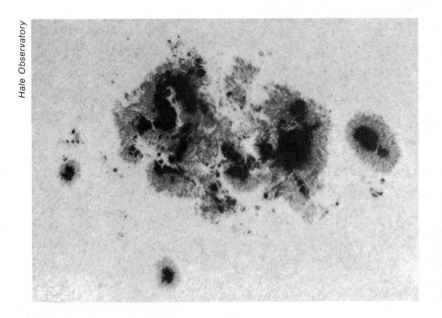

Figure 7–5. The dark floor of a sunspot, the umbra, is surrounded by vertically grooved sides called the penumbra. The grooves of the penumbra seem to be lined up like iron filings on a sheet of paper above a bar magnet.

Scientists think that sunspots are caused by strong magnetic fields below the surface of the sun. They think the magnetic fields are shaped like tubes. These fields become tightly stretched as the sun rotates, sometimes twisting and breaking through the sun's surface. Where the magnetic field pierces the surface, a pair of sunspots form. One sunspot forms where the magnetic field comes out through the surface. Another sunspot forms where the magnetic field goes back in through the surface.

At times there are more sunspots than at other times. In fact, there seems to be a *sunspot cycle* during which the number of sunspots increases and then decreases. It takes eleven years for each sunspot cycle to be completed. Increased sunspot activity seems to be linked to other happenings on the sun and even to changes in weather and communications on the earth.

☐ **Why, do you think, might the sunspot cycle affect the weather and communications on the earth?**

Find Out More

The dark interior of a large sunspot is called an umbra. Sloping upward and outward from the *umbra* is a gray, striped area called a *penumbra*. Using references, find out if all sunspots have these parts.

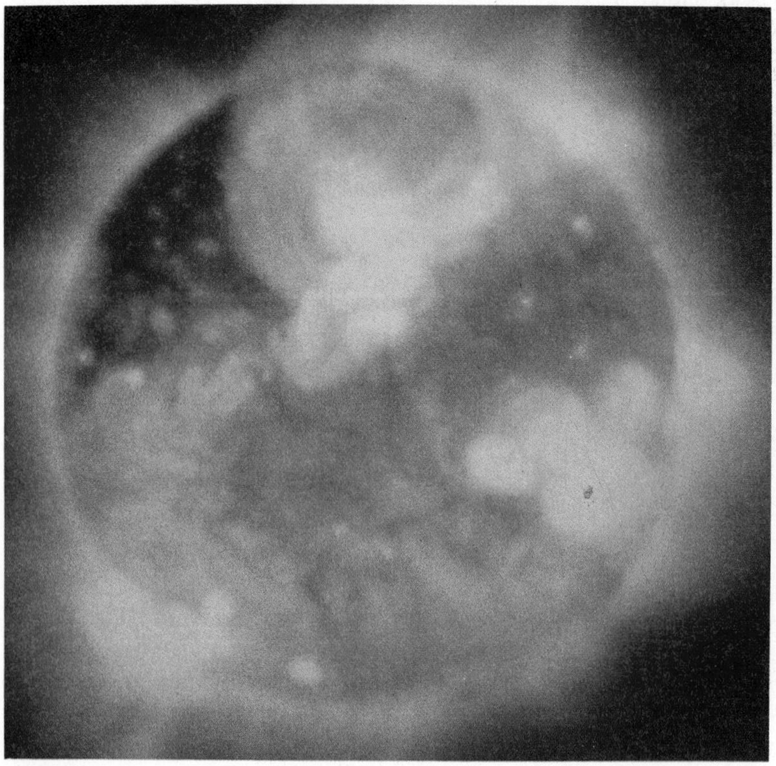

Courtesy of John Davis, American Science and Engineering, Inc., Cambridge, Massachusetts

Figure 7–6. This photograph of the sun, taken during the maximum in a solar cycle, shows many bright, active regions in the sun's atmosphere.

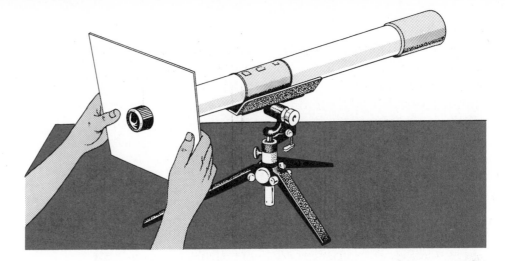

Investigate

**What can you learn
by observing sunspots?**

You will need

pencil, paper, telescope, cardboard, index card

Background

When astronomers noted that sunspots seemed to move across the surface of the sun, they had proof that the sun rotates on its axis. Because the sun is made up of gases, its period of rotation varies with the sun's latitude. The sun rotates once every 25 days at its equator. It rotates once every 34 days at the poles.

Be aware that no one should look directly at the sun even with sunglasses. Permanent eye damage can occur if you look directly at the sun. It is even more dangerous to look at the sun through a telescope or binoculars. There are ways of observing the sun indirectly that will not harm your eyes.

What to do

Put a piece of cardboard around the eyepiece of the telescope. Cut the cardboard 25 cm by 25 cm. Cut a hole in the cardboard the size of the eyepiece. Fit the cardboard snugly around the eyepiece. The cardboard will serve as a shield. With the shield in place, a shadow will be cast around the image of the sun that you project.

Turn your back to the sun. Support the telescope on a stand or on your left shoulder with the objective directed toward the sun as shown. The eyepiece should be aimed toward an index card. By trial and error you should be able to focus a sharp image of the sun on the card.

If the image of the sun is a few centimeters in diameter, you should be able to see sunspots. Have someone draw the sunspots in their exact position on the image of the sun you have projected. Observe the sun indirectly once each day for several days. Notice if the sunspots move. Have someone make a drawing of the sunspots every day.

Now that you have done the investigation

■ How many groups of sunspots did you see on each image of the sun?
■ In which direction did the position of the sunspots change from day to day?

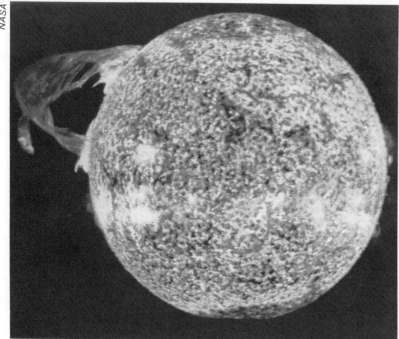

Figure 7–7. Magnetic forces propel a solar prominence, which erupts and grows. The two bases of the prominence are located in the photosphere and in the chromosphere, connected by twisted lines of force.

Solar prominences and flares

Another activity on the sun is in the form of *solar prominences* [PRAHM(-uh)-nuhn(t)s-uhz]. Solar prominences look like flaming arches curving outward for hundreds of kilometers beyond the sun's surface. However, solar prominences are cool, dense masses of gas in the corona. They do not erupt from the sun's surface. They rain down on its surface from the corona.

Solar flares are a kind of solar activity that forms near sunspots. When the magnetic lines of force in a pair of sunspots become intertwined, a spectacular burst of energy may be given off as a solar flare. The energy in a solar flare is released in the form of radio waves, X rays, light rays, and cosmic rays.

Solar flares may last for less than an hour or even for only a few seconds. *Skylab* astronauts photographed a flare that had a temperature of $17\,000\,000°C$ $(30{,}600{,}032°F)$ —hotter than the sun's core. Solar flares are most intense when the sunspot cycle is at its maximum.

Figure 7–8. This colorful picture of a solar flare was electronically processed from a black-and-white photograph that was taken by an astronaut on Skylab. Very bright areas appear as blue, violet, and white. Areas that are less bright appear as red, yellow, and green.

NASA

Solar wind

You know that the sun gives off energy in the form of light and heat. It also gives off gaseous matter from the outermost part of the corona. Most of the matter is made up of electrically charged particles. Scientists call this matter *solar wind*.

Solar wind escapes from the corona through the coronal holes. It escapes from the sun's gravity and races off into space. Solar wind begins at a speed of 500 kilometers (about 310 miles) per second. By the time it comes within 65 000 kilometers (40,300 miles) from the earth, it has slowed to about 50 kilometers (31 miles) per second. Although at this speed solar wind is still traveling fast, it is not a strong wind because of its low density.

After some violent solar activity such as solar flares, the speed of solar wind may double. An increase in the speed of solar wind can be noted by spacecraft as an increase in the magnetic field. Solar winds were first confirmed in 1959 by the Russian spacecraft *Luna 2*.

Solar wind acts as a brake on the sun's rotation. Scientists think that the sun once rotated much more quickly than it does now. It now rotates once every twenty-five days. Solar wind seems to be slowing down the sun's rotation.

☐ **How, do you think, does solar wind escape the sun's gravity?**

Find Out More

The magnetosphere is that region of a planet's upper atmosphere in which the planet's magnetic field controls the behavior of electrically charged particles that come within the boundaries of that magnetic field. Using reference books, find out how the magnetosphere of the earth affects the solar wind. Also find out how the solar wind affects the magnetosphere of the earth.

149

THE SUN'S ENERGY

How does the sun produce its energy?
What is meant by the solar constant?
What is solar energy?
What makes the earth a favorable place for
   living things to thrive?

Fusion

You may wonder how the sun produces energy. For a long time people thought that the sun was burning up its gases. If this were the case, the sun would eventually burn itself to nothing.

It is now generally accepted that the sun produces its energy by a nuclear reaction known as *fusion* [FYOO-zhuhn]. During fusion, the heat at the core of the sun causes the nuclei of atoms of a light element (hydrogen) to fuse, or join, to form nuclei of a slightly heavier element (helium). When fusion occurs, large amounts of energy are given off.

Fusion in the sun comes about in three steps. It is sometimes called a *proton-proton chain of reactions.* In the first step, a hydrogen nucleus, or proton, fuses with another proton. One of the protons loses its charge and becomes a neutron. A *deuterium* [d(y)oo-TIHR-ee-uhm] *nucleus* is then formed. A deuterium nucleus is made up of one proton and one neutron. Deuterium is an isotope of hydrogen.

In the second step, a proton fuses with a deuterium nucleus to make a light form of helium, helium 3. In the third step, two helium 3 nuclei fuse to form helium 4. When this happens, the matter in two protons that are left over is changed into energy.

A great deal of energy is produced during fusion. For every thousand grams of hydrogen used during fusion only seven grams of the proton mass is changed. However, from these seven grams of protons, hundreds of millions of units of energy are produced.

Some of the sun's hydrogen is slowly being used up during fusion. In fact, the sun may be changing billions

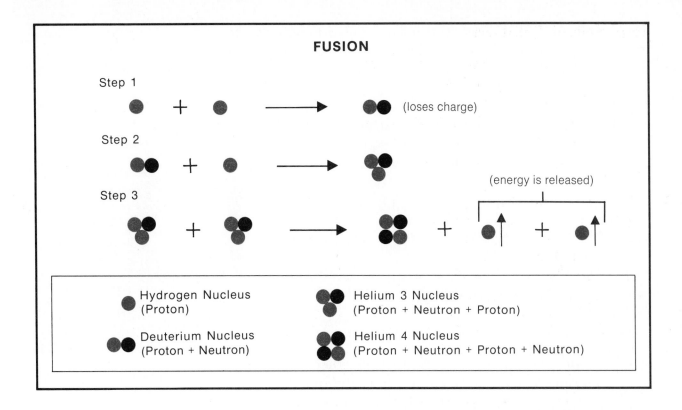

FUSION

Step 1

Step 2

Step 3

(loses charge)

(energy is released)

Hydrogen Nucleus
(Proton)

Deuterium Nucleus
(Proton + Neutron)

Helium 3 Nucleus
(Proton + Neutron + Proton)

Helium 4 Nucleus
(Proton + Neutron + Proton + Neutron)

of kilograms of hydrogen into energy every second. However, this amount of hydrogen is small when compared with the amount of hydrogen in the sun. Fusion can go on at the present rate for another 5 billion years.

☐ **Why, do you think, does fusion occur only on the sun and not on the planets?**

Solar constant

Scientists have been interested in finding out how much energy is given off by the sun. To do so, they measure how much of the sun's energy reaches the earth. Using these measurements, they can figure out the sun's total output of energy.

The amount of solar energy received by each square meter at the top of the earth's atmosphere is called the *solar constant*. Sometimes scientists measure the solar constant in units of power, or kilowatts. The solar constant is 1.36 kilowatts per square meter (1.16 kilowatts

Figure 7–9. Because of very high temperatures in the sun's core, fusion is able to take place there. The chain reactions that occur during fusion make it a very efficient way to produce energy.

To Think About

Some scientists have begun to call the solar constant the *solar parameter* [puh-RAM-uht-ur]. They started doing this when they discovered that the amount of energy received from the sun is not always constant. It varies a little. How might a change in the solar constant affect the climate of the earth?

per square yard). This measurement can be used to figure the total amount of solar energy being given off by the sun. The total amount is 383 million million million million watts.

At times it is useful to measure the solar constant in calories. Calories are a measure of heat. The solar constant is about 2 calories per minute per square centimeter (about 12.9 calories per minute per square inch).

The earth and the sun

Energy used directly from the sun is known as *solar energy*. Enough solar energy reaches the earth's surface in forty minutes to satisfy people's energy needs for an entire year. Some solar energy is used to heat homes and water. Solar energy is also used by solar cells that change sunlight into electricity.

Energy from the sun is important to all living things on the earth. Plants need sunlight to make their food. Both plants and animals need warmth from the sun. The earth's position in the solar system helps living things to receive the energy they require.

Suppose the earth were closer to the sun, as Venus is. The solar constant would be too great for many of the earth's present life forms. What if the earth were farther from the sun, as Mars is? The solar constant would be too small to support life on the earth.

Besides the solar constant, another factor is necessary to keep plants and animals alive on the earth. The earth's atmosphere allows sunlight to pass through and to warm the surface of the earth. However, the sun's warmth would be quickly lost without the blanketing effect of the atmosphere. This effect is known as the *greenhouse effect*.

A greenhouse is a building in which plants can be grown all year round. Its transparent roof lets the sunlight in to warm the air but prevents the heat from escaping. Like the roof of a greenhouse, the atmosphere prevents heat from escaping into space.

□ **Why, do you think, is solar energy not the main source of energy for homes and industry as yet?**

Figure 7–10. Solar panels such as these may be used to supply electrical power for a spaceship.

Find Out More

Green plants store energy from the sun in the food made during photosynthesis. Sometimes this energy remains locked up in the plants for millions of years after the plants become fossilized. Using references, find out how plants become fossilized. Also find out how people use the energy in fossilized plants.

Solar engineers must check their designs. This engineer is checking her latest solar collector.

Photri

Careers

Solar engineer

People have always had the sun working for them. Farmers all over the world make use of the sun for growing their crops. They often use the sun for drying certain crops, such as grains, tobacco, and coffee beans. Many people in the world still preserve their meat and fish by drying them in the sun. Some people harvest salt by evaporating salt water in the sun.

But now more than ever before, people are researching new uses for solar energy. *Solar engineers* design solar water heaters and solar cells that can convert solar energy into electricity. They plan solar ovens for industry and solar panels for spacecraft.

The job of a solar engineer is a challenging

one. Time seems to be running out for most of our present energy sources. Soon the supply may be exhausted. But solar energy will be available for billions of years. Besides, solar energy produces no dangerous pollution or radioactivity. At present, many of the uses of solar energy are expensive. Solar engineers are working on ways to reduce the cost.

In order to become a solar engineer, you need a college degree. You must be skilled in mathematics and physics. If you would like to know more about a career as a solar engineer, you or someone in your class may write to the Solar Energy Institute of America, 1110 Sixth Street, N.W., Washington, DC 20001.

153

Reviewing and Extending

Summing Up

1. Gravity keeps the gases in the sun from escaping. Gas pressure keeps the sun from continuing to collapse.
2. About 71 percent of the sun is hydrogen; 27 percent is helium.
3. The gases in the sun are in the form of a plasma, which is made up of electrically charged particles.
4. The photosphere is covered with large bright regions called plages and small patches called flocculi.
5. The sun's atmosphere consists of three layers: the photosphere, the chromosphere, and the corona.
6. Magnetic lines of force below the surface of the sun break through the sun's surface and form sunspots.
7. A sunspot cycle is completed every eleven years. Solar flares are related to sunspots.
8. Solar wind consists of gaseous matter given off by the sun. Solar wind travels far out into the solar system.
9. The sun produces its energy during a process called fusion. When fusion occurs, hydrogen nuclei are changed into helium nuclei.
10. The solar constant is the amount of solar energy received by each square meter at the top of the earth's atmosphere.
11. Solar energy is energy used directly from the sun.

Checking Up

Vocabulary Write the numerals *1–10* on your paper. Each numbered phrase describes a term from the following list. On your paper, write the term next to the numeral of the phrase that describes it.

solar constant   gravity   flocculi
solar wind   core   chromosphere
solar flares   plages   fusion
convection zone   plasma   sunspots

1. hollow places on the surface of the sun that are made up of cooler gases than those in the surrounding surface
2. large, bright regions on the sun's surface
3. nuclear reaction that produces energy in the sun
4. force that keeps most of the gases in the sun from escaping into space
5. center of the sun
6. red-colored layer of the sun's atmosphere
7. small bright or dark patches on the sun's surface
8. gaseous matter given off from the outermost part of the corona
9. amount of energy received by each square meter at the top of the earth's atmosphere
10. phase of matter made up of electrically charged particles

Knowledge and Understanding   Write the numerals *11–20* on your paper. Beside each numeral, write the word or words that best complete the sentence having that numeral.

11. The matter in the sun is kept from collapsing by a force called (*gravity, gas pressure, weight*).
12. About 71 percent of the sun is made of (*hydrogen, helium, oxygen*).
13. The hottest part of the sun is the (*photosphere, chromosphere, core*).
14. A sunspot cycle is completed every (*seven, eleven, fifteen*) years.
15. Solar wind affects the sun by (*slowing down the sun's rotation, cooling the corona, causing storms on the sun*).
16. When one proton fuses with another proton, and one proton loses its charge, a nucleus of (*hydrogen, deuterium, helium*) is formed.
17. The (*greenhouse effect, solar energy, solar constant*) prevents heat from the earth from escaping into space.
18. The temperature at the core of the sun is (*1 100 000°C, 4 500 000°C, 15 000 000°C*).
19. Fusion can take place on the sun at the present rate for (*1 million, 1 billion, 5 billion*) years.
20. The surface of the sun is the (*photosphere, chromosphere, corona*).

Expressing Yourself   Write a paragraph as an answer to each of the following questions:

21. What are the steps that take place during fusion on the sun?
22. How does the earth's position in the solar system favor the living things that live on its surface?

Doing More

1. Orbiting Solar Observatories (OSOs) orbit the sun while pointing instruments at the sun's surface. Find out when the first OSO was launched. Also find out which important discoveries about the sun were made as a result of the investigations by OSOs.
2. Make a solar collector. Cover a shoe box with black construction paper. Tape a thermometer in the box in a position that will allow you to read the thermometer. Cut a flap in the lid of the box. Keep the flap closed when you are not reading the thermometer. Lift the flap when you wish to read the thermometer.

   Put the box in sunlight. Record the temperature each minute for ten minutes. What happens to the temperature in the box? How might you convert the heat in the solar collector to useful energy?

8   The Earth in Motion

By studying the apparent motions of the stars, scientists are able to learn more about the motion of the earth. How, do you think, can the apparent motions of the stars help scientists do this?

Long ago, many people believed that the earth was the center of the universe. They had a *geocentric* [JEE-oh-SEHN-trihk], or earth-centered, view of the universe. These people also believed that the earth was motionless, with the sun, the stars, the moon, and the planets all moving around the earth.

Today, people know much more about the earth and its motion than did people of long ago. People of today know that the earth is not the center of the universe. And they know that the earth moves in two ways. One way the earth moves is by *rotating*, or spinning on its axis. Another way the earth moves is by *revolving*, or moving in a path through space around the sun.

What forces cause the earth to move? How does the earth rotate? What path does the earth follow as it revolves around the sun? What keeps the earth and the planets moving around the sun? As you study this chapter, you will be learning the answers to these questions and other questions about the movement of the earth.

EXPLORING THE EARTH'S MOTION

*How did Copernicus change the model of our
solar system?*

*What are Kepler's three laws of planetary
motion?*

Who first studied the sky with a telescope?

Copernicus

For many centuries, people accepted without question
the idea that the sky was made up of huge rotating spheres
carrying the sun, the stars, the moon, and the planets
around the earth. It was not until the sixteenth century
A.D. that Copernicus presented a new model for our solar
system. According to Copernicus, the earth and all the
other planets move around the sun.

Many people living at the time of Copernicus could not
accept the idea that the earth was not the center of the
universe. They could not believe that the earth moves and
that it revolves around the sun. It was not until long after
Copernicus died that his ideas were accepted.

☐ **Why, do you think, did people not believe that
the earth is moving?**

Kepler

Another astronomer who helped people understand how
the earth moves was Johannes Kepler (1571–1630). Kepler
used his observations and his understanding of mathematics. He discovered three laws of planetary motion.

The Bettmann Archive   Smithsonian Institution

To Think About

Today it is generally ac-
cepted that the earth revolves
around the sun. What rea-
sons do you think people had
before the time of Copernicus
to believe that the sun revolved around the earth?

*Figure 8–1. Nicolaus Copernicus
(left) and Johannes Kepler (right)
helped to change people's beliefs
about the motions of the planets.*

Kepler's *first law of planetary motion* describes the shape of a planet's orbit. The first law is often called the "law of ellipses" because, as Kepler observed, a planet's orbit is an *ellipse* [ih-LIHPS]. An ellipse is somewhat oval, or egg-shaped, and, unlike a circle, it has two central points. A circle has only one central point. You can see an ellipse in Figure 8–2.

Each central point of an ellipse is called a *focus* [FOH-kuhs]. Kepler's first law states that the orbit of a planet is an ellipse with the sun at one focus. Kepler's first law of planetary motion can be stated as follows:

1. Every planet follows a path, or *orbit*, around the sun. The path of each planet is an ellipse. The sun is at one focus of the elliptical orbit.

Kepler's *second law of planetary motion* describes the speed of a planet in orbit. Kepler studied the time it took Mars to travel from one point to another point in its orbit around the sun. He noted that Mars traveled faster when it was close to the sun than when it was farther away from

Jacqueline Durand

Do It Yourself

Draw the orbit of a planet

According to Kepler's first law, the orbit of a planet is an ellipse. To draw an ellipse, you will need a pencil, a piece of thick cardboard, 2 thumbtacks, and a string 20 cm long. Tie the ends of the string together to form a loop. Push 2 thumbtacks 10 cm apart through a piece of thick cardboard. Each thumbtack will serve as a focus for your ellipse. Slide the string around the tacks, leaving the string slack. Hold a pencil against the string to make the string taut. Now draw an ellipse by keeping the string taut. Draw the sun at 1 focus. On the ellipse, or orbit, draw a planet at the point closest to the sun. Then draw an X on the orbit at the point where the planet would be the farthest from the sun.

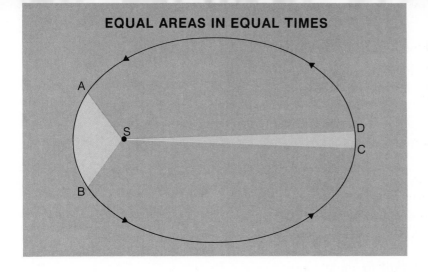

EQUAL AREAS IN EQUAL TIMES

Figure 8–2. A planet moves around the sun in an elliptical, or ellipse-shaped, orbit. It takes a planet the same amount of time to move from point A to point B on its orbit as it does to move from point C to point D. If point S represents the sun, do you think a planet moves faster when it is close to the sun or far from the sun? Why do you think so?

the sun. This observation led Kepler to look for a mathematical explanation.

Kepler noted that a line joining Mars to the sun during the eight weeks when Mars was closest to the sun would cross over a certain area in the ellipse. The line crossed this area when Mars moved from point *A* to point *B* in eight weeks. See Figure 8–2. Kepler computed the area of the shaded part of the ellipse inside points *ABS*.

Next, Kepler noted that a line joining Mars to the sun during the eight weeks when Mars was farthest from the sun would cross over another area in the ellipse. The line crossed the area as Mars moved from point *C* to point *D* in eight weeks. When Kepler computed the area of the shaded part of the ellipse inside points *CDS*, he found this area was equal to *ABS*. The distance from point *A* to point *B* was much greater than from point *C* to point *D*, yet Mars took the same time to travel from point *A* to point *B* as it did from point *C* to point *D*. Having computed the areas, Kepler stated his second law of planetary motion:

> 2. An imaginary line from the center of the sun to the center of a planet crosses over the same area in a given time at any point in the planet's orbit. Planets move faster when they are close to the sun than when they are far away from the sun.

Kepler's second law is based on mathematical reasoning. As you can see, the law is explained only when areas of the ellipse are computed. Kepler's second law of planetary motion is often called the "law of areas."

In working out the *third law of planetary motion*, Kepler studied the information then known about the planets. He noted an interesting fact. The ratio between the time it takes two planets to orbit the sun is proportional to the ratio of the size of the orbits of these two planets. Kepler's third law of planetary motion can be stated as follows:

3. The time it takes for a planet to make one complete revolution around the sun is the planet's *period*. The squares of the planets' periods of revolution are proportional to (have the same ratio as) the cubes of the planets' average distances from the sun.

You may be better able to understand Kepler's third law by working an example. First, square the period of revolution of Jupiter and of the earth. Remember, when you square a number, you multiply it by itself. Note the ratio of the periods when they are squared.

$$\frac{\text{Jupiter } (11.86)^2 \text{ years}}{\text{Earth } (1.0)^2 \text{ years}} = \frac{11.86 \times 11.86}{1.0 \times 1.0} = \frac{140.6}{1.0} = 140.6$$

Now cube the distance of Jupiter and of the earth from the sun. To cube a number, you multiply the number by itself and again by itself. Note the ratio of the distances when they are cubed.

$$\frac{\text{Jupiter } (5.20)^3 \text{ AU}}{\text{Earth } (1.0)^3 \text{ AU}} = \frac{5.20 \times 5.20 \times 5.20}{1.0 \times 1.0 \times 1.0} = \frac{140.6}{1.0} = 140.6$$

Note that you found the same ratio in both cases. You will find that this works when you compare any two planets. Of course, the ratios for the earth and Mars would not be the same as the ratios for the earth and Jupiter. But the ratio between the squares of the periods of the earth and Mars would be the same as the ratio between the cubes of the distances from the sun of the earth and

To Think About

Observatories are places where astronomers view the sky with huge telescopes. Observatories are usually built on high mountains far from cities. Why, do you think, is this so? Why are most observations from the observatories made only at night?

Mars. Kepler's third law can help you to find a planet's average distance from the sun if you know the time it takes for the planet to orbit the sun.

☐ **How could astronomers use Kepler's third law to find out how far a planet is from the sun?**

Galileo

About the same time Kepler was working on his laws, still another astronomer was studying the solar system and the motion of the earth. His name was Galileo Galilei (1564–1642). In 1609, Galileo put several lenses together and built the first telescope used to study objects in the sky.

Galileo's first telescope made objects appear to be three times larger than normal. His later telescopes made objects appear thirty times larger than normal. With his telescopes, Galileo discovered many stars that are too faint to be seen with the eyes alone. Galileo was able to see that the planets are earthlike. He even discovered four of Jupiter's moons. His discoveries helped prove that the earth is a planet and that the earth moves.

Figure 8–3. Sir Isaac Newton constructed one of the first reflecting telescopes to use in his studies. This type of telescope was made with reflecting mirrors and lenses instead of only with lenses, as earlier telescopes were.

NEWTON'S DISCOVERIES

What is Newton's first law of motion?
What is inertia? Gravitation?

First law of motion

Yet another scientist who made discoveries that can explain the motion of the earth was Sir Isaac Newton (1642–1727), an English physicist and mathematician. Newton was born in the year Galileo died. Newton's experiments and his understanding of mathematics helped expand upon the work of both Galileo and Kepler. Kepler, for example, explained how the planets move. But Newton explained why the planets move as they do.

Newton's *first law of motion* explains that force is needed to change the motion of an object. Newton's first law states that if a body is at rest, it tends to stay at rest and that if a body is moving, it tends to keep moving at the

Find Out More

Using references, find out more about Sir Isaac Newton. Newton was famous for his discoveries about motion and gravity. For what other discoveries in science and mathematics is Newton known?

161

Figure 8–4. In what way is inertia affecting the people on this amusement-park ride?

same speed and in a straight line. Of course, this law applies only when there is no interference from outside forces.

Newton's first law of motion is an explanation of a property known as *inertia* [ihn-UR-shuh]. Inertia causes an object at rest to remain at rest and an object in motion to remain in motion. All objects—you, a car, the earth, and the planets—have inertia. To understand how inertia works, suppose you are riding in a car. What happens to you if the car suddenly speeds up? You feel as if you are being pushed backward. You have this feeling because of inertia. The car moves forward, but you tend to keep moving at the same speed you were moving before the car suddenly speeded up. Inertia causes you to feel as if you are being pushed backward.

□ **How, do you think, would inertia affect you if the car stopped suddenly?**

Law of gravitation

Newton's *law of gravitation* [GRAV-uh-TAY-shuhn] is also important to the motion of the planets. This law states that every object in the universe attracts every other object

Figure 8–5. The pull of the earth's gravity causes an arrow to fall back to the earth, instead of traveling in a straight line into space.

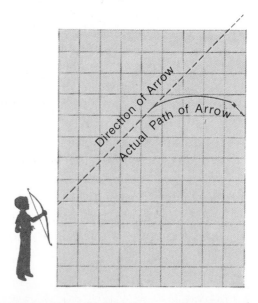

in the universe. Objects pull on one another. The force of attraction between the objects is known as *gravitation*. According to the law of gravitation, the larger the mass of the objects, the greater is the attraction.

The law of gravitation explains why the earth and all the other planets move in orbit around the sun. The sun pulls on the earth and the other planets, keeping them in orbit and causing them to move. The earth's gravitational pull is also known as gravity. The earth's gravity pulls on the moon. Because of this attraction, the moon remains in orbit around the earth.

The pull of gravity can be measured. You measure this pull when you step onto a scale and weigh yourself. *Weight* is a measure of the pull of gravity. Each planet differs in mass from all the other planets. Because of this difference in mass, you would have a different weight on the different planets. On Mercury, for example, your weight would be about a third of your weight on the earth. The earth's mass is eighteen times the mass of Mercury.

Newton's first law of motion and his law of gravitation work together to explain why the earth and the other planets move as they do. According to Newton's first law of motion, the planets move at a uniform speed and in a straight line unless a force acts on the planets and changes the way they move. The law of gravitational attraction explains that the pull of the sun's gravity is the force that causes the earth and the other planets to move in orbits around the sun rather than move in a straight line through space.

ROTATION OF THE EARTH

> *How did Foucault's pendulum prove that the earth rotates on its axis?*
> *In which direction does the earth rotate?*
> *How long does one rotation of the earth take?*

Proof of rotation

As you know, Copernicus and many other early astronomers believed that the earth rotates, or spins, on its axis.

To Think About

The mass of Mars is about one tenth of the mass of the earth. The mass of Jupiter, on the other hand, is about 318 times more than the mass of the earth. Suppose you are on Mars. Would you weigh more or less than you weigh on the earth? Suppose you are on Jupiter. Would you weigh more or less than you weigh on the earth? Explain.

Figure 8–6. The star trails in this picture are the result of the earth spinning on its axis—not the result of the movement of the stars.

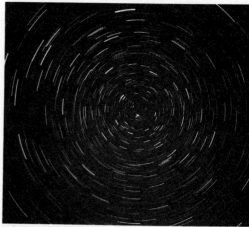

U.S Naval Observatory

Investigate

**In what direction does
the earth rotate?**

You will need

paper, pencil, camera tripod, fast black-and-
white film (ASA 400), camera with a shutter
that can be held open

Background

As you may know, the stars appear to change
their position in the sky throughout the night.
However, the stars are not really moving. They
just appear to move because the earth is rotating on its axis. By observing the way the stars
appear to move, you can find out in what
direction the earth rotates.

What to do

Obtain a camera in which the shutter can be
held open. Select a night when the stars are
bright and your surroundings are dark. Place
fast black-and-white film in the camera. Set the
focus of your camera for the farthest distance
possible. On many cameras this distance is
called infinity. Point your camera to the North
Star. The camera must be mounted on a tripod

or on another steady base so that the camera
does not move.

Make a drawing of the North Star and of
the stars near the North Star. This drawing
shows the position of the stars at the beginning
of this *Investigate*.

Open the shutter of the camera to the widest
opening. Leave the shutter of the camera open
for an hour or two. Then close the shutter,
remove the film from the camera, and have
it developed.

Your photograph will show the apparent
motion of the stars. Compare your photograph
with your drawing of the position of the stars at
the beginning of the *Investigate*. This will help
you find out how the stars seem to have moved.

Now that you have done the investigation

■ Why, do you think, was the North Star used
as the center of the photograph?
■ What causes the apparent circular motion of
the stars?
■ Do the stars seem to move in a clockwise or a
counterclockwise direction?
■ Does the earth rotate in a clockwise or a
counterclockwise direction? How do you know?

164

They were, however, unable to prove this point. The first real proof that the earth does indeed rotate on its axis was not presented until more than 300 years after the death of Copernicus.

In 1851, a French scientist, Jean Foucault (1819–1868), conducted an experiment with a huge pendulum. He suspended a heavy ball by a wire about 60 meters (200 feet) long from the dome of the Pantheon in Paris. Foucault set a pin into the bottom of the ball so that the pin would trace lines into a thin layer of sand on the floor beneath the pendulum. Foucault then started the pendulum swinging.

As time passed, the lines traced by the pendulum moved slowly and steadily in a clockwise direction. See Figure 8–7. Foucault knew that according to Newton's laws of motion the bob of the pendulum should swing in one direction. The pendulum swings in one direction unless a force acts on the pendulum to cause it to change direction. No force was acting on the pendulum, so Foucault had to conclude that the floor was turning under the pendulum. The moving of the lines traced by the pendulum showed that the earth was moving under the swinging pendulum. Foucault's pendulum presented the first proof that the earth rotates.

☐ **Did Foucault's pendulum show that the earth rotates in a clockwise direction or in a counterclockwise direction? Explain.**

How the earth rotates

Foucault's pendulum showed that the earth rotates on its axis. It also showed that the earth moves in a counterclockwise direction, or from west to east. As the earth turns, Japan moves toward California. California moves toward New York. And New York moves toward England. In what direction, do you think, does England move?

The time it takes for the earth to make one rotation has become a standard way to measure time. The time it takes the earth to rotate once on its axis is a *day*. A day is twenty-three hours fifty-six minutes four seconds long.

Find Out More

Foucault designed another experiment to prove that the earth rotates. In this experiment, Foucault used an instrument that he called a gyroscope. Using references, find out what a gyroscope is. Also find out how Foucault used a gyroscope to prove that the earth rotates.

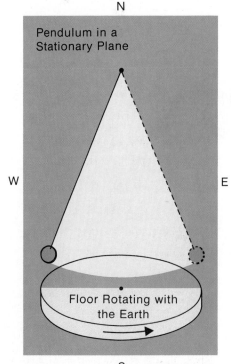

Figure 8–7. As the earth turns in a counterclockwise direction under a pendulum, the lines traced by the pendulum appear to move in a clockwise direction.

165

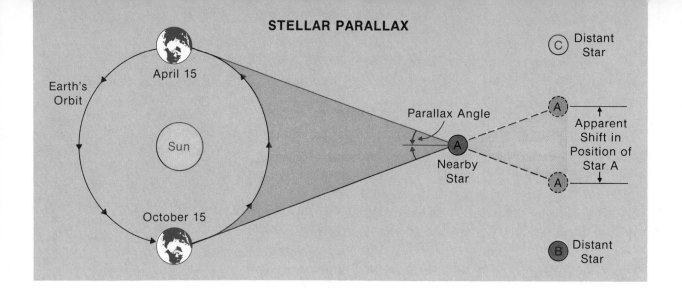

STELLAR PARALLAX

April 15

Earth's Orbit

Sun

October 15

Parallax Angle

A
Nearby Star

C Distant Star

A
Apparent Shift in Position of Star A

A

B Distant Star

THE EARTH IN ORBIT

How does the stellar parallax prove that the earth revolves around the sun?
What is the perihelion? The aphelion?
How long does it take for the earth to make one revolution?

Proof of orbital motion

Astronomers who believed in Copernicus' theory that the earth revolves around the sun wanted to prove that this theory was true. Astronomers knew that on the earth an observer can note a shift in the apparent position of an

Figure 8-8. As the earth moves around the sun from October to April, does the nearby star shown here appear to move up or down?

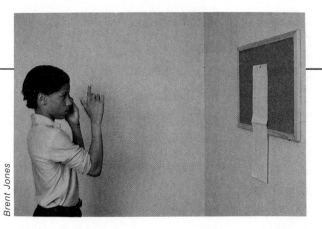

Brent Jones

Do It Yourself
Demonstrate parallax

Pin a narrow strip of paper about 30 cm long in a vertical position on a bulletin board. Stand across the room. Close your left eye and hold up one finger so that it blocks your view of the strip of paper. Now open your left eye and close your right eye. What appears to happen to the strip of paper? How is this like the stellar parallax?

object if the observer sights the object from two different positions. This shift in the apparent position is known as a *parallax* [PAR-uh-LAKS].

The astronomers also knew that if the earth moves from one side of its orbit to the other, there should be an apparent shift in the position of nearby stars. This shift is called the *stellar parallax*. Astronomers tried to prove that the earth revolves by measuring the stellar parallax. Because this shift is so small, it could not be seen with the eye alone or even with early telescopes. The orbital motion of the earth was therefore not proved until 1838. In that year, Friedrich Bessel (1784–1846) was able to measure a shift in nearby stars.

You can understand how the stellar parallax proves the orbital motion of the earth by looking at Figure 8–8. Suppose you observe a nearby star from point *A* on the earth's orbit. Then suppose you observe the same star six months later from point *B* on the earth's orbit. The position of the star in respect to more distant stars will appear to shift. This shift can happen only if the earth moves.

How the earth revolves

By measuring the stellar parallax, Bessel showed that the earth revolves around the sun. He also showed that the earth travels from west to east. That is, it orbits in a counterclockwise direction. Once scientists knew that the earth orbits the sun, they could learn more about the earth's orbit by using Kepler's laws.

Find Out More

There are two different ways of measuring the earth's rotation. Thus there are two different kinds of days. One kind of day is called a solar day. The other kind of day is called a sidereal day. How are these two kinds of days different? Which day do you use? Which day is longer?

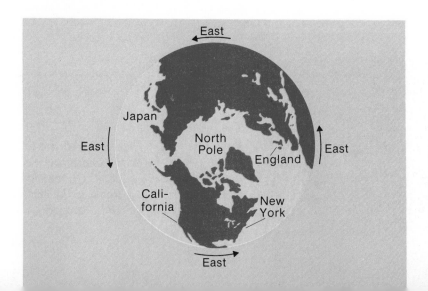

Figure 8–9. The rotation of the earth is shown here as viewed from the North Pole. As the earth turns, in which direction does it carry your school?

According to Kepler's first law, the earth revolves around the sun in an orbit that is an ellipse. Since the sun is at one focus of this ellipse, the earth is closer to the sun at certain times and farther from the sun at other times. About January 3, the earth is closest to the sun. This position is called the *perihelion* [PEHR-uh-HEEL-yuhn]. The distance between the earth and the sun is about 147 million kilometers (91 million miles) at the perihelion.

About July 4, the earth is farthest from the sun. This position is called the *aphelion* [a-FEEL-yuhn]. The distance between the earth and the sun is about 152 million kilometers (94 million miles) at the aphelion. Kepler's third law can be used to show that the average distance between the earth and the sun is about 150 million kilometers (93 million miles).

The earth travels around the sun at an average speed of nearly 107 000 kilometers (66,000 miles) per hour. According to Kepler's second law, the earth travels slowly when it is farther from the sun and faster when it is closer to the sun.

□ **In what month is the earth's motion in orbit the fastest? The slowest? Explain.**

Just as the earth's rotation has become a standard way of measuring time, so has the earth's revolution. The time it takes the earth to travel once around the sun is a *year*. A year is made up of 365.25 days.

To Think About

Kepler's third law of planetary motion can help you to find the earth's average distance from the sun. What other measurement of the earth's orbit can Kepler's third law help you to find?

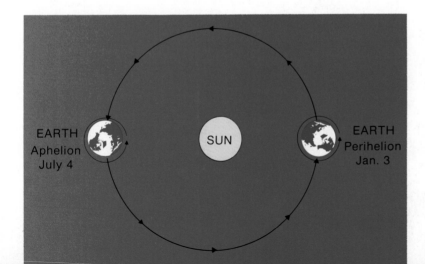

Figure 8–10. The earth is closest to the sun on January 3 and farthest from the sun on July 4. On which two dates, do you think, is the earth's distance from the sun average?

After making certain final adjustments, this astronomer can use the telescope to learn more about the planets and stars. In what ways, do you think, is an astronomer's work important?

Careers

Astronomer

Copernicus, Kepler, and Galileo were all *astronomers*. They were scientists who studied the universe and the laws that govern it. Astronomers are highly skilled scientists who do many different kinds of work.

Astronomers may collect information about the sun, the moon, the stars, or the planets. They may use this information to determine the orbits of the planets and of their moons. Astronomers may also be concerned with studying such things as the brightness of the stars and their distance from the earth. They may also study the makeup of the moon, the planets, and the stars. Astronomers sometimes determine the orbits of comets and asteroids. Some astronomers work in the space program.

The telescope is one of the instruments astronomers use to study the universe. Some astronomers use a radio telescope. Astronomers also use other instruments, such as a *spectrometer* [spehk-TRAHM-uht-ur]. A spectrometer measures the wavelengths of light. Astronomers also use computers to store the information they collect and to calculate such things as orbits and distances.

To become an astronomer, you will need to attend college and study mathematics, physics, and astronomy. You will probably have to study until you have earned an advanced degree. A student in your class might write to the American Astronomical Society, Physics Department, University of Delaware, Sharp Laboratories, Newark, DE 19711, to find out more about becoming an astronomer.

Reviewing and Extending

Summing Up

1. For many centuries, people believed that the earth was the center of the universe and that the earth did not move.
2. Copernicus presented a model of the solar system in which the earth and the planets move around the sun.
3. The orbit of a planet is an ellipse with the sun at one focus.
4. A planet travels slowly when it is far away from the sun and faster when it is near the sun.
5. Galileo was the first to use the telescope to study objects in the sky.
6. Inertia is the property of an object that causes an object at rest to remain at rest and an object in motion to remain in motion.
7. The pull of the sun's gravity causes the earth to orbit the sun rather than to keep moving in a straight line through space.
8. Foucault's pendulum proved that the earth rotates on its axis.
9. The time it takes the earth to rotate once on its axis is a day.
10. The fact that the earth revolves around the sun can be proved by stellar parallax.
11. The earth is closest to the sun at the perihelion of its orbit and farthest from the sun at the aphelion.

Checking Up

Vocabulary Write the numerals *1–10* on your paper. Each numbered phrase describes a term from the following list. On your paper, write the term next to the numeral of the phrase that describes it.

day	Kepler	Galileo
year	circle	inertia
month	rotate	ellipse
Newton	revolve	gravity

1. first astronomer to use a telescope to study the universe
2. shape of the earth's orbit
3. property of an object that causes an object in motion to remain in motion
4. attraction or pull that causes an object to fall to earth
5. time it takes the earth to make one complete revolution
6. stated the law of gravitation
7. to spin on an axis
8. astronomer who discovered three laws of planetary motion
9. to travel in a path around the sun
10. time it takes the earth to make one complete rotation

Knowledge and Understanding Write the numerals *11–17* on your paper. Beside each numeral write the word or words that best complete the sentence having that numeral.

11. The fact that the earth orbits the sun was proved by means of ____.
12. Foucault's pendulum proved that the earth ____ on its axis.
13. Your ____ is a measure of the gravitational attraction between you and the earth.
14. The ____ is the position on the earth's orbit when it is farthest from the sun.
15. The ____ is the position on the earth's orbit when it is closest to the sun.
16. According to Kepler's second law of planetary motion, a planet travels fastest when it is ____ to the sun.
17. Kepler's ____ law of planetary motion compares the ratio of the squares of two planets' periods of revolution and the ratio of the cubes of their average distance from the sun.

Expressing Yourself Write a paragraph as an answer to each of the following questions:

18. Why would your weight on the earth be different from your weight on another planet?
19. What do Kepler's laws tell about the earth's orbit?

Doing More

1. Place a textbook on a sheet of notebook paper. Quickly pull on the paper. What happened to the book? Which law of motion does this demonstrate? Try to think of some other ways to demonstrate this law.

2. Use references to try to find out how the earth's rotation affects the weather on the earth. Also try to find out how the earth's rotation affects characteristics such as the shape of the earth.

The Whirlpool galaxy M51 is one of the millions of galaxies that make up the universe.

9 Beyond Our Solar System

About two hundred years ago astronomers began to understand some important ideas about how the universe is organized. For example, studies begun by one astronomer, Sir William Herschel, and his son John revealed that the stars and other objects in space were not just scattered at random in the universe. Instead the stars and other objects were held together by gravity in a huge system known as a *galaxy* [GAL-uhk-see].

At first it was believed that our galaxy, the Milky Way, contained all the bodies in the universe. Then in 1924 another galaxy outside our own was discovered.

In Chapter 9 you will see that astronomers have since charted over a million galaxies. They believe that there are actually billions more. You may be surprised to find out that some stars in these galaxies are dying, while others are just forming. You may wonder along with scientists, How old is the universe? Does it have any boundaries? These are some questions that will stretch your mind as you "look" beyond our solar system.

STUDYING THE STARS

*What changes are believed to occur in the life
of a star?*

*How are the color and the temperature of a star
related?*

*What unit of measurement is used for the
distance to a star?*

*What is meant by the "absolute magnitude" of a
star?*

Other suns

As you may know, stars are not all alike. They come in various sizes and colors. Our sun is just a medium-sized star. Sirius, the brightest star in the night sky, is another medium-sized star. Medium-sized stars range from one-tenth the size of the sun to ten times its size. Stars that are less than one-tenth the size of the sun are the so-called dwarfs. Some dwarfs are even smaller than the earth. One kind of dwarf, the white dwarf, is a very dense star. It has a mass comparable to the sun, but it is only about as large as the earth.

If a star is ten to one hundred times larger than the sun, it is called a giant star. Larger yet is a supergiant star. A supergiant may be as much as a thousand times the size of the sun. Figure 9–1 lists some giant and some supergiant stars.

The size of a star can reveal something about its age. Scientists believe that a star begins its life as a medium-sized star, expands into a giant, and finally contracts into a dwarf. Such changes are related to a star's production of energy. You may recall that our star, the sun, produces a great amount of heat and light by changing some of its matter into energy. Other stars do the same. When the amount of hydrogen in the center of a star decreases greatly, its core contracts. But its overall size remains the same. The contraction makes the core of the star rise sharply in temperature. The intense heat at the core then

Figure 9–1. Which of these giant and supergiant stars have you heard of before?

SUPERGIANT STARS	GIANT STARS
Rigel	Capella
Deneb	Aldebaran
Betelgeuse	Mira
North Star	Arcturus
Antares	Pollux
Canopus	

pushes on the outer regions of the star, causing these regions to expand. The star keeps growing until it becomes a giant. As the star expands, the matter in its outer region gets thinner and thinner. Because the matter becomes thinned out, the star's surface temperature is lowered. Its color turns red. After a while, the whole star begins to contract. The contraction makes it very dense and hot. It then glows as a white dwarf.

A very large star may shrink to a much smaller size and become much denser than a white dwarf. It becomes so dense that no light at all can escape from its surface. Because of this, the former star is called a *black hole.* A black hole is so dense that a spoonful of its matter may weigh millions of tons! Anything near a black hole would be sucked into it by the force of its tremendous gravity.

These changes occur over millions or even billions of years. How quickly these changes occur depends on the original mass of the star. A star that begins its life with more mass than the sun changes much more quickly than a star with less mass than the sun.

☐ **Why might a larger star change faster than a smaller star?**

Color and temperature of stars

When you look at the stars, almost all of them seem to be shining with a white light. But with a telescope, slight differences in the color of light from certain stars can be noted.

A clue about why stars are of different colors can be gathered by watching a piece of metal being heated. At first the metal glows red. As it becomes hotter, it turns orange, then yellow. Gradually the metal becomes white-hot. If the temperature rises still more, the metal gets blue-white. Scientists know that stars, like metals, vary in color according to their temperature. The hottest stars send out mostly blue-white light.

☐ **Which of two otherwise identical stars do you think would be brighter, a hot star or a cool one? Why?**

Find Out More

A nova is an interesting stage in the life history of some stars. Look in reference books under *novae* (the plural of "nova") to find out about this stage.

174

Distance to stars

When you were studying distances in the solar system, you found that astronomical units (A.U.'s) were easier to work with than kilometers or miles. But when distances beyond the solar system are considered, astronomical units are too small to be helpful. For this reason scientists use a measurement called a *light-year*. A light-year is the distance traveled by light in a year. Nothing in the universe travels faster than light. Light travels about 300 000 kilometers (186,000 miles) per second. At such a speed, light travels about 9.5 trillion kilometers (5.9 trillion miles) in a year.

The nearest star to our solar system is *Alpha Centauri* [AL-fuh sehn-TAWR-ee]. It is actually a group of 3 stars more than 4.3 light-years away. See Figure 9–2 for the distances to some other stars from the earth. The light now seen in the sky from Alpha Centauri was given off by that star group over 4 years ago. If Alpha Centauri would suddenly explode, astronomers wouldn't be aware that it had happened until 4 years from now!

☐ **Close to what important event in history did the light presently seen from the supergiant Betelgeuse [BEET-uhl-JOOS] leave that star? (Use Figure 9–2.)**

TEN BRIGHTEST STARS			
Star	Distance from the Earth (Light-years)	Apparent Magnitude	Absolute Magnitude
1. Sirius	8.8	−1.46	+1.4
2. Canopus	98.0	−0.72	−3.1
3. Alpha Centauri	4.3	−0.01	+4.4
4. Arcturus	36.0	−0.06	−0.3
5. Vega	26.0	+0.04	+0.5
6. Capella	46.0	+0.05	−0.7
7. Rigel	900.0	+0.14	−6.8
8. Procyon	11.0	+0.37	+2.6
9. Betelgeuse	490.0	+0.41	−5.5
10. Achernar	114.0	+0.51	−1.0

Figure 9–2. The first part of this chart gives you information about the distance to some stars. The information in the second part of the chart can be used with "Brightness of stars" on pages 176 and 177.

Brightness of stars

Ancient astronomers thought that the stars were located on a moving sphere that rotated about the earth while the earth stood still. As far as these astronomers were concerned, all the stars were about the same distance from the earth. So they thought that a star's true brightness and size corresponded to the way it looked from the earth. They devised a scale in which a number known as the *magnitude* [MAG-nuh-T(Y)OOD] of a star listed its brightness compared with that of other stars. A very bright star was said to be of a low magnitude. A dimmer star was of a higher magnitude. For example, a star with a magnitude of 1 was much brighter than a star with a magnitude of 10. A star with a magnitude of —2 was brighter than one of —1. Why is this so?

Nowadays we know that all stars are not equal in distance from the earth. And scientists know that distance greatly affects the *apparent magnitude* of a star. The sun has an apparent magnitude of —26.5 because it appears to be the brightest object in the sky. But actually many stars would be far brighter than the sun if they were as close to the earth as the sun is. To determine the true brightness of stars, scientists use a scale giving the *absolute magnitude* of stars. The absolute magnitude gives an idea of the

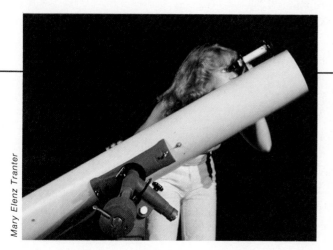

Mary Elenz Tranter

Do It Yourself

Study the stars in the Big Dipper

Look in a reference book to find the names of the stars in the Big Dipper. On a clear night locate the stars of the Big Dipper. Name the stars that seem larger. Name the stars that are brighter. Observe the middle star in the handle of the Big Dipper. What is unusual about this star? Use a telescope to observe the middle star in the Big Dipper. What else do you notice about the middle star?

amount of light that would actually be received from the stars if they were all the same distance from the earth. The sun's absolute magnitude is 5. Such a magnitude shows that the sun is not a bright star after all. Compare the apparent magnitude of some stars with their absolute magnitude in Figure 9–2.

☐ **If two stars look equally bright in the sky, what is the only thing you can know for certain about the two stars?**

To Think About

To understand why some stars shine more brightly than others, think about electric lights you have seen shining. What other factor besides distance and color affects the brightness of a light?

GALAXIES—OUR OWN AND OTHERS

*How did astronomers find out about the shape
   and size of our galaxy?*
*What role did certain variable stars play in
   the discovery of other galaxies?*
What are some shapes that galaxies have?

The Milky Way

The Greeks named the filmy band of stars that they observed in the sky the "Milky Way." They did not realize that the Milky Way was a galaxy nor that our solar system was a part of it. In fact, it was not until two hundred years ago that astronomers discovered that the sun and billions of neighboring stars belonged to one rotating system known as a galaxy. It is now known that tremendous gravitational forces hold the dust, gases, stars, and other bodies of our galaxy together. Modern astronomers, using huge telescopes, have since been able to determine the size and shape of our galaxy.

Astronomers noticed that when they looked toward one part of the Milky Way, there were many stars. When they looked toward another part, there were fewer stars. They gradually came to the conclusion that the area where there were more stars was the center of the galaxy. Further observations revealed the shape of the Milky Way. Our galaxy is like a wagon wheel that bulges out at the center. Extending out from the center are curving arms. This makes the

Find Out More

Like other stars in the galaxy, our sun revolves in an orbit around the center of the Milky Way. Look in reference books to find out how far our sun is from the center of the galaxy and how long the sun and its solar system take to make one complete orbit around the center.

177

Milky Way an open-spiral galaxy such as the one in Figure 9–4.

The Milky Way Galaxy has over 100 billion stars in it. It is so large that it takes light traveling from a star on one side of the galaxy 100,000 light-years to reach the other side!

☐ **Why, do you think, did it take astronomers a long time to realize that our solar system belonged to the Milky Way galaxy?**

Figure 9–3. It isn't possible to see the actual shape of the Milky Way galaxy from a photograph. Only a photograph taken from outside the galaxy would show its actual shape.

Neighboring galaxies

A certain kind of *variable* [VEHR-ee-uh-buhl] *star,* or changing star, was helpful to astronomers in discovering galaxies beyond our own. This kind of variable star is very bright and follows a certain pattern. It is bright for a period, dim for a period, and then bright again. Such a pattern can be used to measure the distance to the star. Astronomers

Tom Stack & Associates

can determine the average absolute magnitude of the star by studying how much time passes between its bright and its dim periods. Then, by comparing the absolute magnitude with the apparent magnitude of the star, the astronomers can tell how far away the star is.

In 1924, a famous astronomer, Edwin Hubble, was studying a distant cloud of dust and gas in space. In the cloud he found some of the variable stars of the kind just mentioned. These variable stars were known to be supergiants, and yet they appeared very faint. Hubble then guessed, correctly, that these stars were very far away. In fact, they were so far away that they could not be in our galaxy. A new galaxy had been discovered! It was named the *Andromeda Galaxy*. Further studies showed that the Andromeda Galaxy is 2 million light-years away. This neighboring galaxy is about twice as large as the Milky Way but is very similar in shape.

Figure 9–4. Spiral galaxies such as the one pictured here have younger stars still forming in the arms of the spiral. Older stars are located in the dense, central part of the spiral.

179

California Institute of Technology and Carnegie Institution of Washington

Many galaxies have since been discovered. Some of them are much closer than Andromeda. The Large and Small Magellanic Cloud galaxies are only about 200,000 light-years away. Studies revealed that our galaxy is part of a group of galaxies known as the *Local Group*. Twenty galaxies are presently thought to belong to the Local Group. There may be more. All galaxies in the Local Group are within 3 million light-years of our solar system.

Figure 9–5. The Andromeda galaxy, visible without a telescope, was thought to be a star by ancient astronomers. The discovery that variable stars can be used to measure huge distances helped the astronomer Edwin Hubble to establish that Andromeda is a galaxy beyond the Milky Way.

More about galaxies

Galaxies do not all have the same shape, as you can see in the pictures on page 181. Their different shapes may be the result of the speeds at which the galaxies began to rotate when they were formed. The amount of dust and gas in the galaxies may also affect their shape. Some astronomers think that all galaxies are about the same age but that the stars within them are of various ages.

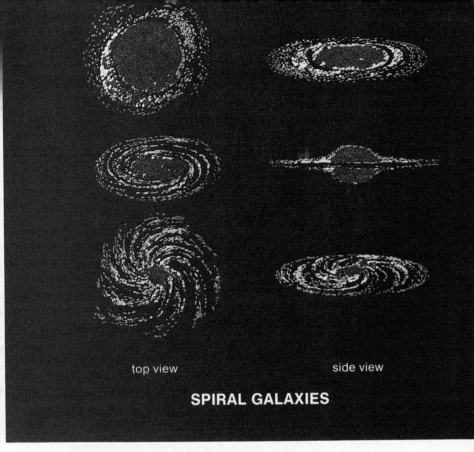

SPIRAL GALAXIES

top view   side view

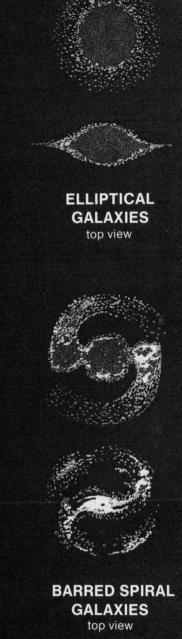

ELLIPTICAL GALAXIES
top view

BARRED SPIRAL GALAXIES
top view

Figure 9–6. Irregular galaxies, which are not pictured here, have no definite shape. What differences do you notice in the shapes of the galaxies pictured here?

GLIMPSING THE UNIVERSE

How have quasars caused scientists to change their idea about the age of the universe?
What are pulsars?
Why do scientists think that the universe is expanding?

New findings

Within the last twenty years, many new discoveries in astronomy have added to our understanding of the universe. One such discovery was that of *quasars* [KWAY-zahrz]. The first quasar was detected by radio astronomers in 1963. The quasar seemed to be a starlike object. And yet its energy output in the form of radio waves was about as large as that of a thousand galaxies. Something that small giving off so much energy had to be very far away.

Since then, hundreds of quasars have been found. One recently discovered quasar is said to be 10 billion light-years from the earth. If that is so, the light reaching the earth now from that quasar left the quasar 5 billion years before our solar system was formed. Astronomers studying that quasar may be looking at something that existed near the beginning of the universe! This would be so if the universe is about 10 billion years old. Some scientists think that the universe may be 14 billion years old.

Another interesting discovery was that of *pulsars* [PUHL-SAHRZ]. A pulsar is a very dense star that sends out radio signals in regular pulses. When the first pulsar was discovered in 1967, it was thought that its signals were from beings in another solar system. This theory is no longer believed to be true. A pulsar's signals seem to be due to the heat and pressure on the atomic particles that make up the star.

☐ **Why do astronomers say that looking at very distant objects in the universe is like looking back in time?**

Figure 9–7. The largest object in the photo on the left is a quasar. The largest object in the photo on the right is a pulsar. Pulsars do not usually emit visible light.

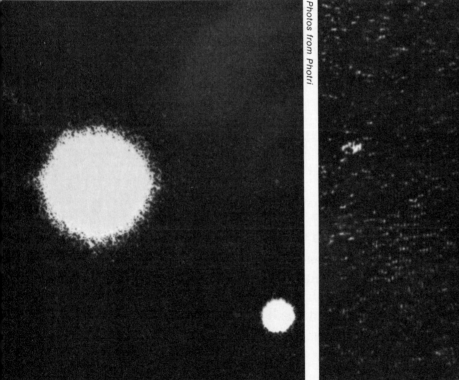
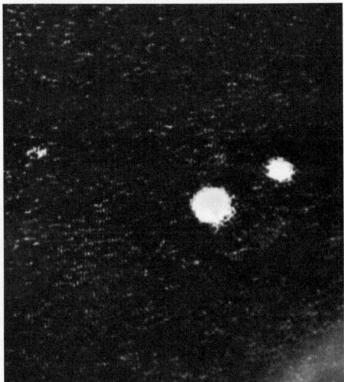

Investigate

How can you tell if a distant moving object is coming toward you or going away from you?

You will need

tape recorder, moving source of sound

Background

Both sound and light travel in waves. Sound waves given off by a stationary object travel outward in all directions at the same rate. But waves given off by a moving object are shorter in the direction of its movement and longer in the direction away from its movement. This is because new waves tend to catch up with the previous waves. This squeezes the front waves and makes them shorter. Just the opposite occurs to the waves behind. Since new waves are moving ahead of the object, there are no new waves to squeeze those behind. And the waves behind get longer. This principle, known as the Doppler effect, can be used to tell if a moving sound is coming toward you or moving away from you. Short waves sound higher. Longer waves sound lower.

Scientists also use the Doppler effect with light waves. As you may know, light separates into a color spectrum when it passes through a prism. The shorter light waves are nearer the blue end of the color spectrum, while the longer light waves are nearer the red end. When the color spectrum is magnified, certain dark lines appear in the color band. When a star is approaching the earth, these dark lines tend to shift toward the blue end of the spectrum ("blue shift"). When a star is traveling away from the earth, the same dark lines shift toward the red end of the spectrum ("red shift").

What to do

Switch a tape recorder on at a place when you can record the sound of a car drawing near to and then passing the recorder. Record the sound made by cars traveling at different speeds. Replay the recording.

Now that you have done the investigation

■ Besides its getting louder or softer, how could you tell when the car was approaching or receding?
■ What change in sound showed differences in the speeds of the various cars?

Changes in the universe

Soon after galaxies were discovered, astronomers noticed that most of the galaxies seem to be moving away from the earth. Later they found that quasars are also moving away at very great speeds. Astronomers concluded from this that the universe is expanding. Some believe that the universe will continue to expand indefinitely. Others think it will reach a certain point and then begin contracting to some original size.

Many scientists use the idea of an expanding universe to support a theory about how the present universe may have begun. These scientists believe that the universe began as a huge fireball. They say the fireball was made of atomic particles that slowly formed some elements, such as hydrogen and helium. After millions of years of expanding and cooling, the matter in the fireball was spread throughout the universe. Then, perhaps as a billion years passed, separate clouds of gas and dust began to form from this matter. Gradually, galaxies and stars developed from these clouds. These galaxies are still expanding away from each other. Scientists call this the big bang theory.

☐ **Even if the universe keeps on expanding, why will people on the earth a million years from now see as many stars as you do today when they look at the sky at night?**

Find Out More

Try to find out about other theories for the beginning of the universe, especially the steady state theory. Look in reference books under *origin of the universe.*

Figure 9–8. According to the big bang theory, the universe is becoming less dense as the galaxies continue to travel away from one another.

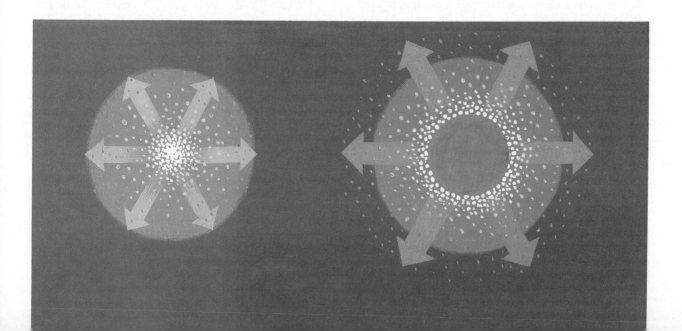

Science writers keep up with the latest discoveries in science by reading current science magazines and books. How else might they keep up with the latest discoveries in science?

Careers

Science Writer

In recent years many new books and magazines about science have been put on display at bookstores. These books and magazines often sell very quickly because people want to know about the latest scientific discoveries. To satisfy these people's desire for reading material, many writers with a knowledge of science have become science writers.

Scientific laboratories employ science writers to explain to the public the experiments carried out at the laboratories. Articles about scientific subjects are regularly written for newspapers and magazines. Similar reports are often prepared for radio and TV news broadcasts. What are some scientific issues you have heard debated by TV panels?

Some writers use their knowledge of science as a background for works intended to entertain people. Many science-fiction writers develop fascinating plots around a future space technology. Other science writers involved in entertainment are those who prepare science documentaries for TV. Newspaper science writers write about events and discoveries in science.

If you like science and enjoy writing, why not consider a career in this field? In college, study the branch of science that most interests you, but try to develop your writing skills at the same time. For more information about a career in science writing, write to the National Association of Science Writers, Post Office Box 294, Greenlawn, NY 11740.

Reviewing and Extending

Summing Up

1. Scientists believe that over billions of years, a star begins as a medium-sized star, expands into a giant star, and then finally contracts into a dwarf.
2. Stars produce a great amount of heat and light by changing some of their matter into energy.
3. Stars with more mass than the sun go through changes more quickly than stars with less mass than the sun.
4. Stars vary in color according to their temperature.
5. Distances beyond the solar system are measured in light-years. A light-year is the distance traveled by light in a year. Nothing in the universe travels faster than the speed of light.
6. The absolute magnitude of a star gives an idea of the amount of light that would actually be received from the star if all stars were the same distance from the earth.
7. Tremendous gravitational forces hold the dust, gases, stars, and other bodies of a galaxy together.
8. Our galaxy, the Milky Way, measures 100,000 light-years across.
9. Astronomers have recently discovered very distant objects in the universe such as quasars and pulsars.
10. According to the big-bang theory, the universe began as a huge fireball of atomic particles that has expanded throughout space. Many scientists think that the universe is still expanding.

Checking Up

Vocabulary   Write the numerals *1–10* on your paper. Each numbered phrase describes a term from the following list. On your paper, write the term next to the numeral of the phrase that describes it.

pulsar	Andromeda	light-year
quasar	Milky Way	white dwarf
color	medium-sized star	Local Group
magnitude	Alpha Centauri	Big Dipper

1. neighboring galaxy
2. star that sends out signals, at regular intervals, that were first thought to be from beings in another solar system
3. galaxy to which our solar system belongs
4. system of twenty galaxies to which our galaxy belongs
5. star having the size of a planet but the mass of our sun
6. first stage in a star's life
7. measure of distances beyond the solar system
8. nearest star to our solar system
9. scale of numbers for comparing the brightness of the stars
10. clue to the temperature of a star

Knowledge and Understanding Write the numerals *11–19* on your paper. Beside each numeral, write the answer that best completes the sentence having that numeral.

11. It is believed that some stars end their life as a (*dwarf, medium-sized, giant*) star.
12. The hottest stars are (*red, yellow, blue-white*).
13. The nearest star is about (*4.3, 30, 100*) light-years from the earth.
14. Nothing in the universe travels faster than (*quasars, pulsars, light*).
15. Scientists think that quasars must be very far away because they are so small and give off (*little energy, very much energy, meteor showers*).
16. Changes occur more quickly in a star with a mass (*greater than, less than, the same as*) the sun's mass.
17. Relying on a theory of the origin of the universe, many scientists believe that all galaxies are about the same (*size, age, shape*).
18. A light-year is (*365 days, a year on the earth, the distance traveled by light in one year*).
19. Scientists believe that the universe began as a (*galaxy, solar system, huge fireball*).

Expressing Yourself Write a paragraph as an answer to each of the following questions:

20. Why can't astronomers depend solely on the apparent brightness of a star in determining its description?
21. What has caused many astronomers to change their idea about the age of the universe?
22. How are astronomers able to "look back" to what was happening billions of years ago?

Doing More

1. Imagine you are a radio astronomer. You have just detected radio signals coming in regular pulses from a distant object in the universe. Write a report for the newspaper about your discovery of the radio signals, adding any possible theories you may have about the "pulsar," as you call it.
2. Discuss with your classmates the possibilities of traveling to another solar system in our galaxy.

Pros and Cons

Space Program—Is It Worth the Cost?

People all over the world have followed with great interest the explorations into space. Within a short time after the beginning of the space age, people walked on the moon. They gathered samples of rock, which are specimens of material on the moon that have not been changed since the time when the moon (and the earth) was formed. In addition, scientific data have been gathered by space probes to other planets, such as Mercury, Venus, Jupiter, and Saturn, that have completely changed our ideas about these planets. Laboratories have been set up on Mars by the *Viking* landers and have carried out complicated experiments that have been monitored from the earth —644 million kilometers (400 million miles) away. More accurate details have been learned about our solar system and the rest of the universe in the past decade than had been discovered in all the years that the science of astronomy has been in existence.

Few will deny that the space program has provided scientists with valuable information about the solar system. But some people look at the problems on the earth and ask, "Is the space program worth the cost?" They point to the conditions of our cities, where many improvements are needed. They say that many people in the world are starving. As the world population increases, it is doubtful that enough food will be produced to meet the demand.

Besides all this, people are faced with other problems. Doctors have still not found cures for many diseases such as cancer and diabetes. Pollution threatens to make the earth unlivable in the future. Our present energy resources may run out before the end of the century. So it is natu-

Much money is needed to clean up and rebuild parts of the large cities in the United States. City governments often cannot afford to do these things on a large scale.

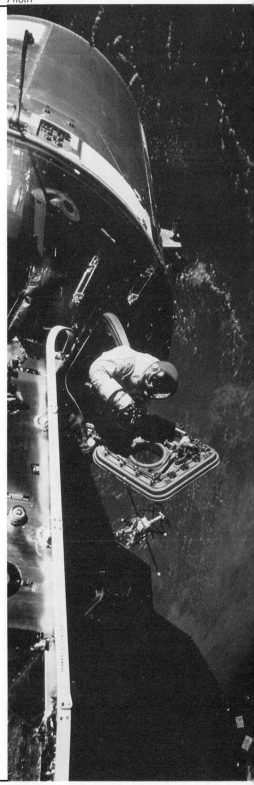

ral for some people to complain that most of the money spent on exploring space could better be used for improving conditions on the earth.

Those in favor of spending money on the space program point to the benefits that have been derived on the earth because of the technology that has been developed for space. Satellites in space provide valuable information for improving food production on the earth. These satellites can note from space when crops are in danger from disease or insects long before such a detection could be made on the earth. There is other valuable information from space that affects our food supplies on the earth. Fertile grazing areas for the use of ranchers can quickly be located from space. For those in the fishing industry, satellites can pinpoint the location of areas rich in nutrients in the oceans of the world. Fish can be found where there is plenty of food for them.

Satellites in space are also monitoring the weather and providing early warnings of hurricanes, floods, and other disasters that have consistently taken their toll in lives and property around the world. Even earthquake prediction has been improved by studies from space.

Communications on the earth have also been improved by satellites in space. Telephone cables had become increasingly overloaded on the earth. And a telephone call to Europe used to be difficult and very expensive. Now, thanks to space technology, communications are better at a fraction of the cost. Perhaps even more important, satellites have permitted interhospital communication to improve health care. Medical examination of patients in

Vast sums of money have been used to send people to the moon and to explore outer space. However, the space program has brought about many discoveries that have been useful for people.

outlying areas has been carried out using TV signals beamed from satellites. This has allowed doctors to treat patients where no medical assistance is available.

As you can see, there are many sides to this question. Ask the members of your family what they think about spending money for the space program. Have the benefits of the program merited future spending in space? Or should scientists concentrate only on the problems here on the earth? What do you think?

Investigate On Your Own

1. Make a model of an expanding universe. Start with a partially inflated balloon. Cover the balloon with dots of black ink evenly distributed over the entire surface. Mark one dot in red. That will represent the earth. The black dots will represent the galaxies beyond the Milky Way. Blow up the balloon. Notice how all the galaxies expand from the earth. In what ways is this model like the expanding universe? In what way is it different from the expanding universe?

2. Pretend you are planning a trip to a planet in another solar system. You are studying the facts known about the planet.

You note that it has an atmosphere with much less oxygen than the earth's. The effect of gravity on the planet is also much less than on the earth. Since it is slightly farther from its star than the earth is from its sun, the planet's temperature is less than the earth's temperature. There is a little water on the planet. Describe the kinds of living things you might expect to find, taking into account the conditions present on the planet.

3. Plan a simple experiment that you will carry out, when you arrive on the planet described above, to determine if there are living things there.

Read On Your Own

Adler, Irving, *The Stars: Decoding Their Messages,* rev. ed. New York: Thomas Y. Crowell Company, 1980.

Readers of this book will discover how astronomers obtain their information about stars, galaxies, and other objects in space.

Asimov, Isaac, *Alpha Centauri, The Nearest Star.* New York: Lathrop, Lee and Shepard Company, 1976.

This interesting book discusses our nearest star group, Alpha Centauri. By means of helpful charts, the author compares Alpha Centauri to various other stars with respect to distance, luminosity, size, and change. A chapter on the possibility of life in the solar systems of other stars is thought-provoking.

Branley, Franklyn M., *Black Holes, White Dwarfs, and Superstars.* New York: Thomas Y. Crowell Company, 1976.

Excellent diagrams, charts, and illustrations convey much information about black holes and white dwarfs. The future of our sun is discussed.

Gallant, Roy A., *Fires in the Sky: The Birth and Death of Stars.* New York: Four Winds Press, 1978.

A wealth of information about the sun, which is used as a basis of comparison with the other stars, is given in this book. Readers learn how matter forms into a star and what causes a star to end its existence. Numerous charts and tables help toward an understanding of many other facts about stars.

Jaber, William, *Exploring the Sun.* New York: Julian Messner, 1980.

This book discusses the features of the sun and how they affect the sun and the earth. Diagrams and photographs help to illustrate these features.

Knight, David C., *The Moons of Our Solar System.* New York: William Morrow and Company, 1980.

This is an easy-to-read study of the moons of our solar system up to and including the findings of the *Pioneer* and *Voyager* space probes.

Provenzo, Eugene F., Jr., and Asterie Baker Provenzo, *Rediscovering Astronomy.* La Jolla, Calif.: Oak Tree Publications, 1980.

The inventions and discoveries that have contributed to our present understanding of astronomy are the topic of this book. Directions for making models of some instruments used in ancient and modern astronomy are given, along with experiments for using the instruments.

Whipple, Fred L., *Orbiting the Sun: Planets and Satellites of the Solar System.* Cambridge, Mass.: Harvard University Press, 1981.

This book provides up-to-date information obtained by means of the American and Russian space programs. A history of our knowledge of the planets brings the reader up to date on the solar system.

Unit 3
ATMOSPHERE AND WEATHER

Without looking outside, can you tell others what the weather is like right now? Is the sun shining? Are there clouds in the sky? Is it raining or snowing? Is it a cold day or a warm day? Chances are, you have a pretty good idea of what the weather is like. Weather is important to you.

Weather is one of the first things you wonder about when you wake up each morning. If it is cold outside, you put on a warm coat. If it is raining, you reach for a raincoat. What are your plans for the day? You may change your plans because of the weather. The weather even has much to do with the way you feel.

On any day of the week, you can easily find out about the weather. You may listen to a weather forecast on the radio or watch a forecast on television. You may look at a weather map in the newspaper. Or you may just look out your window. What is the weather like today?

John Sanford/Photo Network

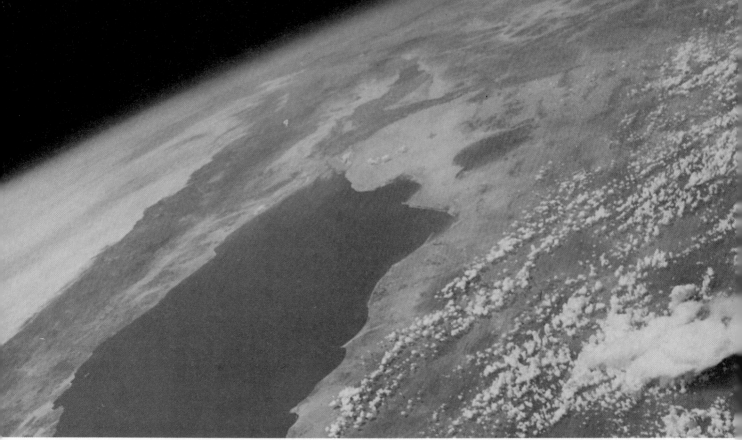

10   Layers of the Atmosphere

When viewed from outer space, the earth's atmosphere often appears to be a glowing blue band. What color do you think the gases that make up the earth's atmosphere really are?

The earth is surrounded by a large ocean of air known as the *atmosphere*. The atmosphere is a part of the earth. It helps make life on the earth possible. The atmosphere provides oxygen for plants and animals. Without oxygen, there would be no living things on the earth. The atmosphere also helps to keep the earth warm. It helps to protect the earth.

The air that makes up the atmosphere is a mixture of gases. Air is about 78 percent nitrogen and 21 percent oxygen. It is 0.033 percent carbon dioxide. There also are trace amounts of argon, neon, helium, krypton, xenon, and hydrogen in air. Water vapor is another gas in the air.

There are five layers of air in the earth's atmosphere. In some layers the air is thinner than in others. The layers are different in other ways, too. How is each layer different from the others? In which layer of the atmosphere do you live? In which layer does weather occur? What is the altitude of the highest layer?

THE UPPER ATMOSPHERE

What are the parts of the upper atmosphere?
What part of the atmosphere continues into space?
How does the thermosphere differ from other layers of the atmosphere?
How is the ionosphere helpful to radio communication?

The exosphere

Imagine that you are in a spacecraft approaching the earth. As you look toward the earth, you can see a hazy blanket of gases above the surface. These gases are the earth's atmosphere. You can see the layers that make up the atmosphere in Figure 10–1.

The part of the atmosphere through which your spacecraft will first pass is the uppermost layer of the atmosphere. This uppermost layer is known as the *exosphere*

To Think About

The atmosphere is made up of colorless gases. But in many photographs taken from outer space, the atmosphere appears to be a glowing blue band. Why, do you think, does the glowing blue band show up in the photographs?

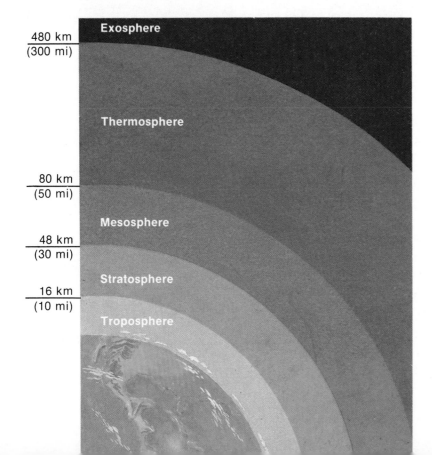

480 km
(300 mi)

Exosphere

Thermosphere

80 km
(50 mi)

Mesosphere

48 km
(30 mi)

Stratosphere

16 km
(10 mi)

Troposphere

Figure 10–1. The earth's atmosphere is made up of five layers. Which is the outermost layer? In which layer do you live?

195

[EHK-soh-SFIH(UH)R]. The exosphere begins in space and continues down to about 480 kilometers (about 300 miles) above the earth.

The air in the exosphere is extremely thin. In fact, the exosphere is made up of only a few molecules of air that are far apart. Because this layer receives the sun's full energy, the molecules of air may become very hot. However, the molecules are so far apart that the exosphere itself is very cold.

☐ **Why, do you think, would there be very little change in the speed of a spacecraft as it enters the exosphere?**

The thermosphere

After passing through the exosphere, your imaginary spacecraft passes into another layer of the upper atmosphere. This layer lies closer to the earth than does the exosphere. It is known as the *thermosphere* [THUR-muh-SFIH(UH)R]. The thermosphere continues down to about 80 kilometers (about 50 miles) above the earth. The air in the thermosphere is thin, but not as thin as the air of the exosphere. Like the exosphere, the molecules in the thermosphere receive the sun's full energy and so they, too, are hot. They are about the same temperature as the molecules in the exosphere.

The sun's energy puts an electric charge on the atoms of air in one part of the thermosphere. These charged atoms are called *ions* [EYE-uhnz]. The part of the thermosphere that contains ions is known as the *ionosphere* [eye-AHN-uh-SFIH(UH)R]. As you can see, the word "ionosphere" comes from the term "ion."

The *ionization* [EYE-uh-nuh-ZAY-shuhn], or charging of atoms, begins at an altitude of about 300 kilometers (about 190 miles). It continues down to an altitude of 50–80 kilometers (30–50 miles). Or, to put it another way, the boundaries of the ionosphere are from 50 to 300 kilometers above the surface of the earth.

Long-distance radio signals can be sent around the world because of the ionosphere. Since radio waves travel in a

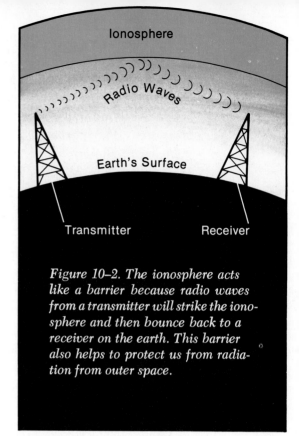

Figure 10–2. The ionosphere acts like a barrier because radio waves from a transmitter will strike the ionosphere and then bounce back to a receiver on the earth. This barrier also helps to protect us from radiation from outer space.

Find Out More

Using references, find out more about *Sputnik*, the first satellite to enter the upper atmosphere. When was it launched? What was learned about the exosphere as a result of this satellite's flight?

Don Lansu

Do It Yourself
Observe the reflection of radio waves

During certain times of the day, radio waves are reflected a greater distance by the ionosphere than during other times of the day. Listen to a radio during the daytime. Use a map to help you find the farthest station you can receive. How far away is this station? Then listen to the radio at night. Use a map to help you find the farthest station you can receive. How far away is this station? When are radio waves reflected a greater distance by the ionosphere? How do you know?

straight line, they do not follow the curvature of the earth. So when the radio waves hit the ionosphere, they are reflected. The ionosphere reflects the radio waves to receivers far away from where they were sent.

Have you ever noticed that radio reception is better at night than during the daytime? At night, the sun's energy is not entering the ionosphere, and fewer ions are formed at night than during the daytime. With fewer ions, the ionosphere rises at night. Because of this rise in the ionosphere at night, radio waves are reflected a greater distance at night than during the daytime.

Figure 10–3. Waves from radio transmitters are reflected by the ionosphere to receivers that are far away. What might happen to long-distance radio communications if the ionosphere were disrupted in some way?

James H. Pickerell

At times, large amounts of the sun's energy enter the ionosphere. When all this energy hits the ions, the tiny particles begin to glow with a green light. This glow can sometimes be seen in the northern sky. This glow is known as the *aurora borealis* [uh-ROHR-uh ʙoʜʀ-ee-AL-uhs], or *northern lights.*

Streamers of light can also be seen in the Southern Hemisphere. The distant southern sky lights up. The glow in the southern sky is known as the *aurora australis* [uh-ROHR-uh aw-STRAY-luhs].

THE MIDDLE ATMOSPHERE

What are the layers of the middle atmosphere?
*Why do most meteors burn up before reaching
   the surface of the earth?*
Why is the ozone layer important?

The mesosphere

As your imaginary spacecraft gets closer to the earth, you pass from the upper atmosphere into the middle atmosphere. The upper layer of the middle atmosphere is known as the *mesosphere* [MEHZ-uh-sғɪʜ(ᴜʜ)ʀ]. The mesosphere continues down to about forty-eight kilometers (about thirty miles) above the earth.

The gases that make up the mesosphere do not receive the sun's full energy. Most of the sun's energy that the gases in the mesosphere can absorb has already been absorbed by the gases in the upper atmosphere. So the mesosphere is cold. The temperature near the top of the mesosphere is only about —93°C (about —135°F).

As you move through the mesosphere toward the earth, you find that the air changes. It gets much thicker. That is, there are more molecules of air, which are closer together.

Rocks, dust, and other objects from outer space enter the earth's atmosphere at great speeds. In fact, scientists think that more than a million billion of these objects enter the earth's atmosphere every day. As these objects fall toward the earth, they collide with molecules of air. This causes the objects to burn.

Figure 10–4. This crater in Arizona is called Meteor Crater. It was formed when a huge meteor hit the earth. The crater is 1 265 meters (4,150 feet) from rim to rim and is 174 meters (570 feet) deep.

Grant Heilman

198

These burning objects can be seen in the sky at night and are often called "falling stars." However, scientists call these burning objects *meteors* [MEET-ee-urz]. Some meteors burn up in the thermosphere. However, a great number of them burn up in the mesosphere.

Only a small number of the largest meteors reach the surface of the earth. The thermosphere and the mesosphere protect the earth from being hit by a great number of meteors. A meteor that gets through the atmosphere and falls to the earth's surface is known as a *meteorite*.

☐ **Why, do you think, do meteors burn up in the mesosphere but not in the exosphere?**

The stratosphere

After passing through the mesosphere, your imaginary spacecraft will pass into another layer of the middle atmosphere. This layer is the *stratosphere* [STRAT-uh-sfih(uh)r]. The stratosphere continues down to about sixteen kilometers (about ten miles) above the earth. The air in the stratosphere is thicker than the air in the mesosphere because the molecules are closer together.

The top of the stratosphere is made up of a form of oxygen called *ozone* [OH-zohn]. The symbol for a molecule of regular oxygen is O_2, but the symbol for a molecule of ozone is O_3. People cannot breathe ozone. In fact, it is a poison. The lower atmosphere is said to be polluted when it contains too much ozone.

Although ozone is a poison, it is also a safeguard for the people on the earth. It absorbs rays from the sun that are harmful to living things. These rays are called *ultraviolet rays*. Without the protection of ozone, life on the earth would soon end.

Because ozone absorbs ultraviolet rays, the upper stratosphere is warmer than the mesosphere. The upper stratosphere is also warmer than the lower stratosphere. The ozone layer has a temperature of 2°C (about 36°F). The temperature at the bottom of the stratosphere is about —55°C (about —67°F).

To Think About

Many meteors have crashed onto the surface of the moon. The meteors have put many craters on the moon's surface. Why, do you think, do more meteors hit the moon than hit the earth?

Figure 10–5. Fluorocarbons from aerosol sprays can rise into the stratosphere and destroy molecules of ozone. Why, do you think, has the use of aerosol sprays containing fluorocarbons been banned?

C. Russell Wood/Taurus

Investigate

Is a meteor shower occurring at this time of year?

You will need

watch, pencil, piece of paper

Background

On a clear night a person can see about five to ten meteors per hour. At certain times of the year, however, there are meteor showers. That is, there are certain times when an unusually large number of meteors enter the earth's atmosphere. One of the strongest meteor showers occurs about the twelfth of August. However, meteor showers occur at other times of the year, too. Scientists believe that meteor showers are caused by particles that break loose from a comet as the comet passes the earth.

What to do

On a clear night, go outside to observe meteors in the sky. It is best to work with a group of three or more people. Try to choose a location away from any bright lights. Bright lights will interfere with your ability to see meteors.

After you have chosen a location for observing meteors, observe the sky for one hour. Meteors usually appear and disappear quickly. So you must pay attention and observe the sky carefully. When anyone in the group sees a meteor, that person should notify the other members of the group and should also record the meteor he or she just observed.

At the end of an hour, add up the total number of meteors observed by your group. Talk with the members of your group and try to decide whether you have observed a meteor shower or just single meteors.

Now that you have done the investigation

■ Why does working with a group help you make a more accurate observation of meteors?
■ Why does bright light interfere with observing meteors?
■ How long was the average meteor in sight?
■ Did you observe a meteor shower? Explain.

THE LOWER ATMOSPHERE

What is a temperature inversion?
What gases make up the troposphere?
Where does weather occur?

Figure 10–6. The high cirrus clouds pictured here are caught in a jet stream. In which direction, do you think, are the clouds being carried?

The tropopause

Your imaginary spacecraft passes from the middle atmosphere into the lower atmosphere. The division between the middle atmosphere and the lower atmosphere is known as the *tropopause* [TROHP-uh-PAWZ]. The tropopause is about sixteen kilometers (about ten miles) above the earth.

As you travel through the stratosphere toward the earth, you begin to feel a change in temperature. The air near the bottom of the stratosphere is colder than the air near the top. But, as you pass through the tropopause, the air gets warmer. The tropopause is a place where the temperature changes.

For the most part, the tropopause is calm. But because of the temperature change within the tropopause, rivers of swiftly moving air are formed. These rivers of air are called *jet streams*. Jet streams flow from west to east. Pilots of jet airplanes often use a jet stream to increase their speed when flying toward the east.

☐ **Why, do you think, do pilots avoid jet streams when flying toward the west?**

Find Out More

During World War II, the Japanese used a jet stream to send balloons armed with bombs to the United States. Using references, find out more about this jet stream and the Japanese attack on the United States.

201

Mary Elenz Tranter

Do It Yourself

Demonstrate the effects of a jet stream

Obtain a string, a blow dryer, a meterstick, a piece of paper, and a paper punch. Punch about twenty holes in the paper. Save the pieces of paper that you make as you punch the holes. Then throw away the paper in which you punched the holes.

Place a string on the floor to mark a starting point. Hold the blow dryer above the string about a meter off the ground. Aim the blow dryer away from you, and turn it on. The fast-moving air from the blow dryer represents a jet stream. Drop pieces of punched paper from above the starting point—first to the left of the blow dryer, then above the air from the blow dryer, and finally to the right of the blow dryer. Measure how far each piece landed from the starting line. What was the effect of a "jet stream"? What effects might a real jet stream have?

The troposphere

After passing through the tropopause, your imaginary spacecraft enters the lower atmosphere. This layer is known as the *troposphere* [TROHP-uh-sғɪн(ᴜн)ʀ]. It is the layer of the atmosphere next to the surface of the earth. It is the layer of the atmosphere in which you live. The temperature of the troposphere is about −55°C (about −67°F) near the top. It rises as you travel toward the earth. The bottom of the troposphere is about the same temperature as the surface of the earth.

The air close to the earth is usually warmer than the air above it. This is because the heat from the earth warms the air close to it. But sometimes, there is a layer of warm air over a layer of cooler air, and there is little or no wind to help the air move around. The cooler air is trapped by the warmer air. This condition is known as a *temperature inversion* [ihn-VUR-zhuhn].

Find Out More

Where, do you think, is the air thinner—at Denver, Colorado, or at Boston, Massachusetts? Why?

What happens when there is a temperature inversion over a city? As you might guess, pollutants, or dust and gases, are released when fuels are burned in the city. These pollutants are warm and rise into the air. But the pollutants can rise only to the level of the warm air. The pollutants became trapped in the air over the city. They will remain trapped until the weather conditions change.

The troposphere is the layer of the atmosphere with the thickest air. It has more molecules of air, closer together, than any other layer of the atmosphere. In fact, more than 80 percent of the molecules of air that make up the earth's atmosphere can be found in the troposphere.

Nitrogen, oxygen, carbon dioxide, and water vapor are some of the gases that make up the troposphere. The makeup of the troposphere is important to all living things. For example, animals need oxygen to stay alive. And plants need carbon dioxide to make food.

If living things use the gases in the atmosphere, you may wonder how the makeup of the atmosphere can stay the same year after year. The answer is that materials are *recycled*, or used over and over again.

One important cycle is the *oxygen cycle*. When animals breathe oxygen, they use it to remove energy from food. But as they produce energy, animals give off a gas called carbon dioxide. Plants use carbon dioxide to make food. As they make food, plants give off oxygen. As you can see, oxygen and carbon dioxide are recycled. The oxygen cycle helps the makeup of the atmosphere stay the same.

Another important cycle is the *nitrogen cycle*. Nitrogen is needed by both plants and animals. But plants and animals cannot use the form of nitrogen that is in the air. Nitrogen must first be changed either by bacteria or by lightning. Then it can be used by plants and animals. When plants and animals die, their tissues decay. This puts nitrogen back into the air.

Weather and the troposphere

Conditions within the troposphere are always changing. These changing conditions are called *weather*. When you

To Think About

Do you think the temperature at the bottom of the troposphere is the same no matter where the troposphere is above the surface of the earth? Why?

Find Out More

Using references, find out about the different ways in which weather acts upon living things. How does weather affect plants? What does it do to animals? How do people react to the weather?

203

think of weather, what do you think about? Chances are, you think of such things as wind, clouds, rain, and snow. Wind, clouds, rain, and snow are conditions of the atmosphere. Each is a part of the weather.

Weather occurs because of the ways that the sun acts upon the atmosphere. The sun's energy, as you know, travels through the earth's atmosphere. Some of the energy is absorbed by and held in the atmosphere and some is reflected back into space. About 53 percent of the sun's energy reaches the earth. See Figure 10–7.

When the sun's energy hits the earth, it heats the earth. The heating of the earth, however, is uneven. Some parts are heated more than other parts. The equator is heated more by the sun than the poles are. And some parts of the earth heat up more quickly than other parts. Land, for example, heats up more quickly than water.

The uneven heating of the earth causes the air in the troposphere to be unevenly heated, too. This causes the air to move in all directions. The movement of air is a weather condition known as *wind*. Conditions within the troposphere may also cause water vapor to change to a liquid or a solid. What weather conditions occur when this happens? What other weather conditions may be caused when the sun acts upon the atmosphere?

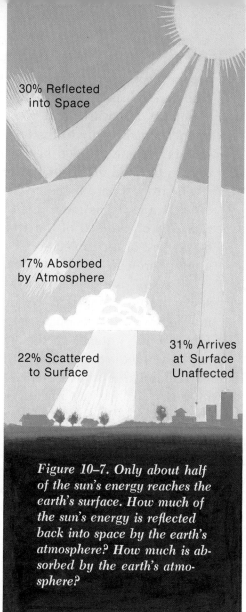

30% Reflected into Space

17% Absorbed by Atmosphere

22% Scattered to Surface

31% Arrives at Surface Unaffected

Figure 10–7. Only about half of the sun's energy reaches the earth's surface. How much of the sun's energy is reflected back into space by the earth's atmosphere? How much is absorbed by the earth's atmosphere?

Figure 10–8. All kinds of weather conditions, even the hurricane pictured here, occur as a result of the sun acting upon the earth's atmosphere.

Thomas Ives

What kinds of props does this television weather forecaster use to help her announce the weather? What other kinds of props have you seen television weather forecasters use?

Careers

Television weather forecaster

There are many ways you can find out about the weather each day. One of the most popular ways to find out about the weather is to watch a weather forecast on television. The announcer who tells you about the weather is the *television weather forecaster.*

The television weather forecaster usually begins the forecast by giving one sentence that tells what the weather will be that day. The forecaster may say, "It's going to be a beautiful day!" Or the forecaster may say, "Get out your umbrella—we're in for a wet one!" Such a statement gives viewers who do not have time to watch the entire forecast an idea about what the weather will be.

The television weather forecaster uses a large map of the country to give more details about the weather. On the map the forecaster shows which areas will be clear and which areas will be cloudy. The forecaster shows where storms are and whether the storms are rainstorms, thunderstorms, or snowstorms. The forecaster may warn people about violent storms.

The forecaster also gives other information about the weather, such as the temperature, and then makes predictions about what the weather will be. Such predictions help people plan what they will wear and do that day.

There are no special requirements to become a television weather forecaster. Many television weather forecasters have a college degree in the study of weather. These forecasters make their own weather predictions. But many television weather forecasters have college training only in television announcing. These forecasters simply announce the weather. A student in your class might write to the National Association of Broadcasters, 1771 N Street N.W., Washington, DC 20036 to learn more about becoming a television weather forecaster.

Reviewing and Extending

Summing Up

1. The earth is surrounded by an ocean of air known as the atmosphere.
2. The earth's atmosphere is made up of five layers—the exosphere, the thermosphere, the mesosphere, the stratosphere, and the troposphere.
3. The exosphere, the uppermost layer of the earth's atmosphere, is made up of extremely thin air.
4. The part of the thermosphere containing large amounts of electrically charged atoms is called the ionosphere.
5. Long-distance radio communication is possible because the ionosphere can reflect radio waves.
6. Objects from space that burn up as they fall through the earth's atmosphere are called meteors.
7. The ozone layer of the stratosphere helps to protect life on earth from the ultraviolet rays of the sun.
8. The tropopause is the division between the middle atmosphere and the lower atmosphere.
9. Jet streams are rivers of swiftly moving air that are formed within the tropopause because of temperature changes.
10. The troposphere is the layer of the earth's atmosphere in which you live and in which weather occurs.
11. Weather occurs because of the ways the sun acts upon the atmosphere.

Checking Up

Vocabulary Write the numerals *1–9* on your paper. Each numbered phrase describes a term from the following list. On your paper, write the term next to the numeral of the phrase that describes it.

ions	exosphere	troposphere
ozone	mesosphere	thermosphere
meteors	ionosphere	stratosphere
weather	tropopause	oxygen cycle

1. form of oxygen that can absorb the sun's ultraviolet rays
2. uppermost layer of the atmosphere
3. objects from space that burn up in the thermosphere or in the mesosphere
4. atoms that are electrically charged
5. division between the middle atmosphere and the lower atmosphere
6. long-distance radio communication is possible because this part of the atmosphere can reflect radio waves
7. layer of the atmosphere that has more molecules of air closer together than any other layer of the atmosphere
8. changing conditions within the troposphere
9. helps the makeup of the atmosphere stay the same year after year

Knowledge and Understanding   Write the numerals *10–16* on your paper. Beside each numeral, write the word or words that best complete the sentence having that numeral.

10. The (*stratosphere, thermosphere, troposphere*) has thinner air and is higher above the earth's surface than the mesosphere.
11. The (*tropopause, ionosphere, troposphere*) is an area of temperature inversion.
12. The atmosphere is made up mostly of (*oxygen, carbon dioxide, nitrogen*).
13. Plants and animals need (*oxygen, carbon dioxide, nitrogen*) but cannot use it in the form in which it occurs in the air.
14. Weather occurs because of the ways the (*sun, earth, ocean*) acts upon the atmosphere.
15. The (*exosphere, mesosphere, troposphere*) is the coldest layer of the atmosphere.
16. The aurora borealis occurs when extremely large amounts of the sun's energy enter the (*ionosphere, exosphere, stratosphere*).

Expressing Yourself   Write a paragraph as an answer to each of the following questions:

17. Why is the ozone layer warmer than the mesosphere or the lower stratosphere?
18. What causes most meteors to burn up as they enter the earth's atmosphere?

Doing More

1. Hold a flashlight a few centimeters away from the equator of a globe. Shine the light onto the equator of the globe. Notice how much light hits the globe at the equator. Now move the flashlight upward so that it is even with the north pole of the globe. Shine the flashlight onto the north pole of the globe. Notice how much light hits the globe at the north pole. How do your findings help explain why the equator is heated more by the sun than the poles are?

2. Using references, find out what effects weather has had in history. For example, how have floods, droughts, blizzards, hurricanes, and tornadoes affected people in the past? How has weather affected the outcome of warfare, such as the battle in the English Channel between the English fleet and the Spanish Armada in 1588, the march of Napoleon's Grand Army into Russia in 1812 and 1813, or the winter at Valley Forge during the Revolutionary War in 1777?

As the air gets very cold quickly, fog may form over the surface of a lake that is warmer than the air. Why, do you think, does fog form?

11 What Makes Up Weather?

You may have read or heard that you live at the bottom of an ocean of air that surrounds the earth. You might say that this ocean of air is constantly changing. That's because the conditions of this "ocean"—temperature, pressure, wind, and moisture—are constantly changing.

You already know about changing air temperatures—from hot to cold and from cold to hot. You may also know about changing air pressures—from high to low and from low to high. You may know about changing winds, too. The amount of moisture in the air also changes. Sometimes the air is very wet, and sometimes it is very dry. What part does each of these conditions play in making up the weather from day to day? What causes these conditions to change? These questions and many other questions that you may have about the conditions of the ocean of air that surrounds the earth will be explored in this chapter.

AIR TEMPERATURE

How is air temperature measured?
*What is the source of heat that keeps the earth
  and the earth's air warm?*
*How is the heating of a greenhouse like the
  heating of the earth's air?*
What causes the convection of air?

By degrees

You probably know what a *thermometer* [thuh(r)-MAHM-uht-ur] is. You can measure the temperature of the air with one. It is marked (calibrated) with one or two scales. The scales that are commonly used are the Fahrenheit scale and the Celsius scale. See Figure 11–1.

A thermometer works on the principle that a rise in temperature causes a liquid or a metal to take up more space. A lowering of the temperature causes the material to take up less space.

Most thermometers are liquid thermometers. They have *mercury* [MUR-kyuh-ree] or alcohol in them. Mercury has a silver color. Alcohol is clear, but a red or blue dye is mixed with it if it is to be used in a thermometer. Why, do you think, is the dye needed?

Runk/Schoenberger/Grant Heilman

Figure 11–1. The thermometer pictured has two temperature scales. One is degrees Celsius (°C) and the other is degrees Fahrenheit (°F). What is the temperature?

209

Jacqueline Durand

Do It Yourself

Change the air temperature with your hand

Look closely at a thermometer. There should be a mark for every degree or for every two degrees on the thermometer. Find the air temperature at the moment. Then place your hand near the bulb of the thermometer, but not touching it. Keep your hand near the bulb for five minutes. At the end of five minutes find the temperature again. What does the warmth of your hand do to the air between the thermometer and your hand?

The source of heat

As you may know, heat from the sun keeps the earth and the earth's air warm. Even though the sun is 150 million kilometers (about 93 million miles) away, the sun gives off so much energy that the earth gets a great deal of heat. You may have felt the rays from the sun heat up your skin or some object. But just how, do you think, do the sun's rays heat the earth's air?

Part of the answer to this question has to do with the *greenhouse effect*. In a greenhouse, rays from the sun pass through the glass panes. The sun's rays are absorbed by plants and other objects inside the greenhouse. These objects, in turn, give off some of this absorbed energy as heat. But the heat that is given off cannot get through the glass panes in the same way that the rays from the sun can get through. The result is that most of the energy that comes through the glass stays inside the greenhouse as heat. In this way, the inside of a greenhouse can be warm on a cool day.

The layers of air above the surface of the earth act in much the same way as the glass panes in a greenhouse. The air allows some of the sun's rays to come to the earth's surface. The earth's surface absorbs most of these rays and becomes warm. The warm earth, in turn, warms the

To Think About

The earth is heated by the sun. But the area between the earth and the sun is very cold. Why is this so?

air next to it. Most of the heat in the earth and in the air is held in by the layers of air above the surface of the earth. In fact, most of the heat is held in by clouds and by tiny drops of moisture in the layers of air. In what way does the air act like a blanket?

Because the layers of air tend to hold in heat, the temperature of the air at night is not a great deal lower than the temperature of the air during the day. But some heat does escape into space. It escapes slowly throughout the night. The coldest part of the day is usually just at dawn before the sun starts warming up the earth's surface again.

☐ **Do you think more heat escapes from the earth on a clear night or on a cloudy night? Why?**

Convection

When air is warmed, it takes up more space and becomes lighter. As it becomes lighter, it rises. Then heavier, cooler air moves down to take its place. Of course, the cool air is then warmed, and it rises as warm air. The warm air eventually becomes cooled and then sinks. As a result of this constant warming, a current of air, or wind, is created. This transfer of heat is called *convection* [kuhn-VEHK-shuhn]. Look at Figure 11–2.

As you may know, the equator receives more rays from the sun than the poles do. The air that is warmed at the equator rises, and the cold air from the poles moves in to take its place. As the warmed air moves toward the poles, it loses its heat, becomes heavier, and sinks.

To Think About

On what side of a building is a greenhouse most likely to be found? Why?

CIRCULATION OF AIR

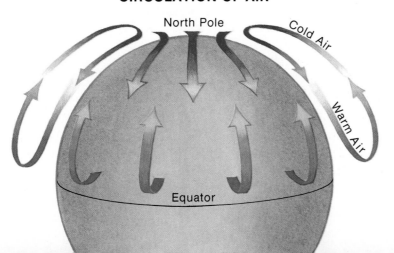

Figure 11–2. If the earth did not turn, the warm air would move to the poles and the cold air would move to the equator. Which kind of air is lighter?

211

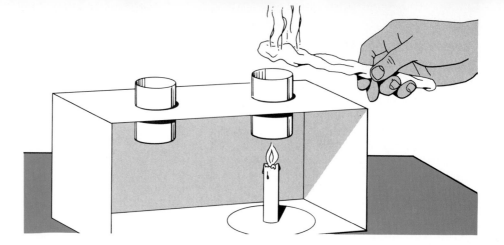

Investigate

How can you show that warm air rises?

You will need

candle, matches, scissors, shoe box, stiff cloth, masking tape, petroleum jelly, 2 thermometers, 2 cardboard tubes

Background

Convection occurs when warm air rises and cooler air moves in to take its place. That is, convection involves the transfer of heat through the movement of air. There are many ways of showing that convection occurs. This investigation shows one of these ways.

What to do

Take the top off a shoe box. Turn the shoe box on its side. Cut two holes in the upper side of the shoe box so that a cardboard tube can fit snugly in each hole. Place a cardboard tube in each hole so that it stands up straight but does not extend into the box very far. If necessary, tape the tubes to the box so that they do not slide down in the holes.

Place a small, lighted candle in the box below one of the holes that contain a cardboard tube. *CAUTION: Keep the candle flame away from the cardboard.* Then coat one end of a stiff piece of cloth with petroleum jelly and light the end that has the jelly on it so that the cloth produces some smoke. Hold the cloth above the cardboard tubes about midway between them. Note what happens to the smoke. Then hold the cloth nearer the tube that the smoke does not go down to see if it will go down that tube. Remove the smoking cloth and hold a thermometer above each tube for two minutes. Record the temperature of each place.

Now that you have done the investigation

■ Did the smoke go down the tube with the lighted candle below it or down the tube without the lighted candle below it?
■ What must have prevented the smoke from going down the tube that it did not go down?
■ Over which tube was the air warmer, the tube with the candle below it or the tube without the candle below it?
■ Did the warm air rise or did the cool air rise? How do you know?

AIR PRESSURE

How is air pressure measured?

What is the effect of temperature on air pressure?

What happens to the air pressure as you go higher and higher above sea level?

Measuring air pressure

As you may know, the air above a given place has a certain amount of weight. The weight of this air presses down on the earth's surface. This causes what is known as air pressure. You usually can't feel air pressure. So you might be wondering how it can be measured. In 1643, an Italian scientist named Torricelli discovered a way. He invented a *barometer* [buh-RAHM-uht-ur], which is an instrument that can measure air pressure.

To make the kind of barometer Torricelli made, you would use a narrow glass tube about eighty-three centimeters (thirty-three inches) long. The tube must be sealed on one end. Fill the tube with mercury and place your finger over the open end. Then turn the tube over and place the end that is sealed by your finger beneath the surface of some mercury in a dish. While holding the tube upright, remove your finger from the open end. Some of the mercury in the tube will drop into the dish. However, most of the mercury in the tube will remain there. Mercury remains in the tube because air pressure, or the weight of air, pushes on the mercury in the open dish. So, the amount of mercury remaining in the tube is a measure of the air pressure. The greater the air pressure, the greater the height of the column of mercury in the tube will be. See Figure 11–3.

To complete the barometer, the tube of mercury must be held up in some way. Also, a ruler must be placed so that the height of the column of mercury in the tube can be measured. If you had such a tube at sea level, the column of mercury would be about seventy-six centimeters (about thirty inches).

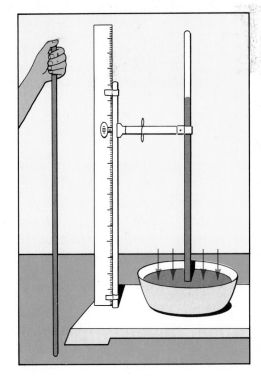

Figure 11–3. The kind of barometer constructed by Torricelli is shown below. Would the height of the mercury in the tube be greater at sea level or above sea level? Why?

Mary Elenz Tranter

Do It Yourself

Make a barometer without using mercury

Obtain a pop bottle, a 1-hole rubber stopper to fit the bottle, some food coloring, a metric ruler, transparent tape, and about 45 cm of glass tubing that has smooth ends. Place about 5 cm of water in the bottle and add a few drops of food coloring to the water. Wet the outside of the glass tubing, and using gloves, carefully slide the tubing through the stopper so that when the stopper is in the bottle, the tubing will extend at least 2 cm below the water. Then place the stopper and tubing in the bottle tightly. Blow air into the bottle through the tubing a little at a time until the level of the colored water in the tubing is about 5 cm above the stopper. Now place a ruler on top of the stopper and tape the ruler to the piece of glass tubing.

Place your barometer in a place in the room where it will not be affected too much by heat, light, or air currents. Measure the height of the liquid at the same time each day for several days. What is the difference in the height of the liquid on a rainy day compared with the height on a sunny day?

Air pressure and temperature

Just as the mercury in a mercury barometer is in a column, the air at any place on the earth can be thought of as being in a column above that place. It is the weight of that column of air that exerts pressure. But the temperature of a column of air has an effect on the pressure caused by that air. Warm air is lighter than cold air. What do you think happens to the air pressure when the air temperature increases?

☐ **If you consider only the temperature of air, where would you say the air pressure would be greater— at the poles or at the equator? Why?**

Find Out More

Using references, find out what an aneroid barometer is. How does this kind of barometer work? How does an aneroid barometer differ from a mercury barometer?

Ed Hoppe Photography

Do It Yourself

Find out the effect of air pressure on a heated can

Take the top off a metal can that has a screw top. *CAUTION: If the can contained a flammable fluid, be sure the can has been rinsed out, dried, and aired out before you use it.* Place 2 or 3 cm of water in the can. Heat the can over a propane burner or a bunsen burner or on a stove or a hot plate until you see steam coming out of the opening. Then screw on the top tightly and use a pot holder to remove the can from the heat. What happens to the can as it cools? How would you explain what happens?

Air pressure and height above sea level

Temperature is not the only thing that affects air pressure. Air pressure becomes less and less as you go higher and higher above sea level. This is because there is less air to "weigh" the higher up you go.

At sea level, the length of a column of mercury in a mercury barometer is about 76 centimeters (about 30 inches). If you were to go straight up about 572 meters (1,875 feet) and measure the air pressure by using a mercury barometer, it would be about 5 centimeters (about 2 inches) less. The air pressure would continue to go down the farther up you go.

☐ **You may have had your ears "pop" as a result of going up or down in an elevator or a plane. Do you think air pressure might have something to do with this? Explain.**

Highs and lows

You may have heard people talk about "highs" and "lows" when they talk about the weather. These people are really talking about regions of high air pressure and regions of low air pressure. A high is the result of a buildup of air.

Find Out More

At the present time, either inches of mercury or millibars are used to describe air pressure. In the future, metric units called pascals may be used. Use references to find out what each of these units is and what the relationship is between them.

The air pressure is higher there than in the regions of air around it. You could think of a high as a hill of air.

In contrast, a low is like a valley of air. The air pressure is lower there than in the regions of air around it. Highs are usually regions of cooler air. What, do you think, might lows be?

WIND

How is wind measured?
What causes the patterns of winds that are observed on the earth?
What part does wind play in the weather where you live?

How wind is measured

As you know, wind is moving air. Wind can be measured in two ways. One of these ways is measuring its direction. To measure the wind's direction, a *wind vane* is used. It points toward the direction from which the wind is coming. See Figure 11–4.

Figure 11–4. A wind vane and an anemometer are pictured below. Which is which? How do you know?

A second way of measuring wind is measuring its speed. To do this, an *anemometer* [AN-uh-MAHM-uht-ur] is used. See Figure 11–4.

The dial on an anemometer shows the speed in miles per hour or in knots. By international agreement, the speed of wind is usually given in knots. A knot is a speed of 1 852 meters (about 6,075 feet or 1.15 miles) per hour. Knots are often used to measure the speed of ships and boats.

Meteorologists [MEET-ee-uh-RAHL-uh-juhsts], or people who study the weather for a living, sometimes use a scale called the *Beaufort* [BOH-furt] *scale* to estimate the speed of the wind in knots. See Figure 11–5. About what is the speed in knots of the wind outside right now? What is its Beaufort number? How do you know?

Figure 11–5. What is the strongest wind that you have ever felt?

ESTIMATING WINDS USING THE BEAUFORT SCALE

Beaufort Number	Wind	Speed in Knots	Effects of Wind	Weather-Map Symbol
0	Calm	0–1	Smoke rises straight up.	 ◉
1	Light air	1–3	Smoke drifts slowly.	◉
2	Light breeze	4–6	Leaves rustle; wind vane moves.	
3	Gentle breeze	7–10	Leaves and twigs move; flag is full.	
4	Moderate breeze	11–16	Small branches move.	
5	Fresh breeze	17–21	Small trees sway.	
6	Strong breeze	22–27	Large branches sway.	
7	Moderate gale	28–33	Whole trees bend.	
8	Fresh gale	34–40	Twigs break off trees.	
9	Strong gale	41–47	Branches break.	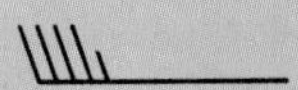
10	Whole gale	48–55	Trees snap and blow down.	
11	Storm	56–63	Widespread damage occurs.	
12	Hurricane	64–71	Extreme damage occurs.	

Do It Yourself

Make a wind vane

Get a square piece of plywood about twice the size of this book and drill a hole in the center of it. Also get a piece of dowel or old broom handle about 45 cm long and about 2.5 cm in diameter. Cut about 30 cm off so that you have 2 pieces of dowel. One piece should be about twice the length of the other. With a screw, attach the larger dowel to the plywood. Drive a small finishing nail (a nail without a large head) partway down into the free end of the dowel. Then drill a small hole midway between the ends of the smaller piece of dowel so that the smaller dowel can be placed over the nail of the larger dowel and can turn freely. Cut a small triangle and a large rectangle out of a piece of stiff cardboard and glue them on the ends of the smaller dowel so that your wind vane looks like the one pictured.

Set your wind vane outside and then use a compass to find out where north is. Look at the pointed end of the wind vane. From which direction is the wind coming? Find out the wind direction at the same time each day and make this a part of your daily weather observations.

Prevailing winds

The direction of major winds on the earth is greatly determined by three things: (1) the air rising at the equator and moving toward the poles; (2) the way the earth *rotates* [ROH-tayts], or turns on its axis; and (3) the buildup of regions of high air pressure. All these things act together so that a certain pattern of winds—called *prevailing* [prih-VAY-lihng] *winds*—is created.

As you know, warm air rising from the equator moves toward the poles, and cooler air moves in to take its place. If the earth were stationary, the air would move from north to south and from south to north, as shown in A of Figure 11–6.

The earth, however, makes one full turn from west to east every twenty-four hours. As the earth rotates, different parts of the earth's surface move at different speeds. The earth's surface moves fastest at the equator. It moves slowest at the poles. The farther you go from the equator toward either pole, the slower the speed is of the moving earth. Therefore, just the rotating of the earth's surface causes the air from the equator to move in the direction shown in B of Figure 11–6.

Not all the air from the equator travels to the poles, however. Regions of high pressure are built up as some of the air from the equator cools and moves closer to the surface. Scientists are not exactly sure why this happens. But as the air builds up in a high, it flows "downhill" away from the high. That is, the air moves from regions of high pressure to regions of low pressure. This causes prevailing wind patterns to be formed as in C of Figure 11–6.

☐ **From what direction does most of the wind come where you live?**

To Think About

How is a turning phonograph record like the rotating earth? What part of the phonograph record would represent the equator? What part would represent a pole?

Figure 11–6. In A, the earth is stationary. In B, the earth rotates from west to east. In C, regions of high air pressure and low air pressure cause prevailing winds on the surface. What kind of region is at the equator?

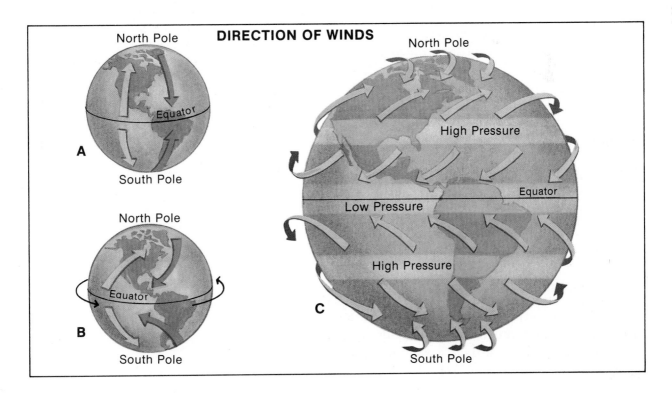

219

Local winds

Most people in the United States live in a region of prevailing westerly winds. Because of this, weather moves across the states from west to east. How, do you think, is information about the weather just to the west of where you live helpful to a meteorologist?

Besides prevailing winds, there are many other things that may affect local winds. Bodies of water, mountains, or buildings may affect them. You may know, for example, that a body of water takes longer to warm up than the land does. The water also takes longer to cool off. The air above the water tends to become the temperature of the water. The air above the land tends to become the temperature of the ground. For this reason, ocean or lake breezes often move toward the land during the day. Breezes tend to move away from the land at night. Near mountains, breezes often move up the mountains during the day. Then breezes tend to move down the mountains at night. How might buildings affect local winds?

☐ **Why do you suppose people go to the beach to cool off in the summertime, even though the water may be too cold for swimming?**

WATER VAPOR

What is relative humidity, and how is it measured?
What are clouds made of?
What are some kinds of clouds that can be observed?
What are some of the forms of precipitation?
What is the water cycle?

The percentage of water vapor

As you may know, the moisture in the air is often called *water vapor* [VAY-pur]. It may also be called *humidity* [hyoo-MIHD-uht-ee]. In fact, you may have heard someone use the term *relative* [REHL-uht-ihv] *humidity*. Whenever that term is used, the person is talking about the amount of water vapor that is in the air compared with the amount that the air could hold at that temperature.

Relative humidity is given as a percentage. For example, suppose a weather report gives the relative humidity as 50 percent. This means that the air is holding half the water vapor that it could hold at that temperature. What would be the percentage if the air held one fourth of the water vapor it could hold?

Temperature affects relative humidity because warm air can hold more water vapor than cold air can. Suppose the relative humidity was 50 percent at a temperature of 20°C (68°F). If the temperature was raised and the amount of moisture remained the same, the relative humidity would become less. This is because the air would be able to hold more water vapor at the higher temperature. But the air would still be holding the same amount of water vapor that it did at the lower temperature. So the amount of water vapor in the air would be less than what it could be. If the temperature was lowered, however, the relative humidity would go up. Why?

When it is raining or when there is early morning dew on the ground, the relative humidity is 100 percent or very nearly 100 percent. This is because the amount of water vapor in the air is very great. But if it is a very dry day, the relative humidity could be as low as 10 percent. What is meant by a relative humidity of 10 percent?

Measuring relative humidity

You may be wondering how relative humidity is measured. To understand how it is measured, you first have to know what happens when water *evaporates* [ih-VAP-uh-RAYTS], or changes from water to water vapor.

When water evaporates, it cools whatever material it is on. That's why you feel cooler when you sweat on a warm day, for example. Your body is acting to keep you cool. But in order to evaporate, water must absorb heat energy from the material it is on. As the water absorbs heat and becomes water vapor, it cools the material.

To Think About

Is the relative humidity likely to be high or low if it is a foggy day? Why do you think so?

Water will evaporate quickly and cool something quickly when the relative humidity is low. This is because the air can hold a great deal more water vapor than it is holding. But when the relative humidity is high, water evaporates slowly and cools something slowly. Why, do you think, does water evaporate slowly when the relative humidity is high?

An instrument known as a *psychrometer* [sy-KRAHM-uht-ur] may be used to measure the relative humidity. The psychrometer has two thermometers on it. One of these thermometers has a bulb that must be kept wet. The bulb of the other thermometer is kept dry. See Figure 11–7.

The cooling that results from evaporating water makes the wet-bulb thermometer show a lower temperature than the dry-bulb thermometer. The difference between the readings of the two thermometers can then be used in a table to find the relative humidity of the air. See Figure 11–8.

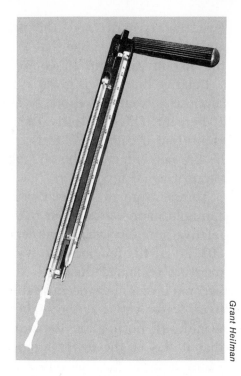

Figure 11–7. Which thermometer is the one that is kept wet? How do you know?

RELATIVE HUMIDITY (in percent)

Dry-bulb temperature (in degrees Celsius)

Difference between readings	30	29	28	27	26	25	24	23	22	21	20	19	18	17	16	15	14	13	12	11	10
1	93	93	93	92	92	92	92	92	92	91	91	91	91	90	90	90	90	89	89	89	88
2	86	86	85	85	85	84	84	84	83	83	83	82	82	81	81	80	79	79	78	78	77
3	79	79	78	78	78	77	77	76	76	75	74	74	73	72	71	71	70	69	68	67	66
4	73	72	72	71	71	70	69	69	68	67	66	65	65	64	63	61	60	59	58	56	55
5	67	66	65	65	64	63	62	62	61	60	59	58	57	55	54	53	51	50	48	46	44
6	61	60	59	58	58	57	56	55	54	53	51	50	49	47	46	44	42	41	39	36	34
7	55	54	53	52	51	50	49	48	47	46	44	43	41	40	38	36	34	32	29	27	24
8	50	49	48	47	46	44	43	42	40	39	37	36	34	32	30	27	26	23	21	18	15
9	44	43	42	41	40	39	37	36	34	32	31	29	27	25	23	20	18	15	12	9	6
10	39	38	37	36	34	33	31	30	28	26	24	22	20	18	15	13	10	7			
11	35	33	32	31	29	28	26	24	22	20	18	16	14	11	8	6					
12	30	28	27	26	24	22	20	19	17	14	12	10	7								
13	25	24	22	21	19	17	15	13	11	9	6										
14	21	19	18	16	14	12	10	8	6												
15	17	15	13	12	10	8	5														

Figure 11–8. If the dry-bulb temperature is 20°C and the difference between the wet-bulb and the dry-bulb readings is 6, the relative humidity is 51%. What must the wet-bulb temperature be?

Do It Yourself

Make a sling psychrometer

Brent Jones

Obtain a flat piece of wood large enough so that 2 thermometers can be mounted on it. If possible, obtain 2 thermometers that have an eye at the top. Fasten the 2 thermometers to the wood by drilling pairs of holes through the wood and attaching the thermometers firmly with wire as shown. One thermometer should extend below the other thermometer as shown at the left. Next, screw a screw eye into the edge of the wood at the middle of one end. Then attach about 50 cm of strong cord to the screw eye.

Wrap and tie a piece of muslin, cheesecloth, or other absorbent cloth around the bulb of the lower thermometer. Then dip the covered end of that thermometer in water. Grasp the cord firmly and whirl your psychrometer around for four or five minutes. This kind of psychrometer is called a sling psychrometer. Record the temperature indicated by each thermometer.

Subtract the temperature indicated on the wet-bulb thermometer from the temperature indicated on the dry-bulb thermometer. Then use the chart on page 222 to find the relative humidity. Find the relative humidity outside at the same time each day.

Clouds

You may have seen clouds form in the sky where there were none before. Clouds do not form unless the relative humidity of the air at the height of the clouds approaches 100 percent. Clouds form from water vapor and dust in the air. These things are in the air all the time. However, clouds form when water vapor is cooled and *condenses* [kuhn-DEHN(T)-suhz], or comes together in tiny drops. The water vapor condenses on the particles of dust in the air. Why, do you think, do clouds usually form high above the earth's surface?

As you may know, there are many different kinds of clouds. However, there are just three major kinds. All other clouds are combinations of these three kinds. The three major kinds of clouds are *cirrus* [SIHR-uhs], *stratus* [STRAYT-uhs], and *cumulus* [KYOO-myuh-luhs]. See Figure 11–9.

Cirrus clouds occur at very high levels in the air. In fact, they occur so high that they are made up of ice. They are white and very thin. Some people call them mare's tails because they make curved shapes in the sky somewhat like a mare's tail.

Stratus clouds, on the other hand, occur at low or middle levels. They may also contain tiny pieces of ice at higher levels or during the winter season. They are often gray and make up a sheet, or layer, across the sky.

Figure 11–9. In the picture at the left, stratus clouds and cumulus clouds are shown. The stratus clouds are the higher clouds. Cirrus clouds are shown in the picture at the right. How would you describe each of these kinds of clouds?

Cumulus clouds also occur at low or middle levels and may contain tiny pieces of ice. They are white to gray and look like piled-up cotton or rolled-up pillows. These three kinds of clouds and the most common combinations of them are illustrated in Figure 11–10.

Figure 11–10. Note the heights, shapes, and names of the clouds. What two kinds of clouds seem to make up cirrocumulus clouds?

TEN KINDS OF CLOUDS

Height in Kilometers

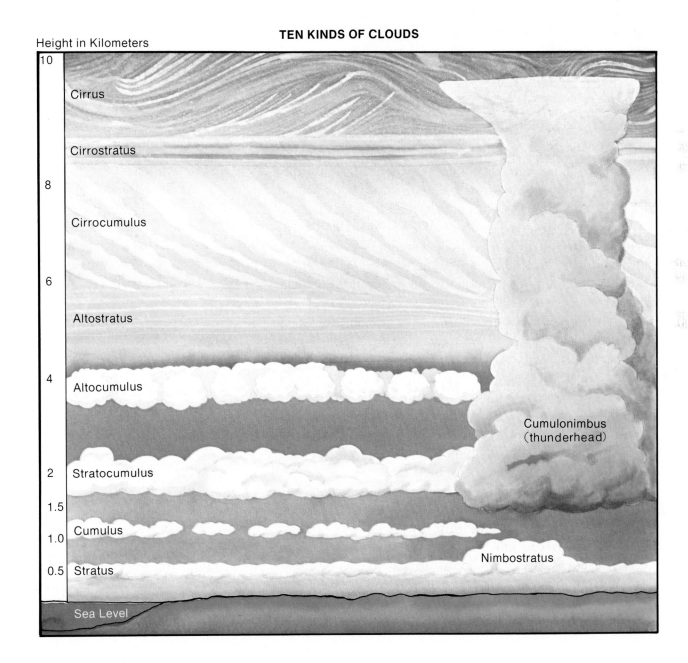

Do It Yourself

Observe clouds

Don Lansu/Action 35 Photography

Observe the clouds in the sky each day. Describe the clouds and try to distinguish the kinds of clouds that you observe. Record your observations and make them a part of your daily weather observations. What clouds indicate that rain or snow is coming within twenty-four hours?

Forms of precipitation

As you know, clouds have water in them. But when clouds have more water in them than they can hold, some of the water falls to the ground as rain, snow, sleet, or hail. You may also know that all the forms of water that fall to the ground are given one name. They are called forms of *precipitation* [prih-SIHP-uh-TAY-shuhn]. What is the most common form of precipitation where you live?

Rain is the most common form of precipitation worldwide. It may occur as a fine drizzle, as very heavy drops, or as something in between. What kind of rain do you see most often?

Rain usually starts out as snow. Snow is formed when water vapor freezes in a part of a cloud that has a temperature below freezing. If the temperature of the air near the ground is at or below freezing, the precipitation reaches the ground as snow rather than rain. If you get a chance to look at snowflakes carefully, you will see that most of them are six-sided ice crystals (six-pointed stars).

Sleet, on the other hand, is frozen raindrops. It can only be formed if there is a layer of warm air over a layer of cold air. As the raindrops fall through the layer of cold air, the raindrops freeze into sleet.

Hail is found only in thunderstorms. Currents of air lift a raindrop high up into a part of the cloud where the temperature is far below freezing. The raindrop freezes and then falls into a lower part of the cloud where water or

Find Out More

Using references, find out how meteorologists explain why precipitation forms in certain clouds and not in others. Also find out more about how precipitation forms. Why is it difficult to learn with certainty what occurs in a cloud to cause precipitation?

James H. Pickerell

Runk/Schoenberger/Grant Heilman

Figure 11–11. Although rain—the most common form of precipitation —is a liquid, some forms of precipitation, such as snow (top) and hail (bottom), are solids. What causes these forms of precipitation to be solids?

snow collects on it. But then it may be lifted back up high in the cloud again. Suppose a hailstone is moved up and down in the cloud many times. What do you think might happen to the hailstone before it eventually reaches the ground?

□ **At what time of year do you think precipitation that starts out as snow would be most likely to come to the ground in some other form? Why?**

The water cycle

As you may know, certain kinds of clouds produce precipitation. These clouds are an important part of the earth's weather. But you may not know that these clouds are a part of a *cycle* [SY-kuhl], or a series of events that occur again and again. This cycle is called the *water cycle*.

In general, the water cycle is the moving of water from the clouds to the land, from the land to the ocean, and from the ocean back into the clouds. See Figure 11–12.

There are many processes that work together to keep the water cycle going. Heat from the sun warms the oceans, causing water to evaporate. Then water vapor condenses on dust particles in the air to form clouds. When the particles are heavy enough, precipitation can fall as rain, snow, sleet, or hail. After the precipitation reaches the land, water flows to the ocean by means of streams and rivers. When it reaches the ocean, some of it evaporates again, continuing the water cycle. In these ways, the water cycle is an important part of the earth's weather.

☐ **What parts of the water cycle can you see? What parts of the water cycle cannot be seen?**

Figure 11–12. Water evaporates from the ocean and eventually helps form clouds. Clouds release their moisture as rain, snow, sleet, or hail. Then the water from precipitation finds its way back to the ocean, thus completing the cycle. How does water get to the ocean?

PARTS OF THE WATER CYCLE

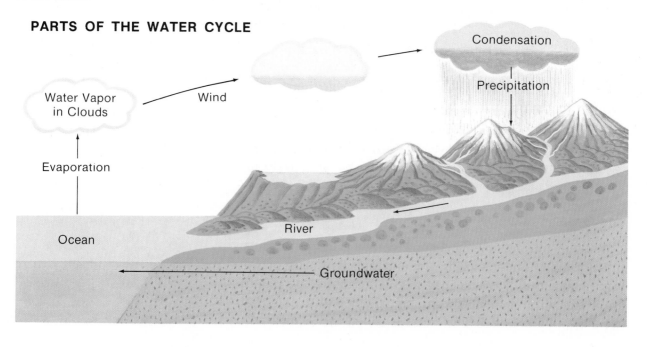

An *air-conditioning and heating technician may be called to help keep a family's home comfortable or may help design heating and cooling systems for office buildings, schools, and hospitals.*

Careers

Air-conditioning and heating technician

When you think of the term "weather," you most likely think of what the weather is like outdoors. You might also give some thought to weather conditions inside your home or school. Air temperature and relative humidity are two conditions of weather that can be observed inside buildings. These indoor weather conditions affect the health and comfort of people who live or work inside large buildings. They are also important because computers and other electronic devices are sensitive to changes in temperature and relative humidity.

One person who helps to control indoor weather conditions is an *air-conditioning and heating technician.* Some air-conditioning and heating technicians are involved in the design of buildings and in the design of heating and cooling systems. These technicians help to make sure that a building can be cooled and heated easily and at a reasonable cost. They also help to make sure that the relative humidity in the building can be kept within a comfortable range. Other air-conditioning and heating technicians install the cooling and heating systems and help to keep these systems working.

If you think that you would like to become an air-conditioning and heating technician, you should study science and mathematics in high school and then attend a technical school. A student in your class might write to the American Society of Certified Engineering Technicians, 2029 K Street, N.W., Washington, DC 20006, for more information about becoming an air-conditioning and heating technician.

Reviewing and Extending

Summing Up

1. There are four major conditions of the air that play a part in the earth's weather. These conditions—temperature, pressure, wind, and moisture—are constantly changing.
2. The earth absorbs the sun's rays and becomes warm, heating the air next to it. Most of this heat is held in by the clouds and the moisture in the layers of air.
3. Warm, light air at the equator rises; cooler, heavier air from the poles comes in to take its place, creating currents of air on the earth.
4. Because air has weight, it presses down on the earth's surface, causing air pressure.
5. Air pressure becomes less and less as you go higher above sea level.
6. Differences in air pressure may result in the formation of regions of high air pressure and regions of low air pressure.
7. The direction of prevailing winds on the earth is determined by (1) air rising at the equator and moving toward the poles, (2) the way the earth moves, and (3) the buildup of regions of high air pressure.
8. Relative humidity is the amount of water vapor in the air compared with the amount of water vapor the air could hold at that temperature.
9. The water cycle is the moving of water from clouds to land, from land to the ocean, and from the ocean back into clouds.

Checking Up

Vocabulary Write the numerals *1–8* on your paper. Each numbered phrase describes a term from the following list. On your paper, write the term next to the numeral of the phrase that describes it.

relative humidity anemometer convection
psychrometer barometer wind vane
precipitation condense evaporate

1. rain, snow, sleet, or hail
2. instrument for measuring air pressure
3. transfer of heat through movement of currents of air
4. instrument for measuring the speed of the wind
5. amount of water vapor in the air compared with the amount of water vapor the air could hold at that temperature
6. instrument for measuring the direction of the wind
7. to change from water to water vapor
8. instrument for measuring relative humidity

Knowledge and Understanding   Write the numerals *9–15* on your paper. Beside each numeral, write the word or words that best complete the sentence having that numeral.

9. Most of the heat that the earth absorbs from the sun's rays is held in because of (*air pressure, the greenhouse effect, the movement of the earth*).
10. The moving of water from the clouds to the land, from the land to the ocean, and from the ocean back into the clouds is known as (*relative humidity, the Beaufort scale, the water cycle*).
11. Air pressure at sea level is (*greater than, the same as, less than*) air pressure at higher altitudes.
12. Most people in the United States live in a region of prevailing (*northerly, westerly, easterly*) winds.

13. The farther you go from the equator toward either pole, the (*faster, slower, stronger*) the speed is of the moving earth.
14. In a mercury barometer, the mercury is held in the column by (*evaporating mercury, pressure of the mercury, air pressure*).
15. One of the reasons why prevailing winds move as they do is that (*the earth rotates from east to west, air rises at the poles and moves to the equator, regions of high air pressure are built up*).

Expressing Yourself   Write a paragraph as an answer to each of the following questions:

16. What is the greenhouse effect? How does the greenhouse effect help the earth stay warm at night?
17. How do cirrus clouds and cumulus clouds differ?

Doing More

1. Try to make a cloud in a jar. Obtain a wide-mouthed jar. Fill the jar with hot water and then carefully pour off about three fourths of the water. Support one or more ice cubes near the mouth of the jar and then hold the jar near a strong light. What causes the cloud to form inside the jar?
2. Collect pictures of different kinds of clouds. What kind of weather does each kind of cloud usually indicate?

12   Forecasting the Weather

Weather forecasts could not have prevented the damage a tornado caused to this neighborhood. In what way, however, might weather forecasts have been helpful to the people who lived here?

Have you ever wished that you could make the weather exactly as you want it to be? Many people have. However, at the present time people can do little to change the weather. Perhaps scientists may be able to change the weather someday. But for now the only thing that scientists can do is to predict the weather with some reliability. And you can only hope for the weather you want.

Many people depend on *weather forecasts* [FOH(UH)R-KASTS], or broadcasts and newspaper reports that give weather predictions. People depend on weather forecasts to help them in planning outside activities and to help them in choosing what clothing to wear. People also depend on weather forecasts to help them in taking care of buildings and other property, in traveling, and in doing many other things. How much do you depend on weather forecasts? In this chapter you will gain an understanding of how weather forecasts are made and how useful they are to you and to other people.

NEED FOR WEATHER FORECASTING

Why are weather alerts necessary?
How do weather forecasts help farmers?
How do weather forecasts help travelers?
How do weather forecasts help you?

Weather alert

Have you ever heard a *weather alert* [uh-LURT] on radio or on TV? If you have, you know that such a broadcast is a warning about the weather that is given to help people. A weather alert warns of a storm, very cold temperatures, very warm temperatures, flooding, or drought. The reason for the warning is that if people know what the weather is likely to be, they can better prepare for it.

A weather alert helps people decide whether or not they should go outside and what they should wear. A weather alert also helps people decide what precautions they should take with regard to property and if they should find a safe place to stay. As you can see, whatever the reason for a weather alert, people are helped by it. Have you ever been helped by a weather alert? If so, how?

To Think About

Under what weather conditions would a home not be a safe place to stay? Why?

Wide World Photos, Inc.

Figure 12–1. A weather alert helps people prepare for very bad weather. One kind of preparation for a hurricane is shown in the picture. What is the boy doing? Why do you suppose it is necessary for him to do this?

233

How forecasts help farmers

Weather forecasts are helpful to farmers. These forecasts help farmers decide when to plant their crops. These forecasts also help farmers decide when to harvest certain crops. Weather forecasts help farmers in other ways, too. What other ways can you think of that weather forecasts may help farmers?

How forecasts help travelers

Weather forecasts are very useful to travelers. For example, suppose you know that there are storms along the route you will be traveling. It might help you decide to spend the night where you were. Or suppose you know that an airport might become snowbound. It might help you decide to postpone a plane trip for a few days.

Weather forecasts also help people who are transporting goods or people. For example, weather forecasts help truck drivers and bus drivers know what the road conditions will be like. Weather forecasts also help railroad engineers, airplane pilots, and ships' captains know what to expect ahead. Why might this be important?

□ **What season of the year do you think is the worst for traveling in your part of the country? Why?**

How forecasts help you

As you may know, people listen to weather forecasts in the evening to find out what the weather will be like the next day. Or they listen to weather forecasts in the morning before they leave home. When do you listen to weather forecasts? Why?

A weather forecast may help you decide if you should wear a raincoat or carry an umbrella. It may help you decide if you should wear boots and gloves. It may also help you decide if you can do something outside or if you should plan to do something inside. It may help you decide many other things, too. What has a weather forecast helped you to decide lately?

Find Out More

Call a radio station or a TV station to find out how many times during the day the station gives information about the weather. What information is given during each broadcast? Where does the information come from?

Do It Yourself

Write to a weather forecaster

Perhaps you have a favorite weather forecaster, or meteorologist. If so, write this person a letter to find out what information he or she uses to forecast the weather. Also ask this person how accurate the weather forecasts are. Why, do you think, is it sometimes difficult to predict the weather?

MAKING A FORECAST

Why is it necessary to collect weather information from different weather stations in order to forecast the weather?
What is an air mass, and how does it move?
What is a front, and how does it move?
How are weather maps used to forecast the weather?

Collecting information

There are weather stations all around the country. These weather stations have instruments for measuring air pressure, temperature, wind direction, wind speed, relative humidity, and precipitation. People who work at a weather station are trained to observe, measure, and report on the weather.

You may be wondering why so many weather stations are needed. The reason is that weather stations help *meteorologists* [MEET-ee-uh-RAHL-uh-juhsts] forecast, or predict, the weather. Meteorologists may use the reported information from many weather stations to forecast the weather for a certain part of the country. They may also use information from *weather satellites* [SAT-uhl-yts], *radiosondes* [RAYD-ee-oh-sahndz], and *radar* [RAY-dahr].

Weather satellites circle the earth and take pictures of it. The pictures show the places that are covered by

Daniel S. Brody

clouds. Radiosondes are weather balloons. They carry instruments for measuring relative humidity, temperature, and air pressure. Radiosondes send out information by radio about the conditions of the air around them. Radar, or *radio detecting and ranging*, can be used to detect clouds and other large objects in the air.

Meteorologists put together the information they receive from weather stations, weather satellites, radiosondes, and radar. They note how the conditions change from hour to hour and from place to place. That is, for each place, they note if the air pressure is rising or falling. They note if the air temperature is going up or down. They note if the winds are changing direction or changing speed. They note if the relative humidity is going up or down. They also note the kind of clouds that cover each place.

Figure 12–2. A Nimbus weather satellite is shown at the left. A radiosonde that is being launched is shown above. Such instruments are being used more and more today. How are weather satellites and radiosondes alike? How are they different?

236

HOW WIND AND AIR PRESSURE MAY INDICATE WEATHER

Wind	Air Pressure	Kind of Weather
SW to NW	Steady near 1018 mb (30.1 in) Rising above 1018 mb (30.1 in) Stationary above 1022 mb (30.2 in) Falling slowly from near 1022 mb (30.2 in)	Fair for 1 or 2 days Fair, but rain in 2 days Fair Fair, rising temperature for 2 days
S to SE	Falling slowly from near 1022 mb (30.2 in) Falling rapidly from near 1022 mb (30.2 in)	Rain within 24 hours Increasing winds, rain soon
SE to NE	Falling slowly from near 1022 mb (30.2 in) Falling rapidly from near 1022 mb (30.2 in)	Rain soon Increasing winds, rain soon
E to NE	Falling slowly, but above 1013 mb (30.0 in) Falling rapidly below 1013 mb (30.0 in)	In summer, rain within 24 hours In winter, rain or snow in 1–3 days Rain soon
SE to NE	Falling slowly below 1013 mb (30.0 in) Falling rapidly below 1013 mb (30.0 in)	Continued rain Rain, high winds
S to SW	Rising slowly	Clearing, fair
S to E	Falling rapidly	Storm
E to N	Falling rapidly	Severe storm
Moves W	Rising	Clearing, fair, cooler

Figure 12–3. What do winds blowing from the south, southwest, or southeast and a rapidly falling air pressure usually indicate? What do winds blowing from a westerly direction usually indicate?

To give you an idea of what changes in certain conditions may indicate, look at Figure 12–3. The combination of wind direction and air pressure usually indicates the kind of weather shown.

Meteorologists know that the weather generally moves from west to east across the United States. Because of this and because they have the weather information from weather stations to the west of a city or town, they can usually forecast the weather for that city or town. Of course, local features such as bodies of water, mountains, and buildings can affect weather and weather forecasts.

But meteorologists take these things into account, based on the way these things have affected the weather before.

☐ **How would a study of the way weather conditions affected the weather on other days help a meteorologist in making a weather forecast today?**

Air masses

You may know that an *air mass* is a large body of air that has certain characteristics. Meteorologists often talk about a warm air mass or a cold air mass. They are talking, of course, about a large body of warm air or a large body of cold air.

An air mass may be quite large. It may cover an area of thousands of square kilometers. But an air mass can still move. In general, it moves from west to east in the United States. It may move at the rate of several hundred kilometers in a day. It may also remain in one place for a time.

An air mass tends to take on the temperature and humidity characteristics of the surface over which it forms. Suppose an air mass formed over the Arctic in winter. The air mass would be very cold and dry. This is because the Arctic is very cold and dry in the winter. But suppose an air mass formed over a warm part of the ocean. The air mass would be warm and have high humidity. What kind of air mass do you think may be affecting your weather right now? Why do you think so?

The center of an air mass is made up of a region of high air pressure. This is because air has been built up to form the center. Meteorologists often call an air mass a high for this reason. On a map that shows lines connecting points of equal air pressure, a high might look like one in Figure 12–4.

Some highs move across the United States. But so do some lows. As you may know, a low is a region of low air pressure. There is usually a low between two widely separated air masses, or highs, of different temperatures. See Figure 12–4.

Find Out More

Using references, find out where air masses that reach the United States come from. Which air masses are most common in the summer? Which are most common in the winter?

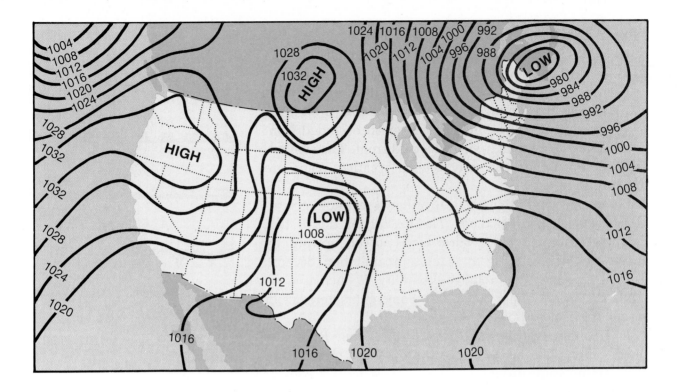

The highs and lows that move across the United States are not the same as the highs and lows that help form prevailing winds. The highs and lows that help form prevailing winds tend to stay in place. The highs and lows that move are related to air masses.

□ **In the lows that move across the United States, air rises and is quickly cooled as it rises. What do you think usually happens to the water vapor in this air? Why?**

Figure 12–4. Each of the lines on the map indicates a particular air pressure in millibars. If the lows and highs move from west to east, is the air pressure over the east coast rising or is it falling?

Fronts

As you have read, air masses move. But air masses, or highs, of different kinds do not usually mix if they come close together. Instead, a *front,* or boundary, forms between them. You might think of a front as a boundary between two nearby highs of different temperatures. Because a cold air mass is heavier than a warm air mass, the edge of the cold air mass stays under the edge of the warm air mass. If the cold air mass pushes forward, it is called a *cold front*. But if the warm air mass pushes forward, it is called a *warm front*. If the boundary doesn't move, it is called a *stationary* [STAY-shuh-NEHR-ee] *front*.

There is also a fourth kind of front, called an *occluded* [uh-KLOOD-uhd] *front*. It occurs when a cold front overtakes a warm front. You might think of an occluded front as a mixture of a warm front and a cold front. The symbols for the fronts that you may see on weather maps are given in Figure 12–5.

Fronts and lows often occur together. Precipitation usually occurs along with them. The reason for this is that in both fronts and lows, warm air is forced upward by cooler air. Warm, rising air causes precipitation because as it gets cooler, its relative humidity is increased so much that water vapor condenses. Some characteristics of fronts are listed below.

1. The temperature on one side of a front is usually much different from the temperature on the other side.

2. Air pressure drops as a front comes in and rises as the front passes.

3. The direction of the wind is much different on each side of a front.

4. The speed of the wind on one side of a front is usually much different from the speed of the wind on the other side.

☐ **Why, do you think, does the air pressure drop as a front comes in?**

Weather maps

If you have watched the news on TV, you have seen people describe the weather by using maps. These people may use symbols for highs, lows, and fronts to describe the weather. Most likely, the person talking about the weather is a meteorologist, or the information about the weather was received from a meteorologist. But the maps you see are not true weather maps. Most people would not be able to understand a true weather map. A weather map from the National Weather Service is shown in Figure 12–6. What information does the map provide?

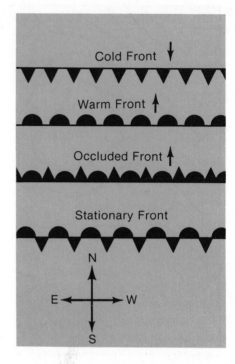

Figure 12–5. Symbols for fronts on a weather map are shown above. The arrows indicate which direction a front is moving. In which direction is each front moving? Why doesn't the last front have an arrow to indicate the direction it is moving?

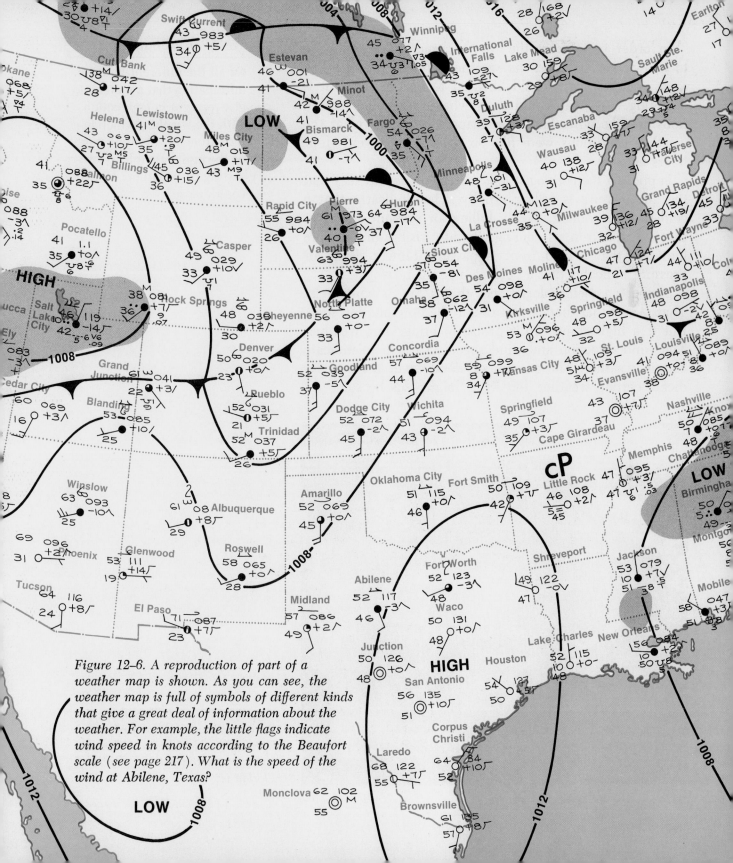

Figure 12–6. A reproduction of part of a weather map is shown. As you can see, the weather map is full of symbols of different kinds that give a great deal of information about the weather. For example, the little flags indicate wind speed in knots according to the Beaufort scale (see page 217). What is the speed of the wind at Abilene, Texas?

In order to forecast the weather, meteorologists have to know in what ways the weather is changing. Two or more weather maps could be used to find out how it is changing. One map could show what the weather conditions are like now. The other maps could show what the weather conditions were like six, twelve, or twenty-four hours ago.

Suppose a meteorologist looks at the maps and sees that the air pressure is falling rapidly. That indicates that a cold front is coming. Slowly falling air pressure indicates that a warm front is coming. Rapidly rising air pressure indicates that a cold front is passing. Slowly rising air pressure indicates that a cold air mass is nearby.

Suppose a meteorologist sees that a low is coming in. That means that there will probably be precipitation soon. But if a high comes in, it probably brings fair weather. The wind direction and wind speed also help to indicate certain weather. The amount of cloud cover helps to indicate certain weather, too. How might this be so?

Courtesy of NOAA/National Climatic Center

To Think About

Of all the different kinds of information that a meteorologist receives in connection with the weather, which information do you think might be the most valuable in forecasting the weather? Why do you think so?

Figure 12–7. A satellite photo of the cloud cover over part of the United States is shown. What do you suppose the swirl of clouds off Florida is?

Investigate

How much does your weather change from day to day?

You will need

newspaper weather maps for two days

Background

The weather maps in a newspaper are not as complex as a meteorologist's weather maps, but they show enough about the weather to make them useful. You can follow the movement of highs, lows, and fronts as they move across the United States. It may even be possible for you to make your own forecast based on the information you can get from the maps.

What to do

Look at the two maps carefully. Keep in mind that in general, the weather moves from west to east. Note the positions of the highs, lows, and fronts on the older weather map. Then plot the highs, lows, and fronts from the newer weather map onto the older weather map.

Draw arrows to show how the highs, lows, and fronts have moved in one day. Note any high or low that has combined with another high or low. Also note any new highs or lows that have formed. Note how the temperature changes after a front passes a weather station. Also note how the wind changes after a front passes.

Now that you have done the investigation

- How did the highs change from one day to the next?
- How did the lows change from one day to the next?
- How did the fronts change from one day to the next?
- If any highs or lows combined, where did they combine?
- If any new highs or lows appeared, where did they appear?
- How did the temperature change after a front passed a weather station?
- How did the winds change after a front passed a weather station?
- How could you figure out how fast a high, a low, or a front moved from one day to the next?

FORECASTING STORMS

What are some common storms, and how can
they be forecast?
When and where does a tornado occur?
How can a tornado be forecast?
When and where does a hurricane occur?
How can a hurricane be forecast?

Some common storms

What is a storm? One dictionary says that a storm is "a disturbance of the atmosphere marked by wind and usually by rain, snow, hail, sleet, or thunder and lightning." But what the dictionary does not say is that a storm is one of nature's strongest forces. A violent storm may cause a great deal of damage. And yet a storm brings needed rainfall for plants and animals. How might a storm be helpful to people?

As you probably know, the most common kinds of storms are rainstorms and snowstorms. These storms are not usually violent storms. But thunderstorms and *blizzards* [BLIHZ-urdz] are violent storms. The kinds of storms you see depend on where you live and the season of the year. What kinds of storms occur where you live?

A rainstorm takes place when warm air rises so high that the clouds that are formed cannot hold their moisture any longer. This warm air can be lifted up in several ways. The air can be lifted up when it is heated by the warm earth or when air masses come together. Or it can be lifted up when it reaches hills or mountains.

When a thunderstorm takes place, warm air rises to a very great height, and a large cloud called a thunderhead is formed. As you may know, thunder, lightning, and heavy rain occur during a thunderstorm. When was the last time you saw a thunderstorm?

A snowstorm is very much like a rainstorm except that the air temperature is below freezing. You may have heard of snowstorms called blizzards. A blizzard is a long-lasting snowstorm that produces driving snow and sometimes sleet.

Find Out More

Using references, find out what causes thunder and lightning. What precautions should a person take during a thunderstorm? Why?

244

Figure 12–8. A cumulonimbus cloud, or thunderhead, is shown in the picture. Its anvil-shaped top indicates what kind of cloud it is. What form of precipitation other than rain may come from such a large cloud?

Artstreet

All these storms form in centers of low air pressure, or lows. If a meteorologist knows from weather maps the speed and direction a low is moving, the meteorologist can forecast a storm for the areas over which the low will probably move.

But suppose weather maps are not available or were not made up within the last few hours. Then the meteorologist can use the changes in air pressure, wind direction, wind speed, kinds of clouds, and relative humidity to help forecast a storm. The meteorologist can also find out what kind of storm it is from the reports given by weather stations over which the storm is passing.

Tornadoes

How much do you know about *tornadoes* [tawr-NAYD-ohz]? Perhaps you have seen one or know someone who has seen one. If so, you know that a tornado is a small storm, but a very violent one. Its winds may be greater than 500 kilometers (about 300 miles) per hour. However, the path of a tornado is, on the average, only about 25 kilometers (16 miles) long and 0.4 kilometers (0.25 miles) wide.

But very little, if any, of a tornado's path touches the ground. In fact, most tornadoes never touch the ground.

However, when one does touch the ground, it causes a great deal of damage to buildings. It also causes injury and loss of life. When, do you suppose, are people most likely to be hurt by a tornado?

A tornado begins high above the earth's surface. It begins when masses and layers of air with very different characteristics come together. Whirling winds and a funnel-shaped cloud are then produced. There have been many ideas about how a tornado forms, but scientists do not seem to agree on any one idea. Why, do you suppose, is it difficult to prove any idea about how a tornado forms?

Most tornadoes occur during the spring in the southern states and during the summer in the midwestern states. They are likely to occur when thunderstorms having a great deal of lightning and hail come into an area. They occur in warm air, either ahead of a cold front or along with a cold front.

A tornado usually travels from the southwest, west, or south. Its forward speed is usually from thirty kilometers (about twenty miles) per hour to sixty kilometers (about forty miles) per hour. Its winds cause a great deal of damage. But damage may also be caused by a drop in air pressure. The low air pressure in the center of a tornado may cause a closed-up building to burst. It bursts from the pressure of the air inside the building.

Meteorologists cannot forecast the exact time or place when a tornado will occur. But they can forecast that in a certain area, say 150 kilometers (about 100 miles) wide and 400 kilometers (about 250 miles) long, a tornado is likely to occur.

It is interesting to note that there are certain patterns in the clouds that may be seen on a radar screen when a tornado is present. The clouds look like the numeral 6. When a meteorologist sees that pattern on the radar screen, the meteorologist reports it. Then a weather alert may be broadcast if one is not already in effect.

☐ **What precautions does your school have in case a tornado or other violent storm occurs during school hours?**

Find Out More

Using references, find out what you should do if there is a violent storm and you are out in the open. Also find out what you should do or tell the driver to do if you are in a car during a violent storm. What should you do if you are home during a violent storm? What is the most important thing to do during any violent storm?

Figure 12–9. Do you know what to do if you see a funnel-shaped cloud like the one pictured? What should you do if you are out in the open?

Devaney

Hurricanes

Another very violent storm is a *hurricane* [HUR-uh-KAYN]. Hurricanes do not occur as often as tornadoes do. But a hurricane is a much larger storm. It may be more than 300 kilometers (about 190 miles) wide and affect a much larger area than a tornado. A hurricane off the east coast of the United States, for example, may affect all the states on the coast.

A hurricane is a storm that begins near the equator. It begins over the open ocean in very warm air. It forms when warm, moist air piles up so high that the wind speeds gradually become faster and faster. Pictures from a satellite show large circular patterns of clouds where a hurricane is present. To be called a hurricane, this storm must have wind speeds of over 120 kilometers (75 miles) per hour. Some of them may even have wind speeds of over 300 kilometers (about 190 miles) per hour near the center, or *eye.* Strangely, however, the winds are calm inside the eye.

Even though its wind speeds are very great, the hurricane itself may move forward very slowly. In fact, the storm may even stop moving forward for a short time. As the hurricane moves closer to a large landmass, however, its forward speed increases. The storm usually breaks up soon after moving over the large landmass.

Most of the hurricanes that come close to the United States form in the Atlantic Ocean. They occur from June through November, but mostly in August, September, and October. On the average, there are six hurricanes each year. Most of them do not cause damage because they stay out over the ocean. What hurricanes do you know about that have caused damage?

As you may know, the winds of a hurricane do a great deal of damage. However, the greatest loss of life during a hurricane is due to drowning. This is because heavy rainfall and large waves during a hurricane cause widespread flooding.

As with tornadoes, meteorologists cannot forecast the exact time or place that a hurricane will occur. But today, hurricanes are observed by satellites and by radar. Ships and airplanes also give reports on them. As a result, the path of a hurricane is easier to forecast than the path of a tornado. That's because a hurricane is such a large storm.

☐ **What, do you suppose, is the best precaution to take if you are near the ocean and you know that a hurricane is coming?**

Even though the whirling wind speeds of a tornado are much greater than those of a hurricane, a hurricane often causes more damage than a tornado. Why, do you think, is this so?

Brent Jones

Do It Yourself

Describe a storm

You have probably seen a thunderstorm. You may also have seen a tornado or hurricane or have seen the damage done by such a storm. Write a description of the storm you saw. If possible, get additional information about it from other people, newspapers, or magazines. What was the thing that impressed you most about the storm?

Modern communication systems help meteorologists receive weather information from across the country. How might access to such information help this meteorologist make weather forecasts?

Careers

Meteorologist

A meteorologist is a scientist who specializes in *meteorology* [MEET-ee-uh-RAHL-uh-jee], or the study of the weather and the air. Of course, a large part of the job of a meteorologist deals with weather forecasting. Because weather sattellites, radar, radiosondes, and many other devices are now used, meteorologists have learned more about forecasting the weather in the last thirty years than in all the years before that. Another reason why so much has been learned about forecasting the weather is that computers are now used to put together thousands of pieces of information in a meaningful way to help meteorologists forecast the weather.

Meteorologists, however, deal with more than just forecasting weather. Meteorologists study many different things about the air and what happens in the air. For example, some meteo-rologists are interested in lightning. They do research to find out more about lightning. Other meteorologists study such things as the effect air pollution has had on weather or the effects the ash from Mount St. Helens has had on weather. The more that meteorologists learn about lightning, air pollution, and the many other things that have to do with weather, the more they learn about the air that surrounds the earth.

Does being a meteorologist sound like an interesting career to you? If you think you might be interested in becoming a meteorologist, you should take courses in science and mathematics. You should also study meteorology in college. A student in your class might write to the American Meteorological Society, 45 Beacon Street, Boston, MA 02108, to find out more about becoming a meteorologist.

249

Reviewing and Extending

Summing Up

1. Weather alerts warn people of a storm, cold temperatures, warm temperatures, flooding, or drought.
2. Weather forecasts help farmers, travelers, and many other people in making their plans.
3. Meteorologists use information from weather stations, weather satellites, radiosondes, and radar to help forecast the weather. In making their forecast, they note how weather conditions change from hour to hour and from place to place.
4. An air mass, or high, is a large body of air that tends to take on the temperature and humidity characteristics of the surface over which it forms.
5. A front is a boundary between two highs.
6. Four kinds of fronts are cold fronts, warm fronts, stationary fronts, and occluded fronts.
7. Fronts and lows often occur together.
8. Storms form in centers of low air pressure, or lows.
9. A tornado is a small, violent storm that produces whirling winds and a funnel-shaped cloud.
10. A hurricane is a large, violent storm with its highest wind speeds near its center, or eye.

Checking Up

Vocabulary   Write the numerals *1–7* on your paper. Each numbered phrase describes a term from the following list. On your paper, write the term next to the numeral of the phrase that describes it.

weather alert   forecast   radar
radiosonde   air mass   front
hurricane   tornado   cloud

1. storm that produces a funnel-shaped cloud
2. violent storm that covers a very large area
3. balloon that carries weather instruments
4. boundary between two air masses of different kinds
5. large body of air that has certain characteristics of temperature and humidity
6. broadcast or newspaper report that gives weather predictions
7. broadcast that warns people about bad weather

Knowledge and Understanding   Write the numerals *8–16* on your paper. Beside each numeral, write the word or words that best complete the sentence having that numeral.

8. If a cold air mass pushes a warm air mass, the front between them is called a (*cold front, warm front, stationary front*).
9. If the boundary between a cold air mass and a warm air mass doesn't move, the front that is produced is called a (*cold front, warm front, stationary front*).
10. Most of the hurricanes that come close to the United States form in the (*Arctic, Atlantic Ocean, Pacific Ocean*).
11. An object that circles the earth and takes pictures of the earth's cloud cover is a (*radiosonde, weather balloon, weather satellite*).
12. People who work at weather stations are trained to observe, measure, and (*change the weather, report on the weather, forecast the weather for a month in advance*).
13. Tornadoes may be spotted on radar when the cloud pattern on the radar screen looks like (*a funnel, an eye, the numeral* 6).
14. If a cold front overtakes a warm front, the mixture of the two fronts is called (*a stationary front, a relative front, an occluded front*).
15. If an air mass is cold and dry, it must have formed over (*the United States, a warm part of the ocean, the Arctic in winter*).
16. One reason why meteorologists can often make correct weather forecasts is that they know that weather moves from (*west to east, north to south, east to west*) across the United States.

Expressing Yourself   Write a paragraph as an answer to each of the following questions:

17. How might weather forecasts be helpful to airline pilots?
18. Why do fronts and lows often bring stormy weather?

Doing More

1. If possible, visit a weather station in your area. How often is each measurement of a weather condition made? What is done with the information that is obtained?
2. Each day for two weeks, listen to the weather forecast for the next day and write down the forecast. Keep a record of the daily weather in your area and compare it with the weather forecast that was given for that day. How often were the meteorologists correct? How often were they incorrect? What sudden changes in weather conditions might account for the times the meteorologists were not correct?

13 Climate and Seasons

On a sunny autumn day you might go outdoors to play a game. What might you plan to do on a snowy winter day? On a rainy spring day? How might the weather affect your plans?

This chapter deals with *climate* [KLY-muht]. Climate is the average of all the weather conditions in a certain place over many years. The climate in a certain place does not change very much from year to year, even though the weather may change a great deal from season to season. So when people talk about climate, they are not talking about the weather on a certain day or in a certain season. Rather, they are talking about the kinds of weather they can expect during the course of many years.

No matter where you live, your climate has a great deal to do with the plant and animal life that is present. Your climate also has a great deal to do with the activities of people. You can find out how climate and seasons affect living things by studying this chapter. You can also find out how and why climates are different from place to place.

WHAT IS CLIMATE?

*What is the difference between weather and
    climate?*
*How does the climate affect the kinds of plants
    that grow in that climate?*
*How does the climate affect the animal life that
    lives in that climate?*
How does the climate affect people's activities?

Weather and climate

Weather, as you may remember, is the sum of all the
conditions of the air that may affect the earth's surface
and its living things. To that definition might be added "at
a given time" or "on a given day." Why do you think such
a phrase might be added?

Climate, of course, is the average of all the weather
conditions in a certain place over many years. Keep in
mind, however, that there may be extreme conditions of
weather that occur in a certain place. Extreme conditions

*Figure 13–1. What kind of climate
permits the type of activity you
see here?*

of temperature might occur within the climate of a northern city. For example, the coldest temperature ever recorded in Chicago, Illinois, was —32°C (—26°F). The warmest temperature was 38°C (100°F). In what parts of the country do you think the extremes would not be as great? Why?

Climate and plant life

As you might guess, the kinds of plants in one climate might be very different from the kinds in another. For example, the desert climate of Arizona, New Mexico, and southern California is very hot and dry much of the year. As a result, the plants that are found in the desert store water and either have no leaves or very small leaves. How would you describe the leaves of a cactus?

In a climate that is very cold and windy much of the year, many of the plants are small and have small leaves. Such plants may produce flowers only every other year because the growing season is short. What state would have large areas with a short growing season? Why?

☐ **What other differences in plants do you know of that may have something to do with the climate?**

Figure 13–2. How do desert plants (left) differ from plants that grow in a colder climate (right)?

Shirley M. Holle

Artstreet

Grant Heilman/Runk/Schoenberger

Do It Yourself

Compare animals in the zoo

Visit a zoo. Look at the animals that normally live in a desert climate. What characteristics do they have in common? Look at the animals that normally live in a cold climate. What characteristics do these animals have in common? What characteristics do animals that normally live in other climates have in common?

Climate and animal life

As you may know, certain animals are well suited to living in a desert climate. These animals conserve water in their body and seek shelter during the hottest part of the day. The gerbil, for example, is such an animal. Gerbils make good pets because they require very little water as long as they get enough to eat.

In a cold climate, the warm-blooded animals grow a great deal of fur before the winter season begins. Some of them also migrate to find food during the winter. Animals like caribou, for example, migrate across frozen, snow-covered lakes in the winter. Where do they find their food?

☐ **What other differences in animals do you know of that may have something to do with the climate?**

Climate and people's activities

The kinds of work people do and the other kinds of activities they do depend a great deal on the climate where they live. For example, people cannot grow oranges in most states because the freezing weather in the winter might kill the trees.

As you know, many people spend a great deal of time outdoors in the summer. But people that live in desert areas may spend a great deal of time indoors during the summer. How would you account for this?

Find Out More

Using references, find out more about the animals that live in one kind of climate. In what ways are these animals well suited to the climate where they live?

255

HOW CLIMATES ARE DIFFERENT

*What things help determine the climate of a
    certain place?*
*What are the major groups of climates in the
    world?*
What is your climate like?

What determines the climate?

As you might guess, there are many things that help
determine the climate of a certain place. One of these
things is the prevailing wind. Mountain ranges and hills,
large bodies of water, ocean currents, the place's distance
from the equator, and its height above sea level also help
determine the climate.

Mountains and hills cause air masses that move toward
them to rise. As an air mass rises and cools, water vapor
condenses and falls to the earth. If the prevailing wind
comes from the west, for example, the rain will fall on the
west side of the mountains. This side of the mountains will
get enough moisture so that crops may be grown. On
the east side of the mountains, however, the climate will
be dry. Why, do you suppose, is this so?

Large bodies of water affect the climate, too. Large
bodies of water have a moderating effect on the temperature. That is, if it is cold inland, the land near a large body
of water will not be as cold as it is inland. If it is hot inland,
the land near the water will not be as hot. So the climate
is usually milder near the water. Inland, however, there
may be great differences between the coldest and warmest
temperatures.

Ocean currents play an important part in determining
the climate, too. For example, you may have heard of the
current called the Gulf Stream. This current moves from
the warm Caribbean area, along the east coast of the
United States, to about Cape Hatteras. Then most of it
moves across the Atlantic Ocean to Europe. Northern Europe would have a colder climate than it has if this warm
current did not reach its coasts.

Find Out More

Using references, find out
the names of the prevailing
winds around the world and
where they are likely to
occur. Where do the names
come from? What do the
prevailing winds have to do
with world climates?

Do It Yourself

Find your latitude

Jacqueline Durand

Obtain a protractor, some tape, a straw, a piece of string about as long as the protractor is wide, and a small weight, such as a fishing weight, that you can tie to the string. Tie the weight to the string and then tape the opposite end of the string to the base of the protractor at its center. When you hold the protractor upside down, the string should cross the 90-degree mark on the curved side of the protractor. Tape the straw to the base of the protractor.

At night, look through the straw at Polaris, the North Star. Have someone note the angle between 90 degrees and the number where the string crosses the protractor (the difference between 90 degrees and the number). This is the angle of Polaris above the horizon. It is equal to the latitude where you are. If each degree of latitude is 111.2 km (about 69.1 miles), how far are you from the equator?

The distance from the equator, or *latitude* [LAT-uh-T(Y)OOD], probably has more to do with the climate at a certain place than anything else. The farther you go from the equator, the lower the average yearly temperature will be. Also, the farther you go from the equator, the larger the yearly temperature range (from warmest to coldest) will be.

The height above sea level of a place also helps determine the climate. The higher you go above sea level, the lower the average yearly temperature will be. You may know that there is snow all year long on the tops of many high mountains, even at the equator. Why do you think the height above sea level of a place affects the temperature as much as it does?

☐ **What things, do you think, help determine the climate where you live? Why do you think so?**

Climates of the world

There are three major groups of climates in the world. These are (1) the *tropical* [TRAHP-ih-kuhl] *climates,* (2) the *middle-latitude climates,* and (3) the *polar* [POH-lur] *climates.* Some people would name a fourth group—the *highland climates.* There are further divisions of each of these major groups.

In tropical climates, the average temperature for any month does not go below 18°C (64°F). As you might guess, these climates are close to the equator.

In middle-latitude climates, the average for the coldest month must be below 18°C (64°F). But the average for the warmest month must be at least 10°C (50°F).

In polar climates, the average for the warmest month is below 10°C (50°F). But highland climates are cold, too. Highland climates are found on mountains and high hills. As you know, the higher you go above sea level, the colder the temperature will be. Because of this, highland climates may change a great deal the higher up you go. At the top of high mountains, highland climates may be much like polar climates.

Your climate

Most areas of the United States have a middle-latitude climate. Look at the map in Figure 13–3. Five of the climates indicated are middle-latitude climates. Keep in mind that many of the lines between climates are not really sharp but that one climate blends into another.

The northeastern quarter of the United States has a *humid continental climate.* This kind of climate has cold winters, hot summers, and over 50 centimeters (20 inches) of rainfall a year. The southeastern quarter of the United States has a *humid subtropical climate.* This kind of climate has mild winters, hot summers, and between 50 and 150 centimeters (20 and 60 inches) of rainfall a year. Which of the states in the southeastern quarter do you suppose have the lowest rainfall? Why?

Most of California has a *Mediterranean climate.* This climate has mild, rainy winters and warm, dry summers.

Find Out More

Look in an atlas or another reference that shows the climates that are grouped under the major climates of the world. How many different climates are there? What are their names? Where are tropical rain forest climates found?

To Think About

Where do you think the term "Mediterranean climate" comes from? What countries in the world do you think have this climate?

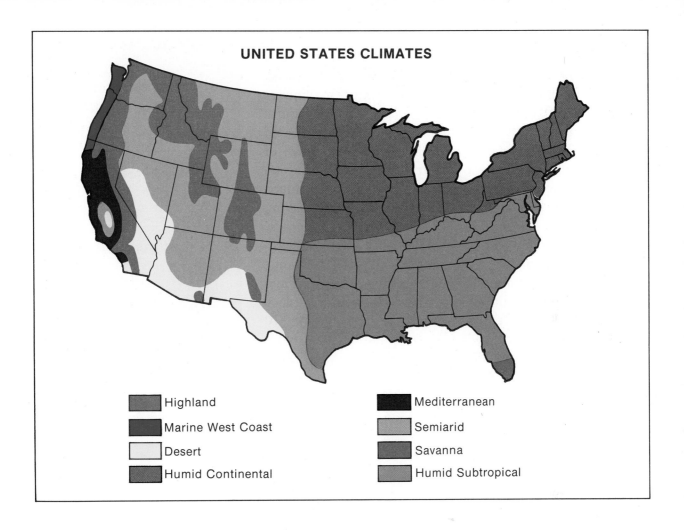

UNITED STATES CLIMATES

Highland

Marine West Coast

Desert

Humid Continental

Mediterranean

Semiarid

Savanna

Humid Subtropical

The coast of Oregon and Washington has a *marine west coast climate*. This climate has mild winters and cool summers.

Except for the Pacific Coast states, the western half of the United States is drier than the eastern half. Notice in Figure 13–3 that the other western states and the eastern part of Oregon, Washington, and California have a mixture of *semiarid climate* and *desert climate*. A semiarid climate is one in which the rainfall is only between twenty-five and fifty centimeters (ten and twenty inches) a year. The rainfall in a desert climate is less than twenty-five centimeters (ten inches) a year. Also, some areas of the western half of the United States have a highland climate.

Figure 13–3. What is the name of the climate where you live? Which states have three or more climates?

259

The climates of Alaska and Hawaii differ from those of the other states. Most areas of Alaska have a polar climate. However, the coast of the lower part of Alaska has a middle-latitude climate. Two of the polar climates of Alaska are the *taiga* [ty-GAH] *climate* and the *tundra* [TUHN-druh] *climate*. The taiga climate has long, cold winters. The summers are warm, but very short. Most of the places that have a taiga climate are covered by forests of conifers. The tundra climate also has long, cold winters. The summer growing season is so short in places having a tundra climate that forests cannot grow there.

Most areas of Hawaii have a tropical climate. It is warm all year in Hawaii. The temperature does not change much between summer and winter or between night and day. But the rainfall may change a great deal from place to place. The rainfall may be only 25 centimeters (10 inches) a year in certain lowlands. But it may be more than 760 centimeters (300 inches) a year in certain highlands. The heaviest rains fall on the northeastern side of each island due to the prevailing wind.

☐ **Do you think the prevailing wind near Hawaii is a westerly wind or an easterly wind? Why?**

Figure 13–4. A scenic picture of Hawaii is shown. What kind of climate would you say Hawaii has?

CHANGING SEASONS

What does the sun have to do with the change of seasons?

How does the change of seasons affect plant life and animal life?

How does the change of seasons affect the activities of people?

Why seasons change

You may know that the earth makes a yearly journey around the sun. The path the earth takes around the sun is called an *orbit* [AWR-buht]. You may also know that an imaginary line running through the earth from the North Pole to the South Pole is called the earth's *axis* [AK-suhs].

The earth rotates about its axis, which is always tilted 23.5 degrees. In the northern half of the earth, the axis always points toward Polaris, the North Star.

Because the earth is in an orbit around the sun, the earth is on different sides of the sun at different times of the year. But remember that in the northern half of the earth, the earth's axis always points toward Polaris. So the axis is tilted toward the sun for part of the year and tilted away from the sun for part of the year. The tilt of the earth's axis and the orbit of the earth around the sun cause the sun's rays to hit the earth at different angles at different times of the year. As you may know, when the sun's rays hit a part of the earth at a more direct angle, the sun warms that part of the earth more. The season of the year depends on the angle at which the sun's rays hit the earth. See Figure 13–5.

At certain times of the year the northern half of the earth receives the sun's rays at a more direct angle. At other times the southern half receives the sun's rays at a more direct angle. At still other times both halves receive the sun's rays equally.

Figure 13–5. The solstices and equinoxes in the northern half of the earth are shown here. How does the position of the northern half of the earth differ from one solstice to the other?

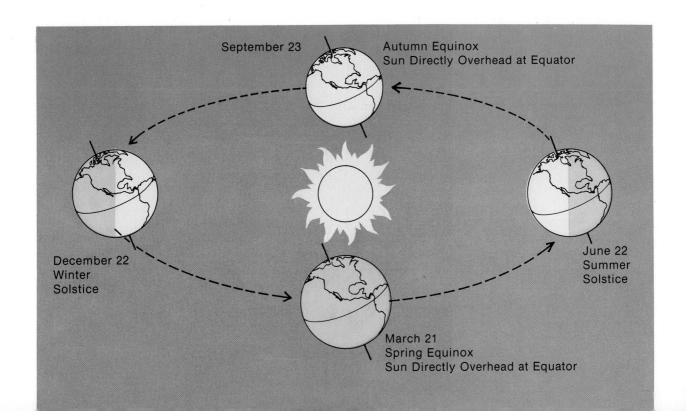

September 23 Autumn Equinox
Sun Directly Overhead at Equator

December 22 Winter Solstice

June 22 Summer Solstice

March 21 Spring Equinox
Sun Directly Overhead at Equator

Perhaps you have heard the words *equinox* [EE-kwuh-NAHKS] and *solstice* [SAHL-stuhs]. These words refer to certain dates in the year and have to do with the seasons. There are two equinoxes a year. One marks the beginning of spring, and one marks the beginning of autumn. The first equinox is March 21 or 22. The second is September 22 or 23. On these two dates of the year, the sun's rays are received at the most direct angle at the equator. So both halves of the earth receive the sun's rays equally.

There are two solstices a year. One marks the beginning of summer, and one marks the beginning of winter. The first solstice is June 21 or 22. The second is December 21 or 22. On each of these dates the sun's rays are received at the most direct angle possible on either the northern half of the earth or the southern half. Which half of the earth receives the rays most directly on June 21 or 22? What season is this? What season is this for the other half of the earth? Why?

☐ **On what date do you think the northern half of the earth has the least amount of daylight? On what date do you think the southern half of the earth has least amount of daylight? Explain.**

When the northern half of the earth has winter, what season does the southern half have? When the northern half has summer, what season does the southern half have? When the northern half has autumn, what season does the southern half have?

Photri.

Figure 13–6. A picture taken north of the Arctic Circle shows the sun at midnight. At what season of the year is the sun visible at midnight? Why?

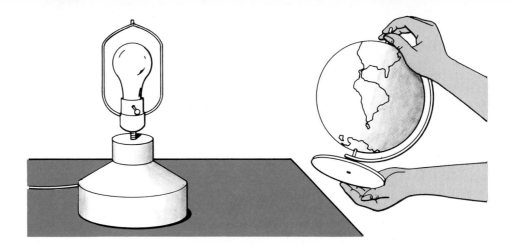

Investigate

How does the path of the earth around the sun cause the change of seasons?

You will need

electric lamp (without a shade), extension cord, globe mounted on a stand

Background

The earth is 150 million km (93 million miles) away from the sun. Because the sun's rays travel such a long distance, they are considered to be parallel when they reach the earth. But because the earth's surface is curved and the earth's axis is tilted 23.5 degrees, the sun's rays do not hit the earth from directly overhead unless a person lives in the latitude near the equator.

What to do

Place the lamp (to represent the sun) on a table or have someone hold the lamp in the middle of a room. You may need an extension cord to use the lamp in the middle of the room. Turn the lamp on and darken the rest of the room. Hold the globe away from the lamp but close enough so that the lamp illuminates part of the globe and the other part is left in a shadow. Without changing the direction that the globe is facing or the angle of the globe's axis, move the globe in an orbit around the lamp. Note the position of the United States at the start of the orbit, at one-quarter orbit, at one-half orbit, at three-quarters orbit, and at full orbit. The start position and the full-orbit position should be exactly the same. Repeat the orbit while rotating the globe on its axis.

Now that you have done the investigation

■ At what point in the earth's orbit is the United States receiving the sun's rays most directly? At what season of the year does this occur?
■ What season of the year in the United States would correspond to the northern half of the earth's being tilted toward the sun?
■ What season of the year would correspond to the northern half of the earth's being tilted away from the sun?
■ In what seasons of the year would the axis of the earth not be tilted either toward the sun or away from the sun?

Seasons and plant and animal life

As you know, climate has a great effect on the plant and animal life in an area. The season of the year also has a great effect on the plant and animal life in an area.

For example, in the middle-latitude climates, winter brings many changes in plants and animals. Many plants and small animals are killed by the first frost. The plants that die leave behind spores or seeds to carry on another year. The animals that die leave behind eggs or young in early stages of growth to carry on another year. The plants and animals that do not die either become dormant or change their activities in some way. Why?

☐ **How do some animals that remain active throughout the winter change their activities?**

Seasons and people's activities

You already know that people's activities change with the seasons. For example, people can't ski or go sledding until winter. People can't go swimming outdoors until summer, unless they have a heated outdoor pool. There are probably many other winter or summer activities you could name, too.

There are also spring or autumn activities. For example, most of the time people can't go canoeing on fast-flowing rivers until spring. Many people can't hike in the woods when the leaves are changing color until autumn. What activities can you do in one season that you cannot do in the others?

Figure 13–7. In certain parts of the world, people can enjoy an autumn scene like the one below. What part of the United States is pictured? Why do you think so?

Grant Heilman

The advice a climatologist gives about weather patterns can help a farmer decide which crops to plant each year.

Careers
Climatologist

Do you think the climate in your area has always been the same? Or do you think the climate may have changed somewhat from the way it used to be years ago? If you do, chances are that you are right. Climate slowly changes through the years. One person who studies the ways climate changes is a *climatologist* [KLY-muh-TAHL-uh-juhst].

A climatologist is a meteorologist with special training. A climatologist studies weather patterns of the past and compares these patterns with today's weather patterns to see how the climate is changing. A climatologist looks for changes in conditions such as wind, temperature, humidity, precipitation, and amount of sunlight. Besides finding out how the climate is changing, a climatologist also looks for the causes of the changes. Climatologists hope they may some-day learn to control some of these changes by studying how climate has changed in the past.

A climatologist's job is important in many ways. For example, climate has much to do with how plants grow in a certain area. Climatologists can give farmers important information about which crops will grow best. Climate also has an effect on the kinds of homes people build. Information from climatologists can be important to builders. In what other ways, do you think, might a climatologist's job be important?

If you think you might be interested in becoming a climatologist, you must first become a meteorologist. Then you must specialize in the study of climates. For information about a career in climatology, a student in your class might write to the American Meteorological Society, 45 Beacon Street, Boston, MA 02108.

Reviewing and Extending

Summing Up

1. The climate in a certain place does not change very much from year to year, even though the weather may change a great deal from season to season within a year.
2. Extreme conditions of weather might occur within the climate of one place and not within the climate of another.
3. The kinds of plants and animals found in one climate might be very different from the kinds found in another climate.
4. The kinds of activities people do may depend a great deal on the climate where they live.
5. The prevailing wind, mountain ranges and hills, large bodies of water, ocean currents, a place's distance from the equator, and its height above sea level help determine the climate.
6. The major groups of climate in the world are the tropical climates, the middle-latitude climates, and the polar climates.
7. There are many different climates across the United States.
8. The angle at which the sun's rays hit the surface of the earth at a certain time determines the season of the year.
9. The season of the year has a great effect on the plant and animal life in an area and on people's activities.

Checking Up

Vocabulary   Write the numerals *1–8* on your paper. Each numbered phrase describes a term from the following list. On your paper, write the term next to the numeral of the phrase that describes it.

middle-latitude climate	earth's orbit	equinox
tropical climate	earth's axis	latitude
polar climate	solstice	climate

1. kind of climate in which the average temperature for any month does not go below 18°C (64°F)
2. distance from the equator
3. kind of climate in which the average temperature for the warmest month is below 10°C (50°F)
4. imaginary line running through the earth from the North Pole to the South Pole
5. average of all the weather conditions in a certain place over many years
6. date on which the sun's rays are received at the most direct angle at the equator
7. yearly journey that the earth makes around the sun
8. date on which the sun's rays are received at the most direct angle possible on one half of the earth

Knowledge and Understanding Write the numerals *9–17* on your paper. Beside each numeral, write the word or words that best complete the sentence having that numeral.

9. If a moist wind reaches some mountains from the west, rain will fall on the (*west, east, south*) side of the mountains.
10. Most areas of the United States have a (*marine west coast, middle-latitude, humid continental*) climate.
11. The northern half of the earth's axis is always pointed toward (*the North Pole, the sun, Polaris*).
12. In the northern half of the earth, the sun's rays are received at the most direct angle on (*June 21, September 22, March 21*).
13. Most areas of Alaska have a (*tropical, middle-latitude, polar*) climate.
14. Most of California has a *tropical, subtropical, Mediterranean*) climate.
15. (*A mountain, Wind, Water*) has a moderating effect on the temperature and climate of a place that is close by.
16. Most of the western states have a mixture of semiarid, desert, and highland climates. Because of this, the western half of the United States is (*drier, colder, damper*) than the eastern half.
17. The higher above sea level a place is, the (*lower, higher, more variable*) the average yearly temperature will be.

Expressing Yourself Write a paragraph as an answer to each of the following questions:

18. Why do some parts of the earth obtain more energy from the sun in the summer season than they do in the winter season?
19. Why does northern Europe have a climate similar to that of the northeastern quarter of the United States, even though northern Europe is at a higher latitude?

Doing More

1. Place soil in 2 boxes that are alike. Measure the temperature of the soil in each box. Then prop up 1 box so that it receives the direct rays of the sun. Let the other box rest on the ground. Measure the temperature of each box of soil after 30 minutes. Do the temperatures of the 2 boxes differ after 30 minutes? Explain.
2. Make clay models of the earth to show how the earth looks as seen from the sun at the solstices and equinoxes in its orbit.

Lou Jones

Bill Means

Teenagers that live in a climate that has warm, sunny summers are able to enjoy going to the beach. In what kind of climate, do you think, are teenagers able to enjoy winter sports?

14   Weather and People

Wherever you live, you probably have observed that the weather keeps changing from day to day. On some days, the skies are bright and sunny. Other days are dark and cloudy. The winds pick up speed and then slow down. The temperature goes up and down. The conditions of weather are constantly changing.

You must adjust to the weather as you go through your daily activities. The weather can affect what you wear, what you do, and even how you feel. How is the way you dress in the winter different from the way you dress in the summer? What does the weather have to do with your plans for a picnic or a backyard barbecue? Are you likely to be more cheerful on a bright, sunny day or on a day when the skies are dark and overcast with clouds?

Because weather is important to everyone, some scientists are looking for ways to control the weather. They are asking many questions about the weather. What causes the weather to change? How can rain be made to fall from clouds in the sky? What can be done about fog and frost? How has the earth's climate changed from year to year? What might cause changes in the climate? You will find the answers to questions such as these in this chapter.

WEATHER AND YOU

What does the weather have to do with what you wear?
How does the weather help you decide what you will do after school?
What does the weather have to do with how you feel?
How does the weather help determine where you live?

What you wear

What kinds of clothes do you wear to the beach in the summer? What kinds of clothes do you wear on a warm, rainy day? What kinds of clothes do you wear on a winter day? These questions should help you see that the weather on a given day in the place where you live has a great deal to do with what you will probably wear.

You dress for comfort and also for current styles. That is, you want to be comfortable in what you wear. But at the same time you want to look nice. If you had a choice, would you rather dress to be in style or dress for the weather? Why?

Gene Harris/Meyers Photo Art

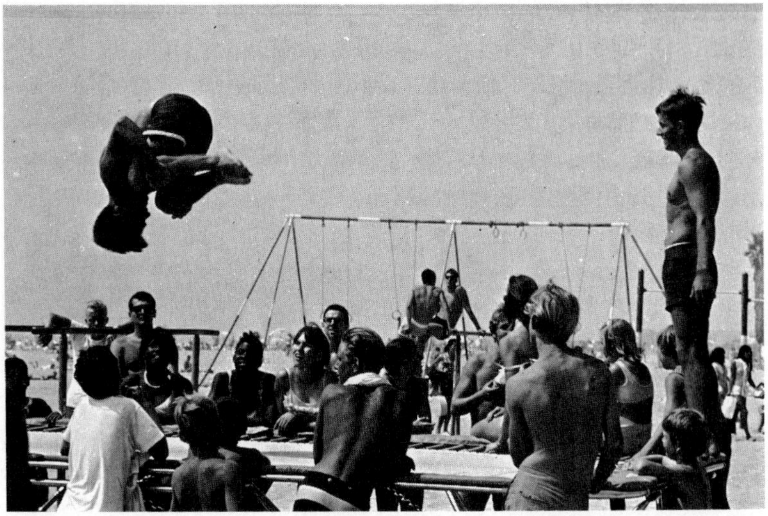

Figure 14–1. When it is winter where you live, under what conditions would you be able to do the things these boys are doing?

Figure 14–2. What game are these boys playing? What do you think the weather is like where they are playing? Why do you think so?

What you do after school today

What are you going to do after school today? Chances are, no matter how you answer this question, the weather has something to do with it. For example, if it was raining outside, you would probably rather play basketball inside than play baseball outside. But if it was sunny and warm outside, you would probably want to play baseball or take part in some other outdoor activity. How might the weather affect what you will do today?

How often have you had to postpone an outdoor activity because of the weather? Or how often have you decided to do something outside because the weather was so nice? Of course, how many outdoor activities you can take part in depends on the season. In the winter season, for example, you might take part in many indoor activities. In the summer you might want to be outside most of the time. Which season—winter or summer—seems longer to you? Why?

How you feel

Do you sometimes feel better on a sunny day than you do on a cloudy or rainy day? Many people do. A sunny day may seem to make everything brighter and more agreeable

Find Out More

Take a survey among people of different ages to find out what they like to do on a sunny day. Also find out what they like to do on a rainy day. Find out which kind of activity—the sunny-day activity or the rainy-day activity—they like to do better. Could you have predicted their choice for the better-liked activity? Why or why not?

to you. You may not only feel better but you may also work harder and play harder. Is it sunny or cloudy outside right now? How does this weather make you feel?

If the weather is bad, some people might have pain in the joints of their body or have headaches. Some people become hard to get along with. People are often not as happy, especially if the bad weather continues for more than a day or two. Why do you think this might be true?

The amount of moisture in the air has a lot to do with how you feel. For example, sometimes the air has a great deal of moisture in it. Your body does not give off as much heat in moist air as it does when the air is dry. Would you say that you feel comfortable or uncomfortable on a very moist and warm summer day?

Sometimes the air is very dry. Then your skin might also be very dry. Dry skin might make you want to scratch yourself a great deal. If the air is cold as well as dry, your lips might become chapped. The inside surfaces of your nose and throat might become dry and a little bit sore. These surfaces lose some of their moisture to the dry air. Would you say that you feel comfortable or uncomfortable on a very dry and cold winter day?

☐ **Based on what you know about the weather at different seasons of the year and how you feel at different seasons of the year, during which season or seasons of the year do you think people would be the healthiest? Why?**

Photri

Figure 14–3. What kind of weather does this boy see? How do you think it makes him feel?

271

Jacqueline Durand

Do It Yourself

Observe the daily weather

Make daily observations of the weather throughout your study of this unit. If you can, record the temperature, humidity (moisture), air pressure, direction of the wind, and condition of the sky (cloudy, partly cloudy, or clear), and record if there is rain or snow. If you cannot make all these observations yourself, you may wish to get some of them from a daily newspaper or a daily weather report. Also make a note of how you feel each day. In general, what does the weather have to do with how you feel?

Where you live

Many people have moved to Hawaii, to California, to the Southwest, to the Gulf states, or to Florida. Perhaps you or people you know have moved to one of these states. One of the reasons that many people have moved to these states is that the year-round weather is warmer in these places than where they used to live. Also, the weather does not change a great deal from season to season.

Some people prefer to live in an area where the weather changes a great deal from season to season. These people may like the spring and fall seasons and may enjoy winter sports. Do you know people who prefer to live in an area where the weather changes a great deal from season to season? If so, what do you think their reasons are for living in the area they live in?

☐ **Many people enjoy warm weather for most of the year. Some of these people may also enjoy being able to ski not far from where they live. Where are people most likely to find warm weather where they live and ski slopes close by?**

To Think About

Suppose you had a choice of where you could live. Where would that be? What factors do you think would influence your decision? What part would weather play in the decision you would make?

272

CONTROLLING WEATHER

*How might watching the world's weather help in
  controlling the weather?*
*What is cloud seeding, and how does it change
  the weather?*
*What is the effect of hail on crops, and how can
  hail be prevented?*
How may fog and frost be controlled?

World weather-watch

Today, satellites are being used more and more to watch
the weather around the world. The reason for using satellites is that scientists believe that hurricanes and other
severe weather may be forecast with more accuracy if a
world weather-watch is kept. A world weather-watch is
the constant watching of weather around the world. Satellites and radiosondes can be used to take pictures of
clouds and to record temperatures and pressures throughout the world. This weather information can then be put
into computers. Millions of bits of information can be
analyzed in a short time. Accurate weather forecasts can
then be made.

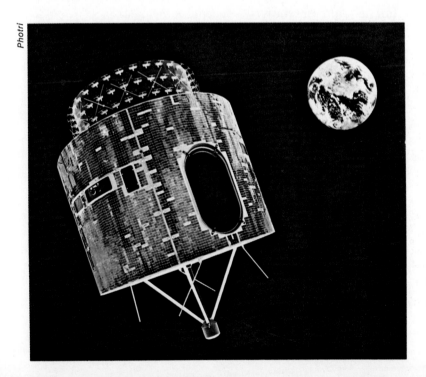

Photri

*Figure 14–4. This weather satellite
takes pictures of the earth every
thirty minutes. It also receives and
transmits weather information. How
are pictures of the earth helpful
to meteorologists?*

273

The problem in making forecasts for several days ahead of time is that small disturbances in the air may quickly change and become large ones. Lately, however, scientists have gained a better understanding of the forces that affect the weather and cause such disturbances. A world weather-watch using computers can be used to spot such disturbances and to forecast what will happen to them. Someday it may even be possible to control such disturbances. Then severe weather will occur less often.

☐ **What kinds of severe weather do you think should be controlled? Why do you think so?**

Cloud seeding

It has been known since 1946 that certain clouds may be seeded. Tiny grains of very cold materials such as dry ice may be scattered in a cloud from an airplane to make the cloud produce rain or snow. *Dry ice* is frozen carbon dioxide. Making rain or snow may help drought-stricken farmers and ranchers.

But you may be wondering how cloud seeding produces rain or snow. The very cold grains provide surfaces on which the water vapor in the cloud can condense. When enough tiny water drops condense on a grain, the large drop or ice crystal that forms will fall as rain or snow.

Figure 14–5. Some of the clouds in the picture have been seeded with dry ice from an airplane. As a result, there is a "hole" in the clouds. What probably happened to the cloud material at that place?

Wide World

Jacqueline Durand

Do It Yourself

Try to seed some air

Obtain a large, clear, plastic bag. Blow up the bag and then close the bag with a rubber band or a twist tie. Place the bag in a freezer for at least one day. Then remove the bag and open it just enough to be able to blow into it. Blow your breath into the bag until it is filled. Then close the bag quickly. What do you see inside the bag? Were you able to seed the air inside the bag? Explain.

Even though cloud seeding may help some people, cloud seeding may also cause problems. For example, suppose a cloud is seeded to provide moisture that is needed in a certain area. Also suppose that the cloud might have provided moisture in another place if the cloud had not been seeded. In other words, the moisture in the cloud was "stolen" by cloud seeding. How do you think such a problem can be settled?

☐ **On what kinds of particles do you think water vapor usually condenses in a cloud?**

Preventing hail

Hail can damage crops such as wheat and corn. In fact, insurance companies pay out millions of dollars every year due to crop damage from hail. Because of this damage, scientists are trying to find out how to prevent hail. There has been some success.

Hail is produced in thunderstorm clouds. These clouds can be seeded. Seeding increases the number of grains around which the tiny water drops can condense and form ice crystals. Then a large number of small ice crystals can be formed instead of a small number of large ice crystals. The small crystals usually melt before they reach the ground. What, do you suppose, might be a problem in seeding thunderstorm clouds?

To Think About

Do you think there should be laws regarding cloud seeding? Why or why not?

Controlling fog

Fog can be dangerous on a highway. It can also be dangerous over an airport or a harbor. Fog is really made up of clouds near the earth's surface. Because of this, fog may be controlled in several ways.

One way to control fog is to spray dry-ice pellets into the fog. Tiny water drops condense on the pellets and cause ice crystals to grow. The ice crystals soon become so large that they fall to the ground, carrying some moisture out of the fog with them. So, the fog is lessened.

Another way to control fog is to spray liquid propane fuel into the air. Tiny water drops condense on the propane. Still another way is to seed the fog with very tiny grains of table salt. The salt combines with water vapor to form drops of brine. The drops of brine fall to the ground. Other chemicals besides table salt have also been seeded in clouds to control fog.

☐ **If a portion of fog is seeded, that part forms a clear pocket. If some movement of air occurs, what do you suppose will happen to the clear pocket? Why?**

Controlling frost

Have you heard about frost damage to crops? If you have, you may know that frost can destroy orchard crops, for example. Frost may occur on a cold, clear night during the growing season. As you know, clear weather at night means that more heat can escape from the earth than on a cloudy night. So, one of two things might be done to prevent frost. Either (1) the temperature of the air might be raised or (2) smoke might be created to hold in the heat.

The temperature of the air may be raised by using oil heaters placed around an orchard. Or a gas flame on the ends of long stationary or revolving pipes may be used.

Smoke may be created by burning certain materials. *Smudge pots* are used for this. Smudge pots are pots filled with oily materials, old rubber, or damp leaves that burn

Find Out More

Table salt is a hygroscopic, or water-attracting, compound. Using references, find out what other materials are hygroscopic. Do you think these materials could also be used for fog control? Why or why not?

Wide World

slowly and put smoke into the air. Smudge pots are placed near an orchard on the side from which the wind is blowing so that the smoke will be carried over the orchard. The smoke forms a protective layer that prevents loss of heat from the ground. Why, do you suppose, are smudge pots usually used at night?

Figure 14–6. A pear orchard is pictured at night. Do you think the above scene may take place at any time of the year? Why?

CHANGES IN THE EARTH'S CLIMATE

What is some evidence for past changes in the earth's climate?

How might changes in the earth's orbit affect the climate?

How does air pollution affect the climate?

Climates of the past

Scientists have discovered that the earth's climate, or the climates throughout the earth, have changed from time to time. For example, great sheets of ice once covered at least half of North America. What does this tell you about North America's climate in the past?

Figure 14–7. A coral fossil, Halysites, is pictured. Such fossils are found in climates where living corals cannot be found today. Why, do you suppose, is this so?

Dr. H. Wirth/ZEFA

Fossils of coral, an animal that lives only in warm seawater, have been discovered in the rocks of Greenland. Today, Greenland is an island almost completely covered by ice. What does this tell you about Greenland's climate in the past?

Scientists study past climates in many different ways. For example, scientists study such things as deep-sea cores, ice cores, and tree rings. See Figure 14–8. All these studies seem to show that the climate is always changing. Of course, such changes are noticeable only over a period of many years.

Scientists say the earth's climate is now warm. In fact, from 1850 to 1940 the average air temperature of the earth was slowly rising. Temperature records kept in many different places show this. Since 1950, however, the average air temperature has been slowly falling.

☐ **What do you think a falling average air temperature might indicate about the earth's climate in the near future?**

Find Out More

Using references, find out what you can about the fossils that exist in the sedimentary rocks of Greenland, Antarctica, and other places that are very cold today. What have scientists learned about past climates from such fossils?

278

Grant Heilman   Dr. P. Schoeck/ZEFA

Changes in the earth's orbit

Some scientists believe that changes now taking place in the shape of the earth's orbit around the sun will lead to ice sheets covering many places on the earth again. These scientists found that there are certain changes taking place in the earth's orbit. They wondered if there might be a relationship between past climates and these changes. So, they studied the records of climates in deep-sea cores and compared these records with the changes in the earth's orbit. They found that the two matched. Because of this, these scientists believe the earth will continue cooling slowly for the next 20,000 years. If what they say is true, what do you suppose the earth's climate will be like at the end of that time? Why?

Changes caused by air pollution

Air pollution may cause changes in the cycle of the earth's climate. It is known that volcanoes sometimes

Figure 14–8. Tree rings and ice from a glacier help scientists discover what past climates were like. What does each ring in a tree stump indicate? What does each layer of ice indicate?

cause air pollution. The eruption in 1980 of Mount St. Helens, a volcano in Washington, is one example. The eruptions of volcanoes place great amounts of dust into the air. This dust can lower the amount of sunlight reaching the earth's surface. Tree rings and temperature records show that this dust affects the earth's climate. For example, the summer of 1816 in New England was unusually cold. This cold weather was caused by a thick layer of dust in the air that came from Mount Tambora, a volcano in the Dutch East Indies, which erupted in 1815. What effect, do you think, might the eruption of Mount St. Helens have on the earth's climate?

People can also cause air pollution. People place great amounts of dust into the air when they burn fuels. Like volcano dust, this dust can affect the climate. The carbon dioxide and other gases placed into the air when people burn fuels can also affect the climate. For example, carbon dioxide helps cause the greenhouse effect. So, the more carbon dioxide that is in the air, the warmer the air is likely to be.

☐ **The earth's climate may be in a cycle of cooling caused by changes in the earth's orbit. If this is true, what effect do you think dust and carbon dioxide are having on this cycle?**

Mary Elenz Tranter

Do It Yourself

Find out about air pollution in your area

Many places have an air-pollution problem. You can find out about air pollution in your area by doing a test. Take a clean sheet of white paper outside and use masking tape to tape it to a windowsill or to a light pole. Carefully spread a thin layer of petroleum jelly on the paper. Take the paper in after a few days. Compare the paper with a clean sheet. How dirty is the air? What, do you think, causes the air to be dirty?

Courtesy of Department of the Air Force

Photri

Information gathered by weather reconnaissance pilots and obtained from satellite photographs are used by the National Weather Service to issue hurricane warnings.

Careers

Weather reconnaissance pilot

As you know, hurricanes are violent storms. Each year they cause millions of dollars of damage and sometimes cause the loss of many lives. Scientists are interested in learning how to predict hurricanes and how to control hurricanes. One person who is helping scientists learn more about hurricanes is the *weather reconnaissance pilot*.

Weather reconnaissance pilots fly airplanes into hurricanes. They are sometimes called "hurricane hunters." Much of the time these pilots fly in areas where hurricanes are likely to develop. They observe and report the weather conditions in these areas. But the real job of weather reconnaissance pilots begins when a hurricane develops. It is the job of these pilots to fly specially equipped airplanes right into the eye, or the calm center, of the hurricane to gather information.

The information gathered by weather reconnaissance pilots helps meteorologists make accurate forecasts about the path of the hurricane. These forecasts can help save many lives. In the 1930's and the early 1940's, hurricanes caused an average of 160 deaths each year. But when pilots began to fly into hurricanes to help predict the hurricane's path, the average number of deaths dropped to only 4. Weather reconnaissance pilots also gather information that can help scientists learn more about hurricanes. With the right information, scientists may one day learn how to control these storms.

Most weather reconnaissance pilots get their training in the armed forces. In fact, most of the weather reconnaissance pilots are air force pilots. For further information a student might write to USAF Recruiting Service, Wright-Patterson Air Force Base, OH 45899.

Reviewing and Extending

Summing Up

1. The weather affects what you wear on a given day, what you do after school, how you feel, and where you live.
2. A world weather-watch may be used to make weather forecasts for several days ahead of time and to spot disturbances in the weather.
3. Satellites are being used to observe the weather around the world.
4. Certain clouds may be seeded with tiny grains of very cold materials to make the clouds produce rain or snow.
5. Thunderstorm clouds may be seeded to prevent hail. Fog may also be controlled by seeding.
6. To control frost, either (1) the temperature of the air is raised or (2) smoke is created to hold in the heat.
7. Scientists have much evidence that shows the earth's climate has changed in the past. This evidence includes fossils; deep-sea cores, ice cores, and tree rings; and evidence of great sheets of ice that covered large parts of the earth.
8. Some scientists believe that changes now taking place in the shape of the earth's orbit around the sun will lead to ice sheets covering many places on the earth again.
9. Air pollution caused by volcanoes or caused by the activities of people may affect the earth's climate.
10. Mount St. Helens is a volcano that has recently caused air pollution.
11. The more carbon dioxide placed into the air, the warmer the air is likely to be.

Checking Up

Vocabulary Write the numerals *1–10* on your paper. Each numbered phrase describes a term from the following list. On your paper, write the term next to the numeral of the phrase that describes it.

carbon dioxide	sulfur dioxide	weather
cloud seeding	air pollution	coral
weather-watch	smudge pots	cores
thunderstorms	dry ice	hail

1. condition that may be caused by dust from volcanoes or by people burning fuels
2. gas that helps hold in the earth's heat by means of the greenhouse effect
3. scattering tiny grains of very cold materials, such as dry ice, in a cloud to make the cloud produce rain or snow.
4. storms that can produce hail
5. taking pictures of clouds and recording the air temperature and air pressure throughout the world by means of satellites and radiosondes
6. burn slowly and produce smoke that is used to control frost
7. affects what you wear, what you do, and how you feel
8. large ice crystals
9. frozen carbon dioxide
10. fossils of a sea animal discovered in rocks in Greenland

Knowledge and Understanding Write the numerals *11–18* on your paper. Beside each numeral, write the word or words that best complete the sentence having that numeral.

11. Since 1950, the average air temperature of the earth has been slowly _____.
12. To control frost in an orchard, _____ may be created by burning certain materials in smudge pots.
13. One reason why many people have moved to Hawaii, to California, to the Southwest, to the Gulf states, or to Florida is that the weather is _____ in those places.
14. If the air has a great deal of moisture in it, your body gives off _____ heat than it does when the air is dry.
15. When the weather is bad, some people might have pain in the joints of their body or have _____.
16. Changes now taking place in the shape of the earth's _____ around the sun may lead to ice sheets covering many places on the earth again.
17. Weather information is put into _____ so that it can be analyzed in a short time and weather forecasts can be made.
18. Crops, such as wheat and corn, are often damaged by _____ during storms.

Expressing Yourself Write a paragraph as an answer to each of the following questions:

19. How does cloud seeding produce rain or snow and yet serve to control hail and fog?
20. The oldest living pine trees are about 4,500 years old. How can dead pines that lived between 4,000 and 8,000 years ago be used to find out what the earth's climate was like 8,000 years ago?

Doing More

1. Take a survey in your area to find out the different sources of air pollution. If possible, try to find out exactly what is causing the air pollution. What do you think could be done to control each source of air pollution? How do you think the air pollution affects the weather in your area?

2. Try to find out what the government officials in your area are doing about the problem of air pollution. What are the laws against air pollution? How are these laws enforced? Should new laws against air pollution be passed? What can concerned citizens do to help officials?

Pros and Cons

**Weather—Should It
Be Controlled?**

As you have read in this unit, some weather control is possible now. Even more control may be possible in the future. Some people think weather should not be controlled. They point out, for example, that advance warnings are usually given for severe weather so that people can prepare for it. But people who think weather should be controlled say that even though advance warnings help people protect themselves and their property, there is still far too much storm damage.

People who think weather should not be controlled point out that in certain areas of the country severe storms provide needed moisture. If the storms were controlled, they say, there might not be enough moisture reaching all the areas that need it. But people who think weather should be controlled say that in many cases there are other ways of providing moisture. They also believe that even if there was no other way of providing moisture, it would be better to have some areas run short of moisture than to have the damage caused by severe storms.

Those in favor of controlling weather state that more moisture could be provided for certain areas by cloud seeding. This might avoid the problem of drought. But

Certain chemicals or very cold materials, such as dry ice, may be scattered from an airplane to seed clouds and cause rain to fall. Why do some people object to seeding clouds?

people who object to weather control maintain that if moisture was taken out of the air in some areas, other areas downwind might not get enough rainfall.

The people who are in favor of leaving weather alone state that there would be legal battles if weather was controlled. This is because the people whose farms and ranches were downwind from areas in which seeded clouds released most of their moisture would not receive enough precipitation. These people would complain that they were being robbed of their livelihood. The charge would also be made that certain areas were "stealing" the precipitation that belonged to other areas. People in favor of leaving weather alone say that the costs of such legal battles would be great. They feel that it might be far less costly just to leave the weather alone.

Those in favor of controlling weather say that moisture in the air does not "belong" to anyone. However, to avoid a possible problem in this regard, some of these people believe that the control of weather should be left up to the government and not to individuals or to private enterprise. Of course, some people believe that the moisture in the air belongs to everyone and that it should not be controlled.

Cumulonimbus clouds, or thunderhead clouds, occur naturally in many parts of the United States. What problem might result if such clouds do not occur often enough in a certain area?

What do you think should be done about the problem of controlling weather? Is there an easy answer to this question? Should weather be controlled as much as possible, or should it be controlled part of the time? Should it be controlled at all? If weather should be controlled, who should control it? Many arguments other than those given here could be presented. What do your parents or other adults think? What do your classmates think?

Investigate On Your Own

1. Make a barometer with two jars. Fill a tall, widemouthed jar about half full of water. Then fill a narrow jar (such as an olive jar) about a fourth full of water. Seal the narrow jar with a stopper. Invert the narrow jar into the widemouthed jar. The narrow jar should be able to float freely in the widemouthed jar. Remove or add water to the jars so that the water levels in both jars will be equal when the narrow jar floats in the widemouthed jar. Your barometer is now ready to use. Observe your barometer twice a day. If the air pressure is rising, the water level in the narrow jar will be higher than in the widemouthed jar. If the air pressure is falling, the water level in the widemouthed jar will be higher. How would you explain this?

2. Place two ice cubes on a plate. Then sprinkle salt on one of the ice cubes. Observe the ice cubes to see which cube melts faster. Of what value is the effect you observed for clearing snowy or icy streets?

3. If you live in an area where snow falls in the winter, you may wish to examine snowflakes. Let some snowflakes fall on a piece of dark cloth. Use a strong magnifying glass or the low power of a microscope to examine the snowflakes. You may wish to draw the patterns of as many snowflakes as you can. How many snowflakes have exactly the same shape and pattern?

4. The temperature at which condensation occurs (called the dew point) in a sample of air doesn't change unless moisture in the air itself changes. Place a thermometer in a can of water that is about half full. Then add some ice to the water. Watch for the first appearance of moisture on the sides of the can and note the temperature. Empty the can and dry it off. Then spray water several times into a large, nearly closed cardboard box that has been placed on its side. Place water, ice, and a thermometer in the can again and place the can in the box. Again watch for the first appearance of moisture on the sides of the can and note the temperature. Was the temperature at which moisture appeared the same as before? Explain.

Read On Your Own

Alth, Max, and Charlotte Alth, *Disastrous Hurricanes and Tornadoes*. New York: Franklin Watts, Inc., 1981.

The true stories of some of the most disastrous hurricanes and tornadoes are presented along with a scientific description of each of these violent kinds of storms.

Cosgrove, Margaret, *It's Snowing!* New York: Dodd, Mead & Company, 1980.

The formation of snow, the structure of snow crystals, the importance of snow, and the destructive nature of snow are some of the topics included in this book. The book suggests ways to play safely in the snow.

Gallant, Roy, *Earth's Changing Climate*. New York: Four Winds Press, 1979.

The earth's changing climate and some possible causes for such changes are explored in this book. The book explains many natural forces, such as sunspots and cosmic dust clouds. It includes a discussion of how people affect the environment and the weather.

Heuer, Kenneth, *Rainbows, Halos, and Other Wonders: Light and Color in the Atmosphere*. New York: Dodd, Mead & Company, 1978.

The magic of rainbows, halos, coronas, mirages, and other effects of light and color in the atmosphere are explained in easy-to-understand language. Excellent photographs add interest to this book.

McFall, Christie, *Wonders of Dust*. New York: Dodd, Mead & Company, 1980.

Sources of dust from within the earth to outer space are discussed in this book. The book explains dust storms and the effects of dust on the weather.

Witty, Margot, and Ken Witty, *A Day in the Life of a Meteorologist*. Mahwah, N.J.: Troll Associates, 1981.

A day in the life of a Philadelphia weather forecaster is briefly described in this book. Photographs of radar images, satellite pictures, and weather maps enhance the text.

Unit 4
WATER ON THE EARTH

When you look at a globe of the earth, you can see that most of the earth is covered by water. Almost all of the water is in the ocean. This water contains salt and other minerals. If you were to taste this water, you might call it salty. Water in rivers and lakes contains much less salt and fewer minerals. Compared with seawater, most water in rivers and lakes would be called fresh. Fresh water is an important resource that can be used in many different ways. In what ways do you use fresh water?

People have always been challenged by new frontiers. Columbus and other explorers sailed across an unknown ocean to find new lands. Early settlers in America traveled west across plains as vast as an ocean. In fact, their shiplike covered wagons were called prairie schooners. Recently, scientists have launched satellites and other spacecraft to learn more about frontiers in space. Today, the earth's ocean offers a new and challenging frontier. What do you think some of the challenges of the ocean might be?

Photri

15 The Chemistry of Water

Many particles of water are part of a spray of water. But the tiny particles you see in a spray are not the smallest particles of water. You could not even see them with a magnifying glass.

Have you ever looked closely at a picture in a comic book or in a newspaper? Without a magnifying glass, the picture appears to be made either of shades of black and white or of shades of colors. With a magnifying glass, however, you can see that the shades are made up of tiny dots of ink.

Looking at water is somewhat like looking at that picture. The "tiny dots" that make up

water are, however, too small to be seen. Fortunately, scientists have learned how to study things that are too small to be seen. What they learned when they studied the makeup of water turned out to be rather interesting. What things do you know about the makeup of water? What do you suppose you might learn about water if you were able to take a closer look at it?

MAKEUP OF WATER

*What "building blocks" make up everything
around you?*
What two gases combine to form water?
*What are some characteristics of the gases
that form water?*

Building blocks of all things

Everything around you is made up of certain kinds of "building blocks." For example, from a distance a brick wall looks different from the way it looks when you are close to it. When you are close to the wall, you are able to see the bricks and the mortar that make it up. The matter that makes up everything around you is similar to a brick wall. For example, all matter is made of separate particles held together in some way. But these particles are too small to be seen without using special microscopes. These particles are called *molecules* [MAHL-ih-kYOO(UH)LZ]. Molecules, like the bricks of the wall, are tiny particles that make up matter.

Molecules, like the bricks in the wall, usually consist of even smaller particles. These smaller particles are called *atoms* [AT-uhmz]. In some kinds of matter, each molecule

Figure 15–1. This picture was taken by using a field-ion microscope. It shows the location of atoms on the point of a needle made of tungsten.

Photri

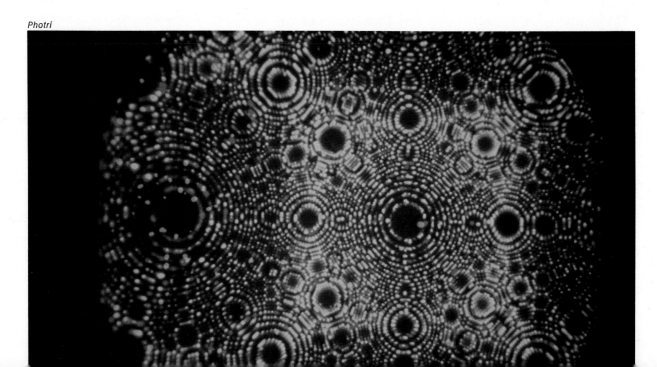

consists of a single atom, and each molecule is made of the same kind of atom. Iron and copper are examples of such matter. Most matter consists of molecules with two or more atoms. The atoms of these molecules may be alike. For example, oxygen molecules have two oxygen atoms joined together. However, matter usually consists of molecules with two or more different kinds of atoms joined together. A salt molecule, for example, consists of one atom of sodium and one atom of chlorine.

☐ **How is a molecule of copper different from a molecule of salt?**

Elements and compounds

When you look at silver, aluminum, mercury, or carbon, you are looking at some kinds of matter in which the molecules are alike. The molecules of these kinds of matter consist of only one kind of atom. For example, molecules of silver consist only of atoms of silver. Matter of which the molecules consist only of one kind of atom is called an *element* [EHL-uh-muhnt]. Only a few kinds of matter are found as elements in or on the earth. In addition to those elements mentioned above, a more complete list of the elements found in or on the earth is given in the table in Figure 15–2.

Most matter on the earth consists of molecules of two or more different kinds of atoms. Such molecules are called *compounds* [KAHM-POWNDZ]. There are several thousand known compounds.

To understand better the difference between elements and compounds, think about water. By just looking at water, it is impossible to determine whether water is an element or a compound. But scientists have found that water is a compound. A water molecule consists of atoms of the elements *hydrogen* [HY-druh-juhn] and oxygen. Hydrogen and oxygen are, by themselves, gases. But when two atoms of hydrogen combine with one atom of oxygen, they form the compound called water. If the symbols H and O are used to represent these two gases, then a molecule of water may be represented by the formula H_2O.

(*Text continues on page 294.*)

Figure 15–2. Which of the elements in this list have you seen? Where might you be able to see these elements?

SOME ELEMENTS FOUND IN OR ON THE EARTH

Carbon	Mercury
Copper	Neon
Gold	Nitrogen
Helium	Oxygen
Hydrogen	Silver
Lead	Sulfur

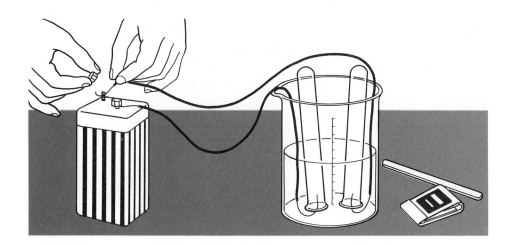

Investigate

What elements make up water?

You will need

water, beaker, matches, wood splint, 6-volt dry cell, insulated copper wire, sodium-carbonate solution, 2 test tubes

Background

Oxygen and hydrogen are clear, colorless gases. But there is a way to tell them apart. If a flame is held near the opening of a test tube of hydrogen, the hydrogen burns with a *pop*. The way to test for oxygen is to start a wood splint burning and blow out the flame so the wood is just a glowing ember. Then pass the glowing end into the test tube. If oxygen is present, the wood will burst into flame.

What to do

Pour water into a beaker until it is about half full. Fill two test tubes with water and place them in the beaker as shown. Use your thumb to keep the water in each tube as you put it in the beaker. Pour 15 ml of sodium-carbonate solution into the water in the beaker.

Scrape the insulation from each end of two pieces of copper wire. Bend one end of each piece of copper wire into a hook, and slip the hook end into each of the test tubes. Connect the other end of each wire to the dry cell as shown.

Observe the bare part of the wire inside the test tubes. Also observe the area near the top of each tube. After fifteen minutes, disconnect the wires. Pick up the test tube with the most gas in it. Keep the tube closed. Light a wood splint. After you turn the tube over, remove your thumb. Hold the burning splint near the opening of the tube. Be careful to keep the opening pointed away from anyone. Test the other tube with a glowing splint.

Now that you have done the investigation

■ What appeared in the test tubes during the fifteen minutes?
■ What gas do you think was in the first tube you tested? Explain your answer.
■ What gas do you think was in the second tube you tested? Explain your answer.
■ What elements do you think make up water?

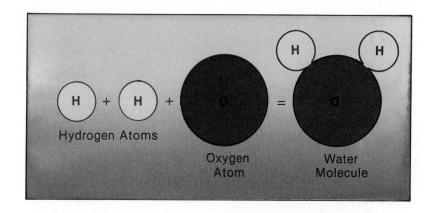

Figure 15-3. In this drawing, circles are used to show how atoms combine to form a molecule of water. The shape of the water molecule helps give the molecule some important qualities.

You might be interested in knowing another way of showing how hydrogen combines with oxygen to form water. Let two small circles represent hydrogen atoms. Let a larger circle represent an oxygen atom. Look at Figure 15-3 to see how these atoms would combine to form a molecule of water. Notice the position of the two hydrogen atoms on the oxygen atom. Their position gives the water molecule a certain shape—somewhat like the ears on an animal's head. Scientists were able to determine the shape of a water molecule through the use of a technique called X-ray diffraction. Scientists also used special microscopes to determine the shape of a water molecule by studying the shapes of snowflakes as they form. The shape of a water molecule helps give the molecule some important qualities that will be discussed later.

☐ **What is the difference between an element and a compound?**

More about hydrogen and oxygen

Hydrogen gas and oxygen gas are very important to us because they form molecules of water. However, it was not in water that hydrogen and oxygen were first discovered.

Hydrogen was first discovered during an experiment by Henry Cavendish in 1766. He made the gas in his laboratory by dropping pieces of zinc into an acid. During the chemical change that resulted, a colorless and odorless

Find Out More

Use reference materials to help you find out who first produced water in a laboratory by combining hydrogen gas and oxygen gas. What method was used to produce the water?

gas (hydrogen) was given off. Another scientist by the name of *Lavoisier* [luhv-WAHZ-ee-AY] called the gas hydrogen. In Greek, the word "hydrogen" means water producer. Hydrogen was given this name because whenever hydrogen was burned with air inside a container, drops of water formed inside the container.

Like hydrogen, oxygen is a colorless and odorless gas. As a gas, oxygen is present in the air you breathe. However, it was not its presence in air that led to its discovery. Oxygen gas was first made in a laboratory by Karl Wilhelm Scheele sometime between 1770 and 1773. He did this by heating certain compounds that contained oxygen. The heating caused a chemical change and freed the oxygen from the compounds. In 1774, Joseph Priestley also made oxygen in a similar way. Priestley made oxygen gas in his laboratory by focusing the sun's rays onto mercuric oxide. The heat caused oxygen to be given off. Later, Lavoisier (the same scientist who named hydrogen) gave the name "oxygen" to the gas that had been prepared.

Today, hydrogen and oxygen are used in certain industrial processes and in laboratory research. Much of the hydrogen and some of the oxygen that is used are prepared from water. One way of preparing these gases uses a method similar to the one used in the *Investigate* on page 293.

page 293.

To Think About

Mercuric oxide consists of the elements mercury and oxygen. If Priestley produced oxygen gas during his experiments, what other kind of matter, do you think, was also produced?

Figure 15–4. Priestley (left) is shown making a discovery about the importance of oxygen to living things. What do you think he discovered? Lavoisier (below) is shown testing air to see if it contains oxygen. What do you think he found?

Historical Pictures Service

The Bettmann Archive

PROPERTIES OF WATER

What are the three phases of water?
What is heat capacity?
*What are two characteristics of water that are a
result of molecules of water holding tightly
together?*
*What property of water makes it able to dissolve
various kinds of matter?*

How water occurs

Water is present all around you. However, the water
around you does not always look the same. Some water
around you is *liquid* [LIHK-wuhd]. Some water is *solid*
[SAHL-uhd]—in the form of ice. And some water is in the
form of a *gas.* Water as a gas, called *water vapor* [VAY-
pur], cannot be seen. However, you become aware of water
vapor when air containing it begins to cool. As air cools,
water vapor forms tiny droplets of liquid water, forming
either clouds or steam. Clouds and steam, of course, can
be seen.

Scientists use the term *phase* [FAYZ] to refer to the form
in which matter occurs. Ice is the solid phase of water.
Water is the liquid phase. Water vapor is the gas phase.

Grant Heilman

*Figure 15–5. Water around you may
be in the form of a solid, a liquid, or a
gas. What phases of water are
pictured here?*

Although water does not look the same in its three phases, each consists only of water molecules. At any one time, water can be found on the earth in all three phases. This *property* [PRAHP-urt-ee], or characteristic, of water—that of occurring naturally on the earth in three different phases —is unusual. In fact, water is the only matter that has this property.

The fact that water occurs naturally in all three phases on the earth is important in many ways. Water in its liquid phase is needed by all living things. Water as a liquid is necessary for many processes in living things. In Chapter 11, you may remember reading that water vapor is an important factor in our daily weather. In what ways does water as a solid affect people?

Though water is found in all three phases on the surface of the earth, water also changes from one phase to another. For example, you know that adding heat to ice causes the ice to melt. When ice melts, it changes into water. Heat may also cause water to boil. Then the water changes into water vapor. What, do you suppose, might cause water vapor to change back into water? What causes water to change into ice?

Heat capacity of water

Have you ever walked barefoot along a sandy beach on a sunny day? Perhaps the sand was so hot that you had to run to the water to keep your feet from getting burned. Once in the water, you may have noticed that the water felt cool. Though the hot sun was heating both the water and the sand, the water felt cooler than the sand.

If you were to take the same walk at night, you would notice that the sand felt cooler than the water. But using a thermometer to compare the temperature of the water during the day with its temperature at night might surprise you. The temperature of the water at night would be about the same as its temperature during the day. That is, water seems to keep its heat, whereas sand seems to lose its heat, even though neither is receiving any more heat from the sun. This property of matter—the ability to keep the heat

Find Out More

As water cools to 4°C (39°F), it becomes more dense. From 4°C to 0°C (39°F to 32°F), which is the freezing range, water becomes less dense. This means that ice is less dense than very cold water. Use reference materials to help you find out more about what happens to the water in bodies of water as it freezes. What might happen to the living things in bodies of water if ice were more dense than cold water?

it has received—is called *heat capacity* [kuh-PAS-uht-ee]. You might also say that any matter having a high heat capacity, such as water, has the ability to absorb large amounts of heat without becoming much warmer.

Water has a higher heat capacity than most other kinds of matter. For example, a greater amount of heat is needed to warm water than is needed to warm most other kinds of matter. Suppose you had a kilogram (about 2.2 pounds) each of water, gold, and iron. All are at —273°C (—460°F). If all three were heated equally, the gold would begin to melt at 1 102°C (2,016°F). But after the same period of time, the ice would only be —184°C (—300°F). Later, when the iron finally began to melt at 1 299°C (2,370°F), the ice would have reached only 0°C (32°F)!

The heat capacity of water makes water important for several reasons. For example, when water is sprayed onto burning wood, the water can take away enough heat from the wood so that the wood stops burning. In another situation, water can take away heat from one place and then give up some of that heat in another place. For example, in an auto, water in the cooling system takes heat away from the engine to keep the engine from getting too hot. It releases this heat through the radiator. During cold months, this hot water can be used to heat the air inside the auto to make the air more comfortable for the driver and passengers.

To Think About

How, do you suppose, does water's high heat capacity enable a body of water, such as a lake, to keep the nearby air temperature from having extreme changes? How might a body of water influence weather changes close to it?

Figure 15–6. These fire fighters are using an important property of water to fight a fire. What is the property, and how does it help fight the fire?

Brent Jones

298

Why water holds together

Another unusual property of water is that its molecules hold tightly together. The reason water molecules are able to hold tightly together is because they have *polarity* [poh-LAR-uht-ee]. That is, every water molecule has oppositely charged poles, just as a magnet has different magnetic poles at each end.

A water molecule's polarity is a result of its shape. Earlier in this chapter you learned that a water molecule has a certain shape. Water molecules have a shape in which the two hydrogen atoms bulge from one end of the oxygen atom. One effect of this shape is a distribution of charges as shown in Figure 15–7. These charges are part of the hydrogen atoms and the oxygen atom that make up the molecule. The hydrogen side of the water molecule has a positive charge. The oxygen side of the water molecule has a negative charge. As a result of this polarity of charges, water molecules hold very tightly together. See Figure 15–7.

The fact that water molecules hold very tightly together gives water two important characteristics. One of these important characteristics of water is *surface tension* [TEHN-chuhn]. The surface tension of water may be observed at a dripping faucet. As a drop of water begins to leave the faucet, the water stretches into a long drop of

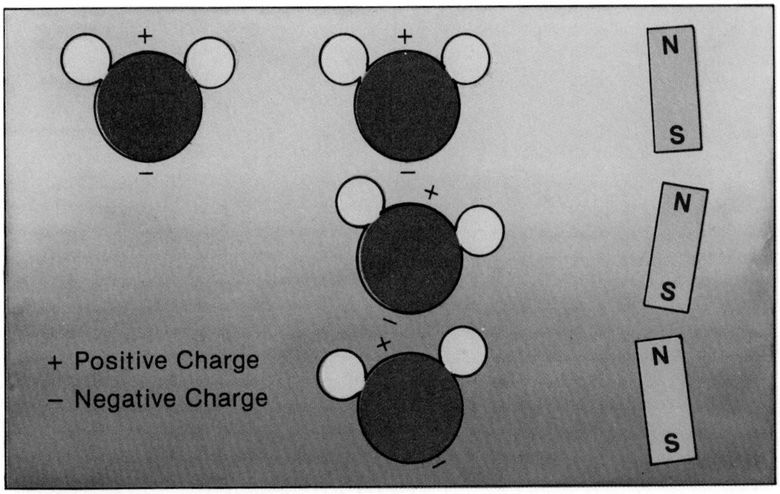

Figure 15–7. The polarity of water molecules, resulting from the opposite charges on each end of a water molecule, causes water molecules to hold together in a way that is similar to the way magnets hold together.

+ Positive Charge
− Negative Charge

water. As the drop falls from the faucet, the water forms into the shape of a ball. The water forms into a ball because the molecules at the surface of the drop hold tightly together.

The surface tension of water may be observed in another way. Carefully place a needle or a razor blade on the surface of a bowl of water. The needle or the razor blade floats on the surface because of surface tension. That is, the water molecules at the surface hold together so tightly that they can support certain objects. Even some insects are able to walk on the surface of water because of its surface tension.

The second important characteristic of water is *capillarity* [KAP-uh-LAR-uht-ee]. Capillarity is the ability of a liquid to climb up a surface against the pull of gravity. Look carefully into a glass of water. You can see that the water is higher around the edges where it touches the surface of the glass. The capillarity of water is the reason why water can climb up the surface of the glass. The capillarity of water also helps water move through the soil and up into plants.

☐ **What, do you think, causes raindrops to be shaped like a ball?**

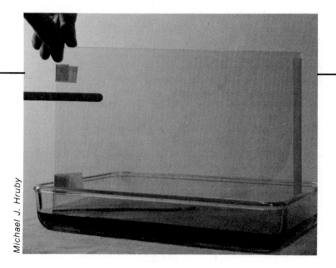

Michael J. Hruby

Do It Yourself
Observe capillarity

Obtain two sheets of clean, flat glass. Both pieces should be at least 30 cm by 20 cm. Hold the two sheets together and tape them together along one side. Insert a small piece of wood or cardboard between the sheets along the second side before taping the second side together. Stand the two sheets on end in a pan or tray of water. What happens to the water between the sheets of glass? Along which side does the water climb the highest? Explain.

Solutions

Perhaps the most remarkable property of water is its ability to *dissolve* [dihz-AHLV], or break apart, many kinds of matter. Water dissolves rocks as it washes over the land and seeps through the ground. Water also dissolves the nutrients that all living things need. It dissolves and carries the nutrients in soil to growing plants. Once inside the plants, water carries the dissolved nutrients to the cells within the plants. Water also helps dissolve the food that people and animals eat and helps carry the nutrients that make up food to the cells of the body.

The polarity of water molecules is, for the most part, responsible for dissolving many kinds of matter. The molecules of most kinds of matter are not held together as tightly as are the molecules of water. As a result, the charges of water molecules are able to break apart the molecules of many kinds of matter with which the water comes into contact.

An important result of the ability of water to dissolve matter is the formation of many *solutions* [suh-LOO-shuhnz]. A solution consists of two or more different kinds of matter in which one kind of matter dissolves in the other. When you dissolve sugar in water, you are making a solution.

You are probably familiar with many solutions that are made by water. Most of the drinks you like are solutions of water. For example, soft-drink manufacturers dissolve sugar, different flavorings, and carbon-dioxide gas in water to make a variety of soft drinks. Many foods are solutions made with water. Most instant broths and soups, for example, are made by dissolving powdered foods in water. Many of the things you use are solutions made with water. Many glues and pastes are solutions of water. Watercolors and some kinds of paints are also solutions. Even many cleaning solutions and the acid in a car's battery are solutions made with water.

There are many solutions of water that are found in nature. The liquid part of blood is a solution of certain salts and proteins. Sap in plants is also a solution. Salt

Figure 15–8. This soft drink is a solution. What is a solution, and what might be some kinds of matter that make up this solution?

Alfa

301

water is a natural solution that fills the oceans. The water that you get from faucets in your home is a solution. This water can, in fact, contain many dissolved minerals.

Water that contains many dissolved minerals is called *hard water*. Long ago, people noticed that clothes washed in water having many minerals did not feel soft. They felt stiff, or hard. Also, they were hard to clean. For these reasons water with many minerals is called hard water. However, clothes washed in water having few minerals, such as rainwater, felt soft. They were also easy to clean. Years later, people discovered that the minerals in hard water caused soap used in washing the clothes to collect in the clothes. The soap gave the clothes the hard feeling.

The minerals in hard water also cause problems in tea-kettles, hot-water tanks, and other places where water is heated. Heating the water so that some of it evaporates causes the minerals to be left behind. These minerals cause problems as they accumulate. Where else, do you suppose, might hard water cause problems?

☐ **If the rain that falls to the earth is soft water, how does it become hard water?**

Mary Elenz Tranter

Do It Yourself

Try making some hard water

Hard water is made in nature when water flows over or through certain kinds of rocks. Hard water can also be made in another way. Use a straw to exhale into a beaker of limewater (calcium hydroxide). The limewater will appear milky from the formation of calcium carbonate. If you add some soap to this solution, the scum that forms indicates that the water is hard. If you heat this water, most of the calcium carbonate falls to the bottom of the beaker. What might happen if hard water was heated in a hot-water tank or in a boiler over a period of years?

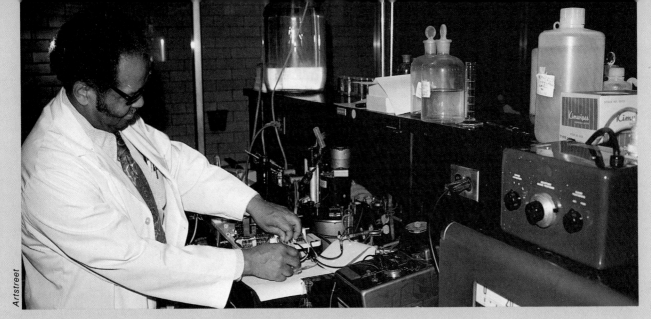

Why is it important for the inorganic chemist pictured here to know what minerals are in the water used in cooling equipment?

Artstreet

Careers

Inorganic Chemist

Most fresh water has some minerals dissolved in it. However, even small amounts of minerals can be a problem when water is used in certain ways. One way in which water is used a great deal is for cooling. Certain industrial processes use great amounts of water for cooling. During such processes much water evaporates. As the water evaporates, the minerals in the water are left behind. These minerals can accumulate and cause problems in the equipment. Fortunately, an *inorganic* [IHN-AWR-GAN-ihk] *chemist* [KEHM-uhst] knows how to control this problem.

An inorganic chemist would know what chemicals might be added to water to keep the water from losing its minerals while inside certain cooling equipment. That person also needs to know what chemicals might prevent

organisms from growing in the water used in cooling equipment. An inorganic chemist's job is important because minerals and organisms can cause serious problems in cooling equipment. For example, such things can block tubes and pipes inside the equipment. It is very costly to have such equipment cleaned. Such blockages may also cause damage to expensive equipment.

An inorganic chemist must know the chemical and physical properties of water. That person must also understand how different chemicals affect the properties of water and of minerals dissolved in water. Do you think you might like to be an inorganic chemist someday? If so, you will need a college education with most of your training in the science of chemistry.

Reviewing and Extending

Summing Up

1. Scientists use the term "molecules" to describe the tiny particles that make up matter.
2. Atoms are tiny particles that make up molecules.
3. An element is any matter in which the molecules of that matter consist only of one kind of atom.
4. A compound consists of two or more different kinds of atoms joined together.
5. A water molecule consists of two atoms of hydrogen and one atom of oxygen.
6. Water is the only kind of matter that occurs naturally in three phases—solid, liquid, and gas.
7. Heat capacity is the ability of matter to keep the heat it has received. Water has a high heat capacity.
8. An important property of water is that its molecules are held tightly together. Water's surface tension and capillarity are two characteristics of that property.
9. Water molecules are held tightly together because of their polarity. This property of water is also responsible for water's ability to dissolve many kinds of matter.

Checking Up

Vocabulary   Write the numerals *1–8* on your paper. Each numbered phrase describes a term from the following list. On your paper, write the term next to the numeral of the phrase that describes it.

atom   element   hydrogen
salt   compound   molecules
phase   polarity   property

1. tiny particle that makes up molecules
2. tiny particles that make up matter
3. kind of matter that has only one kind of atom in its molecule
4. any matter consisting of two or more kinds of atoms joined together
5. one of the two gases that, when joined together, make up water
6. form in which matter occurs
7. characteristic of matter
8. having oppositely charged poles

Knowledge and Understanding   Write the numerals *9–15* on your paper. Beside each numeral, write the word or words that best complete the sentence having that numeral.

9. Water is said to be hard if it has many (*hydrogen atoms, nutrients, minerals*) dissolved in it.

10. The fact that a kettle used to boil water will become hot long before the water in it is warm is an example of the (*capillarity, heat capacity, surface tension*) of water.

11. An important result of the ability of water to dissolve many different kinds of matter is the formation of many (*solutions, atoms, molecules of hydrogen and oxygen*).

12. The (*capillarity, hardness, surface tension*) of water may be demonstrated by floating a razor blade on the surface of a bowl of water.

13. The (*polarity, color, size*) of water molecules causes water molecules to hold together in a way that is similar to the way magnets hold together.

14. When two atoms of hydrogen combine with one atom of oxygen, the result is a (*mixture, phase, molecule*) of water.

15. The reason why water is able to dissolve so many different kinds of matter is (*that water molecules have the property of polarity, hydrogen and oxygen are atoms, that water is present on the earth in three phases*).

Expressing Yourself   Write a paragraph as an answer to each of the following questions:

16. Which of the properties of water might be useful in considering the use of water in the cooling system of an automobile engine? Explain how the property is useful.

17. Would it be better to use hard water or soft water in a boiler system used to heat a building? Explain.

Doing More

1. A quick and easy way to determine if water has minerals dissolved in it is by heating the water and causing it to evaporate. Place a few drops of water from your faucet on a small piece of clear glass. Carefully place the glass in the oven and turn the heat on low. After the water has evaporated, turn off the oven and allow the glass to cool. Remove the glass and study the area from which the water evaporated. Are there any minerals left on the glass? What color are they?

2. Find out about your community water supply. Does your community water department have to remove any minerals from your water supply? If so, how is this done? Are any materials added to your water supply? Which are added and for what purposes are they added?

*Water is important to people all over the earth.
In this picture, water is being raised from a well so
that it can be used to irrigate crops. How do you
use water?*

16 Fresh Water

Early people always lived near sources of fresh water. They lived close to such sources because they could only store and carry small amounts of water. They used jars made of clay and bags made of animal skin to store and carry their water. Later, the Romans built cities that were often great distances from sources of fresh water. But they built canals and aqueducts to bring water from lakes and rivers into the cities. These structures were built so well that some of them are still in use today, several hundreds of years later.

When the American pioneers crossed the Missouri River, they entered a dry land. They soon learned that finding fresh water meant the difference between life and death. Today, the people of every nation are still concerned with supplying their need for fresh water. In this chapter you will learn about some of the sources of fresh water that are available for people to use.

SURFACE FRESH WATER

Where does the water that becomes runoff, and
*   later flows in streams and rivers, come from?*
What is a watershed?
How is a pond different from a lake?
Why are glaciers and ice caps possible sources
*   of fresh water?*

Runoff and rivers

You have probably watched rain falling. During a light rain, most of the water may soak into the ground. But if the rain is heavy, not all the water can soak into the ground. Some of the water flows over the surface of the land. Rainwater that flows over the surface is called *runoff*.

Runoff always flows from higher places to lower places. As the runoff flows over the land, water begins to drain into lower places. This draining forms small streams of water. Many small streams flow into larger streams and rivers. The rivers then flow into lakes or into oceans. However, whether or not a river is useful as a source of fresh water depends chiefly on two factors—its rate of flow and the amount of water in the river.

ZEFA

Figure 16–1. Rain, melting snow, and ice produce the runoff that forms the stream you see here. Where do you suppose the water will go from here?

The water in some rivers flows much faster than it does in other rivers. The rate of flow depends upon the slope of the land over which a river flows. For example, suppose the level of the land drops one meter (about one yard) over a distance of one kilometer (0.6 mile). A river flowing over this land would drop one meter per kilometer. The *gradient* [GRAYD-ee-uhnt], or slope of the river, would be one meter per kilometer. A river's gradient indicates how fast the water in the river flows. If its gradient was two meters per kilometer (about two yards per 0.6 mile), a river would flow faster. How would a river flow if it had a smaller gradient than one meter per kilometer?

As said before, the rate of flow of a river is important in terms of the river's usefulness as a source of water. Generally, if the rate of flow is fast, the river provides a large amount of water. However, such water often carries with it large amounts of sand and mud. If the rate of flow is slower, less water may be provided. However, the water may be clearer. Of course, clear water is more useful than muddy water as a source of water for people.

☐ **Although rivers with a fast rate of flow are often muddy, some are still used as sources of fresh water. How might such water be made useful as a source of fresh water for people to use?**

Have you ever traveled along a river or seen pictures taken at different places along a river? If so, you know that the amount of water in a river seems to vary at different places. However, the amount of water is almost always greater toward the end of a river. The amount of water in a river may also vary during the year because of changes in rainfall. At what time of the year is rainfall heaviest where you live?

A river in which there is little change in the amount of water is usually a dependable source of water. Most often, a large river is a more dependable source than a small river. The total amount of water supplied by rivers is not as great as from other sources. But rivers are important because they are often the only dependable sources of water available in some areas.

Watersheds and floodplains

Of all the water that falls to the earth, about 25 percent stays on the surface of the land in the form of runoff. Some of the runoff from the land drains into rivers. The area of land that is drained by a river is known as the river's *watershed*. Scientists study watersheds in order to help determine how much surface water is available for people's needs.

Generally two different watersheds are separated from each other by a high area of land. Such a high area of land is called a *divide*. The Great Divide in the Rocky Mountains separates the watershed of the Columbia River from the watershed of the Mississippi River.

The Mississippi watershed is the largest watershed in the United States. At one time, almost 40 percent of the Mississippi watershed was covered with trees. Today, only 4 percent of that land is covered with trees. Trees help protect the land from uncontrolled runoff. The soil that is held by the roots of trees helps the ground hold water for a longer period of time.

Because many areas have fewer trees today, runoff from rain and snow has frequently become uncontrolled. Uncontrolled runoff can cause much damage to the land. For example, much topsoil may wash away from land where trees have been cut down. Some scientists estimate that

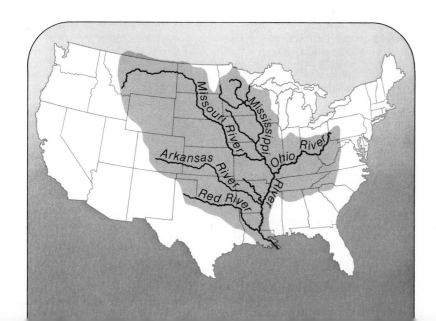

Figure 16–2. The shaded area on the map is the area that is drained by the Mississippi River. This watershed is sometimes called the Mississippi River Drainage. Do you live in this watershed?

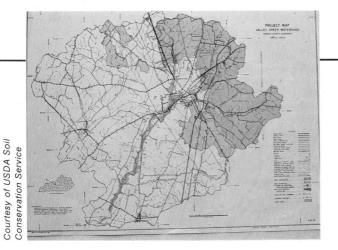

Do It Yourself

Study a watershed

Study the watershed where you live. Maps of the watershed in which your community is located may be available from your state's department of agriculture or department of geology. Using a map, trace the path that water takes from the watershed to a body of fresh water, such as a river or a lake. Continue this path all the way to your home. What makes a watershed good in terms of supplying enough water for a community?

one result of this loss of protection has been the loss of 25 percent of the land's topsoil. Just as important, however, is the fact that uncontrolled runoff usually causes a river's supply of fresh water to be irregular and, thus, undependable.

Uncontrolled runoff often leads to flooding. Floodwaters generally carry so much topsoil that the water is muddy. Muddy water is not very useful for people to use as a source of water. After a flood, much of the topsoil is left on the land that was flooded. This land is called a *floodplain*. For thousands of years the Egyptians depended upon the yearly floods of the Nile River to add rich topsoil to their farms. As soon as the floods were over, they planted their crops. Even though the topsoil that remains on floodplains is usually rich, most farmers today do not want to depend on flooding for rich soil.

Ponds and lakes

All the runoff from a watershed does not drain into streams and rivers. A great deal of the runoff from a watershed drains into ponds and lakes as well. In fact, there is 100 times more water in ponds and lakes than in streams and rivers.

If you were asked to explain the difference between a pond and a lake, you would probably say that a pond is smaller than a lake. But there are large and small ponds as well as large and small lakes.

Generally, ponds are smaller and contain less water than lakes. However, area and volume are not the most important factors. A pond is usually considered to be much shallower than a lake. A *pond* is so shallow that some sunlight can reach the bottom. A *lake* nearly always has some deep places where no sunlight can reach the bottom. Since some sunlight can reach the bottom of ponds, ponds most often have many water plants growing in them.

Ponds are not important as sources of fresh water for people. But ponds are sometimes used on farms as sources of water for animals. Large ponds are also used in some places for recreation. In what ways might a large pond be used for recreation?

Lakes are the most widely used sources of fresh water for people. If you were to look at a map of the United States, you would see that the lake with the largest surface area in the world is Lake Superior. Lake Superior is larger in area than the combined area of the states of Connecticut, Massachusetts, New Hampshire, New Jersey, and Rhode Island. However, for depth and volume, Lake Baikal in Russia holds the record. The deepest part of Lake Baikal is 1 620 meters (5,315 feet). In contrast, Lake Superior's deepest part is only 406 meters (1,333 feet). Because Lake Baikal is so deep, its volume is very great. Lake Baikal holds as much fresh water as the five Great Lakes in North America plus *all* the rivers in the world!

In many areas of the country, people have created lakes as sources of water. Huge dams have been built across rivers to help provide additional sources of fresh water. The lakes, called *reservoirs* [REHZ-uh(r)v-wAHRz], that form behind these dams are sometimes quite far away from the cities that use the water. For example, the reservoirs that provide water for the city of New York are more than 160 kilometers (100 miles) away.

□ **Are there any reservoirs where you live? If so, how far away are they?**

Find Out More

Most of the freshwater lakes in the northern part of the earth have been formed by giant glaciers that once existed. How do glaciers form lakes? In what other ways are lakes formed? Use reference materials to help you find out what ways lakes are formed. See if you can find out how the following lakes were formed: Lake Champlain; Crater Lake; Lake Manitoba; Lake Mead; Lake Titicaca, South America; and Lake Victoria, Africa.

UNDERGROUND FRESH WATER

What is groundwater?

How does groundwater sometimes reach the surface of the earth?

In what ways do people get water from under the ground?

Down it goes

You have read that some rain becomes runoff and flows into rivers and lakes. But some of the rain soaks into the soil. After soaking into the soil, some of the water stays in the soil and is used by growing plants. However, much of the water keeps moving down through the sand and the gravel below the soil. Rainwater that soaks into the earth is called *groundwater*. As a source of fresh water, groundwater is plentiful. In fact, scientists believe the amount of groundwater is thirty-five times greater than the amount of water in all the rivers and lakes.

Groundwater also moves down through certain kinds of rock. It can do this because of the tiny open spaces in the rock. Rock with such spaces is said to be *permeable* [PUR-mee-uh-buhl]. Two examples of permeable rock are sandstone and limestone. These kinds of rock are layered and contain many tiny cracks and spaces. These cracks and spaces generally contain great amounts of water. Layered rock that contains much water is called an *aquifer* [AK-wuh-fur].

Eventually the downward movement of water stops. The movement stops when water meets impermeable rock. Shale is an example of impermeable rock.

☐ **What, do you suppose, makes shale and certain other rock impermeable?**

Moving along

After the downward movement of groundwater stops, it may still move in another way. After soaking down into an aquifer, groundwater may move through the aquifer and across the surface of impermeable rock. Groundwater flows through some aquifers at a rate of only several centimeters (a few inches) a day. In other aquifers, the groundwater may move at a rate of six to nine meters (seven to ten yards) a day.

The diagram in Figure 16–3 shows a cross section of the earth just below the surface. The part of the ground in which all the tiny openings are filled with water is called the *zone of saturation* [SACH-uh-RAY-shuhn]. That is, the ground is filled with water. The top of this zone is called the *water table.*

The water table can rise and fall. Heavy rain or melting snow can raise the water table. Dry spells or heavy use of groundwater can lower the water table. If the water table falls too low, wells can go dry. Also, some trees and certain plants will die because water can no longer reach their roots. Along the coast, salt water can move through the ground and replace missing fresh water. Then wells near the coast contain salt water instead of fresh water. What would happen if the water in your home changed from fresh water to salt water?

To Think About

Why might it be important to know how rapidly groundwater moves in an aquifer before a person drills a well?

Figure 16–3. This cross section shows how water is present in the earth as groundwater. What is the top of the groundwater called?

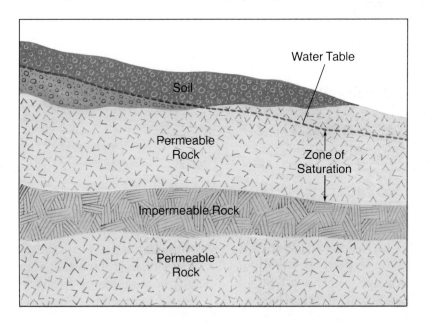

313

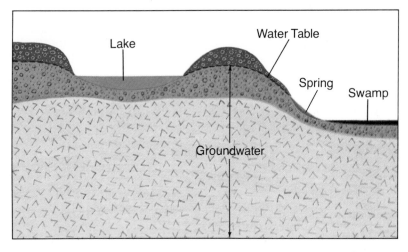

Figure 16–4. In some places, the water table may appear at the surface. What are some of these places?

Out it comes

Groundwater may stay in the ground from a few hours to thousands of years. However, water can come out of the ground in a number of ways. If groundwater is at or close to the surface, the water table may be seen as a swamp. In many places, the land dips below the water table. In such places small lakes or ponds are found. If the water table comes out of the side of a hill, the groundwater will flow out of the ground. This flow of water is called a *spring*. Many streams and springs depend upon the water table for some of their water. The drawing in Figure 16–4 shows how the water table might look if you could see into the ground.

In some places in the ground, an aquifer becomes sandwiched between two layers of rock that are impermeable. The impermeable layers act like the walls of a pipe. They prevent the escape of the water to the surface. When this happens, the water in the aquifer may be under great pressure. If a well is drilled into the aquifer, the water may flow up to the surface because of the great pressure below. The water will continue to flow if there is enough rainfall to keep the water under pressure. Such a flowing well is called an *artesian* [ahr-TEE-zhuhn] *well*. The water

Find Out More

The name "artesian" comes from the Artois province in France, where such wells were first discovered in about the year 1100. Find out more about artesian wells. Try to find out more about how they occur and where they are found throughout the world. Also find out how important they are as a source of fresh water for people.

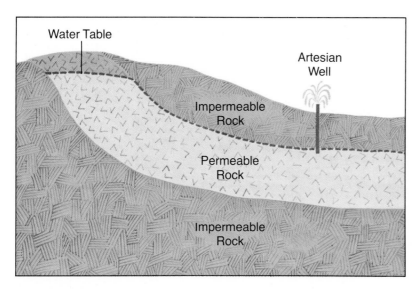

Figure 16–5. This cross section shows how water flows from an artesian well. What would happen to an artesian well if no rain fell for a long time at the place where water enters the aquifer?

pressure depends upon the difference in height between the well and the place where the water enters the aquifer. See Figure 16–5.

Pumping it up

In some areas of the earth, there are no lakes, rivers, and springs from which people can get water. In those areas, holes may be dug or drilled down to the water table. Such a hole is called a *well*. A well will contain water as long as the water table remains high enough. Years ago, wells were dug by hand and were not very deep. Wells today are drilled by machine and are often very deep. The water is pumped out of a well either by hand, windmill, or motor.

Pumping water from a well lowers the water table around the well. Wells that supply water for homes generally do not lower the water table very much. Wells used for irrigation or industry, however, may pump so much water that the water table is lowered over a large area. Some people believe that the water table in many places is much lower today than it was a few years ago.

(*Text continues on page 317.*)

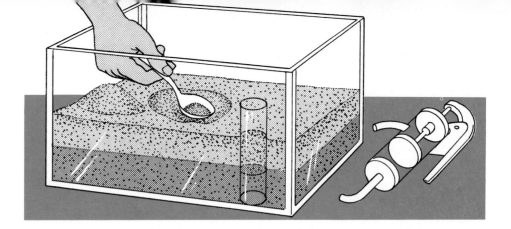

Investigate

How does lowering the water table affect the water level in nearby ponds and lakes?

You will need

sand, beaker, food coloring, sprinkling can, aquarium tank, large-diameter glass or plastic tube, lift pump or siphon to fit the tube

Background

The level of water in some ponds, streams, small lakes, and wells is determined by the level of the water table. Pumping water out of the ground tends to lower the water table, sometimes causing small ponds and lakes to become dry. Rainwater is responsible for adding water to the ground and tends to cause the water table to rise.

What to do

Place the glass tube in a corner of the aquarium. Add sand to the aquarium until it is half full. Do not put any sand in the tube. Add water to the aquarium until you see water halfway up into the sand. The top of the water in the sand represents the water table below the surface of the ground.

Dig out some of the sand in the aquarium until a "pond" appears. Using the lift pump in the glass tube, remove some of the water from the tube. The glass tube can be thought of as a well. Observe the level of the water in the pond. Continue to remove the water from the "well" and observe the level of the water in the pond.

Pour water into the well until water again appears in the pond. Mix a few drops of food coloring with some water in a sprinkling can and sprinkle it over the sand. Wait a few minutes and then take some water out of the well, using the lift pump. Observe the color of the water.

Now that you have done the investigation

■ When some of the sand was dug out to form a pond, what determined the height of the water in the pond?
■ When the lift pump was used to remove some of the water from the well, what happened to the level of the water in the pond? What happened to the level of the water in the well?
■ After sprinkling colored water and waiting a few minutes, what did you observe as you took some water out of the well? What seems to be responsible for raising the water table?

There are some areas where groundwater is being pumped out faster than it can be replaced. In these areas, the water table is getting lower every year. If the water table gets too low, streams and springs that depend upon the water table may stop flowing. The loss of streams and springs can cause problems for wildlife. Even some plants growing near these sources of water might be affected. How might you be affected if the water table where you live got too low?

☐ **What might be some reasons why more water is being used today than ever before?**

THE WATER CYCLE

What is the water cycle?
What effect does the water cycle have on the purity of water?

Water gets around

Suppose you were asked the question, Where does water come from? How would you answer? If you said that water comes from rivers, you would be partly correct. This answer, however, leads to another question, Where does the water in the rivers come from? If you said the water comes from rain, you would be partly correct again. But where does the rain come from? A good answer to this question would be the oceans. Clouds form over the oceans as water *evaporates* [ih-VAP-uh-RAYTS], or changes into a gas. Where does the water in the oceans come from? Looking at a map or a globe shows you that some of the water in the oceans comes from rivers.

Besides answering such questions, suppose you tried to draw a picture of where water comes from. Your drawing would show that water gets around. Your picture might show that some of the water rises into the air. Water rises into the air when it evaporates. The energy of the sun causes water to evaporate. Some of the water in the air falls back to the earth as rain or snow. Much of this water becomes runoff and eventually returns to the ocean. Water

Figure 16–6. *The cool air in this mountain area has caused some of the moisture in the air to form drops that are so large that they appear as fog or mist. Where have you seen fog or mist?*

follows this series of events again and again. A series of events that occurs again and again is called a *cycle* [SY-kuhl]. Your picture of where water comes from, then, would show the *water cycle*. See Figure 16–7.

A complex cycle

Although the water cycle may seem quite simple, it is not. And some parts of the water cycle would not be easy to show in a picture. For example, of all the water that evaporates from an ocean, most of it falls back into the ocean. Also, some of the water in the water cycle does not come from the ocean. Some of the water evaporates from plants, animals, and water on the earth's surface. Some water even evaporates from glaciers and ice caps. But with enough time, water will follow a general cycle from the ocean, to the air, to the land, and back to the ocean. How might you be affected if the water cycle somehow came to a stop?

(*Text continues on page 320.*)

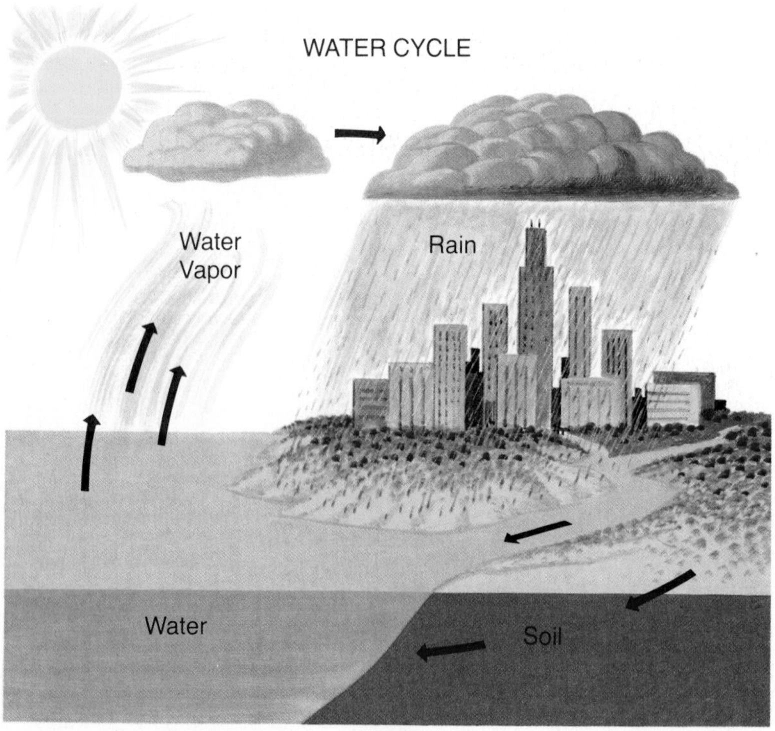

To Think About

For every 100 L of water falling as rain or snow on the oceans, 109 L evaporate from the oceans. Why, then, don't the oceans dry up?

WATER CYCLE

Water Vapor

Rain

Water

Soil

Figure 16–7. All water comes from the ocean and is returned to it in the continuous water cycle. What are some ways in which water returns to the ocean?

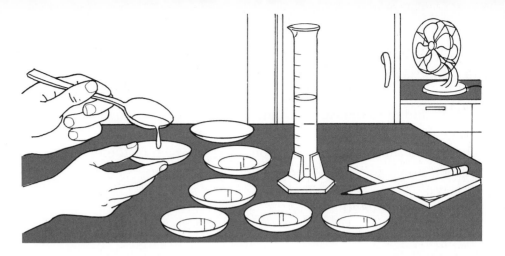

Investigate

What factors affect the rate of evaporation of water?

You will need

water, electric fan, refrigerator, pencil and paper, graduated cylinder, 7 watch glasses

Background

A very important step in the water cycle takes place when water evaporates and enters the air. Most of the water in the air has evaporated from the oceans. Some water has evaporated from lakes, rivers, and damp soil. A little water even evaporates from plants and animals on the earth's surface. In each of these examples, certain factors affect the rate at which water will evaporate. These factors are related to the movement of air and/or the temperature of air.

What to do

Pour 2.5 ml of water in each of seven watch glasses. Set three watch glasses where the temperature is the same. However, the first watch glass should be where the air is quiet. The second watch glass should be in a slight breeze, and the third should be in rapidly moving air. Carefully place the watch glasses so that you can use the electric fan to produce the breeze and the rapidly moving air. Record the length of time it takes for the water to evaporate from each watch glass.

Place the fourth watch glass in a warm place (40 to 45°C or 104 to 113°F). The fifth watch glass should be kept at room temperature (21°C or 70°F). The sixth should be placed in a refrigerator and the seventh in a freezer. Again record the time it takes for the water to evaporate from each watch glass.

Now that you have done the investigation

■ From which of the first three watch glasses did the water evaporate first?
■ What would you say about the relationship between the rate of evaporation and the movement of air?
■ From which of the last four watch glasses did the water evaporate first?
■ What would you say about the relationship between the rate of evaporation and the temperature of air?

As water is carried along by the water cycle, it changes in many ways. In an ocean, water is a liquid. As water evaporates, it changes into a gas—water vapor. Before water vapor can fall to the earth, it must change back to a liquid (rain) or a solid (snow or ice). These changes are simply changes in phase. When have you observed each of these phases?

Water gets reused

Some further changes take place in water as it is carried along in the water cycle. Ocean water is salty. But as water evaporates, the salt is left behind. Water that falls as rain, snow, or ice is almost pure water. It is safe to use.

After fresh water has been on the earth's surface for a while, it may not be safe to use. While fresh water is on the surface, it "picks up" many things that make it unsafe to use. You will read about some of these things in the next chapter. Fresh water must be made safe before it can be used. Fresh water is made safe by cleaning it and treating it. Once cleaned and treated, it is safe to use in cities, homes, and industries.

Thus, the water cycle helps change water so that it can be used over and over again. Salt water cannot be used by plants and animals on the land. People cannot use salt water, either. But fresh water can be used. And after water has been used, the water cycle helps "clean" it so that it can be used again.

☐ **At what places in the water cycle might water be safe to use? When might water not be safe to use?**

Grant Heilman

Figure 16–8. Although water in the ocean is salty, it is the source of all fresh water on the earth. How does it get to be fresh? What happens to the salt?

In order to test water to see if it is safe to use, a limnologist must make a chemical analysis of the water. Why might such an analysis be important?

Careers

A Limnologist

Many towns and cities were started along rivers and lakes. In the early days, the water was used for drinking, cooking, and bathing. However, you would not want to drink water from most rivers and lakes today. The reason for this is that many different wastes from farms, cities, and towns are dumped into the water. Many industries also put their wastes into the water. The result is that the water has many chemicals and microorganisms in it. Some of the chemicals and microorganisms that have become a part of the water might be dangerous to people.

Perhaps you are wondering who tests the water for chemicals and microorganisms. A *limnologist* [lihm-NAHL-uh-juhst] is qualified to make such tests. A limnologist tests rivers, lakes, streams, ponds, and other bodies of fresh water. Such a person knows which chemicals

and microorganisms are normally found in water and which occur in polluted water.

Some of the materials that are in water may be seen if you hold a test tube of water taken from a river or lake up to a light. But the chemicals and microorganisms cannot be identified without performing certain chemical tests or microscopic observations. Many bodies of water are tested on a regular basis to make sure that there are no dangerous pollutants in the water.

You probably agree that the work of a limnologist is an important job. A limnologist is interested in the chemical, physical, and biological conditions of all kinds of fresh water. Do you think you might want to be a limnologist someday? If so, you will need a college education with training in the sciences of chemistry and biology.

Reviewing and Extending

Summing Up

1. Rainwater that flows over the surface of the land is called runoff. Runoff helps form streams, rivers, ponds, and lakes.
2. Whether or not a river is important as a source of fresh water depends upon two factors—its rate of flow and the amount of water in the river.
3. The area of land that is drained by a river is known as the river's watershed. Two different watersheds are separated from each other by a high area of land that is called a divide.
4. Lakes are more widely used than rivers as sources of fresh water for people because lakes contain more water.
5. In some places huge dams have been built across rivers to form bodies of water called reservoirs. The reservoirs help to provide an additional source of fresh water to large cities.
6. Rainwater that soaks into the earth is called groundwater.
7. Groundwater that is at the surface or close to the surface can appear as a swamp, a pond, or a lake.
8. Groundwater can flow out of the ground as a spring or as an artesian well.
9. Groundwater can be pumped from the ground in various ways, but pumping too much water can lower the water table.
10. In the water cycle, water follows a general movement from an ocean, to the air, to the land, and back to an ocean.
11. The water cycle helps change water so that it can be used over and over.

Checking Up

Vocabulary Write the numerals _1–8_ on your paper. Each numbered phrase describes a term from the following list. On your paper, write the term next to the numeral of the phrase that describes it.

well   aquifer   watershed
cycle   gradient   floodplain
spring   evaporate impermeable

1. slope of a river
2. land drained by a river
3. land on which topsoil has been deposited by floods
4. layered rock that contains much water
5. flow of groundwater out of the ground
6. hole dug or drilled down to the water table
7. change into a gas
8. series of events that will occur again and again

Knowledge and Understanding   Write the numerals *9–16* on your paper. Beside each numeral, write the word or words that best complete the sentence having that numeral.

9. Groundwater is able to flow (*along the top of, downward through, sideward through*) impermeable rock such as shale.
10. Two watersheds are generally separated by a high area of land called a (*gradient, floodplain, divide*).
11. Huge dams have been built in some places to provide additional sources of fresh water. These sources are called (*floodplains, reservoirs, ponds*).
12. The top of the zone of saturation is called (*the water table, a spring, a gradient*).
13. An artesian well will flow as long as there (*are impermeable rock layers for water to move through, is enough rainfall to main-tain pressure, are oceans to provide enough water*).
14. Rainwater that flows over the surface is called (*a gradient, groundwater, runoff*).
15. Rainwater that soaks into the earth is known as (*permeable water, groundwater, saturation*).
16. One important result of the (*water cycle, zone of saturation, floodplain*) is that water is "cleaned" enough to be reused.

Expressing Yourself   Write a paragraph as an answer to each of the following questions.

17. What is the main difference between a pond and a lake?
18. What are the differences and similarities between a spring, a drilled well, and an artesian well?

Doing More

1. What is the source of water for your community? Visit the water department for your community and find out what problems there are concerning the source(s) of water, the storage of water, and the usage of water for your community. What future problems are anticipated, and what steps are being taken for future demands?

2. Make a model of a water table by filling a clear glass or plastic container with sand. Pour water into the container until the water is almost to the top. Dig out a shallow hole in the sand so that you can see the water. What would you need to do to make the water table rise? To make the water table drop?

Grant Heilman

Mountain streams provide fresh water for many communities. Why can't mountain streams supply enough water for everyone's needs?

17 The Supply of Fresh Water

Each year people use more water than in the past. People use a great deal of water in their homes. Water is being used for irrigation in order to grow the food people need. Greater amounts of water than ever before are being used by industry to produce the goods people want. So much fresh water is being used today that getting enough water for everyone has become a problem.

Enough rain falls on the earth each year to satisfy everyone's need for fresh water. But rain does not fall evenly over the earth. Some places get more fresh water than is needed, but other places do not get enough water.

People do many things to provide themselves with fresh water. They drill wells, build long pipelines, trap runoff from rains, and change seawater into fresh water. In this chapter you will read about some of the problems in supplying people with fresh water. You will also look at some of the things that make some sources of fresh water unsuitable for people to use.

UNEVEN DISTRIBUTION OF WATER

*What are some reasons for differences in rainfall
over different areas of the earth?*
*Which continents have many lakes and rivers?
Which continents have few?*
*What are some problems people have in getting
fresh water?*

Rainfall over the earth

Water is a part of a water cycle on the earth. Scientists
say there is a kind of balance in the water cycle. The
amount of water that evaporates from the earth is equal
to the amount that falls back to the earth. But this balance
is not true for all land areas. Just as rain does not fall
evenly all over the earth, water is not evaporated evenly
all over the earth.

Worldwide, the average amount of rainfall on the land
is more than 80 centimeters (32 inches) a year. In fact, the
rainfall on all the land during a year is enough to provide
every person on the earth with more than 84 000 liters
(over 22,000 gallons) of water! Of course, this is only an
average. Rainfall varies from about 250 centimeters (100
inches) a year in the tropics to less than 2.5 centimeters
(1 inch) a year in some desert areas.

Generally, the places where many people live get enough
rainfall for their needs. Places such as Europe, India,
Southeast Asia, most of China, northwestern Russia, and

Find Out More

In most parts of the earth,
rainfall is seasonal. But in
certain areas of the earth,
such as in the watershed of
the Amazon River, rain falls
every day of the year. Use
reference materials to help
you find out more about differences in rainfall on the
earth. Find out about mon-
soons, flash floods, and oro-
graphic rains. Find out what
these things are and where
they occur.

WORLD RAINFALL DISTRIBUTION

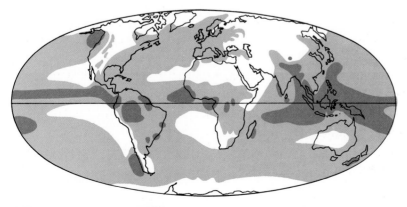

Heavy Rainfall   Moderate Rainfall   Light Rainfall

*Figure 17–1. The distribution of
rainfall is indicated by different
colors. Which areas of the earth have
heavy rainfall? Which areas have
light rainfall?*

325

most of the United States get enough rainfall. But about half the land on the earth does not get enough rainfall for the needs of large numbers of people. These places are the Middle East, northern Africa, central Australia, and most of Asia.

Rainfall in the United States

Overall, there is plenty of water for people living in the United States. The average amount of rainfall in the United States is more than seventy-five centimeters (thirty inches) a year. This amount is close to the average for the earth. Like many other places on the earth, the rainfall over the United States is not distributed evenly. Most of the states east of the Mississippi River get more than seventy-five centimeters (thirty inches) of rainfall a year. This is more than enough to grow crops. But large areas west of the Mississippi River get less than twenty-five centimeters (ten inches) of rainfall a year. Most crops will not grow well in these areas unless irrigation is used.

The Pacific Northwest gets much more rainfall than the average for the country. Along the northwestern coast, moist air from the Pacific Ocean moves against the western side of the Cascade Mountains. As the air rises over the mountains, the moisture condenses. As a result, between 350 and 375 centimeters (140 and 150 inches) of rain falls there each year. Some parts of Hawaii get even more rain

Figure 17–2. The distribution of rainfall in the United States is indicated by different colors. What amount of rainfall does Chicago receive?

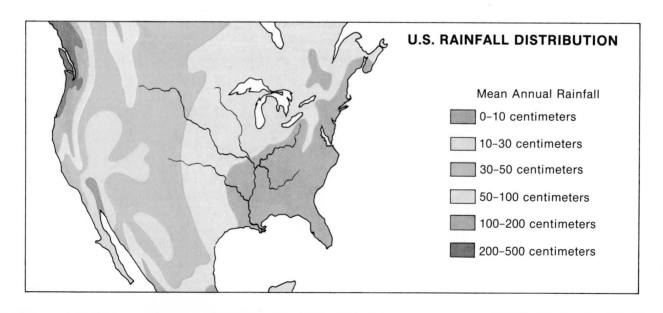

U.S. RAINFALL DISTRIBUTION

Mean Annual Rainfall

0–10 centimeters

10–30 centimeters

30–50 centimeters

50–100 centimeters

100–200 centimeters

200–500 centimeters

than the Pacific Northwest. Mount Waialeale in Hawaii averages 1 150 centimeters (460 inches) of rainfall a year!

☐ **On the average during the year, how much rain falls where you live?**

Lakes and rivers

When you look at maps that show the lakes and rivers of the earth, you might notice that there are great areas that do not have any lakes. The only exceptions might be those lakes made by damming a river. Large lakes in South America are rare. The same is true for Australia and much of Africa and Asia. In fact, of all the continents, North America has the greatest number of lakes. These lakes range from small to very large.

☐ **What are some of the largest lakes you know of in the United States? What are some of the smallest?**

Every continent except Antarctica has important rivers. Almost all these rivers start in mountain regions. Most of them flow through humid lands. Two important exceptions are the Nile and Colorado rivers. These rivers flow mostly through dry lands. Rivers that flow through dry lands are important because they are often the only source of water in those places.

Many rivers are important simply because they supply people with water. Some are also important because they

S. Vidler/Leo de Wys Inc.

Do It Yourself

Compare lakes and rivers of continents

Use geography books to help you list the important lakes and rivers on each continent (excluding Antarctica). Which continent has the most lakes? Which has the fewest? Which has the most rivers? Which has the fewest? Which continent has the largest lake? Which has the longest river? Which river carries the most water?

have made possible both cheap transportation and the generation of electric power. In North America, the Mississippi River is the most important river. In South America, the Amazon River is the most important river. The important rivers of other continents are the Nile in Africa, the Ob in Asia, and the Murray in Australia. What is the largest river near where you live?

Problems in getting water

As a result of the uneven distribution of water, people try different ways to get the water they need. They may have to build dams across rivers to create reservoirs that can provide enough water for their needs. But they may also have to have the reservoir some distance away. Or they may have to drill wells. All these efforts can lead to certain problems in getting fresh water.

One problem in trying to get water is that dams, reservoirs, and *aqueducts* [AK-wuh-DUHKTS] are costly to build. Aqueducts are channels that carry water from one place to another. Some countries do not have enough money to build dams, reservoirs, and aqueducts.

Compared with the uneven distribution of rainfall, of lakes, and of rivers, the distribution of groundwater seems to be more even. But in many areas of the world it is difficult and costly to drill wells to get to the groundwater. In many parts of the world, people must spend half their time carrying water from wells for their own needs. They may also have problems in getting enough water for their animals and crops.

Another problem people have in getting enough water is *water rights,* or the right to use a certain source of water. In certain areas of the United States, water is scarce because of little rainfall and because many people use the water. When such conditions exist, there is a problem of who has the right to use what little water there is. Water rights are especially complicated if the source of water involves two or more states or two or more countries.

☐ **Where do people in the area in which you live get their water?**

Find Out More

In many dry parts of the earth, wells have been the only source of water for thousands of years. Two famous old wells are Jacob's Well in Palestine and Joseph's Well in Egypt. Using reference materials, find out how old and how deep these wells are. Then find out if there are any wells where you live. If there are wells near you, compare their depth with the depth of these two old wells.

Figure 17–3. Hundreds of years ago, The Romans built aqueducts, such as the one shown here, to carry water to their cities.

Gary Milburn/Tom Stack & Associates

IMPROVING DISTRIBUTION AND SUPPLY

How can the building of dams, reservoirs, and aqueducts help solve the problem of getting enough water?

How can wells that have gone dry be made to supply water once again?

What are two possible sources of water that might be used to solve some of our water-shortage problems?

Getting more water

Because of a growing population in our country and the use of greater amounts of water, many towns and cities are having water shortages, or problems in getting enough water. Many small towns and cities get their water from wells. But these communities have had to drill more wells to get the water they need. Some have also had to drill their old wells deeper in order to get more water.

Large cities often need to do more than drill wells. For example, Los Angeles is a large city that is solving the problems of getting more water. Many dams, reservoirs, and aqueducts have been built in California to carry water to the people of Los Angeles. Large amounts of water are also needed for irrigation in the area around Los Angeles. Agreements have been reached with nearby states to use some of the water from the Colorado River.

Recently, Los Angeles has also considered the idea of getting water from Oregon, Washington, and Idaho. Many other cities have also tried to get more water by building dams, reservoirs, and aqueducts. What other areas do you know of besides Los Angeles that have tried to get more water by such costly means?

Recharging wells

Growing communities that use wells to get their water have had to pump greater amounts of water from their wells. But overpumping can remove so much groundwater that the wells become dry. One solution to this problem is

To Think About

To keep from having water shortages, many communities have built large water-storage tanks that are able to hold large amounts of water. What advantages, if any, are there in building water-storage tanks instead of reservoirs? What disadvantages are there?

Figure 17–4. In order to get more water for people, dams like the one pictured here have been built. How is water stored in the town or city where you live?

R. A. Parker/Cyr Color Photo Agency

329

to drill deeper wells. But doing this costs money. A less costly practice is *recharging wells*. Recharging consists of replacing some of the lost groundwater so that the wells can produce water once again.

Two ways of recharging wells are used today. One way is by spreading wastewater over the land. Wastewater may be spread out over a large land area by using ditches. In time, the wastewater soaks into the ground. As the wastewater filters through the gravel and sand in the ground, it becomes fairly clean and then becomes part of the groundwater.

Another way to recharge wells is by pumping either wastewater or the extra water from a flooded lake or river into the ground. In this case, however, the water is not clean, and it will have to be treated before it can be used for drinking.

The purpose of recharging wells by replacing the groundwater is not only to raise the water table but also to store extra water in the ground for dry times when the water will be needed. If the extra water were stored on the surface, evaporation would cause much of the water to be lost.

☐ **Why might water pumped from a recharged well probably need to be treated or cleaned before being used for drinking? Why wouldn't the same thing have to be done if the water was to be used for irrigation?**

Figure 17–5. Two ways of recharging wells by replacing lost groundwater are illustrated here.

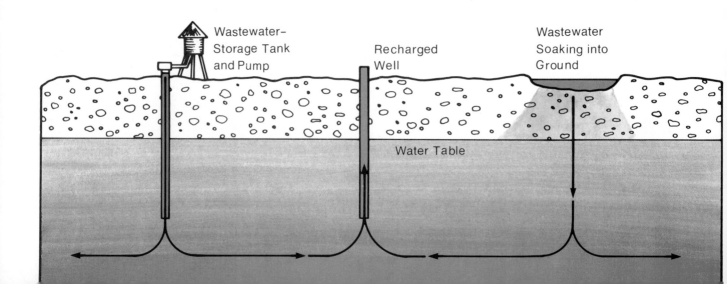

Wastewater–
Storage Tank
and Pump

Recharged
Well

Wastewater
Soaking into
Ground

Water Table

Figure 17–6. Some scientists have suggested using icebergs as a source of fresh water. What might be some advantages and disadvantages in using icebergs?

Finding new sources

There are two possible solutions that could be used to solve some of our water-shortage problems. One possible solution is to get some of our fresh water from the polar ice caps. According to one estimate, 75 percent of all the fresh water on the earth is present in the ice caps. Thus, the amount of fresh water available at the polar regions is great.

The ice that makes up the ice caps originally fell to the earth as frozen fresh water in the form of snow or sleet. An ice cap is, therefore, almost completely free of salt and other minerals. It is believed that an iceberg from an ice cap could be towed into the currents of the Pacific Ocean and floated to a warmer area. Once there, the iceberg could be melted and used for drinking water. It has been calculated that water obtained in this way might cost less than the water now being used in southern California!

A second possible solution to some of our water problems is to *desalinate* [dee-SAL-uh-NAYT], or remove the salt from, seawater. Fresh water may be obtained from seawater in several different ways. These ways involve using either heat or electricity. Some processes remove the salt from the water. Others remove water from the salt. But whatever process is used, it is costly.

☐ **What might be some examples of places where the cost of desalinating seawater would be worthwhile? What are some examples of places where desalinating would not be worthwhile?**

Find Out More

Using reference materials, find out how fresh water is made from salt water on a large scale. Look under the heading *Water* for the subheads "Desalting," "Desalination," "Distillation," "Electrodialysis," and "Freezing."

331

Investigate

What is one way fresh water can be made from salt water?

You will need

tape, table salt, shallow pan, bright light, widemouthed jar, clear plastic bag

Background

Salt water contains a variety of materials. The most important of these materials is salt. The salt that is dissolved in salt water keeps people from using the water in industry, for crops, and in their home. If the salt could be easily removed from salt water in large amounts, there would be large amounts of fresh water available for our use. You can find out one way to make fresh water from salt water by doing this activity.

What to do

Make a salt solution in the widemouthed jar by mixing 9 g of salt in 250 ml of water. This solution is about as salty as seawater. Taste the water to find out how salty it is. Then set the jar in the center of the shallow pan. Place the open end of the plastic bag over the top of the jar. Use the tape to hold the bag in place. Support the bag above the jar so that the bag does not fall over. Shine the light at the surface of the water. After several minutes, water should begin to collect on the inside of the bag. Droplets will move down the outside of the jar into the pan. When enough water has collected in the pan, taste the water.

Now that you have done the investigation

■ How did the water that was in the widemouthed jar taste?
■ How did the water that was collected in the shallow pan taste?
■ How long did it take to collect enough water in the shallow pan for you to taste?
■ Would the use of a bright light be helpful in obtaining a large amount of fresh water? Why or why not?

OTHER NATURAL PROBLEMS

*In nature, what things affect the quality of
water?*

*What problems with water result when rivers
overflow their banks?*

*What problems with water result when water
causes erosion?*

*How does a drought affect plant life, animal life,
and people?*

Water quality

Besides the uneven distribution of water on the earth,
there are other problems with fresh water in nature. One
important problem is *water quality*, or water purity. The
quality of water is partly determined by the amount of
minerals and gases dissolved in the water. Pure water, of
course, contains no dissolved matter. Although rainwater
contains dust and gases from the air, it is sometimes
thought of as being pure water.

If you were to look at some groundwater, you might
think that it is almost pure. However, because groundwater soaks through soil and rock, it generally has many
dissolved minerals called *salts* in it. Salts commonly found
in groundwater contain the elements calcium, sodium, potassium, and chlorine. Water having more than 500 parts
per million (ppm) of salt is generally not used by people
in their homes. This is equal to 500 grams of salt dissolved
in 1 000 000 grams of water.

Unfortunately, much groundwater has more than 500
ppm of salt. Thus, many people cannot use groundwater
as their source of water. These people must either use other
sources of water or bring in water from areas farther away.
One other possibility is to remove the dissolved salts from
the water. Of course, doing any of these things can be
costly.

Most people in large cities use water from lakes or rivers
as their source of water. In fact, of the 300 largest cities in
the United States, most use water from lakes or rivers as
their chief source of supply. Generally, this water contains

Find Out More

Use reference materials to
help you find out about saline
water. What is saline water?
Where is saline water found
as groundwater? Are there
any surface sources of saline
water? If so, where are such
surface sources located?

fewer dissolved minerals than groundwater does. This is because lakes and rivers are supplied by runoff. Rainwater that becomes runoff does not spend enough time in the ground to dissolve many minerals. However, water from lakes and rivers may have sand and silt in it. It is also likely to have more *organic* [awr-GAN-ihk] *material*, or material from living things, than groundwater does. Such water must be treated and filtered before it can be used.

□ **What are some examples of organic material that might be found in lakes and rivers?**

Flooding and erosion

From time to time you may have heard news about a flash flood. A flash flood is usually caused by a heavy rainstorm in mountainous or hilly areas. If the ground is hard and dry and if the rain comes down fast, the ground may not be able to soak up much rainwater. This water may flow downhill so fast that plants are uprooted or buried.

A flood can happen in almost any low-lying area. A flood may occur if there is a large amount of rainfall within a short time. A flood may also occur when it rains for several days without stopping. What may happen to the homes in a low-lying area if there is a flood?

Large rivers, such as the Ohio River and the Mississippi River, sometimes overflow their banks. A large amount of rainfall or the sudden melting of snow and ice often causes flooding of these large rivers. Although large rivers seldom have flash floods, the floods from large rivers often cause a great deal of property damage. Large areas of land near the rivers may become covered by water. Families may be forced to leave their homes. Crops that become covered by water for too long may die. What else do you think may happen when rivers flood?

Another problem with flooding is that water can pick up and carry great amounts of mud, silt, and disease-causing germs. These materials can make the use of the water difficult or impossible for most purposes.

□ **At what time of year are floods caused by melting snow and ice most likely to occur? Why?**

Figure 17–7. Flooding is a problem for animals because they could drown if the water gets too deep. Why might flooding be a problem for plants?

334

Jacqueline Durand

Do It Yourself
Look at river water

Tie a long string around the neck of a glass jar. While standing on a bridge that crosses a river or while standing along the bank of a river, carefully lower the jar into the water. Collect some water by allowing water to flow into the jar. Remove the jar from the river and set the jar someplace where it will not be disturbed for several hours. Then look at the bottom of the jar. What do you see?

Slowly pour the water from the jar. Then put your fingers into the material at the bottom of the jar. Rub your fingers together. What does the material feel like? Look at some of this material under a magnifying glass or a microscope. What does the material look like? How do you think homes that were flooded by river water would look after the water was gone?

Another problem caused by heavy rainfall and flooding is soil erosion. This loss of soil is, perhaps, the most important natural problem caused by moving water. Bridges, highways, and homes can be repaired or rebuilt, but soil cannot be repaired or rebuilt. It takes many thousands of years to make soil. And the soil that is lost can never be replaced. Unfortunately, about one third of the soil of the United States has been lost as a result of erosion.

Droughts

As you have read, rainfall is not always constant or dependable. Sometimes there is very little rainfall over a long time. People may say they are having a *drought* [DROWT(H)]. A drought is a period of time in which rainfall is absent or much less than usual. Most of the time a drought does not last long. But sometimes a drought lasts for months or years. When a drought lasts for a long time, all life in the area of the drought is affected. Many animals and plants die because they cannot get enough water for their needs. Dead plant materials such as grasses, leaves, and bushes become so dry that forest fires start easily. Such fires often kill many animals and plants.

From 1931 to 1938 there was a severe drought in the Great Plains. The drought became so severe that people named that area of our country the Dust Bowl. The name was used because the plowed soil, unprotected by plants, was carried up into great dust clouds by the wind. As a result, many farms were abandoned, and many people moved out of the area. Some people believe this may happen again in some places if the soil is not protected.

WATER TREATMENT

What are some things that people of long ago did to make water safe to drink?
How does a water-treatment plant make water safe to drink?

History of water treatment

People have learned that it is not enough simply to have a source of fresh water. The water must also be clean enough for their use. Many people who lived a long time ago knew that some sources of water could make them sick. As early as 2000 B.C., people in India knew that water could be made safe to drink if it was treated in certain ways. For

Find Out More

Where are droughts most likely to occur in the United States? Why do you think so?

Figure 17–8. The device shown here was used to purify water for German troops during World War I.

The Bettmann Archive

example, people were told to treat their drinking water by boiling it. Two thousand years ago, people in China and Egypt put alum into tubs of dirty water to make the water safer to use. Roman soldiers were told to mix wine with their drinking water to keep from becoming sick when they were in cities other than Rome.

In 1855, the city of London began filtering its water through sand filters. The practice of filtering water began in the United States about 1870. But for years, many people still did not think it was important to filter their water. Then in 1892, many people living in Hamburg, Germany, became sick from *cholera* [KAHL-uh-ruh], a disease caused by certain germs in unfiltered drinking water. Hamburg used unfiltered water from the Elbe River. At the same time, the people across the river in the city of Altona did not get sick, because the drinking water of Altona had been filtered.

In 1909, people began to use small amounts of *chlorine* [KLOH(UH)R-EEN] to kill certain germs in their water. The practice of adding this chemical to treat water is called *chlorination* [KLOHR-uh-NAY-shuhn]. Chlorine has been found to be especially useful in killing germs that cause *typhoid* [TY-FOYD] *fever*. For example, in 1900 there were more than 35,000 cases of typhoid fever throughout the world. Today, less than 500 cases are reported each year.

☐ **Why, do you think, did some people living in Hamburg, Germany, in 1892 think it was not important to filter water?**

Safe enough to drink

Today, many communities have a *water-treatment plant* to make their drinking water safe. Treatment at such a plant may consist only of chlorination. But treatment may involve other kinds of processes as well. These processes include filtering and settling. Communities that use groundwater may just add chlorine because groundwater is generally safe enough to drink.

To Think About

Why, do you suppose, are cases of typhoid fever still being reported throughout the world?

Figure 17–9. The water-treatment-plant worker pictured here is checking the purity of samples of water in order to determine how much chlorine must be added to make the water safe to use.

Gerry Souter/Atoz Images

337

But suppose a city gets its water from a river or a lake. Water from such sources often contains sand, silt, and organic matter. Some of this organic matter may be algae and bacteria. The water may also have a bad taste and a bad odor. Before entering the water-treatment plant, the water must pass through screens. The screens remove most of the larger things from the water, such as branches, cans, and bottles. Next, the water is mixed with chemicals. Some of these chemicals are called *coagulants* [koh-AG-yuh-luhnts]. Coagulants are small, sticky particles. Bacteria, mud, and other materials stick to the particles. The water is pumped to large tanks where those particles slowly sink to the bottom.

The water is then filtered through beds of sand and gravel that trap many of the remaining particles and bacteria. After filtering, the water flows to huge tanks for a final chlorine treatment that kills any remaining bacteria. Finally, the water is safe enough to drink.

Some water-treatment plants do other things to the water. For example, the water may be sprayed into the air. In the process, the oxygen in the air helps remove the bad taste and odor. Sometimes chemicals are added to the water to help keep water pipes from rusting. Also, many treatment plants add a substance called a *fluoride* [FLU(-UH)R-YD] to their water to help reduce tooth decay in the community.

Find Out More

In some parts of the United States, fluorides are a natural part of the water that people use. However, in many communities a fluoride is added to the water. Use reference materials to find out what amount of fluorides are added to a community's water and how it compares with the amount of fluorides present where fluorides are found naturally. How effective are fluorides in preventing tooth decay?

Jacqueline Durand

Do It Yourself
Make some muddy water clean

One of the first steps taken to purify the water in a water-treatment plant can be done very easily. Make or collect 2 L of muddy water and divide the liquid into 2 containers. Add about 112 g of alum (from a drugstore) to one of the containers. Then add a few drops of ammonia, so that the water changes red litmus paper to blue, and stir the mixture. Observe the 2 containers of muddy water. In which container do the small particles settle to the bottom sooner? How do you explain these results?

338

The work done by a hydrologist can be important in determining where to drill for water. What kind of work does a hydrologist do?

Grant Heilman

Careers

Hydrologist

If you wanted to find a source of groundwater, who would you ask for help? Perhaps you would ask a *hydrologist* [hy-DRAHL-uh-juhst] to help you. A hydrologist studies the properties of water and the distribution and location of sources of water. Part of a hydrologist's job is finding groundwater. The hydrologist must also be able to determine how much water is available underground.

To find groundwater, the hydrologist collects and organizes a great deal of information. For example, the hydrologist keeps records of where wells have been drilled, how much water each well produces, and the quality of water pumped from each well. Whenever a new well is drilled, the hydrologist adds information about the well to the records. These records help determine the best places to drill new wells.

A hydrologist sometimes relies on geologists and chemists for help. A geologist may help the hydrologist figure out which *aquifer* [AK-wuh-fur], or rock layer that contains groundwater,

might be best to use as a source of groundwater. A chemist might help the hydrologist decide whether or not the water from an aquifer is good enough to use. The hydrologist might also get information about groundwater by visiting recorder wells. These are wells that have recording instruments attached to them. These instruments tell about changes in the level of the water table at certain locations. All this information helps homeowners, farmers, well drillers, and others to drill a well in the best location.

If the work of a hydrologist appeals to you, you should first get a high-school education. It is also important for you to like to work with different kinds of tools and scientific instruments. To have the opportunity to do many interesting kinds of work in hydrology, you need a college education.

For information about a career in hydrology, a student in your class might write to the American Geophysical Union, 1909 K Street, N.W., Washington, DC 20006.

Reviewing and Extending

Summing Up

1. Rainfall, lakes, and rivers are unevenly distributed over the earth.
2. People in many areas of the earth have problems in getting enough water for their needs. This is also true of many towns and cities in the United States.
3. Building dams, reservoirs, and aqueducts helps get more water to certain areas.
4. Recharging wells, using water from polar ice caps, and desalinating seawater are other possible solutions to the problem of water shortage.
5. Dissolved salts and organic materials are things that affect the quality of water in nature.
6. Flooding and erosion cause problems with bodies of water by making the use of the water difficult and by removing soil.
7. Droughts cause problems because living things cannot get enough water.
8. Many people who lived a long time ago knew that some sources of water could make them sick. This knowledge led to the practices of filtering water and adding chlorine to water.
9. Most communities use a water-treatment plant to make their drinking water safe.

Checking Up

Vocabulary   Write the numerals *1–6* on your paper. Each numbered phrase describes a term from the following list. On your paper, write the term next to the numeral of the phrase that describes it.

silt   aqueduct   desalinate
cholera   coagulant   organic material
drought   reservoir   evaporate

1. channel that carries water from one place to another
2. disease caused by certain germs in unfiltered drinking water
3. material from living things
4. to remove the salt from seawater
5. chemical that forms sticky particles in water
6. period of time during which rainfall is absent or much less than usual

Knowledge and Understanding   Write the numerals *7–14* on your paper. Beside each numeral, write the word or words that best complete the sentence having that numeral.

7. Chlorine is added to water in a water-treatment plant to (*kill germs, reduce tooth decay, form coagulants*).

8. A growing population and the use of greater amounts of water causes (*drought, water shortages, erosion*).

9. Although it is unevenly distributed, the average annual rainfall in the United States is about (*75 centimeters, 130 centimeters, 455 centimeters*).

10. The continent with the greatest number of lakes is (*Africa, South America, North America*).

11. The loss of soil because of (*drought, aqueducts, erosion*) is one of the most important problems caused by water in nature.

12. To correct the problem of overpumping, wells are often (*capped, recharged, reversed*).

13. The serious drought which occurred in the 1930's caused the Great Plains region of the United States to be called the (*Dust Bowl, Great Desert, Drought Land*).

14. Water is filtered in a water-treatment plant in order to (*control cholera, control flooding, desalinate the water*).

Expressing Yourself Write a paragraph as an answer to each of the following questions:

15. How does the distribution of groundwater differ from the distribution of rainfall, of lakes, and of rivers? What problems might people have in trying to use each of these as a source of fresh water?

16. Do you think that using icebergs to supply fresh water to major cities along the coast is a good idea? If so, explain why. If not, explain why not.

Doing More

1. Prepare a report on your community's water supply. Where does the water come from? How is it treated to make it clear and safe? If water shortages ever occur in your community, what does the community do about them? What do you think might be done to improve the supply of water for your community?

2. Try to imagine how much water people waste as well as ways in which water might be conserved. Estimate the volume of water you use in a day. How much do you waste? Multiply these amounts by the number of people who live in your community. Make a list of ways to reduce your own wasting of water. Report your study to the class.

Steve Lissau/Photri

Waves may have a great deal of energy. But what causes a wave to curl and spill like the wave pictured here?

18 Oceans and Seawater

People have always asked questions about the ocean. Many persons have asked, "Why is the ocean salty?" Others have asked, "What causes waves and currents?" In order to answer such questions, people have studied the ocean. The study of the ocean is called *oceanography* [OH-shuh-NAHG-ruh-fee]. Many studies of the ocean are going on today.

As you may know, the world's ocean is large. But the ocean is not just a large body of water. The ocean has different kinds of salts in it. Also, the water in the ocean is always moving.

Did you know that there are mountains, valleys, and plains on the seafloor? How are these features like similar features on land? What are some of the salts found in seawater? What causes waves, and how do they move? As you study this chapter, you will discover the answers to many questions such as these.

PROPERTIES OF SEAWATER

What causes the ocean to be salty?
How does the salinity of the ocean change from place to place?
How does the temperature of the ocean change from place to place?

To Think About

How would you explain why seawater is so much more salty than water in streams and rivers?

What makes seawater salty?

Have you ever tasted seawater, or water from the ocean? If you have, you know that it can be very salty. About 75 percent of the salts in seawater is *sodium chloride* [SOHD-ee-uhm KLOH(UH)R-YD]. Sodium chloride is the name of the salt you know as table salt. But seawater also has many other kinds of salts in it. Some of the other salts in seawater are listed in Figure 18–1.

How much of a sample of seawater is made up of salts? Scientists say that in every 1 000 grams (about 2.3 pounds) of seawater, there are about 35 grams (about 1.23 ounces) of salts. In other words, the total amount of salts in a sample of seawater, or its *salinity* [say-LIHN-uht-ee], is 35 parts per thousand. This is often written as 35 ppt.

But where, do you suppose, do all the different salts in the ocean come from? The answer is that most of them come from streams and rivers that flow into the ocean. As precipitation falls on the land, the salts that are in the soil and rocks are slowly washed out. The water with the salts in it runs into streams and rivers and finally gets to the ocean. Year after year salts are carried to the ocean in this way. What do you think happens to these salts when the water evaporates from the ocean?

How does the salinity change?

During the 1800's, the salts in samples of seawater from different places in the world's ocean were studied carefully. It was found that the salinity of seawater is always between 32 ppt and 38 ppt. It was also found that the

Figure 18–1. Which is the second most common salt in seawater?

SALTS IN SEAWATER	
Salt	Grams per liter
Sodium Chloride	27.213
Magnesium Chloride	3.807
Magnesium Sulfate	1.658
Calcium Sulfate	1.260
Potassium Sulfate	0.863
Calcium Carbonate	0.123
Magnesium Bromide	0.076
Total—	35.000

amounts of the different salts in seawater always stay about the same.

Even though the salinity of water in the ocean stays about the same, there are some differences from place to place. For example, where rivers enter the ocean, the salinity can drop to between 32 ppt and 35 ppt. Why, do you suppose, is the salinity lower at such places?

The salinity of a certain part of the ocean also depends on evaporation. In places where there is a great deal of evaporation, the salinity is higher than 35 ppt. For example, the dry climate in the area of the Mediterranean Sea means that there is a great deal of evaporation there. There is also very little rainfall occurring in this area. Because of this, the salinity of the Mediterranean Sea stays about 38 ppt.

Scientists are not sure whether or not the ocean is getting more salty. They do know, however, that some salts settle to the bottom and some stay in the water. They also know that salts are used by animals for making their shells, bones, and flesh. For example, the element *calcium* [KAL-see-uhm] reaches the ocean in the salts called calcium sulfate and calcium carbonate. But calcium doesn't seem to build up in the ocean. Instead, it is used by clams, oysters, snails, and corals to make their shells or other hard body parts.

☐ **Do you think the water along the coast of the Gulf of Mexico is more salty or less salty than the water in the middle of the Atlantic Ocean? Explain.**

Figure 18–2. Although the Mediterranean Sea contains a great deal of water, the salinity of its water is very high. Why is this so?

Temperature of the ocean

The temperature of seawater is usually between 0°C and 30°C. But there are some warmer and colder areas in the ocean. For example, most of the surface of the Arctic Ocean is frozen all year. The freezing point of fresh water is 0°C, but the freezing point of seawater is about −2°C. The salts in seawater help lower the freezing point.

Seas and coastal waters are often warmer than the middle of the ocean. This is because seas and coastal waters are not deep. They can be heated more easily by the sun than the deep ocean can. Also, because the water does not circulate very much in seas and coastal waters, they are easier to warm. The waters of the Red Sea and the Persian Gulf, for example, often reach a temperature of 35°C.

In parts of the ocean where the water is deep, there are usually 3 temperature layers. The first layer is at the surface. It is called the *surface layer.* This layer may be 200 meters (about 650 feet) thick. The water in this layer is warmed by the sun's rays. It is usually well mixed, too. Why, do you think, is the water in this layer well mixed?

Below the surface layer is the *thermocline* [THUR-muh-KLYN]. This is a thin layer of water. The temperature in this layer drops rapidly the deeper you go. You might think of the thermocline as the boundary between the warm water above and the cold water below.

Below the thermocline is the *deep zone.* Very little sunlight reaches this zone. Because of this, the water stays

To Think About

How would you compare the extreme air temperatures over land to the extreme temperatures of seawater? What might account for the difference?

Runk/Schoenberger/Grant Heilman

Figure 18–3. Some water samplers have thermometers on them. Why might an oceanographer want to know the temperature of the area where a water sample was taken?

cold in this zone. Generally, the temperature in the ocean becomes a little colder the farther down you go.

You may know that on land, mountains and rivers can act as barriers to animals. Most animals cannot cross these barriers. It is interesting to note that there are barriers in the ocean, too. Barriers resulting from temperature sometimes form in the ocean. One such barrier extends around the earth at about latitude 55 degrees south. At this latitude, the cold water from Antarctica meets the warm water from the equator.

The place where the cold water and the warm water meet is called the *Antarctic convergence* [kuhn-VUR-juhn(t)s]. Here, the warm water and the cold water seem to flow side by side with very little mixing. In most cases, ocean animals on one side of the convergence are different from those on the other side. Only a few kinds of ocean animals are able to survive on both sides of the convergence.

☐ **Warm water is more salty than cold water. Do you suppose that the difference in salinity of the waters on either side of the convergence also acts as a barrier? Why or why not?**

Find Out More

Use references to find out which animals are able to survive on both sides of a convergence. Are they the animals you expected? Explain.

Do It Yourself

Demonstrate the freezing point of seawater

Dissolve 35 g of table salt in 965 ml of water. This water will then have about the same salinity as seawater. Now fill a cup, jar, or beaker about ¾ full with tap water. Then fill another cup, jar, or beaker with the same amount of "seawater." Place a thermometer in each container and place both containers in a freezer. Record the temperature in each container every 5 minutes until both liquids are frozen. At what temperature does water from the tap freeze? At what temperature does "seawater" freeze? Which temperature is lower?

Jacqueline Durand

MOVEMENT OF SEAWATER

*What causes waves to form on the surface of
the ocean?*
How do waves move across the water?
*How do waves cause changes on the coastlines
of continents?*
*What are the different kinds of ocean currents,
and what causes these currents?*

What causes waves?

Have you ever watched waves move across a large body
of water, such as a lake or an ocean? You probably wondered what made the waves. Most waves are caused by
wind. As wind blows across a large body of calm water, it
makes small ripples in the water at first. Then larger ripples
may form and begin to grow into larger and larger waves.

The size of waves depends on how hard and how long
the wind blows. The size of waves also depends on the
distance the wind blows over the water.

Wind is not the only cause of waves in the ocean. Waves
can also be caused by earthquakes, volcanic eruptions, and
landslides that take place underwater. These three causes
of waves may disturb the water a great deal. You could
think of each earthquake, eruption, or landslide as creating
a kind of shock wave in the water. A large wave at the
water surface that results from such a shock wave is called
a *tsunami* [(t)su-NAHM-ee].

Some tsunamis are known to have traveled thousands of
kilometers at a rate of 750 kilometers (about 470 miles) an
hour. Tsunamis are very high waves when they reach the
shore. They are sometimes over 30 meters (about 100 feet)
high. As you might guess, waves this high might cause a
great deal of damage. Also, many people may be drowned
if they are not warned that these waves are coming.

How do waves move?

If you have ever watched waves move in the middle of a
lake or out in an ocean, you might think that a large amount

Find Out More

In 1946 an earthquake that
took place underwater near
the Aleutian Islands caused
tsunamis over 32 meters
high on nearby Unimak
Island. The waves also traveled 3 700 kilometers to
Hawaii. There, waves
smashed into Hilo, Hawaii,
killing 59 people. Using reference books, find out more
about tsunamis. How large
are tsunamis in the middle
of the ocean?

of water moves with each wave. But this is not so. In fact, very little water moves. If you have ever watched a bobber used for fishing as it moves with a wave, you know that it moves up and down. But it does not move forward with the wave unless there is also a current in that direction.

All waves at the surface have the same general shape as they move. The high point of a wave is the *crest*. The low point is the *trough* [TRAWF]. The distance from any crest to the next crest or from any trough to the next trough is called a *wavelength*. In fact, the distance between any point on a wave and the corresponding point on the next wave is a wavelength. See Figure 18–4.

Another word used in describing waves is *frequency* [FREE-kwuhn-see]. The frequency is the number of waves that pass a certain point in a certain amount of time. See Figure 18–5.

As ocean waves move, they have energy. The amount of this energy depends on the height of the waves, the frequency of the waves, and the wavelength. But as the waves enter shallow water, the frequency becomes less. This is partly because the lower part of the waves drags along the ocean bottom, so that the waves lose some of their energy. Also, water returning from waves that have already reached the shore interferes with the incoming waves, causing them to lose energy. When this happens, the crest of each wave overtakes the trough, and the wave breaks. Such waves are called *breakers*. These are the kind of waves that people who like surfing, or riding the surf on a surfboard, look for.

☐ **Do you think surfing would be better on beaches with long, sloping bottoms or on beaches where the bottom drops off rapidly? Explain.**

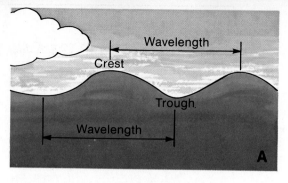

Figure 18–4. In A, the crest, the trough, and the wavelength of waves are indicated. Using the drawing, how would you describe half a wavelength?

Figure 18–5. In B, the dotted line marks the start of a series of waves. In C, the crest of the first wave has traveled forward as far as the position shown in one second. Since two waves have passed the dotted line, what is the frequency of the waves?

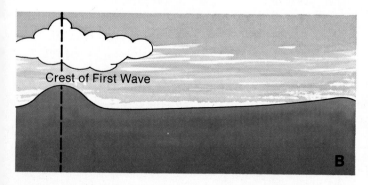

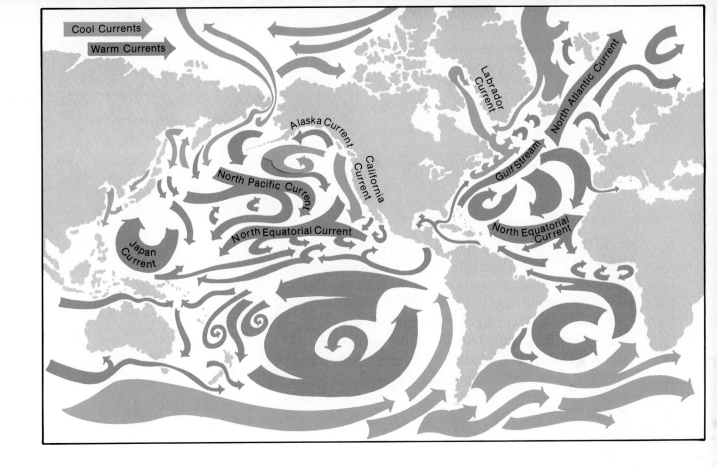

Cool Currents →
Warm Currents →

Alaska Current

Labrador Current

North Atlantic Current

North Pacific Current

California Current

Gulf Stream

Japan Current

North Equatorial Current

North Equatorial Current

Surface currents

As you know, waves move *across* water. But currents move *in* water. One kind of current that moves in water is caused by the wind. This current is known as a *surface current*. Because winds are moving masses of air, they do not affect water more than a few meters below the water's surface. Surface currents are often the same year after year. See Figure 18–6.

The kinds of winds that have the greatest effect in creating surface currents are the *prevailing* [prih-VAY-lihng] *winds*. Such winds move great distances. Prevailing winds from the west, called *westerlies*, affect the weather in most of the United States.

Warm prevailing winds called *trade winds* help create the surface current known as the *Gulf Stream*. In the Atlantic, trade winds push a warm-water current from the

Figure 18–6. Some of the surface currents in the ocean are indicated. What surface currents are near the United States? Which of these are cold currents?

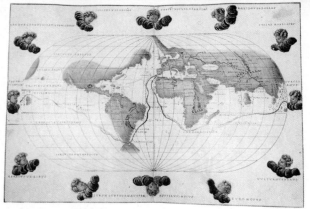

Figure 18–7. This ancient map shows important winds as small heads around the edge of the map.

equator into the area between the western tip of Cuba and Yucatán, Mexico. There, this current meets water from the Gulf of Mexico, so that a new current—the Gulf Stream— turns eastward around the southern tip of Florida. The Gulf Stream flows north along the United States coastline to Cape Hatteras. Near this point, it turns northeast and crosses the Atlantic. This warm current brings warm water to the coasts of northern Europe. The warm water helps give northern Europe a warmer climate than it would otherwise have.

Density currents

Scientists have found that there are large ocean currents far below the water's surface. These currents are called *density* [DEHN(T)-suht-ee] *currents*.

As you may know, cold water weighs a little more than an equal volume of warm water weighs. Scientists say that cold water has a higher density than warm water. Because cold water has a higher density, it sinks. Warm water, being lighter, rises.

In the ocean, water is heated near the equator and other warm areas. As water is heated, it takes up more space and rises to the surface. Then it moves away from the warm areas because of surface currents. Water from areas like Antarctica and Greenland is cold. Because this water is cold, it sinks. The cold, deep density currents move in the opposite direction from the surface currents.

☐ **Where do you think most density currents begin in the northern half of the earth?**

Investigate

How do temperature and salinity change the density of water?

You will need

balance, food coloring, graduated cylinder, glass-marking pencil, pot holders or insulated mitt, hot plate or other source of heat, 2 test tubes, 6 beakers

Background

When the amount of salt in water or the temperature of water is changed, the water's density is also changed. Water that is more dense tends to sink below water that is less dense. When this happens in the ocean, one layer of water can sometimes flow above another layer, with very little mixing.

What to do

Label 4 of the beakers A through D. Using a balance, place 8 g of salt in beaker A. Then measure 195 ml of water with the graduated cylinder and place the water in beaker A. Add 2 or 3 drops of food coloring to the water, and mix. Place the same amount of water in beakers B, C, and D. Add 2 or 3 drops of food coloring

to beaker D and place it in a freezer for 30 minutes.

Keep beaker B at room temperature. Heat the water in beaker C until it is almost boiling.

Label the test tubes 1 and 2. Place each tube in an empty beaker so that each tube rests on a slant. Then fill tube 1 about half full of water from beaker A. Very slowly, finish filling the slanted tube with water from beaker B. Observe what happens.

Fill tube 2 about half full of water from beaker C. Very slowly, finish filling the slanted tube with water from beaker D. Observe what happens.

Now that you have done the investigation

- What happened in test tube 1?
- What happened in test tube 2?
- Which is more dense, pure water or salty water?
- Which is more dense, cold water or warm water?
- How does this investigation illustrate how density affects water in the ocean?

351

Tidal currents

All along the coasts of the ocean, water levels rise and fall twice each day. Each large rise in the water level is called *high tide*. Each large fall in the water level is called *low tide*. The current created by the moving water of a tide is sometimes called a *tidal current*.

In most coastal areas there are two high tides and two low tides each day. In some places there may only be a small change in the water level. But in other places, such as narrow bays, the difference between high and low tides may be as much as fifteen meters (about fifty feet).

In order for tides to take place, large amounts of water must be moved. This movement of water is caused chiefly by the moon's gravity pulling on water in the ocean. See Figure 18–8.

Because the earth rotates on its axis, the moon constantly changes its position with respect to any spot on the earth. This constant change is why the tides rise and fall. For example, two views of the rotating earth are shown in Figure 18–9. In the first view, the moon attracts the earth, so there are high tides at W and Y and low tides at X and Z. In the second view, the earth has rotated a quarter turn. There are now high tides at X and Z and low tides at W and Y. Since the earth rotates once every twenty-four hours, how many high tides would you expect at one place in a day? Why?

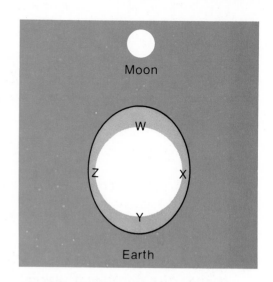

Figure 18–8. High tides occur on the side of the earth toward the moon and on the side of the earth opposite the moon. Why do the tides occur as shown?

Figure 18–9. Where do you think the high tides and low tides would occur if the earth rotated another quarter turn after the second view shown?

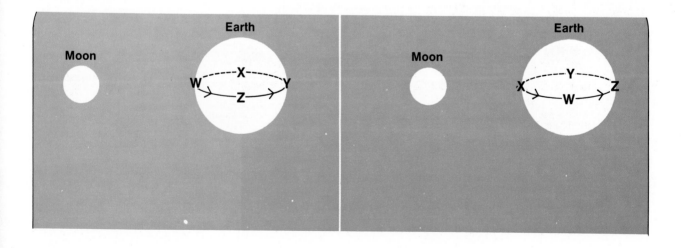

THE SEAFLOOR

What is the seafloor next to the continents like?
What part of the seafloor is flat?
What part of the seafloor has mountains and
  valleys?

Continental shelf and slope

Suppose the Atlantic Ocean could be drained so that you could walk from any place on the east coast of the United States to any place along the coast of Europe. What would your journey be like? First, you would walk across the *continental* [KAHNT-uhn-EHNT-uhl] *shelf*. A continental shelf is an area of the seafloor next to a continent. The shelf gently slopes downward. In fact, it usually slopes about 2.25 meters for every kilometer (12 feet for every mile).

As you might guess, the continental shelf is not the same width all the way around the United States. Off the coast of San Francisco, for example, the shelf is only about 48 kilometers (30 miles) wide. Off the coast of Boston, the shelf is about 415 kilometers (260 miles) wide.

If you continued walking toward Europe, you would eventually come to what is called the *shelf break*. Here, the slope suddenly begins to get steeper. This is where the continental shelf ends. It is still not very deep here compared with the great depths of the sea. It may be from 40 meters (130 feet) deep to 500 meters (1,600 feet) deep at the shelf break.

The *continental slope* begins at the shelf break. This area drops down about 95 meters per kilometer (about 500 feet per mile). It drops down to 4 or 5 kilometers (about 13,000 to 16,000 feet) below sea level. You might think of the continental shelf and the continental slope as parts of a continent that are below sea level.

Abyssal plain and mountain ridges

If you walked all the way down the continental slope, you would come to the *abyssal* [uh-BIHS-uhl] *plain*. The

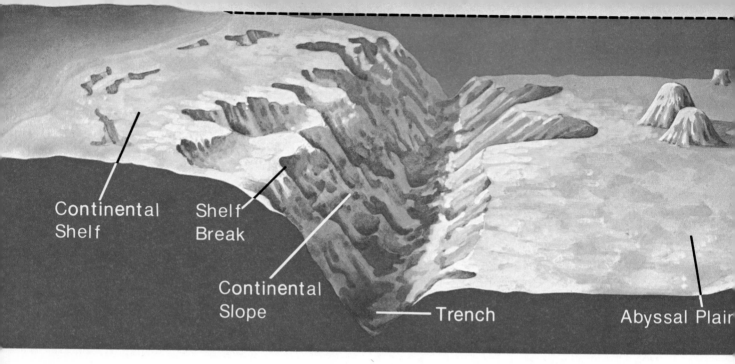

Continental Shelf

Shelf Break

Continental Slope

Trench

Abyssal Plain

abyssal plain is very flat. It makes up about a third of the seafloor.

If you continued your journey to Europe, you would probably see a few mountains rising from the abyssal plain. Such mountains are called *seamounts* [SEE-MOWNTS]. They are formed by underwater volcanoes. Some seamounts rise more than a kilometer (over 3,000 feet) above the abyssal plain. Some of them are so tall that they extend above the surface of the water.

> ☐ Mauna Kea is a volcano on Hawaii that rises 4 205 meters (about 13,796 feet) above sea level. The part of this volcano below sea level extends downward another 6 000 meters (about 19,500 feet). Since Mount Everest is 8 848 meters (29,028 feet) tall, about how much taller is Mauna Kea than Mount Everest?

After you had walked many kilometers on the abyssal plain, the seafloor would start to become rough and hilly. The rough and hilly seafloor would be very similar to foothills at the base of mountains on land. But these underwater foothills belong to a series of mountains that are

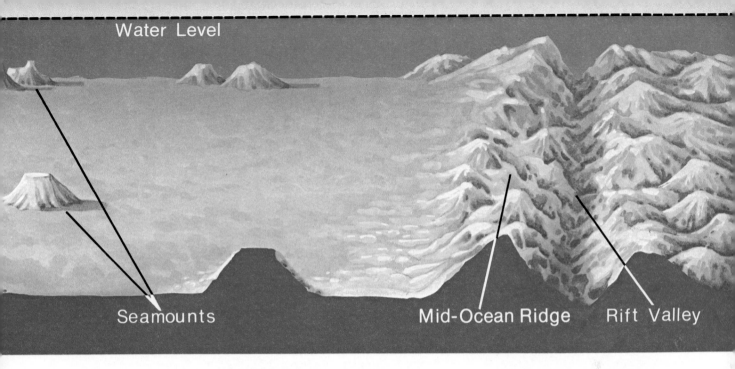

Water Level

Seamounts   Mid-Ocean Ridge   Rift Valley

taller than many mountains or volcanoes on land. Some of the mountains are 6.4 kilometers (about 4 miles) above the abyssal plain.

The series of underwater mountains forms a long *ridge,* or range of mountains. In fact, scientists say that there is a long ridge of mountains near the center of each of the large oceans. The ridge in the Atlantic Ocean, called the *Mid-Atlantic Ridge,* is probably the best known.

Rift valleys and trenches

If you were able to cross these mountains on your journey toward Europe, you would find that there is a long, deep valley in the middle of the Mid-Atlantic Ridge. This kind of valley is called a *rift valley.* Scientists have found that the rift valley is an area of earthquake activity. In fact, the rift valley seems to be an area of weakness in the earth's crust.

At this point in your journey you would be only about halfway to Europe. The last half of your journey would be like the first half, only in reverse. There would be mountains, foothills, an abyssal plain, a continental slope, and a continental shelf.

Figure 18–10. Features of the sea-floor are illustrated on these two pages. What might each of these features be called if they occurred on land?

To Think About

Do you suppose the ridges in the oceans have any effect on density currents? Why or why not?

Throughout the Atlantic Ocean, in general, the seafloor follows the kind of pattern described. But in some places in the Atlantic Ocean there are deep valleys called *trenches*. Trenches are deep, V-shaped cuts in the seafloor. They are long and narrow and have steep sides.

The Pacific Ocean has many more trenches than the Atlantic Ocean. The Mariana Trench is located near the Mariana Islands in the Pacific Ocean. The bottom of this trench is 11 033 meters (36,198 feet) below sea level. This is the deepest known place in the ocean.

☐ **The Pacific Ocean has many more volcanoes and earthquakes than the Atlantic Ocean does. Why, do you think, does the Pacific Ocean also have more trenches than the Atlantic Ocean?**

Find Out More

Using references, find out how the depth of the Mariana Trench was determined. Do any ocean animals live that far down?

Jacqueline Durand

Do It Yourself

Make a profile of a "seafloor"

Mark off a 12-meter-long piece of string in half-meter intervals. Have 2 classmates tie the ends of the string to 2 broomsticks. The string should be tied at the same height on each pole. Have your classmates move to opposite sides of the classroom, hold the poles vertically, and stretch the string tightly between the poles. The string represents the surface of the ocean. The floor and the furniture in the room represent the "seafloor."

You should use a meterstick to measure the "depth" or distance between the string and the floor and between the string and the furniture in the room. Make a measurement at each interval of the string and record your measurements. When you finish measuring at all the intervals, draw a profile of the "seafloor." What might the tallest piece of furniture you measured represent in the ocean? Would it be difficult to make a complete map of the room using profiles? How could the profile you made be improved?

Chemical oceanographers often carry out their work on ships, using many different kinds of equipment.

Careers

Chemical oceanographer

Far below the surface of the ocean are many valuable minerals and metals. Some of these minerals make up the mud on the seafloor. Certain metals occur as nodules on the seafloor. The location and composition of these materials are being studied by scientists. One kind of scientist who studies these materials is a *chemical* [KEHM-ih-kuhl] *oceanographer*. Chemical oceanographers are scientists who study the chemistry of seawater and ocean sediment. These scientists also study the chemical reactions that take place in the ocean.

Most chemical oceanographers do research by making observations and conducting experiments at sea. They may study, collect samples, and work on data while on board a research vessel. They may also use aircraft and various types of underwater craft. They generally use special instruments to measure and record their findings. Special cameras with bright lights may be used to photograph the seafloor. Sound-ing devices may also be used to measure, map, and locate ocean materials. Sometimes many samples of sediments and ocean life are collected by means of these devices.

Many chemical oceanographers, however, work in laboratories on land. To present the results of their studies, they write reports and prepare charts. Sometimes the reports are prepared for the company that employs the scientist. At other times the reports are prepared for printing in scientific journals.

The minimum requirement for becoming a chemical oceanographer is a bachelor's degree with a major in oceanography and a minor in chemistry. However, most jobs in research and teaching require graduate training in oceanography or a basic science.

For information about a career as a chemical oceanographer, a student in your class might write to the American Society for Oceanography, 845 Main Building, Houston, TX 77002.

Reviewing and Extending

Summing Up

1. The salinity of seawater is about thirty-five parts per thousand.
2. The amounts of the different salts in seawater always stay about the same.
3. The deeper you go in the ocean, the colder the water becomes.
4. Most waves are caused by wind.
5. All waves have the same general shape.
6. The amount of energy that waves have depends on the height of the waves, the frequency of the waves, and the length of the waves.
7. Waves move across water, but currents move in water.
8. Three kinds of currents in the ocean are surface currents, density currents, and tidal currents.
9. Cold water has a greater density than warm water. Because of its density, cold water sinks.
10. The features of the seafloor include the continental shelf, the continental slope, the abyssal plain, seamounts, ridges, rift valleys, and trenches.

Checking Up

Vocabulary Write the numerals *1–11* on your paper. Each numbered phrase describes a term from the following list. On your paper, write the term next to the numeral of the phrase that describes it.

crest
trough
tsunami
salinity
trenches

frequency
seamounts
deep zone
thermocline
abyssal plain

surface layer
tidal currents
density currents
continental shelf
continental slope

1. high point of a wave
2. wave caused by an underwater disturbance
3. measure of the amount of salts in seawater
4. deep currents in the ocean
5. area of the seafloor next to a continent
6. mountains formed by underwater volcanoes
7. warmest part of the ocean
8. low point of a wave
9. thin layer of water that forms a boundary between the warm water and the deep zone
10. deep valleys in the ocean
11. number of waves that pass a certain point in a certain amount of time

Knowledge and Understanding Write the numerals *12–20* on your paper. Beside each numeral, write the word or words that best complete the sentence having that numeral.

12. Most waves in the ocean are caused by (*earthquakes and landslides, the moon, the wind*).
13. The distance from the crest of a wave to the crest of the next wave is called a (*breaker, trough, wavelength*).
14. The tidal movement of water is caused chiefly by (*the moon's gravity, temperature, the sun's gravity*).
15. Two words that may be used to describe density currents are (*cold and swift, warm and deep, cold and deep*).
16. The abyssal plain on the seafloor is generally (*hilly, flat, mountainous*).
17. As they move, all waves at the surface have (*the same general shape, the same wavelength, the same frequency*).
18. The amounts of the different salts in seawater (*change constantly, stay about the same, cause different kinds of currents*).
19. Because cold water has a higher density than warm water, cold water (*flows faster, rises quickly, sinks*).
20. The salinity of the ocean is likely to be higher where there (*is much evaporation, are many fish, are swift currents*).

Expressing Yourself Write a paragraph as an answer to each of the following questions:

21. Would long, rolling waves have a higher or lower frequency than short, choppy waves? Explain.
22. What are some of the reasons for the range of salts in seawater to be from 33 ppt to 38 ppt?

Doing More

1. Using references such as encyclopedias and library books, find out what the following instruments are and what they are used for: fathometer, bathythermograph, Nansen bottle, tide gauge, bathysphere, wave recorder, and hydrophone.
2. Go to a lakeshore or to a seashore and observe the way the waves move to the shore. Then observe a wind vane to determine the direction of the wind. What is the relationship between the way the waves move to the shore and the direction of the wind?

19 Resources of the Ocean

Oil is an important resource that everyone needs. Offshore rigs like the one pictured above are used to obtain oil from rock layers beneath the seafloor.

There are more than 4 billion people living on the earth today. This number is growing larger each year. This means that more and more food, fresh water, oil, metals, and other materials are needed each year to meet the needs of people.

How will the needs of people be met in the future? Many people think that more and more of the things people need will come from the ocean. For this reason many people are trying to find ways to make greater use of the resources of the ocean.

What things do people get and use from the ocean today? What are some ways in which people may use the ocean in the future? Why must people be careful about the ways they use it? You can find the answers to these questions in this chapter.

FOOD FROM THE OCEAN

What kinds of food come from the ocean?
How do people get food from the ocean today?
*How might people get food from the ocean in
    the future?*

Kinds of food from the ocean

What does the word "seafood" mean to you? If you
are like most people, you probably think of certain kinds
of fish and shellfish as being seafood. However, the word
"seafood" could be used to describe any plant or animal
that comes from the ocean and is used for food by people.

People eat more fish than any other kind of seafood.
Tuna, herring, cod, halibut, sole, and mackerel are important fish used for food in all parts of the world. Other
fish, such as shark and swordfish, are also used for food in
many countries. Some of these fish are eaten as fresh
fish. However, most of the fish caught in the ocean are
processed in some way. They may be frozen, canned, dried,
or used to make fish sticks or fish patties.

Harrison Forman

*Figure 19–1. Seafood is an impor-
tant part of the diet of many people.
How many different kinds of seafood are being sold in this market-
place?*

361

Many kinds of fish that are caught are not eaten directly. These fish can be used in another way. For example, they can be made into fish flour. Fish flour will keep for a long time without spoiling. It can be added to other foods to provide materials people need to eat in order to be healthy. At present, very little fish flour is used by people for food. Most is used in animal food. Some is also added to soil in which crops are grown. But, fish flour may become an important food for people in the future.

Shellfish are another kind of seafood eaten by people. Favorite shellfish include clams, oysters, crabs, and lobsters. Octopus and squid are also eaten in some places.

Seaweeds, such as sea lettuce and Irish moss, are eaten in some countries. Some seaweeds are used in salads or in soups. A certain kind of seaweed is made into a bread known as *laver* [LAY-vur] *bread*. Laver bread looks like a small cake or roll having a jellylike inside. In most countries, however, seaweeds themselves are not eaten. Instead, substances made from seaweeds are used in making other foods. One such substance is *carrageenan* [KAR-uh-GEE-nuhn]. Carrageenan is used in making ice cream and creamy salad dressings.

In some places the meat of seals and of whales is used for food. Whale fat, called *blubber* [BLUHB-ur], is also used in making margarine and cooking oil.

☐ **What kinds of seafood have you eaten?**

Phil Degginger

Do It Yourself

Find out what kinds of seafood are in the stores around you

Visit a local grocery store or supermarket. Find out what kinds of seafood are sold in the store. Also find out how the seafood has been processed. That is, note whether it is fresh, frozen, canned, or dried. Make a list of the kinds of seafood and the ways it has been processed. Report your findings to the class.

Figure 19–2. Scallops are often gathered from the seafloor by using shovellike dredges.

Getting seafood today

At one time all seafood was gathered from its natural habitat. Clams, oysters, and seaweed were gathered by wading through water close to the shore. Most fish were caught in small boats close to shore. A few large ships hunted fish far out in the ocean. Fish caught from these ships were cleaned and packed in salt to keep them from spoiling.

Today most fish are caught far out in the ocean. However, people now use ships that are like floating factories. Fish caught from these ships can be frozen or canned right on the ships. Also, planes are used to spot large schools of fish. This means that ships do not have to sail over large parts of the ocean just looking for fish. Instead, such ships can be directed to places where large numbers of fish can be caught.

People are also raising some kinds of seafood in the ocean in much the same way as plants and animals are raised on farms. At present clams, oysters, and some kinds of seaweed are being raised. People are also looking for ways to raise crabs, lobsters, and fish in the ocean.

Getting seafood in the future

The number of people living on the earth is growing larger every year. This means that more food is needed each year. Long ago people found they could get more

Find Out More

Use references such as encyclopedias to find out how different kinds of seafood such as seaweed, fish, and whales are harvested. Report your findings to the class.

food by farming than they could by hunting. Today many people believe that the ocean will supply more and more food in the future. But, in order to get more food from the ocean, new ways of getting that food will have to be developed. One possible way to get more food from the ocean is by using *mariculture* [MAR-uh-KUHL-chur], or sea farming.

The greatest amount of mariculture is done in the Orient. There, people grow seaweeds, oysters, shrimp, and several kinds of fish. Seaweeds are grown on nets held by poles in shallow water along the coasts. Oysters usually live on the bottom of shallow coastal areas. However, they can also be grown fastened to wooden poles or on hanging ropes. Shrimp and fish are grown in large ponds or in pens made by surrounding a part of the sea with fine nets.

One problem with mariculture today is that people must catch young plants and animals in order to raise them. Many people are looking for ways to breed these living things the way land farmers breed their animals and plants. Perhaps someday people will not have to depend on catching the young of living things from the ocean in order to raise them.

☐ **What other problems might people have to solve before they can raise large amounts of seafood by mariculture?**

Artstreet

Figure 19–3. Seaweed farms, such as this one, provide one kind of seafood. What other kinds of seafood might people raise using mariculture?

FRESH WATER FROM THE OCEAN

What is solar distillation?
What is one problem with solar distillation?
*What other methods are being used to get fresh
    water from salt water?*

Using the sun

Many places on the earth have little or no fresh water. Some of these places are near the ocean. However, seawater is too salty for people to use. In order to get fresh water from the ocean, plants must be built that *desalinate* [dee-SAL-uh-NAYT], or remove the salt from, the seawater. There are several ways by which seawater can be desalinated. All of these ways involve the use of some form of energy.

One possible way to desalinate seawater is by using energy from the sun. This way is called *solar distillation* [SOH-lur DIHS-tuh-LAY-shuhn]. In a solar distillation plant, a large tank or basin is filled with seawater. The tank is covered by a clear, slanting roof. Heat from the sun causes water to *evaporate* [ih-VAP-uh-RAYT], or change to a gas. This gas is called *water vapor* [VAY-pur]. The water vapor rises and begins to collect on the roof. There, the vapor forms drops of fresh water. These drops of water move down the slanting roof and fall into another tank.

Today, people living on some of the islands in the Pacific Ocean use solar distillation to get fresh water from seawater. However, there are problems in producing fresh water by solar distillation. For example, a tank having a surface area a little smaller than a city block could only produce about 25 000 liters (7,000 gallons) of fresh water a day. This would only be enough water for about thirteen people at the rate water is used by people in the United States.

☐ **What other problems can you think of that might result from depending upon solar distillation for fresh water?**

Investigate

How can you get fresh water by solar distillation?

You will need

pie plate, clear glass mixing bowl, small dish, salt

Background

The sun gives off great amounts of energy. Some of this energy reaches the surface of the earth. People have been trying to find ways to use this energy from the sun. One way energy from the sun is being used today is to get fresh water from seawater. You can find out how energy from the sun can be used to get fresh water from "seawater" by doing this activity.

What to do

Make a salt solution by mixing 9 g of salt in 240 ml of water. This solution is about as salty as seawater.

Set a pie plate near a sunny window. Place a small dish in the pie plate and fill the dish with the salt solution. Taste the salt solution. Now place the clear glass bowl upside down over the dish. The bowl should fit inside the rim of the pie plate. Observe the bowl and dish at various times during the day. Taste the water that collects in the pie plate.

Now that you have done the investigation

■ How did the water you placed in the dish taste?
■ How did the water that collected in the pie plate taste?
■ How long did it take to collect enough water in the pie plate for you to taste?
■ Would solar distillation be useful where a large amount of fresh water was needed? Why or why not?

Other methods of desalination

Solar distillation is only one of several different ways to desalinate seawater. There are several other methods in use. One method that is widely used is called *flash distillation*.

In a flash distillation plant, water is changed quickly into steam without boiling the water. This is done by letting heated water flow into a chamber in which the air pressure is low. The steam rises in the chamber, cools, and changes back into water. This water, which is fresh water, is collected. See Figure 19–4.

In desalination plants that use flash distillation, the seawater passes through several chambers. Fresh water is collected from each one. So, such plants can produce large amounts of fresh water. The flash distillation plant at Key West, Florida, produces more than eight million liters (about two million gallons) of fresh water each day.

Figure 19–4. In a flash distillation plant, salt water is heated at A. As it flows through each chamber, some of the water changes to vapor. The vapor is cooled by the coils at B, which contain cooler incoming salt water. The cooled vapor then forms drops of fresh water.

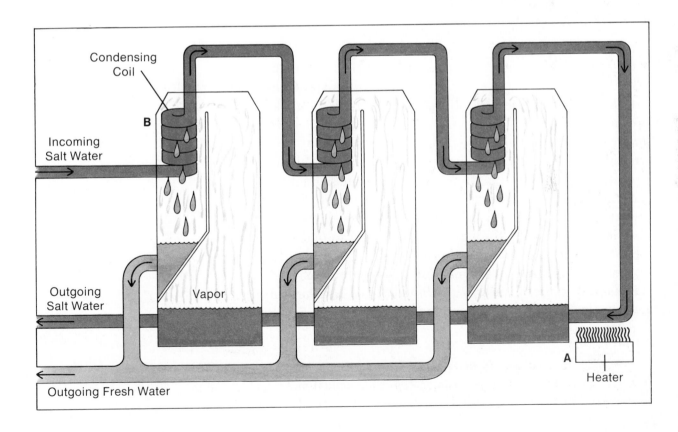

Two other ways of getting fresh water from seawater are *freezing* and *reverse osmosis* [rih-VURS ahz-MOH-suhs]. When water freezes, the ice that forms is pure water. However, salt crystals are trapped between ice crystals. The salt is separated from the ice by washing the ice with fresh water. This method uses large amounts of energy. It also requires large amounts of fresh water.

Osmosis is a process by which water moves through a *membrane* [MEHM-brayn], or thin sheet of material. A reverse osmosis desalination plant uses a chamber that is divided into two parts by a membrane that allows water, but not salt, to pass through. There is fresh water on one side of the membrane and salt water on the other. Normally, fresh water would flow through the membrane into the salt water. However, by increasing the pressure on the saltwater side of the tank, water can be made to move from the saltwater side to the freshwater side. This is reverse osmosis.

Many places in the Great Plains area have water that is not as salty as seawater but that is far too salty for people to use. Such water is said to be *brackish* [BRAK-ihsh] *water*. One method that has proved useful for desalinating brackish water is *electrodialysis* [ih-LEHK-troh-dy-AL-uh-suhs]. When salt dissolves in water, it breaks up into two kinds of electrically charged particles called *ions* [EYE-uhnz]. Salt breaks up into sodium ions and chloride ions. The electrodialysis process uses a large chamber divided into three parts by two membranes. Each of these membranes lets one kind of ion pass through it. An electric current is passed through salt water in this chamber. Sodium ions pass through one membrane to one side. Chloride ions pass through the other membrane on the opposite side. The water remaining in the center part of the chamber is fresh water. The United States government runs an electrodialysis desalination plant in Webster, South Dakota.

☐ **In what way is the electrodialysis process similar to the reverse osmosis process of desalination? In what way is it different?**

Figure 19–5. This desalination plant in Kuwait is one of the largest in the world. Why might the country of Kuwait want or need a large desalination plant?

MATERIALS FROM THE OCEAN

Why are offshore oil wells needed?
Where are offshore wells located?
What are some problems with drilling oil wells
offshore?
What metals are being mined from the ocean?
How might manganese nodules be removed
from the seafloor?

The need for oil

You may have heard the saying "The world runs on oil." This saying becomes easier to understand when you think about the many products that come from oil. When oil is pumped out of the ground and refined, people get such products as gasoline for cars, jet fuel for airplanes, and diesel fuel for trucks. People also get other oil products such as heating oil, kerosene, and fuels for industry. What oil product have you used lately? Do you think you could get along without it?

In the past, most of the oil wells in the world have been drilled on land. You may have seen oil wells in states like

Figure 19–6. Drilling for oil can be hard and dangerous work. What, do you think, are some of the benefits for people who do this kind of work?

369

Louisiana, Oklahoma, and Texas. As you might guess, scientists do not think they have discovered all the places where oil is to be found under the land. However, they have probably discovered most of the rich ones and the ones that will be easiest to drill. Some of the richest oil wells are in Saudi Arabia, Iraq, Iran, Java, Mexico, Colombia, and Venezuela. Most people believe the world's oil needs will continue to grow.

☐ **Why, do you think, will the world's oil needs continue to grow? What must be done to supply these needs?**

Offshore oil wells

Scientists discovered many years ago that the rock layers of the continental shelf were usually the same as those on the nearby land. This discovery led them to believe that if they found oil in the rock layers on land, they would also find oil under the continental shelf. This was later found to be true. In fact, in many cases there was found to be more oil in the rock layers under the ocean than in the same rock layers on land. What might be one reason for this?

Today, there are many offshore wells in places like the Persian Gulf and the North Sea. Many offshore wells have also been drilled off the coasts of California, Texas, and Louisiana. In the Gulf of Mexico, scientists found oil near large *salt domes.* You might think of salt domes as hills of salt that exist within the rock layers of the earth. Salt domes may be found in rock layers on land and under the ocean.

Before the salt domes were formed in the earth, layers of oil-bearing rock had formed on top of deep layers of salt. But pressure deep inside the earth caused the salt to push upward through the oil-bearing rock toward the surface. The pushed-up salt formed domes. Salt domes are sometimes more than a mile across. When the salt domes formed, oil was trapped next to the domes. Scientists look for the salt domes because they know they will find oil and gas trapped nearby.

Figure 19–7. Why are offshore oil wells such as this one important to people today?

370

The first major offshore wells were drilled off the coast of Venezuela in the 1930s. These wells were drilled in only a few feet of water. Today, wells are drilled far out in the sea. Some are so far from the shore that they cannot be seen from land. Oil wells are also being drilled in deep water. In fact, wells are now being drilled in the continental slope at depths of 180 meters (600 feet) to 300 meters (1,000 feet). Today, offshore oil wells account for over 22 percent of the world's oil production.

Many problems had to be overcome before offshore oil wells could become productive. Drilling platforms had to be made strong enough to withstand hurricane winds and waves. The drilling platforms that rest on the bottom are now used for wells where the water is up to 180 meters (600 feet) deep. Wells that have to be drilled in deeper water now require a floating vessel of some kind. Such a vessel may be kept in place by anchors and motors. Otherwise, high winds and waves may move the vessel. But plans are underway to build taller platforms—up to 300 meters (1,000 feet).

There are other problems with offshore wells, too. People and supplies have to be carried back and forth from the shore to the drilling station. Also, the people who work on the drilling platform have to be constantly on the alert for oil spills. Why are oil spills a problem in ocean areas?

☐ **Why, do you think, may taller platforms that rest on the seafloor soon be built?**

Materials dissolved in seawater

You have probably seen at least one kind of mine. Perhaps it was a copper mine or a gold mine. At the turn of the century, many people began to mine large amounts of gold and silver in the southwest United States. They hunted for places where these valuable metals could be found in the ground. Today, scientists are beginning to look to the ocean to help supply people with many different metals and other materials. The ocean is proving to be a large storehouse of many materials that people need.

To Think About

More oil remains to be discovered on land. If it is less costly to drill on land, why are so many wells being drilled offshore?

371

Do It Yourself

Recover salt from salt water

Mix 15 ml of salt in a liter of water. What do you think would be the cheapest and easiest way to recover the salt from the water? Try it and see. What do you think would be two ways of speeding up the process? Try them and see. What are the advantages and disadvantages of each of these ways of recovering salt from seawater? Of the three ways you tried, which one was the most expensive?

More gold exists in the water of the ocean than has ever been mined on land. In fact, scientists say there are about 6 kilograms (13 pounds) of gold in every cubic kilometer (0.25 cubic mile) of seawater. This seems like a large amount of gold until you learn an important fact. That fact is that it would take almost 400 million liters (over 100 million gallons) of seawater to produce 1 gram (0.04 ounce) of gold! Using today's methods, it would be much too costly to recover the gold from seawater.

Using today's methods, it would also cost too much to recover most of the other materials, such as silver, that are dissolved in seawater. Only a few, such as salt, bromine, barium, and magnesium, are presently being recovered. Most of the world's supply of magnesium comes from seawater.

Manganese nodules from the ocean

Certain useful materials may be obtained from the seafloor. For example, scientists have found that the element *manganese* [MANG-guh-NEEZ] is found in clumps, or *nodules* [NAHJ-oo(uh)lz], on the seafloor in many parts of the world. As you may know, manganese is used to help make steel.

A manganese nodule may be as small as a pea or as large as a potato. These nodules are found in water that

372

is 1 500 to 5 500 meters (5,000 to 18,000 feet) deep. Scientists think that in certain places there are many thousands of tons of these nodules covering the seafloor. Other important metals are also found in these nodules. These metals include copper, iron, cobalt, and nickel.

In 1976, a team of scientists found a large number of very pure manganese nodules near the Mid-Atlantic Ridge. Their studies indicated that these nodules were made near hot springs in the seafloor. These scientists believe that hot springs carry manganese out of the hot rocks below. As the water cools, the nodules form.

Scientists have been trying several ways to remove the nodules. One of these ways is by using submarines, either with or without people aboard. Another way scientists have been trying to remove the nodules is by using long, flexible hoses that suck up the nodules like a vacuum cleaner picks up dirt. The hose carries the nodules to a waiting ship. What might be a problem in removing the nodules with a hose?

Find Out More

Using references, find out what magnesium is used for. Also find out how it is recovered from seawater. Why is magnesium recovered from seawater rather than from magnesium ore found on land?

Wide World

Figure 19–8. Huge scoops such as this one are dragged along the seafloor in some places to recover manganese nodules. Why are people interested in finding new ways to get these nodules from the seafloor?

Figure 19–9. Large dredges similar to the harbor dredge pictured here might be used to recover certain materials from the seafloor near the coast.

Other materials from the ocean

All the elements that make up the minerals in the earth's crust can be found in seawater. Among these elements are iron, zinc, silver, gold, copper, and manganese. It is costly to remove gold and silver from the ocean, but manganese can be removed without a great cost. A chemical process is used to recover the manganese. Iodine, magnesium, and bromine can be taken from the salt in seawater.

Large amounts of almost pure copper have been found in the Atlantic Ocean. At the present time, however, there is no way to bring this copper up because it is at depths up to 2 100 meters (7,000 feet). Nickel and cobalt also are deep within the ocean.

As you can see, many different kinds of materials are being removed from the ocean. In the future, many more materials will be removed. Some scientists believe there is a danger in this. Perhaps removing these materials may harm the ocean and its life if it is not done properly. In what ways do you think removing materials from the ocean may cause harm?

PRESERVING THE OCEAN

*What resources in the ocean are already in
danger of being used up?*
*What animals in the ocean are among the world's
endangered species?*
*How can people save the endangered animals in
the ocean?*

Can the ocean continue to help supply our needs?

As you know, the ocean provides many of the things we need, such as food, minerals, and oil. But you may wonder how long the ocean's supply of these things will last. It depends. Some things that the ocean now provides, such as crude oil, gas, and minerals, have hardly been touched. These resources have a good chance of lasting quite a while. But certain kinds of fish from the ocean are already in danger of being overfished. Overfishing in some parts of the ocean began about eighty years ago. It was noticed

Scott Ransom/Taurus

Figure 19–10. Sea otters often eat sea urchins. In large numbers, sea urchins often destroy large amounts of seaweed. How can preserving sea otters be helpful to people?

then that, even though fishing operations were increased, fewer fish of certain species were caught. This was alarming and caused some countries to place an annual catch limit on these species.

Endangered species

Until recently, too many whales had been caught every year. Now the number of certain whales—blue, right, gray, humpback, and bowhead—in the ocean is far too few. These whales are now among the endangered species. No one is allowed to catch these whales until their number builds up again. This will take many years.

Besides food sources, other life in the ocean is sometimes destroyed by overfishing. Certain dolphins are often found swimming together with tuna fish. As soon as fishers see the dolphins, they let down their nets to catch the tuna. But they also unintentionally catch many dolphins in their nets, killing thousands of these playful, intelligent animals every year. The dead dolphins have no commercial use. To save what dolphins they can, tuna fishers have to use extra time and effort to allow the dolphins to escape.

☐ **What other animals that live in the ocean are in danger of being overhunted?**

Do It Yourself

Make a study of whales

Using references such as *National Geographic,* find out which species of whales can be hunted legally. Find out how many of each of these species of whales can be caught each year. Give a report on whales. Tell the class where various species of whales can be found and what products people use from whales. Why is it difficult for marine biologists to study whales?

A marine biologist may study the living things of the ocean while they are in the ocean or take them back to a laboratory to be studied later.

Careers

Marine Biologist

A *marine biologist* is a scientist who studies the life in the ocean. The word "marine" means relating to the sea. Marine biologists classify marine plants and animals and seek to learn how the plants and animals live. They study the relationships among living things in the ocean. Marine biologists are also known as biological oceanographers.

Marine biologists often go to sea to make direct observations of plants and animals. They sail on research vessels and use deep-sea nets to capture life from the ocean. With diving equipment, the biologists also dive into the water to make firsthand observations. Once they have been at sea, the marine biologists return to their specially equipped laboratories. In the laboratory, they make detailed observations and carry out many experiments.

Through their study of marine plants and animals marine biologists have learned a great deal about the human body. The organs in the human body are much like the organs in an animal. For example, marine biologists have learned how nerve cells work by studying the squid's nerve fibers. They have observed the mechanical, chemical, and electrical responses of nerves. Marine biologists have learned about viral and bacterial infections through a study of corals, seaweed, and sea cucumbers.

An inexpensive booklet, *Training and Careers in Marine Science*, is available from the International Oceanographic Foundation, 3979 Rickenbacker Causeway, Virginia Key, Miami, FL 33149. You and others in your class might like to read the booklet to find out more about marine biologists.

Reviewing and Extending

Summing Up

1. Foods that people get from the ocean include fish, shellfish, seaweeds, seals, and whales.
2. Large factory ships that can process the catch are used for fishing today. Airplanes are often used to spot large schools of fish and direct the ships to where the fish can be caught.
3. In the future, people may use mariculture to get more food from the ocean.
4. A solar distillation plant uses energy from the sun to get fresh water from seawater.
5. Flash distillation, freezing, reverse osmosis, and electrodialysis are other processes used to desalinate salt water.
6. The need for oil is growing each year. Offshore oil wells account for over 22 percent of the world's oil production today.
7. Many minerals are dissolved in seawater. However, only a few, such as salt, bromine, barium, and magnesium, are presently being recovered from seawater.
8. Manganese nodules are found in many places on the seafloor. Because manganese is important in making steel, people are trying to find ways to get these nodules.
9. Overfishing began about eighty years ago. If overfishing is allowed to continue, too few fish may be caught to meet the needs of people.
10. Large amounts of copper have been found in the Atlantic Ocean, but at the present time there is no way to bring the copper to the surface because it is at a depth of up to 2 100 meters (7,000 feet).
11. Whales are now among the endangered species in the ocean.
12. Some scientists believe it is dangerous to remove too many materials from the ocean.

Checking Up

Vocabulary Write the numerals *1–6* on your paper. Each numbered phrase describes a term from the following list. On your paper, write the term next to the numeral of the phrase that describes it.

carrageenan brackish osmosis mariculture
desalinate nodule evaporate salt dome

1. clump of manganese on the seafloor
2. substance made from seaweed and used in making foods such as ice cream and creamy salad dressing
3. water that is not as salty as seawater but is too salty for people to use
4. sea farming
5. process by which water moves through a membrane
6. change into a gas

Knowledge and Understanding Write the numerals *7–16* on your paper. Beside each numeral, write the word or words that best complete the sentence having that numeral.

7. A (*solar distillation, flash distillation, reverse osmosis*) desalination plant uses energy from the sun to get fresh water from salt water.
8. Oil is being pumped from offshore oil wells in the rock layers under (*forests, mountains, continental shelves*).
9. The fat from whales, called (*blubber, laver, carrageenan*), is used in making some margarines.
10. A (*desalination plant, nodule, salt dome*) is a hill of salt found within the rock layers of the earth.
11. Laver bread is made from (*fish, shellfish, seaweeds*).
12. Most of the world's supply of (*magnesium, gold, manganese*) comes from seawater.
13. When salt dissolves in water, it breaks up into two kinds of electrically charged particles called (*nodules, ions, membranes*).
14. Overfishing results in catching (*more, larger, fewer*) fish.
15. Oil and gas are often found where (*nodules, salt domes, continental shelves*) have been pushed up into layers of oil-bearing rock.
16. An element that can be removed from the ocean with little cost is (*gold, copper, magnesium*).

Expressing Yourself Write a paragraph as an answer to each of the following questions:

17. Since there is so much gold in seawater, why do people not get the gold they need from the ocean?
18. How is salt water changed to fresh water in a flash distillation plant?

Doing More

1. Grow several bean plants in two separate containers. Water the plants in one container with fresh water. Water the plants in the other container with salt water. Observe and describe what happens to the plants in each container.
2. Fill a pail full of water. Pour some sand into the bottom of the pail. Try to remove the sand from the pail by using a siphon such as the kind used to clean fish tanks. How can siphons be used to get materials from the seafloor?

Pros and Cons

The World Ocean—Whom Does It Belong To?

The world ocean covers over 70 percent of the earth's surface. For thousands of years, people have used the ocean for fishing and for travel. Before 1945, the laws of the ocean were accepted by almost all countries. That is, along the shores of most continents and islands there was a 12-mile (19-kilometer) limit. Within the limit, coastal countries owned the fish and minerals and could inspect foreign ships to prevent smuggling and enforce health regulations. But they could not prevent ships of other countries from moving about within most of this limit. The ocean beyond this limit was free to all nations to sail, fish, explore, and dump all kinds of wastes.

After 1945, many countries began turning to the ocean to help feed their growing population and to obtain raw materials for their industries. Modern technology also became responsible for an increased interest in the ocean. Through technology, oil companies were able to drill wells anywhere in the continental shelf. Mining companies could sweep up minerals from the seafloor. Modern fishing vessels could haul in whole schools of fish with huge nets. As a result, the ocean became so valuable that many

These people are using a large net to catch fish just off the coast of Mexico. Why might they not be interested in an extended 200-mile (about 320-kilometer) limit for fishing?

countries began to extend their limit to 200 miles (320 kilometers).

Perhaps you are wondering what difference it makes when a country extends its limit to 200 miles (320 kilometers). When a country extends its limit, many questions are raised. First of all, would extending the limit give countries the right to restrict ships from sailing within the new limit? If it would, as much as 50 percent of the ocean in which ships now sail freely could become closed to shipping. Second, would a country's ownership of a tiny speck of land give it rights to great areas of the ocean? Third, how would the ocean around scattered islands, such as those in the Caribbean, be divided? Fourth, from what point along the shore would the new limit be determined—low tide, high tide, or somewhere else? Fifth, just what rights and responsibilities regarding fish, minerals, and pollution would countries have within the extended area of water along their shoreline? Finally, and perhaps most important of all, what rights would land-locked countries and poor countries have in regard to fish and minerals in the ocean?

Many fishing companies use modern equipment to catch and process large amounts of fish. Why might the owners of these companies want an extended limit for their fishing boats?

As a result of all the unanswered questions regarding the use of the ocean, people from many countries are meeting in order to write a treaty to end misuses of the ocean such as pollution and to settle conflicts over navigation and territorial rights, fishing rights, and rights to minerals on the seafloor. How would you answer some of these questions? Whom do you think the ocean belongs to? What responsibilities do you think go along with the use of the ocean?

Investigate On Your Own

1. One way in which oceanographers obtain samples of materials from the seafloor is by using a core sampler. A simple core sampler can be made from a length of metal tubing such as a pipe. Using a hammer, pound your piece of pipe down into the soft edge of the ocean, a lake, or some other body of water. Pull out the pipe and, using a round stick, carefully push your sample out of the pipe in order to study the material. What do you observe? Do you see any living things in your sample? Do you see any differences between the top and the bottom of your sample? Do you think you can draw any conclusions about the floor of the entire body of water from the results obtained from this one test? Why or why not?

2. One important measurement that many oceanographers make is the temperature of the water. Use a minimum-maximum thermometer to determine the temperature of the water in the ocean or in some other body of water. Such a thermometer is set up to record the minimum and maximum temperatures of air or water. A hardware store may carry this kind of thermometer. Tie a long cord to the top of the thermometer. Lower the thermometer to different depths in the water. Make sure that you reset the thermometer after each trial. Allow the thermometer to remain at each depth for at least five minutes. What temperatures do you observe at different depths? What do you think will happen to the temperature deeper in the water?

Read On Your Own

Aylesworth, Thomas G., *Storm Alert: Understanding Weather Disasters.* New York: Julian Messner, 1980.

Thunderstorms, tornadoes, hurricanes, and other weather disasters are the topics of this book. The author deals with what causes storms and what takes place during storms. The book includes information about weather disasters that have occurred in different parts of the world.

Barry, James P., *The Great Lakes.* New York: Franklin Watts, Inc., 1976.

This book illustrates and describes the geography of the Great Lakes, the history of the Great Lakes, and the past and present uses of the Great Lakes. Pollution in the Great Lakes is also discussed.

Fodor, R. V., *Angry Water: Floods and Their Control.* New York: Dodd, Mead & Company, 1980.

Among the topics in this book are causes of floods, protection from floods, and ways to prevent floods.

McFall, Christie, *Underwater Continent—The Continental Shelves.* New York: Dodd, Mead & Company, 1975.

This book is about continental shelves. Fishing, mining, archaeology, and water movement are also considered.

McGovern, Ann, *The Underwater World of the Coral Reef.* New York: Four Winds Press, 1976.

The author makes it clear that a coral reef is a part of an underwater community. This community is fully described.

Unit 5
THE CHANGING EARTH

The earth is always changing. You have probably seen some of the ways in which the earth has changed. Houses and shopping centers have been built where there were once open fields. Large open-pit mines have been dug in the earth. All these changes are caused by people. But not all changes in the earth are caused by people.

Some changes in the earth are caused by natural forces. Erosion, volcanoes, and earthquakes cause changes in the earth. Wind, water, and masses of ice act upon the surface of the earth and cause erosion. You may have seen examples of erosion. But there are other changes in the earth that you may not have seen. For example, scientists say that the continents are slowly moving in response to natural forces within the earth. They also say that as a result of the moving of the continents, volcanoes and earthquakes change the earth.

Changes caused by natural forces have been happening for billions of years. As you study this unit, you will be reading about some of the ways natural forces have changed the earth in the past and how they are changing and shaping the earth even today.

Bert Van Bork/Root Resources

This scene shows organisms that lived more than 400 million years ago on the floor of a warm, shallow sea. Which of these organisms are living today?

20 Geologic History

Suppose you could travel back in time millions of years. You would see a much different looking earth than you see today. Many of the animals and plants you would see would be quite different from those living today. Even the surface of the earth would look somewhat different if you went back far enough in time.

Scientists have described many changes that have taken place on the earth. How have scientists learned about these changes? When did major changes in the surface of the earth take place? How did these changes affect living things? You can find answers to these and other questions about the history of the earth in this chapter.

EVIDENCE OF CHANGE

What is a fossil?
How do fossils show that the earth has changed?
How do rocks show that the earth has changed?
How do scientists find out the age of a rock?

Fossils as clues to the past

The earth is undergoing many changes today. Some of these changes affect living things. For example, if a swamp dries up, plants and animals that lived in the swamp will no longer be able to live there.

Scientists believe that the same kinds of changes that are taking place today have been going on for millions of years. These changes have made the earth what it is today. But the earth must have been quite different millions of years ago.

It is not easy to find out what the earth was like long ago. Scientists do not have a time machine to help them see what the earth was like. Instead, scientists must search for clues about the earth's history in the earth's rocks. Some of the clues come from *fossils* [FAHS-uhlz].

A fossil, you may remember, is the impression, the remains, or any other evidence of a living thing that has been preserved in the earth. Many fossils are the hard parts of animals or plants. That is, they are shells, bones, teeth, seeds, or wood. Fossils of worms, jellyfish, and leaves are often preserved only as outlines in a rock. A few fossils are footprints or other signs of an animal left in mud that later changes into rock.

Some living things that have left fossils were like animals and plants living today. Others were quite different. Scientists often compare fossils to living animals and plants. In this way they learn how the kinds of living things on the earth have changed. However, fossils can tell scientists much more about the past history of the earth. For example, fossil corals have been found in Scotland, Canada, and the northern part of the United States. Living corals are found only in warm, shallow seas. Scientists think

Find Out More

Even though a great many fossils have been found, scientists still think of fossils as being rare. Use references such as encyclopedias and books on fossils to answer the following questions: How are fossils formed? Which kinds of living things are most likely to leave fossils—those that have hard parts or those that have only soft bodies?

that the fossil corals must also have lived in warm, shallow seas. The fossil corals tell scientists that Scotland, Canada, and the northern part of the United States must have been covered by warm, shallow seas at one time.

Fossils give other clues about the changes in the earth. Fossils of a certain small animal are found in South America and in Africa. Scientists are sure this animal could not have crossed a wide ocean. Many scientists think this shows that South America and Africa were once joined together. They say that these fossils are found far apart today because the plates of the earth's crust have moved, causing South America and Africa to move apart.

☐ **How would you explain finding layers of rock containing fossils of sea animals above and below a layer of rock containing fossils of land animals?**

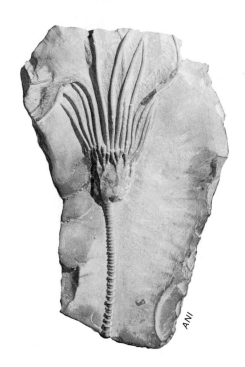

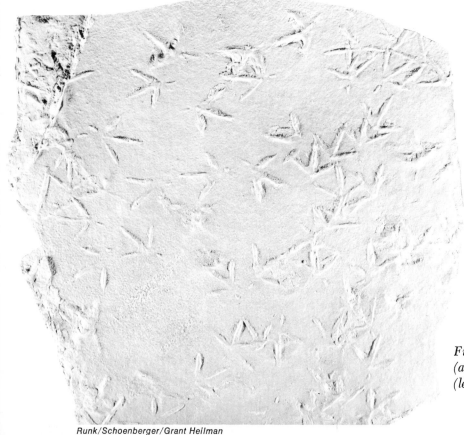

Figure 20–1. How is the fossil crinoid (above) like the fossil bird tracks (left)? How are the fossils different?

Runk/Schoenberger/Grant Heilman

Cameramasters

You can probably find rocks in which there are fossils around your home and school. You should look for limestone, marble, sandstone, and shale. These rocks are often mined and used to make such things as gravel, windowsills, and wall facings. Examine pieces of gravel, wall facings, and windowsills made from such rocks around your home or school. Look for shapes in the rocks that appear to be fossils. Use reference books on fossils to try to identify those you find.

Rocks as clues to the past

Studying fossils is one way to learn how the earth has changed. However, fossils are not found in many kinds of rock. Igneous and metamorphic rock contain few, if any, fossils. Why, do you think, is this so?

The different kinds of rock found in the earth form under different conditions. So, rock can also be used as clues to learn about the past history of the earth. For example, limestone is formed in shallow ocean water. Limestone may be changed into marble. Finding limestone or marble in a place tells a scientist that that place must once have been covered by a shallow sea.

Limestone and marble are not the only kinds of rock that are used to learn about past changes in the earth. Granite and gneiss are important rocks of mountains. These two kinds of rock are often clues that tall mountains may once have stood where there are flat plains today.

Scientists can even tell if a place was hot and dry or cold and wet from studying rock. As water moves over rock and soil, the water dissolves certain kinds of matter. If the water then flows through a place that is hot and dry, the water evaporates. The dissolved matter is left behind, forming sedimentary rock and salt deposits.

Figure 20–2. How might this glacier cause changes in these mountains over a long period of time?

When weather is cold and wet over a long period of time, large amounts of snow fall. In time the snow may pack together, forming a thick sheet of ice. Pressure from more and more snow may cause the ice sheet to begin to move. Such a moving ice sheet is called a *glacier* [GLAY-shur]. As a glacier moves, it picks up and carries rocks and soil. The rocks and soil leave scratches in rock over which they move. The rocks and soil are dropped in places where the glacier melts. Rocks and soil dropped in this way form low, rounded hills. These hills are called *moraines* [muh-RAYNZ].

Several times in the past huge glaciers have covered large parts of the earth. These times are known as *ice ages.* During the last ice age most of Europe, Canada, and the northern half of the United States was covered by glaciers. During earlier ice ages parts of Africa, India, South America, and Australia were covered by glaciers.

☐ **Where are glaciers found today?**

390

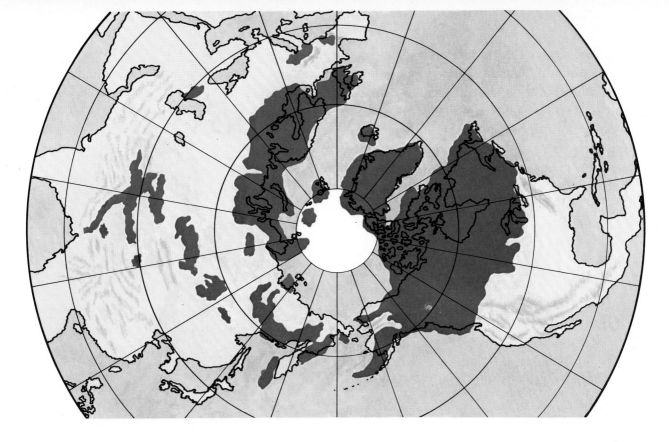

Measuring the age of rock

When sedimentary rocks are being formed, new layers of sediment are deposited on top of older sediment. So, younger layers of sedimentary rock are usually found on top of older ones. Fossils found in younger sedimentary rock are younger than fossils found in older rock. But knowing that one fossil is younger than another does not tell you how many years old each fossil is.

Scientists do have a way of telling about how many years ago a fossil was formed. They do this by finding out the age of rock found along with a fossil.

Certain kinds of matter found in rock are *radioactive* [RAYD-ee-oh-AK-tihv]. Radioactive matter changes into a different kind of matter that is not radioactive. Each kind of radioactive matter makes this change over a different length of time. Scientists test a rock to find out how much radioactive matter is present in the rock. They also test to find the amount of new matter that has been formed

Figure 20–3. This map shows what parts of the earth were covered by glaciers during the last Ice Age. Was the place where you live covered by glaciers at that time?

as the radioactive matter has been changed. By comparing the two amounts and by knowing how long it takes for a given amount of the radioactive matter to make this change, scientists can find out the age of a rock.

One major problem is that only igneous rock can be dated this way. However, igneous rock is often found over, under, or mixed with sedimentary rock. Therefore, scientists can tell much about the age of sedimentary rock and of any fossils in it by finding out the age of the igneous rock around it.

GEOLOGIC HISTORY OF THE EARTH

How old is the earth?
How has the surface of the earth changed
during its long history?
What changes in living things are found in the
fossil record?

Geologic time

Time is measured in many different units. The smallest unit of time you probably use is the second. The longest is probably a year. You may think that a hundred years is a very large amount of time and that a second is a very small amount. And yet, a hundred years in the history of the earth is a smaller amount of time than one second is in a person's whole lifetime.

The history of the earth is described in terms of *geologic* [JEE-uh-LAHJ-ihk] *time.* A million years is a very small amount of geologic time. Much of the known history of the earth is described in terms of tens or hundreds of millions of years. The whole history of the earth is described in thousands of millions of years. Scientists believe the earth is about 4,600 million years old. A thousand million is equal to a *billion* [BIHL-yuhn]. So, the earth could also be described as being 4.6 billion years old.

☐ **What are some other things you have heard of described in terms of millions? In terms of billions?**

To Think About

Suppose you found a number of very unusual fossils in limestone. None of the rock above or below the limestone was igneous. What is one way you could learn how long ago the fossils were formed?

To Think About

Suppose you were to mark dots on a piece of paper, making 1 dot every second. How long would it take you to make a million dots if you could make 1 dot after another without ever stopping? How long would it take you to make 4,600 million dots?

ERAS OF GEOLOGIC TIME	
Era	**Began**
Precambrian [pree-KAM-bree-uhn]	4.6 billion years ago
Paleozoic [PAY-lee-uh-ZOH-ihk]	570 million years ago
Mesozoic [MEHZ-uh-ZOH-ihk]	225 million years ago
Cenozoic [SEE-nuh-ZOH-ihk]	65 million years ago

Figure 20–4. Several eras take their names from the dominant life forms during that era. What were the dominant life forms during the Paleozoic Era (ancient life), the Mesozoic Era (middle life), and the Cenozoic Era (modern life)?

Scientists divide geologic time into four parts called *eras* [IHR-uhz]. The table in Figure 20–4 gives the name of each era and when each began.

Changes in the crust

The Precambrian Era lasted almost 4 billion years. This is about 88 percent of all geologic time. During this time the first oceans and *continents* [KAHNT-uhn-uhnts], or large landmasses, were formed. Scientists think that the continents were much smaller than they are today. New crust was added to the edges of each continent over many millions of years. Some of the new crust was igneous rock. Some of it was sedimentary rock formed from matter that was weathered from the continents. During this time several large mountain ranges were formed, but they have since worn away. The Laurentian Mountains of Quebec, Canada, were formed during this era. Today, all that is left of these mountains is a hilly plain with crests that are about 900 meters (3,000 feet) tall.

The Paleozoic Era began about 570 million years ago. During this era, changes took place in the crust of the earth. Several mountain ranges were formed during this time. The Caledonian Mountains of Scotland and the Acadian Mountains of Canada were formed about 400 million years ago. The Ural Mountains between European Russia and Siberia were formed about 300 million years ago. About 270 million years ago, the Allegheny Mountains in North America were formed. Many scientists think these mountains formed as different continents were joined together.

Find Out More

The Paleozoic Era, the Mesozoic Era, and the Cenozoic Era are usually divided into smaller units of time called periods. Use references such as geology books to find out the names of the periods. Prepare a chart showing each era and its periods. Explain your chart to other members of your class.

There were other changes in the crust during the Paleozoic Era. From time to time shallow seas and deep oceans covered much of North America and Europe. Large amounts of sediments were carried into the seas. In time, these sediments changed into sedimentary rock. Scientists can tell much about these seas from the rock that was formed in them. However, scientists do not know why seas covered the continents. Some scientists think the land sank below sea level. Others think that the water level in the oceans rose.

The Mesozoic Era began about 225 million years ago. At this time, most of the continental lands were above sea level. These lands remained above sea level throughout most of this era. Some scientists believe that there was only one continent during the early part of the Mesozoic Era. They call this supercontinent *Pangaea* [pan-JEE-uh].

Several important changes in the crust took place during the Mesozoic Era. Mountain ranges began to form along the west coast of North America and South America. There were also great numbers of volcanic eruptions on all lands. The Rocky Mountains were formed about 130 million years ago.

Many scientists describe another important change as taking place during the Mesozoic Era. This change is the breakup of Pangaea that began 180 million years ago. When this happened, 2 supercontinents formed—*Gondwanaland* [gahn-DWAHN-uh-LAND] and *Laurasia* [loh-RAY-zha]. An oceanic waterway called the *Tethys* [TEE-thuhs] *Sea* separated the 2 continents.

Throughout the Mesozoic Era, important changes were taking place on Gondwanaland and Laurasia. Gondwanaland was breaking apart to form the lands known today as Africa, South America, Australia, Madagascar, Antarctica, the Falkland Islands, and parts of India. Laurasia was breaking apart to form North America, Greenland, Europe, and Asia. Figure 20–5 shows some of the stages in the breakup of Pangaea.

☐ **How would the forming and the breaking up of Pangaea affect the oceans of the earth?**

To Think About

How might the different continents have been brought together to form Pangaea? What might have caused Pangaea to break up?

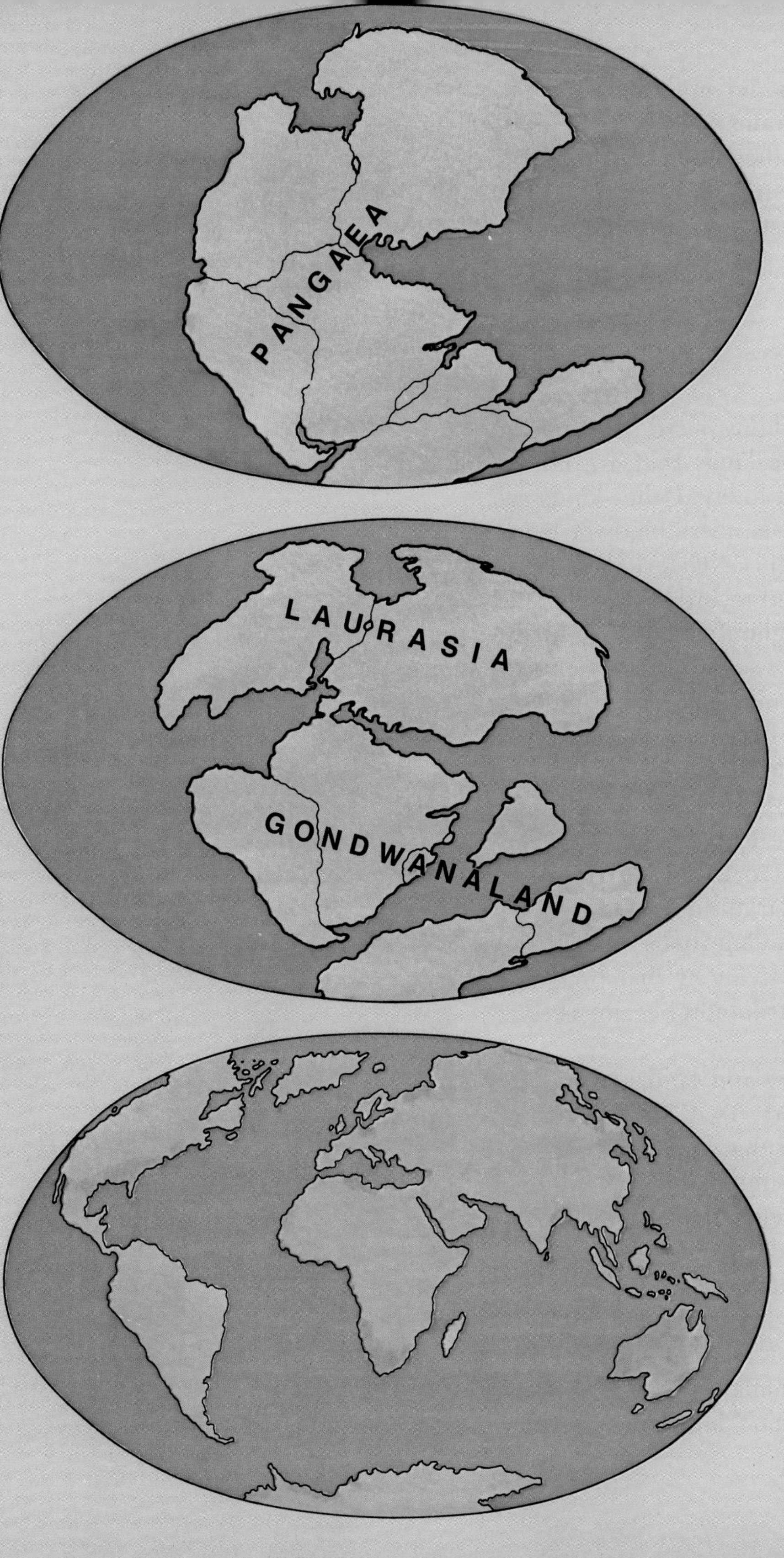

200 Million Years Ago

135 Million Years Ago

Today

Figure 20–5. How have the different landmasses that make up the continents today changed their position since the breakup of Pangaea?

The Cenozoic Era began about 65 million years ago. During this time, the tallest mountains found on the earth today were formed. These include the Himalayas, the Alps, and the Sierra Nevadas. South America and North America were joined together when the Isthmus of Panama was formed during this era.

Changes in living things

Many different kinds of living things have lived on the earth during its long history. Some kinds that are known from very old fossils are still living today. Other kinds are no longer living on the earth. That is, these kinds of living things have become *extinct* [ihk-STIHNG(K)T]. All these fossils form a fossil record. The fossil record shows changes in the kinds of living things throughout the history of the earth.

The oldest known fossils date from the Precambrian Era. Some of them formed more than 3 billion years ago. All of these fossils are of simple, one-celled living things. A few fossils of jellyfish and wormlike animals have been found in rocks dating from the end of the Precambrian Era.

Fossils first became common in rocks dating from the beginning of the Paleozoic Era. Large numbers of fossils from this time are of sea animals having shells. One of the most important groups of animals living at that time was the *trilobites* [TRY-luh-BYTS]. The trilobites became extinct about the end of the Paleozoic Era.

The oldest fossils of fish, insects, and land plants date from the middle of the Paleozoic Era. Two other groups of animals appeared toward the end of this era. These animals are the *amphibians* [am-FIHB-ee-uhnz] and the *reptiles* [REHP-tuhlz]. Living amphibians include frogs and toads. Living reptiles include snakes, lizards, and crocodiles. Most of these animals are much smaller than the amphibians and reptiles that lived during the Paleozoic Era.

When the Mesozoic Era began, many kinds of animals from the Paleozoic Era had become extinct. Different groups of animals and plants became important. One of

Figure 20–6. Which animals living today, if any, look like this fossil trilobite?

ANI

Figure 20–7. Do you think this dinosaur was a plant eater or a meat eater? Why do you think so?

the most important groups was the *dinosaurs* [DY-nuh-SAW(UH)RZ]. Dinosaurs are thought to have been reptiles.

Most people think of dinosaurs as being very large animals. Some were quite large. But many dinosaurs were small. Some were no larger than a chicken. Each kind of dinosaur had its own way of life. Some were plant eaters. Others were meat eaters. Most lived on land. A few could fly. There were even fishlike dinosaurs that lived in the ocean. In other words, dinosaurs lived in every way known for living animals of today.

Three other important groups of living things are first known from rocks of Mesozoic age. These groups are flowering plants, birds, and *mammals* [MAM-uhlz]. The oldest mammal fossils are of small mouselike and ratlike animals. Living mammals include dogs, horses, elephants, and people.

Dinosaurs became extinct at the end of the Mesozoic Era. Mammals and birds became the important animals of the Cenozoic Era. During this time there were many changes in the kinds of mammals living on the earth. Horses changed from tiny mammals to the larger mammals we know today. Many strange, giant-sized mammals lived and became extinct. Early people may have caused some of them to become extinct by overhunting. The oldest humanlike fossils date from about 2 million years ago.

Investigate

How can you show events in the history of the earth?

You will need

tape, paper, pencil, meterstick, reference books on geology

Background

It is not always easy to realize the great amounts of time that are involved in the history of the earth. One way to do so is to diagram events on a time line. A time line has a scale in which a given length represents a certain number of years. In making your time line, 1 mm will be used to represent 1 million years.

What to do

Cut strips of paper about 10 cm wide. Tape several strips together until you have a strip that is 4.6 m long. Using 1 mm to represent 1 million years, mark the information from the table on your strip. Each date is given in millions of years ago. Use this book and other reference books to mark in other dates you think are important.

Now that you have done the investigation

- What length on your time line represents the time from the beginning of earth history to the time fossils became common?
- What information other than what is in the table did you add to your time line?
- How does a time line help you show the great length of geologic time?

Date	Label	Date	Label
4,600	Beginning of the earth's history	325	Reptiles
4,000	Oldest rock	290	Allegheny Mountains
3,000	Oldest fossils	200	Pangaea
600	Fossils become common	180	Pangaea began breaking up
410	Land plants	135	Dinosaurs
400	Caledonian Mountains	130	Rocky Mountains
380	Insects, amphibians	2	People

CHANGING CONDITIONS

What changes in the air may have taken place?
What changes in the water may have taken place?
How is the climate thought to have changed?

Changes in the air

The air is made up of many different gases. About four fifths of the air is *nitrogen* [NY-truh-juhn]. Two other gases in the air that are important to living things today are *oxygen* [AHK-sih-juhn] and *carbon dioxide* [KAHR-buhn dy-AHK-syd]. Almost all living things use oxygen to get energy from their food. Plants and plantlike protists use carbon dioxide to make food.

Scientists think that the makeup of air may have been different during the early history of the earth. For example, certain kinds of rock can form only when oxygen gas is present. However, these kinds of rock do not seem to have been formed earlier than 2.5 billion years ago. Oxygen gas, or free oxygen as it is sometimes called, may not have been part of the air at that time.

If free oxygen became an important part of the air about 2.5 billion years ago, living things probably caused this change. Certain one-celled living things use sunlight in making food. As they make food, they give off oxygen. Certain old fossils look like tiny living things called *monerans* [muh-NIHR-uhnz]. For this reason, scientists think some early living things made their own food and gave off oxygen. If so, these early living things caused an important change in the air.

☐ **How might free oxygen becoming part of the air have caused changes in living things?**

Figure 20–8. Fossil algae such as those shown here may be more than one meter (about three feet) across.

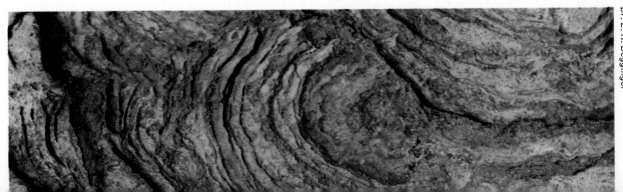

Dr. E. R. Degginger

Changes in the water

The water in rivers and in most lakes is fresh water. The water in the oceans is salt water. The terms "fresh water" and "salt water" are used to refer to the amount of salt dissolved in water. Fresh water has only a very small amount of salt in it. Salt water has more than three times the salt found in fresh water.

Today there are many kinds of animals and plants that live in water. Some live only in fresh water. Some live only in salt water. A few live in places where rivers flow into the oceans. The water in such places is more salty than fresh water but less salty than seawater.

As a rule, living things that live only in fresh water cannot live in salt water. Those that live only in salt water cannot live in fresh water. This is due to differences in the body of each of these living things.

The oldest fossils have been found in rocks that were formed in oceans. But scientists are not sure if these early oceans were as salty as the oceans are today. Some even think that the water in the early oceans was fresh water. Therefore, scientists do not know if early living things lived in fresh water or in salt water. If the early oceans were fresh water, some living things must have changed

Cameramasters

Do It Yourself

Observe the effect of salt water on an Elodea leaf

Elodea is a freshwater plant often used in aquariums. Place an *Elodea* leaf on a microscope slide. Cover the leaf with a coverslip and observe the leaf cells through a microscope.

Lift the coverslip and cover the leaf with a solution of very salty water. Wait a few minutes and again observe the leaf cells through the microscope. What changes, if any, did you observe in the cells of the leaf? What might happen to living things that were used to fresh water if the water became salty?

in order to be able to live in oceans that are salty today. If, on the other hand, the early oceans were salty, some living things must have changed in order to be able to live in freshwater lakes and rivers. Of course such changes must have taken place slowly over many hundreds of millions of years.

Changes in the climate

Suppose you tell a friend that the temperature is 25°C (77°F) and that it is raining where you live. You would be describing the weather. However, you might describe where you live as having cold winters, cool springs and falls, and hot summers. In this case, you would be describing the *climate* [KLY-muht]. Climate is a general weather pattern for a place over a number of years.

Each part of the earth has its own climate. However, many of these places have had very different climates in the past. For example, less than 20,000 years ago most of Canada and the northern part of the United States was covered by thick glaciers. These places had a climate somewhat like that of Antarctica and northern Alaska today.

There have been several ice ages during the long history of the earth. Places that are hot and dry today, such as the Sahara Desert, were once covered by large glaciers. On the other hand, many places that are cold today once had warmer climates. Fossils of tropical plants have been found in Greenland. Today, most of Greenland is covered by thick glaciers.

Animals and plants living today live in many different climates. As a rule, living things suited to live in one kind of climate do not live in places having a very different climate. That is, those that live in the tropics do not live in the arctic, and so on.

Over millions of years, the climate in many places has changed. As the climate changed, the kinds of animals and plants able to live in those places also changed. Scientists have found clues to many such changes in climate in the fossil record.

Find Out More

Use references such as encyclopedias and biology books to compare mammoths and mastodons with elephants. Where did the mammoths and mastodons live? Where do elephants live today? How does the appearance of mammoths and mastodons differ from that of elephants?

For example, at one time there were tropical forests in what is now Pennsylvania. Millions of years later, cool-climate plants such as oaks and maples had replaced the tropical trees. Oaks and maples are able to live in a cooler and drier climate. During the ice ages, glaciers moved down from the north. Part of Pennsylvania was covered by ice. The rest of it was too cold for oaks and maples to grow. The oaks and maples died out in that area. Of course, this change did not happen overnight. It took thousands of years. During that time, some of the oaks and maples were still growing and forming seeds. The seeds were carried long distances by wind and water. Some of these seeds began to grow in somewhat warmer land to the south. As the climate changed, the glaciers melted. In time, Pennsylvania again became warm enough for oaks and maples to grow there.

☐ **What things might happen to animals living in a given place as the climate slowly changes?**

Figure 20–9. Would you expect to find tropical trees or glaciers in Pennsylvania today? Why or why not?

Atoz Images

Artstreet

402

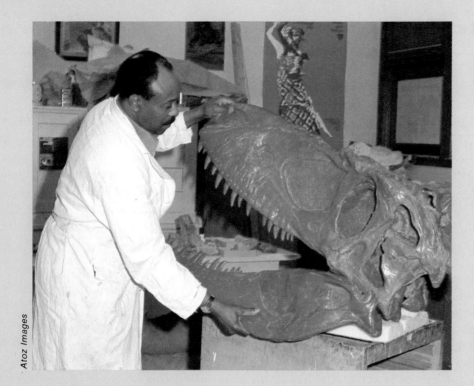

Many paleontologists work for museums. In addition to studying fossils, they prepare exhibits to show other people what they have learned.

Careers

Paleontologist

Have you ever wondered what dinosaurs were really like? Many scientists have. Scientists who study living things of the past, such as dinosaurs, are called *paleontologists* [PAY-lee-AHN-TAHL-uh-juhsts]. For many years paleontologists thought dinosaurs were cold-blooded reptiles. That is, they were something like the snakes, lizards, and crocodiles living today. In recent years new evidence about dinosaurs has been discovered. For example, some dinosaur bones look like the bones of warm-blooded animals such as birds, dogs, cats, and people. So, many dinosaurs may have been warm-blooded. Some seem to have taken care of their young.

What became of the dinosaurs? Paleontologists do not know. They only know that the dinosaurs disappeared about 65 million years ago. Perhaps someday you might want to become a paleontologist. Perhaps you will study dinosaurs and try to find out what happened to them. If so, you will have to learn a great deal about fossils. You will also need to know something about the different kinds of animals living today.

To find out about the career of a paleontologist, a student in your class might write to the American Geological Institute, 5205 Leesburg Pike, Falls Church, VA 22041.

Reviewing and Extending

Summing Up

1. A fossil is the impression, the remains, or any other evidence of a living thing that has been preserved in the earth.
2. Scientists study fossils and the different kinds of rock found in the earth to try to find out how the earth has changed throughout its history.
3. In order to find out the age of rock, scientists measure both the amount of radioactive matter and the amount of new matter formed by radioactive matter that has changed.
4. The history of the earth is measured in geologic time. The earth is thought to be 4,600 million (4.6 billion) years old.
5. Geologic time is usually divided into four eras—the Precambrian Era, the Paleozoic Era, the Mesozoic Era, and the Cenozoic Era.
6. There were major changes in the earth and in the kinds of living things during each era.
7. Scientists believe that there have been major changes in the makeup of the air, in the amount of salt in seawater, and in the climates of different parts of the earth throughout geologic time.
8. Changes in the air, the water, and the climate may have had many different effects on the different kinds of living things on the earth.

Checking Up

Vocabulary Write the numerals 1–8 on your paper. Each numbered phrase describes a term from the following list. On your paper, write the term next to the numeral of the phrase that describes it.

fossil	extinct	dinosaur
billion	climate	Pangaea
carbon dioxide	trilobite	oxygen

1. number equal to a thousand million
2. the impression, the remains, or any other evidence of a living thing that has been preserved in the earth
3. gas of the air used by living things to get energy from food
4. general weather pattern for a place over a number of years
5. important group of animals that lived during the Mesozoic Era
6. term used to describe animals and plants no longer living on the earth
7. name that is given to a supercontinent that scientists think existed about 200 million years ago
8. important group of animals that lived during the Paleozoic Era

Knowledge and Understanding Write the numerals *9–18* on your paper. Beside each numeral, write the answer that best completes the sentence having that numeral.

9. During the last ice age, huge sheets of ice called (*moraines, glaciers, gneiss*) covered the northern half of the United States.
10. The earth is thought to be (*65; 600; 4.6*) billion years old.
11. Scientists divide geologic time into parts called (*eras, seconds, fossils*).
12. The name (*Gondwanaland, Laurasia, Siberia*) is used for an early continent that is thought to have included what today are Africa, South America, Australia, Antarctica, and India.
13. One gas in the air that appears to have become part of the air about 2.5 billion years ago and is important to living things today is (*oxygen, nitrogen, carbon dioxide*).
14. The oldest known fossils are about (*3,000; 300; 30*) million years old.
15. Finding granite and gneiss in a place that has flat plains is a clue that once there may have been (*seas, rivers, mountains*) in that place.
16. Mammals became an important group of living things during the (*Precambrian, Paleozoic, Cenozoic*) Era.
17. The longest era in geologic history is the (*Precambrian, Paleozoic, Mesozoic*) Era.
18. Toward the end of the Paleozoic Era two groups of animals appeared. These were the amphibians and the (*jellyfish, fish, reptiles*).

Expressing Yourself Write a paragraph as an answer to each of the following questions:

19. How would you explain the fact that many fossils of sea animals are found throughout the Rocky Mountains?
20. How does the fossil record show changes in the earth?

Doing More

1. Form some clay into a block about 15 cm square and about 5 cm thick. Press an item such as a shell, a stick, or your hand into the clay. Gently remove the item you pressed into the clay. Mix some plaster of paris, and pour it into the impression in the clay. Set the clay aside until the plaster dries. Gently remove the plaster object from the clay. Show the "fossil" of your object to the class.
2. Use references such as geology books and books on fossils to find out what kinds of living things lived during each era. Make a chart showing the different eras and some of the living things that lived during each era.

G. R. Roberts

The world-famous Wellington fault line in New Zealand separates two blocks of the earth's crust in almost a straight line.

21 Plate Tectonics

Think about a dinner plate. It is thin, flat, and rigid. A dinner plate can give you an idea of the makeup of the earth's crust. Earth scientists now believe the earth's *crust,* or outer layer, is made up of seven major plates and at least twenty smaller plates. Like a dinner plate, each of the earth's plates is thin, flat, and rigid.

Not only do scientists think the earth's crust is made up of plates, but they believe the plates are slowly moving. Keep in mind that, if the plates move, the continents must move with them. The idea of moving plates is a part of a widely accepted theory about the earth's crust today.

The theory is not as simple as it might sound because scientists do not know all there is to know about the moving plates. The theory of *plate tectonics* [tehk-TAHN-ihks], or the idea that the earth's crust is made up of rigid plates that fit together and move slowly, is still rather new.

The theory of plate tectonics is based on another theory known as the theory of *continental* [KAHNT-uhn-EHNT-uhl] *drift.* According to this theory, the continents have drifted from the places in which they were once located. You can learn more about the moving plates of the earth's crust by studying this chapter.

CONTINENTAL DRIFT

Who started the theory of continental drift?
What evidence did Wegener obtain from fossils
and continental shelves?
How do rocks and past climates support the
theory of continental drift?

Drifting continents

You read in Chapter 20, "Geologic History," that many scientists believe there was only one continent at the end of the Paleozoic Era. They call this supercontinent *Pangaea*. They think Pangaea broke up and drifted apart to form the continents of today. But who first proposed this idea and what evidence was used to back it up?

The modern theory of plate tectonics was started by a German astronomer and meteorologist named Alfred Wegener (1880–1930). He presented his ideas on what came to be known as *continental drift* in 1912. But these ideas were not generally accepted in the years that followed because Wegener could not fully explain the cause of the drifting continents. Also, many people simply did not believe that the continents could move. In fact, Wegener ideas were laughed at by some people. As a result, his ideas were largely ignored until the 1960's.

□ **Would you say that Alfred Wegener was probably a scientist whose ideas were ahead of his time? Explain.**

Wegener's evidence

Like a few other scientists of his time, Wegener noticed that if it were not for the Atlantic Ocean, the coastlines of several of the present-day continents would fit together. But Wegener also compared the edges of the *continental*

Historical Pictures Service

Figure 21–1. Alfred Wegener was trained as an astronomer, but he spent most of his life working as a meteorologist. He is best remembered for his theory of continental drift, which has little to do with either astronomy or meteorology.

shelves, or undersea platforms of the continents, rather than just the coastlines. He found that the continental shelves fit together even better than the coastlines. Then he began to look for other bits of evidence to show that the continents were once connected.

The fossils found on present-day continents provided further evidence. For example, Wegener knew that fossils of *Mesosaurus* [MEHZ-uh-SAWR-uhs], a small reptile that lived about 270 million years ago, are found only in South Africa and in Brazil. He believed that these land areas must have been connected at one time because this animal could not have crossed the ocean.

Fossils of *Lystrosaurus* [LIHS-truh-SAWR-uhs] a sheep-sized reptile that lived in Antarctica, Africa, and India about 200 million years ago, are recent discoveries in support of Wegener's theory. This animal had to have lived in a climate warmer than Antarctica is today. Like *Mesosaurus*, it could not have crossed the ocean.

As another bit of evidence, Wegener recognized that the rock of the continents is lighter than the rock of the sea-floor. This difference in rock is one thing that sets the seafloor apart from the surface of the continents.

In Wegener's time and for many years afterward, many scientists believed there once were land bridges between

MESOSAURUS

Figure 21–2. Mesosaurus *was a small, crocodilelike reptile. Do you think such an animal could have crossed thousands of miles of ocean?*

Mary Elenz Tranter

Do It Yourself

Fitting continents together

Use a piece of thin paper to trace the outline of the world's continents from a world map. The outline of the continents should be close to their true shape as shown on a globe.

Use scissors to cut out the tracings of the continents. Paste or glue each of the continents to a sheet of thin cardboard. Cut out each of the continents from the thin cardboard. Then arrange the continents as they are on the world map and move them together so that they form one super-continent. Which continents seem to fit together well? Which continents do not?

the continents. They believed the bridges later sank into the ocean. But Wegener knew that the rock of the continents had to be lighter than the rock of the seafloor. He was sure the land could not sink into the seafloor. It could not sink into a material that was heavier than itself.

Additional evidence comes from the kinds of rock found on today's continents. Wegener knew that large amounts of the same kind of rock could be found on the continents of Africa and South America exactly where they would be found if the continents once fit together. Wegener believed that the rocks matched, just as if a person were to fit torn pieces of a newspaper together by matching their edges and checking to see whether or not the lines of print ran smoothly across.

Climate as evidence

Several years after stating his theory, Wegener studied past changes in world climate. Glaciers, he noticed, left evidence of a change in climate. A glacier forms in a cold climate. But the deposits that some glaciers left on the earth many years ago are now found in warm climates. Did the deposits move from one climate to another by means of continental drift?

Salt beds and coal beds provided Wegener with more evidence. Salt beds are formed by the evaporation of salt water. This evaporation can only take place in a hot, dry climate. It cannot take place in the cool, moist places where many salt beds can now be found. Coal forms in a hot, wet climate. But many coal beds are now found in cooler climates.

All together, the evidence of past climates makes little sense unless one accepts the idea of continental drift. Continental drift explains the present location of salt beds, coal beds, and certain glacial deposits. Wegener was the first person to use the name "Pangaea" for a supercontinent. This name means "all land" in Greek.

□ **Why, do you suppose, did Wegener use the name "Pangaea" for the supercontinent?**

To Think About

Coal is a plant material that has been changed in many ways to form solid fuel. Why, do you think, is it believed that coal was formed in places that were hot and wet?

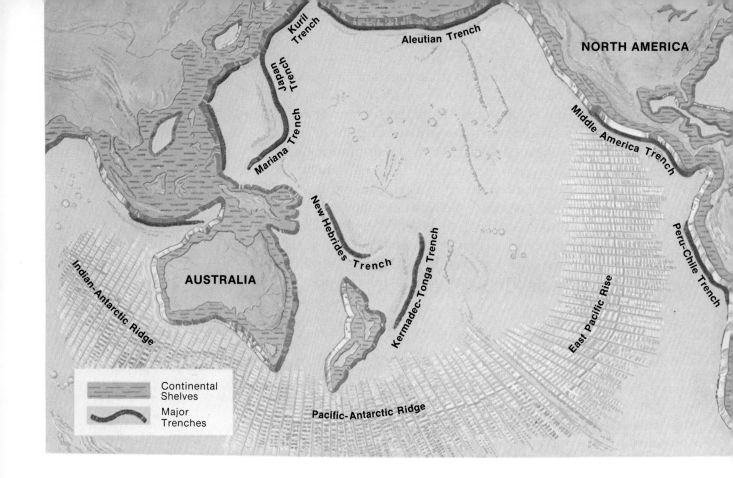

SEAFLOOR SPREADING

What is a ridge on the seafloor?
What is a trench on the seafloor?
What is a rift valley?
How has radioactive dating helped scientists discover where seafloor spreading occurs?
Why have scientists now accepted the idea of continental drift?
What is paleomagnetism?

Figure 21–3. This map shows and names many features of the seafloor that are always covered by water. Which features of the seafloor are the most prominent?

Ridges and trenches

Many maps show the continents of the earth in great detail. But few maps show the seafloor. The maps that do show the seafloor show that, like the continents, the seafloor has flat areas, mountainous areas, and deep valleys.

410

Mountain ranges are important features of both the continents and the seafloor. In many places on the seafloor, mountain ranges extend for great distances. The longest of these ranges is found in the middle of the Atlantic Ocean. This range of mountains is called the *Mid-Atlantic Ridge*. Other long mountain ranges below the ocean surface are also called *ridges*. How many other ridges are shown in Figure 21–3?

In addition to the ridges, there are deep valleys, or *trenches*, in the oceans. Most trenches are found in the Pacific Ocean. The deepest of these is the *Mariana* [MAR-ee-AN-uh] *Trench*. The Mariana Trench is located just east and south of the Mariana Islands. How many other trenches are shown in Figure 21–3?

Forming new crust

In recent years, scientists have been able to get rock

To Think About

In addition to the ridges in the ocean at which magma forms new rock, where else on the earth's crust is new rock formed? What is this new rock called?

samples from different parts of the seafloor. Radioactive dating has shown that the rock samples are of different ages. The rocks from near the ridges are not as old as those from farther away. In fact, the farther away from the ridges the rocks are, the older they are.

From rock samples scientists have learned that two plates of the earth's crust are moving apart at each of the ridges. Each plate spreads out from a valley, called a *rift valley*, found in the center of the ridge. The rift valley runs the length of the ridge. It is partly formed by *faults*, or cracks that form in the earth's crust.

The seafloor is being pushed upward within the rift valley. With this push, the seafloor sometimes bulges and cracks. Molten rock comes up from the mantle and fills the crack in the rift valley. As the molten rock cools and hardens to form new seafloor crust, it pushes the older seafloor crust away on both sides of the ridge. This forming of new seafloor crust along the ridge is called *seafloor spreading*.

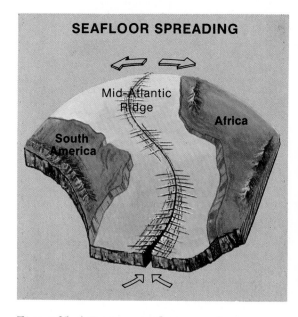

SEAFLOOR SPREADING

Figure 21–4. *Because seafloor spreading takes place, whole continents are pushed apart and new seafloor crust is formed.*

☐ **Suppose seafloor spreading at the Mid-Atlantic Ridge goes along at the rate of 5 centimeters (2 inches) a year. How long would it take for a width of 5 meters, or 500 centimeters (200 inches), of new rock to form?**

Seafloor cycle

As new seafloor crust forms at the ridges, older seafloor crust is pushed toward the trenches (located near continental coastlines). At the trenches, seafloor crust sinks into the mantle of the earth. So, the earth's seafloor is in a cycle—the forming of new crust at the ridges and the sinking of old crust at the trenches.

As the old seafloor crust sinks into the mantle, it becomes molten once again. It becomes a lighter part of the mantle. In time, the lighter, molten rock of the mantle rises to the surface at the ocean ridges. The cycle keeps going. The new rock hardens. Millions of years later, it sinks into the mantle when it reaches the trenches.

When seafloor spreading was discovered, many earth scientists changed their mind about continental drift. They realized that Wegener had been right. If a continent rests on a large plate and that plate moves because of seafloor spreading, then the continent must move along with the plate. Scientists now accept the idea of continental drift.

Paleomagnetism

Other signs of seafloor spreading have been discovered. For many years scientists have known that igneous rock, or rock formed from magma, is weakly magnetic. This rock is magnetic because it has some iron in it. Before magma cools, the bits of iron in the rock are free to turn. Because the earth behaves like a giant magnet, the turning bits of iron line up with the earth's magnetic field. The iron particles point toward the north magnetic pole.

By using a device called a *magnetometer* [MAG-nuh-TAHM-uht-ur], scientists have found that new rock formed near the ridges lines up with the north magnetic pole. But rock farther away from the ridges does not. This older rock lines up in a different way. The farther from the ridge the rock is, the older it is.

The direction of the magnetism of the old rocks is known as *paleomagnetism* [PAY-lee-oh-MAG-nuh-TIHZ-uhm]. If rock of a certain paleomagnetism is found 1 000 kilometers

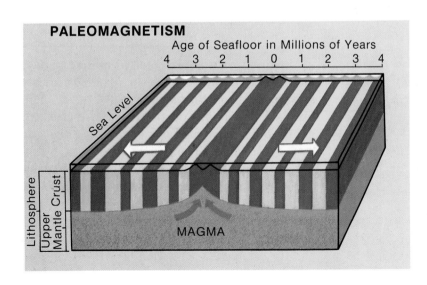

Figure 21–5. *Strips of seafloor from both sides of a ridge match one another. Where are the oldest rocks of the seafloor in relation to a ridge? Where are the youngest rocks?*

413

(600 miles) to one side of a ridge, rock of the same paleo-magnetism is found 1 000 kilometers (600 miles) on the other side. The strips of rock match each other.

The magnetic rocks were formed in the rift valley, a part of the ridge. The difference in the magnetism of the rocks away from the ridge is evidence of seafloor spreading. It also is a sign of continental drift. Paleomagnetism shows the direction in which the rocks move.

Scientists also believe that the earth's magnetic field has reversed itself from time to time in the past. That is, north has been south, and south has been north. In fact, studies of paleomagnetism on different rocks of the continents and of the seafloor show that the earth's magnetic field has reversed many times in the past.

Scientists do not know why the magnetic field of the earth reverses. But some scientists believe the reversal may be caused by changes in the way the earth rotates. Some believe it may also be caused by changes in the earth's *core,* or center, which is believed to be made up of a great deal of iron.

☐ **Why, do you think, can scientists find a continuous record of reversals of the earth's magnetic field on the seafloor?**

Find Out More

Use references to find out when scientists think the earth's magnetic field was last reversed. Also try to find out what the average length of time for a reversal is. Are we overdue or not overdue for a reversal?

Ed Hoppe Photography

Do It Yourself

Compare a bar magnet's magnetic field with the earth's magnetic field

Obtain a bar magnet, some iron filings, and a large piece of paper. Place the magnet on a flat surface and place the paper on top of the magnet. Sprinkle iron filings on the piece of paper and gently tap the paper. Look at the pattern made by the iron filings. The pattern made by the iron filings shows the magnetic field of the magnet. The earth's magnetic field is similar to that of a bar magnet. The bar magnet has a north pole and a south pole; so does the earth. In regard to magnetism, in what other ways are the bar magnet and the earth alike? Different?

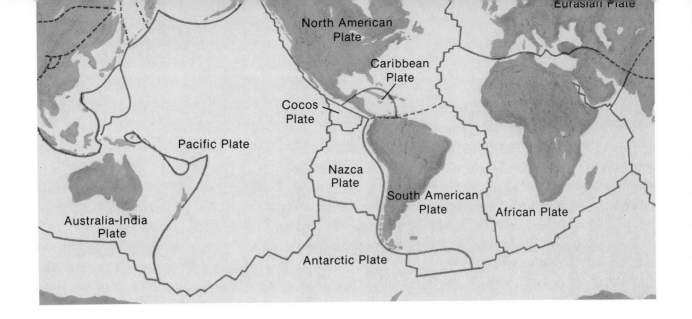

Figure 21–6. *Study the map of the boundaries of the major plates of the earth's crust. Why, do you think, do scientists believe that certain boundaries are fairly accurate?*

PLATES OF THE EARTH'S CRUST

What are the seven major plates of the crust?

How do scientists think convection currents cause seafloor spreading and plate movement?

What causes faults on the earth's crust?

Where do many of the faults occur on the crust?

Plate boundaries

Scientists now have a great deal of evidence that the plates of the earth's crust are moving. But how many major plates are there? What are their boundaries?

Some of the boundaries between plates are at the ridges on the seafloor where new rock is forming. Other boundaries are at the trenches where part of the crust is sinking. Still others are on land. The major plates of the earth's crust and their boundaries are shown in Figure 21–6. The plates are the following:

Australia-India Plate   African Plate   Eurasian Plate
North American Plate   Pacific Plate   Antarctic Plate
South American Plate

☐ **Of the seven major plates, which one consists mostly of seafloor?**

To Think About

The boundaries between plates change with the passing of time. Can a plate of the earth's crust also change its shape with the passing of time? Explain.

415

Convection currents

Many scientists believe the core of the earth is hot. They also believe that the mantle of the earth is hot and that parts of it may flow. Because there is heat within the earth, many scientists believe there are *convection currents* [kuhn-VEHK-shuhn KUR-uhnts] within the earth. These currents may help to explain why there is seafloor spreading and why the plates of the earth's crust move.

To understand how convection currents work, think about water being heated in a pan. Water near the bottom of the pan becomes hot before the water near the surface does. The hot water rises through the cooler water to the surface. As the hotter water reaches the surface, it cools slightly. At the same time, the cooler water that was at the top moves to the bottom of the pan, where it is heated. These movements of water are convection currents.

In the earth, the convection currents are believed to be an interaction between the *magma* [MAG-muh], or molten rock within the earth, and the soft rock of the mantle. Scientists know that the mantle is hot and that this rock behaves somewhat differently from the way the cooler rock of the crust behaves. Some scientists believe that some of this hot rock can flow without having melted. That is, it behaves somewhat like soft tar.

(*Text continues on page 418.*)

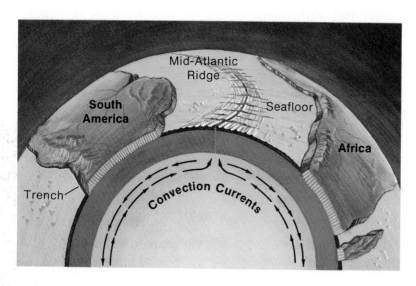

Figure 21–7. Under what features of the earth's crust does magma rise? Under what features of the crust does rock sink into the mantle?

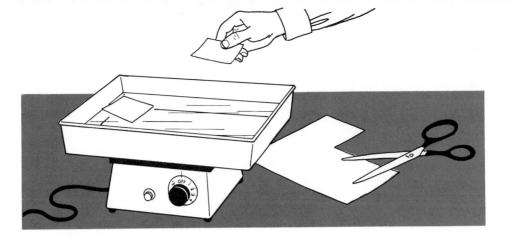

Investigate

How can you show how convection currents from the mantle might affect the surface of the earth?

You will need

scissors, hot plate, piece of typing paper, Pyrex dish or metal baking pan that is much larger than the surface of the hot plate

Background

One explanation of the forces that cause the plates of the earth's crust to move is that these forces result from convection currents. Convection currents are used every day in cooking. In fact, convection currents can be observed when you boil water.

In this activity you will observe how convection currents in a pan of water that is being heated may cause movements at the surface of the water. If the water is heated from below, the bottom part of the water will become heated first. Then the water from the bottom will begin to move toward the surface by means of convection currents.

What to do

Fill the pan about half full of water and place it on the hot plate. The water represents the mantle of the earth and the hot plate represents the hot core of the earth.

Use the scissors to cut two squares out of the white paper. The squares should be about 8 cm x 8 cm or larger. The pieces of paper represent the earth's crust. Place the two pieces of paper on the surface of the water but do not let the top side of the pieces of paper get wet. Move the pieces of paper so that they are touching each other on one edge. They should be together in the center of the pan. Turn the hot plate to low heat and watch what happens to the pieces of paper in the pan as the water warms up.

Now that you have done the investigation

■ What happened to the pieces of paper as the convection currents began moving water to the surface?

■ With what part of the earth's crust might you compare the places where the two squares were joined?

■ If the sides of the pan represent the trenches of the ocean, what would happen to the moving pieces at these places?

Scientists have suggested that convection currents are formed in the mantle. These convection currents cause hot, partly melted mantle rock to rise, to move some distance under the plates of the crust, and then to sink. As the hot rock flows beneath the crustal plates, the plates are made to move. See Figure 21–7.

Faults

Up to now, you have been reading about seafloor spreading and moving crustal plates. But other things happen in the earth's crust, too. Plate tectonics involves more than seafloor spreading and moving plates. For example, there are faults that occur on the earth's crust. Faults are breaks in the crust.

Changes in the earth cause the rock of the crust to be pushed and pulled in different directions. The pushes and pulls, or *forces*, acting on the crust cause rock to bend. If the amount of force is great enough, the rock breaks. Each break is a fault.

A fault divides the rock into two parts. Forces acting on the two parts push them in different directions. At the same time, the surfaces of the rock on each side of the fault

Figure 21–8. Places where earthquakes occur on the earth are indicated. Do more earthquakes seem to occur in the continents or in the seafloor?

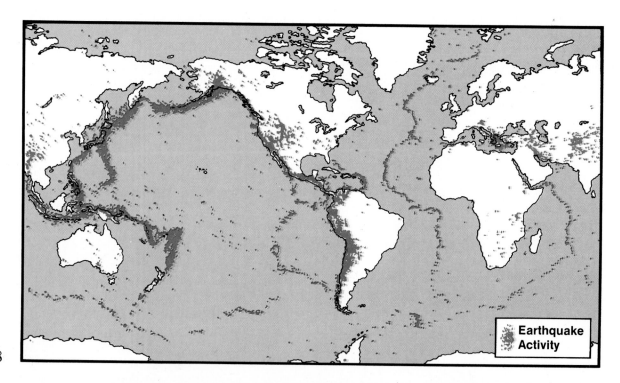

Earthquake Activity

rub against each other. Whenever rock surfaces rub together, there is *friction* [FRIHK-shuhn]. Friction is a force that keeps two objects that rub together from moving.

Stress builds up in rock that is being pushed by one force and is being kept from moving by friction. When the amount of stress becomes great enough, the rock moves along the fault. That is, the rock moves whenever the amount of force pushing the rock overcomes the friction acting on the rock. When the rock moves, there is an *earthquake* [URTH-kwayk].

Many earthquakes occur on the seafloor. Many of these shake the earth at the ridges, where seafloor spreading is under way. But many also occur at the trenches, where part of the crust is sinking into the mantle. See Figure 21–8. Compare the boundaries of the plates of the crust in Figure 21–6 and the points of earthquake activity in Figure 21–8.

☐ **Most of the new rock is being added to the crust in the Atlantic Ocean, whereas most of the trenches where part of the crust is sinking into the mantle are in the Pacific Ocean. How might this affect the size of each of the oceans over millions of years?**

MOUNTAIN-BUILDING ACTIVITY

What is a divergent boundary? A convergent boundary?

How does the idea of moving plates explain how some mountains are formed?

What are two explanations of why the land rises and sinks other than by movements of the plates of the earth's crust?

Mountains and faults

The idea that the plates of the earth's crust move has been used to explain how mountains and other surface features of the earth may form. The plates may move apart, collide with each other, or slide past each other. In each case, the moving plates cause changes in the earth's crust.

Find Out More

One important site of major earthquakes in the United States is the San Andreas Fault in California. Use references such as encyclopedias and magazines to find out about the San Andreas Fault. Where is the San Andreas Fault located? Is it a single fault, or is it made up of many faults?

A boundary separates two plates when they come close to each other. The boundary between plates that move apart is known as a *divergent* [duh-VUR-juhnt] *boundary*. Sometimes two plates bump against each other, or *collide*. The boundary between colliding plates is called a *convergent* [kuhn-VUR-juhnt] *boundary*.

When two plates move apart at an ocean ridge, magma rises from the mantle to the surface. In other words, a volcano erupts. Lava flows on the seafloor and, in time, a volcanic mountain is formed. The ocean ridges are made up largely of such mountains.

Mountains are also formed when two plates collide. When the plates come together, the edges of the plates are bent and folded. See Figure 21–10. With this bending and folding, rocks pile up and form mountains. Earth scientists believe the Alps and the Himalayas were formed in this way. The collision of two plates also formed the Appalachian Mountains a long time ago.

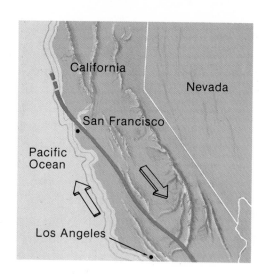

Figure 21–9. This illustration shows how the Pacific Plate and the North American Plate are moving, one in regard to the other, in California. How, do you suppose, do scientists know about the movements of these plates?

G. R. Roberts

Figure 21–10. Some folded limestone rocks in England are pictured. Note the people at the very top of the rock formation. How would you describe the forces within the earth that can cause rock to bend in this strange way?

In some places, two crustal plates slide past each other. A large fault—the cause of many earthquakes—often lies between the sliding plates. The San Andreas Fault in California is an example of such a fault. This long fracture extends more than 1 200 kilometers (750 miles) from northern California to the southern part of the state.

The crust along the coast from San Francisco to the Gulf of California rides on the Pacific Plate. The part of the state east of the San Andreas Fault rides on the North American Plate. The Pacific Plate is moving slowly toward the northwest, and the North American Plate is moving slowly toward the southwest. See the map in Figure 21–9.

☐ **If the North American Plate and the Pacific Plate continue to move as they are now moving, where will the land now occupied by the city of Los Angeles be at some time in the future? Explain.**

To Think About

The Pacific Plate is thought to be moving toward the northwest. The North American Plate is thought to be moving toward the southwest. What effect might these two movements have on the state of California?

Mary Elenz Tranter

Do It Yourself

Show how moving plates may form mountains by folding

Using 3 different colors of clay, make 6 slabs, 2 of each color, about 10 cm wide by 12 cm long and about 1 cm thick. Make 2 blocks by placing the different-colored clay slabs on top of one another as shown in the illustration. Think of these blocks as plates of the earth's crust. Each layer of colored clay represents a different rock layer.

Place a square piece of waxed paper on a flat surface, and place the two blocks of clay on the waxed paper. Slowly push the two blocks together. Notice what happens to the clay as the blocks are pushed together. In what way or ways does what happens to the clay resemble what happens to rock when mountains are formed by folding? Suppose the bottom layer of clay represents the oldest rock and the top layer of clay represents the youngest rock. How would you explain finding older rock on top of younger rock in mountains that had been formed by folding?

Rising and sinking land

Not all scientists agree that mountains and other features of the earth have been formed as a result of the movements of the plates of the earth's crust. In fact, even the scientists who believe that the plates move have not been able to explain how the Rocky Mountains and the plateau in which the Grand Canyon is found could have been formed by plate movements.

People have known for many years that the surface of the land may rise or sink. For example, there are several old buildings in Italy that were once on dry land but have since sunk below the surface of the seawater. In Norway, there are rings fastened into cliffs that were once used to tie up ships. These rings are now far above the level of the water.

Scientists have several explanations of why the land rises and sinks. One explanation takes into account the effects of weathering and erosion. Weathering and erosion remove matter from one place and carry it to another place. After thousands of years, places from which a great deal of matter has been removed by weathering and erosion push down with less force. But the places where weathered matter has been deposited push down with more force. In time, the surface rises or sinks until the forces are again in balance. Such changes in the balance of forces may cause the earth's surface to be bent and faulted. Mountains may be formed as a result.

Many scientists think there is another explanation for rising and sinking land. They believe that rising magma causes some of the uplift, or pushing up, of the earth's surface. They suggest that large amounts of magma push up toward, but do not reach, the earth's surface. This causes large areas of land to be uplifted. To maintain the balance within the earth, other areas of land have to sink. Scientists think that much of the land in the western part of the United States was uplifted in this way.

☐ **What reasons can you give to explain why scientists do not agree on what causes large areas of land to be uplifted?**

R. Thompson/Taurus

Figure 21–11. The Grand Canyon is evidence of land that had been rising for many years. Scientists believe that the Colorado River could not have cut into the rock so deeply unless the land was rising at the same time that the river was cutting through the rock.

Find Out More

Using references, find out how much the Scandinavian countries have been rising along the coasts each year. What do scientists think is the cause of the rising land?

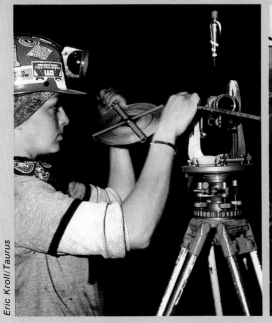

Careers

Mining Engineer

A mining engineer has the responsibility of coordinating the surveying, the mining, and the transporting of ore. Why are these jobs more difficult if the ore is obtained from the seafloor?

The ridges of the seafloor are rich in minerals that come from magma. These minerals will be mined in the future as the need for certain minerals increases. *Mining engineers* are concerned with the mining of minerals that are present on the seafloor. The kind of mining that will have to be done on the seafloor will be much different from the kind that is usually done on land.

Mining engineers supervise mining operations and are responsible for mine safety. But it is unknown at the present time what the best way of mining the seafloor is. The mining engineer will have the responsibility of selecting the methods to be used in mining the minerals and in transporting them to the surface (either to waiting ships or via a pipeline to a nearby continent). Mining engineers also make surveys of the amounts of minerals in a particular location in order to try to figure out if it will be profitable to obtain minerals at that location.

If the idea of being a mining engineer appeals to you, you should take as much mathematics as possible. Physics and chemistry are the most valuable sciences for a mining engineer, although the earth sciences are also valuable. Some college courses are needed. Most positions require a bachelor's degree or a higher degree in engineering. Some colleges and universities require that a person take more than a four-year program for a degree in engineering. But sometimes a student can work part-time as a mining engineer and take engineering courses at a nearby college at the same time to get his or her degree.

The career of a mining engineer will be a good one for the future because more metals from minerals will be needed. If these minerals cannot be obtained from the land or from the seafloor, they may even have to be obtained from the moon or from nearby planets.

Reviewing and Extending

Summing Up

1. The theory of plate tectonics is the idea that the earth's crust is made up of rigid plates that fit together and move slowly.
2. Alfred Wegener proposed the idea that the continents of the earth move—the theory of continental drift.
3. As evidence of continental drift, Wegener used the edges of the continental shelves, the fossils on different continents, and the rocks on different continents.
4. Many scientists disagreed with Wegener during his lifetime, but seafloor spreading now supports his theory.
5. Paleomagnetism has helped to show that seafloor spreading occurs.
6. Earth scientists believe that convection currents provide the force that moves the crustal plates.
7. The movement of crustal plates causes volcanoes and earthquakes.
8. The coming together of two crustal plates builds mountains.
9. A divergent boundary lies between two crustal plates that are moving apart.
10. A convergent boundary lies between two crustal plates that are colliding.
11. A large fault lies between two crustal plates that are sliding past each other.
12. Land may rise and sink as a result of weathered matter being moved from one place to another and as a result of magma pushing up toward the earth's surface.

Checking Up

Vocabulary   Write the numerals *1–10* on your paper. Each numbered phrase describes a term from the following list. On your paper, write the term next to the numeral of the phrase that describes it.

plate	Pangaea	plate tectonics
fault	trenches	seafloor spreading
magma	friction	continental shelves
ridges	paleomagnetism	convection currents

1. undersea platforms of the continents
2. deep valleys on the seafloor
3. idea that large plates of the earth's crust move
4. mountainous areas on the seafloor
5. direction of the magnetism in old rocks
6. break in the earth's crust
7. molten rock that is formed in the mantle
8. single continent believed to have existed in the past
9. fact that now supports the theory of continental drift.
10. force caused by the rubbing of two objects against each other

Knowledge and Understanding Write the numerals *11–17* on your paper. Beside each numeral, write the word or words that best complete the sentence having that numeral.

11. The plates of North America and Eurasia are (*moving toward the poles, sinking, moving apart*).
12. When the plates of two continents are pushed together, the result is the formation of (*mountains, trenches, new crust*).
13. The San Andreas Fault is located between the North American Plate and the (*South American Plate, Pacific Plate, Mexican Plate*).
14. The force that is believed to move the plates of the earth's crust is (*gravity, heat and pressure, convection currents*).
15. The ridges of the seafloor are places where the earth's crust is (*sinking, spreading apart, coming together*).
16. The idea of continental drift was revived when rock samples from the seafloor were (*dated, moved, worn away by erosion*).
17. The idea of continental drift was proposed by (*San Andreas, Pangaea, Wegener*).

Expressing Yourself Write a paragraph as an answer to each of the following questions:

18. How has paleomagnetism been used to discover facts about the past positions of the poles of the earth?
19. What are two explanations, other than plate movements, of why land areas rise or sink?

Doing More

1. Use references such as encyclopedias, magazine articles, and books about rocks and minerals to find out what kinds of rocks and minerals are believed to form on the seafloor in connection with the ridges. What amounts of these rocks and minerals form at the ridges as compared with the amounts formed on land areas? What agreements might have to be made between nations as a result of the facts you have read about?

2. Using clay and two large, flat pieces of wood, make a model of a portion of the seafloor. Use the illustrations in this chapter as your guide. You should show what happens at a plate boundary on your model. What part of the seafloor does your model represent? What is happening to the earth's crust at this place? How would you use your model to explain the movements of the plates of the earth's crust?

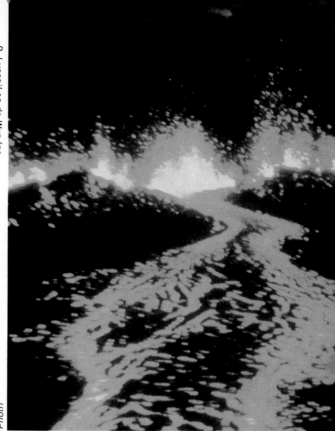

P. Lucas/Leo de Wys Inc.

Photri

Lava flowing down the side of a volcano and earthquake damage to a city are pictured. Which of these, do you think, is the more destructive?

22 Eruptions and Quakes

Have you heard about the Mount St. Helens *volcano* [vahl-KAY-noh] in the state of Washington? Almost everyone has. Also, have you heard about the major earthquake in Guatemala in 1976? Perhaps not, but you have certainly heard about earthquakes. If you live in a part of the country in which earthquakes are common, chances are you have felt an earthquake, too.

Both volcanoes and earthquakes have a great deal to do with plate tectonics, or the slow moving of the plates of the earth's crust. In fact, the moving of the plates causes vol-canoes and earthquakes. If you have never seen a volcano or felt an earthquake, you have a great deal to learn about them. Even if you have seen or felt them in the past, you probably have some questions about volcanoes and earthquakes.

How are volcanoes formed? What kinds of materials come from volcanoes? What different kinds of volcanoes are known to exist? What causes earthquakes? How are earthquakes detected far from their source? Many questions about volcanoes and earthquakes are answered in this chapter.

VOLCANOES

What is a volcano? How does it form?
Where are most of the volcanoes in the world found?
How are magma and lava different from each other?
What is a volcanic eruption?
What kinds of volcanic rocks may come out of the earth during a volcanic eruption?

How volcanoes form

In Chapter 21, you read about the moving plates of the earth's crust. You also read about trenches and magma. All these things have a great deal to do with plate tectonics and how volcanoes form.

A *volcano* may be described as a vent, or opening, in the earth's crust from which molten rock and gases come out. It may also be described as the cone or mountain that is made up of some of the rock and other materials that come out of a vent.

Volcanoes begin deep in the earth. They are caused by the movement of the earth's crustal plates. Most of the volcanoes in the world are found near trenches. You may remember that trenches are the places where one plate is bending downward and moving beneath another plate. See Figure 22–1.

Figure 22–1. What, do you think, is the relationship between the crust that moves down into the mantle at a trench and the magma that later comes to the surface?

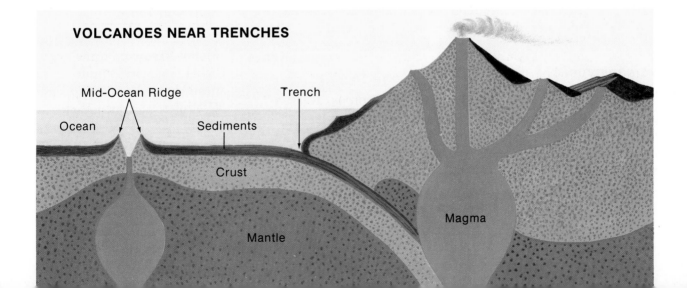

VOLCANOES NEAR TRENCHES

Mid-Ocean Ridge

Trench

Ocean

Sediments

Crust

Magma

Mantle

Volcanic action often marks the edges of the plates that are coming together. Scientists believe that this is because the material from the crust melts as it moves down into the hot mantle. Because the melted material from the crust is lighter than the material in the mantle, it later moves up from the mantle and into the crust as magma.

In time, the pressure of the gases in the rising magma may help to push the magma to the surface. The melting and breaking of the rock of the crust occurs as this happens. When the magma reaches the surface, a volcano *erupts* [ih-RUHPTS]. Rock and other materials may be tossed out suddenly and often violently. This is how a volcano forms.

Magma and lava

Molten rock beneath the surface of the earth is called *magma*. But when magma reaches the surface, or when it is erupted from a volcano, it becomes *lava*. Lava may flow out of a volcano. But it may also flow out of cracks in the earth's surface. In each case the lava cools and becomes solid rock.

Lava is not the only thing that comes out of a volcano. Water in the form of steam rises from the vent. Certain kinds of gases, dust, and ash may also come out. A *volcanic eruption* [vahl-KAN-ihk ih-RUHP-shuhn] occurs when lava, steam, gas, dust, or ash come out of a volcano.

☐ **What might the presence of large amounts of steam in a volcanic eruption indicate about the presence of water in the surface rocks near a volcano?**

Volcanic rocks

Often the first sign of a volcanic eruption is a large column of steam, gases, dust, and ash. This column moves up into the air and may be carried great distances by the wind. Larger pieces, such as *cinders* [SIHN-durz] and *bombs,* may come out after the lighter materials. Cinders are ashlike pieces of rock that are hot but not burning. Bombs are rounded pieces of red-hot rock that are larger

To Think About

Crystals of minerals are found in some lavas that have cooled but not in others. What may happen to crystals in lavas that cool very quickly compared with those in lavas that cool very slowly?

Find Out More

Study a map of Italy. Find Mount Vesuvius on the map. What large city is built near Mount Vesuvius today? Use references such as encyclopedias to find out more about Mount Vesuvius. When did it last erupt? Might it erupt again? If so, what might happen to the people who live near it?

than cinders. Both cinders and bombs fall to the surface near the volcano and add to its size.

Finally, the lava itself may rise through the opening. Most of the lava piles up around the opening of the volcano. It flows over the older rock and the surrounding land. If the eruption continues off and on for several years, the lava may form a tall mountain.

Dust, ash, cinders, and bombs are different-sized forms of volcanic rock. Ash, cinders, and bombs may pile up to help form the cone of a volcano. Or, large amounts of land around a volcano may be covered by thick layers of this matter. In fact, enough matter may come out of a volcano to bury a city. Several cities have been buried in the past. The cities of Pompeii and Herculaneum were buried during an eruption of Mount Vesuvius in A.D. 79. In recent times, towns and villages in Mexico and Iceland have also been buried.

Several kinds of rock may form from lava. The rock may be in the form of *basalt* [buh-SAWLT], which is dark-colored. Also, it may be in the form of *rhyolite* [RY-uh-LYT], which is a rock that is much like granite. The rock may even be in the form of *pumice* [PUHM-uhs], which is full of little holes and very light in weight.

☐ **Pumice is often used in a powdered form for smoothing and polishing metals. Why, do you suppose, is pumice used for this purpose?**

Figure 22–2. What effect might this volcano have on the lives of the people who live near it?

Figure 22–3. A part of the city of Pompeii is pictured. This Roman city was covered by volcanic ash for almost 1700 years. The vegetation that you see grew after the city was uncovered.

Camerique

Do It Yourself
Study pictures of volcanoes

Obtain as many pictures of volcanoes and volcanic areas as you can. Observe how each volcano has changed the surface of the earth. How many different kinds of changes can you identify? What changes, other than those shown by the pictures, could be caused by volcanoes? Select the most interesting pictures and prepare a bulletin-board display of the effects of volcanoes.

KINDS OF VOLCANOES

About how many active volcanoes are there in the world?

How is a shield volcano formed?

What materials make up a cinder cone?

What materials make up a composite volcano?

What happened to the surrounding landscape when Mount St. Helens erupted on May 18, 1980?

Volcanoes of the world

There are about 500 *active volcanoes* on the earth. Although there may be many years between eruptions, volcanoes are called active if they have erupted within historic time. Many other volcanoes are said to be *extinct* [ihk-STIHNG(K)T], or no longer active. There is no record of them erupting, and weathering and erosion have had time to wear them down somewhat. Still others are said to be *dormant* [DAWR-muhnt], or "sleeping." The dormant volcanoes are believed to be able to erupt again someday.

Volcanoes are found in many different places on the earth. Look at Figure 22–4. Notice that some volcanoes are found on continents. But others are found on islands in the oceans. In fact, many of these islands are really the tops of huge volcanic mountains that formed on the sea-

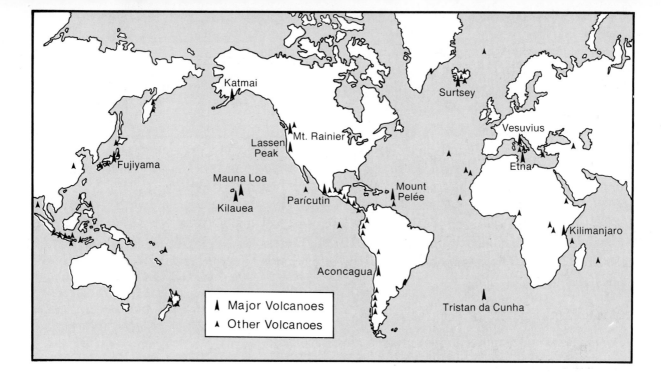

Figure 22–4. *Which of the volcanoes shown on this map have you heard about?*

floor. Iceland and Hawaii are islands that were formed in this way.

☐ **Volcanoes in Iceland and Hawaii erupt every few years. How might this affect the size of these islands?**

There are also volcanic mountains under water. These mountains are known as *seamounts* [SEE-MOWNTS]. Some seamounts are high, but because the ocean is deep where they are found, they do not stick out above the surface of the water. Those that do stick out, of course, are volcanic islands.

Shield volcanoes

One kind of volcano is known as a *shield volcano*. This kind of volcano often forms volcanic islands or seamounts.

The kind of lava that comes from shield volcanoes forms basalt. It flows out quietly from long, thin cracks in the earth. As the lava flows, it spreads out over a wide area. You could think of the lava as forming sheets of rock. In time, these sheets build up into a high structure. If it is high enough, an island is formed.

A shield volcano does not have a peak or steep sides as some volcanoes do. Instead, it has a rounded top or a flat top. This is the reason it has the name "shield." From the top, it looks like a shield. Even without a peak, a shield volcano can be very high.

Each of the Hawaiian Islands is formed by one or more shield volcanoes. The highest of these is Mauna Kea. Its summit is more than 4 200 meters (13,800 feet) above sea level. But it also has a large part of its overall height below sea level. If you add the part of it that is below sea level to its height, Mauna Kea is more than 10 000 meters (33,000 feet) high. This is much higher than other kinds of volcanoes are.

Figure 22–5. Mauna Kea is pictured. It is the highest volcano in Hawaii, but it is considered a dormant volcano. Its sister volcanoes Mauna Loa and Kilauea are active volcanoes.

Cinder cones

A *cinder cone* is much different from a shield volcano. For one thing, it is much smaller in size. It also has a different shape, and it is made up of pieces of lava rather than sheets of lava. A cinder cone is really a cone-shaped hill. It is made up of ash, cinders, bombs, and other pieces of rock tossed out by the eruption.

Most cinder cones are between 60 and 120 meters (200 and 400 feet) high. But they may also be as much as 450 meters (1,500 feet) high. A cinder cone often has a *crater* [KRAYT-ur], or bowl-shaped opening, at the top.

Groups of cinder cones may occur over a wide area of land. For example, there is a group of them north and east of Lassen Peak in northern California. There is also a group of them surrounding the San Francisco Peaks in northern Arizona.

□ **From where, do you suppose, did cinder cones get their name?**

Composite volcanoes

A *composite* [kahm-PAHZ-uht] *volcano* is a combination volcano. The cone is formed by layers of ash, cinders, and bombs and by layers of rock from lava flows.

The lava from a composite volcano often comes out of cracks along the sides of the cone. But the ash, cinders, and

To Think About

Which kind of volcano—a shield volcano, a cinder cone, or a composite volcano—do you think releases the most material? Why?

bombs come out of a crater. All these outpourings pile up to form the cone. The cone may be more than 3 500 meters (12,000 feet) high. It is also very wide. It may be more than 16 kilometers (10 miles) wide at the base.

Mount Hood, in Oregon, is a large composite volcano. So is Fujiyama, in Japan. The cones of such volcanoes are very steep at the top. Many of them also have small glaciers on them.

Composite volcanoes are not as quiet as the shield volcanoes. In fact, composite volcanoes are often very explosive. They may toss out large pieces of rock. They may also release great clouds of ash and dust.

☐ **How would you classify Mount St. Helens—as a shield volcano, as a cinder cone, or as a composite volcano? Why?**

Composite volcanoes may have a *caldera* [kal-DEHR-uh]. A caldera is a large crater. It is formed by the collapse of the center of a volcano or by a great explosion. The caldera has steep sides. Crater Lake, Oregon, is in a caldera. Scientists believe that it was formed when the cone of a volcano collapsed.

The eruption of Mount St. Helens

Like Mount Hood and Mount Rainier, Mount St. Helens is a composite volcano because it has layers of lava and layers of ash, cinders, and bombs. Mount St. Helens is one of a chain of fifteen active volcanoes that extends from northern California to Canada. Any of these volcanoes may erupt at any time.

Many people thought of Mount St. Helens as simply a mountain until it erupted in 1980. It had been quiet for 123 years. But scientists knew that it would erupt again. It has erupted several times since 1980. Scientists believe that it will continue to erupt for several more years.

There were warnings before Mount St. Helens erupted. For example, there were small earthquakes in the area in March of 1980. Smoke and large cracks were seen on March 27. In early April, there were earthquakes of a kind that occurs when there is magma beneath the surface. In

Breck Kent

Figure 22–6. Crater Lake, Oregon, is pictured. The lake is in a caldera. The island in the center, called Wizard Island, is the result of an eruption that occurred after the caldera was formed.

Find Out More

Use references to find out about the eruption of Krakatoa in 1883. What made this eruption one of the worst in history?

433

Figure 22–7. One of the later eruptions of Mount St. Helens and some of the destruction caused by earlier eruptions are pictured.

Michael O'Leary/Picture Group   Ray Atkeson/Photri

late April, the north side of the mountain started to bulge. On May 18, the pressure was just too much, and part of the mountain exploded.

During the 1980 eruption, 49 people were killed or listed as missing. These people were buried or suffocated by the ash. Ash and dirt moved down from higher ground into nearby rivers, blocking the rivers and causing floods. The water in the rivers became so hot that millions of fish were killed. Also, millions of trees were knocked down by the force of the explosion.

The eruption of Mount St. Helens was only a medium-sized eruption. But some of the ash from this volcano was carried around the world by prevailing winds. So much ash fell nearby that travelers were stranded because of slippery roads and automobile accidents. In time, however, the ash from this volcano will become a part of the soil and will enrich the soil.

Kevin Schafer/Tom Stack & Associates

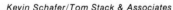

Do It Yourself

Make a model

Using references, try to find out some of the specific effects of the 1980 Mount St. Helens eruption on the mountain itself. Make a clay model to illustrate the mountain before the eruption and then make another model to show what happened to the mountain as a result of the eruption.

EARTHQUAKES

What causes earthquakes?
How does a seismograph work?
*What are seismic waves and how can they be
    used to detect an earthquake?*
How might earthquakes be predicted?

Causes of earthquakes

As you know, an earthquake is a shaking and trembling of the earth. Scientists think there may be as many as one million earthquakes in a year. Most earthquakes are barely felt, if at all. But some earthquakes are so strong that they destroy homes and buildings and break pipelines.

Many earthquakes are caused by changes in the layer of the earth that extends from the surface to a depth of 60 kilometers (about 40 miles) below the surface. This is the earth's crust. As the plates of the crust move, rocks in the crust crack. They crack because they are being pushed and pulled in different directions. If the amount of force on them is great enough, the rocks break and the crust moves. Such a break is known as a *fault*.

U.S. Geological Survey, Department of the Interior

Figure 22–8. What kind of damage resulted when this earthquake struck Anchorage, Alaska, in 1964?

435

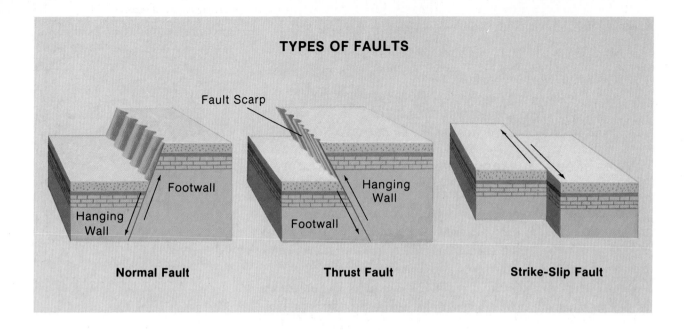

TYPES OF FAULTS

Fault Scarp

Footwall

Hanging Wall

Normal Fault

Hanging Wall

Footwall

Thrust Fault

Strike-Slip Fault

When a fault takes place, there is a sudden slip between two large blocks of rock. Three kinds of faults may occur —*normal faults*, *thrust faults*, and *strike-slip faults*. In normal faults and thrust faults, one block of rock slips upward and the other slips downward.

The block of rock that overhangs the fault surface is called the *hanging wall*. The block of rock that is below the fault surface is called the *footwall*. A normal fault produces a footwall that appears to have moved up. A thrust fault produces a hanging wall that appears to have moved up. When the fault occurs at the earth's surface, the wall of the block of rock that moves upward forms a *fault scarp*. See Figure 22–9.

A strike-slip fault occurs when one block of rock slides past another one without any up-and-down movement. This kind of fault is in a horizontal plane. See Figure 22–9.

☐ **Of the three kinds of faults, which two are more likely to produce mountains?**

Perhaps the most well-known fault in the United States is the San Andreas Fault. This fault is located on a line running roughly north-northwest from the Gulf of Cali-

Figure 22–9. In two of the types of faults illustrated, blocks of rock move up or down, causing a fault scarp to form. In the third type (above), blocks of rock move in a horizontal plane.

To Think About

A fault scarp that is produced when the hanging wall moves up does not generally last very long. Why, do you think, is this so?

fornia to a point along the coast near San Francisco. The San Andreas Fault is a strike-slip fault. It marks the boundary between the North American Plate and the Pacific Plate.

Measuring earthquakes

The movement along a fault that causes an earthquake also causes *seismic* [SYZ-mihk] *waves,* or earthquake waves, in the earth. These waves move in the solid earth. The instrument used to measure seismic waves is a *seismograph* [SYZ-muh-GRAF]. Scientists learn about all the earthquakes on the earth by using seismographs.

A seismograph has a pen or other marker fastened to a heavy weight. The weight is fastened to a spring. The tip of the pen touches a slowly turning drum covered with paper. When the ground moves, the pen marks the paper with wavy lines. The paper that has the wavy lines on it is called a *seismogram* [SYZ-muh-GRAM]. The seismogram is a scientist's record of the seismic waves from an earthquake.

Figure 22–10. A part of the area through which the San Andreas Fault passes is pictured. Where, do you suppose, is the fault?

Figure 22–11. Two types of seismographs are illustrated. Why are two types needed to record earth movements?

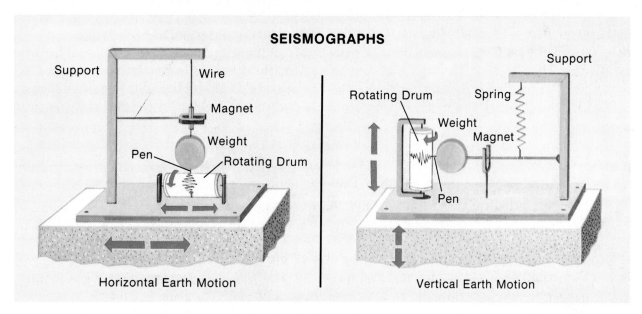

SEISMOGRAPHS

Support Wire Magnet Weight Pen Rotating Drum

Horizontal Earth Motion

Rotating Drum Spring Support Weight Magnet Pen

Vertical Earth Motion

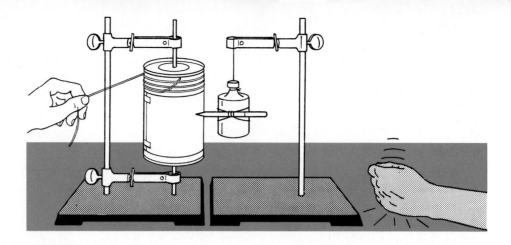

Investigate

How does a seismograph record the shaking of the ground?

You will need

nail, string, weight, hammer, white paper, felt-tip pen, wire cutter, masking tape, ring-stand ring, wire coat hanger, large juice can with holes in the top, 2 ring stands, 2 burette clamps

Background

A seismograph is made up of a turning drum and a marker mounted in a frame. The marker is fastened to a weight that is supported by a spring. When the earth shakes during an earthquake, the frame and the drum shake. But the weight and the marker do not move when the ground shakes. This is because they are supported by a spring instead of being fastened directly to the frame of the seismograph.

What to do

With a hammer and a nail, punch a hole in the center of each end of the can. Wrap the sides of the can with white paper, and tape the paper in place. Cut a long, straight piece of wire from a wire hanger. Put the wire through the holes in the can. Tape one end of a long piece of string to one end of the can. Wrap the string around the can several times. Using a ring stand and two clamps, set the can and wire on a table as shown in the diagram. This will be your seismograph drum.

Tape a felt-tip pen to a heavy weight. Use a piece of string to hang the weight from the ring or clamp of a second ring stand as shown in the diagram. The string will take the place of a heavy-duty spring. Place this ring stand so that the tip of the pen touches the drum.

Pull the string to make the drum turn slowly. After the drum has begun to turn, you or a classmate should hit the table to make it shake. Look at the line made by the pen on the paper.

Now that you have done the investigation

■ What kind of line was made on the drum before you made the table shake?
■ What kind of line was made on the drum when the table was shaking?
■ Will this kind of seismograph record a shaking from side to side as well as a shaking up and down? Try it and find out.

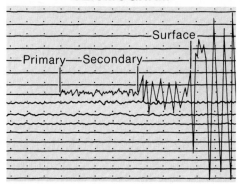

Scientists have discovered that there are three kinds of seismic waves. They call these waves *P waves*, *S waves*, and *L waves*. P waves move faster than the other two. They are the first to appear on a seismogram after an earthquake. They move all the way through the earth. P waves are also called *primary waves* or *push waves*. See Figure 22–12.

S waves are slower than P waves. S waves do not travel through the core of the earth because the outer part of the earth's core is liquid. These waves are also known as *secondary waves*, *shake waves*, *shear waves*, or *transverse waves*. See Figure 22–13.

L waves are the slowest of the seismic waves. They move only at the surface of the earth. But these waves can travel for great distances. Sometimes they circle the earth several times. There are two kinds of L waves, or *surface waves*. They are known as *Love waves* and *Rayleigh waves*. See Figure 22–13.

Scientists know how fast P waves and S waves move through the earth. By measuring the distance between marks made by P waves and S waves on a seismogram and by using a certain formula, scientists can find out how far away the earthquake occurred. They decide how strong

Figure 22–12. On a seismogram, the slowest waves have the largest amplitude, or distance up or down from a center line.

Figure 22–13. Look at the illustration of how different seismic waves move in the earth. Try to picture the movement of each wave by looking at the blocks, which would be of equal sizes if no seismic waves were passing through.

SEISMIC WAVES

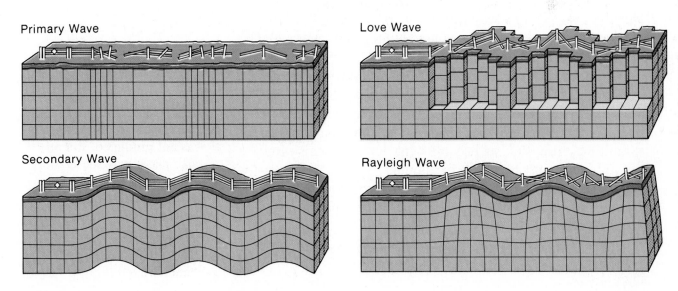

Primary Wave

Love Wave

Secondary Wave

Rayleigh Wave

the earthquake was by measuring the height of the wavy lines. They can find out the location of an earthquake by computing the distances of the earthquake from three reporting stations and then plotting this information on a map.

The strength of earthquakes is often described in terms of the *Richter* [RIHK-tur] *scale*. This scale is based on information from seismograms. The smallest earthquake that can be felt is measured at 1.5 on this scale. Earthquakes measured at less than 5.0 cause little damage at the surface of the earth. Earthquakes of 7.0 or more, on the other hand, usually cause a great amount of damage.

The largest earthquakes ever recorded measured 8.9 on the Richter scale. One of these earthquakes occurred near the border between Colombia and Ecuador in South America in 1906. Another occurred in Japan in 1923. The famous San Francisco earthquake of 1906 was rated at 8.3. The Tangshan, China, earthquake of 1976 had a rating of 8.2.

Predicting earthquakes

About 500,000 people lost their life in the earthquake that struck Tangshan, China, in 1976. A great many people live in places that may have destructive earthquakes. For this reason, many people are trying to find out as much as they can about earthquakes. From what they learn, people may be able to find a way to *predict* [prih-DIHKT] earthquakes. That is, they may be able to tell that an earthquake is going to occur before it happens.

Scientists have discovered that certain kinds of changes can often be observed before an earthquake begins. The water in wells often becomes muddy. The amount of radon, a gas, in the water may become greater. The ground above a fault may rise, sink, or become bent. Even animals often act differently just before an earthquake. Scientists are trying to find a way to predict earthquakes by observing such changes as these. They hope that predicting earthquakes will save many lives.

☐ **How might lives be saved by predicting earthquakes?**

Find Out More

The earthquake at Tangshan was not predicted. But an earthquake was successfully predicted in Liaoning Province, China, in 1975. As a result, many lives were saved. Using references, find out how Chinese scientists predicted this earthquake.

440

Seismologists use many instruments to study earth movements. Some of the information they obtain must be fed into a computer at the National Earthquake Information Service in Golden, Colorado.

Careers

Seismologist

One of the most exciting careers in the earth sciences today is that of the *seismologist* [syz-MAHL-uh-juhst]. Seismologists are scientists who learn about the earth by studying the different seismic waves produced by earthquakes. At one time most seismologists were concerned only with the study of earthquakes. But this is not the case today.

Many seismologists are trying to find out just what happens to cause the plates of the earth's crust to move and cause earthquakes. They hope that from such studies they will learn how to predict and possibly control the earthquakes that occur in the places where many people live.

The study of earthquakes has helped seismologists locate the edges of the plates. Further studies have shown that earthquakes occur at different depths in the crust. The deepest earthquakes occur in places near the ocean trenches. This fact has led seismologists to believe that the trenches are places where one plate is bending and moving beneath another plate.

Perhaps you would like to be a seismologist and study the moving plates and other interesting things about the earth. If so, you will need to take many college-level courses in the earth sciences and physics. A seismologist needs to know a great deal about rocks and minerals and the structure of the earth.

For information about a career as a seismologist, a student in your class might write to the American Geophysical Union, 1909 K Street, N.W., Washington, DC 20006.

Reviewing and Extending

Summing Up

1. A volcano is a vent in the earth's crust from which molten rock and gases come out. It is also the cone or mountain that is made up of the materials that came out of the vent.
2. Most of the volcanoes in the world are found at the edges of plates where one plate is bending downward and moving beneath another plate.
3. A volcanic eruption occurs when lava, steam, gas, dust, ash, or other material comes out of a volcano.
4. Dust, ash, cinders, and bombs are different-sized forms of volcanic rock. Basalt, rhyolite, and pumice are certain kinds of rock that may form from lava.
5. Shield volcanoes are volcanoes that often form volcanic islands and seamounts. They have a rounded top or a flat top because the lava from them forms sheets of rock.
6. Cinder cones are made up of ash, cinders, bombs, and other pieces of rock. They often have a crater at the top.
7. Composite volcanoes are explosive volcanoes made up of layers of rock from lava flows and layers of ash, cinders, and bombs.
8. Mount St. Helens is a composite volcano that had been quiet for more than 100 years before it erupted in 1980.
9. Most earthquakes are caused by faults along plate boundaries. These faults are normal faults, thrust faults, and strike-slip faults.
10. There are three kinds of seismic waves—P waves, S waves, and L waves. They move at different speeds in the earth and can be used to detect the strength and the location of an earthquake.
11. Scientists are trying to find ways to predict earthquakes.

Checking Up

Vocabulary Write the numerals *1–10* on your paper. Each numbered phrase describes a term from the following list. On your paper, write the term next to the numeral of the phrase that describes it.

bombs	cinders	rhyolite
basalt	dormant	seamounts
crater	caldera	seismogram
pumice	extinct	seismograph

1. word that describes "sleeping" volcanoes
2. ashlike pieces of rock that are hot but not burning
3. large crater that is formed by the collapse of the center of a volcano or by a great volcanic explosion
4. volcanic rock that is full of little holes and is very light in weight
5. rounded pieces of red-hot rock
6. dark volcanic rock
7. volcanic mountains that are under water
8. instrument that scientists use to measure seismic waves
9. volcanic rock that is much like granite
10. paper that is a scientist's record of the waves from an earthquake

Knowledge and Understanding Write the numerals *11–18* on your paper. Beside each numeral, write the word or words that best complete the sentence having that numeral.

11. A volcano that has layers of lava and layers of ash, cinders, and bombs is a (*composite volcano, shield volcano, cinder cone*).
12. The movement of rock along a fault causes earthquake waves, or (*volcano waves, seismic waves, Richter waves*), to travel within the earth.
13. Most of the active volcanoes in the world are located near (*seamounts, fault scarps, trenches*).
14. A kind of fault that occurs when one block of rock slides past another one in a horizontal plane is a (*normal fault, thrust fault, strike-slip fault*).
15. Any volcano that has not been known to erupt and has been worn down somewhat by weathering and erosion is said to be (*dormant, extinct, sleeping*).
16. The fastest waves that travel in the earth are the (*L waves, S waves, P waves*).
17. A (*volcanic eruption, dormant volcano, caldera*) occurs when lava, steam, gas, dust, or ash comes out of a volcano.
18. A kind of volcano that has a rounded or a flat top and from which lava spreads out and forms sheets of rock is known as a (*composite volcano, shield volcano, cinder cone*).

Expressing Yourself Write a paragraph as an answer to each of the following questions:

19. What is the difference between a normal fault, a thrust fault, and a strike-slip fault?
20. What were the warnings of the Mount St. Helens eruption of May 18, 1980?

Doing More

1. Using clay and a large, flat piece of wood, make a model of a convergent boundary. A convergent boundary is a trench and the land nearby, including the volcanoes. Use the illustrations in this chapter and Chapter 21 as your guide. Include a cutaway view in your model to show how the lighter material from the seafloor trenches may move back to the earth's surface as magma and then come out as lava. What parts of the earth are involved in your model?
2. Using references such as encyclopedias, magazine articles, and books about the earth, find out which volcanoes are active in North America at the present time. Also find out which volcanoes are now believed to be extinct. What parts of North America have active volcanoes now as compared with those having active volcanoes at the start of the Cenozoic Era? The Mesozoic Era?
3. Using references, find the location of the most-active faults in North America. What is the relationship, if any, between the most-active faults and the most-active volcanoes?

Photri

This mountain climber is using cracks and pits in the rock to climb the mountain. What caused the cracks and pits to form in the rock?

23 Weathering and Erosion

If you look at a mountain from a distance, the mountain may appear to be smooth. But is any mountain really smooth? Mountains often have a rugged, or rough, surface. In fact, the closer you get to a mountain, the more rugged it looks. If you climb a mountain, you will find that it is covered with soil and pieces of broken rock.

If you examine the pieces of rock as you climb, you will notice that they are not smooth. Instead, the rock surfaces are cov-

ered with many pits, scratches, and cracks. The natural process by which rock and other materials are changed and broken down is known as *weathering*.

Weathering brings about many changes on the surface of the earth. For example, weathering breaks rock down into soil. The breakdown of rock into soil is an example of *physical* [FIHZ-ih-kuhl] *weathering*. Physical weathering changes the surface of the earth. It is one of the topics of this chapter.

WEATHERING

What is physical weathering?
How does physical weathering change rock?
What is chemical weathering?
How does chemical weathering change rock?
*What two soillike particles result from
   weathering?*

To Think About

In the United States, winds generally blow from west to east. Which side of a mountain—the western side or the eastern side—would be more likely to show the greater amount of weathering? Why?

Physical weathering

Physical weathering breaks matter into pieces that are smaller in size. From the word "weathering," you might guess that it has something to do with weather. In a way, this is so. Wind, water, and changes in temperature all help to cause physical weathering.

There are several ways in which physical weathering may take place. For example, as wind blows, it picks up tiny grains of sand. The sand may blow across the surface of a rock and scratch it. In time, the sand will help to wear away the surface of the rock.

Perhaps the greatest cause of physical weathering is water. Water from rain, rivers, streams, and oceans may flow over rock. This water may carry sand and small pieces of rock that grind against larger pieces of rock. The grinding causes the larger pieces of rock to wear away. Water may also fill tiny cracks in rock and then freeze. As water changes to ice, it *expands* [ihk-SPANDZ], or takes up more space. As the ice expands, it pushes against the rock, causing the rock to break.

Changes in temperature may also cause physical weathering. Heat does not move through rock easily. As the outside of a rock gets hot, it expands. But the inside of a rock does not get hot as fast as the outside. So the inside of a rock does not expand as fast as the outside. The differences in temperature may cause the outside surface of the rock to crack.

☐ **What examples of physical weathering have you seen?**

Figure 23–1. Bryce Canyon in Utah contains many interesting rock formations. What name is given to the natural processes that shaped these formations?

Alan Pitcairn/Grant Heilman

445

Chemical weathering

A second kind of weathering is known as *chemical* [KEHM-ih-kuhl] *weathering*. In chemical weathering, there is a change in the kinds of minerals that make up a rock. For example, because of chemical weathering, the minerals in granite that are called feldspars are changed into clay minerals.

Water is one of the causes of chemical weathering. One way in which water causes chemical weathering is known as *hydration* [hy-DRAY-shuhn]. Hydration takes place when minerals in rock combine with water. As the minerals combine with water, they are removed from the rock. As a result, there is a change in the makeup of the rock. The rock may crumble, breaking apart bit by bit.

Air is also a part of chemical weathering. Some of the carbon dioxide in the air dissolves in raindrops, causing a weak acid known as *carbonic acid* [kahr-BAHN-ihk AS-uhd] to form. The rain then falls to the ground. The carbonic acid slowly dissolves parts of certain kinds of rock. For example, rock such as limestone will dissolve in weak carbonic acid. This process of dissolving rock is known as *carbonation* [KAHR-buh-NAY-shuhn].

A process known as *oxidation* [AHK-suh-DAY-shuhn] also causes chemical weathering. Oxidation takes place when a substance combines with oxygen. For example, iron in surface rock may combine with oxygen in the air. This combination produces iron oxide. Rust is another name for iron oxide, and it is one product of chemical weathering. You may have observed rust on the metal rail of an outside stairway in your neighborhood. Oxidation caused the rail to rust.

Plants and animals also help bring about both physical and chemical weathering. Tiny roots grow into small cracks in rock. As the roots grow, they can cause enough force to crack the rock. The roots of many plants also make an acid that dissolves certain kinds of rock. Even the tiny lichens and mosses that grow on rock help to break it apart. If the rock that is being broken apart is granite, then grains of quartz will be formed.

Figure 23–2. The red color on the rock shown here is due to iron oxides. The iron oxides were deposited when the iron oxides settled out of the water that carried them.

To Think About

Air is important in chemical weathering because it contains water vapor. In factory areas, air may also contain corrosive gases. Among these gases are acid-forming oxides of sulfur and nitrogen. What effect could the air around factories have on stone in nearby buildings?

446

Obtain four or five bean seeds and soak them for a day before doing this activity. The next day, add enough plaster of paris to water in a small milk carton to form a thick plaster about 2 or 3 cm deep. Push the presoaked bean seeds into the wet plaster. Allow the plaster to set and harden. Cut away the paper carton as soon as the plaster has hardened. Observe what happens to the block of plaster as the seeds begin to sprout. How might your observations explain how plants cause weathering in nature?

Ants, earthworms, and larger animals tunnel through soil. Water and air move down through the tunnels to places near rock, which is then broken up by chemical weathering. The materials left by animals may also contain acids that dissolve certain minerals in rock.

☐ **What are some examples of larger animals that burrow into the soil?**

The results of weathering

Certain particles remain after rock has been broken down. These particles consist of grains of certain minerals. One kind of particle that remains from weathering is *sand*. Sand is made up of grains of quartz. These grains are released from rock during the decomposition of other minerals in the rock. The quartz grains may collect as sand deposits, or they may help make up soil.

Another kind of particle that remains from weathering is *clay*. Minerals called feldspars are changed into clay minerals during hydration. Clay is made up of very fine particles that help to make up soil.

Sand and clay do not break down any further. They also tend to remain in the soil that forms when rock is broken down. As a result, sand and clay are two important parts of most soils.

SOIL AND SOIL TYPES

How do plants help in the formation of soil?
How do soil horizons differ?
What happens when leaching occurs?
What is one basis for the classification of soil types?

Formation of soil

Weathering is the process that causes a rock to break down into smaller and smaller pieces. Also, weathering causes the kinds of minerals that make up the rock to be changed. As rock is broken down, soil is formed. The soil-making process goes through many different steps over many years. In fact, the making of a centimeter of soil may take 500 years.

The first step in forming soil takes place when solid rock, called *bedrock,* is broken into pieces by weathering. Weathering of bedrock over a long time results in a mixture of smaller pieces of different sizes. These pieces of rock begin to make up a layer above the bedrock. See *A* and *B* in Figure 23–3. The amount of weathered rock increases over the years. Keep in mind that the pieces of rock near the surface are the smallest pieces, because there is more weathering at the surface than beneath it.

Figure 23–3. Soil forms when bedrock (A) is broken down (B) into small pieces. Humus develops (C) as plants and animals add organic matter to the weathered rock. A layer of minerals and clay forms by leaching. (D)

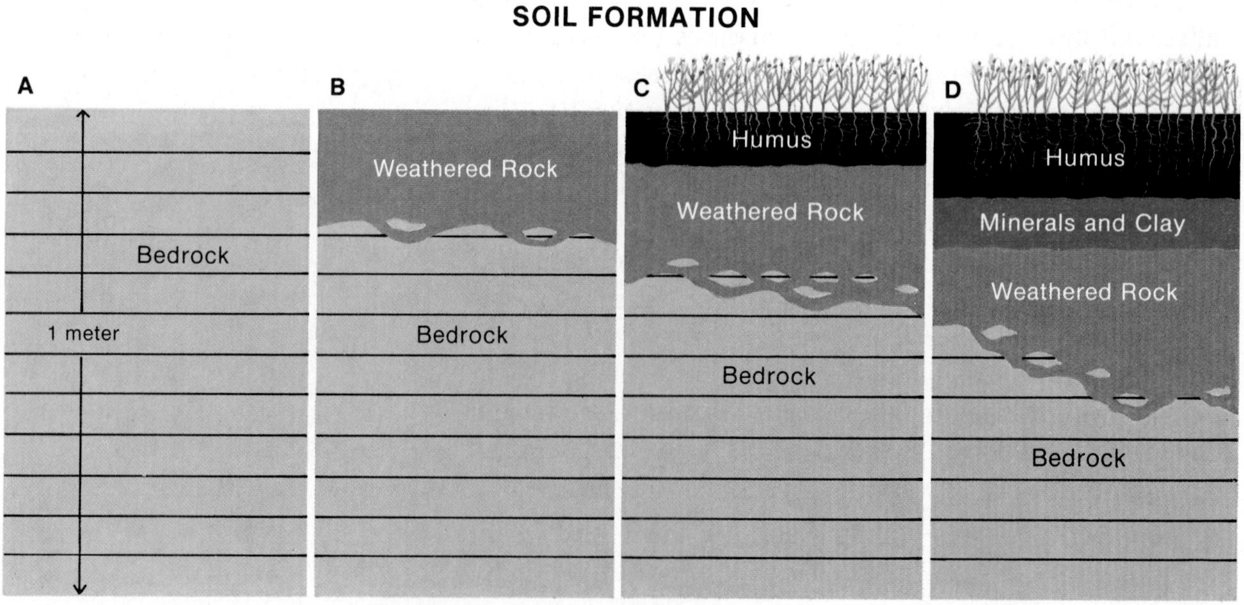

SOIL FORMATION

After a while, plants begin to grow in the weathered rock. See *C* in Figure 23–3. As more and more plants grow and die, the decaying plant material, called *humus* [HYOO-muhs], begins to form another layer. After water from rain and snow has passed through this layer for some time, certain materials are dissolved out of the humus and washed down to a lower layer. This process is called *leaching.*

Clay minerals and iron oxide are washed down into the weathered-rock layer by means of leaching. Clay makes up the smallest particles of soil. The clay minerals, iron oxide, and other materials begin to form still another layer. See *D* in Figure 23–3.

☐ **What might happen to the downward movement of water as the layer of clay and other materials becomes larger?**

Soil horizons

Although most soil forms in a similar way, the various layers of soil are different from one another. Suppose you were to dig into soil. If you dig deep enough, you might be able to see that each soil layer has a slightly different color. If you could dig down to the bedrock, you would see other differences, too.

Soil scientists have used machines to dig down to the bedrock in thousands of places. In almost every place they dug, they found three layers. These three layers of soil, called *horizons* [huh-RYZ-uhnz], are different from one another in many ways. See *D* in Figure 23–3.

The first soil horizon, or *A horizon,* is at the top. The color of this layer is generally dark gray or black. Its dark color is caused by the humus from decayed plants and animals. This soil horizon may also be sandy because clay has been leached out. Other minerals that are easily dissolved may have been leached out, too. The A horizon may be from a millimeter to many centimeters thick.

The *B horizon* is just below the A horizon. This soil horizon has more clay than the A horizon because the clay has been added to it from the layer above. The color of the B horizon is from brown to red because of the iron

Figure 23–4. Soil horizons can easily be seen in excavations such as the road cut you see here. Do you think this A horizon is thick or thin?

Grant Heilman

449

oxides carried down from the A horizon. Also, the B horizon contains minerals from the layer above and from the bedrock below. This horizon may be from a few centimeters to a few meters thick. Together, the A horizon and the B horizon make up the true soil.

The *C horizon* is the lowest layer. It is just above the bedrock. This layer is made up of partly weathered rock. The color of this layer is determined by the color of the bedrock. The C horizon is known as *subsoil*.

Soil types

The type of soil at a certain place is determined mostly by the climate. The following paragraphs describe some soil types that are based on the climate in which the soil was formed.

One type of soil is *grassland soil*. It covers the United States from the eastern forests to the Rocky Mountains. Grassland soil has large amounts of humus in it. The humus was formed by the many different grasses that covered this area for many years. Humus makes the soil very fertile. Grassland soil also receives a great deal of rain. As a result, plants grow well.

Another kind of soil is *forest soil*. Most forest soil is located in the eastern and southern parts of the United States. Trees grow well in forest soil. However, minerals are leached deeply into the B horizon of a forest soil because of heavy rainfall. As a result, the A horizon in a forest soil is rather thin.

Find Out More

Look for a place nearby where you can observe the materials beneath the soil. Such a place might be the side of a gully, a stream bank, or an excavation for a road or building. What materials did you find beneath the soil?

Figure 23–5. The kinds of plants that grow in grassland soil and forest soil are shown here. Which soil, do you suppose, has the thicker A horizon?

Larry Thorngren/Tom Stack & Associates

Dr. E. R. Degginger

Do It Yourself
Compare plant growth in various soils

How do different kinds of soil affect the growth of plants? Fill a flowerpot with soil from one of the following places: (a) soil from an old fence row, field, or pasture that has never been plowed; (b) soil from an eroded hillside; (c) subsoil from a depth of about a meter (the subsoil may be taken from a bank at the side of a road where the different layers of soil can easily be seen); (d) desert soil or sand. Fill a second, or possibly a third, flowerpot with soil from another of the places above. Plant three beans in each flowerpot. Keep the beans watered and place the pots where they will receive some sunshine and be warm. Also place three or four beans in cotton and keep them moist. Keep a record of how fast the beans in each pot grow. Compare these plants with the growth of the beans in the cotton.

Desert soil is found in the dry regions of the western United States. Because of the small amount of rainfall in a desert, leaching does not take place in a desert soil. Although it receives little water, a desert soil is rich in minerals. Desert soil is thin, and few plants grow in it, largely because of the lack of rain.

Figure 23–6. Desert soil is pictured here. Since there is very little rainfall in desert areas, the B horizon is not well formed.

451

EROSION AND DEPOSITION

What is erosion? Deposition?
How does moving water change the land?
How do waves change the coastline?
How does wind change the land?

Changing the earth's surface

Weathering occurs whenever wind, water, temperature, and living things act on rock and break it down. Weathering changes rock to soil. But weathering and soil formation are not the only ways that the surface of the earth is changed.

The earth's surface is also changed by *erosion* [ih-ROH-zhuhn]. Erosion is the moving of soil, sand, and weathered rock from one place to another over the surface of the earth. When erosion stops, a process of settling out known as *deposition* [DEHP-uh-ZIHSH-uhn] takes place. The important causes of erosion and deposition are moving water and wind.

Moving water

Most erosion occurs because of water. Much of the water that flows over the land comes from rainfall. Rain that falls on soil covered with growing plants usually soaks into the ground. But sometimes so much rain falls in a short time that the ground cannot soak up the rain as fast as it falls. Of course, rain also falls on rock, which does not soak up much water.

If water cannot soak into the ground, it moves over the surface. As water moves over soil and pieces of rock, it picks some of them up and carries them along. The steeper the path that the water follows, the faster the water moves. Fast-moving water will pick up and carry larger pieces of rock and more soil than will slow-moving water.

As water moves over the land, material carried by the water also wears away rock and soil. The path of the water is made wider and deeper. In time, the path may become a riverbed. At first, the river erodes the rock below it more than it does the rock on either side. It forms a narrow river valley having high, steep sides.

As times passes, the moving water erodes more rock and soil along the sides of the river. The river valley becomes wider. As the water erodes the land, the land becomes less steep. The water moves more slowly and carries fewer large pieces of rock. In fact, material carried by the water may begin to settle to the bottom of the riverbed. There the material begins to block part of the flow of the water. The water may have to form a new path as it moves around this material. In time, the river follows a winding path instead of a straight one.

Eventually the water in the river flows into the ocean. By the time the water reaches the ocean, it is moving slowly. Soil and small pieces of rock carried by the water settle to the bottom near the mouth of the river. After thousands of years, this material builds up large areas of land. Such land is called a *delta* [DEHL-tuh]. New Orleans is built on part of the delta formed by the Mississippi River.

☐ **Other than the kind of erosion that forms riverbeds, what kinds of erosion caused by water can you identify?**

Figure 23–7. This river has formed a winding path because of the materials that it picks up, carries, and later drops.

Investigate

How does moving water change the surface of the earth?

You will need

sand, gravel, beaker, large baking pan

Background

As water flows over the surface of the earth, it moves stones and soil from one place to another. In this way, the shape of the land is changed. How the land is changed depends upon whether the water is flowing down steep mountains, down low hills, or over flat plains.

What to do

Make a small hill of sand and small pieces of gravel in a baking pan. Make this hill as tall and as steep as possible. Fill a beaker with water. Slowly pour the water on the top of the hill. Notice what happens as the water runs down the sides of the hill.

Now shape the sand and gravel into a low, round hill. Use your finger to make a gully in one side. Again, fill the beaker and pour water on the hill. Note what happens as the water flows down the sides of this hill.

Next, flatten the sand so that it forms an almost-flat surface. Fill the beaker and pour the water onto the sand at one end of the pan. Note how the water flows over this surface.

Now that you have done the investigation

■ What happened to the sides of the steep hill as water flowed down them?
■ What happened as water flowed down the low, round hill?
■ How did moving water affect the almost-flat surface?
■ Which kind of surface in nature—steep mountainside, low hill, or flat plain—would most likely undergo the greatest amount of erosion?

Figure 23–8. *What is happening to the parking lot pictured here? Why is it happening?*

To Think About

How do waves move materials away from a coastline? How do waves add materials to a coastline?

Waves

Whenever waves roll onto the shore, the shape of the coastline is changed. You can prove this to yourself. If you visit the same shore two or three years in a row, you will notice that many changes have taken place.

Some forms of erosion and deposition are probably the first changes that you will notice along the shore. This is not unusual because, in time, waves can undercut even the strongest shores. In fact, waves can even move and break up heavy rocks. Moving water alone can wear away

Figure 23–9. *The beating of waves on these rocks will cause the rocks to wear away in time. Where might the rock particles be deposited?*

455

Figure 23–10. These sand dunes are big and cover a large area. What caused these dunes to form?

large rocks. But most of the time small pieces of sand or rock help the water do the work by rubbing and pounding against the large rocks.

Waves often carry large amounts of sand, stones, and bits of shell along with them. These materials can either be taken away from an area or be added to it, depending on the movement of waves. Beaches often become smaller or larger over time because of wave movement.

Wind

Water is not the only cause of erosion and deposition. Wind can pick up soil that is not covered by growing plants. Strong winds can carry large amounts of soil long distances. If too much of the soil is blown away, plants may not be able to grow. The soil blown away from one place is deposited in other places. It may cover and kill the plants growing there. In these ways, large areas of land may become wastelands.

In deserts and near some beaches, strong winds pick up and carry sand. Sand moved by the wind may form hills called *dunes*. Some dunes move as the wind carries sand in one direction. Some of these dunes may even cover large plants and roads.

☐ **What effect, do you think, might wind erosion and deposition have on people living in the area where the erosion occurs?**

Find Out More

Find out how farmers prevent the erosion of soil in their fields. How do they prevent water erosion? What do they do to prevent wind erosion? To find out about wind and water erosion on a farm, you might talk to a farmer. Or you might read an article on farming in an encyclopedia.

456

These soil scientists are doing field surveys in order to help farmers use the soil on their farms in more efficient ways.

Careers
Soil scientist

Suppose you were thinking of buying a farm and you wanted to check on the quality of the soil. Then you would probably want to talk to a *soil scientist*. A soil scientist knows about the physical, chemical, and biological characteristics of soil. Soil scientists try to find out the composition, distribution, and classification of different soils in order to help people use them in wise and productive ways.

Soil scientists do much of their work outside. They often walk over fields and talk with farmers. They also give advice on what crops to grow, how to drain water from fields, and what fertilizers to use. They may use chemicals to test a soil to find out what minerals are needed to improve the soil. Then they suggest various ways to improve the soil.

Soil scientists may work for private businesses, such as fertilizer companies, or for private research laboratories. Some of them work for real-estate firms or state road departments. Others work for park departments or for farm-management agencies.

A degree in agronomy (crop science) or soil science is necessary to become a soil scientist. If you are interested in a career in soil science, you might try working part-time, weekends, or summer vacations on a farm. Another idea would be to join a 4-H Club or the Future Farmers of America.

For information about a career as a soil scientist, a student in your class might write to the U.S. Department of Agriculture, Washington, DC 20250.

Reviewing and Extending

Summing Up

1. Physical weathering is a process by which rock and other materials are broken into smaller pieces. Wind, water, and changes in temperature all help to cause physical weathering.
2. Chemical weathering is a process that changes the kinds of minerals that make up rock. Carbonation, oxidation, and hydration are three kinds of chemical changes that cause rock to weather.
3. Two kinds of particles that result from the weathering of rock are sand and clay.
4. The formation of soil takes place over a long time and is the result of weathering, plant growth, and leaching.
5. Layers of soil called horizons develop during the formation of soil.
6. The type of soil in a certain place is determined mostly by the climate.
7. Some types of soils in the United States are grassland soil, forest soil, and desert soil.
8. The surface of the earth is changed by erosion and by deposition.
9. Moving water is an important factor in the erosion of land surfaces and in the deposition of eroded material on land surfaces.
10. Waves cause erosion and deposition along coastlines.
11. Wind is another factor that causes erosion and deposition.

Checking Up

Vocabulary   Write the numerals *1–9* on your paper. Each numbered phrase describes a term from the following list. On your paper, write the term next to the numeral of the phrase that describes it.

dune   bedrock   hydration
humus   erosion   oxidation
subsoil   delta   deposition
horizon   feldspar   carbonation

1. hill of sand formed by wind
2. solid rock that is the source material for soil
3. name given to any of the three layers of soil that result during the formation of soil from bedrock
4. moving of soil, sand, and weathered rock from one place to another
5. decaying plant material in soil
6. settling out of material that is carried by water or wind
7. chemical change in which a weak acid causes certain rock to dissolve
8. horizon of weathered rock
9. mineral that changes to clay mineral as a result of weathering

Knowledge and Understanding Write the numerals *10–20* on your paper. Beside each numeral, write the word or words that best complete the sentence having that numeral.

10. The most important result of the weathering of rock is the (*release of oxides by leaching, formation of soil, erosion that occurs*).
11. Generally, most erosion occurs because of (*water, wind, leaching*).
12. Certain materials in soil may move down into the (*B horizon, C horizon, bedrock*) as a result of leaching.
13. Rock in which changes in the kinds of minerals are taking place is said to be undergoing (*erosion, mechanical weathering, chemical weathering*).
14. The layer of soil in which most of the decayed plant and animal parts are found is the (*A, B, C*) horizon.
15. A soil that contains much humus is (*grassland soil, desert soil, forest soil*).
16. Soil that has developed over a long time generally has (*one, two, three*) layers.
17. The part of the air that is involved in oxidation is (*oxygen, nitrogen, carbon dioxide*).
18. Carbonation occurs when minerals combine with (*oxygen, water, carbon dioxide*).
19. Soil in dry climates is rich in minerals because (*it lacks horizons, little leaching occurs, much leaching occurs*).
20. Subsoil is the name given to the (*A, B, C*) horizon of soil.

Expressing Yourself Write a paragraph as an answer to each of the following questions:

21. How would you explain the statement that erosion tends to level the land?
22. What problems might result with the minerals in a soil if farmers irrigate their fields too often?

Doing More

1. Find out how contour farming affects the rate of erosion. Make a mound of soil in each of two pie tins or baking pans. Use a stick or a pencil to dig furrows that run from the top to the bottom of the mound of soil in one pan. In the other pan, make furrows that circle the mound of soil. Use a watering can to sprinkle a can of water over each mound. In which pan does the water carry more soil to the bottom of the pan? How should a hill be plowed by a farmer?
2. Read about oxbow lakes in reference books. Write a report about where such lakes are found, how they form, and why they have such a name. You may wish to give the report to the class.

In many places thick sheets of ice slowly move down to the sea. How does the surface of this ice sheet look? Why might it look that way?

24 Glaciers

Twenty thousand years ago, great sheets of ice covered the northern part of the earth. This period of time in the earth's history is known as the *ice age*. During the ice age, the climate was much different from what it is today. The winters were long, and the summers were short. Ice covered much of the earth's surface.

Great sheets of ice spread across nearly all of Europe, Canada, and the northern half of the United States. If you now live in the North, the spot where you are standing was probably covered by ice many years ago.

The ice was about 660 meters (about 2,000 feet) thick and slowly moved. Such thick sheets of moving ice are called *glaciers* [GLAY-shurs].

Today, glaciers no longer cover such places as Boston and Chicago. But glaciers can still be found in many parts of the earth. In fact, three fourths of all the fresh water in the world is frozen in glaciers. How have glaciers formed? How have they helped to shape the land? You will find the answers to questions such as these as you study this chapter.

KINDS OF GLACIERS

What are the two major kinds of glaciers?
How does a mountain glacier differ from a
*   piedmont glacier?*
How do icebergs form?

High-altitude glaciers

Glaciers occupy nearly 15 million square kilometers (nearly 6 million square miles) of the earth's surface. The average glacier is about 125 meters (about 400 feet) thick. As you might guess, so much ice can form only in cold places. Glaciers can be divided into two major groups according to where they form.

One major kind of glacier is the *high-altitude glacier.* As its name implies, a high-altitude glacier forms high above sea level. At high altitudes, the temperatures are cold, and there is a great deal of snowfall. A high-altitude glacier is often described as being a "river of ice."

One kind of high-altitude glacier is the *mountain glacier,* or *alpine glacier.* An alpine glacier forms near the top of a mountain and moves slowly down the mountainside.

☐ **Where do you think alpine glaciers might be found? Explain.**

Another kind of high-altitude glacier is the *valley glacier.* A mountain glacier becomes a valley glacier when it moves

Find Out More

Using references, find out more about the ice age. What four glacial periods made up the ice age? What were the three interglacial periods called? What kinds of animals lived during the ice age that no longer live today? What kinds of animals survived the ice age?

Tom Bean/Tom Stack & Associates

Figure 24–1. Why, do you think, is a high-altitude glacier often described as a "river of ice"?

461

down a mountain through a mountain valley. Often two or more valley glaciers join to form a larger valley glacier. Valley glaciers can be found in the United States in the mountains of Colorado, Oregon, Washington, and California. More than one glacier can be found on some mountains. For example, twenty-eight valley glaciers move down Mount Rainier in Washington.

Still another kind of high-altitude glacier is a *piedmont* [PEED-mahnt] *glacier*. A piedmont glacier differs from other high-altitude glaciers in that it is a slow-moving cake of ice. When one or more valley glaciers reach the bottom of a mountain, they form a piedmont glacier. Today, piedmont glaciers can be found in Alaska, Greenland, and Iceland.

High-latitude glaciers

Another major kind of glacier is the *high-latitude glacier*. This kind of glacier forms near the North and South poles. At high latitudes, the temperatures are below freezing all

To Think About

Even though a piedmont glacier is a high-altitude glacier, it is more often called a "puddle of ice" than a "river of ice." Why, do you think, is this so?

Figure 24–2. The ice cap at the South Pole of the earth is an example of a high-latitude glacier.

Photri

year round. There is a large amount of snow each year, and little melting can be observed from year to year.

Unlike glaciers that form at high altitudes, glaciers that form at high latitudes are sheets of ice. They are thick at the center and thin at the edges. High-latitude glaciers are most often called *ice sheets,* or *ice caps.* When ice sheets are large enough to cover much or all of a continent, they are called *continental glaciers.* Continental glaciers cover the North and South poles and most of Greenland and Antarctica.

Icebergs

As you may know, *icebergs* are huge pieces of ice floating in the ocean. Icebergs are really pieces of glaciers that flow until they reach the ocean. These glaciers break off in pieces that drop into the ocean.

Some valley glaciers flow until they reach the ocean. Such glaciers are known as *tidewater glaciers.* Where tidewater glaciers meet the ocean, there are high cliffs of ice. These cliffs form when large pieces of ice break off the glacier and fall into the water as icebergs.

Some continental glaciers also flow until they reach the ocean. In fact, some continental glaciers reach out over the ocean for many kilometers. The overhanging ice is known as an *ice shelf.* An ice shelf in Antarctica reaches out over the ocean for about 640 kilometers (about 400 miles).

A piece of ice sometimes breaks off an ice shelf. When this happens, a large iceberg drops into the ocean. Such an iceberg is known as a *tabular* [TAB-yuh-lur] *iceberg.* A tabular iceberg that was 332 kilometers (about 200 miles) long and 96 kilometers (about 60 miles) wide was once found in the Antarctic Ocean.

Icebergs may travel for years and for thousands of kilometers before they melt. The huge blocks of ice can be dangerous to ships. A ship is damaged and may sink when it crashes into an iceberg. The United States Coast Guard has an Iceberg Patrol that locates icebergs and warns ships of their positions.

Find Out More

Using references, find out more about icebergs. Why are some icebergs so dangerous to ships? How are icebergs useful today? How do scientists think icebergs might be useful in the future? What is a bergy bit? What is a growler?

Figure 24–3. The seals pictured here are using a tabular iceberg as a place to rest.

Richard Harrington/Photo Trends

463

Jacqueline Durand

Do It Yourself

Observe how icebergs float

Obtain a spoon; cold water; table salt; a clear glass, a glass jar, or a beaker; and an odd-shaped chunk of ice. Fill the jar or beaker about half full of cold water. Add some table salt and stir until the salt dissolves. Continue adding salt to the water until no more salt will dissolve. Carefully place a chunk of ice in the salt water. Observe the ice from the side through the jar or beaker.

Make a drawing that shows the shape of the ice in side view and at the waterline. How much of an iceberg floats above the surface of the ocean? How much of an iceberg is hidden below the surface? Why, do you think, are ships that seem to be a safe distance from an iceberg sometimes damaged or sunk by the iceberg?

ORIGIN AND MOVEMENT OF GLACIERS

How does a glacier form?
How does a glacier differ from an ice field?
What causes a glacier to move?

Formation of glaciers

Glaciers form either in high altitudes or in high latitudes. Many glaciers form near the North and South poles, but some glaciers also form in high mountains—even in warm places. For example, there are glaciers on mountains in Mexico and Africa.

The time it takes for a glacier to form depends on many things. It depends on the amount of snowfall and on the temperature. A glacier may form in just a few years, or it may take hundreds of years to form.

A glacier begins as a large mass of snow called a *snowfield*. The snow in a snowfield builds up in layers, year after year. As the snow builds up, it slowly begins to change. The snow on the surface begins to press down on the snow beneath it. This pressure makes the snow near the bottom of the snowfield hard and icelike.

As the temperature changes, the snow in a snowfield melts and freezes. Water from melting snow, or *meltwater*, also helps change the snowfield. Meltwater drains down to the icelike snow at the bottom of the snowfield. It freezes and makes the bottom of the snowfield even more icelike. In this way, a snowfield may become an ice field.

An ice field is not yet a true glacier. The ice field must build up over the years until it is heavy enough to move. That is, it must be about 62 meters (about 200 feet) thick, or about as high as a 20-story building. When the ice begins to move, a true glacier has formed.

Movement of glaciers

The ice in a glacier moves for the same reason water in a river flows. It moves because of gravity. The force of gravity causes a valley glacier to move down a mountain. It causes the ice in the center of an ice sheet to move down toward the edges of the ice sheet.

The movement of glaciers seems to come about in two ways. Some of the movement is a slipping motion known as *basal* [BAY-suhl] *slip*. As a glacier slips, it brings along some rocks and dirt. The rocks and dirt become frozen into the glacier. The rocks and dirt give the glacier a bottom that is like sandpaper. As the glacier slips, it wears away the ground.

Rocks that were once frozen into a glacier are easy to identify. They have a flattened side called a *facet* [FAS-uht]. This flattened side is often covered with scratches called *striae* [STRY-ee]. Striae are the result of rocks within a glacier rubbing against rocks beneath the glacier.

□ **Why, do you think, do rocks that were once frozen into the bottom of a glacier have a facet?**

For the most part, however, the movement of a glacier occurs by *internal flow*. Internal flow is much like the flow

Figure 24–4. A glacier once flowed over the rock pictured here. Why, do you think, does this rock have striae?

Artstreet

465

of a river. The movement is deep within the ice in an area called the *zone of flow*. The ice above the zone of flow breaks easily. However, because of the pressure caused by the heavy ice above it, the ice in the zone of flow does not break easily. Instead, it can bend without breaking. Because of the pressure, the ice molds itself into the shape of the land. See Figure 24–5.

As a glacier moves, the ice in the zone of flow moves, changes shape, and flows. But the ice on the surface cannot move or bend without breaking and as a result cracks, or *crevasses* [krih-VAS-uhs], form in the surface of the glacier. Some crevasses are small cracks, but other crevasses are more than 31 meters (100 feet) across and 62 meters (200 feet) deep.

To Think About

Scientists have drilled holes through certain glaciers to obtain ice cores for study. What kinds of things do you think scientists might be able to learn from studying the layers of glacial ice cores?

Figure 24–5. Ice in the zone of flow shapes itself to the land as a glacier moves. What happens to ice in the zone of fracture?

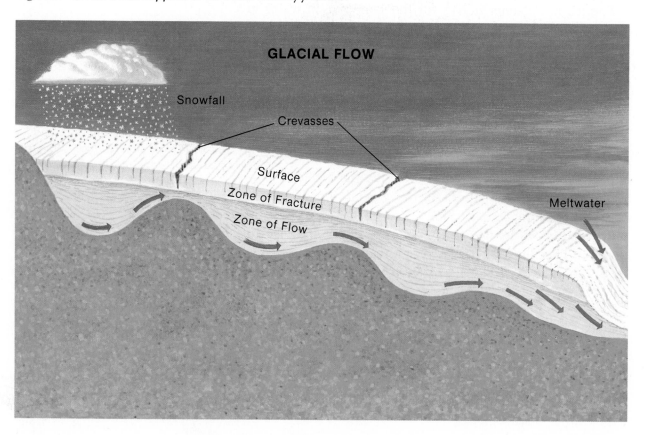

GLACIAL FLOW

Snowfall

Crevasses

Surface
Zone of Fracture
Zone of Flow

Meltwater

Figure 24–6. Stakes pounded into a glacier (left) show how the glacier moves (right). Which part of a glacier moves the fastest?

Different parts of a glacier move at different speeds. This was discovered when scientists learned to measure the rate of flow of a glacier. To measure a glacier's rate of flow, scientists pounded stakes in a straight line across a glacier. As the glacier moved, the stakes at the center moved farther than the stakes at the sides. See Figure 24–6.

The ice in the center of a glacier moves faster than the ice at the sides or on the bottom. This happens because the sides and the bottom of a glacier scrape against the ground as a glacier moves. But the ice in the center of a glacier is free to flow. Friction slows the flow of the sides and the bottom of a glacier. Friction does not, however, slow the flow of the ice in the center of a glacier nearly as much.

Glaciers move slowly. Most glaciers move less than 30 centimeters (1 foot) per day. The rate of movement is faster in summer and slower in winter because high temperatures make the ice more flexible. Thicker glaciers move faster than do thin glaciers because thick ice exerts more pressure and helps the ice to flow. One of the fastest moving glaciers is in Greenland. This glacier moves between 48 meters (about 160 feet) and 62 meters (about 200 feet) each day.

Find Out More

Using references, find out more about other features of glaciers. What is a moulin? What happens when a glacier is calving? What are retreating glaciers? What are galloping glaciers?

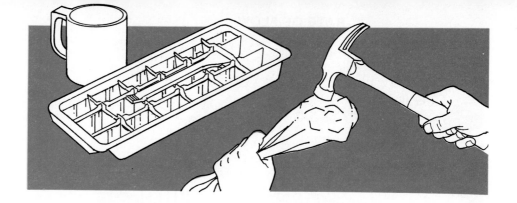

Investigate

What physical properties does ice have?

You will need

cup, hammer, shallow pan, heavy metal key, piece of cloth, piece of brick or some other heavy object, 6 ice cubes

Background

Ice has many surprising properties. Since glaciers are made up of ice, understanding the properties of ice can help you to better understand glaciers and how they are able to flow.

What to do

Wrap two ice cubes in a piece of cloth. Use a hammer and hit the ice cubes several times. Open the cloth and notice what has happened to the ice cubes. Place the remaining ice into a cup and wait two or three minutes. Notice what has now happened to the ice. Record your observations.

Place two ice cubes in a shallow pan. Put a piece of brick or another heavy object on one ice cube. Wait two or three minutes. Notice which ice cube melts faster. Also notice where the melting seems to be taking place. Record your observations.

Place two more ice cubes in a shallow pan. Place a heavy metal key on top of one ice cube. Put the pan in the freezer and leave it overnight. Examine the ice and notice the location of the key. Record your observations.

Now that you have done the investigation

- What happened when you hit the ice with a hammer?
- What happened when you allowed pieces of ice to touch one another in the cup?
- What two properties of ice do hitting ice and allowing pieces of ice to touch one another demonstrate?
- Does ice with a weight on it seem to melt faster or slower than ice without a weight on it?
- Where does the most melting seem to take place when ice has a weight on it?
- How is ice with a weight on it like ice at the bottom of glacier?
- Do you think the movement of a glacier begins at the top of the glacier or at the bottom? Why?
- Where in the ice did you find the key?
- How, do you think, does ice flow around an object?

HOW GLACIERS SHAPE THE LAND

In what two major ways do glaciers shape the land?

How does a glacial valley differ from a river valley?

What are drumlins? Eskers? Kames?

Glacial erosion

As a glacier moves over the land, it changes and shapes the land. Many mountain peaks, valleys, hills, and lakes are the work of glaciers. Glaciers can shape the land in two major ways.

One way in which glaciers can shape the land is by *glacial erosion* [ih-ROH-zhuhn]. The bottom of a glacier is much like sandpaper. As the glacier moves, it takes soil and rocks along with it, and it wears away the land beneath it. With all this erosion, there is a change in the land.

A landform that glaciers can make by glacial erosion is a bowl-shaped hollow near the top of a mountain. This hollow is called a *cirque* [SURK]. A cirque is formed at the

Mary Elenz Tranter

Do It Yourself

Observe glacial erosion

Obtain clay, sand, water, plasterboard, small rocks, and a small plastic container. Put a layer of sand and small rocks on the bottom of the container. Pour water into the container to a depth of 3 cm. Put the container into a freezer until the water freezes. The block of ice, sand, and rocks represents a glacier.

Flatten some clay. Rub the ice block over the clay, with the sand-and-rock side down. Record your observations. Also rub the block of ice over the plasterboard. Record your observations. What effects, do you think, does a glacier have as it passes over soil and soft rocks? Over hard rocks?

469

Figure 24–7. A glacier can hollow out a cirque (left) or carve a valley (right) by glacial erosion. Is the valley V-shaped or U-shaped?

place where a glacier begins. Meltwater from the glacier drains into cracks in the rock below. As the meltwater freezes, it breaks the rock into many pieces. These pieces of rock then freeze into the glacier. When this process happens again and again, the cirque becomes larger and larger.

Another landform glaciers can make by glacial erosion is a rough, steep mountain peak called a *horn*. Such a rough, steep peak is all that is left of a mountaintop when a number of cirques form close together. One example of a horn is the Matterhorn in Switzerland.

Still another landform produced by glacial erosion is a *mountain valley*. As a glacier moves down a mountain, it can wear away rocks to form a valley. The shape of a mountain valley made by a glacier differs from the shape of one made by a river. A mountain valley that is carved by a river is V-shaped. But a mountain valley that is made by a glacier is U-shaped.

Yet another landform produced by glacial erosion is a steep valley into the ocean. Such a valley is called a *fjord* [fee-AW(UH)RD]. As you know, some glaciers flow until they reach the ocean. Sometimes these glaciers carve a deep valley. When the glacier melts, the ocean flows in and fills the valley, forming a fjord. A fjord has steep walls and deep water. One fjord in Norway has cliffs 914 meters (about 3,000 feet) high. Its water is 1 219 meters (about 4,000 feet) deep.

Find Out More

Using references, find out more about how the Great Lakes were formed. When were they formed? What role did glacial erosion play? How did the Great Lakes become filled with water?

Glacial deposits

A second way in which glaciers can shape the land is by *glacial deposits.* As you know, rocks and dirt are frozen inside glaciers. Another name for such rocks and dirt is *glacial drift.* As a glacier melts, it leaves, or deposits, its glacial drift. Glaciers can make many landforms by glacial deposits. Because mountain glaciers and continental glaciers are so different, they make different landforms.

One landform mountain glaciers can make by glacial deposits is a *moraine* [muh-RAYN]. The word "moraine" is a French word that means "debris deposited by a glacier." Glaciers can make different kinds of moraines.

A *terminal* [TURM-nuhl] *moraine* is a glacial drift left at the end, or *snout,* of a glacier. A terminal moraine is a ridge of rocks and dirt shaped like a half moon. The points of the moon show the direction from which the ice flowed.

A *lateral* [LAT-uh-ruhl] *moraine* is a ridge of glacial drift left at the sides of a glacier. Since a lateral moraine is left at the sides of a glacier, it shows the path of the glacier. When two or more glaciers flow together, their lateral moraines join to form a *medial* [MEED-ee-uhl] *moraine.* See Figure 24–8.

A *ground moraine* is glacial drift left by the bottom of a mountain glacier. Instead of being a ridge, a ground

To Think About

If a large glacier has two medial moraines, how many smaller glaciers made up that glacier? How do you know?

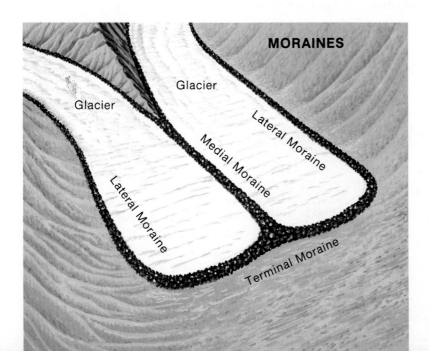

MORAINES

Glacier

Glacier

Lateral Moraine

Medial Moraine

Lateral Moraine

Terminal Moraine

Figure 24–8. Drift deposited when a glacier melts forms lateral moraines, terminal moraines, and medial moraines. Where does the material in the moraines originally come from?

471

moraine is a layer of rocks and dirt. A ground moraine is not often more than a meter (about three feet) deep.

Continental glaciers also make certain landforms by glacial deposits. See Figure 24–9. One such landform is *till*. Till is the name given to the drift left by the bottom of an ice sheet. Sometimes till is shallow, but till can be hundreds of meters deep. Much of the fertile soil in the Middle West is made of till.

Another landform a continental glacier can make by glacial deposits is a *drumlin* [DRUHM-luhn]. A drumlin is a long hill made of till deposited around a large rock. It is shaped like an egg cut in half the long way. The long end of a drumlin points towards the direction the ice was moving.

Still other landforms a continental glacier can make by glacial deposits are *eskers* [EHS-kurs] and *kames* [KAYMZ]. An esker is a long, winding hill made of glacial drift carried by rivers flowing through tunnels in the ice. A kame is a small cone-shaped hill made of glacial drift carried by meltwater flowing down into a crevasse.

☐ **Do you think landforms indicate that a glacier once covered the area where you live? Explain.**

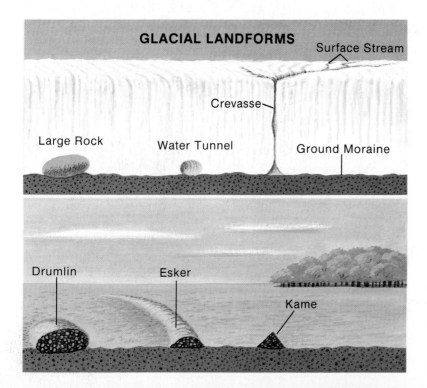

Figure 24–9. The features of a glacier (above) and the resulting glacial landforms (below) are shown. What causes a kame to form? An esker? A drumlin?

An ice-patrol officer helps to locate icebergs and determine their size.

Courtesy of U.S. Coast Guard

Careers

Ice-patrol officer

In 1912 a ship, the *Titanic*, rammed into an iceberg and sank in the Atlantic Ocean. Some people from the ship were saved. But 1,517 people died in the icy water. The next year, in 1913, the International Ice Patrol was formed. It is the job of the Ice Patrol to locate icebergs and to help ships avoid crashing into them. One member of the Ice Patrol is the *ice-patrol officer.*

Some ice-patrol officers work aboard iceberg patrol ships. Other officers work aboard aircraft. Ice-patrol officers seek to keep the waterways safe for ships of all countries. For example, an officer may order that a dye be dropped onto an iceberg so that the iceberg can be tracked and easily identified by its color.

Officers also order their crew to figure the speed of icebergs and to determine the direction in which icebergs travel. The information is sent by radio to all the ships at sea. In some cases, an officer may order that dynamite be used to help break up an iceberg.

The Ice Patrol does most of its work in the North Atlantic Ocean. The patrol works from about March until July. Not only does this job keep an officer away from home for a long time, but the job is dangerous, too. Under certain conditions, such as fog, icebergs are difficult to spot. Sometimes an iceberg will break apart, and the pieces will bob up and down violently. Sometimes, as an iceberg melts, it will suddenly turn in the water, endangering nearby ice-patrol ships.

To become an ice-patrol officer, you must first become an officer in the United States Coast Guard. You may become an officer by attending the United States Coast Guard Academy. Or you can take a special officer-training course after you graduate from college. You must then apply to work with the Ice Patrol. For further information, a student in your class might write to Commandant (G-PMR), United States Coast Guard, Washington, DC 20590.

Reviewing and Extending

Summing Up

1. A glacier is thick, moving ice.
2. Two major kinds of glaciers are glaciers that form at high altitudes and glaciers that form at high latitudes.
3. Mountain glaciers, alpine glaciers, valley glaciers, and piedmont glaciers are high-altitude glaciers. An ice sheet is a high-latitude glacier.
4. When an ice sheet is large enough to cover much or all of a continent, it is called a continental glacier.
5. An iceberg is a piece of a glacier that breaks off and floats in the ocean.
6. When an ice field builds up year after year and can move, it is called a glacier.
7. Gravity causes a glacier to move.
8. The internal flow of a glacier takes place within the zone of flow.
9. The rocks and dirt frozen within a glacier are called glacial drift.
10. Glaciers can shape the land by glacial erosion and by glacial deposits.

Checking Up

Vocabulary Write the numerals *1–10* on your paper. Each numbered phrase describes a term from the following list. On your paper, write the term next to the numeral of the phrase that describes it.

cirque   lateral   piedmont
facet   drumlin   terminal
kame   crevasse   tidewater
fjord   striae   continental

1. kind of moraine that is left along the sides of a valley glacier
2. long hill made of till deposited around a large rock by a continental glacier
3. crack in the surface of a glacier
4. kind of glacier that is formed when one or more valley glaciers reach the bottom of a mountain
5. kind of moraine that is left at the snout of a valley glacier
6. bowl-shaped hollow formed by a glacier near the top of a mountain
7. valley glacier that flows until it reaches the ocean
8. flattened side of a rock frozen into the bottom of a glacier
9. steep valley into the ocean with high cliffs and deep water
10. scratches on the flattened side of a rock once frozen into a glacier

Knowledge and Understanding Write the numerals *11–17* on your paper. Beside each numeral, write the word or words that best complete the sentence having that numeral.

11. High-latitude glaciers form (*in the mountains, near the poles, near the ocean*).
12. Another name for a mountain glacier is (*an alpine, a terminal, a tabular*) glacier.
13. When a continental glacier reaches out over the ocean, it is called an (*ice cap, ice sheet, ice shelf*).
14. Today continental glaciers cover most of (*Greenland, Canada, the Rocky Mountains*).
15. The (*center, bottom, side*) of a glacier moves faster than the rest of a glacier.
16. A horn forms where a number of (*drumlins, cirques, moraines*) are close together.
17. Eskers and kames are formed by (*glacial deposits, drumlins, glacial erosion*).

Expressing Yourself Write a paragraph as an answer to each of the following questions:

18. In what two ways can icebergs form?
19. How does a snowfield change into a glacier?

Doing More

1. Find pictures of at least three different mountains in books or magazines. Look at each picture carefully. Are glaciers present on any of the mountains? If so, how many glaciers do you see? What features of the glaciers can you see? If the mountains pictured do not have glaciers, did the mountains have a glacier or glaciers at some time in the past? What landforms that have been made by glaciers can you see?
2. Use modeling clay to make a model of a mountain. Carve valleys and hollows to represent various landforms that could be created by a mountain glacier. Include the plain below the mountain as part of your model. Mold landforms on the plain to represent glacial deposits. Be sure to include features such as cirques, horns, terminal moraines, and lateral moraines. Label each landform in your model. Then share your model with your classmates and discuss how each landform was made by a mountain glacier.

Pros and Cons

**Earthquakes—Should People Be Told
That One Is Predicted if Scientists Are
Not Absolutely Sure That One Is Going
to Occur?**

A map of the known earthquake epicenters in the United States would show you that most earthquakes occur in the western states and Alaska. However, there have been many earthquakes in the eastern states, the midwestern states, and the southern states, too. In fact, in 1811 and 1812 three of the most destructive earthquakes in American history occurred in southeastern Missouri and Arkansas near the Mississippi River. In fact, they actually shifted the course of the river.

Earth scientists say that earthquakes could occur at any time near many of the heavily populated areas of the United States. If an earthquake that registered 6.0 or greater on the Richter scale were to occur near any large center of population, houses and other buildings would be destroyed. Many lives would be lost.

Earthquakes have been successfully predicted in China. For example, in February 1975 an earthquake was predicted for southern Liaoning Province in China. Because people were moved outdoors to fields and parks, tens of thousands of lives were saved when the violent earthquake occurred. But in the summer of 1976, the people of Kwangtung Province spent two months living in tents, and an earthquake did not occur. These people had to be

Part of a seismologist's job is to monitor earthquake activity. Each of the recorders pictured records information on earthquakes from a different part of the country. Someday it may be possible to predict earthquakes with the help of such recorders.

cared for during this two-month period, but all the trouble was for nothing.

Suppose an earthquake is predicted for a heavily populated area in the United States. People would be told to leave their homes. They would be moved or told where to drive, and they would have to be fed. Many temporary shelters, such as tents, would be set up. Hospital and sanitary facilities would be provided in an outdoor setting. State and local governments would provide this care for all the people.

What about stores, businesses, and factories? These workplaces would have to be shut down. Then all the stores, businesses, factories, and homes would have to be guarded to protect them against looting. The National Guard would probably be called up.

Many people would say that all this help is necessary to protect people from the dangers of injury and loss of life. In fact, no one would argue about the prediction if the earthquake actually occurred. But suppose the predicted earthquake did not occur? What would people say then? Stores would lose some of their sales, businesses would be put behind schedule, factory output would be stopped for a time, and all the companies would lose money.

A severe earthquake can cause extensive damage to a nearby highway system, particularly if large bridges are a part of that system. How would an earthquake warning have helped people before the earthquake damage in the picture occurred?

Do you think that earth scientists would be praised for their efforts to save people from an earthquake if the earthquake did not actually occur? Would you be willing to predict an earthquake if there was a small possibility that there would be no earthquake? Would you be willing to leave an area a second or a third time if an earthquake did not occur when it was predicted previously? Talk to other people in your class about these questions. What do you think should be done if scientists think an earthquake is likely to occur within a few days in the area in which you live?

Investigate On Your Own

1. As you have read, carbon dioxide mixes with water in the air to form a weak acid. This same weak acid is found in soda pop. You can test the effect of weak acids in causing weathering by using clear soda pop, which is sold under the name "soda water" or "sparkling water." First examine some small pieces of rock with a magnifying glass. Place the pieces into a jar filled with soda water. Cover the jar and set it aside for two or three days. At the end of that time, examine the pieces of rock again. How did the weak acid affect the pieces of rock that were left in the jar?

2. Use reference books on fossils to find out what kinds of organisms were important during the different eras of the history of the earth. Make models of several important fossils out of such material as clay, plaster of paris, or papier-mâché. Label each of your models with the name of the fossil it represents and the era in which that organism lived. Display your models along with those of your classmates.

3. Geysers and hot springs were not mentioned in Chapters 21 and 22. But these are interesting features of the earth's crust. Use references to find out where they occur and what causes them. What do these features have to do with geothermal energy? How is a geyser like a volcano?

4. Obtain a coiled spring, such as a toy that "walks" down the stairs. You and your partner should each hold one end of the coiled spring on a wooden or tiled floor about 3 m apart. One of you should hold his or her end of the spring in one position while the other person moves the other end of the spring forward and back one time in one quick motion. Note the wave that travels the length of the spring and back. This is a P wave. Now move one end of the spring from side to side one time in one quick motion. This is an S wave. Which wave travels faster?

Read On Your Own

Asimov, Isaac, *How Did We Find Out About Earthquakes?* New York: Walker and Co., 1978.

Topics in this book include the structure of the earth, the causes of earthquakes, and plate tectonics. The instruments used to detect earthquakes are clearly described.

Fodor, Ronald V., *Earth in Motion: The Concept of Plate Tectonics.* New York: William Morrow and Company, Inc., 1978.

Excellent drawings assist the author in describing the origin of the idea of continental drift, the structure of the earth, the evidence for plate tectonics, and some of the applications of what scientists now know about the movements of the earth's crust.

Gallant, Roy A., *Earth's Changing Climate.* New York: Four Winds Press, 1979.

Part of this book deals with what changes are occurring in the earth's magnetic field. The author also describes how scientists are able to tell what kinds of changes took place in the earth's climate in the past.

Goldner, Kathryn Allen, and Carol Garbuny Vogel, *Why Mount St. Helens Blew Its Top.* Minneapolis: Dillon Press, Inc., 1981.

The events of May 18, 1980, are given first. Then an explanation of volcanoes in general is provided. The question of whether Mount St. Helens is going to blow its top again is explored.

Kiefer, Irene, *Global Jigsaw Puzzle: The Story of Continental Drift.* New York: Atheneum Publishers, 1978.

The history of the development of the theory of plate tectonics is given in an interesting and informative way. Well illustrated, this book points out clearly how scientists' ideas change with new discoveries.

Nixon, Hershell H., and Joan Lowery Nixon, *Glaciers: Nature's Frozen Rivers.* New York: Dodd, Mead & Company, 1980.

Many interesting photographs help this book bring excitement to the study of glaciers. The formation, features, and movement of glaciers are clearly explained.

Thackray, John, *The Earth and Its Wonders.* New York: Larousse and Co., Inc., 1980.

In this book, the author describes geological processes, the composition of the earth, the history of the earth, earthquakes, volcanoes, geysers, and hot springs. Excellent illustrations are used throughout the book.

Walker, Bryce, and the Editors of Time-Life Books, *Earthquake.* Alexandria, Virginia: Time-Life Books Inc., 1982.

Excellent photographs and interesting and informative chapters dealing with what happens during earthquakes are presented. Stories of how people prepare for and react to earthquakes are given. Up-to-date activities of scientists in studying earthquakes and attempting to predict earthquakes are described.

Unit 6
THE EARTH'S RESOURCES

The earth and all its resources are important to you and to other people. In fact, people depend on the earth's resources. Trees are used to make lumber that is used for building homes. Rocks, such as sandstone, marble, and slate, are important building materials, too. Soil is used to grow crops. Minerals taken from the earth are used to make steel for cars, copper for pipes, and aluminum for beverage cans. The list can go on and on.

Some of the earth's resources are limited. That is, once they are used up there will be no more. For example, there will be no more oil to drill for when all the oil has been taken from the earth. But other resources are not so limited. They can be replaced. After trees are cut down, seedlings can be planted to replace the cut-down trees.

As you study this unit, you will be learning about many of the earth's resources that people depend on. You will also be learning how taking these resources from the earth can disfigure the land and how changing these resources into useful products can pollute the air and water.

Artstreet

Coal is an important resource obtained from the earth. Coal that lies near the surface is removed by a process called strip mining. How has strip mining changed the land in the picture?

25 Treasures of the Earth

The earth is a great storehouse. Within parts of the earth, there are many treasures, or natural resources. Among the natural resources are air, water, food, fuels, minerals, living things, and living space. We hardly could live from day to day without food and water. Other natural resources are also important to life and to living things.

Many natural resources can be found on the surface of the earth. For example, the water in a stream and the trees in a forest are on the surface. Other natural resources are beneath the surface. Coal is one natural resource that is taken from mines beneath the surface. Air and the gases in air are found in the atmosphere. Natural resources can also be taken from the oceans.

Some of the natural resources that we use will be used up someday. These resources are nonrenewable. They cannot be replaced. For example, petroleum is a nonrenewable resource. Once it is taken from the ground, it cannot be replaced. Other resources are renewable resources. For example, plants and animals are two kinds of renewable natural resources.

REUSABLE RESOURCES

What are resources?
*What is meant by reusable resources, and what
    are some examples of them?*
*What is meant by renewable and nonrenewable
    resources?*

Kinds of resources of the earth

In discussing the earth as our environment, people often
use the word *resources* [REE-soh(UH)RS-uhz]. Resources
are all the natural materials and features of the earth that
help support life and satisfy people's needs. Air, water, and
soil are examples of resources that help support life. Materials that are used to make buildings, clothes, and radios
are examples of resources used to satisfy people's needs.
What might some of these materials be?

There are different kinds of resources. Some resources,
namely air and water, can be used over and over again.
These are called *reusable* [ree-YOO-zuh-buhl] *resources.*
Some resources, such as trees and farm animals, can be
replaced as they are used. These are known as *renewable*
[rih-N(Y)OO-uh-buhl] *resources.* Other resources, such as
soil and land, cannot be replaced as they are used. These
are *nonrenewable resources.*

Each of the resources used for energy also falls into one
of these groups. Energy resources, however, will be treated
as a separate group in this chapter.

    ☐ **Even though some resources can be reused or
replaced, why do you think it is important to make
wise use of all resources?**

Water as a reusable resource

When you think about the ways you use water every day,
it may be hard to think of it as a reusable resource. For
example, when you wash something, the water comes to
you out of the faucet. After you use the water, it goes down
the drain and makes its way to a river, lake, or ocean. This
may seem like a one-way trip. But water from a river, lake,

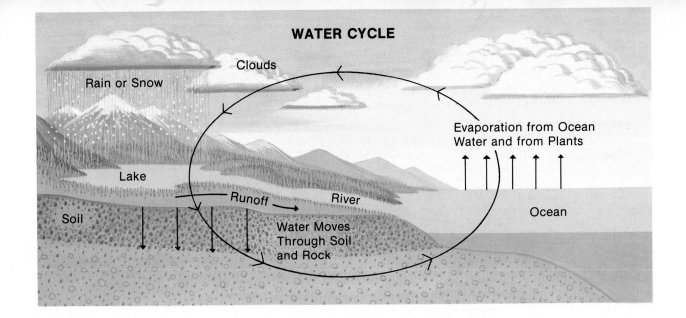

WATER CYCLE

Clouds

Rain or Snow

Evaporation from Ocean
Water and from Plants

Lake

Runoff

River

Ocean

Soil

Water Moves
Through Soil
and Rock

or ocean gets used again. Many things, however, must happen to this water before it can be used again.

Water can be used again and again because of something in nature called the *water cycle* [SY-kuhl]. Basically, the amount of water on the earth stays the same. But because of the water cycle, the water is always moving. Let's take a look at the water cycle. See Figure 25–1.

As you may remember, about 70 percent of the earth's surface is covered by water. Most of this water is salt water in the oceans. As water in the oceans is heated by the sun, it *evaporates* [ih-VAP-uh-RAYTS]. That is, it changes into the form of a gas. This gas, called *water vapor* [VAY-pur], rises and becomes part of the air. When this happens, salt from the ocean water is left behind.

As water vapor rises, it becomes cooled and helps form clouds. These clouds are blown over the land. When enough water vapor collects in the clouds and when they become cool enough, the water vapor turns into rain or snow. Rain and snow help fill the rivers and lakes that supply cities, homes, and industries with water. And water from most rivers and lakes finds its way back into the oceans.

Thus, the water cycle is completed, allowing water to be used over and over again. Of course, water must be made safe before it can be used in cities, homes, and

Figure 25–1. Besides helping to renew the supply of water for people, how else do you think the water cycle is important?

industries. This is usually done in water-treatment plants. And after use, water from these places must be treated again before it is returned to the environment. This is usually done in sewage-treatment plants. What things can you think of that might interfere with the water cycle?

Air as a reusable resource

In studying air as a reusable resource, it's necessary to consider the different parts of air separately. Just like water, some parts of air go through a natural cycle.

Air is made up of a mixture of gases. By volume, about 78 percent of air is made up of *nitrogen*. About 21 percent is *oxygen*. The remaining 1 percent is made up of *argon, carbon dioxide, helium, hydrogen,* and other gases. As far as living things are concerned, the three most important gases in air are nitrogen, oxygen, and carbon dioxide.

Nitrogen helps make up the cells of living things. Living things, however, do not get nitrogen directly from air. Look at the picture of the nitrogen cycle on this page. Certain bacteria that live in soil and in some plants can combine nitrogen from air with other chemicals. The nitrogen and chemicals are combined to make compounds known as *nitrates* [NY-TRAYTS]. Nitrates provide plants with the nitrogen they need to grow. How do you think animals get nitrogen?

Figure 25–2. *Why, do you suppose, must the nitrogen depleted from farm soil often be replaced by means of fertilizers rather than by relying on the nitrogen cycle?*

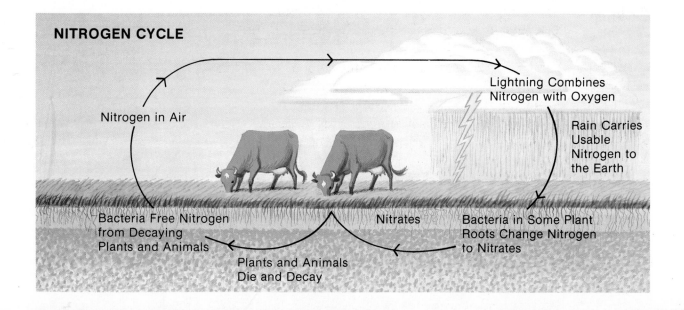

NITROGEN CYCLE

Nitrogen in Air

Lightning Combines Nitrogen with Oxygen

Rain Carries Usable Nitrogen to the Earth

Bacteria Free Nitrogen from Decaying Plants and Animals

Nitrates

Bacteria in Some Plant Roots Change Nitrogen to Nitrates

Plants and Animals Die and Decay

There is another way in which nitrogen from air gets into soil. During thunderstorms, electricity from lightning causes nitrogen to form a compound with oxygen. This compound is then carried to soil by rain.

As plants and animals die and decay, they become part of soil. Certain bacteria in soil help cause plants and animals to decay. As they decay, the nitrogen that was part of their body is given off as a gas into the air. Thus, the nitrogen cycle is completed, allowing nitrogen to be used again.

Oxygen and carbon dioxide are involved in a combined cycle. Oxygen from the air is needed to help utilize food in the cells of plants and animals. As oxygen is used by the cells, many "waste" products are formed. One of these is carbon dioxide. Carbon dioxide is a compound of carbon and oxygen.

Plants, however, also use carbon dioxide from the air in making their food. As carbon dioxide is used by plants, the carbon becomes part of the food. Oxygen is given off and becomes part of the air. The picture on this page helps show how oxygen and carbon dioxide can be used again and again. In what ways do different living things take in and give off these gases?

Figure 25–3. Plants and animals that live in water also rely on the carbon dioxide/oxygen cycle. How, do you think, does the cycle in water differ from the cycle on land?

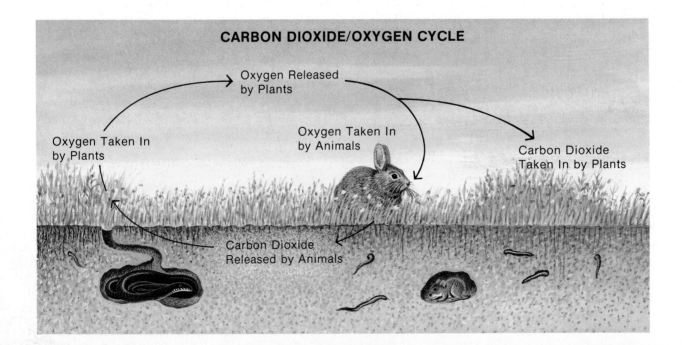

CARBON DIOXIDE/OXYGEN CYCLE

Oxygen Released by Plants

Oxygen Taken In by Plants

Oxygen Taken In by Animals

Carbon Dioxide Taken In by Plants

Carbon Dioxide Released by Animals

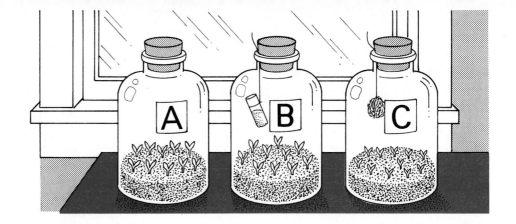

Investigate

What happens to plants when they don't get enough oxygen or carbon dioxide from the environment?

You will need

steel-wool pad; caustic soda (drain cleaner); small pill bottle; garden soil; string; rubber gloves; small spoon; 3 clear-glass jars with stoppers; about 30 fast-growing seeds such as radish, bean, or mustard

Background

Some of the specific growth requirements of green plants may vary. But oxygen and carbon dioxide seem to be needed by all green plants.

What to do

Soak the seeds in water for two or three hours. Label the jars A, B, and C. Put some moist soil in the bottom of each jar. Spread about ten seeds on the soil in each jar. Put a stopper firmly in jars A and B. Tie a string around the steel-wool pad. Moisten the pad and suspend it in jar C as shown. The steel wool will form rust (iron combined with oxygen), thus using up the oxygen in the jar. Put a stopper firmly in jar C. Place the jars in a warm spot where they will get a small amount of light. Note any differences in the seeds after two or three days. Answer the first set of questions below before going on. Jar C will not be used again.

When the seeds have sprouted, take the stopper out of jars A and B. Make sure the soil is moist. Put on the rubber gloves and carefully fill the pill bottle with caustic soda, using the spoon. Caustic soda will burn the skin, so be careful not to get any on your skin. Wash well with water if you do. Caustic soda removes carbon dioxide from the air. Suspend the open pill bottle in jar B as shown. Put the stoppers back in. Place jars A and B where they will get the same amount of fairly bright light, but don't let them get too warm. Compare the growth of the plants in these jars after two or three days.

Now that you have done the investigation

■ What differences did you notice between the seeds in A and B and those in C? What may have caused any differences?
■ What differences did you notice between the plants in jars A and B? Explain any differences.

RENEWABLE RESOURCES

What are some examples of renewable resources?
How is each of these resources important?

Plants as a renewable resource

Think about some of the ways plants are important to you as a resource. Many of the foods you like are made from plants. Lumber from trees is used to make houses and furniture. Some of the clothes you wear are made from cotton plants. Many medicines are made from plants. Which plants do you know of that provide food or medicine?

One of the characteristics of plants and other living things is that they are able to *reproduce* [REE-pruh-D(Y)OOS]. That is, they can produce new living things like themselves. Trees, for example, grow seeds. Under proper conditions, these seeds can grow into new trees. Therefore, as trees are cut down and used as a resource, they can be replaced, or replanted. This is why trees and other plants are known as a renewable resource.

In many cases, such as with certain trees and crops, people may need to collect and plant the seeds. Scientists have even been able to produce special *breeds,* or kinds, of plants. For example, the reproduction of two kinds of corn plants can be controlled. The seed that results from this produces a breed of corn plant with characteristics of both parent plants. How might this be important?

But many plants, such as wild plants, produce seeds and new plants naturally. What might keep a plant or a group of plants from remaining a renewable resource?

Animals as a renewable resource

Animals are also important to you as a resource. Many animals provide meat and other foods. What kinds of meat do you like to eat? Many things, such as clothes and soap, are made from animals. What things do you use that are made from animals?

Grant Heilman

Figure 25–4. In much the same way that some other resources are involved in a cycle, plants and animals are involved in a food cycle. How are these chickens involved in the food cycle?

Through the years, people have tamed many of the animals that are used as a resource, such as sheep and pigs. People have also produced many special breeds of animals, such as certain kinds of chickens and cattle. What other tame or specially bred animals do you know of?

☐ **What do you think are some of the advantages of having tame or specially bred animals?**

To Think About

Living things that are not raised by people are called *wildlife*. What examples of wildlife do you know of? In what ways is wildlife a resource?

NONRENEWABLE RESOURCES

What are some examples of nonrenewable resources?
How is each important?

Land as space for living

Think for a moment about being in two different environments. One is a city with many buildings and streets. The other is a country road alongside open fields that stretch as far as you can see. In the first environment, you might feel that each person has only a small amount of space in which to live and move about. You might think that there is very little space left for more people. In the second environment, you might feel that a person could have all the space he or she wants. You might wonder if people could ever run out of space!

Phil Degginger

Do It Yourself

Compare some of the ways land is being used

Obtain a camera and take pictures of places that show different ways in which land in your environment is being used. If you can't get a camera, cut pictures from magazines and newspapers. Make a display, collage, or scrapbook. Which pictures do you think show land being used wisely? Unwisely? What improvements in land use might you suggest?

Both examples help illustrate the difference in the amount of living space in different environments. Both help point out a resource that is sometimes taken for granted or not generally thought of as a resource. This resource is land. There are many ways in which land is needed to provide space. Land is needed for building homes and cities. It is needed for roads and parks. In what other ways is land needed?

Land is an example of a nonrenewable resource. Unlike a renewable resource, a nonrenewable resource cannot be replaced as it is used up. The processes that have formed a nonrenewable resource, such as land, have for the most part been completed. And land that provides space for a building, for example, basically can't be used for anything else. What are some examples around you of more and more land being used?

Grant Heilman

Figure 25–5. What uses of land are shown here? How might the use of some of this land change in the future?

Soil for growing things

In addition to providing living space, land is important in another way. It contains soil that helps support life on the earth. Soil provides a "foothold" for the roots of plants. It supplies nutrients needed for plant growth. It also holds water and air that are needed by plants. Animals and people depend on plants or on animals that eat plants for all of their food. Which animals do you know of that eat only plants? Only animals? Both?

There are many kinds of soil. Basically, each kind of soil was formed from the rocky materials of the earth. These materials have been broken down through millions of years. Some soil also contains the decayed remains of plants and animals.

The forces that form soil are still at work. However, it takes thousands of years to form 2.5 centimeters (1 inch) of soil! So soil is thought of as a nonrenewable resource. In what ways does soil get "used up" or lost?

The soil over the surface of the earth averages 61 to 91 centimeters (2 to 3 feet) deep. The most fertile of this soil, called *topsoil*, is usually less than 30 centimeters (1 foot) deep. Many areas of the United States at one time had 23 to 30 centimeters (9 to 12 inches) of fertile topsoil. Through years of use and misuse, the amount has dropped to 15 centimeters (6 inches) or less in many places.

Figure 25–6. What differences do you notice between the topsoil (left) and the loamy soil (right)? Which would be better for growing plants? Why?

Grant Heilman

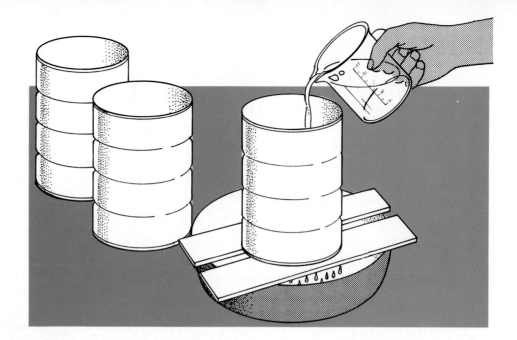

Investigate

How can you compare the water-holding capacity of soils?

You will need

different kinds of soil, coffee can for each kind of soil, fine screening for the bottom of each can, hammer, small nail, boards to support the coffee cans, bowls large enough to hold ½ L of water

Background

The capacity to absorb and hold water is an important characteristic of soil. It is important not only in supplying plants with water but also in preventing flooding and erosion. So the water-holding capacity of soil helps determine its value as a resource. However, different kinds of soil can hold more water than others.

What to do

With the hammer and nail, punch a number of small holes in the bottom of each of the coffee cans. Be sure to punch the same number of holes in each can. Line the bottom of each can with the screening. Fill each can about half full with a different kind of soil. Support the cans with the boards as shown. Place a bowl under each of the cans. Pour ½ L of water into each of the cans of soil. Watch what happens to the water poured into each can of soil.

Now that you have done the investigation

■ Which soil holds water best?
■ Which soil drains the fastest?
■ On which soil does the water stay the longest before soaking in? How might this be a problem?
■ What things about the makeup of each soil do you think cause them to have different water-holding capacities?

Minerals for making things

Throughout history, people have made use of materials from the earth to make their life easier. Tools made of flint, bronze, copper, and iron have been found in homes of ancient people. The materials for these tools were made of *minerals* [MIHN(-uh)-ruhlz] from the earth. Generally, minerals can be thought of as the solid, nonliving, natural materials found in the earth. The earth's supply of minerals was formed over millions of years. Therefore, minerals are a nonrenewable resource.

You learned about minerals in your study of Chapter 2, "Minerals." In studying minerals further, you will be looking upon minerals as a natural resource. Minerals have many uses, and they should be used with care. As nonrenewable resources, many minerals can be used up someday. They should not be used carelessly. Minerals should not be wasted.

Many resources, such as air and soil, are readily available for use. But minerals must first be mined, or taken from the earth. Minerals that are mined are often called *ores*. Some ores, such as copper ore and iron ore, are often found at or near the surface. They can be mined by a surface method such as open-pit mining. Other minerals, such as silver and lead ore, are often found deep inside the earth. They must be mined by a method such as shaft mining.

Most minerals must also be refined before they can be used. That is, impurities such as waste rock in the ore must be removed. For example, copper ore is crushed and screened. Chemicals are added to help remove some of the impurities. Then it is heated, and more chemicals are added until the desired purity is reached.

After some minerals are refined, they are combined with other minerals. A combination of two or more minerals, usually metals, is called an *alloy* [AL-oy]. For example, after iron ore is refined, metallic minerals such as chromium or nickel might be added to form an alloy of steel. What things do you use that are made of steel?

□ **What do you think is the advantage of alloys?**

H. Armstrong Roberts

Figure 25–7. An open-pit copper mine is shown here. What are some advantages to this kind of mine? Some disadvantages?

Find Out More

There are many minerals that are used to make alloys of steel. Find out what some of these minerals are and what useful properties they give to steel. Also find out which other kinds of alloys are commonly used. You may want to use reference books to help you.

ENERGY RESOURCES

What is energy, and in what ways is it important to people?

What are some of the resources that are used for energy?

Energy and people

Picture in your mind for a moment people doing the following things: dancing, riding a bus, frying a hamburger, huddling around a campfire to keep warm. Though each thing is different, each has something in common. Each involves *energy* [EHN-ur-jee]. What things do you do that involve energy?

You've probably heard the word "energy" used in many ways. Energy is usually defined as the ability to do work or to cause change. When you dance or ride a bike, you are doing work. As you grow, your body changes. What other examples of work and change can you think of?

There are different kinds and sources of energy. In order for you to grow and change, for example, you need *chemical energy* from *food*. To cook food, you need *heat energy* from *gas* or *electricity*. To run a bus requires heat energy and *mechanical energy* from burning *gasoline*. To make steel for buses and other things requires large amounts of heat energy from *coal*.

Without energy, all our activities would come to a stop. Though it is unlikely that people will soon run out of energy resources, there are many problems related to energy. People in some countries do things that require more energy than people in other countries do. For example, the United States has 6 percent of the world's population. But its businesses, industries, and transportation use about 32 percent of the total energy used throughout the world! As other countries become more developed, what do you suppose will happen to their energy needs? Another problem is that the supply of energy resources is unevenly distributed throughout the earth. Perhaps the main problem is that most of the earth's supply of resources now used for

To Think About

Many of the things that you do or use each day are part of what is known as your *life-style*. For example, the kind of clothes you wear, what you do for recreation, and how you travel from place to place are all part of your life-style. To a great extent, people's life-styles depend on the resources—especially energy resources—that are available. Explain how this might be so for the examples given above. What other examples can you think of in which people's life-styles depend on the resources available to them?

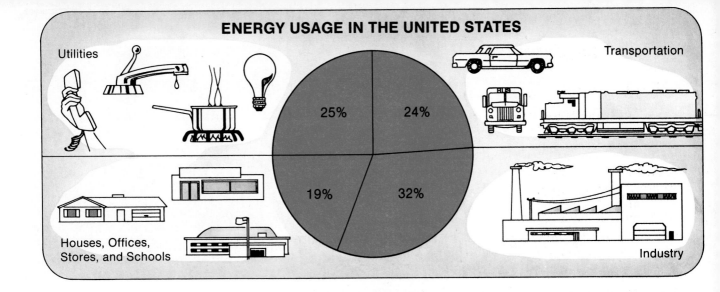

ENERGY USAGE IN THE UNITED STATES

Utilities

Transportation

25%

24%

19%

32%

Houses, Offices, Stores, and Schools

Industry

energy is limited. The rest of this chapter will help you take a closer look at each of the different energy resources.

Figure 25–8. In what ways are the uses of energy shown here important to you?

☐ **In what ways do you suppose uneven world distribution of energy resources is a problem?**

Fossil fuels

There are many plants growing throughout the world today. But millions of years ago there were even more plants. And for a long time, much of the land was swampy. As plants died, they fell into the swamps and became covered with water. This kept them from decaying. Slowly, the swamps began to fill in with mud. Then layers of rock began to form over the dead plants. Through the years, the weight of the mud and rock squeezed the plants together. Because of this and certain chemical changes, the plants became hardened into a rocklike material known as *coal.*

As you probably know, plants use sunlight in making food. When this happens, energy from the sun is stored in the plants. The remains of plants that make up coal still have this stored energy. When coal is burned, this energy is released. Energy from burning coal is mainly used to run most of the electric-power plants around the world. Why do you think coal is often called a *fossil* [FAHS-uhl] *fuel?*

Figure 25–9. (Top) Bituminous coal, or soft coal, is the most widely used coal in power plants and in industry. (Middle) Lignite, or brown coal, has a high percentage of water, which makes it a poor fuel. But lignite may become more important as a fuel if other kinds of coal become scarce. (Bottom) Anthracite, or hard coal, produces almost no smoke when burned, but it lies deeper in the earth than bituminous coal.

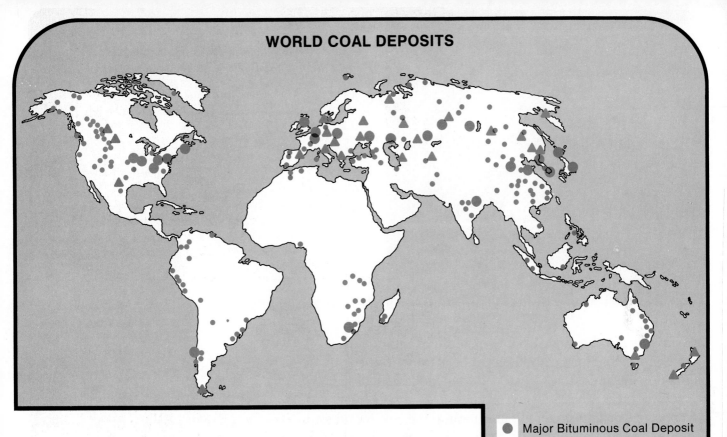

WORLD COAL DEPOSITS

● Major Bituminous Coal Deposit
· Minor Bituminous Coal Deposit
● Major Anthracite Deposit
· Minor Anthracite Deposit
▲ Lignite Deposit

So far, coal and other fossil fuels have been the most abundant energy resources. Figure 25–10 shows the location of major coal deposits around the world. Coal deposits vary in thickness from 2.5 centimeters (1 inch) to 30 meters (100 feet). Most coal is mined from deposits that are from 76 to 240 centimeters (2½ to 8 feet) thick. Some coal is close enough to the surface to be mined by strip mining. Most coal, however, lies far below the surface. It is mined by underground-mining methods.

There are two other resources known as fossil fuels. They are *oil* and *natural gas*. People are not exactly sure how oil and natural gas were formed. It is thought that they began to form millions of years ago at a time when most of the earth was covered by oceans. Tiny ocean plants and animals died and collected in great numbers on the ocean floor. Through the years, they became covered with sand and other materials from the ocean. These materials eventually formed layers of rock that squeezed the plants and animals together. The plants and animals also underwent

Figure 25–10. What are some advantages of having an abundant supply of coal in an area? Some disadvantages?

Figure 25–11. Which of these products made from coal have you used? What others do you know of?

many chemical changes. Some of these changes caused oil to be formed. Some caused natural gas to be formed.

Both oil and natural gas collected in layers of underground rock. These layers of rock are usually made of sandstone or limestone. Oil and natural gas are found and mined mainly by underground-drilling methods. Though formed from ocean plants and animals, why, do you think, can oil and natural gas be found under dry land today?

Many things are made from oil and natural gas. Oil is used mainly to make fuels, grease, and oil for engines. Natural gas is used to heat homes and other buildings.

☐ **Would you consider fossil fuels a reusable, renewable, or nonrenewable resource? Why?**

Nuclear energy

Many of the resources used for energy, such as wood, coal, and oil, have been known to people for a long time. And it's relatively easy to release the energy from these resources simply by burning them. But the development of another kind of energy, *nuclear* [N(Y)OO-klee-ur] *energy,* has an interestingly different history.

In 1896, the French scientist Antoine Henri Becquerel was working with some uranium ore and photographic plates. One day he left a piece of the ore on top of the plates.

By chance, he put them in a drawer where it was dark. Later, he developed one of the plates. To his surprise, he found an image of the piece of uranium ore! He accidentally found that the uranium gave off energy that caused the image to appear.

This opened the door for many ideas and discoveries about the relationship of matter and energy. In 1905, Albert Einstein stated his famous Special Theory of Relativity. The theory stated that there are great amounts of energy locked in matter. For a long time, people had suspected that matter was made up of small parts called *atoms* [AT-uhmz]. From various bits of evidence, scientists in the early 1900's began to put together a model of what they thought an atom was like. Figure 25–12 shows what an atom is thought to look like. Why, do you think, are people not exactly sure what an atom looks like?

The center of the atom is called the *nucleus* [N(Y)OO-klee-uhs]. It is made up of particles known as *protons* [PROH-TAHNZ] and *neutrons* [N(Y)OO-TRAHNZ]. The nucleus of each *element* [EHL-uh-muhnt] has a different total of protons and neutrons. Another part of an atom is the electron. Electrons whirl around the nucleus. An element is a substance made up of only one kind of atom.

The particles in the nucleus are held together by a strong force. In certain elements, however, some of these particles escape as energy. These elements are said to be *radioactive* [RAYD-ee-oh-AK-tihv]. It was radioactive energy from uranium that caused the image of the piece of uranium ore to appear on Becquerel's photographic plate.

The amount of energy that is given off naturally by radioactive elements is small. A goal of scientists in the 1930's was to find a way to release the great amounts of energy in matter that were suggested by Einstein's theory. In 1939, experiments were done in which the nucleus of a uranium atom was bombarded with neutrons. The result was the *fission* [FIHSH-uhn], or splitting, of the uranium atom. When a uranium atom is fissioned, atoms of two lighter elements are formed. But more important, two or three free neutrons and a great amount of energy are given off.

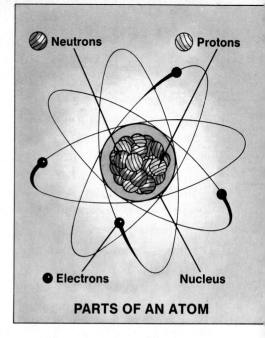

PARTS OF AN ATOM

Neutrons   Protons

Electrons   Nucleus

Figure 25–12. The nuclei of the heaviest elements, such as uranium (below), contain the largest amounts of energy. Why, do you think, is this so?

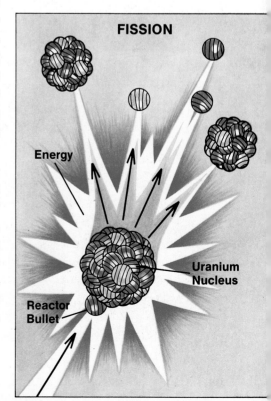

FISSION

Energy

Uranium Nucleus

Reactor Bullet

In 1942, scientists built the first *nuclear reactor* [ree-AK-tur]. In it, they were able to produce a controlled nuclear *chain reaction.* That is, the free neutrons of one fissioned uranium atom were allowed to fission other uranium atoms, and so on. If a chain reaction is uncontrolled, the energy is released all at once. An atom-bomb explosion is an example of this. But in a controlled reaction, the energy is released slowly. This energy can be used in many ways. The main use of energy from nuclear reactors is to heat water to make steam. The steam is then used to make electricity. What are some other uses of nuclear energy?

At present, about 10 percent of the electric power in the United States comes from nuclear reactors. One advantage of nuclear reactors is that a huge amount of energy can be released from a small amount of fuel. Some people think that nuclear energy is fairly safe and low in pollution compared to other sources of energy. However, other people do not. Problems of nuclear reactors include thermal pollution of water, radioactive-waste disposal, and possible scarcity of fuel in the future. Tons of uranium ore must be mined to produce even a small amount of fissionable uranium. Scientists are working on ways to improve nuclear reactors.

Find Out More

There are many areas of research concerning nuclear energy. These include developing fusion reactors rather than fission reactors, using fuels other than uranium, and improving the safety of reactors. Using reference materials, find out the significance and current status of research in these and other areas of nuclear energy. You may also want to write to the Energy Research and Development Administration, Washington, DC 20545.

Thomas M. Pantages

Do It Yourself

Compare an uncontrolled and a controlled chain reaction

Set up about twenty dominoes in a triangle as shown. Each domino represents a uranium atom. Start a chain reaction by knocking over (fissioning) the domino (atom) that stands alone. How long does it take for all the atoms to be fissioned in this uncontrolled chain reaction?

Set up the dominoes again. This time use a ruler to keep some of the atoms from fissioning until you want them to. How does this represent a controlled chain reaction? Try finding out how a chain reaction is controlled in a nuclear reactor.

Solar energy

Of all the energy resources, perhaps the most noticeable and the most elusive is energy from the sun. Energy from the sun is often called *solar* [SOH-lur] *energy*. It is noticeable because it is around you almost every day. It keeps the earth warm enough for life. It gives light for plants to grow. It is elusive because people have not yet found practical and inexpensive ways to capture it for other uses.

Solar energy comes to the earth as light and heat. This light and heat come about because of nuclear reactions that take place on the sun. Unlike fission, which is the splitting of atoms, the reactions on the sun combine atoms. The sun is made up almost entirely of the gases hydrogen and helium. There is extreme heat and pressure in the center of the sun. Under these conditions, hydrogen nuclei are combined. They form the slightly heavier element helium. This combining is known as *fusion* [FYOO-zhuhn].

The fusion of elements produces even greater amounts of energy than the fission of elements. The sun is a huge furnace, about 1.3 million times the size of the earth. In

Figure 25–13. The panel of mirrors shown here focuses rays from the sun into a solar furnace. The furnace can reach about 3 302°C (5,975°F)—hot enough to melt a plate of steel in a minute!

Gerolf Kalt/ZEFA

40 minutes, the sun sends to the earth's surface as much energy as people use to run factories, machines, and vehicles and to heat buildings for a year!

One of the main problems in trying to capture solar energy is that it is spread out across the surface of the earth. The sun does not shine enough on any one place. What are some other problems with capturing solar energy that you can think of?

One device used for collecting solar energy is the *flat-plate collector*. It has a black metal plate that absorbs sunlight. The heat made by the sunlight is removed from the plate by water or some other liquid. The heated liquid can be used to heat water and air in a building.

Another device for collecting solar energy is the *solar furnace*. Mirrors or lenses are used to focus sunlight on a small area. Some solar furnaces can produce temperatures hot enough to melt steel! What might be some possible uses of a solar furnace?

Electricity can be produced from sunlight by means of a *solar cell*. A solar cell is a kind of battery made of special material. When light shines on this material, electricity is made. Many satellites in space are powered by solar cells. Why do you suppose solar cells are particularly suited for satellites?

□ **Would you consider solar energy a reusable, renewable, or nonrenewable resource? Why?**

Other energy resources

Besides those energy resources talked about so far, there are others used to produce electric power. Some power plants make use of the energy of moving water. These power plants have a dam built across a river. The dam has gates that allow water to pass through. The force of this moving water turns large wheels. The wheels, in turn, cause *electric generators* [JEHN-uh-RAYT-urs] to spin. Electricity made in this way is known as *hydroelectric power*. Hydroelectric power is a cheap source of electricity. What parts of the world do you suppose rely on hydroelectric power?

(*Text continues on page 504.*)

Figure 25–14. Hydroelectric power plants supply only about 2 percent of the world's electric power. In the future, do you think more of the world's electric power will have to come from hydroelectric power plants? Why?

Phil Degginger

502

Investigate

How can you make your own solar furnace?

You will need

reflecting material such as aluminum foil, large bowl or other object with a curved surface, coat hanger, thermometer, small piece of dark paper, 2 jars of water

Background

The earliest known use of a solar furnace is thought to have occurred in 214 B.C. The Greeks are said to have set fire to Roman ships by using mirrors to focus the sun's rays on them. Since then, many experimental solar furnaces have been built.

What to do

Line the inside of the bowl with foil, shiny side out. Bend the coat hanger so that it can support the bowl on its side. On a sunny day, place the bowl so that it catches rays from the sun. The curved surface of the bowl will focus the rays at a certain spot in front of the bowl. Move the piece of dark paper slowly away from the front of the bowl to find this spot.

Place a jar of water at this spot. You'll have to experiment with the placement of the bowl and the jar. For example, you may have to put the bowl on the ground and suspend the jar from a chair or table as shown. Set the other jar in the sunlight and record the temperature of both jars of water. Do this every ten minutes for at least an hour.

Now that you have done the investigation

■ How warm did the water get from your solar furnace?
■ What are some of the advantages of heating water this way? Some of the disadvantages?

Many people have seen the erupting of gushers of hot water and steam called *geysers* [GY-zurz]. In Italy in 1905, the first electric-power plant was built to utilize steam from the earth. Such heat energy from the earth is known as *geothermal* [JEE-oh-THUR-muhl] *energy*. More recently, other countries, including the United States, have developed geothermal-power plants. Geothermal energy is a very clean source of power as far as pollution is concerned.

The inside of the earth is very hot. It's hot enough to boil water. In some places, water seeps underground and becomes heated to the boiling point. Sometimes, great pressure within the earth pushes the water to the surface where it changes to steam. In other cases, the pressure is less and allows the water to change to steam below. Then it rises to the surface. In any case, the force of this steam can be used to run electric generators. The most promising places for geothermal power are areas near volcanoes. Why might this be so?

Figure 25–15. What might be some advantages of geothermal power plants such as this one? Some disadvantages?

Coal miners remove underground coal from the earth. They often have to work in poorly lighted, cramped quarters.

Careers
Coal miner

A coal miner goes into a mine deep beneath the surface of the earth and removes coal. In the past, miners used a method known as *conventional mining*. In conventional mining, a *cutting-machine operator* uses a chain saw to remove coal from a seam in the earth. The *continuous-mining* method eliminates the drilling and blasting operations of conventional mining.

A key worker in the continuous-mining method is the *continuous-mining-machine operator*. The continuous-mining-machine operator sits in a cab and operates levers. When a lever is pulled, the coal is ripped out from the seam and loaded onto a conveyor or a shuttle car. The conveyor belt or shuttle car takes the coal to the surface.

Many workers are employed in the operation of a coal mine. One of the workers is the *fire boss*. Before the miners are allowed to go underground, the fire boss inspects the work area. The fire boss inspects the area for inadequate ventilation, a loose roof, and dangerous gases. If there seems to be a danger in the work area, the fire boss will not allow the miners to enter the mine.

Miners usually begin their work as helpers. They help experienced miners and learn the skills that are needed to work a mine. With experience, miners can move up to higher-paying jobs. With college work, they can receive a certificate in mine technology. For information about the work of a miner, a student in your class might write to the United Mine Workers of America, 900 15th Street, N.W., Washington, DC 20005.

Reviewing and Extending

Summing Up

1. Resources are all the natural materials and features of the earth that help support life and satisfy people's needs.
2. Reusable resources are those that can be used over and over again.
3. Air and water are reusable resources.
4. Renewable resources are those that can be replaced as they are used.
5. Plants and animals are renewable resources.
6. Nonrenewable resources are those that cannot be replaced as they are used.
7. Land, soil, minerals, and certain energy resources are nonrenewable resources.
8. Energy is the ability to do work or to cause change.
9. Energy resources include fossil fuels, nuclear energy, solar energy, hydroelectric power, and geothermal energy.

Checking Up

Vocabulary Write the numerals *1–10* on your paper. Each numbered phrase describes a term from the following list. On your paper, write the term next to the numeral of the phrase that describes it.

geothermal energy   fission   minerals
nonrenewable resources   fusion   nucleus
hydroelectric power   element   fossil fuels
reusable resources   energy   solar energy

1. splitting of atoms
2. matter made up of only one kind of atom
3. center of an atom
4. combining of atoms
5. solid, nonliving, natural materials in the earth
6. coal, soil, minerals
7. ability to do work or to cause change
8. energy from the sun
9. energy from moving water
10. air and water

Knowledge and Understanding Write the numerals *11–21* on your paper. Beside each numeral write the word or words that best complete the sentence having that numeral.

11. A resource that can be replaced as it is used is known as a _____ resource.

12. Land is an example of a _____ resource.
13. The most abundant gas in air is _____.
14. The soil, including the topsoil, over the surface of the earth averages about _____ to _____ centimeters deep.
15. Minerals that are mined are often called _____.
16. Water is always moving and can be used again and again because of the _____.
17. Plants and animals are renewable resources because of their ability to _____.
18. The great amount of energy in the nucleus of a heavy element can be released by _____.
19. Coal and oil are _____ fuels.
20. Solar energy falls on the earth as heat and _____.
21. Heat energy from deep within the earth is _____ energy.

Expressing Yourself   Write a paragraph as an answer to each of the following questions:

22. What things might help determine the kind of energy resource that is used to produce electricity in a given area? Be sure to give some examples.
23. What are some of the advantages and disadvantages of each energy resource?

Doing More

1. One of the characteristics of soil that affects plant growth is pH, or the degree of acidity or alkalinity of the soil. Obtain various soil samples and small jars with lids. Put a teaspoon of soil in each jar. Fill each jar about halfway with distilled water. Shake each jar for a minute. Let the soil settle. Test the pH of the soil solutions with litmus paper or some other pH indicator. Find out which plants prefer acid or alkaline soil. You might ask a farmer or look in references. Find out what can be done if soil is too acidic or too alkaline.

2. Make a collection of minerals or things made of minerals. List the uses of each mineral and the properties that make it useful. For example, graphite that is used in pencils is soft and leaves a mark when used for writing.

Kevin Horan/Picture Group

26 People and the Environment

In the rain forests of Brazil many trees are being cut down to clear the land for farming. Do you think this change will be helpful or harmful to the environment?

Some years ago, a mountain that was almost entirely made up of iron ore was discovered in Western Australia. Miners have been using large machines to break up the mountain to get the ore ever since. By the year A.D. 2000, this mountain may no longer be standing.

In the rain forests of Brazil, many trees are being cut down, and the land is being cleared to make room for farming. However, in that part of Brazil, the land supports crops only for a few years. After a few years, the farmers are forced to move on, leaving behind barren land that is subject to the forces of erosion.

Leveling a mountain and cutting down forests are only two ways people change the earth. In what other ways do people cause changes? Are all the changes that people cause helpful, or have some changes turned out to be harmful? This chapter can help you find answers to these questions and to other questions about how people have changed the earth.

CHANGING THE SURFACE

What are natural resources?

How can mining cause changes in the surface of the earth?

How does building homes and cities cause changes in the surface of the earth?

Why are people causing greater changes in the surface of the earth than ever before?

Natural resources and people

People need and use many different materials from the earth. Think of some of the things you need and use. You could not live without oxygen and water. You also need food. Your food comes from plants and from animals that eat plants. Plants need certain materials from soil in order to grow. Some things you use, such as coins and glasses, are made from materials found within the crust of the earth. Materials from the earth that people need or use are called *natural resources* [NACH-(uh-)ruhl REE-soh(UH)RS-uhz].

Perhaps the most widely used natural resources for making things are minerals, fossil fuels, and trees. Metal, cement, glass, and chemicals are made from minerals. The fossil fuels are coal, oil, and natural gas. They are called fossil fuels because they are thought to have formed from the remains of living things. Fossil fuels are used to make many important products. They are also used for heating buildings and for running cars, trucks, and other vehicles. Trees are used for lumber and for making paper, paint thinner, and many chemicals.

Effects of getting resources

As you may know, minerals and fossil fuels are found within the crust of the earth. In order to get these resources, people must use some form of mining. Salt, sulfur, and oil are often pumped to the surface from deep wells. Minerals and coal that lie far below the surface are mined by digging tunnels. Minerals and coal that lie close to the surface are mined from large open pits. Each of these ways

Find Out More

Use references such as encyclopedias to find out what products are made from coal, from oil (petroleum), and from natural gas. Make a display showing some of the products made from these fossil fuels.

of getting minerals and fossil fuels causes changes in the surface of the earth.

For example, coal is often found as a seam between layers of other kinds of rock. When coal is mined from an open pit, miners must often dig up large amounts of the other kinds of rock to reach the coal. This rock is dumped in piles near the mine. Such piles may become large hills. In time, the mine area will have many deep pits surrounded by hills of broken rock. Few plants will grow in such places.

Lumbering results in a different kind of change in the surface of the earth. Most trees that are cut down for lumber grow in forests on hillsides and on mountainsides. The roots of these trees help hold the soil in place. However, the branches of the trees may be so close together that little sunlight reaches the forest floor. As a result there may be few plants other than trees growing in the forest. If large numbers of trees in a given place are cut down, there may be too few plants left to keep the soil from being eroded by water or by wind. The soil may be carried into rivers, making the water very muddy. Some soil may be deposited on top of plants in other places. This soil may kill these plants. How might the surface of the earth be affected in those places?

☐ **How might erosion that could result from lumbering be prevented?**

Brent Jones

Do It Yourself

Find out what natural resources are found in your state

Use references about natural resources to find out which of the following resources—minerals, trees for lumber, and fossil fuels—are found in your state. What are the most important resources of your state? Make a map that shows where each of the important resources that come from your state is found. Find out what is being done so that the surface of the earth is changed as little as possible in obtaining these resources.

Effects of building homes and cities

Perhaps you have watched people putting up buildings. If so, you know that the first thing that happens is that trees and other large plants are cut down. The topsoil is scraped off the land. A hole for a foundation may be dug into the earth. Such changes for one or two buildings do not cause a great amount of change in the surface of the earth. But think about how many buildings make up the cities or towns near where you live. And, think about how many cities and towns there are over the surface of the entire earth!

A city or a town is made up of more than homes and other buildings. There are also streets, parking lots, and underground pipes to carry water and wastes. There may also be underground tanks to store water and fuel. Each time one of these things is built, people scrape and dig into the surface of the earth.

☐ **What other changes might people make in the surface as a result of building homes and cities?**

To Think About

What new buildings, streets, or other things have you seen being built? How has the building of these things caused changes in the surface of the earth?

Alan Pitcairn/Grant Heilman

Figure 26–1. What changes in the earth have resulted from people digging these oil wells?

511

Figure 26–2. How does building a subway cause changes in the earth?

More people, more changes

People have been digging up certain resources, such as stone and ores of metals, from the earth for thousands of years. In doing so, people have caused changes in the surface of the earth. However, until fairly recent times few of these changes have been as great as those being made today.

One reason for this is that long ago people did not have large machines run by engines. Machines that are run by engines have come into use only in the last 200 years. Another reason is that there are more people living on the earth today than there were many years ago. With more people living today, more resources are needed to meet their needs. Getting more resources leads to greater changes in the surface of the earth. It also means that such changes are made at a faster rate than they have ever been made before.

512

CHANGING THE SOIL

How does poor soil differ from rich soil?
How do growing plants affect soil?
How can farming cause changes in soil?

Makeup of soil

One of the most important resources of the earth is soil. People depend on soil to grow the plants they use for food, for making some kinds of cloth, and for wood. However, there are many different kinds of soil on the earth. Not all kinds of soil can be used to grow plants.

As you may know, soil is made up of bits of weathered rock and the remains of living things. The part of soil that comes from weathered rock is known as *mineral matter*. The part of soil that comes from the remains of living things is called *organic* [awr-GAN-ihk] *matter*. Different kinds of soils differ in the kinds of mineral matter and the amount of organic matter present.

Figure 26–3. In what way have people caused changes in part of this dry desert land?

Soils may further be described as rich or poor. Rich soil contains many different kinds of mineral matter as well as large amounts of organic matter. Poor soil may be lacking in mineral matter, in organic matter, or in both. Few plants grow well in poor soil.

Plants and soil

As you may know, plants need many different substances in order to grow and to form seeds. Some of these come from the mineral matter and the organic matter in soil. They are dissolved in water in soil. Plants take in water containing these substances through their roots.

Suppose plants only *took* matter from soil in which they grow. In time that soil would become poor soil. That is, the mineral matter and the organic matter that plants need in order to grow would be used up. In nature, this seldom happens. As plants die, their remains become part of soil. In this way, much of the mineral and organic matter used by the plants is returned to the soil. Freshly weathered rock adds more mineral matter. The remains of animals also add more organic matter to soil. Therefore, mineral matter and organic matter are always being added to soil in nature.

☐ **In what way is the use of mineral matter and of organic matter by plants part of a cycle?**

Find Out More

Use references such as geology books to find out more about different kinds of soil. —loamy soil, sandy soil, and clayey soil. How do these soils differ? What are some other terms used to describe different kinds of soil?

S. Rannels/Grant Heilman

Figure 26–4. Fungi, such as these mushrooms, help return materials to the soil when the fungi break down leaves and other remains of living things. What happens to the mushrooms when they die?

514

Investigate

What happens to plants grown in soil lacking mineral and organic matter?

You will need

sand, scissors, bean seeds, garden soil or potting soil, 2 small milk cartons

Background

There are many different kinds of soil. Each kind differs in the kind of weathered rock material and the amount of organic matter present. For example, tropical soils often contain little organic and little mineral matter. Desert soils usually have very little organic matter but large amounts of mineral matter. However, the mineral matter is not always in a form that plants can use. You can find out how the amount of mineral and organic matter in soil affects the growth of plants by doing this activity.

What to do

Cut off the tops of two small milk cartons. Fill one of the cartons with sand. Sand contains little or no mineral matter in a form that plants can use and no organic matter. Fill the other carton with rich garden or potting soil. Such soil has a great deal of mineral matter and organic matter. Plant three or four bean seeds in each carton. Water each carton with equal amounts of water and set the cartons in a well-lighted place. Observe the seeds as they begin to grow and for a week or two afterward. [Note: During the first few days of their growth, the beans will be using food stored in their seeds.]

Now that you have done the investigation

■ What happened to the bean plants growing in the sand after they had used up the food stored in their seeds?
■ What happened to the bean plants growing in the soil after they had used up the food stored in their seeds?
■ What difference, if any, did you observe between the plants growing in soil and the plants growing in sand?
■ How does a lack of mineral and organic matter in soil affect the growth of bean plants?

People have always depended on plants for much of their food. At one time all food from plants came from wild plants. Later people learned how to grow certain kinds of plants for food. However, growing plants for food often leads to changes in the soil.

Long ago, there was a great amount of land that could be used to grow plants for food. There were also fewer people living on the earth. People chopped down and burned the wild plants to clear land. Then they planted crops in the cleared land. The parts of the crops people did not use were fed to animals or burned. No plant remains were added to soil. In time, soil used in this way would no longer produce enough food to feed the people living there. Then the people would move away to new land.

Today there are many more people living on the earth. Most soil that can be used for farming is being used to grow crops. Farmers can no longer move away if soil becomes too poor to grow large amounts of crops. For this reason, farmers have had to learn what kinds of matter plants need to grow. This matter can then be added to soil as *fertilizer* [FURT-uhl-EYE-zur]. This helps to keep soil useful for growing crops.

Besides using up matter that plants need to grow, farming can lead to other changes in soil. Soil that is to be used for farming is often covered by growing plants. The roots of these plants hold soil in place and keep it from being lost through erosion. In farming, the soil is plowed. This destroys the wild plants that hold soil in place. This also results in breaking soil up into very fine pieces. Many kinds of crops are planted far apart. The roots of these plants do not hold soil in place as well as the roots of plants that grow close together. Also, during much of the year, there are no plants covering soil used to grow crops. As a result, much soil may be lost through erosion.

☐ **What ways can you think of in which farmers might prevent soil erosion?**

Photri

J. G. Zimmerman/Alpha Photo Associates, Inc.

Figure 26–5. What are some things farmers can do to prevent erosion by wind and by water?

CHANGING THE AIR AND THE WATER

Why are air and water important resources?
How do people cause changes in the air?
How do people cause changes in the water?

Two important resources

As you know, people need and use many different resources. Minerals are used to make metals, glass, and many other things. Fossil fuels are used to make heat and electricity. Soil is used to grow plants. In each case, the resource is used to produce something that people can use.

There are two resources that people use directly. These are air and water. People need oxygen to live. They get oxygen by breathing air. People also need to drink a certain amount of water each day to be healthy. Furthermore, water that people drink must be fresh. It must also be clean. People cannot use water that has too much salt or that has harmful substances in it.

Many of the things people do, however, cause changes in the air and in the water people need in order to be healthy. Some of the ways people change the air and the water can be harmful to people and to other living things.

☐ **What problems might result from harmful changes in the air or in the water?**

Changing the air

There are many ways in which the air might be changed. A volcanic eruption can add large amounts of ashes, water, and different gases to the air. However, volcanic eruptions do not happen very often. Therefore, they do not make lasting changes in the air. On the other hand, people are adding matter to the air day after day. This causes some very great changes in the air in some places.

One way that people cause changes in the air is by burning fossil fuels. These fuels are burned to produce electricity. They are burned to heat homes and other buildings. They are also burned to run cars, trucks, and large machines. As fossil fuels burn, they give off smoke, water, and gases. These kinds of matter are usually given off into the air.

One kind of matter given off into the air by burning fossil fuels is the gas carbon dioxide. Growing plants take carbon dioxide from the air to make food. However, there are fewer growing plants in large cities than there are in small towns or in open country. Therefore, a large amount of this gas tends to remain in the air over cities. The carbon dioxide mixes with water in the air to form an acid. This acid can damage buildings and be harmful to plants.

Find Out More

Smog is or has been a major problem in cities such as Los Angeles and London. Use references such as encyclopedias to find out more about smog. What is smog? What are people in Los Angeles and in London doing to solve this problem?

518

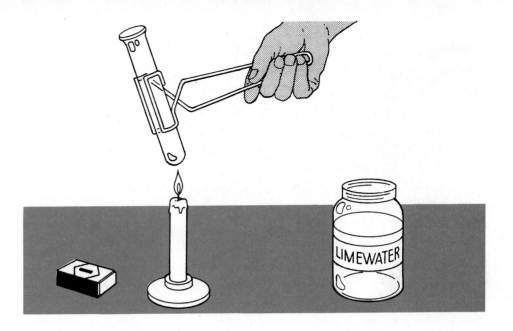

Investigate

What are some of the kinds of matter given off into the air by a burning fuel?

You will need

limewater, small jar, wax candle, candleholder, cold test tube, test-tube holder, matches

Background

Oil is used to make many products that can be used as fuels. Among these are gasoline, kerosene, heating oil, and candle wax. Each gives off certain kinds of matter as it burns. You can identify some of the kinds of matter given off by a burning fuel by observing a burning candle in this activity.

What to do

Set a candle in a candleholder and light the candle. Use a test-tube holder to hold a cold test tube over the flame. Notice what, if any, kinds of matter collect on the bottom and the sides of the test tube.

Set a small jar of limewater near the candle. Hold the test tube so that the open end of the test tube is over but not quite covering the flame. After about one minute put the open end of the test tube into the jar of limewater. Notice if the limewater around the open end of the test tube becomes cloudy. Limewater turns cloudy when carbon dioxide is present.

Now that you have done the investigation

■ What, if any, kinds of matter collected on the outside of the cold test tube?
■ Did the limewater become cloudy? If so, what gas did you collect in the test tube?
■ What kinds of matter did you observe being given off into the air by the burning candle?

Changing the water

People need water to drink, to grow food, and to make things they use. For these reasons, people have often settled near lakes and rivers. However, people have not always taken care of these sources of water.

For example, people have been dumping their garbage and other wastes into lakes and rivers for hundreds of years. Long ago, this seldom caused major problems. There were fewer people living on the earth then. Therefore, there was also much less waste than there is today.

Today, there are many more people living on the earth. Greater amounts of waste are dumped into rivers and lakes. Some kinds of factory wastes are especially harmful to living things. Plants and animals may no longer be able to live in these lakes and rivers. Furthermore, these wastes must be removed from the water so that it is safe for people to drink.

□ **What problems have you heard about that resulted from the practice of dumping wastes into lakes and rivers?**

Artstreet

Figure 26–6. How has dumping garbage into the water led to changes in the water?

Grant Heilman

How is the soil conservationist helping these farmers?

Careers

Soil Conservationist

Most people in this country live in cities and towns. These people depend on farmers to grow the food they need. In order to grow enough food to feed the millions of people who live in cities and towns, farmers must take care of their soil.

Many people work at finding ways to help farmers take care of their soil. Some of these people are *soil conservationists* [KAHN(T)-sur-VAY-sh(uh-)nuhsts]. Soil conservationists work with farmers to help them find ways to prevent erosion and make the best use of their land. Soil conservationists also study changes in soil and try to find ways of improving poor soil.

Soil conservationists have a college degree in *agronomy*, or crop science. That is, they have studied new and better ways of growing crops. If you would like to know more about the kind of work that soil conservationists do, you or someone in your class should write to the Soil Conservation Society of America, 7515 Northeast Ankeny Road, Ankeny, IA 50021.

Reviewing and Extending

Summing Up

1. Materials from the earth that people use are called natural resources.
2. People have caused many changes in the surface of the earth in getting resources such as minerals and fossil fuels and in building homes and cities.
3. People are causing changes in the surface of the earth at a faster rate today than ever before because there are many more people living today and because more resources are needed to meet the needs of people today.
4. Soil is important because people depend on soil to grow the plants they use for food.
5. People cause changes in soil when they do not replace the kinds of matter used by growing plants and when they break up soil by plowing.
6. Air and water are two resources people use directly. Some of the things people do cause changes in the air and in the water.
7. One way people change the air is by burning fossil fuels.
8. People cause changes in the water when they dump garbage and other wastes into water. Some of these wastes are harmful to living things.

Checking Up

Vocabulary   Write the numerals *1–5* on your paper. Each numbered phrase describes a term from the following list. On your paper, write the term next to the numeral of the phrase that describes it.

natural resources	fossil fuel	mineral matter
organic matter	rich soil	carbon dioxide

1. term used to describe coal, oil, and natural gas because they are thought to have formed from the remains of living things
2. one of the gases given off by burning coal, oil, or natural gas
3. part of soil that comes from the remains of living things
4. materials from the earth that people need and use
5. part of soil that comes from weathered rock

Knowledge and Understanding   Write the numerals *6–18* on your paper. Beside each numeral, write the word or words that best complete the sentence having that numeral.

6. People use some form of (*mining, farming, manufacturing*) in order to get mineral resources and fossil fuels.
7. Two resources that people use directly are water and (*air, soil, iron ore*).
8. Breaking up (*soil, ores, minerals*) into fine pieces is a change that results from plowing.

9. (*Fertilizers, Minerals, Trees*) are an important resource used for making paper, paint thinner, and many chemicals.
10. One reason that changes in the surface of the earth are being made at a faster rate than before is that (*minerals are easier to find, many more people are living today, fewer kinds of resources are being used today*).
11. When plants die, much of the mineral and the organic matter used by plants is (*given off into the air, dumped into the lakes, returned to the soil*).
12. Some kinds of factory wastes dumped into lakes and rivers (*are especially harmful to living things, help keep the environment clean, slow down production at the factory*).
13. A kind of matter that is added to soil in order to help keep the soil useful for growing crops is (*fossil fuel, iron ore, fertilizer*).
14. Minerals and coal that lie close to the surface are mined from large (*wells, open pits, tunnels*).
15. Soils that contain large amounts of (*mineral and organic matter, sands, carbon dioxide*) are said to be rich soils.
16. When people burn fossil fuels, they change the (*soil, air, water*).
17. Much mineral matter is added to soil by (*rain, wind, weathered rocks*).
18. After trees are cut down in a forest, (*soil increases in organic and mineral matter, soil may be carried away by wind and by water, soil is not affected*).

Expressing Yourself   Write a paragraph as an answer to each of the following questions:

19. What actions of people lead to an increase in the amount of erosion?
20. What problems might result when farmers do not take care of the soil?

Doing More

1. Find out how different ways of plowing affect the rate of erosion. Make a mound of soil in each of two pie tins or baking pans. Use a stick or a pencil to dig furrows running from the top to the bottom of one mound. Make furrows running around the other mound. Use a watering can to pour water over each mound gently. In which of the two pans does the water carry more soil to the bottom of the pan?
2. Use references such as encyclopedias and magazine articles to find out what kinds of gases are given off by burning fossil fuels. How do these gases cause changes in the quality of the air? Which of these gases are most harmful to living things?

Grant Heilman

Air, water, and land are being polluted or have been polluted in the area pictured here. What are some of the things that cause this pollution?

27 Environmental Pollution

Your environment affects the kind of life you lead. Your health and even your personality may depend on the environment that surrounds you. Sometimes matter *pollutes* [puh-LOOTS] the environment, or makes it unclean or even unsafe for you and other living things.

People talk more about the topic of *pollution* [puh-LOO-shuhn] than ever before. Pollution is the fouling of the environment. Documentaries on radio and TV, articles in newspapers and magazines, and political speeches devote much time to problems

caused by pollution. Government agencies have been formed to deal with these problems.

Pollution is not something new. People and other living things have always polluted the environment. However, in the past the problems were not as serious as they are now.

What are some kinds of pollution? Why does pollution cause greater problems today than it did many years ago? Has technology caused some pollution? What can be done about pollution? These are some questions about pollution discussed in this chapter.

Devaney

Figure 27–1. One cause of air pollution is automobile exhaust. If
the exhaust is blue in color, it
means that a great deal of hydrocarbons are being put into the air.
What do you think can be done
about such pollution?

AIR POLLUTION

What are some causes of air pollution?
What is an inversion?
What are some ways in which technology may
be used to control air pollution?

Must we have dirty air?

The air is a very important part of our environment.
In fact, our life depends on air. When we breathe, we
take air into our body to get the oxygen we need. When
we look at the things around us, we are looking through
air. As we move about, we are moving through air. Having
clean air is good for everyone.

But the air is not always clean. People often make the
air dirty, or polluted. For example, you have seen smoke
coming from a chimney. You have seen smoke coming
from an automobile tail pipe. You have probably smelled
these things too. The smoke you have seen and smelled
is something that does not belong there. The smoke is
called a *pollutant* [puh-LOOT-uhnt].

(*Text continues on page 527.*)

Figure 27–2. Which of these pollutants have you seen being put into the air?

In sunlight, nitrogen dioxide combines with hydrocarbons to form smog. Smog irritates the eyes and harms the lungs. It also harms plants.

Sulfur dioxide combines with oxygen and water vapor to form sulfuric acid, which harms the lungs and corrodes metal.

Particulates harm the lungs, make it difficult to see clearly, and affect the weather.

Hydrocarbons harm plants.

Sulfur dioxide harms the lungs.

Carbon monoxide gets into the blood through the lungs. It causes headaches and dizziness.

Nitrogen dioxide harms the lungs of animals. It also harms plants.

Mercury harms the brain and nerves.

Hydrocarbons
Nitrogen dioxide
Carbon monoxide

Sulfur dioxide
Nitrogen dioxide

Acid rain kills fish and other water life, harms plants, and wears away stone and brick.

Particulates
Mercury

Burning of trash and garbage

Automobiles, buses, trucks, trains, and planes

Office buildings, homes, and factories

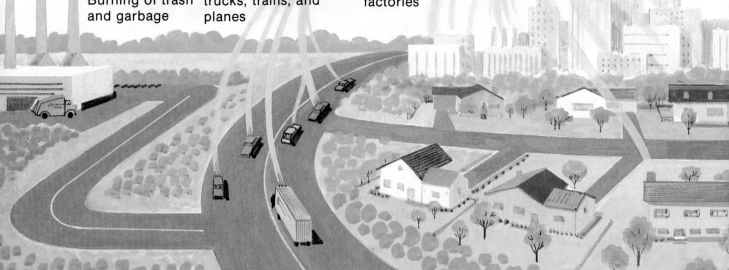

Without the smoke from burning fuels, the air would be cleaner. But if fuels were not burned, we might not have warm homes in the winter. We might not have electricity to light our homes, offices, schools, and factories. We would not be able to use automobiles, buses, trains, and planes for going places.

Can we have clean air and still do everything we want to? That's a good question. Many people think we can. Scientists are working on ways to have clean air without giving up the way of life we are used to. Everyone can benefit by knowing more about air pollution and ways of controlling it.

☐ **What are some air pollutants you can see? What are some you can smell?**

Some causes of air pollution

Most air pollution results from burning. You can probably think of many examples of burning. Fuels are burned in automobiles, buses, trucks, trains, planes, and boats. Much of the electricity we use is generated by burning coal or oil. Many homes have furnaces that burn fuel oil or natural gas.

Whenever a fuel is burned, some kind of pollutant is formed. Too often the pollutants are released into the air. The pollutants can be in many different forms. Some are invisible gases. Others, such as black smoke, are easily seen. Some are *particulates* [pur-TIHK-yuh-luhts], or tiny particles of solid or liquid matter.

Another kind of pollutant from burning fuels is the gas *sulfur dioxide* [SUHL-fur dy-AHK-syd]. This gas combines with water vapor in the air to form an acid. Rain that falls downwind from where fuels are burned will have some of this acid in it. Scientists believe acid rain may be very harmful to crops. They also believe acid rain helps wear away stone and brick. What do you suppose happens to monuments and buildings after many years of acid rain?

Another kind of burning also puts pollutants into the air. The burning of garbage and trash puts particulates

To Think About

Automobile engines that are not properly adjusted do not burn fuels as completely as these engines would if they were properly adjusted. As a result, such engines cause a lot of air pollution. But all automobile engines get out of adjustment when parts become worn. How, do you think, can we make sure that people have their engines properly adjusted?

into the air. Small amounts of mercury are sometimes put into the air by the burning of garbage and trash too.

Not all air pollution is caused by people. Even if there were no people, the air would not be perfectly clean. Volcanoes put great amounts of gases and dust into the air. Forest fires put smoke and gases into the air. The wind can blow dust, sand, and soil particles many miles through the air.

☐ **Have you ever seen dust in the air due to a windstorm? If so, where do you think the dust came from?**

Weather and air pollution

Sometimes weather conditions can help cut down on the amount of pollutants in the air. Wind can blow away polluted air. Rain and snow carry pollutants to the ground. However, we cannot depend on the weather to stop air pollution. In some places—especially cities—pollutants are put into the air faster than they are carried away, even under normal conditions.

The weather does not always help cut down on pollution. Sometimes a weather condition called an *inversion* [ihn-VUR-zhuhn] can increase the amount of pollutants in the air.

During an inversion, a layer of cool air is trapped near the surface of the earth. This happens when there is a quick drop in temperature near the surface. Then, a layer of warm air is above a layer of cool air.

(*Text continues on page 530.*)

Artstreet

Figure 27–3. In an inversion a boundary exists between a layer of warm air above and a layer of cool air below. Where is this boundary in the picture?

Investigate

What is an inversion like?

You will need

pin, ice cubes, large plastic bag, large aquarium tank, food coloring or ink, hot and cold water

Background

It is hard to see an inversion taking place in the air because the warm air layer looks just like the cold air layer. It would be much easier to see an inversion if the layers were of different colors. You can make an inversion in water, using water of different colors. Perhaps doing this will help you understand what an inversion in air is like.

What to do

Fill the tank about three-fourths full of cold water. Add the ice cubes to the water in the tank. Allow the ice cubes to melt for several minutes, causing the water to become even colder.

Fill the plastic bag with hot water. *CAUTION: Do not use water so hot that it will burn your skin.* Place a few drops of food coloring or ink into the hot water. Carefully seal the plastic bag in some way so that very little air is left in the bag.

Take the ice cubes out of the tank. Then put the plastic bag filled with hot water into the tank. The plastic bag should be at or near the top of the cold water in the tank. Wait until the water in the tank is calm. Then stick the pin into the plastic bag in several places. Record what happens to the hot water.

Now that you have done the investigation

■ Did the hot water move from the top of the tank? Why or why not?
■ Did the cold water move from the bottom of the tank? Why or why not?
■ How would you explain what happened to the hot water and the cold water in the tank?

An inversion is not always a problem. But when pollutants are constantly being added to the air, the inversion does not allow them to escape. The air close to the surface becomes highly polluted. This polluted air can be dangerous for people and other living things. For example, in 1952 there was a serious inversion in London, England. The inversion lasted several days. Pollution became so bad that three thousand to four thousand people died. There have been other such incidents, too.

Controlling pollution

Most air pollution is caused by the activities of people. Most of these activities involve the use of fuel-burning engines. So, some people think that technology is the cause of air pollution. The use of engines, together with the fact that there are many more people living today than in the past, is partly the cause of air pollution. But science and technology can also help control air pollution.

The exhaust gases from older automobiles contain many harmful pollutants. But automobiles made today have many pollution-control devices. See Figure 27–4.

Burning coal to make electricity can cause air pollution in the form of smoke. Burning fuel in furnaces and burning trash can also cause pollution. This kind of pollution

Find Out More

Serious inversions have happened in the United States. For example, there was a serious inversion in Donora, Pennsylvania, in 1948. Using references, find out what happened during this inversion. How many days did it last? How many people died as a result of it? What was the source of most of the air pollution?

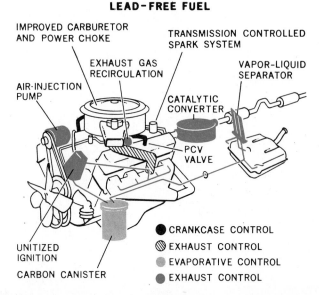

EMISSION CONTROL SYSTEM
LEAD-FREE FUEL

IMPROVED CARBURETOR AND POWER CHOKE

TRANSMISSION CONTROLLED SPARK SYSTEM

EXHAUST GAS RECIRCULATION

VAPOR-LIQUID SEPARATOR

AIR-INJECTION PUMP

CATALYTIC CONVERTER

PCV VALVE

UNITIZED IGNITION

CARBON CANISTER

● CRANKCASE CONTROL
◎ EXHAUST CONTROL
● EVAPORATIVE CONTROL
● EXHAUST CONTROL

Figure 27–4. Diagrams like this one, showing pollution-control devices, may be found in the Owner's Manual of a new automobile. Why are pollution-control devices needed on automobiles today?

can be controlled. One way is to use a device called a *scrubber* [SKRUHB-ur]. Steam and other chemicals clean the gases as they pass through the scrubber.

Another way to clean smoke is with an *electrostatic precipitator* [ih-LEHK-truh-STAT-ihk prih-SIHP-uh-TAYT-ur]. These devices remove particulates. The tiny pieces of pollutant are attracted to a metal plate because of the electric charge on the plate.

Technology is being used to control pollution in yet another way. Scientists and engineers are trying to find new sources of energy and power. For example, solar energy and fuel cells are being studied. If they could become very efficient, the amount of fuel burned would be much smaller than it is now. Air pollution, in turn, would be much less. Several different kinds of low-pollution engines are also being tested. If these engines could be perfected, air pollution would be cut down.

The ways of controlling air pollution are often costly. One reason automobiles cost more today is that so many pollution-control devices have been added to them. Adding scrubbers and electrostatic precipitators to buildings is also costly. Using new sources of energy and power may be costly too.

☐ **Do you think having cleaner air is worth these extra costs? Explain.**

WATER POLLUTION

What are some causes of water pollution?
What is eutrophication?
What are some ways in which technology may be used to control water pollution?

The goal—clean water

Water, like air, is a very important part of the environment. All living things need water to live. Most living things—including people—need clean water to live. If you have ever looked at a map of the United States, you may

Find Out More

There are other sources of energy that may help us control pollution. Using references, find out what geothermal energy is and where it is being used to generate electric power. Also find out what areas in the world may be good for the construction of power plants that can use geothermal energy. Why are some areas better than others?

have noticed that many large cities are located near a river or a lake. Cities first started in these places because the river or the lake provided transportation and was a good place to get water.

Today, many cities are faced with a special problem. Their supply of water is not clean. Their water is becoming polluted in one way or another. The pollutants come from many different places. The pollutants get into the water in many different ways. It seems as if water pollution becomes worse whenever many people live close together.

Since more and more people are living in cities, finding ways to cut down on water pollution is very important. But before water pollution can be cut down, water pollution must be understood. What are some pollutants in the water? Where do they come from? How can they be controlled? If answers to all these questions can be found, everyone will benefit by having cleaner water.

☐ **Do you think everyone is concerned about having clean water? Why or why not?**

Figure 27–5. Small streams often become polluted when people dump garbage and junk into them. What has caused the water in the picture to become polluted?

Some causes of water pollution

Many kinds of water pollution come from the activities of people. That is why the water near cities, in general, is more polluted than the water in places where fewer people live.

One kind of pollution is *sewage* [SOO-ihj]. Sewage is the waste material carried away by sewers. This includes body wastes, garbage that has been ground up by garbage disposals, and detergents from washing.

Body wastes and garbage are sometimes called *organic* [awr-GAN-ihk] *pollutants*. The term "organic" is used to mean matter that is living or comes from living things. A body of water such as a river or a lake can take in some organic matter without becoming polluted. That is, the water seems to clean itself.

The cleaning takes place in several different ways. Oxygen in the water combines with the organic matter, causing the matter to change into other substances. In addition, certain bacteria in the water feed on the organic matter and remove it in that way. Some heavy particles settle to the bottom and stay there.

Sewage may cause serious changes in water. As sewage in water decays, it uses up much oxygen. Besides, sewage provides added nutrients for plantlike protists in the water called *algae* [AL-jee]. The algae multiply rapidly—more rapidly than the fish can eat them. Many algae die and decay. Their decay uses up more oxygen. Without plenty of oxygen, the fish in the water die and also decay. This process of change in the water is known as *eutrophication* [yu-TROH-fuh-KAY-shuhn].

Detergents in sewage also speed up eutrophication. So do fertilizers that wash into water from fields and lawns. Detergents and fertilizers speed up eutrophication because they have chemicals called *phosphates* [FAHS-FAYTS] in them. It is the phosphates that help algae grow.

☐ **Have you seen bodies of water that you think are polluted? If so, why do you think the water is polluted?**

To Think About

What are some natural forms of water pollution— that is, water pollutants that are not caused by people? What do you think happens to these pollutants? Why?

Figure 27–6. What evidence is there that eutrophication has changed the water shown here? What kinds of pollutants cause eutrophication?

Arstreet

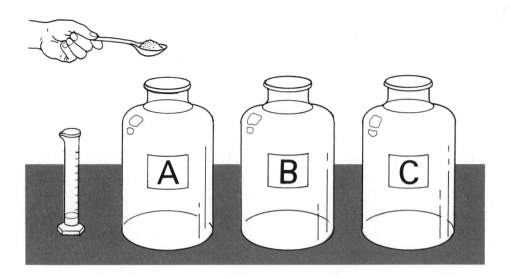

Investigate

How do detergents and fertilizers affect how fast algae will grow?

You will need

distilled water, laundry detergent, lawn fertilizer, teaspoon, pond water, graduated cylinder, marking pencil, 3 gallon jars

Background

Distilled water is about as pure as water can be. Very few algae would grow in distilled water because of the lack of nutrients. On the other hand, pond water usually contains organic matter in the form of decaying leaves, twigs, and other plant materials. As you may know, pond water often looks very clear. But even though pond water looks clear, it usually contains organic matter that allows many algae to grow there.

What to do

Label one jar *A*, another *B*, and another *C*.

Fill each jar to 2 cm from the top with distilled water. Then add a spoonful of detergent to jar *A*. Add a spoonful of fertilizer to jar *B*. Leave jar *C* as it is.

Next, measure about 10 ml of pond water in the graduated cylinder, and add this amount to jar *A*. Add the same amount to each of the other jars. Leave the jars uncovered, and set them in a well-lighted place for 2 weeks. At the end of that time, compare the 3 jars. Record your observations.

Now that you have done the investigation

■ Did more algae grow in some jars than in others? If so, which jars?
■ What might cause more algae to grow in some jars than in others?
■ Based on what you have learned, what might happen to a body of water if large amounts of detergents and fertilizers were added to it? Explain.

Sewage treatment

Because it causes water pollution, untreated sewage should not be put into streams, rivers, and lakes. But what should be done with sewage? Most cities and towns change sewage so that it is less likely to cause pollution. The changing of sewage into less harmful kinds of matter is called *sewage treatment* [TREET-muhnt].

There are three steps in treating sewage. The first step is *primary* [PRY-MEHR-ee] *treatment*. In this step, the sewage passes through a coarse screen. The screen removes large objects. Then the sewage goes into a large tank where sand, soil, and other small particles are allowed to settle out. Primary treatment removes only solid organic matter. In places where the number of people is small, primary treatment may be good enough. But further steps are usually needed.

The second step in treating sewage is called *secondary* [SEHK-uhn-DEHR-ee] *treatment*. During this step, bacteria eat up to 90 percent of the organic matter in the sewage. After bacteria work on the sewage for several hours, the solid matter is allowed to settle out. This solid matter is called *sludge* [SLUHJ].

In some places secondary treatment is enough to avoid water pollution. The water that is left after the sludge settles out is treated to kill bacteria. Then the water is put into a stream, a river, a lake, or an ocean.

In some places secondary treatment is not enough. Many kinds of harmful chemicals are not removed by secondary treatment. A third step is needed to remove these pollutants from sewage. The third step is called *tertiary* [TUR-shee-EHR-ee] *treatment*. After secondary treatment, the amount of pollutants left in the water is small. You might think that removing this small amount would not be very costly. This is not true. The cost of tertiary treatment is greater than the total cost of primary and secondary treatment.

Tertiary treatment removes almost all the pollutants. After tertiary treatment, the water that once had sewage in it is sometimes clean enough to drink.

Find Out More

To find out about an excellent facility for sewage treatment, write to the South Lake Tahoe Chamber of Commerce, Inc., P.O. Box 3418, South Lake Tahoe, California 95705. Ask them to send you information about wastewater purification at Lake Tahoe.

A. Courtesy of Sewerage Commission of the City of Milwaukee, Milorganite Division
B & C. Daniel Brody

D & E. *Photri*

Figure 27–7. *Some stages in sewage treatment are pictured. Sewage passes through a screen (A). Small particles are allowed to settle out (B). The sewage is aerated by spraying it into the air (C). After bacteria have worked on the aerated sewage, sludge is allowed to settle out (D). Treated water is stored in a holding pond (E) before being put into a stream or lake.*

Taurus

Do It Yourself
Visit a sewage-treatment plant

Get permission to visit a sewage-treatment plant in your area. Find out what steps in sewage treatment are taken in the plant. Also try to find out what happens to the extra sewage if the amount of sewage is greater than what the treatment plant can handle. Try to follow what happens to the sewage during each step or have someone at the plant explain what happens during each step. How pure is the water that is released from the plant?

LAND POLLUTION

What is the cause of land pollution?
How are things recycled in nature?
How can people help in the recycling of used materials?

What is land pollution?

Have you ever seen a junkyard? Have you ever seen a garbage dump? Have you ever seen a street littered with paper? If you have seen any of these things, you have seen land pollution.

Land pollution is often caused by things that people throw away. As you know, people throw away things made of paper, wood, glass, plastic, or metal. They also throw away food wastes.

Land pollution, like other kinds of pollution, seems to be a bigger problem today than it was many years ago. You can probably think of some reasons why. One reason is that there are more people today. The greater the number of people, the greater the number of things that are thrown away.

Another reason has to do with the kinds of things that people throw away. People have always thrown things away, but the kinds of things they throw away today are different. Today, for example, we throw away many glass bottles and jars. We also throw away bottles, bags, and other containers made of plastic.

Glass and plastic are two substances that do not break down easily in nature. They tend to stay the way they are. For example, suppose you are in a park and you drop a plastic bag on the ground. If no one picked it up, the bag would just stay there for years. Imagine the mess that would result if a lot of people littered the park with plastic bags. Unless someone cleaned up the mess, the bags would clutter up the park.

Littering the park with bags made out of paper would be bad, too. But after several weeks, the paper would start to disappear. It does not really disappear, however. Instead, it becomes a part of the soil. This happens because paper is a kind of material that is said to be *biodegradable* [BY-oh-dih-GRAYD-uh-buhl]. The word "biodegradable" means that the material can be broken down easily in nature. Usually the breaking down is because of the action of bacteria or molds.

☐ **What materials, other than glass and plastic, are not biodegradable?**

Natural recycling

To some extent, the land part of the environment can clean itself, just as the water part can. That is, many waste products can be *recycled* [ree-SY-kuhld] in nature. Recycling means changing some used material into a form that can again be useful.

Paper and garbage can be recycled in nature. These materials break down and become a part of the soil. After they break down, they supply some of the chemicals that green plants need to grow. But this kind of recycling takes time. In places where many people live close together—in cities, for example—more garbage is made than can be recycled in nature. In cities, then, getting rid of garbage can be a problem.

Land pollution from garbage is a very ugly kind of land pollution. Have you ever seen garbage piled up in an

Figure 27–8. This is a picture of a biodegradable milk carton. Why, do you suppose, is the milk carton called biodegradable?

538

alley? If so, you know that garbage can be ugly. It also has a bad smell. Furthermore, if garbage is not covered, it becomes a health problem. It attracts rats and insects that carry disease.

Even if garbage is hauled away, it has to be taken somewhere. In many cities garbage is taken to a place where it can be dumped on vacant land. Then it may be burned or it may just be allowed to rot. Of course, piles of garbage that are not covered provide homes for rats and insects.

A better way to get rid of garbage is in a *sanitary* [SAN-uh-TEHR-ee] *landfill*. A sanitary landfill is a place set aside for careful filling. After garbage is dumped at this place, bulldozers spread out the garbage. The garbage is covered with a layer of dirt at the end of each day.

As time passes, the garbage in the deeper layers is naturally recycled. It becomes a part of the soil.

☐ **Why, do you think, is a sanitary landfill covered with a layer of dirt each day?**

Help in recycling

Glass and plastic break down very slowly, if at all. Other materials are also slow to break down. Old tires, aluminum cans, and worn-out cars and appliances are not recycled very fast by natural processes. What can be done with such things?

Figure 27–9. Getting rid of garbage is a big job, requiring machines and land space. What happens when garbage is not picked up and disposed of properly?

Unfortunately, these kinds of things are often just left in the environment. They are ugly. They make the land unfit for other uses, such as recreation or the growing of food. In other words, they pollute the land.

Even though nature does not recycle these items, people can recycle them. That is, the used materials can be put into some form that can again be useful.

Many communities have recycling centers. Maybe you have taken glass bottles and jars to such a center for recycling. Most of the glass is melted and then made into glass bottles and jars again.

As you know, paper is recycled in nature. But people use so much paper that natural recycling is not fast enough. Also, there is a shortage of paper in this country. So, paper is recycled to make new paper. You may have seen a book, newspaper, or magazine that was printed on recycled paper. Perhaps you have seen a label such as "Recycled Paper" or "This book is printed on recycled paper."

Scrap metal, such as aluminum and iron, can be recycled too. Perhaps you have taken used cans to a recycling center. Like glass, scrap metal is taken to a place where it is melted and used to make metal objects, such as cans, again.

☐ **What other things can you think of that people can recycle?**

Find Out More

Using references, find out what has to be done to paper in order to recycle it. How does the cost of recycling paper compare with the cost of producing paper from trees?

Brent Jones

Do It Yourself

Visit a junkyard

Look for a junkyard near your home. You may have to go to an out-of-the-way area to find one. If you can, look through the whole junkyard. What kinds of things may be found in the junkyard? Try to find out how long some of the junk has been in the yard and what may eventually happen to it. How is a junkyard like a recycling center?

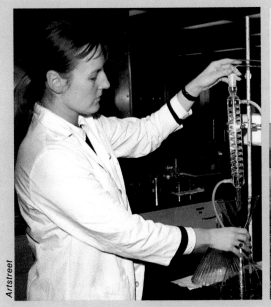

Artstreet

Robert Buchbinder

The environmental technician on the left assists in determining the quality of the water being used in a city. The technician on the right checks out a complaint against a factory that is causing excessive air pollution.

Careers

Environmental technicians

Some people devote their lives to improving the environment. *Environmental technicians* [tehk-NIHSH-uhnz] belong to a group dedicated to this task. Environmental technicians must be qualified to use scientific and engineering theories to improve the air, the water, and other parts of the environment.

The technicians may operate or supervise a water-treatment system, insuring that the drinking water in an area meets certain health standards. They regulate the flow of water from wells, rivers, and lakes to the water-treatment plants. They also check that water filters are operating efficiently.

The efforts of some environmental technicians are directed toward making the environment beautiful. The planting of trees and shrubs may come under their supervision. Or

they may foster attractive highway systems by maintaining roadside grasses and flowers.

Other environmental technicians work for a government agency. If this is the case, their role may be to monitor the pollutants being sent into the air by mills and factories. Environmental technicians may also evaluate and help control noise caused by cars and airplanes.

If you would like to become an environmental technician, you should first complete two years of study at a junior college or a technical school. To qualify for a government position, you must also pass a civil-service examination. For more information about the career of an environmental technician, someone in your class may wish to write to the National Environmental Health Association, 1600 Pennsylvania Street, Denver, CO 80203.

Reviewing and Extending

Summing Up

1. Most air pollution results from burning fuels.
2. Weather conditions affect air pollution.
3. Air pollution may be controlled by using certain pollution-control devices and by using new sources of energy power.
4. Many kinds of water pollution come from the activities of people.
5. A body of water can take in some organic matter without becoming polluted.
6. Water pollution from sewage may be controlled by treatment plants.
7. Land pollution is often caused by things that people throw away.
8. Paper and garbage can be recycled in nature.
9. People can recycle glass and scrap iron.

Checking Up

Vocabulary Write the numerals *1–10* on your paper. Each numbered phrase describes a term from the following list. On your paper, write the term next to the numeral of the phrase that describes it.

pollutant
inversion
electrostatic
  precipitator

algae
sludge
sewage
organic

recycling
eutrophication
biodegradable
sanitary landfill

1. anything in air, in water, or on land that causes pollution
2. name given to the waste material that is carried away by sewers
3. living or coming from living things
4. place set aside for careful filling with garbage that will be naturally recycled
5. broken down easily in nature
6. process of change in a body of water after sewage has been poured into it
7. plantlike protists that grow in great numbers in polluted water
8. device that is used to remove particulates from smoke
9. changing a used material into a form that can again be useful
10. layering of air, so that pollutants are trapped near the earth

Knowledge and Understanding Write the numerals *11–20* on your paper. Beside each numeral, write the word or words that best complete the sentence having that numeral.

11. All the pollutants in sewage may be removed by (*primary, secondary, tertiary*) treatment.

12. Not all air pollution is caused by people. Volcanoes, wind, and (*hydrocarbons, forest fires, inversion*) also place pollutants into the air.
13. As a problem, land pollution seems to be (*bigger than, smaller than, the same as*) it was many years ago.
14. A device called (*a scrubber, a sludge, an inversion*) can be used to clean the gases that come from burning fuel in furnaces and from burning trash.
15. Water cleans itself of small amounts of organic matter because (*algae, bacteria, fish*) eat most of the organic matter.
16. Glass and plastic are two widely used substances that (*break down in nature, are biodegradable, are not recycled very fast by natural processes*).
17. Air pollutants can build up to dangerous levels (*when winds blow gases and dust long distances, during an inversion, as a result of tertiary treatment*).
18. Detergents and fertilizers speed up the growth of algae in water because they contain (*oxygen, phosphates, mercury*).
19. After bacteria work on sewage in water for several hours, the solid matter, called (*particulates, plastic, sludge*), is allowed to settle out.
20. Black smoke can be seen because it contains (*particulates, bacteria, phosphates*).

Expressing Yourself   Write a paragraph as an answer to each of the following questions:

21. Why do changes in pollution control often require a long time before they are put into effect?
22. What does the presence of a large amount of algae in water indicate about the water?

Doing More

1. Look around your community to see what different kinds of pollution you can find. Make a list of the kinds of pollution that you find and where you find them. For example, is garbage or litter to be found anywhere? Are any chimneys or smokestacks pouring particulates into the air? Is there junk lying around? List each thing that you find.

2. Smear petroleum jelly on several pieces of cardboard. Leave each piece of cardboard in a different place. For example, you might leave one near a chimney, one on a playground, and one near a busy street. After one hour, look at the pieces of cardboard. Where did the material on each piece of cardboard come from?

Artstreet

Obeying the speed limit is a good way to conserve fuel. How many people, do you think, make an effort to conserve fuel in this way?

28 Protecting Our Environment

Until recently, few people worried about the way resources were being used or about changes being made in the earth. They did not worry about the increasing numbers of people on the earth. Most people believed that there would always be enough resources to meet their needs. They thought that the changes made in the earth had to be accepted as part of the way they lived.

Today many people realize that we are using up certain resources very fast. They believe that we must make changes in the way we live if we are to enjoy life in the future. Why are we beginning to worry about the way we use resources? What changes in the way we live might help protect our environment in the future? You can find out by reading this chapter.

NEED FOR PLANNING

Why should people plan how to use resources?
*Which resources are renewable, and which are
    nonrenewable?*
*What effect does the number of people living on
    the earth have on the use of resources?*

Why plan ahead?

Many newspaper headlines in recent years have been
about shortages of food, water, and oil. That is, at times
there has not always been enough food, water, or oil to
meet all of the needs of people in some places. Does this
mean that these resources are being used up?

The resources of the earth are *limited* [LIHM-uht-uhd].
That is, there is only a certain amount of each kind of resource available. Therefore, if resources are not used wisely,
some of them could be used up within a very short period
of time. And, once resources such as oil, coal, and minerals

*Figure 28–1. How do posters such
as this one encourage people to plan
how to use resources?*

are used up, they will be gone forever. Planning how to use each kind of resource will make it possible for people to continue using resources for many years in the future.

☐ **What shortages have you read about or heard about in recent years?**

To Think About

Would you group soil with the renewable resources or with the nonrenewable resources? Why?

Renewable and nonrenewable resources

In planning how to use resources wisely, people must know what kind of resource they are using. In general, resources can be divided into two groups. One group is made up of *renewable* [rih-N(Y)OO-uh-buhl] *resources.* The other is made up of *nonrenewable* [NAHN-rih-N(Y)OO-uh-buhl] *resources.*

Renewable resources are those that can be replaced even as they are being used. Plants are a good example of a renewable resource. Seeds of plants that are used can be planted to grow more of the same kind of plant. Farm animals are also a renewable resource. What other kinds of resources are renewable resources?

Nonrenewable resources are those resources that cannot be replaced. Fossil fuels and minerals are nonrenewable resources. Once they are removed from the earth, they cannot be replaced. What other kinds of resources are nonrenewable resources?

☐ **How might the way people plan to use a renewable resource differ from the way they might plan to use a nonrenewable resource?**

How many is too many?

One thing that needs to be considered in planning how to use resources wisely is the number of people living on the earth. About 200 years ago there were less than 700 million people living on the earth. Today, there are more than 4 billion people. More resources are needed to meet the needs of this greater number of people. Therefore, resources are being used at a faster rate.

Some people think that there are too many people on the earth compared with the limited amount of resources available. They point out that if there were fewer people, there would be more resources for each person.

Not everybody thinks that there are more people living on the earth than the earth can support. Some people think that there are enough resources to support many more people. However, in order to provide for more people, people must plan to make wiser use of resources than they have up to the present time. This means resources cannot be wasted. It also means getting and using resources in ways that change the earth as little as possible.

MAKING WISER USE OF RESOURCES

How can people conserve resources?
What is meant by recycling, and how can
recycling help to conserve resources?
How can restoring the land help to conserve
resources?

Resources for the future

In order to have the resources we will need in the future, we must learn to use resources so that the resources are neither destroyed nor wasted. That is, we must find ways to *conserve* [kuhn-SURV] resources.

One way for people to conserve resources is for each person to use less of a given resource. For example, heating a home to 20°C (68°F) uses less fuel than does heating a home to 22°C (72°F). Several people traveling together in one car use less gasoline than they would if each person drove his or her own car.

Another way people can conserve resources is to use plentiful resources instead of less plentiful ones wherever possible. For example, pots and pans can be made from either aluminum or iron. However, there is far more aluminum in the earth than there is iron. So, making pots and pans out of aluminum helps to conserve iron.

☐ **What are some things people could do to conserve water?**

Cameramasters

Do It Yourself

**Help people learn how to
conserve resources**

Read newspaper and magazine articles on
methods people are using to conserve resources.
Select a resource that you think is important to
conserve. Make a poster to show people how
they can help to conserve that resource. See if
you can display your poster for many people
to see.

Recycling of materials

Resources such as oil and coal can be used only once.
Therefore, they should be used very wisely. Some materials
made from resources of the earth can be used more than
once. That is, certain materials can be *recycled* [ree-SY-
kuhld]. Materials that can be recycled include metal, glass,
and paper.

Recycling helps to conserve resources. For example, there
are only small amounts of gold and silver ores in the earth.
Recycling these metals means that less of these two ores

Grant Heilman

*Figure 28–2. The metals used in mak-
ing automobiles are being shredded
for recycling. How does recycling
metals help to conserve resources?*

548

need to be mined. But there is plenty of aluminum ore in the earth. Recycling is not as important in conserving this resource. However, it takes less energy from fuel to recycle aluminum metal than it takes to make the metal from the ore. So, recycling aluminum helps to conserve fuel.

Restoring the land

There is no way to get minerals and fossil fuels out of the earth without causing changes in the surface. In the past, people made such changes without thinking about using that land in the future. As a result much of the land around mines became wasteland and was useless to people. Furthermore, soil that eroded from such land often made streams and rivers muddy.

Land that is used for mining does not have to be left as a wasteland. Such land can be restored. Restoring such land involves leveling the surface and covering it with soil. Grass is often used to hold the soil in place. Later, trees or crops may be grown in the soil. In this way, land that was once mined may become useful as parkland or farmland.

☐ **What resources are likely to be conserved by restoring land?**

To Think About

There is enough sand on the earth to make all the glass that people will need for many years to come. Trees used in making paper are a renewable resource. Why, then, do many people think these materials should be recycled?

Photri

Figure 28–3. How has strip mining changed this land? What further changes might take place if this land is not restored?

CONSERVING WILDLIFE

What is wildlife?
Why is wildlife disappearing from the earth?
What are three reasons for conserving wildlife?
How can wildlife be conserved?

Why conserve wildlife?

One resource that is in danger of disappearing from the earth is *wildlife*. Wildlife can be defined as those living things that are not raised by people for a purpose. Wild animals, such as jackrabbits, white-tailed deer, and timber wolves, are wildlife. Many plants and trees are wildlife, too.

Many kinds of wildlife are dying out, or becoming *extinct* [ihk-STIHNG(K)T]. Since 1600, more than 200 species of wildlife have vanished. The great auk, the Florida black wolf, and the dodo bird are examples of wildlife that can no longer be found living on the earth. Nearly 700 additional species of wildlife are in danger of becoming extinct. These plants and animals are called *endangered species*. The brown pelican, the whooping crane, and the elephant are examples of endangered species.

Wild plants and animals are dying out because of changes people are making in the environment. Increasing numbers of people need space in which to live, so land is being cleared to make room for cities. More people need food, and as a result land is also being cleared for farming. In addition, people are causing more air and water pollution. Some kinds of wildlife can survive the changes people are making in the environment. But many kinds cannot.

There are several reasons why it is important to conserve wildlife. One reason is that wildlife is a valuable resource. Trees, for example, are a source of wood for building houses and making paper. Other important products, such as alcohol, charcoal, turpentine, and maple sugar, also come from trees. Trees and other wild plants are sources of fruit and nuts. Some wild animals, such as ducks, fish, and deer, are important sources of meat.

Another reason wildlife should be conserved is that wildlife provides natural beauty. Each wild plant and

Brown pelicans, whooping cranes, and elephants are some endangered species. Using references, find out more about which other kinds of wildlife are also endangered. Also find out if any of the endangered species can be found in your area.

Figure 28–4. Even though the eagle is one of the largest and most powerful birds in the world, it is an endangered species. What factors, do you think, have caused our national bird to become endangered?

animal is special in its own way. Each helps to make the environment beautiful. Many people value the wide variety of wildlife on the earth. These people believe that all the different kinds of wild plants and animals help to make life pleasant.

Still another reason wildlife should be conserved is to maintain the balance of nature. Every living thing plays a part in the life of every other living thing. For example, many birds depend on insects for food, and many insects depend on plants for food. Suppose some kind of pollution killed all the birds in a certain area. What might happen to the number of insects in that area? What might happen to farmers' crops in that area? As you can see, if the balance of nature is destroyed, all other kinds of living things— including people—are affected.

☐ **What, do you think, is another reason for conserving wildlife?**

Ways to conserve wildlife

Usually when people realize that a certain kind of wildlife is in danger, they try to do something to help that kind of wildlife survive. To conserve wildlife, people must keep wild plants and animals from being destroyed or killed. People must also protect the natural environment of these plants and animals.

People can help conserve wildlife by passing certain laws. Laws against hunting wild animals or picking wild flowers can protect many kinds of wildlife. Laws against mining or changing the land in other ways help to maintain the places where wildlife live, or their *habitats* [HAB-uh-TATS]. Antipollution laws help wildlife have fresh air to breathe, clean water to drink, and food that is free from poisons.

Another way people can help conserve wildlife is to set aside certain areas for wildlife. Two kinds of areas people set aside that help protect wildlife are national parks and wildlife refuges.

There are forty-eight national parks in the United States today. Originally, the national parks were not set aside just to protect wildlife. The national parks were set aside to conserve beautiful or unusual areas of the country. Grand Canyon National Park, Crater Lake National Park, and Yellowstone National Park are some examples. To keep the condition of the national parks unspoiled, however, it is important to maintain the balance of nature. Wildlife is protected in the national parks as a means of maintaining the balance of nature.

The United States also has more than 600 wildlife refuges. These areas were set aside to serve as homes for wildlife. Certain refuges were especially set aside to protect endangered species. For example, the Pelican Island Refuge, off the coast of Florida, protects brown pelicans.

☐ **Why, do you think, is protecting the natural environment of wildlife an important part of conserving wildlife?**

Grant Heilman

Do It Yourself

Find out about wildlife refuges in your area

Write to the Fish and Wildlife Service, Department of the Interior, Washington, DC 20240, to find out about wildlife refuges and other nearby areas that protect wildlife. If possible, plan a class visit to such an area. What kinds of plants and animals are protected in the area? Make a map showing the location of nearby wildlife refuges. Show your map to the class and discuss the kinds of wildlife that are protected in each nearby refuge.

Robert Buchbinder

How are these city planners working to try to make the environment better for people?

Careers

City planner

A great many people live and work in cities. In order to be a good place in which to live, a city needs to provide many services for the people who live there. A city must also provide a healthy and pleasing environment for people. Planning ways to make a city a good place for people to live and work is the job of a city planner.

In order to become a city planner, a person needs to know about a great many different things. For example, most cities have zoning laws. These laws state where factories, stores, and homes may be built within the city. They also state how tall a building may be built within the city. City planners need to be able to work with such laws in meeting the needs of people. They also need to understand how governments operate and how to work within a budget. And, city planners need to understand how changes that result from building cities might affect people and the earth.

Perhaps someday you might wish to work in this field. If so, you will need to learn about architecture, engineering, economics, law, and politics. You will probably also need to take special courses in city planning. A student in your class might write to the American Planning Association, 1313 East Sixtieth Street, Chicago, IL 60637, for further information about becoming a city planner.

Reviewing and Extending

Summing Up

1. The resources of the earth are limited. If resources are not used wisely, some of them may be used up within a short period of time.
2. Renewable resources are those that can be replaced even as they are being used. Nonrenewable resources are those that cannot be replaced.
3. The number of people living on the earth has increased from less than 700 million to more than 4 billion within the last 200 years.
4. Because there are greater numbers of people living on the earth today than in the past, more resources must be used to meet people's needs.
5. Conserving resources means using resources in such a way that the resources are neither destroyed nor wasted.
6. Recycling is one way to help conserve resources.
7. Land that has been strip-mined can be restored by leveling the surface and covering it with soil. Such restored land can then be used as parkland or as farmland.
8. Wildlife should be conserved because it is a valuable resource, it provides outdoor recreation and sport, it provides natural beauty, and it is needed to maintain the balance of nature.
9. Wildlife is protected in national parks and wildlife refuges. Laws protect wildlife.

Checking Up

Vocabulary   Write the numerals *1–8* on your paper. Each numbered phrase describes a term from the following list. On your paper, write the term next to the numeral of the phrase that describes it.

recycle	extinct	renewable
refuges	conserve	endangered
restore	wildlife	nonrenewable

1. areas set aside to protect wildlife
2. to use a material more than once
3. resources that cannot be replaced
4. to die out and no longer be found living on the earth
5. to use in a way that neither destroys nor wastes a resource
6. resources that can be replaced as they are being used
7. wildlife that is in danger of becoming extinct
8. living things not raised by people for a purpose

Knowledge and Understanding Write the numerals *9–17* on your paper. Beside each numeral, write the word or words that best complete the sentence having that numeral.

9. Minerals and fossil fuels are (*renewable, nonrenewable, reusable*) resources.
10. There are about (*4 million, 400 million, 4 billion*) people living on the earth today.
11. One material that can be recycled is (*aluminum metal, coal, oil*).
12. Heating a home to 20°C instead of to 22°C is one way to (*recycle, conserve, restore*) fuel.
13. Plants are an example of a (*renewable, nonrenewable, reusable*) resource.
14. The place where a kind of wildlife lives is its (*reserve, refuge, habitat*).
15. A (*whooping crane, jackrabbit, brown pelican*) is not an endangered species.
16. To conserve wildlife, people must protect both wildlife and its (*resources, wasteland, environment*).
17. Leveling certain areas and covering them with soil is one way to (*recycle, restore, revive*) land.

Expressing Yourself Write a paragraph as an answer to each of the following questions:

18. How does the number of people living today affect the way resources are used?
19. How can restoring land that has been used for mining be helpful to people?

Doing More

1. Use references, such as encyclopedias, to find out about uses for either oil or coal other than as fuels. Collect small samples, package labels, or magazine illustrations of these products. Make a poster or bulletin-board display showing the different uses of either oil or coal.

2. Find out about the laws your city or state government has passed to protect wildlife. You should be able to get this information from your public library. You may also be able to find out about such laws by talking to your city council representative or other city official. Report your findings to the class.

Pros and Cons

Changes in the Earth—What Kinds Should Be Made?

Every living thing on the earth causes some changes in the earth. However, people are able to make more changes and greater changes than any other kind of living thing. Furthermore, people are able to decide what kinds of changes they will make in the earth.

What kinds of changes should people make in the earth? Not everyone agrees about the changes that should be made. For example, in the 1890's the United States government set aside millions of acres of forestlands to provide lumber and wood products for the people of this country. Many of these areas are known as national forests. Today more than half of the best trees for lumber are found in national forests. People do not agree, however, on how such forestlands should be used. Some people want to cut more and more trees from the forests to provide lumber to build new homes. As you might guess, cutting so many trees would change the forestlands greatly. Other people do not agree that more trees should be cut. These people point out that forestlands provide natural beauty, areas for recreation, and homes for many kinds of wildlife. These people do not believe that cutting down forests is a kind of change that should be made in the earth.

Many of the changes being made in the earth today are the result of the great increase in the population and of

Because the population is growing, more and more land must be used to provide housing. Apartment buildings can provide more housing on a given area of land than can single-family dwellings.

changes in the way people live. The greater population means that more space in which to live, more fuels, more minerals, and more land on which to grow food are needed. Meeting each of these needs means that many choices have to be made as to how land should be used. And, the use of land almost always brings about changes in the earth.

For example, people need both food and housing. Some people want a house with a large yard. Land to build such houses is only found outside of cities today. However, most of this land is also good farmland. Should people demand large houses with large yards even though it means large amounts of good farmland must be used for this purpose? Or should people think in terms of smaller homes and yards, which would use up less land? What do you think?

Having enough land to grow all the food needed for people today is becoming more and more of a problem. Most of the good farmland in the world is producing as much food as it can. Therefore, soil from land that has not been used to grow crops before must be used. Many desert areas have become important farmlands today. Rivers have been dammed to store water to irrigate desert farms. This water is then piped to the farms.

Land that was once used to grow crops is now used to build homes. Which use is more important today? Which use will be more important in the future? Explain.

One problem is beginning to develop from farming these desert lands. All fresh water contains small amounts of salt. When a river flows to the ocean, little of this salt remains on the land. However, most of the water used to irrigate desert farmland evaporates. When water evaporates, it leaves some of the salt behind. Over many years, desert farmland may become too salty for crops or any other plants to grow. Should people risk making desert land salty and useless for growing food in the future in order to get more food today?

As you can see, people are making great changes in the earth today. Even greater changes might be made in the future. But what kinds of changes should be made? Should the size of the population be controlled to help control the kinds of changes made in the earth? If so, how? These are questions that will need to be answered in the near future. What do you think about these questions and others you may have about people and changes in the earth?

Investigate On Your Own

1. Try to find out if your town or city has a recycling center and, if so, where the recycling center is located. Recycling centers are often listed under the heading "Recycling" in the Yellow Pages of the telephone directory. Also find out what kinds of materials your local recycling center collects, and find out if there is any special way that materials should be prepared for collecting. Report your findings to the class. Perhaps you and your classmates can organize a drive to collect and turn in one of these kinds of materials.

2. Make a list of all the ways you and your family use energy in a single day. Meet with your family and discuss your list of energy uses. Try to determine some of the ways that you and your family might be wasting energy. Also try to plan some ways that you and your family might be able to conserve energy in the future.

Read On Your Own

Branley, Franklyn M., *Feast or Famine? The Energy Future*. New York: Thomas Y. Crowell Co. Publishers, 1980.

The author begins by describing today's energy resources. He then assesses each energy resource as an option for the future. The author discusses the pros and cons of using nuclear power.

Graham, Ada, and Frank Graham, *Careers in Conservation*. San Francisco: Sierra Club Books, 1980.

This book uses vignettes to introduce readers to a wide variety of conservation careers. Among the individuals featured in this book are the woman who manages Central Park and a young couple who work in a canyon in Arizona. Individuals featured discuss such topics as their difficulty in finding a job in conservation and the rewards of their job.

McClung, Robert M., *Vanishing Wildlife of Latin America*. New York: William Morrow & Co. Inc., 1981.

After describing the environment and the natural history of Latin America, the author presents the story of some of the native animals that are now endangered species. More than half of the animals described in this book are mammals. There are many pictures of animals in the book.

Pringle, Laurence, *Lives at Stake: The Science and Politics of Environmental Health*. New York: Macmillan, Inc., 1980.

This book examines environmental factors that affect human health. Factors such as chemical poisons in the air and the water, food additives, and noise are included. The author discusses each factor and the ways that scientists and politicians propose to deal with it.

Pringle, Laurence, *What Shall We Do With the Land? Choices for America*. New York: Thomas Y. Crowell Co. Publishers, 1981.

This book explores the pros and cons arising out of our use of land. Pringle describes our use of farmlands, forests, mountains, and coasts. He examines the reasons why we use land as we do. Pringle also explores what the results of today's land use might be in the future.

Satchwell, John, *Energy at Work*. New York: Lothrop, Lee & Shepard Books, 1981.

This book examines the complex topic of energy in an easy-to-understand way. Solar energy, nuclear energy, hydroelectric energy, geothermal energy, and energy from fossil fuels are discussed. Ways to conserve each form of energy are described. A simple energy game involves readers and adds interest to the book.

COMPUTERS

Programs to Accompany the Units

in

Experiences in Earth-Space Science

Contents

Using Computers in Earth-Space Science

Computers are used in earth-space science for two main purposes: (1) to solve problems and (2) to store and organize large amounts of information. In either case, a computer program is needed to tell the computer what to do.

On the following pages are several computer programs. These programs are designed to help you understand some of the key ideas in this book. By studying the programs, typing them into a computer, and running them, you will gain an understanding of how a program directs a computer to solve a science problem or to store and organize science information.

The following programs are written in the computer language called BASIC, which stands for Beginners' All-purpose Symbolic Instruction Code. These programs are written so that they can be used with most kinds of microcomputers (such as Apple, TRS-80, IBM PC and PCjr, Commodore, and Atari). However, the programs may not take advantage of certain capabilities of the particular brand of computer you are using. You are encouraged to look for ways to improve the programs so that they make use of the special features of your computer.

Entering information

Many of the programs require entering information into the computer. To enter information, type the necessary information and then press either RETURN, ENTER, or ↵ (depending on the computer). Also, when "press <RETURN>" appears as a message on the screen, just press RETURN, ENTER, or ↵ (depending on the computer).

Using a printer with the programs

The programs on the following pages were designed to display information on a video monitor. However, the programs can be altered to produce a printed copy of the screen displays.

If you have an APPLE computer, add the two lines below to each program.

90 PR#1

900 PR#0

If you have a TRS-80, ATARI, or IBM computer, add a new program line after every program line that contains the command PRINT. The new line should be identical to the line that precedes it; however, the command PRINT should be replaced with LPRINT.

Example: 140 PRINT "2. SPEED"   ◄ existing line

145 LPRINT "2. SPEED"   ◄ new line

If you have a COMMODORE 64 computer, add the two lines below to each program.

90 OPEN 4

900 CLOSE 4

Also add a new program line after every program line that contains the command PRINT. The line should be identical to the line that precedes it; however, PRINT should be replaced with LPRINT.

Example: 140 PRINT "2. SPEED"   ◄ existing line

145 LPRINT "2. SPEED"   ◄ new line

If you have a COMMODORE VIC 20 computer, follow the directions for the Commodore 64 described above; however, change OPEN 4 to OPEN 1 and CLOSE 4 to CLOSE 1.

NOTE: Be sure your printer is connected properly and turned on.

E-notation

When a program makes the computer do calculations, sometimes the numbers that result are very large. When the computer has to print numbers that are equal to or greater than 1 million, it uses a form called E-notation. In this notation, the number 1 million (1,000,000) appears as $1E + 06$. This means "the number 1 followed by 6 zeros." In E-notation 45 trillion is written $4.5E + 13$.

Correlation of the Programs to Units in *Experiences in Earth-Space Science*

Program	Unit
Mineral Classification	1
Calculating Air Distances	1
Planet Mass	2
Solar–System Distances	2
Speed of the Earth	2
Windchill	3
Predicting Storms	3
Melting Polar Ice	4
Electricity Usage and Waste	6
Air Pollutants	6

MINERAL CLASSIFICATION

Minerals have certain kinds of properties. These properties can help you identify minerals that you find. This program produces a chart that classifies minerals according to their properties. The program lists in columns the type of mineral, the color of the mineral, the streak made by the mineral on a streak plate, the mineral's hardness, the mineral's luster, and the mineral's type of cleavage.

```
100  REM ***MINERAL CLASSIFICATION***
110  DIM A$(10,6)
120  FOR Q = 1 TO 24 : PRINT : NEXT Q
130  PRINT TAB( 5); " MINERAL CLASSIFICATION"
140  PRINT TAB( 9); " BY PROPERTIES"
150  PRINT
160  PRINT "MINERAL"; TAB( 13);"COLOR"; TAB( 27);"STREAK"
170  FOR I = 1 TO 40
180  PRINT "-";
190  NEXT I
200  PRINT : PRINT
210  FOR J = 1 TO 8 : K = 1
220  READ A$(J,K)
230  IF A$(J,1) = "LAST" THEN GOTO 260
240  K = K + 1: IF K < = 6 THEN GOTO 220
250  NEXT J
260  FOR J = 1 TO 8
270  PRINT A$(J,1); TAB( 11);A$(J,2); TAB( 27);A$(J,3)
280  NEXT J : PRINT
290  INPUT "PRESS <RETURN> TO VIEW OTHER PROPERTIES.";Z$
300  FOR I = 1 TO 10: PRINT : NEXT I
310  PRINT "MINERAL"; TAB( 12);"HARDNESS"; TAB( 22);"LUSTER"; TAB
     ( 32); "CLEAVAGE" : PRINT
320  FOR I = 1 TO 40: PRINT "-";: NEXT I: PRINT" "
330  FOR J = 1 TO 8
340  PRINT A$(J,1); TAB( 15);A$(J,4); TAB( 25);A$(J,5); TAB( 32);A$(J,6)
350  NEXT J : PRINT
360  PRINT " NM=NONMETALLIC "
370  PRINT " MET=METALLIC "
380  DATA TALC,GRAY TO SILVER,WHITE,1,NM,GOOD
390  DATA GALENA,GRAY,GRAY,2.5,MET,PERFECT
400  DATA HALITE,WHITE-COLORLESS,COLORLESS,2.5,NM,PERFECT
410  DATA CALCITE,WHITE-COLORLESS,WHITE OR GRAY,3,NM,PERFECT
420  DATA GRAPHITE,STEEL GRAY-BLK,BLACK,1 TO 2,MET,PERFECT
430  DATA MAGNETITE,BLACK,BLACK,6,MET,POOR
440  DATA MUSCOVITE,BLK-BRN-GRAY,COLORLESS,2.5 TO 3,NM,
     PERFECT
450  DATA QUARTZ, CLEAR-WHITE,COLORLESS,7,NM,POOR
460  DATA LAST
```

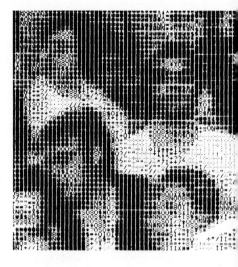

Correlates with Chapter 2,
"Minerals," pages 34–38

563

CALCULATING AIR DISTANCES

This program can calculate the air distances between many places in North America. However, you must know the latitude and the longitude of each place. You can look up the latitudes and longitudes of various cities on a map or a chart. Latitudes and longitudes are also listed in some atlases. Since all cities in North America lie in north latitudes and west longitudes, no directional information needs to be used in this program.

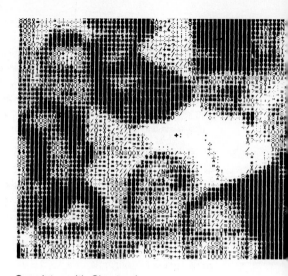

Correlates with Chapter 4, "Mapping the Earth," pages 70–76

```
100   REM ***CALCULATING AIR DISTANCES***
110   FOR Q = 1 TO 24 : PRINT : NEXT Q
120   DEF FN AC(X) = ATN (( SQR (1 - X * X)) / X)
130   R = 1.745329E - 02
140   PRINT "THE AIR DISTANCE BETWEEN TWO CITIES": PRINT "CAN BE
      CALCULATED FROM THEIR LATITUDE"
150   PRINT "AND LONGITUDE."
160   PRINT "LOOK UP THE LATITUDE AND LONGITUDE IN"
170   PRINT "DEGREES AND MINUTES FOR EACH CITY."
180   PRINT "NEXT TO THE QUESTION MARK, ENTER THE"
190   PRINT "NAME OF THE CITY AND ITS LATITUDE AND"
200   PRINT "LONGITUDE AS IN THE EXAMPLE BELOW."
210   PRINT : PRINT "? CHICAGO,41,49,87,37": PRINT
220   PRINT "ENTER THE NAME OF THE FIRST CITY"
230   PRINT "AND ITS LATITUDE AND LONGITUDE IN"
240   PRINT "DEGREES AND MINUTES."
250   PRINT
260   INPUT S$,A1,A2,B1,B2
270   PRINT
280   PRINT "ENTER THE NAME OF THE SECOND CITY AND": PRINT "ITS
      LATITUDE AND LONGITUDE IN DEGREES"
290   PRINT "AND MINUTES."
300   PRINT
310   INPUT D$,C1,C2,D1,D2 : PRINT
320   A = A1 + A2 / 60
330   B = B1 + B2 / 60
340   C = C1 + C2 / 60
350   D = D1 + D2 / 60
360   AR = A * R:BR = B * R:CR = C * R:DR = D * R
370   X = ( SIN (AR) * SIN (CR) + COS (AR) * COS (CR) * COS (DR - BR))
380   DIST = 1.853915 * 60 * FN AC(X) * 57.2958
390   DIST = INT (DIST + .5)
400   PRINT "THE AIR DISTANCE FROM ";S$: PRINT "TO ";D$;" IS ";DIST;
      " KILOMETERS.": PRINT : PRINT
410   PRINT "DO YOU WANT TO DETERMINE ANOTHER": INPUT
      "DISTANCE? ENTER Y OR N.";A$
420   PRINT : PRINT : PRINT : IF A$ = "Y" THEN GOTO 220
```

PLANET MASS

You learned about the planets in the solar system and their differences in mass in Chapter 5. In this program, a chart that displays the mass of each planet is produced. The computation of each planet's mass is based on the ratio of its mass to that of the earth. The mass (in kilograms) of each planet is given in E-notation, which is explained on page 562.

```
100   REM ***PLANET MASS***
110   FOR I = 1 TO 24 : PRINT : NEXT I
120   PRINT "AFTER THE NAME OF EACH PLANET APPEARS,"
130   PRINT "ENTER THE RELATIVE MASS OF THE PLANET AS"
140   PRINT "GIVEN ON PAGE 100 OF EXPERIENCES IN"
150   PRINT "EARTH-SPACE SCIENCE."
160   PRINT
170   FOR I = 1 TO 9
180   READ A$(I)
190   PRINT : PRINT A$(I)
200   PRINT : INPUT P(I)
210   LET M(I) = (5.979E + 24) * P(I)
220   NEXT I
230   FOR I = 1 TO 24 : PRINT : NEXT I
240   PRINT TAB( 15);"PLANET SIZE"
250   PRINT : PRINT
260   PRINT "PLANET"; TAB( 12);"MASS OF"; TAB( 29);"PERCENTAGE OF"
270   PRINT TAB( 12);"PLANET (KG)"; TAB( 29);"EARTH'S MASS"
280   PRINT "-----------------------------------"
290   FOR I = 1 TO 9
300   PRINT A$(I); TAB( 12);M(I); TAB( 30);P(I) * 100; TAB( 37);"%"
310   NEXT I
320   DATA MERCURY,VENUS,EARTH,MARS,JUPITER,SATURN,URANUS,
      NEPTUNE,PLUTO
```

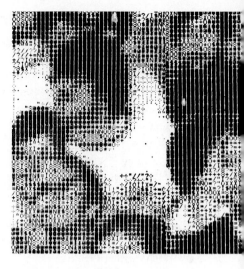

Correlates with Chapter 5, "The Solar System," pages 99–103

DOING MORE

1. Modify line 320 in the program so that it will list the earth's moon. Use reference materials to help you find the ratio of the mass of the moon to that of the earth.

2. Change the program so that the planets are listed in order of size. The information needed to modify the program can be found on page 100 of your text.

3. Use reference books to help you find out how the mass of an object in space can be determined. How might the mass of the sun be determined? Explain.

SOLAR-SYSTEM DISTANCES

In Chapter 5, you learned about distances between the sun and the nine planets in the solar system. This program will create a chart that compares the average distances between the sun and the planets. The chart will also show the average distance between the earth and each planet.

```
100   REM ***SOLAR SYSTEM***
110   REM ***DISTANCES***
120   FOR Q = 1 TO 24 : PRINT : NEXT Q
130   PRINT TAB( 9);"PLANET CHART"
140   PRINT : PRINT : PRINT
150   PRINT TAB( 16);"MILLIONS OF KM": PRINT
160   PRINT TAB( 16);"FROM"; TAB( 26);"FROM"
170   PRINT "PLANET"; TAB( 16);"SUN"; TAB( 26);"EARTH"
180   PRINT "---------------------------------"
190   FOR I = 1 TO 9
200   READ A$(I),B(I),C(I)
210   PRINT A$(I); TAB( 16);B(I); TAB( 26);C(I)
220   NEXT I
230   DATA MERCURY,58,92
240   DATA VENUS,108,42
250   DATA EARTH,150,0
260   DATA MARS,228,78
270   DATA JUPITER,780,630
280   DATA SATURN,1 430,1 280
290   DATA URANUS,2 870,2 720
300   DATA NEPTUNE,4 500,4 350
310   DATA PLUTO,5 900,5 750
```

Correlates with Chapter 5, "The Solar System," pages 103–105

DOING MORE

1. Modify the program so that it will list, in another column, a comparison of average distances between the orbits of adjacent planets.

2. The moon is a satellite of the earth. Other planets have more than one satellite. Modify the program so that it will list the average distances of various satellites from their planets.

3. Use reference materials to help you find out about distances outside the solar system. How far is it to the nearest star? The nearest galaxy? The nearest solar system?

SPEED OF THE EARTH

You already know that the earth is moving around the sun, or revolving, in an orbit. As the earth revolves, it moves at a great speed through space. While traveling on the earth's surface, perhaps you have wondered how your rate of travel compared with that of the earth around the sun. The program below will help you calculate the amount of time required to cover certain distances by car. This program will also compare the distance a person travels in a car with the distance the earth travels during the same time.

```
100  REM ***SPEED OF THE EARTH***
110  FOR Q = 1 TO 24 : PRINT : NEXT Q
120  PRINT "THIS PROGRAM TELLS HOW LONG IT WOULD"
130  PRINT "TAKE YOU TO TRAVEL A GIVEN DISTANCE AT"
140  PRINT "THE SPEED THE EARTH REVOLVES AROUND "
150  PRINT "THE SUN.": PRINT
160  PRINT "ENTER A DISTANCE BETWEEN 100 KM AND"
170  PRINT "18 000 KM, BUT ENTER ONLY THE NUMBER."
180  INPUT KM
190  PRINT
200  PRINT "TRAVELING AT 80 KM PER HOUR, YOU WOULD"
210  PRINT "TAKE ";KM / 80;" HOURS TO TRAVEL ";KM;" KM."
220  PRINT
230  S = KM * .033
240  PRINT "TRAVELING AT THE SPEED OF THE EARTH,"
250  PRINT "YOU WOULD TAKE ";S;" SECONDS TO TRAVEL"
260  PRINT KM;" KILOMETERS."
270  PRINT
280  PRINT "IN ";S;" SECONDS, THE EARTH"
290  PRINT "TRAVELS ";KM;" KILOMETERS."
300  PRINT
310  PRINT
320  PRINT "WOULD YOU LIKE TO TRY AGAIN?"
330  INPUT "ENTER Y OR N. ";GO$
340  IF GO$ = "Y" THEN GOTO 160
```

Correlates with Chapter 8, "The Earth in Motion," pages 166–168

DOING MORE

1. Modify the program so that it will compare the distance the earth travels with the distance another planet travels in the same period of time.

2. Use reference materials to help you find out how scientists have been able to determine the speed of the earth as it travels around the sun.

WINDCHILL

The computer program printed below will help you better understand what effect the wind has on how the air temperature feels to you. A temperature representing the combined effect of air temperature and wind is sometimes called a windchill. This program will display a chart in which the air temperature is a variable and various wind speeds and the windchills for those speeds are listed.

```
100   REM ***WINDCHILL***
110   FOR Q = 1 TO 24
120   PRINT
130   NEXT Q
140   PRINT "AIR FEELS COLDER ON EXPOSED SKIN WHEN"
150   PRINT "THERE IS WIND. THE COMBINED EFFECT OF"
160   PRINT "AIR TEMPERATURE AND WIND SPEED IS "
170   PRINT "THE WINDCHILL. ENTER A NUMBER THAT"
180   PRINT "REPRESENTS A TEMPERATURE BETWEEN 0 AND"
190   PRINT "70 DEGREES FAHRENHEIT."
200   PRINT
210   INPUT F
220   PRINT
230   PRINT
240   PRINT "WINDCHILL WHEN THE AIR TEMPERATURE"
250   PRINT "IS ";F;" DEGREES FAHRENHEIT."
260   PRINT
270   PRINT "MPH";,"WINDCHILL"
280   PRINT "---","--------"
290   FOR V = 5 TO 40 STEP 5
300   LET W = INT (.0817 * (3.71 * SQR (V) + 5.81 - .25 * V) * (F - 91.4) + 91.4)
310   PRINT TAB( 1);V; TAB( 20);W
320   NEXT V
330   PRINT
340   PRINT "WOULD YOU LIKE TO TRY AGAIN?"
350   INPUT "ENTER Y OR N. ";GO$
360   IF GO$ = "Y" THEN GOTO 110
```

Correlates with Chapter 11,
"What Makes Up Weather?"
pages 216–220

PREDICTING STORMS

Most people agree that there is a real need for accurate weather forecasting. Such forecasting can help people in work, play, and travel. Various data about the condition of the air must be collected and studied before an accurate forecast can be made. The computer program printed below predicts how long a storm will last before breaking up. The prediction is based on a computation involving the diameter of the storm.

```
100   REM ***PREDICTING STORMS***
110   FOR Q = 1 TO 24
120   PRINT
130   NEXT Q
140   PRINT "THE DIAMETER OF A STORM CAN BE USED TO"
150   PRINT "PREDICT HOW LONG THE STORM WILL LAST."
160   PRINT
170   PRINT "ENTER A DIAMETER BETWEEN 2 KM AND 100 "
180   PRINT "KM. ENTER ONLY THE NUMBER."
190   PRINT
200   INPUT D
210   PRINT
220   PRINT
230   LET T = INT (60 * SQR ((D * D * D) / 885))
240   PRINT "THE STORM WILL LAST APPROXIMATELY "
250   IF T < 120 THEN PRINT T;" MINUTES ";
260   IF T > = 120 THEN PRINT INT ((10 * T + 0.5) / 600); " HOURS ";
270   PRINT "IF IT IS ";D;" KILOMETERS IN "
280   PRINT "DIAMETER."
290   PRINT
300   PRINT
310   PRINT
320   PRINT "WOULD YOU LIKE TO TRY AGAIN?"
330   INPUT "ENTER Y OR N. ";GO$
340   IF GO$ = "Y" THEN GOTO 170
```

Correlates with Chapter 12, "Forecasting the Weather," pages 244–248

DOING MORE

1. Call the weather bureau in your area to find out how professional meteorologists use computers in forecasting the weather. If you could get the right kinds of information, could you use a computer to help forecast the weather? Explain.

2. Graphics are used to display weather information on computers. Use references to answer the following questions: What kinds of graphics would be most helpful to a meteorologist? Why?

MELTING POLAR ICE

One possible solution to our water-shortage problem is to use icebergs as a source of fresh water. Large icebergs could be broken off ice caps, towed to warmer areas, and melted. There has been a natural increase in the rate of ice-cap melting in recent years. The increase is probably a result of an increase in carbon dioxide in the atmosphere. Huge amounts of carbon dioxide are constantly being released into the atmosphere by the burning of fossil fuels. Carbon dioxide traps the heat caused by the earth's absorption of solar radiation instead of letting it be radiated into space. In this program, you will see what effect increases in carbon dioxide have on the level of the sea.

```
100   REM ***MELTING POLAR ICE***
110   FOR I = 1 TO 24
120   PRINT
130   NEXT I
140   Y = 1985:TCHANGE = .0425
150   PRINT "AN INCREASE IN CO2 IN THE ATMOSPHERE"
160   PRINT "CAUSES A GLOBAL RISE IN TEMPERATURE."
170   PRINT "THIS INCREASE IN AIR TEMPERATURE CAUSES"
180   PRINT "MELTING OF THE POLAR ICE, WHICH RESULTS"
190   PRINT "IN AN INCREASE IN SEA LEVEL."
200   PRINT : PRINT "THIS PROGRAM IS BASED ON A 1.70-PARTS-"
210   PRINT "PER-MILLION INCREASE IN CO2 PER"
220   PRINT "YEAR."
230   PRINT
240   PRINT : PRINT "DO YOU WANT TO INCREASE THE AMOUNT"
250   PRINT "OF CO2?": PRINT
260   INPUT "ENTER Y OR N. ";A$
270   IF A$ < > "Y" THEN GOTO 320
280   PRINT : PRINT
290   PRINT "WHAT IS THE AMOUNT OF INCREASE"
300   PRINT "(PPM)? ";: INPUT TINCREASES
310   TCHANGE = TINCREASES * .0425 / 1.7
320   PRINT
330   RISE = TCHANGE * 3 / .0425
340   PRINT "HOW MANY CENTIMETERS DO YOU WANT THE"
350   PRINT "SEA LEVEL TO RISE?"
360   PRINT : INPUT "ENTER ONLY THE NUMBER. ";R
370   IF R > = 8000 THEN GOTO 470
380   PRINT
390   PRINT "IT WILL TAKE "; INT (10 * (R / RISE) + .5) / 10 ;" YEARS FOR"
400   PRINT "THE SEA LEVEL TO RISE ";R;" CENTIMETERS."
410   PRINT
420   PRINT "DO YOU WANT TO ENTER ANOTHER CHANGE"
430   PRINT "IN SEA LEVEL?"
440   PRINT : INPUT "ENTER Y OR N. ";D$
```

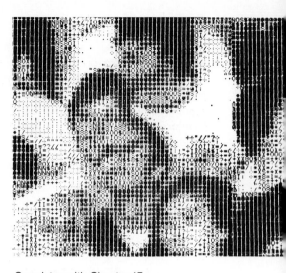

Correlates with Chapter 17, "The Supply of Fresh Water," pages 331–332

```
450   IF D$ = "Y" THEN GOTO 240
460   GOTO 560
470   PRINT
480   PRINT "IF THE ICE CAPS MELT COMPLETELY, THE"
490   PRINT "SEA LEVEL WILL RISE 8 000 CM, OR 80"
500   PRINT "METERS."
510   PRINT : PRINT
520   PRINT "DO YOU WANT TO TRY ANOTHER AMOUNT?"
530   INPUT "ENTER Y OR N. ";B$
540   IF B$ = "Y" THEN GOTO 240
550   GOTO 560
560   PRINT
570   PRINT "TO FIND OUT HOW MUCH THE SEA LEVEL"
580   PRINT "WILL RISE BETWEEN THIS YEAR AND A FUTURE": PRINT
      "YEAR, ENTER A FUTURE YEAR."
590   PRINT
600   INPUT "FOR WHAT YEAR DO YOU WANT AN ANSWER? ";FY
610   IF FY < Y THEN GOTO 800
620   PRINT
630   LET CHECK = RISE * (FY - 1985)
640   LET Z2 = RISE * (FY - Y)
650   IF CHECK > = 8000 THEN GOTO 750
660   PRINT "BY THE YEAR ";FY;" SEA LEVEL WILL HAVE"
670   PRINT "RISEN"; INT (Z2);" CM."
680   PRINT
690   PRINT "DO YOU WANT TO ENTER ANOTHER FUTURE"
700   PRINT "YEAR? "
710   PRINT
720   INPUT "ENTER Y OR N. ";C$
730   IF C$ = "N" THEN GOTO 820
740   GOTO 590
750   PRINT "BY THE YEAR ";FY;" THE ICE CAPS WILL HAVE"
760   PRINT "COMPLETELY MELTED, AND SEA LEVEL"
770   PRINT "WILL HAVE RISEN 8 000 CENTIMETERS."
780   GOTO 680
790   PRINT
800   PRINT "YOUR YEAR IS NOT A FUTURE YEAR. TRY AGAIN."
810   GOTO 590
820   END
```

ELECTRICITY USAGE AND WASTE

When you travel on a bus, energy is needed to move the bus. The energy is supplied by petroleum. When you make a cake, energy is needed to mix the ingredients and bake them into a cake. In most cases you are using some kind of fossil fuel when you use energy. The fossil fuel used may be petroleum, natural gas, or coal. Since the supplies of fossil fuels are limited, people would be wise not to waste them. This program calculates how much energy is wasted when a light bulb is left burning.

```
100   REM ***ELECTRICITY USAGE AND WASTE***
110   FOR I = 1 TO 24: PRINT : NEXT I
120   PRINT "BULB SIZE"; TAB( 13);"COST"; TAB( 23);"COST"; TAB
      ( 33);"COST"
130   PRINT "IN WATTS"; TAB( 13);"DAY"; TAB( 23);"MONTH"; TAB
      ( 33);"YEAR"
140   PRINT "--------------------------------------"
150   READ CU,FC,SC
160   FOR J = 1 TO 3 : READ H(J) : NEXT J
170   FOR I = 1 TO 6 : READ A(I)
180   PRINT A(I); TAB( 12);
190   FOR J = 1 TO 3
200   LET R(I) = H(J) * (A(I) / 1000)
210   IF R(I) < = CU THEN C(I) = R(I) * FC
220   IF R(I) > CU THEN C(I) = CU * FC + R(I) - CU * SC
230   IF I > 1 THEN GOTO 270
240   PRINT "$"; INT (100 * C(I) + .5) / 100;
250   IF J < > 3 THEN PRINT ".......";
260   GOTO 290
270   PRINT "$"; INT (100 * C(I) + .5) / 100;
280   IF J < > 3 THEN PRINT ".......";
290   NEXT J
300   PRINT
310   NEXT I
320   DATA 2000,.04381,.05043
330   DATA 24,720,8760
340   DATA 7.5,40,60,75,100,150
```

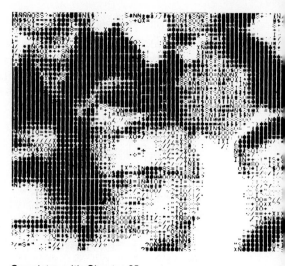

Correlates with Chapter 25, "Treasures of the Earth," pages 494–504

DOING MORE

Modify the program so that it reflects the actual electrical rates in the area in which you live. To do this you will need to change the cost of electricity per kilowatt-hour (kwh). You must change the values of FC and SC in line 320. FC is the cost per kwh below or at a certain usage level, and SC is the cost per kwh above the same level.

AIR POLLUTANTS

You read about air pollution and its effects on people in Chapter 27. You also read about some causes of air pollution. There are two types of pollutants in the air—particulates and gases. This program will produce a chart of various air pollutants. You will be able to use this data to make predictions.

```
100   REM ***AIR POLLUTANTS***
110   FOR I = 1 TO 24
120   PRINT
130   NEXT I
140   DIM A$(5),B(5),C(5),R(5),P(5),D(5),E(5),F(5)
150   PRINT "BELOW IS A CHART SHOWING CHANGES IN"
160   PRINT "AMOUNTS OF CERTAIN POLLUTANTS IN THE"
170   PRINT "AIR BETWEEN 1970 AND 1980 (IN MILLIONS"
180   PRINT "OF METRIC TONS). THESE CHANGES TOOK"
190   PRINT "PLACE AS A RESULT OF THE CLEAN AIR ACT"
200   PRINT "OF 1970."
210   PRINT
220   PRINT "POLLUTANT"; TAB( 21);"1970"; TAB( 31);"1980"
230   PRINT "-----------------------------------"
240   FOR I = 1 TO 5
250   READ A$(I),B(I),C(I)
260   PRINT A$(I); TAB( 20);B(I); TAB( 30);C(I)
270   NEXT I
280   PRINT
290   INPUT "PRESS <RETURN> TO CONTINUE.";PAUSE$
300   FOR I = 1 TO 24
310   PRINT
320   NEXT I
330   PRINT
340   PRINT
350   FOR I = 1 TO 5
360   PRINT "POLLUTANT"; TAB( 20);"1970"; TAB( 30);"1980"
370   PRINT "-------------------------------------"
380   PRINT A$(I); TAB( 20);B(I); TAB( 30);C(I)
390   PRINT
400   PRINT "AT THIS RATE OF CHANGE, WHAT WOULD BE"
410   PRINT "THE AMOUNT OF ";A$(I);" IN THE"
420   PRINT "AIR IN THE YEAR 1990?";
430   INPUT R(I)
440   PRINT
450   PRINT "AT DOUBLE THIS RATE OF CHANGE, WHAT"
460   PRINT "WOULD BE THE AMOUNT IN 1990?";
470   P(I) = ( INT (P(I) * 10)) / 10
480   INPUT P(I)
490   R(I) = ( INT (R(I) * 10)) / 10
```

Correlates with Chapter 27, "Environmental Pollution," pages 525–531

```
500   PRINT
510   PRINT
520   PRINT
530   PRINT
540   NEXT I
550   PRINT : PRINT : PRINT
560   PRINT "POLLUTANT"; TAB( 20);"CORRECT"; TAB( 30);"YOUR"
570   PRINT " 1990"; TAB( 20);"ANSWERS"; TAB( 30);"ANSWERS"
580   FOR I = 1 TO 40: PRINT "-";
590   NEXT I
600   PRINT
610   FOR I = 1 TO 5
620   D(I) = C(I) / B(I)
630   E(I) = ( INT (C(I) * D(I) * 10)) / 10
640   F(I) = ( INT (C(I) * D(I) * D(I) * 10)) / 10
650   PRINT A$(I); TAB( 20);E(I); TAB( 30);R(I)
660   PRINT "(DOUBLE RATE)"; TAB( 20);F(I); TAB( 30);P(I)
670   PRINT
680   NEXT I
690   END
700   DATA CARBON DIOXIDE,110.9,85.4
710   DATA SULFUR OXIDES,27.9,23.7
720   DATA ORGANIC COMPOUNDS,27.1,21.8
730   DATA PARTICULATES,17.6,7.8
740   DATA NITROGEN OXIDES,18.5,20.7
```

574

Software Suggestions and Bibliography

If you are looking for other software programs that are related to the units studied in *Experiences in Earth-Space Science,* you may find the following programs interesting:

Unit 1   *Rock Cycle*   This program, with the help of color graphics, helps you to understand how rocks are formed. Educational Computing Systems, Inc. Disk; Apple II series (48K)

Unit 2   *Astronomy—A Voyage Through Our Solar System*   By means of this program you can take a trip through the solar system and learn about the planets and their moons. Concept Educational Software. Disk or cassette; TRS-80 III, 4 (16K)

Unit 3   *World Clock*   Here's a program that shows each planet in relation to the sun and to the other planets, while at the same time explaining the change of seasons on the earth. COMPress. Disk; Apple II series (48K)

Unit 4   *The Water Cycle*   This program will help you to visualize and work with the water cycle by doing experiments on the computer. Educational Computing Systems, Inc. Disk; Apple II series (48K)

Unit 5   *Earth Science*   One program on this disk can be used when you study about earthquakes. (Other programs on the disk calculate solar distance and Ursa rotation.) Minnesota Educational Computing Consortium. Disk; Atari 400, 800 (48K)

Unit 6   *Acid Rain*   With this program you can explore what happens to the aquatic environment as a result of air pollution. Diversified Educational Enterprises, Inc. Disk; Apple II series (48K)

Reading About Computers

Corbett, Scott, **Home Computers.** Boston: Little, Brown and Company, 1980.

Besides making you aware of the many uses of home computers, this book has an excellent chapter on the role of computers for a family in the future.

D'Ignazio, Fred, **Messner's Introduction to the Computer.** New York: Julian Messner, 1983.

If you want to know something about the history of computers and about the people responsible for developing them, you will find this book interesting.

Smith, Brian Reffin, **Introduction to Computer Programming.** London: Usborne Publishing, Ltd., 1982.

Each time this book explains one of many programs, it asks you to write a similar program. You'll enjoy the clever illustrations.

Software Suppliers

COMPress
P.O. Box 102
Wentworth, NH 03282

Concept Educational Software
P.O. Box 6184
Allentown, PA 18001

Diversified Educational Enterprises, Inc.
725 Main Street
Lafayette, IN 47906

Educational Computing Systems, Inc.
136 Fairbanks Plaza
Oak Ridge, TN 37830

Minnesota Educational Computing Consortium
3490 Lexington Avenue, North
Saint Paul, MN 55122

GLOSSARY

When certain science words or words related to science topics are used for the first time in this book, or in some cases for the first time in a unit, they are spelled in a special way to help the reader learn how to say them. These words are also spelled in this way in this Glossary. The special spellings always appear in [ ]. When a word has two or more syllables, certain syllables are stressed more than others. In the special spelling of a word, the syllable stressed the most is spelled in large capital letters. The syllable stressed second most is spelled in small capital letters. The syllable or syllables not stressed are spelled in small letters. If there are ( ) around one or more letters within the [ ], those letters may or may not be said.

Below is a list of the letter or letters used for the special spellings. Next to each letter or letters is a description of the way the letter or letters should be said.

a . . . . . *a* in *hat* [HAT]	eh . . . . *e* in *let* [LEHT]	sh . . . . . *sh* in *she* [SHEE]
ah . . . . *a* in *father* [FAHTH-ur] and *o* in *hot* [HAHT]	eye . . . . the first *i* in *iris* [EYE-ruhs]	u . . . . . *u* in *put* [PUT] and *oo* in *foot* [FUT]
aw . . . *a* in *all* [AWL] and *o* in *order* [AWRD-ur]	g . . . . *g* in *go* [GOH]	uh . . . . *u* in *cup* [KUHP]
	ih . . . . *i* in *hit* [HIHT]	ur . . . . . *er* in *term* [TURM] and *ir* in *sir* [SUR]
ay . . . . *a* in *face* [FAYS]	oh . . . . *o* in *open* [OH-puhn]	y . . . . . *i* in *nice* [NYS]
ch . . . . *ch* in *child* [CHYLD] and in *much* [MUHCH]	oo . . . . *oo* in *food* [FOOD] and *u* in *rule* [ROOL]	z . . . . . *s* in *atoms* [AT-uhmz]
ee . . . . . *e* in *equal* [EE-kwuhl]	ow . . . . *ou* in *out* [OWT]	zh . . . . . *s* in *treasure* [TREHZH-ur]
	oy . . . . *oi* in *voice* [VOYS]	
	s . . . . . *s* in *say* [SAY]	

A

Absolute magnitude: the amount of light that would be received from a star if all stars were the same distance from the earth

Abyssal [uh-BIHS-uhl] **plain:** a flat plain that makes up about one third of the seafloor

Acid rain: a rain containing an acid formed by sulfur dioxide gas and water vapor or by nitrogen dioxide gas and water vapor

Air mass: a large body of air

Alloy [AL-oy]: a mixture of two or more metals or a mixture of a metal and another substance

Anemometer [AN-uh-MAHM-uht-ur]: an instrument that is used for measuring the speed of wind

Anthracite [AN(T)-thruh-SYT] **coal:** hard coal; coal with the highest carbon content

Aphelion [a-FEEL-yuhn]: the point in a planet's orbit at which the planet is farthest from the sun

Apogee [AP-uh-jee]: the point in the orbit of the moon or of an artificial satellite at which the orbiting object is farthest from the center of the earth

Apparent magnitude: the brightness that a star appears to have in the sky in comparison with other stars

Aqueduct [AK-wuh-DUHKT]: a channel that carries water from one place to another

Aquifer [AK-wuh-fur]: the layered and permeable rock, such as sandstone and limestone, that contains groundwater

Artesian [ahr-TEE-zhuhn] **well:** a well having flowing water from an aquifer that contains water that is under pressure

Asteroids [AS-tuh-ROYDZ]: the small planets that are in orbit between Mars and Jupiter and in certain other parts of the solar system

Asthenosphere [as-THEHN-uh-SFIH(UH)R]: the flexible second layer of the earth's mantle

Astronomical unit: a unit of length, used in astronomy, equal to the distance from the earth to the sun

Astronomy [uh-STRAHN-uh-mee]: the study of the stars and of other objects in space

Atmosphere [AT-muh-SFIH(UH)R]: the layer of air around the surface of the earth; the layer of gases surrounding a planet or a star

Atom [AT-uhm]: a tiny particle that makes up molecules of matter

Axis [AK-suhs]: (of the earth) an imaginary line running through the earth from the North Pole to the South Pole, on which the earth rotates; (in a crystal) an imaginary line extending from one side of a crystal to the other side of a crystal

B

Barometer [buh-RAHM-uht-ur]: an instrument that is used for measuring air pressure

Batholith [BATH-uh-lihth]: a thick block of igneous rock

Beaufort [BOH-furt] **scale**: a scale that is used to estimate the wind's speed in knots

Big bang theory: the theory that the universe began as a huge fireball and gradually formed into separate clouds of gas and dust that later became the galaxies, the stars, and the planets

Biodegradable [BY-oh-dih-GRAYD-uh-buhl]: a term used to describe substances easily broken down by natural processes, usually by bacteria or molds

Biosphere [BY-uh-SFIH(UH)R]: the thin layer of the earth in which living things exist

Bituminous [buh-T(Y)OO-muh-nuhs] **coal**: soft coal; coal that is harder than lignite but softer than anthracite

Black hole: a former star that has become so dense that anything nearby is pulled toward it by its tremendous gravity

Blizzard [BLIHZ-urd]: a violent snowstorm

Bomb: a rounded, red-hot piece of rock that comes out of a volcano

Brackish [BRAK-ihsh] **water**: water that is less salty than seawater but too salty for people to use.

C

Caldera [kal-DEHR-uh]: a large crater formed by the collapse of the center of a volcano or by a great volcanic explosion

Capillarity [KAP-uh-LAR-uht-ee]: the ability of a liquid to climb up a surface against the pull of gravity

Carbon dioxide [KAHR-buhn dy-AHK-syd]: a gas in the air that is used by plants to make food; a gas that is a pollutant from burning fuels; a gas that causes the greenhouse effect

Cenozoic [SEE-nuh-ZOH-ihk] **Era**: the present era in the earth's history, which began approximately 65 million years ago

Chain reaction: a nuclear reaction in which neutrons given off during the fission of one atom cause the fission of other atoms

Chlorination: the practice of adding chlorine to water in order to purify the water

Chlorine [KLOH(UH)R-EEN]: a chemical used to kill certain germs in water

Cholera [KAHL-uh-ruh]: a disease caused by certain germs in unfiltered drinking water

Chromosphere [KROH-muh-SFIH(UH)R]: the second layer of the sun's atmosphere

Cinder [SIHN-dur]: a hot, ashlike piece of rock that comes out of a volcano

Cinder cone: a small, cone-shaped hill that is made up of cinders and ash and that is formed by a volcanic eruption

Cirrus [SIHR-uhs] **clouds**: one of the three major kinds of clouds, occurring at high levels in the air

Cleavage [KLEE-vihj]: the ease with which and the way in which a mineral splits

Climate [KLY-muht]: the average of all the weather conditions in a certain place over many years

Cloud seeding: the scattering of certain materials in a cloud to make the cloud produce rain or snow

Coagulant [koh-AG-yuh-luhnt]: a chemical that forms small, sticky particles that remove bacteria, mud, and other materials from water in water-treatment plants

Cold front: a front in which a mass of cold air pushes forward under a mass of warmer air

Cold layer: the temperature layer in the ocean that is below the thermocline; the lowest temperature layer in the ocean

Composite volcano: the kind of volcano that has layers of lava and layers of ash, cinders, and bombs

Compound [KAHM-POWND]: a material whose molecules consist of two or more different kinds of atoms

Condense [kuhn-DEHN(T)S]: to come together in tiny

drops, such as the coming together of molecules of water vapor on the particles of dust in the air

Conserve [kuhn-SURV]: to use something in such a way that it is neither wasted nor destroyed

Continental [KAHNT-uhn-EHNT-uhl] **drift, theory of:** the theory that the continents move

Continental shelf: the edge of each continent that is below the ocean surface

Continental slope: an area around a continent that begins at the edge of the continental shelf and extends downward to the seafloor

Contour [KAHN-tu(uh)r] **map:** a flat map that shows elevation

Convection current [kuhn-VEHK-shuhn KUR-uhnt]: the circular movement that results as matter is heated and rises, becomes cooler and sinks, becomes heated and rises again

Convergent [kuhn-VUR-juhnt] **boundary:** a boundary between crustal plates that are colliding

Core: the central part of the planets and of the sun

Corona [kuh-ROH-nuh]: the outer region of the sun's atmosphere

Crater [CRAYT-ur]: a hollow in the surface of a planet made by impact with bodies such as small asteroids that crossed the planet's path

Crest: the high point of a wave

Crevasse [krih-VAS]: a crack in the surface of a glacier

Crust: the layer of rock just below the earth's surface

Crystal [KRIHS-tuhl]: the definite solid structure of a mineral

Cumulus [KYOO-myuh-luhs] **clouds:** one of the three major kinds of clouds, occurring at low or middle levels in the air; may contain tiny pieces of ice

Current [KUR-uhnt]: a large stream of moving water in the ocean

D

Delta [DEHL-tuh]: an area of land built up from soil deposited at the mouth of a river

Density [DEHN(T)-suht-ee]: the amount of matter present in a given volume

Deposition [DEHP-uh-ZIHSH-uhn]: the settling out of soil, sand, and weathered rock carried during erosion

Desalinate [dee-SAL-uh-NAYT]: to remove the salt from seawater or salt water

Dike: a large mass of igneous rock that forms when magma from a batholith cuts across rock layers and hardens

Dissolve [dihz-AHLV]: to cause to break apart, as certain liquids break apart certain kinds of matter

Distortion [dihs-TAWR-shuhn]: an error in size or shape on a map projection

Divergent [duh-VUR-juhnt] **boundary:** a boundary between crustal plates that are moving apart

Divide: a high area of land separating two adjacent watersheds

Drought [DROWT(H)]: a period of time in which rainfall is absent or is much less than usual

E

Earth-moon system: the earth and the moon considered as a single body in relation to the sun

Earthquake [URTH-kwayk]: a shaking or rolling of the ground caused by movement of rock along a fault

Eclipse [ih-KLIHPS]: the shadowing or hiding of one body in space by another body in space

Electrodialysis [ih-LEHK-troh-dy-AL-uh-suhs]: a method of desalinating water by using an electric current

Element [EHL-uh-muhnt]: any matter that is made up of atoms of only one kind

Elevation [EHL-uh-VAY-shuhn]: the height of the land above sea level

Ellipse [ih-LIHPS]: the oval shape of a planet's orbit

Endangered: a term used to describe living things that are in danger of becoming extinct

Energy [EHN-ur-jee]: the ability to do work to cause change

Environment [ihn-VY-ruhn-muhnt]: the surroundings of living things; includes all the things that can be seen, heard, felt, smelled, and tasted

Equator [ih-KWAYT-ur]: the parallel on a globe that is drawn halfway between the North and South poles and that is marked 0°

Equinox [EE-kwuh-NAHKS]: one of two dates during the year when the sun's rays are received at the most direct angle at the equator; the beginning of spring or the beginning of autumn

Era [IHR-uh]: a major division of geologic time

Erosion [ih-ROH-zhuhn]: the moving of soil, sand, and weathered rock from one place to another

Eutrophication [yu-TROH-fuh-KAY-shuhn]: a process of change that may occur in water after sewage has been poured into the water

Evaporate [ih-VAP-uh-RAYT]: to change from a liquid to a gas

Exosphere [EHK-soh-SFIH(UH)R]: the uppermost layer of the atmosphere

Expand [ihk-SPAND]: to take up more space

Extinct [ihk-STIHNG(K)T]: the term used to describe kinds of organisms that are no longer living on the earth

Extrusive [ihk-STROO-sihv]: a term used to refer to igneous rock formed on the earth's surface

F

Facet [FAS-uht]: the flattened side of a rock that was once frozen into a glacier

Fault: a break in the earth's crust

Fertilizer [FURT-uhl-EYE-zur]: a substance used in farming to help crops grow; can lead to water pollution if washed into nearby rivers and lakes

Fission [FIHSH-uhn]: the splitting of an atom

Flash distillation [DIHS-tuh-LAY-shuhn]: a method of desalinating water by using low pressure

Fluoride [FLU(-UH)R-YD]: a substance added to drinking water to help reduce tooth decay

Fossil [FAHS-uhl]: the impression, the remains, or any other evidence of a living thing that has been preserved in the earth

Fossil fuel: a fuel—such as coal, oil, or natural gas—that is thought to have formed from the remains of living things

Frequency [FREE-kwuhn-see]: the number of waves that pass a certain point in a certain amount of time

Friction [FRIHK-shuhn]: a force that keeps objects that rub together from moving

Front: a boundary between two air masses of different temperatures

Fusion [FYOO-zhuhn]: the combining of hydrogen nuclei to form helium nuclei

G

Galaxy [GAL-uhk-see]: a huge system of stars held together by gravity

Geologic [JEE-uh-LAHJ-ihk] **time:** the time during the long history of the earth

Geothermal [JEE-oh-THUR-muhl] **energy:** the heat energy from the earth's interior

Geyser [GY-zur]: a gusher of hot water and steam that erupts from a hole in the ground

Glacier [GLAY-shur]: a large, moving mass of ice

Globe: a map drawn on a sphere

Gondwanaland [gahn-DWAHN-uh-LAND]: the name given to an early continent thought to have been made up of the land areas known today as Africa, South America, Australia, Madagascar, the Falkland Islands, Antarctica, and India

Gradient [GRAYD-ee-uhnt]: the slope of a river

Gravitation [GRAV-uh-TAY-shuhn]: the force of attraction between bodies in space

Greenhouse effect: the effect of holding in the heat that the earth absorbs from the sun's rays

Grid lines: a system of lines on a globe that are used to find places

Groundwater: the water that soaks into the earth; a source of fresh water for people to use

H

Hard water: water that contains many dissolved minerals

Heat capacity [kuh-PAS-uht-ee]: the ability of certain kinds of matter to absorb heat without becoming much warmer

High: a region of high air pressure caused by a buildup of air

High tide: a rise in water level caused by the moon's gravity

Horizon [huh-RYZ-uhn]: (of the earth) the place where the earth's surface seems to meet the sky: (in the soil) one of the three different layers of soil

Humidity [hyoo-MIHD-uht-ee]: the moisture, or water vapor, in the air

Humus [HYOO-muhs]: the decaying plant material found in soil

Hurricane [HUR-uh-KAYN]: a slow-moving, violent storm that covers a large area

Hydroelectric power: the power produced by water turning large wheels that cause electric generators to spin and produce electricity

Hydrosphere [HY-druh-SFIH(UH)R]: the water on the earth

I

Ice age: a period of time when large areas of the earth were covered by huge glaciers

Iceberg: a piece of a glacier floating in the ocean

Igneous [IHG-nee-uhs] **rock:** the rock that is formed from cooled lava or magma

Inertia [ihn-UR-shuh]: a force that tends to keep something at rest or moving in the same direction unless some other force is exerted on it

Inland waterway: a body of water such as a canal, a river, or a lake

Intrusive [ihn-TROO-sihv]: a term used to refer to igneous rock formed within the earth

Ion [EYE-uhn]: an electrically charged atom

Ionosphere [eye-AHN-uh-SFIH(UH)R]: a part of the thermosphere in which the atoms of the air are electrically charged

J

Jet stream: a swiftly moving river of air within the tropopause

L

Laccolith [LAK-uh-LIHTH]: an igneous rock formation that looks like the cap of a large mushroom

Lake: a body of fresh water that has some deep places where no sunlight can reach bottom

Latitude [LAT-uh-T(Y)OOD]: the distance in degrees north or south of the equator

Laurasia [loh-RAY-zha]: the name given to an early continent thought to have been made up of the land areas known today as North America, Greenland, Europe, and Asia

Lava [LAHV-uh]: the molten rock at the surface of the earth that comes from a volcano

Leaching: the carrying down of certain materials by water to lower layers of soil

Legend [LEHJ-uhnd]: the part of a map that explains the meaning of the symbols used on that map

Light-year: the distance traveled by light in a year

Lignite [LIHG-NYT]: brown coal; the softest coal

Lithosphere [LIHTH-uh-SFIH(UH)R]: the outer shell of the earth that includes the crust and the first layer of the mantle

Local Group: a group of galaxies to which the Milky Way belongs

Longitude [LAHN-juh-T(Y)OOD]: the distance in degrees east or west of the prime meridian

Lunar [LOO-nur] **eclipse:** an eclipse of the moon caused when the earth is directly between the sun and the moon

Luster: the property of having a shine or a lack of shine; one physical property of a mineral

M

Magma [MAG-muh]: the molten rock below the surface of the earth

Magnetic declination [DEHK-luh-NAY-shuhn]: the angle of difference between a magnetic needle and true north

Magnetosphere [mag-NEET-uh-SFIH(UH)R]: a region surrounding the earth that is affected by the earth's magnetic field

Magnitude [MAG-nuh-T(Y)OOD]: a scale used for describing the brightness of stars

Manganese nodule [MANG-guh-NEEZ NAHJ-oo(uh)l]: a clump of the element manganese found on the seafloor

Mantle: the layer of the earth just below the crust

Map projection [pruh-JEHK-shuhn]: a transfer of features from the curved surface of a globe to a flat surface

Maria [MAHR-ee-uh]: the dark, low plains on the surface of the moon

Mariculture [MAR-uh-KUHL-chur]: the raising of ocean plants or animals by ocean-farming methods

Mascon (MAS-KAHN): a lump of extra matter beneath large maria on the moon

Mass: the amount of matter in an object

Meltwater: the water that comes from melting snow

Membrane [MEHM-BRAYN]: a thin sheet of material

Mercury [MUR-kyuh-ree]: a silver-colored liquid used in thermometers

Meridian [muh-RIHD-ee-uhn]: a grid line that runs north and south on a globe

Mesosphere [MEHZ-uh-SFIH(UR)R]: (of the earth) the third layer of the mantle; (of the atmosphere) the layer between the stratosphere and the thermosphere

Mesozoic [MEHZ-uh-ZOH-ihk] **Era:** an era that began about 225 million years ago and ended about 65 million years ago

Metamorphic [MEHT-uh-MAWR-fihk] **rock:** existing rock that has been changed into a new kind of rock by heat and pressure

Meteor [MEET-ee-ur]: an object that burns as it falls through the atmosphere toward the earth's surface; a falling star

Meteorite [MEET-ee-uh-ryt]: a meteor that gets through the atmosphere and falls to the earth's surface

Meteorology: the science of studying the air and the weather

Mid-Atlantic Ridge: a long mountain range in the middle of the Atlantic Ocean; a place where seafloor spreading occurs

Milky Way: the galaxy of which our solar system is a part

Mineral: a solid, formed in nature, that has a definite chemical makeup and structure and that does not contain organic materials

Moho: the boundary between the rock of the crust and the denser rock of the mantle

Molecule [MAHL-ih-KYOO(UH)L]: the smallest particle of any kind of matter

Moraine [muh-RAYN]: the rocks and soil deposited by a glacier

N

Natural [NACH-(uh-)ruhl] **resource:** a material from the earth that people need or use

Neutron [N(Y)OO-TRAHN]: a particle found in the nucleus of an atom

Nitrogen [NY-truh-juhn]: a gas that makes up about fourth fifths of the air

Nonrenewable [NAHN-rih-N(Y)OO-uh-buhl] **resource:** a resource, such as soil and land, that cannot be replaced as it is used

Nuclear [N(Y)OO-klee-ur] **energy:** the energy given off by changes in the atoms of radioactive matter

Nuclear reactor [ree-AK-tur]: a place in which a controlled nuclear chain reaction is allowed to occur

Nucleus [N(Y)OO-klee-uhs]: the center of an atom

O

Occluded [uh-KLOOD-uhd] **front:** a front that forms when a cold front overtakes a warm front

Orbit [AWR-buht]: the path traveled by one body in its revolution around another body, such as by a planet around the sun or a moon around a planet

Ore: a mineral that is mined

Oxygen [AHK-sih-juhn]: a gas in the air that is used by almost all living things to get energy from their food; released into the air by plants as they make food

Ozone [OH-ZOHN]: a special form of oxygen that forms a layer within the stratosphere and that absorbs ultraviolet rays from the sun

P

Paleomagnetism [PAY-lee-oh-MAG-nuh-TIHZ-uhm]: the direction of the magnetism of old rocks, showing that the poles have shifted from the time that the rocks hardened; evidence for seafloor spreading

Paleozoic [PAY-lee-uh-ZOH-ihk] **Era:** an era that began about 570 million years ago and ended about 225 million years ago

Pangaea [PAN-JEE-uh]: a single continent thought to have existed near the end of the Paleozoic Era

Parallel [PAR-uh-LEHL]: a grid line that runs east and west on a globe

Perigee [PEHR-uh-jee]: the point in the orbit of the moon or of an artificial satellite at which the orbiting object is closest to the center of the earth

Perihelion [PEHR-uh-HEEL-yuhn]: the point in a planet's orbit at which the planet is closest to the sun

Permeable [PUR-mee-uh-buhl]: a term used to describe rock that has tiny open spaces and cracks into which water may move

Phase [FAYZ]: the form—solid, liquid, or gas—in which matter occurs

Phases: the changes in the way the moon looks from the earth

Phosphate [FAHS-FAYT]: a kind of chemical in wastewater that cannot be removed by primary and secondary treatments

Photosphere [FOHT-uh-SFIH(UH)R]: the visible surface of the sun; the first layer of the sun's atmosphere

Physical [FIHZ-ih-kuhl] **map:** a flat map that shows surface features by the use of different shadings of color

Plages [PLAHZH-uhz]: the large, bright regions on the surface of the sun

Planet [PLAN-uht]: a large, massive object in the solar system that travels in orbit around the sun

Plasma: a gas with an electric charge

Plates: the parts into which the crust of the earth is divided

Plate tectonics [tehk-TAHN-ihks], **theory of:** the theory that the earth's crust is made up of rigid plates that fit together and move slowly

Polarity [poh-LAR-uht-ee]: a property of matter whereby each molecule has oppositely charged poles

Pollution [puh-LOO-shuhn]: the fouling of the environment

Pond: a body of fresh water that is so shallow that some sunlight can reach bottom

Precambrian [pree-KAM-bree-uhn] **Era:** the era of geologic time before 570 million years ago

Precipitate [prih-SIHP-uht-uht]: a substance separated from a solution by means of a chemical or a physical change

Precipitation [prih-SIHP-uh-TAY-shuhn]: any form of water that falls to the ground

Predict [prih-DIHKT]: to tell if something is going to occur before it happens

Pressure [PREHSH-ur]: a force acting on something

Prevailing [prih-VAY-lihng] **wind:** a wind that moves a great distance in roughly the same direction

Prime meridian: the meridian line on maps and globes that runs through London, England, and is marked 0°

Property [PRAHP-urt-ee]: a characteristic of matter

Proton [PROH-TAHN]: a particle found in the nucleus of an atom

Psychrometer [sy-KRAHM-uht-ur]: an instrument used to measure relative humidity

Pulsar [PUHL-SAHR]: a very dense star that sends out radio signals in regular pulses

Q

Quasar [KWAY-ZAHR]: a distant, starlike object that sends out great amounts of energy in the form of radio waves

R

Radar [RAY-DAHR]: a device that can be used to detect clouds and other large objects in the air

Radioactive [RAYD-ee-oh-AK-tihv] **material:** a kind of matter in which some particles escape from the nuclei of the atoms as energy; may be used to measure the age of rock

Radiosonde [RAYD-ee-oh-SAHND]: a weather balloon that carries weather instruments and that sends out information about the conditions of the air around it

Radio telescope: an instrument that receives radio waves from distant objects

Recharging: a method of replacing groundwater lost because of overpumping

Recycle [ree-SY-kuhl]: to process in order to use more than once

Relative [REHL-uht-ihv] **humidity:** the amount of water vapor in the air compared with the amount that the air could hold at that temperature

Relief [rih-LEEF] **map:** a map that is not flat; represents mountains, valleys, ridges, and other surface features that appear on an area of land

Renewable [rih-N(Y)OO-uh-buhl] **resource:** a natural resource, such as a tree, that can be replaced as it is being used

Reproduce [REE-pruh-D(Y)OOS]: to produce new living things of the same kind

Reservoir [REHZ-uh(r)v-WAHR]: a lake that forms behind a dam that has been built across a river to provide additional sources of fresh water for people

Resource [REE-SOH(UH)RS]: a natural material or feature of the earth that helps to support life and satisfy people's needs

Reusable [ree-YOO-zuh-buhl] **resource:** a resource, such as air and water, that can be used over and over again

Reverse osmosis [rih-VURS ahz-MOH-suhs]: a method of desalinating water by using high pressure to force water through a membrane

Revolution: a complete orbit

Richter [RIHK-tur] **scale:** a scale used to describe the strength of an earthquake

Rift [RIHFT] **valley:** a valley that forms when rock along a fault is pulled apart; found in the middle of a ridge

Rock: a mass of strong material, usually made up of one or more minerals

Rock cycle [SY-kuhl]: a term used to mean the continuous changing of rock into other kinds of rock

Rotate [ROH-TAYT]: to turn on an axis

Runoff: the rainwater that flows over the land's surface

S

Salinity [say-LIHN-uht-ee]: the total amount of salt in a sample of seawater; a measure of the amount of salt in seawater

Salt: a mineral that is dissolved in groundwater and in seawater

Salt dome: a hill of salt that exists within rock layers of the earth

Sanitary [SAN-uh-TEHR-ee] **landfill:** a place for burying solid wastes

Satellite [SAT-uhl-YT]: a body that orbits a larger body in space

Scale: the part of a map that shows how much of the earth's surface is represented by a given measurement on the map

Seafloor spreading: a process by which rock matter is added to the edges of crustal plates as the plates move apart

Seafood: any plant or animal that comes from the ocean and is used for food by people

Seamount [SEE-MOWNT]: an underwater mountain that is formed by an underwater volcano

Sediment [SEHD-uh-muhnt]: the material carried and deposited by wind, water, or glaciers

Sedimentary [SEHD-uh-MEHNT-uh-ree] **rock:** the rock that is formed when sediments are packed together and become hard

Seismic [SYZ-mihk] **wave:** the form in which energy given off by an earthquake moves through the earth

Seismograph [SYZ-muh-GRAF]: an instrument used to measure seismic waves

Sewage [SOO-ihj]: the used water and other liquid wastes carried off by sewers and sometimes dumped into bodies of water

Sewage treatment: the changing of sewage into less-harmful kinds of matter

Shield volcano: the kind of volcano that has a rounded or flat top from which lava spreads out and forms sheets of rock

Sialic [sy-AL-ihk] **layer:** the layer of rock that makes up the continents

Sill: an igneous rock formation that is a tablelike block of rock

Simatic [sy-MAD-ihk] **layer:** the layer of rock that is beneath the seafloor

Smudge pot: a pot that is used for burning certain materials in order to control frost

Sodium chloride [SOHD-ee-uhm KLOH(UH)R-YD]: the salt known as table salt

Solar distillation [SOH-lur DIHS-tuh-LAY-shuhn]: a method of desalinating water by using the sun's energy

Solar eclipse: an eclipse of the sun that occurs when the moon is directly between the sun and the earth

Solar energy: the energy from the sun

Solar prominence [PRAHM(-uh)-nuhn(t)s]: a flamelike projection of gases on the sun

Solar system [SIHS-tuhm]: the sun and the objects that revolve around it

Solar wind: the hot gases that expand away from the surface of the sun

Solstice [SAHL-stuhs]: one of two dates during the year when the sun's rays are received at the most direct angle possible on either the northern half or the southern half of the earth; the beginning of summer or the beginning of winter

Solution [suh-LOO-shuhn]: a substance that consists of two or more different kinds of matter, one of which dissolves in another

Sphere [SFIH(UH)R]: a ball shape; a term generally used to represent the earth's shape

Spicules [SPIHK-yoo(uh)lz]: the jets of hot gases that look like flaming fingers within the chromosphere

Stationary [STAY-shuh-NEHR-ee] **front:** a front that forms when the boundary between two different air masses does not move

Stratosphere [STRAT-uh-SFIH(UH)R]: the layer of the atmosphere that extends from the top of the troposphere to the mesosphere

Stratus [STRAYT-uhs] **clouds:** one of the three major kinds of clouds, occurring at low or middle levels in the air

Stellar parallax [PAR-uh-LAKS]: an apparent shift in the position of nearby stars that is used to prove the revolution of the earth

Stock: a small batholith

Streak: the color of the powder that is left by a mineral when that mineral is rubbed across a piece of white, unglazed porcelain

Striae [STRY-ee]: the scratches on a rock that was once frozen into a glacier

Sulfur dioxide [SUHL-fur dy-AHK-syd]: a gas from burning fuels that is a pollutant; combines with water vapor in the air to form acid rain

Sunspots: the hollow places in the sun's surface gases that look like dark spots on the sun

Surface: the outer layer of soil, rock, and water of the earth

Surface layer: the temperature layer in the ocean near the water's surface

Surface tension [TEHN-chuhn]: a characteristic of water whereby water molecules hold very tightly together

Symbol [SIHM-buhl]: a drawing or a mark used to show a certain feature on a map

T

Temperature [TEHM-puh(r)-CHU(UH)R]: a way of describing how warm or how cold something is

Temperature inversion [ihn-VUR-zhuhn]: a weather condition in which a layer of warm air lies over a layer of cooler air; little or no wind is present to help air circulate

Thermocline [THUR-muh-KLYN]: a temperature layer in the ocean that is very thin and that forms the boundary between the warm water above and the cold water below

Thermosphere [THUR-muh-SFIH(UH)R]: the layer of the atmosphere between the exosphere and the mesosphere

Tidal current: a kind of current caused by the moving water of a tide

Tide [TYD]: a rising and falling of the water's surface on the ocean and on bodies of water that are connected to the ocean

Topographic [TAHP-uh-GRAF-ihk] **map:** a map that shows surface features

Topography [tuh-PAHG-ruh-fee]: the surface features of an area

Topsoil: the surface soil; the most fertile part of soil

Tornado [tawr-NAYD-oh]: a small, but very violent, storm with very high winds that produce a funnel-shaped cloud

Tree ring: a ring that can be observed when a tree stump is studied; represents one year's growth, during which the tree adds a new layer

Trench: a deep, V-shaped valley in the seafloor; a place where one plate is bending downward and moving beneath another plate

Tropopause [TROHP-uh-PAWZ]: the division between the stratosphere and the troposphere

Troposphere [TROHP-uh-SFIH(UH)R]: the layer of the atmosphere that is closest to the surface of the earth

Trough: the low point of a wave

Tsunami [(t)su-NAHM-ee]: a very high wave that reaches the shore and that is caused by an underwater earthquake or landslide

U

Ultraviolet rays: rays from the sun that are harmful to livings things; absorbed by the ozone layer

V

Van Allen belts: two layers of the magnetosphere in which electrically charged particles are trapped

Volcanic eruption [vahl-KAN-ihk ih-RUHP-shuhn]: the bursting of gases and magma through the earth's surface layer of soil and rock

Volcanic neck: an igneous rock that forms in the part of the channel found within the volcano itself

Volcano [vahl-KAY-noh]: a vent, or opening, in the earth's crust from which lava, gases, and other materials come out; a cone or a mountain made up of rock and other materials that have come out of a vent

W

Water cycle: the movement of water from the ocean to the sky, to the land, and back to the ocean over and over again; allows water to be used again and again

Water pollution [puh-LOO-shuhn]: the fouling of water so that the water contains so much waste that it is unclean or dangerous for many uses

Water quality [KWAHL-uht-ee]: the purity of water

Water rights: the authority to use a certain source of water

Watershed: the area of land that is drained by a river

Water table: the top of the zone of saturation

Water-treatment plant: a plant that filters and treats water in order to make it clean and safe to use

Water vapor [VAY-pur]: the moisture in the air; water in the form of a gas

Wavelength: the distance between any point on a wave and the corresponding point on the next wave

Weather: the changing conditions within the troposphere that may affect the earth's surface and living things

Weather alert [uh-LURT]: a radio or TV broadcast about the weather that warns of a storm, very cold temperatures, flooding, or drought

Weather forecast [FOH(UH)R-kast]: a broadcast or a newspaper report that gives weather predictions

Weathering: the natural process by which rock and other materials are broken apart

Weather map: a current map of the weather, used by a meteorologist to help forecast the weather

Weather satellite [SAT-uhl-yt]: an object that circles the earth and takes pictures of it to aid in weather forecasting

Wildlife: kinds of living things that are not raised by people for a purpose

Wind vane: an instrument that is used to measure the wind's direction

World ocean: a term that refers collectively to the Atlantic Ocean, the Pacific Ocean, and the Indian Ocean

World weather-watch: the constant watching of the weather around the world by using satellites and radio-sondes

Z

Zone of flow: an area deep within a glacier, where the ice is flexible and where the flow of the glacier takes place

Zone of saturation [sach-uh-RAY-shuhn]: the part of the ground in which all the tiny openings are filled with water

Lake: 311, 327, 520, *ill.* 314

Land: pollution of, 537–540, *ill.* 539; as resource, 489–490, *ill.* 490; restoration of, 549, *ill.* 549; use of, 556–557, *ill.* 556, 557

Lateral moraine: 471, *ill.* 471

Latitude: and climate, 257; definition of, 71, *ill.* 71

Laurasia: 394, *ill.* 395

Lava: 132, 428–429, 431–434

Lavoisier: 295, *ill.* 295

Leaching: 449

Legend: of a map, 76

Lightning: nitrogen and, 203

Light-year: 175

Lignite: 57

Limestone: 55, 59, 389, 446

Limnologist: 321, *ill.* 321

Lithosphere: 14–17, 33

Local group: 180

Longitude: definition of, 71, *ill.* 71

Love wave: 439–440, *ill.* 439

Low: 215–216, 219, 238–239, *ill.* 219, 239

Lumbering: 510

Lunar eclipse: 135, *ill.* 135

Lunar soil: 128

Luster: of minerals, 35

L wave: 439–440, *ill.* 439

Lystrosaurus: 408

M

Magma: 15, 33, 49–52, 416, 422, 428, 433

Magnetic declination: 25–26

Magnetic field: of earth, 24–26, *ill.* 23; and sunspots, 146

Magnetic pole: of earth, 24–25

Magnetometer: 29, 413

Magnetosphere: 26–28, *ill.* 26

Magnitude: 176–177

Manganese: 372–373, *ill.* 373

Mantle: of earth, 17–18, 412, 416, 418–419, *ill.* 17, 19; of moon, 132, *ill.* 132; of planets, 108, *ill.* 108

Map: contour, 79, *ill.* 79; distortion, 73; language of, 75–76; physical, 79, *ill.* 79; projection, 71–74, *ill.*

71, 72, 73, 74; relief, 78, *ill.* 78; topographic, 78, *ill.* 78, 79. *See also* Weather map.

Marble: 59, 389

Maria: 127

Mariana Trench: 410, *ill.* 410

Mariculture: 364, *ill.* 364

Marine biologist: 377, *ill.* 377

Mars: 102, 108, 112–114, 118, 120; and Kepler's laws, 158–159

Mascon: 132

Mass: definition of, 99; and motion of solar system, 102–103

Medial moraine: 471, *ill.* 471

Mediterranean climate: 258, *ill.* 259

Meltwater: 465, 470, *ill.* 466

Membrane: definition of, 368

Mercury: 102, 111, 113, 117, 163

Meridian: 71, *ill.* 71

Mesosaurus: 408, *ill.* 408

Mesosphere: as layer of atmosphere, 198–199; as layer of earth, 18, *ill.* 17

Mesozoic Era: 394, 397

Metamorphic rock: 48, 59–60, 389

Metamorphism: 59

Meteor: 198–200, *ill.* 199

Meteorite: 199

Meteoroid: 102

Meteorologist: 217, 235–242, 249, *ill.* 249

Meteorology: 249

Methane: 107, 114–115, 120

Microbe: in atmosphere, 11

Mid-Atlantic Ridge: 355, 410, *ill.* 355, 410, 412, 416

Middle-latitude climate: 258–259

Milky Way: 172, 177–178, *ill.* 178

Mineral: 32, 509–510, 546, *ill.* 45; as crystals, 38–41, *ill.* 40, 41; definition of, 32; formation of, 33–34; and hard water, 302; identification of, 37–38, *ill.* 38; as ores, 42–43, *ill.* 43; properties of, 34–37, *ill.* 36; as resource, 493, *ill.* 493; in seawater, 374; in water, 21, 333; and weathering, 446–447

Mining engineer: 423, *ill.* 423

Moho: 17, *ill.* 17, 18

Mohorovičić discontinuity. *See* Moho.

Molecule: definition of, 291–292; of water, 292–295, *ill.* 294

Moon: definition of, 117; of earth, 118, 124–136, 352, *ill.* 10, 127, 132, 134, 135, 352; of planets, 118–120, *table* 118

Moonquake: 131–132

Moraine: 390, 471, *ill.* 471

Mountain: formation of, 419–422

Mountain glacier: 461, 471–472

Mountain valley: 470

Mount St. Helens: 280, 426, 433–434

N

National park: 552

Native metal: 42

Natural gas: 497–498

Natural resource: 509–512, *ill.* 511, 512; definition of, 509. *See also* Resource.

Neap tide: 127

Neptune: 102, 108–109, 114–115, 117, *ill.* 109

Neutron: of atom, 499, *ill.* 499

Newton, Sir Isaac: 161–163

Nitrate: 485

Nitrogen: 11, 107, 399, *table* 11. *See also* Nitrogen cycle.

Nitrogen cycle: 203, 485–486, *ill.* 485

Nodule: definition of, 372

Nonrenewable resource: 489–493, 546; land as, 489–490, *ill.* 490; minerals as, 493, *ill.* 493; soil as, 491, *ill.* 491

Northern lights: *See* Aurora borealis.

Nuclear energy: 498–500, *ill.* 499

Nuclear reactor: 500

Nucleus: of atom, 499, *ill.* 499

O

Obsidian: 50, *ill.* 50

Occluded front: 240

Temperature: of ocean, 344–346, ill. 345

Temperature inversion: 203

Terminal moraine: 471

Thermocline: 345

Thermometer: 208, ill. 208

Thermosphere: 196–198

Third law of planetary motion: 160–161

Thrust fault: 436, ill. 436

Thunderstorm: 244, ill. 245; and nitrogen, 486

Tidal current: 352, ill. 352

Tide: 126, 352, ill. 127, 352

Tidewater glacier: 463

Till: from glaciers, 472

Time. See Day; Geologic time; Year.

Titan: 119–120, 125

Titanic: 473

Topography: 78–88; definition of, 78; of East, 82–83, ill. 83; importance of, 81–82; of Midwest, 86, ill. 86; of South, 83, ill. 83; of West, 86–87, ill. 87; of West Coast, 88, ill. 88

Topsoil: definition of, 491, ill. 491; and floods, 310

Tornado: 245–246, ill. 247

Trade wind: 349

Tranquilityite: 130

Tree rings: and climate, 278, ill. 279

Trench: 356, 410–411, 427, ill. 354, 410, 416

Trilobite: 396

Triton: 125

Tropical climate: 258, 260

Tropopause: 201

Troposphere: 202–204

Trough: of water waves, 348, ill. 348

True north: 25

Tsunami: 347

Tundra climate: 260

Typhoid fever: 337

U

Ultraviolet rays: 199

Uranus: 102, 108–109, 114–115, 117–118, 120, ill. 109, 117

V

Valley glacier: 461–462

Van Allen belts: 28, ill. 27

Venus: 102, 108, 111, 113–114, 117

Vibrations: of moon, 131–132

Volcanic eruption: 428–429, 433–434, 518

Volcanic neck: 52, ill. 52

Volcanic rock: 428–429

Volcano: 426, 518, ill. 431; formation of, 427–429, ill. 427; kinds of, 430–434; on planets, 111; underwater, 354

W

Warm front: 240

Water: 290–294, ill. 290; and climate, 256; improving distribution of, 329–332; makeup of, 21–22, 291–295, ill. 294; natural problems with, 333; of past, 400–401; pollution of, 531–536, ill. 532, 533, 536; properties of, 296–302, ill. 299; as resource, 483–485, 520, ill. 484, 520; uneven distribution of, 325–328, ill. 325; and weathering, 445–446, 452–453

Water cycle: 227–228, 317–320, 325, 484–485, ill. 228, 317, 318, 320, 484

Water quality: 333–334

Water rights: 328

Watershed: 309, ill. 309

Water table: 313, 315, ill. 313, 314, 315

Water treatment: 336–338; history of, 336–337, ill. 336; modern, 337–338, ill. 337

Water-treatment plant: 337–338

Water vapor: 220–228, 296, 317–318, 365, 484, ill. 318; and clouds, 223–225, ill. 224, 225; definition of, 220–221

Wave: cause of, 347; movement of, 347–348, ill. 347, 348; and weathering, 455–456

Wavelength: of water waves, 348, ill. 348

Weather: 13, 146, 203–204; and air pollution, 528, ill. 528; and climate, 253–254; controlling, 273–276; definition of, 203–204; effects on people, 269–272, ill. 269, 270, 271

Weather alert: 233, ill. 233

Weather forecast: 232, 234; making of, 235–242, 244–248, 273–274

Weathering: 42, 53, 422; chemical, 446–447, ill. 446; definition of, 42, 444; physical, 444–445, ill. 445; results of, 447; and soil formation, 448–449, ill. 449

Weather map: 240–242, ill. 241

Weather reconnaissance pilot: 281, ill. 281

Weather satellite: 235–236, 273, ill. 236, 242, 273

Wegener, Alfred: 407–409, 413, ill. 407

Weight: definition of, 163

Well: water, 315–316, 329; oil, 369–371, ill. 360, 369, 370; recharging of, 330, ill. 330. See also Artesian well.

Whale: 362

Wildlife: as resource, 550–552

Wildlife refuge: 552

Wind: 204, 216–220; and convection, 211; definition of, 204; and hurricanes, 247; local, 220; measuring, 216–217, ill. 216, table 217; prevailing, 218–219, ill. 219; and tornadoes, 245; and weather forecasting, table 237; and weathering, 445, 456; westerly, 349

Wind vane: 217

World ocean: 20, 380–381, ill. 380, 381

World weather-watch: 273–274

Y

Year: definition of, 168

Z

Zone of flow: 466, ill. 466

Zone of saturation: 313, ill. 313